Dictionary of Literary Biography

Documentary Series

1 *Sherwood Anderson, Willa Cather, John Dos Passos, Theodore Dreiser, F. Scott Fitzgerald, Ernest Hemingway, Sinclair Lewis,* edited by Margaret A. Van Antwerp (1982)

2 *James Gould Cozzens, James T. Farrell, William Faulkner, John O'Hara, John Steinbeck, Thomas Wolfe, Richard Wright,* edited by Margaret A. Van Antwerp (1982)

3 *Saul Bellow, Jack Kerouac, Norman Mailer, Vladimir Nabokov, John Updike, Kurt Vonnegut,* edited by Mary Bruccoli (1983)

4 *Tennessee Williams,* edited by Margaret A. Van Antwerp and Sally Johns (1984)

5 *American Transcendentalists,* edited by Joel Myerson (1988)

6 *Hardboiled Mystery Writers: Raymond Chandler, Dashiell Hammett, Ross Macdonald,* edited by Matthew J. Bruccoli and Richard Layman (1989)

7 *Modern American Poets: James Dickey, Robert Frost, Marianne Moore,* edited by Karen L. Rood (1989)

8 *The Black Aesthetic Movement,* edited by Jeffrey Louis Decker (1991)

9 *American Writers of the Vietnam War: W. D. Ehrhart, Larry Heinemann, Tim O'Brien, Walter McDonald, John M. Del Vecchio,* edited by Ronald Baughman (1991)

10 *The Bloomsbury Group,* edited by Edward L. Bishop (1992)

11 *American Proletarian Culture: The Twenties and The Thirties,* edited by Jon Christian Suggs (1993)

12 *Southern Women Writers: Flannery O'Connor, Katherine Anne Porter, Eudora Welty,* edited by Mary Ann Wimsatt and Karen L. Rood (1994)

13 *The House of Scribner, 1846-1904,* edited by John Delaney (1996)

14 *Four Women Writers for Children, 1868-1918,* edited by Caroline C. Hunt (1996)

15 *American Expatriate Writers: Paris in the Twenties,* edited by Matthew J. Bruccoli and Robert W. Trogdon (1997)

16 *The House of Scribner, 1905-1930,* edited by John Delaney (1997)

17 *The House of Scribner, 1931-1984,* edited by John Delaney (1998)

18 *British Poets of The Great War: Sassoon, Graves, Owen,* edited by Patrick Quinn (1999)

19 *James Dickey,* edited by Judith S. Baughman (1999)

See also DLB 210, 216, 219, 222, 224, 229

Yearbooks

1980 edited by Karen L. Rood, Jean W. Ross, and Richard Ziegfeld (1981)

1981 edited by Karen L. Rood, Jean W. Ross, and Richard Ziegfeld (1982)

1982 edited by Richard Ziegfeld; associate editors: Jean W. Ross and Lynne C. Zeigler (1983)

1983 edited by Mary Bruccoli and Jean W. Ross; associate editor Richard Ziegfeld (1984)

1984 edited by Jean W. Ross (1985)

1985 edited by Jean W. Ross (1986)

1986 edited by J. M. Brook (1987)

1987 edited by J. M. Brook (1988)

1988 edited by J. M. Brook (1989)

1989 edited by J. M. Brook (1990)

1990 edited by James W. Hipp (1991)

1991 edited by James W. Hipp (1992)

1992 edited by James W. Hipp (1993)

1993 edited by James W. Hipp, contributing editor George Garrett (1994)

1994 edited by James W. Hipp, contributing editor George Garrett (1995)

1995 edited by James W. Hipp, contributing editor George Garrett (1996)

1996 edited by Samuel W. Bruce and L. Kay Webster, contributing editor George Garrett (1997)

1997 edited by Matthew J. Bruccoli and George Garrett, with the assistance of L. Kay Webster (1998)

1998 edited by Matthew J. Bruccoli, contributing editor George Garrett, with the assistance of D. W. Thomas (1999)

1999 edited by Matthew J. Bruccoli, contributing editor George Garrett, with the assistance of D. W. Thomas (2000)

Concise Series

Concise Dictionary of American Literary Biography, 7 volumes (1988-1999): *The New Consciousness, 1941-1968; Colonization to the American Renaissance, 1640-1865; Realism, Naturalism, and Local Color, 1865-1917; The Twenties, 1917-1929; The Age of Maturity, 1929-1941; Broadening Views, 1968-1988; Supplement: Modern Writers, 1900-1998.*

Concise Dictionary of British Literary Biography, 8 volumes (1991-1992): *Writers of the Middle Ages and Renaissance Before 1660; Writers of the Restoration and Eighteenth Century, 1660-1789; Writers of the Romantic Period, 1789-1832; Victorian Writers, 1832-1890; Late-Victorian and Edwardian Writers, 1890-1914; Modern Writers, 1914-1945; Writers After World War II, 1945-1960; Contemporary Writers, 1960 to Present.*

Concise Dictionary of World Literary Biography, 20 volumes projected (1999-   ): *Ancient Greek and Roman Writers; German Writers; African, Carribbean, and Latin American Writers.*

Dictionary of Literary Biography® • Volume Two Hundred Thirty-One

British Novelists Since 1960
Fourth Series

Dictionary of Literary Biography® • Volume Two Hundred Thirty-One

British Novelists Since 1960
Fourth Series

Edited by
Merritt Moseley
University of North Carolina at Asheville

A Bruccoli Clark Layman Book
The Gale Group
Detroit • San Francisco • London • Boston • Woodbridge, Conn.

Matthew J. Bruccoli and Richard Layman, Editorial Directors
C. E. Frazer Clark Jr., Managing Editor
Karen L. Rood, Senior Editor

Printed in the United States of America

The paper used in this publication meets the minimum requirements of American National Standard for Information Sciences–Permanence Paper for Printed Library Materials, ANSI Z39.48-1984.∞™

Library of Congress Cataloging-in-Publication Data

British novelists since 1960. Fourth series / edited by Merritt Moseley.
p. cm.–(Dictionary of literary biography: v. 231)
"A Bruccoli Clark Layman book."
Includes bibliographical references and index.
ISBN 0-7876-4648-2 (alk. paper)
1. English fiction–20th century–Bio-bibliography–Dictionaries. 2. Novelists, English–20th century–Biography–Dictionaries. 3. English fiction–20th century–Dictionaries. I. Moseley, Merritt, 1949– . II. Series.

PR881.B734 2000
823'.91409'03–dc21 00–057300
[B] CIP

10 9 8 7 6 5 4 3 2 1

To
Alec, Sue, Anna, and Will
Robert and Heidi.

Contents

Plan of the Series

The advisory board, the editors, and the publisher of the *Dictionary of Literary Biography* are joined in endorsing Mark Twain's declaration. The literature of a nation provides an inexhaustible resource of permanent worth. We intend to make literature and its creators better understood and more accessible to students and the reading public, while satisfying the standards of teachers and scholars.

To meet these requirements, *literary biography* has been construed in terms of the author's achievement. The most important thing about a writer is his writing. Accordingly, the entries in *DLB* are career biographies, tracing the development of the author's canon and the evolution of his reputation.

The purpose of *DLB* is not only to provide reliable information in a convenient format but also to place the figures in the larger perspective of literary history and to offer appraisals of their accomplishments by qualified scholars.

The publication plan for *DLB* resulted from two years of preparation. The project was proposed to Bruccoli Clark by Frederick G. Ruffner, president of the Gale Research Company, in November 1975. After specimen entries were prepared and typeset, an advisory board was formed to refine the entry format and develop the series rationale. In meetings held during 1976, the publisher, series editors, and advisory board approved the scheme for a comprehensive biographical dictionary of persons who contributed to North American literature. Editorial work on the first volume began in January 1977, and it was published in 1978. In order to make *DLB* more than a reference tool and to compile volumes that individually have claim to status as literary history, it was decided to organize volumes by

topic, period, or genre. Each of these freestanding volumes provides a biographical-bibliographical guide and overview for a particular area of literature. We are convinced that this organization—as opposed to a single alphabet method—constitutes a valuable innovation in the presentation of reference material. The volume plan necessarily requires many decisions for the placement and treatment of authors who might properly be included in two or three volumes. In some instances a major figure will be included in separate volumes, but with different entries emphasizing the aspect of his career appropriate to each volume. Ernest Hemingway, for example, is represented in *American Writers in Paris, 1920–1939* by an entry focusing on his expatriate apprenticeship; he is also in *American Novelists, 1910–1945* with an entry surveying his entire career, as well as in *American Short-Story Writers, 1910–1945, Second Series* with an entry concentrating on his short stories. Each volume includes a cumulative index of the subject authors and articles. Comprehensive indexes to the entire series are planned.

Since 1981 the series has been further augmented by the *DLB Yearbooks,* which update published entries and add new entries to keep the *DLB* current with contemporary activity. There have also been *DLB Documentary Series* volumes which provide biographical and critical source materials for figures whose work is judged to have particular interest for students. One of these companion volumes is devoted entirely to Tennessee Williams.

We define literature as the *intellectual commerce of a nation:* not merely as belles lettres but as that ample and complex process by which ideas are generated, shaped, and transmitted. *DLB* entries are not limited to "creative writers" but extend to other figures who in their time and in their way influenced the mind of a people. Thus the series encompasses historians, journalists, publishers, book collectors, and screenwriters. By this means readers of *DLB* may be aided to perceive literature not as cult scripture in the keeping of intellectual high priests but firmly positioned at the center of a nation's life.

DLB includes the major writers appropriate to each volume and those standing in the ranks behind them. Scholarly and critical counsel has been sought in deciding which minor figures to include and how full their entries should be. Wherever possible, useful references are made to figures who do not warrant separate entries.

Each *DLB* volume has an expert volume editor responsible for planning the volume, selecting the figures for inclusion, and assigning the entries. Volume editors are also responsible for preparing, where appropriate, appendices surveying the major periodicals and literary and intellectual movements for their volumes, as well as lists of further readings. Work on the series as a whole is coordinated at the Bruccoli Clark Layman editorial center in Columbia, South Carolina, where the editorial staff is responsible for accuracy and utility of the published volumes.

One feature that distinguishes *DLB* is the illustration policy—its concern with the iconography of literature. Just as an author is influenced by his surroundings, so is the reader's understanding of the author enhanced by a knowledge of his environment. Therefore *DLB* volumes include not only drawings, paintings, and photographs of authors, often depicting them at various stages in their careers, but also illustrations of their families and places where they lived. Title pages are regularly reproduced in facsimile along with dust jackets for modern authors. The dust jackets are a special feature of *DLB* because they often document better than anything else the way in which an author's work was perceived in its own time. Specimens of the writers' manuscripts and letters are included when feasible.

Samuel Johnson rightly decreed that "The chief glory of every people arises from its authors." The purpose of the *Dictionary of Literary Biography* is to compile literary history in the surest way available to us—by accurate and comprehensive treatment of the lives and work of those who contributed to it.

The *DLB* Advisory Board

Introduction:
Reviewing and Publicizing British Novels

In Britain as anywhere else the crucial elements of the enterprise that is the contemporary novel are writers and readers. Without either of them novels will not exist, or will not exist for long. But it would be naive or purist to remain unaware of the other, perhaps annoyingly obtrusive, parts of the transaction. Among these are merchandising–the operation of bookstores, the promotion and advertising of books by publishers, even the placement of authors on television and radio programs, and the commissioning of seductive cover art for paperbacks.

Merchandising is the responsibility of businesses; publishers are businesses ("like any other," some of them insist, though many readers still prefer to think of publishing as different from selling gelatin or socks); and the publishing business, "like any other," has come under increasing pressures to conglomerate, rationalize, maximize profits, and cut marginal products from the line. The decision of the Oxford University Press, announced in November 1998, to cancel at one stroke its entire list of contemporary poetry, was a stunning example. The poetry list was not even losing money, and the press is very rich (in July 1999 it passed on £87 million in profits to the university). The decision was greeted by most observers as a Philistine maneuver unworthy of a great university press, but defended in the usual terms–the low turnover of poetry and the need to concentrate on more-popular titles, presumably anthologies such as *The Oxford Book of Animal Poems*.

Book reviewing occupies a more complex niche in the world of books or the literary establishment. The reviewer is not working for the publisher and, though he or she presumably favors a healthy trade in books, is (when writing for an ethical reviewing outlet) immune to obvious commercial pressures on the expression of critical judgment. Francis Wheen, an experienced literary journalist, provides a grimmer vision of the reviewing establishment in *Lord Gnome's Literary Companion* (1994), insisting that it is almost impossible to escape conflicts of interest, from the simple kind in which one is asked to review the book of a friend or enemy, to a more complex kind, resulting from media integration;

the reviewer for the *Sunday Times* is aware that its owner, Rupert Murdoch, also owns HarperCollins publishers, one of the largest conglomerates. Wheen attributes the compromised reviewing establishment to "the network of debts and allegiances that is literary London, bearing in mind that 'London' in this sense reaches out to include even our promising young writer in Warrington"–that is, the remoter reaches of the provinces.

In *A Vain Conceit: British Fiction in the 1980s* (1989), D. J. Taylor, a prolific reviewer as well as a novelist, has analyzed the state of literary journalism with some care. He draws the boundaries liberally:

> the literary establishment has innumerable redoubts: the English departments of provincial universities, an Oxbridge common room or two, elegant houses in Campden Hill Square, cramped metropolitan flats harbouring junior playwrights, gloomy bedsitters in Camden Town containing X the aspirant novelist whose 800-page handwritten manuscript An Ill Wind has just come back from its seventeenth publisher and who pays the rent by writing reviews for the *London Magazine*.

Despite this large and miscellaneous world, Taylor believes that "the English novel is consistently let down by a deferential reviewing establishment with an engrained reluctance to condemn inferior work": that reviewing "is a racket, a pleasant and sweetly conducted racket, but a racket all the same, in which everybody more or less knows everybody else and gamely conspires in mutual backslapping."

This depressing perception of literary reviewing comes, in both cases, from insiders, and it may be that a certain amount of personal dissatisfaction or even bad conscience has led to such sweeping generalizations. From another perspective, that of the reader and purchaser of English fiction, reviews do not seem so compromised. Whatever the mixture of motives in their authors–deference, fear, desire to sell a book to one of the decreasing number of publishers, personal feelings for the author–nevertheless, book reviews provide the most unbiased public information available to the prospective reader.

Reviewers in Britain are often novelists themselves. Though it is no longer possible to make a living just from reviewing books, as it was in the days of George Orwell and Cyril Connolly, it is apparently still an attractive way of earning additional money, even for the novelist whose sales would seem to make it unnecessary. Prolific novelists such as Anita Brookner and Julian Barnes appear often as reviewers in a variety of journals. Jonathan Coe, Nicholas Shakespeare, Shena Mackay, and Isabel Colegate, all included in this volume, review regularly. Ferdinand Mount is both a prolific novelist and the editor of one of the most important reviews, the *TLS,* just as Martin Amis, Julian Barnes, and Sebastian Faulks, among the outstanding post–1980 British novelists, also spent time as literary editors for daily newspapers or fortnightly reviews while beginning their careers in fiction.

Two ways in which the literary establishment stakes out its positions—both always involving reviewers and both occupying the contested ground somewhere between objective criticism (if such a thing exists) and book marketing—are the awarding of literary prizes and the annual naming of books of the year. The big literary prizes given annually are the Booker Prize (one winner chosen from a shortlist of six novels), the Whitbread Award (four winners, two of them novels), and the Orange (one winner, chosen from a shortlist for which only women are eligible). The judging panels mix the creative, the critical, and the commercial. For instance, the judges for the 2000 Whitbread novel of the year are novelist Robert Harris, Hartley Moorhouse of Borders Books, and broadcaster Jenni Murray; for the Whitbread First Novel Award, they are authors Kate Saunders and Nigel Williams and Erica Wagner, the literary editor of *The Times.* The 1999 Booker Prize was judged by Gerald Kaufman (chairman), a politician; Boyd Tonkin, the literary editor of *The Independent;* Natasha Walker, a literary journalist, mostly for *The Guardian;* John Sutherland, a don at London University; and Shena Mackay, a novelist. That political and other extraliterary considerations sometimes shape decisions in such competitions, that axes are ground and compromises occur, is obvious. In many cases members of the judging panel have already reviewed one or more of the books before they are listed for the Booker, and, though the situation is usually considered unethical, it is hard to see how a busy literary journalist can always avoid it. (For a fuller treatment of British literary prizes, see *DLB Yearbook: 1998,* pp. 210–214.)

The autumn closing dates of eligibility for the major prizes help to dictate the publication dates of promising literary fiction in Britain, and the winter is generally a slower time. This circumstance may be partly why so many magazines and newspapers fill their books pages, between late November and the end of the year, with books of the year, though Wheen offers a different explanation: "Editors like them because they don't have to pay for them. Contributors like them because it's flattering to be asked and they can conspicuously do favours. Booksellers like them because they come at Christmas, helping baffled donkeys spend their money." For whatever reason, they are a nearly universal feature of newspapers and magazines with serious books sections. The custom is that each contributor names about three books; sometimes the third is an "overrated" book, so only two are recommended. Variations include the people who vote for old books on the grounds that they have only now gotten around to reading them, the people who ostentatiously name only books not available in England or even in English (Anthony Burgess was famous for this practice), and those who contrive to praise themselves. The most brazen instance was that of Jeanette Winterson, who in 1992 used her space to announce that "My own *Written on the Body* is this year's most profound and profoundly misunderstood book. A fiction which dismantles the scaffolding of the 19th century novel, replacing time, place, situation, character, even gender, with an intense consciousness." Winterson made herself ridiculous by transgressing the unwritten rules that would have allowed her to praise another novelist who in turn praised her, but not to praise her own book directly.

Acknowledging the foibles of reviewers, especially novelist-reviewers, and the human temptations and conflicts to which reviewers and literary editors are necessarily subject must not obscure the breadth and, in some cases, depth of the opportunities for a good book to be well reviewed. A major novel by an established writer, published by a frontline press, will usually receive many reviews, written by well-qualified reviewers, in daily, weekly, and monthly publications. All the broadsheet or quality newspapers do a good job of reviewing such books. For instance, J. M. Coetzee's *Disgrace,* the eventual 1999 Booker Prize winner, was reviewed, between June 26 and August 21, in *The Daily Telegraph, The Scotsman, The Independent, The Guardian, The Sunday Times, The Observer, The Irish Times,* and *The Times,* as well as the July *Literary Review.* All of these reviews were stand-alone features between six hundred and one thousand words in length. In almost every case there was another story when *Disgrace* made the Booker shortlist (announced in late August), another handicapping the respective candidates, another at the time of its award (in November), and at least one more on reactions to that award. *The Indepen-*

dent published its books of the year compilation on November 20; five contributors mentioned *Disgrace*. (That two of them—Boyd Tonkin and Shena Mackay—were also Booker judges perhaps made it mandatory that they honor Coetzee.) Coetzee is more self-effacing than many authors (for instance, he did not come to the Booker ceremony) and he lives in South Africa, so the quality papers carried fewer features and interviews than is often the case with celebrated literary fiction and its authors. The author interview is often interspersed with a review of the novel and constitutes a quasi-review with more overtones of biography, personality, and celebrity than the standard sort.

The list of newspapers reviewing *Disgrace* is a good guide to the sites where novel reviewing is given most importance. Though some of the tabloid or mass-market papers (for instance, *The Evening Standard*) have books sections, the most serious reviewing is in the broadsheets. *The Times* runs books sections twice a week, on Thursday and Saturday; *The Guardian* on Saturday; *The Independent* on Saturday; the Sunday-only papers, *The Observer* and *The Sunday Times*, both have book review sections. *The Sunday Times*, while in some ways exemplary, also manages to cause unease among observers of the literary picture. Its books supplement is a separate, sixteen-page section; its example is credited with causing other newspapers to expand their review section. Likewise, *The Sunday Times* increased the compensation for reviewers. Wheen, writing in 1994, claimed that "in the mid–1980s, largely to keep up with Rupert Murdoch's *Sunday Times,* many national newspapers belatedly started paying their reviewers properly: contributors who had been accustomed to receive £50 [about $80] for a 700–word review suddenly found that it was now worth £200 [about $320]." These developments should be welcome—Wheen writes that "as we lurch towards the new, bookless millennium, literature and its service industries are in surprisingly robust financial health"—and the unease may be attributable to other factors. One is the ownership of *The Sunday Times* (as well as the daily *Times*): Rupert Murdoch's News Corporation, which also owns *The Sun* (Britain's most successful and most lowbrow daily tabloid); its Sunday counterpart, *The News of the World;* various satellite television companies; and HarperCollins publishers—as well as America's Fox television network, *TV Guide, The New York Post,* and a large slice of U.S. publishing.

The Sunday Times books section may seem superficially like *The New York Times Book Review*. It has a major review that occupies the front page; inside are additional full-length reviews, best-seller lists, and brief reviews. The difference is in scope. During the month of September 1999, *The Sunday Times* averaged fourteen full reviews a week, including eleven full reviews of novels, two of which were of mystery and detection. In the same month *The New York Times Book Review* ran between thirteen and twenty-four full reviews a week, with no fewer than four novels reviewed and no more than nine. Likewise, though *The New York Times Book Review* seems to devote most of its attention (like *The Sunday Times*) to nonfiction, there is a less perceptible agenda to the featured nonfiction. In *The Sunday Times* the featured review is often of a book that has recently been or is currently being serialized in another section of the paper. The newspaper's interests in royal biography, particularly if discreditable, and in other sorts of popular scandal are heavily represented in the choice of which books deserve reviewing. The front page of the 19 September 1999 issue, for instance, is devoted to *The Mistress* by Victoria Griffin; nothing suggests that it was the most important book published that week, but it did provide an opportunity to print five photographs of famous mistresses (including Monica Lewinsky, Marilyn Monroe, and a naked Nell Gwyn), and the review is written by Margaret Cook, the spurned wife of an unfaithful Labour minister.

The most crucial difference between *The Times* and *The Sunday Times* and *The New York Times* is in their influence. *The New York Times* is one of three major English-language daily newspapers in New York, the capital of American publishing, and the only one of them to be taken seriously for its cultural commentary. Thus, its reviews have a significance out of all proportion to the circulation of the newspaper, the wisdom of its reviewers (no matter how wise), or any other matter. By contrast, the United Kingdom has many national newspapers, all published in London but distributed to the whole country. *The Times* is older than *The Independent* and *The Sunday Times* is more financially stable than *The Observer,* but it is by no means the "newspaper of record," either for news or for reviewing, that *The New York Times* is.

The Sunday Times has three features not found in its American counterparts. One of these is John Carey's "Books of the Century," a sort of ongoing revaluation of worthy titles, complete with ordering information. Another is the anonymous diary, including news from the world of books and booksellers, gossip about critics and prize judges, and funny blunders. (The diary is a regular feature of many British publications; *The Guardian* books page has one by "The Loafer," *The Telegraph,* one by "Newman Noggs.") The most useful column in *The Sunday Times* is "Harvey Porlock," which is a review of reviews. Usually examining the treatment given to two books each week, Porlock provides a cross-section of responses (including those in his own newspaper); among other things he almost always demonstrates that critical opinion in Britain is far from uniform and certainly far from uniformly deferential. In addition he brings out the small examples of snideness, the blind spots, and the occasional hypocrisies of reviewers. A typical comment: "Several of Strong's reviews have been unattractively personal. '*The Spirit of Britain* is a topdown cultural history. Unfortunately, Sir Roy has so little up top himself that he is not the man for his self-appointed job,' sneered Eric Griffiths in *The Guardian*." Porlock's subjects are in rough proportion to the contents of the books section, that is, mostly about nonfiction titles.

As for the weekly press, Harvey Porlock has commented:

> How is fiction faring these days? The answer depends on which literary magazine you read. *The London Review of Books* virtually ignores it altogether—of 42 titles covered in the last three issues, the novel was represented by an unlikely trio of Thomas Harris, Zoe Heller and Ernest Hemingway. *The Literary Review* tends the other way, with critic after critic showering extravagant praise on the month's offerings.

The London Review of Books is a counterpart and offshoot of *The New York Review of Books;* like that magazine, it was founded during a newspaper labor dispute—in this case, during the 1979 lockout by which Rupert Murdoch broke the power of the newspaper unions, moved his operations out of Fleet Street, and earned the undying enmity of the British Left. For six months *The London Review of Books* appeared as an insert in *The New York Review of Books;* since 1980 it has been a fortnightly. Like its American counterpart, it features long and ruminative essays and a powerful and polemical letters section. It does not do a good job of reviewing fiction, however. A typical issue (25 November 1999) included poems, letters, reviews of nonfiction, and a diary, but nothing about the novel.

Similarly preoccupied, though not to the same extent, is the weekly *Spectator*. For years it was one of a pair of weeklies, the other being *The New Statesman* founded by famous Fabian Socialists, including Bernard Shaw. *The Spectator* was conservative, *The New Statesman* liberal to radical. Each carried political commentary, columns (including the essential diary), and a good selection of reviews. *The New Statesman* has fallen on hard times and changed its name and ownership frequently; though it still reviews books, they are, as one might expect, heavily tilted toward politics and history. The same is true in *The Spectator*. In one month in 1999 there were forty-four books reviewed, eleven of which were novels; however, of those eleven, three titles were American (including one posthumous Hemingway novel), two Indian, one Russian, and one French. Thus an average of one British novel a week earned a review.

The situation is marginally more encouraging in the most estimable British review, the *TLS*. (Though part of the Times/News Corporation empire and thus also owned by Rupert Murdoch, the *TLS* is not in any real sense a supplement to *The Times* and has a sufficiently independent identity.) The *TLS* appears weekly and is usually thirty-six or forty pages long. It typically runs forty to forty-four book reviews, in addition to letters to the editor, competitions, poems, commentary, and diary features. Of these, six or seven are typically fiction reviews, though, since the *TLS* also regularly notices American, European, and subcontinental titles, there are not six or seven reviews of contemporary British fiction. The current editor of the *TLS* is Ferdinand Mount (see entry in this volume), who, in addition to being a political commentator for *The Sunday Times* and (during the Thatcher years) a political operative for the Conservative Party, is also a novelist. Whether Mount's editorship has made the journal more sensitive to fiction, or profuse in reviewing it, is not clear, though Ian McIntyre has praised Mount for improving it in at least one respect: "Over the past seven years he has been conducting a highly successful irrigation programme at the *TLS,* territory previously notorious for its aridity."

Perhaps the most generous reviewing of contemporary British novels appears in *The Literary Review,* a monthly journal of modest circulation, edited by Auberon Waugh. Waugh occupies a peculiar position in the British book world. He is primarily a columnist and editor, and a humorous or satiric commentator notable for his intransigent opposition to the main lines of modern culture (he is particularly scathing on the influence of American culture on Europe, affecting to blame AIDS and other ills on "hamburger gases"). He writes a column for each issue of *The Literary Review* called "From the Pulpit," expressing his views on a variety of topics, including the excesses of feminism, the desirability of returning to "poetry that rhymes, scans and makes sense" (there is a "real poetry" competition in each issue, limited to poems of this sort), and the "lunatic preferences of so many politically and socially disoriented English teachers." Literacy is on the wane, Western civilization under attack from the Left, from the United States, from political correctness; novels, Waugh reckons, may continue to be published, but he will publish no more (he is the author of five) because of the critical standards imposed by politicized socialist reviewers.

Despite the gloomy view of the world and the world of letters delivered from the pulpit, the rest of the magazine is full of enthusiasm for books and particularly for fiction. A typical issue might consist of fifty or so reviews, in the course of which between fifteen and twenty fiction titles will be reviewed, some of them, indeed, American or otherwise non-British; but in terms of percentage of space devoted to contemporary fiction, *The Literary Review* is doing a better job than any of its competitors, which Waugh dismisses briskly in an editorial explaining why publishers should advertise in his journal:

Literary Review is not the only magazine catering for those interested in literature. There is also the *Times Literary Supplement,* taken by many libraries and no doubt read by some of the academics who wish to write for it, and the *London Review of Books,* said to be read by many Americans in London who mistake it for the *New York Review of Books,* some of whom might well buy books occasionally. . . . There is still good money to be made from publishing good books. There are still people waiting to buy them, although with the new emphasis on serialisation, it would seem that many publishers have forgotten about selling books which cannot be packaged like tomatoes.

No survey of the means of reviewing and otherwise bringing to light new British fiction is complete without mentioning the broadcast media. Both radio and television devote more attention to reviews, author interviews, and other "notices" of contemporary novels and novelists than their counterparts in the United States. The shows include *Bookmark* on BBC-2 and *Omnibus* on BBC-1 as well as *Late Review* on BBC-2 and *Book Choice* on Channel 4 (all television); radio programs devoted to books include *Books & Company* and *Open Book.*

One of the main venues for such notice is *The South Bank Show,* produced by London Weekend Television and broadcast on ITV. Its presenter for many years has been Melvyn Bragg (now Lord Bragg), well-known as a broadcaster (he has also contributed to *Start the Week* and *The Lively Arts* on the BBC) and novelist. *The South Bank Show* is not a program about literature, but it has featured many authors in sympathetic and, most important, long interviews accompanied by analysis and appreciation of their work. Inevitably, the reception of *The South Bank Show* has been affected by people's feelings about Melvyn Bragg, who is one of those nearly ubiquitous figures—playwright and screenwriter, author of sixteen novels and many nonfiction books, Labour party supporter (ennobled by Prime Minister Tony Blair), friend of Princess Diana—who provoke resentment. His 1999 novel, *The Soldier's Return,* received mostly good reviews, but as Harvey Porlock noted, it was "the first Bragg novel for years that has been reviewed without pointless, chippy references to the author's broadcasting persona." That *The South Bank Show* appears on Independent Television, along with *Mad about Pets* and *Who Wants to Be a Millionaire?,* provides license for those who wish to dismiss Bragg as a populist middlebrow; but his television show undoubtedly reaches millions of viewers who read none of the books sections of the quality newspapers, not to mention the low-circulation journals like *The Literary Review* and *The New Statesman.*

One other site for reviewing is quite different from all the others: *Private Eye,* a fortnightly satirical magazine. Francis Wheen, whose jaundiced assessment of English reviewing has been cited already, is the editor of *Lord Gnome's Literary Companion,* a compilation of *Private Eye* reviews from the 1980s and 1990s; in his preface he attributes the fact that most best-selling novels are never reviewed at all to the failure of literary editors to understand the reading public. He continues:

> This is where *Private Eye* comes in. The "Literary Review" page at the back of the magazine is just as likely to notice Jack Higgins or Catherine Cookson as Iris Murdoch or Sir Kingsley Amis. Whatever the genre there is a willingness to appraise critically. More importantly, it attempts to explain the unseen forces that police this literary culture—the literary agents, the editorial directors, the hype-merchants, the back-scratchers.
>
> In keeping with *Private Eye* tradition, the articles are anonymous. Just as the news pages of the *Eye* have long provided a sanctuary for stories that journalists are unable to get into their own newspapers, so the literary section allows professional reviewers a freedom that they can't find in the other papers for which they write. . . . The whole point of the "Literary Review" page is that there are no sacred cows, no inhibitions, no special favours, no treacly euphemisms. Messy work, but someone's got to do it.

In practice, as one might expect, the freedom from inhibitions and the anonymity of reviewers permit a greater vigor in mostly negative criticism, ranging from characterizations such as "Bill Buford, a portly American braggart" to more analytical passages: "the conspiracy to promote Jeanette Winterson as a major talent continues—one of the most culpable examples of the present tendency to judge a book by criteria other than the ability of the author to write." In practice *Private Eye* does devote more attention than other reviewing media to best-sellers—almost always deriding them, but it derides most of the books which come under its purview. Years ago, Auberon Waugh, at one time the most influential fiction reviewer in Britain, declared that "the key quality in reviewing is not judiciousness or erudition or good taste, least of all is it moderation. It is liveliness of response." In the "Literary Review" section of *Private Eye* (without doubt named for the magazine edited by Waugh, a longtime contributor to *Private Eye* himself), there is no shortage of that quality.

What is in short supply is coverage. *Private Eye* appears twenty-six times a year and its "Literary Review" usually notices one book, not always a novel. *The Literary Review* itself may notice two hundred novels in a good year, with others reviewing novels in the proportions listed above. But of course this number is an infinitesimal proportion of the novels actually published. With the number of volumes of serious literary fiction published in the United Kingdom each year probably between six thousand and ten thousand, brief reflection on even the two to four fiction titles a week reviewed in *The Sunday Times,* or the fifteen a month in *The Literary Review* and the lesser numbers in *The London Review of Books* will show how inadequate this coverage would be to the supply of new books, even if each of these publications reviewed entirely different books instead of demonstrating the remarkable overlap of the books each editor judges worthy of review.

What this overview suggests, finally, is that while book reviewing provides an important service to the book-buying public, it is less crucial in promoting the distribution of literature than, presumably, reviewers and their editors would like. At one end of the spectrum are the books that are seldom reviewed but sell in the hundreds of thousands anyway, and thus are review-proof or review-independent—the works of Catherine Cookson, Danielle Steele, and Stephen King—and all those which, though not blockbusters, fall into the genre category: mysteries, romances, science fiction, and so on, to which *The Telegraph* devotes a one-sentence plot summary, more than most other quality newspapers give them. Again, Francis Wheen is acute on this phenomenon. "In their own way," he writes, "literary editors are as out of touch with the reading public as any Eng. Lit. lecturer. Many of the authors who regularly dominate the best-seller lists— Jean M. Auel, Shaun Hutson, Barbara Taylor Bradford, Delia Smith, Rosemary Conley—are *never reviewed at all.*" A review of two novels by Jack Higgins and Frederick Forsyth picks up the theme:

> One of the ironies of the book trade in this country is that most of the attention is paid to the books that nobody buys. The young novelist commended by the Sunday newspaper as "a writer to watch out for," the biographer neatly anatomising some Bloomsbury hanger-on: both may receive plenty of review coverage, both add lustre to a publisher's list, but nobody much will actually pay money for their work.
>
> The great British book-buying public reserves its book tokens for the great stodgy monsters that will pay a publisher's Garrick Club bill long after the slim first novels are nestling in the remainder bin.

An illustration from a recent best-seller list reinforces the point. The ten best-selling fiction titles include a murder mystery, a thriller, a historical romance set in Napoleonic times, and a novel about sex among the polo-playing set, all of which are installments in ongoing series. There is another historical romance, a contemporary romance about a woman involved in a love triangle, and a novel by a popular newspaper columnist. There are, in addition, three "literary" novels—Joanne Harris's *Chocolat,* shortlisted for the Whitbread Award for best novel; Ahdad Soueif's

The Map of Love, shortlisted for the Booker Prize; and J. M. Coetzee's *Disgrace,* the Booker winner.

These three books received enormous publicity in the books pages, being widely reviewed, discussed as potential prizewinners, and named in books of the year features. A more characteristic best-seller, however, is— for instance—Bernard Cornwell's *Sharpe's Trafalgar,* the newest in a series about an officer named Sharpe fighting in Wellington's army. Though it is regularly mentioned in newspaper lists of best-seller, there is no indication that it was reviewed anywhere, a fact which has apparently not affected its success. Jilly Cooper's *Score,* the sexy polo novel, did receive some reviews, mostly negative. As Harvey Porlock commented, "Nothing enrages critics more than the review-proof popular author. They rant, they mock, they stamp their feet—and yet still the author's latest blockbuster soars effortlessly to the top of the bestseller list." *Score* soared in spite of sarcastic notices in *The London Evening Standard* and *The Daily Mail* (both tabloid newspapers) and *The Daily Telegraph;* it was also reviewed in *The Sunday Telegraph* and (favorably) in *The New Statesman.*

David Caute, who is the subject of an entry in this volume, wrote a novel in 1998 that illustrates some of the unpredictable features of the book publishing, reviewing, and selling arts. *Fatima's Scarf,* his latest book in a long career, is a long and dense work focusing on an Egyptian/British novelist whose book outrages Muslims worldwide and especially in the fictional north England town of Brudderford. The middle section of the novel, a magic-realist meditation on author Gamal Rahman's life and recent Egyptian history, is not unlike the style of Salman Rushdie, and the plot obviously alludes to the Rushdie case and the outcry against his novel *The Satanic Verses* (1992).

Fatima's Scarf was rejected by twenty-five publishers, and while there may be many reasons for declining to publish a long novel by a novelist who is far from Jilly Cooper's degree of popularity, Caute attributed much of their reluctance to cowardice: not so much fear of Muslim reaction but fear of irritating Salman Rushdie. At least one publisher, in her letter of rejection, admitted she was unwilling to risk her relationship with Rushdie.

In the end Caute published the novel himself, under the imprint of Totterdown Books. He paid some £14,000 ($22,000) to publish it and arranged distribution through a small company, aided by his own appeals to bookshops. Perhaps assisted by Caute's own record as a writer (and critic—he is the former literary editor of *The New Statesman*), his book received reviews in the *Daily* and *Sunday Telegraph, The Literary Review, The New Statesman, The Guardian, The Observer, The Times, The Sunday Times,* and *The Independent,* as well as Scottish newspapers, including *The Herald* of Glasgow and *The*

Scotsman. With the exception of negative reviews in *The New Statesman* and *The Independent* (whose reviewer, novelist and activist Tariq Ali, seems to be the inspiration for one of the characters in the book) the reviews were strongly positive. Many of them were written by fellow novelists, such as Amanda Craig, Allen Massie, and Maggie Gee; Melanie Phillips, lead reviewer for *The Observer,* praised the novel highly. In another unusual development, the judging panel for the 1998 Booker Prize requested or "called in" *Fatima's Scarf* (novels are usually nominated by their publishers), and it appeared on the "long list" of about twenty titles from which the shortlist and winner were duly chosen.

Thus, the quality and importance of *Fatima's Scarf* overcame the reluctance of publishers; it was nominated for the most important British literary award and was reviewed in all the important outlets and praised by important literary voices. Nevertheless, paperback publishers shied away, and when the paperback version of the novel appeared in spring of 1999, the imprint was, once again, Totterdown.

A more ordinary story is that of a book at the other end of the spectrum from the unreviewed or irrelevantly reviewed blockbusters, one of the hundreds or thousands of novels that are of the same type as those widely reviewed, and may even be of the same quality, but which, for some reason, fail to rise to critical visibility. Candida Crewe's 1998 novel, *The Last to Know,* belongs to this latter category. Published by Century, it is a mainstream novel about a man's mysterious decision to disappear, leaving his wife in the dark and, eventually, his almost equally unmotivated decision to return to her. It is a good book. Crewe was the author of five previous novels, a regular reviewer and journalist for a range of London broadsheets, and the daughter of two writers, thus hardly estranged from the literary world. Her novel was never featured on *The South Bank Show* and was not nominated for any of the major (or, for that matter, minor) literary awards. It was reviewed by *The Independent,* given 182 words as part of a "summing-up-several-books-not-worthy-of-their-own-reviews" column; in a similar column in *The Telegraph,* it received 221 words. In 1999 *The Times* devoted all of 76 words to the paperback of *The Last to Know.* Yet, perhaps the most important fact about this shortlist of critical notices is that the book did appear in a paperback edition. Reviews are important. But even modest, midrange novels can succeed without much merchandising help from reviews, which, considering how few books receive it, is a reassuring fact.

—Merritt Moseley

Acknowledgments

This book was produced by Bruccoli Clark Layman, Inc. Karen L. Rood is senior editor. Carol Fairman was the in-house editor. She was assisted by Charles Brower and Karen L. Rood.

Production manager is Philip B. Dematteis.

Administrative support was provided by Ann M. Cheschi, Dawnca T. Williams, and Mary A. Womble.

Accountant is Kathy Weston. Accounting assistant is Amber L. Coker.

Copyediting supervisor is Phyllis A. Avant. The copyediting staff includes Brenda Carol Blanton, Melissa D. Hinton, William Tobias Mathes, Jennifer S. Reid, Nancy E. Smith, and Elizabeth Jo Ann Sumner. Freelance copyeditor is Rebecca Mayo.

Editorial associates are Michael S. Allen, Margo Dowling, Richard K. Galloway, and Michael S. Martin.

Layout and graphics supervisor is Janet E. Hill. The graphics staff includes Karla Corley Brown and Zoe R. Cook.

Office manager is Kathy Lawler Merlette.

Photography editors are Charles Mims, Scott Nemzek, and Paul Talbot.

Digital photography supervisor is Joseph M. Bruccoli. Digital photographic copy work was performed by Abraham R. Layman.

SGML supervisor is Cory McNair. The SGML staff includes Linda Dalton Mullinax, Frank Graham, Jason Paddock, and Alex Snead.

Systems manager is Marie L. Parker.

Typesetting supervisor is Kathleen M. Flanagan. The typesetting staff includes Sarah Mathes, Mark J. McEwan, Patricia Flanagan Salisbury, and Alison Smith. Freelance typesetters are Wanda Adams and Vicki Grivetti.

Walter W. Ross did library research. He was assisted by Steven Gross and the following librarians at the Thomas Cooper Library of the University of South Carolina: circulation department head Tucker Taylor; reference department head Virginia W. Weathers; Brette Barclay, Marilee Birchfield, Paul Cammarata, Gary Geer, Michael Macan, Tom Marcil, Rose Marshall, and Sharon Verba; interlibrary loan department head John Brunswick; and Robert Arndt, Jo Cottingham, Hayden Battle, Barry Bull, Marna Hostetler, Marieum McClary, Erika Peake, and Nelson Rivera, interlibrary loan staff.

Dictionary of Literary Biography® • Volume Two Hundred Thirty-One

British Novelists Since 1960
Fourth Series

Dictionary of Literary Biography

Peter Ackroyd
(5 October 1949 –   )

Andrew Biswell
University of Warwick

See also the Ackroyd entry in *DLB 155: Twentieth-Century British Literary Biographers.*

BOOKS: *Ouch* (London: Curiously Strong Press, 1971);

London Lickpenny (London: Ferry Press, 1973);

Notes for a New Culture: An Essay on Modernism (London: Vision Press, 1976; New York: Barnes & Noble, 1976);

Country Life (London: Ferry Press, 1978);

Dressing Up, Transvestism and Drag: The History of an Obsession (New York: Simon & Schuster, 1979; London: Thames & Hudson, 1979);

Ezra Pound (London: Thames & Hudson; 1980); republished as *Ezra Pound and His World* (New York: Scribners, 1980; London: Thames & Hudson, 1987);

The Great Fire of London (London: Hamilton, 1982; Chicago: University of Chicago Press, 1988);

The Last Testament of Oscar Wilde (London: Hamilton, 1983; New York: Harper & Row, 1983);

T. S. Eliot (London: Hamilton, 1984; New York: Simon & Schuster, 1984);

Hawksmoor (London: Hamilton, 1985; New York: Harper & Row, 1985);

Chatterton (London: Hamilton, 1987; New York: Grove, 1988);

The Diversions of Purley and Other Poems (London: Hamilton, 1987);

First Light (London: Hamilton, 1989; New York: Grove Weidenfeld, 1989);

Dickens (London: Sinclair-Stevenson, 1990; New York: HarperCollins, 1990);

Introduction to Dickens (London: Sinclair-Stevenson, 1991; New York: Ballasting, 1992);

Peter Ackroyd (courtesy of the author)

English Music (London: Hamilton, 1992; New York: Knopf, 1992);

The House of Doctor Dee (London: Hamilton, 1993; London & New York: Penguin, 1994);

Dan Leno and the Limehouse Golem (London: Sinclair-Stevenson, 1994); republished as *The Trial of*

Elizabeth Cree: A Novel of the Limehouse Murders (New York: N. A. Talese / Doubleday, 1995);

Blake (London: Sinclair-Stevenson, 1995; New York: Knopf, 1996);

Milton in America (London: Sinclair-Stevenson, 1996; New York: Nan A. Talese, 1997);

The Life of Thomas More (London: Chatto & Windus, 1998; New York: Nan A. Talese, 1998);

The Plato Papers: A Novel (London: Chatto & Windus, 1999); republished as *The Plato Papers: A Prophecy* (New York: Nan A. Talese, 2000);

Secret London (London: Sinclair-Stevenson, forthcoming 2000).

Peter Ackroyd's novels and biographies have consistently hovered on the boundaries of conventional literary form. While his historical novels characteristically assume the disguise of an imaginary journal or confessional narrative presented as a "discovered" manuscript, his biographical works have increasingly made use of the devices of fiction—most conspicuously in *Dickens* (1990), a predominantly nonfiction work that includes significant fictional and autobiographical interludes. The majority of Ackroyd's novels share an overriding preoccupation with an individual who is imaginatively in touch with the past of London, or of England in general. These fictions usually employ some element of the magical or the supernatural to effect an intense, hallucinatory convergence of past and present.

Ackroyd offers his readers a series of almost spiritual meetings with a bygone England. His histories have consistently refused to confront the uncomfortable realities of industrialized England and of its attempt to construct a global empire. These aspects of nineteenth-century England are replaced in Ackroyd's worldview by a vastly energetic "sub-magic realism," which speaks in powerful ways to his large and loyal readership. Some critics, however, distrust Ackroyd's writings, fiction and nonfiction alike, for the liberties they take with history. They have also faulted his "unscholarly" obsession with the "hidden" London that stands solidly at the center of each novel.

Peter Ackroyd was born in Paddington Hospital on 5 October 1949, the only son of Graham Ackroyd and Audrey Whiteside. His parents separated a short time after his birth, and he settled with his mother in East Acton, where he lived in a council house near Wormwood Scrubs jail until the age of seventeen. Nothing is known about Graham Ackroyd. Audrey Whiteside worked as a personnel officer for a firm that made metal boxes. Their son was educated by Benedictine monks at Saint Benedict's School in the Borough of Ealing, on the western edge of Greater London, at the end of the District Line on the London underground railway system. His interest in the geography of London began at an early age. As he told Francis Gilbert in 1999, "My grandmother would often take me into the City and show me things like the Old Curiosity Shop in Portsmouth Street, Holborn—which isn't actually the original shop that Dickens based his novel upon. This was something I found out when I was researching my biography of Dickens."

In 1968 Ackroyd enrolled at Clare College, Cambridge, where he took a degree in English in 1971. As a working-class student funded by a local authority grant, Ackroyd found the transition to Cambridge life difficult at first. According to Gilbert, Ackroyd tried to disguise his London accent when he arrived at the university: "I spent hours trying to get certain vowel sounds right. I still sometimes get them wrong and slip into Cockney." After graduation, Ackroyd was awarded a Mellon Fellowship at Yale University, where he spent two years doing graduate work. He returned to England in 1973 as literary editor of *The Spectator,* a right-wing weekly political magazine. In 1978 he became joint managing editor at *The Spectator,* a post he held until 1982, when he resigned to write full time. By then he had completed one novel, *The Great Fire of London* (1982); the publisher Hamish Hamilton had given him a contract to write a book about T. S. Eliot; and he was about to start another novel, *The Last Testament of Oscar Wilde* (1983).

Ackroyd is reticent about the details of his private life, but it is known that for many years he shared a house with his partner, Brian Kuhn. After Ackroyd won several lucrative literary prizes, he and Kuhn left London in 1990, moving first to a cottage in Lyme Regis and then, in 1993, to a large house in north Devon, with a swimming pool, lake, and park. When Kuhn died from an AIDS-related illness in 1994, Ackroyd sold his Devon property and moved back to London. He currently lives in Islington, a fashionable district of north London.

Ackroyd started out as a poet, but his poetry consistently failed to attract readers. Most of the poems that Ackroyd chose to include in his collected poems, *The Diversions of Purley and Other Poems* (1987), are parodies or satires, ironic and dislocated utterances deprived of any concrete sense of who is speaking or to whom. The closing lines from "The first axiom" offer a characteristic example of Ackroyd's playful strangeness: "and so to bed, and so to bed, and so to bed, and so to bed / ouch / whatisthislifeiffullofcarewehavenotimeto / the supreme penalty / is is is is." The narrative poems, though more rewarding, are few in number. A poem called "The novel" seems to offer a proleptic commentary on some of Ackroyd's later fiction and biographies, particularly when the poem speaks of trying to celebrate prominent literary figures: "Ah these people, I wish I could immortalise them / like Ronald Firbank or even Graham Greene . . . well, / their breath can be traced like pale branches, / here today and gone tomorrow." Ackroyd has published no original poetry since *The Diversions of Purley and Other Poems,* but he integrates verse into his novels by writing poems in the voices of fictional characters. The most noteworthy example is the long poem written in imitation of William Blake, which appears in *English Music* (1992).

Ackroyd's illustrated biography *Ezra Pound* (1980), published in Thames and Hudson's Literary Lives series, is a courageous attempt to explain the Poundian aesthetic for the benefit of readers coming to the author of *The Cantos* (1948) for the first time. As a chronological narrative of the events of Pound's long life, this book is a model of brevity. There is informative discussion of the Vorticist movement and the background to the pioneering World War I magazine *Blast!* Ackroyd is extremely cautious in his critical judgments of Pound's poems, and he stops well short of saying, as other critics (notably Anthony Julius) have claimed, that the monstrous hatreds of fascism stand firmly at the heart of Pound's mature poetic. As a critical biography, *Ezra Pound* seems a little cursory if read alongside Humphrey Carpenter's later, full-length biography, *A Serious Character: The Life of Ezra Pound* (1988); but Ackroyd's book successfully established him as a chronicler of the Modernist period.

Ackroyd's first novel, *The Great Fire of London* (1982), is playful and intelligent; yet, its cleverness is not quite enough to sustain it as a novel. The book is tightly linked to Charles Dickens's *Little Dorrit* (1857) and details the modern-day attempts of Spenser Spender to make a motion-picture adaptation of Dickens's novel. The cast is an odd collection of eccentrics, drawn in the Dickensian style. Audrey Skelton, a deranged telephone operator, is so fascinated by Amy Dorrit (the "Little Dorrit" of the title) that she believes herself to be in touch with Amy's ghost, whom she contacts during a séance. One recurring theme is the extent to which London has changed since the age of Dickens: an amusement arcade now stands on the site of the old Marshalsea Prison, where William Dorrit was imprisoned in Dickens's book.

Many of the elements of Ackroyd's later fiction are present in his first published novel: the intersection of past and present, the detailed London urban setting, strong echoes of the works of Dickens, a talent for mimicry, and a concern with recording everyday speech. *The Great Fire of London* was respectfully reviewed as a good Dickensian pastiche, but it did not generate the level of excitement that greeted Ackroyd's more-mature novels.

Ackroyd's second novel, *The Last Testament of Oscar Wilde* (1983), is his first mock autobiography. The book

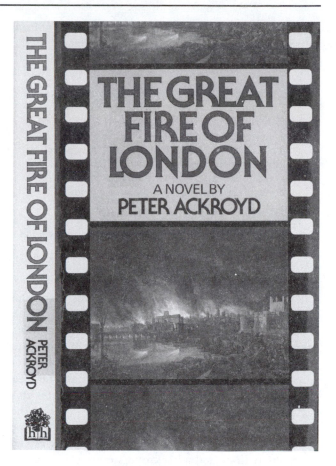

Dust jacket for Ackroyd's first novel (1982), about an attempt to make a movie version of Charles Dickens's novel Little Dorrit (1857)

is supposedly a journal that Oscar Wilde kept secretly between his arrival in Paris after being released from Reading Gaol, where he had served a sentence of hard labor for sodomy, and his death on 30 November 1900. The novel is a richly imaginative blend of recorded fact and Wildean epigrams, demonstrating Ackroyd's ability to enter into the language and mindset of his historical subject. Although the novel sustains a voice approximating that of the Irish playwright for nearly two hundred pages, Ackroyd's Wilde never quite matches the epigrammatic wit of the original. Writing for *TLS: The Times Literary Supplement* (28 April 1989), critic Claude Rawson estimated that the fictional Wilde "strikes me as being about 70 per cent convincing to knowing readers and probably more to others." Andrew Hislop, also writing in *TLS* (15 April 1983) went further to claim that *The Last Testament* was "consummate ventriloquism, so Wildean that it was easy to forget that it was make-believe and the result of research, hard work and a brilliant ear."

The novel is at its best when it deals in a general way with the sexual morality of late Victorian England

and criticizes the hypocrisy that lay behind the judicial persecution of Wilde and other homosexuals of the period. As Ackroyd's Wilde says,

> My affection for Lord Alfred Douglas gave a beauty and a dignity to the love between men which the English could not look upon without horror: that is why they sent me to prison. I could have had all the renters I wanted; the boys who sell themselves in Southwark or Clerkenwell are of no account, and it was only to be expected that I would shower red gold upon them in exchange for their pale bodies. That, after all, is the theory of capitalism. But that I should have conceived of a higher love, a love between equals–that they could not accept, for that there would be no forgiveness.

Ackroyd's next book was a biography of *T. S. Eliot* (1984), a project that aroused the displeasure of the poet's widow and literary executor, Valerie Eliot. The Eliot Estate refused Ackroyd permission to quote from Eliot's published work, except for the purposes of comment in a critical context. There was a blanket interdiction on quoting any of Eliot's unpublished letters or private papers. The likely explanation for this lack of co-operation is that Valerie Eliot was at the time preparing her edition of *The Letters of T. S. Eliot,* volume 1 of which appeared in 1988. The irony of these restrictions is that Ackroyd's extremely successful biography in many ways prepared the reading public for Valerie Eliot's edition of the letters and boosted the sales of her book.

Ackroyd's book manages to give a full portrait of its subject. Cleverly negotiating the serious restrictions imposed on his methodology, Ackroyd relied on the sharpness of his judgments to build a critical case, and the emerging portrait of Eliot is far from hostile. The book is especially memorable for its illuminating account of Eliot's first marriage, to Vivien Haigh-Wood. Ackroyd regards Vivien Eliot as an artist in her own right and sympathetically details her descent into madness, though he also takes care not to demonize Eliot as an unsympathetic husband, as other, less-fair-minded commentators have done.

Scholars still regard this biography as a key reference point in Eliot studies. *T. S. Eliot* was awarded the Whitbread Prize for the best biography of 1984 and was joint winner of the prestigious William Heinemann Award of the Royal Society of Literature.

Hawksmoor (1985), Ackroyd's earliest significant novel, is about the imagined history of London, insisting–perhaps a little too loudly, at times–on mystical connections between the past and present. In this case church architecture of the early eighteenth century provides the link between two temporally distant narratives. In the first narrative, told in what is intended to

sound like eighteenth-century English, architect and devil worshiper Nicholas Dyer and his assistant, Walter Pyne, build seven London churches in accordance with a 1711 Act of Parliament, which dictated that the city should be reconstructed following the Great Fire of 1666. In the twentieth-century narrative with which it is counterpointed, an urban detective, Nicholas Hawksmoor, investigates several ritual killings that have taken place in the churches in question. The chapters alternate between these two time periods, and the linking passages depend on verbal puns and echoes: for example, a conversation about time at the end of one section leads reasonably and smoothly into a discussion of clocks in the next.

Behind the novel stands the historical architect Nicholas Hawksmoor (1661–1736), whose six London churches, including Christ Church in Spitalfields, are noted examples of English vernacular Baroque, described by Sir Nikolaus Pevsner, in his *An Outline of European Architecture* (1942), as "megalomaniac" and "perverse." Ackroyd attributes passages from Hawksmoor's letters to his fictional architect and adds a seventh, imaginary church to Dyer's output, Little St Hugh in Blackstep Lane, built on the site of an ancient Druid temple and later the meeting place of a group of Satanists. Each of Dyer's churches is in fact consecrated to evil spirits by a human sacrifice made in its foundations.

Dyer and the twentieth-century Hawksmoor (whose stories turn out to be interdependent) stalk each other until, in the ambiguous final chapter, the detective at last confronts the old artificer, and the two men become one. Hawksmoor reads an incantation from Dyer's book of verses, ending with the words: "I saw a man who is not, nor ever could he be, / Hold up your hand and look, for you are he." He then sees a devilish shadow that has taken on his own image. "And when they spoke, they spoke with one voice."

Ackroyd's note of acknowledgment states that the version of history presented in this novel is entirely his invention, and he admits a specific and important debt to the poet, novelist, and self-styled "psycho-geographer" Iain Sinclair, whose book-length poem, *Lud Heat* (1975), first directed his attention to the strange characteristics of London churches. Sinclair has written on themes that are extremely close to those of Ackroyd's novels, including Jack the Ripper, the Dickensian reaches of the Thames downriver, necromancy, conspiracy, and strange disappearances. (Sinclair's works, which are consistently darker, more squalid, and more despairing than Ackroyd's, have just begun to find a popular readership.) In Sinclair's book of illustrated essays, *Liquid City* (1999), he identifies Ackroyd as one of the monuments of London. It is clear that these two men perceive London in similar ways.

Ackroyd's previous research on T. S. Eliot has a slight but perceptible influence on *Hawksmoor:* Dyer has a servant whose name is Eliot, and the book includes various Eliotian meditations on time as well as references to "hollow men," and other half-lines and phrases from Eliot's poems. As critic and novelist Alan Hollinghurst has pointed out in *TLS* (27 September 1985), "the essence of Dyer's possession of Hawksmoor is the simultaneity of experiences centuries apart, to which Dyer's churches are perversely capable of granting access—as all great art may be thought to transcend time." There are also recondite architectural allusions that the general reader may fail to recognize. For example, at one point in his journal Dyer writes that "Curved lines are more beautiful than Straight," a deliberate reversal of Sir Christopher Wren's statement, in one of his *Tracts,* that "Strait Lines are more beautiful than curved." Ackroyd demands a high level of literary competence from his readers if they are to apprehend the full complexity of his text at such moments.

Most of the critics agree that the eighteenth-century chapters of *Hawksmoor* are linguistically more lively than the twentieth-century detective narrative. Interviewed by *The New York Times,* in 1996, Ackroyd explained that he had spent four months in the British Library reading early-eighteenth-century printed books and the Nicholas Hawksmoor papers. He stated: "I wanted to assimilate the voice of the time, to train myself so I could write in that style without self-consciousness. . . . I'm not sure whether it's a historical novel set in the present or a contemporary novel set in the past. That's one of the puzzles the book sets for itself." *Hawksmoor* was awarded the Whitbread Award and the Guardian Fiction Prize for 1985.

Chatterton (1987), which was highly successful from a commercial point of view, is (along with *Hawksmoor*) a central work in the Ackroyd canon, the novel in which he articulates his thesis about the presence of the past most intelligently. The point of departure for the novel is the biography of the British poet and forger Thomas Chatterton (1752–1770), whose death by suicide was commemorated by Samuel Taylor Coleridge in his "Monody on the Death of Chatterton" (1794). Henry Wallis's painting *The Death of Chatterton* (1856)—for which the writer George Meredith served as the painter's model—is a cultural icon on prominent display in the Tate Gallery in London, and Ackroyd's novel examines the process whereby Chatterton's life and death have been appropriated into an English myth of unfulfilled literary potential and Romantic early death.

The central idea of Ackroyd's *Chatterton* is that the forger succeeded in faking his death in 1770 and lived on into old age. The protagonist in the twentieth-cen-

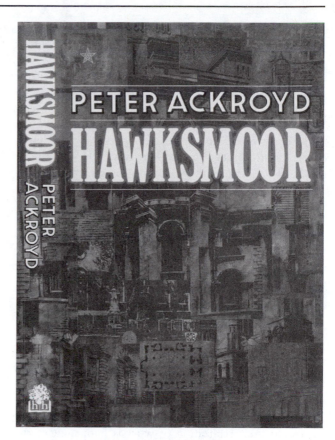

Dust jacket for Ackroyd's 1985 novel, in which a central character is based in part on architect Nicholas Hawksmoor (1661–1736), designer of six London churches

tury narrative, writer Charles Wychwood, becomes intrigued by the apparent discovery of a portrait of the elderly Chatterton and searches in Bristol for unpublished manuscripts to prove that the poet did not die at the age of eighteen. Wychwood suffers from a brain tumor, and his perceptions are distorted to such an extent that he may not be a reliable witness. Furthermore, the papers he finds may be the work of a second forger, and the novel cleverly demands that the reader evaluate evidence, manuscripts, forgeries, and (by implication) the notion of "the authentic." Such questions show Ackroyd to be working firmly in the self-referential tradition. Furthermore, by placing the daring question "What if . . . ?" at the forefront of this novel, Ackroyd established a formula that sustained him throughout the speculative novels he wrote after *Chatterton,* up to and including *Milton in America* (1996).

Chatterton was a critical success and did much to consolidate Ackroyd's reputation in Great Britain. Martin Dodsworth, reviewing the novel in *TLS* (11 September 1987), wrote that it was "ingenious and extraordinarily self-sustaining, not to say self-conscious. . . . All about the fiction there lie hints of an uncertainty not kept fully at bay, and never more so than in the final pages." After the publication of *Chatterton,* several years passed before Ackroyd produced another novel as strikingly original.

In *First Light* (1989) novelist Thomas Hardy stands behind the narrative, and his presence is so crucial to the plot that one thinks of him as a controlling intelligence. The story takes place in Hardy's Wessex; two of the characters have the surname Clare (after Angel Clare in Hardy's 1891 novel, *Tess of the D'Urbervilles*), there is a dog named Jude (after the title character of *Jude the Obscure,* 1895), and the action of the book mirrors that of an earlier Hardy novel, *Two on a Tower* (1882).

First Light concerns the archaeological discovery of an ancient burial site. Within the tomb is a sophisticated planetarium of uncertain origin, which might be the final resting place of the astrologer Merlin or the elusive burial place of Arthur (who is thought, in some versions of the myth, to have been the King of Wessex). The tomb is mysterious and perhaps haunted: strange voices are heard at the site, and items mysteriously disappear. Nearby, as in Hardy, there is a tower called Swithin's Column (named for the astronomer in *Two on a Tower*), where a death takes place. It is as if the characters unknowingly re-enact Hardy's pre-existing literary text, and their realization of what is happening is the pivotal moment of the book.

First Light is Ackroyd's first novel to be set entirely outside a city, and several reviewers made scathing remarks about the implausible dialect spoken by the rustic "peasant" characters. Yet, the book is convincing in its depiction of gay and lesbian characters, whose colloquial and eccentric language is recorded with relish and enthusiasm, in much the same manner as Dickens's characterizations. This novel is also not preoccupied, as had been Ackroyd's previous books, with the question of individual artistic genius, and thus it represents a change of direction. Despite these innovations, the critics agree that *First Light* is an artful and ambitious failure, probably because it strays too far from the urban setting that generally forms the backbone of Ackroyd's fiction.

Dickens (1990) is a big book in every sense: a 1,195-page biography that took five years to research and write. Its subject is the novelist who documented more of London than any other nineteenth-century writer, and the vast scale of Ackroyd's portrait is in part an act of homage to the size of Dickens's reputation. The prologue, which deals with the death of Dickens in 1870, is written as a parody of Dickens's sentimental style: "Charles Dickens was dead. He lay on a narrow green sofa—but there was room enough for him, so spare had he become—in the dining room of Gad's Hill Place. He had died in the house which he had first seen

as a small boy and which his father had pointed out to him as a suitable object of his ambitions." After this bravura opening, the book settles into an old-fashioned biographical narrative, untroubled by any literary theory that an academic biographer might have brought to bear on such a subject.

It is easy to see why the prospect of writing a biography of Dickens attracted Ackroyd, and some of the similarities between these two novelists are worth noting. Both fascinated by London, they also share an interest in the supernatural, a good ear for dialogue, and a conviction that time and history are important themes for the novelist. The first chapter of Dickens's *Bleak House* (1853) shows how alike Ackroyd's and Dickens's imaginations can be on occasion: "Implacable November weather. As much mud in the streets, as if the water had but recently retired from the face of the earth, and it would not be wonderful to meet a Megalosaurus, forty feet long or so, waddling like an elephantine lizard up Holborn-hill." One might usefully compare this passage with one of Matthew Palmer's visions in Ackroyd's *The House of Doctor Dee* (1993): "About a year ago I was walking by the Thames. Do you know, near Southwark? When suddenly I thought I saw a bridge of houses. A shimmering bridge, lying across the river. . . . It was like a bridge of light. It only lasted for a moment, and then it was gone. But there was, for that moment, a bridge connecting two shores."

The facts of Dickens's life are well known to most British readers, and one would be surprised, given the existence of a large and energetic scholarly tradition, if Ackroyd had discovered anything genuinely new about the Victorian novelist. Yet, *Dickens* is worth reading for its passages of imaginative reconstruction, the most prominent of which is the biographical symposium (described as "a true conversation between imagined selves") in chapter 14. Chatterton, Eliot, Dickens, and Wilde sit down to discuss literature, biography, and history. "If William Blake were here—" says Dickens at one point. "He will be joining us shortly," replies Chatterton. This chapter enlivens the narrative and offers important examples of Ackroydian self-criticism and parody.

In a somewhat daring gesture, the "author" interviews himself four-fifths of the way through the biography (in chapter 29), providing a summary of the construction of the book that is illuminating from a biographical point of view:

Take the example of footnotes. I was determined not to have any at all but then, in the last stages of composition, my nerve failed. I certainly did not intend to sit down and list every source for every quotation but I did compromise: I wrote little essays on my sources for

It would be out of place here to list the "literature of London" scripts because to a large extent it represents the literature of England; few novelists, poets and dramatists have not been touched by London. So we may name Chaucer, Shakespeare, Dickens, Pope, Dryden, Johnson, Blake, ~~Spen~~ and to myriad other writers who comprise a distinct and distinctive London world. That is matter of another book. All I wish to do here is list specific debts, to writers and to books mentioned in the course of my narrative. ~~I feel of one~~ ~~Thackeray~~ on ~~great~~ obligation to Thomas More, William Mole and Charles Dickens who have helped to fashion ~~my vision~~ London; to Greg ~~Arthur Machen~~ Charles Lamb, ; Ned Gissey ~~De Quincey~~; Wordsworth and the urban pilgrims I owe a great debt. I have alluded in this biography

Page from the manuscript for Ackroyd's biography of Dickens (Collection of Peter Ackroyd)

each chapter. In a way this is a sort of confidence trick I felt compelled to perform because instinctively I felt that a book without footnotes would not be taken seriously. Now I know scholarly footnotes themselves have always been a sort of trick, an academic habit established upon the nineteenth-century illusion that scholarship can fulfil the demands of science and based, too, upon the nineteenth century preoccupation with *origins.* Theoretically I knew all of that, but practically I was still under the influence of that derelict and now often farcical practice. So I did it. I put them in.

In this digression Ackroyd also claims that writing the life of T. S. Eliot had been "a breeze" in comparison to writing about Dickens, principally because relatively little was known about Eliot's biography, whereas a great deal was known about Dickens. The other chief difficulty was Dickens's immense literary productivity: it took Ackroyd three or four months to work through the novels (not counting the letters or journalism), whereas, he claims, it is possible to read all Eliot's poetry and plays in a long weekend.

Ackroyd's anxiety that he might be thought unscholarly seems to have been unfounded, since this complaint was seldom voiced in the reviews of *Dickens.* It is likely that his pre-emptive self-criticism answered possible objections before the publication of the work, and *Dickens* entered the hardback best-seller lists. Yet, his biographical speculations did raise certain scholarly questions: Ackroyd argues that Dickens's long extramarital association with the actress Ellen Ternan was entirely chaste. He found it "almost inconceivable" that the couple ever had sexual relations. However, a few months after Ackroyd's book appeared, Claire Tomalin published new evidence in her *The Invisible Woman: The Story of Nelly Ternan and Charles Dickens* (1990) that cast Ackroyd's conclusions into doubt, and he was forced to retract the suppositions he had made about the relationship between Dickens and Ternan.

Ackroyd's next novel was published in 1992. *English Music* sets itself a fairly straightforward task in that the central character, Timothy Harcombe, is a medium—a man of psychic gifts whose trances and otherworldly journeys conveniently include snatches of recollected former lives intersecting with English composers of the past, who form the ostensible subject of the novel. In this novel Ackroyd presents an Anglicized version of South American magic realism. As in *First Light,* his writing encompasses rural England, and his version of pastoral is surprisingly uncomplicated. The idyll is untroubled, the landscape a reflection of what are clearly (to Ackroyd) crucial painters of the past: Thomas Gainsborough, William Blake, and Blake's follower Samuel Palmer. The paradigmatic moment occurs when Timothy walks into *Early Morning* (1857), a

well-known painting by Palmer, which has become a talisman of lost rural England.

This novel displays Ackroyd's unevenness at its most extreme. He explores the English past in the approximate style of the period in question, so there are sections of the book that are intended as pastiches of the Sherlock Holmes stories or Lewis Carroll's *Alice's Adventures in Wonderland* (1865), and there is even a "missing" chapter from Dickens's *Great Expectations* (1861). Chapter 16 is a protracted and dull parody of Blake's prophetic books. Yet, it is followed, characteristically, by a beautifully written section, in which the stage medium is revealed as a true magician who apparently has the power to raise the dead. The ending demonstrates that Ackroyd can construct a climactic scene that compels the belief of even the most unwilling reader.

James Wood's hostile review for *The Guardian* (21 May 1992) detailed his objections to *English Music:* "Those who dismissed Peter Ackroyd's last novel, *First Light,* as one of the worst ever written will now be chastely aware that such judgements can be too hasty. For who at that time could have envisaged the rich, denuding, *final* badness of his latest, *English Music?* It is a book that exhausts all negative superlatives. Marked by Ackroyd's usual failings—that flapping language that hits nothing precisely or uniquely, those papery characters that are little more than tissues of implausibility and authorial will—this novel has a simple-mindedness that is new." Although there were other, more sympathetic, reviews, Wood's outrage indicates how troubling Ackroyd's fiction had become to the literary establishment by the early 1990s.

In *The House of Doctor Dee* (1993) the connections between past and present are more elusive than elsewhere in Ackroyd's work. Dreams, glimpses, and half-seen figures perceived by Matthew Palmer, a young man in contemporary London, take possession of a wholly fictional house built on the supposed site of an earlier house, now demolished, belonging to the historical Renaissance astrologer and magician John Dee. Ackroyd sets his book in Clerkenwell, an area he knew well from the period when he was working on *The Spectator.* Yet, John Dee actually lived at Mortlake, and records show that his first wife died long before 1581, the year in which the Dee section of the narrative takes place. These and other elementary historical errors in the novel were catalogued by Christopher Howse in a 24 September 1993 letter to *TLS. The House of Doctor Dee* is far from being Ackroyd's most-successful historical novel, but it is not without its attractions as a well-plotted ghost story. Nevertheless, as Howse's letter showed, this book raised difficult questions about Ackroyd's seemingly cavalier approach toward archival research and scholarly accuracy.

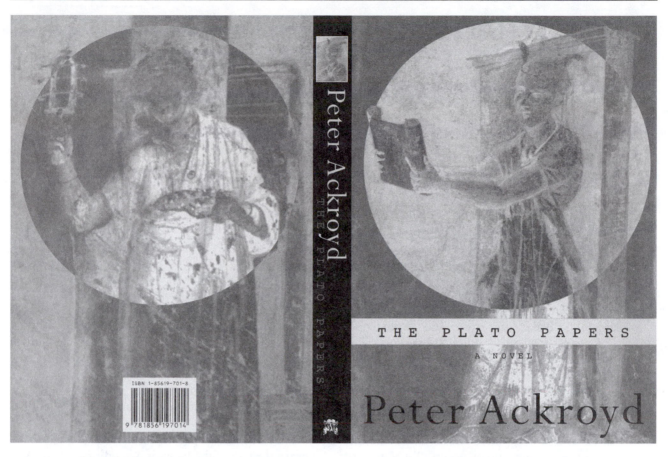

Dust jacket for Ackroyd's 1999 novel, in which a twenty-second-century scholar attempts to piece together a history of the twentieth century from fragmentary evidence left after a nuclear holocaust

Dan Leno and the Limehouse Golem (1994), republished in the United States as *The Trial of Elizabeth Cree: A Novel of the Limehouse Murders* (1995), is perhaps the lightest of Ackroyd's novels. It attempts to bring together two elements of late-nineteenth-century London: the popular music hall and the vicious killings of prostitutes in Whitechapel by Jack the Ripper. Karl Marx and the novelist George Gissing are also given minor roles in Ackroyd's sensational and preposterous story. In this novel Ackroyd sets up a problem that is never fully resolved: how can Marxist economics or literary realism make sense of a series of supernatural killings? Ackroyd seems to have been undecided about whether the novel should be a ghost story with significantly unanswered questions or a realistic detective thriller in which everything is finally explained in the final chapter according to rational causes and effects. The reader is left with a chain of inexplicable coincidences; yet, whether these imply underlying order or chaos is difficult to say. The general critical view is that *Dan Leno and the Limehouse Golem* is an interesting, if deeply frustrating, minor work.

Blake (1995), by contrast, is a diligently researched and clear-sighted biography that builds a convincing and accessible portrait out of the often impenetrable critical commentary of other Blake scholars. In fact, Ackroyd's interpretation of Blake's life helps readers to a fuller understanding of *English Music* because the biography allows them to see how poetry, dream visions, and the visual arts, taken together, represent a mystical continuum of Englishness in Ackroyd's imagination.

In preparing his material for *Blake,* Ackroyd read widely in Blake criticism, and he makes intelligent use of Roman Jakobson's theories and other semiological readings of Blake's art and poetry. Prior to Ackroyd's *Blake,* there was no reliable popular biography, and the book continues to be important as a beginner's introduction to the poet. The original hardback edition, designed by Craig Dodd, incorporates many of Blake's illustrations into the main body of the text, blending words and images in a way that is entirely appropriate to Ackroyd's overall argument about the arts.

Milton in America (1996), another of Ackroyd's speculative novels, is above all a remarkable piece of impersonation that seeks to answer the question of what would have happened if the poet John Milton had fled England at the Restoration of King Charles II and made a new life among the Puritans in New England. This question is worth asking; as William Riley Parker's two-volume *Milton: A Biography* (1968; revised by Gordon Campbell, 1996) makes clear, Milton would almost certainly have been tried and executed as a regicide if he had not been completely blind by 1660. In Ackroyd's version of events, Milton travels to America by sea with a young companion, Goosequill, who acts as the poet's eyes.

As Jonathan Bate pointed out in his review in the *Sunday Telegraph* (31 August 1996), the springboard for this novel is Ackroyd's biography of Blake. Like Milton, Blake was a political radical who looked back fondly to the reforming spirit of Oliver Cromwell's Commonwealth. Blake also wrote and illustrated a strange prophetic book titled *Milton* (1804–1808), the original source for the nationalistic English hymn "Jerusalem." Ackroyd's version of Milton is essentially a Blakean dream vision rather than an attempt at biographical accuracy and should be read as such.

In Ackroyd's imaginative reconstruction of history, Milton is invited by the Puritans to become the leader of their new colony and draws up a list of unmerciful punishments for various misdemeanors, including whipping for prostitutes and burning for sodomites. He regards Native Americans as little more than "heathen rabble," so it is left to Goosequill to befriend them and learn their language. Temptation, however, is not far away in this version of an unfallen Garden of Eden, and there is a strong danger that Milton—who, as one character suggests, is possibly guilty of the sin of pride—will fall spectacularly from grace. When he goes on an excursion among the Native Americans, the lure of earthly delights presents itself in the form of a powerful distilled spirit and an attractive young girl. Milton's newly established paradise may not survive if he gives in to these temptations.

The tortuous plot of *Milton in America,* as it flips through various narrators and periods in time, is an achievement in itself, but the real cleverness of Ackroyd's writing may be measured in terms of structure and literary style. It becomes clear to the attentive reader that the novel is composed along Miltonic lines: the War in Heaven between the good and evil angels is parodied, and the text is crammed with quotations from Milton's works, ending with the words: "The blind man wandered ahead and, weeping, through the dark wood took his solitary way," an echo of the final lines from Milton's epic poem *Paradise Lost* (1667),

which paradoxically remains unwritten in Ackroyd's alternative "biography."

Yet, this book is more than an ironic exercise in allusion and erudition. In the impassioned speech of his Puritan characters, Ackroyd captures the tone of seventeenth-century anti-Catholic discourse: "Their arrows borrowed from the savages will lose their golden heads, their purple robes will untwine, their silken beads will slip their knots. God's people of New England will clean out that hole of Satan in our midst. The chosen race will be saved!" As a sustained act of literary homage and impersonation, it is hard to imagine this novel being bettered.

Ackroyd's next endeavor, *The Life of Thomas More* (1998), is an ambitious biographical project flawed by one crucial omission; Ackroyd appears not to have read any of More's works in the original Latin. Although he gives an extensive secondary bibliography of English-language works and translations, Ackroyd is left with the impossible task of trying to view one of the best Latinists in Europe exclusively through the medium of English. He often falls into general speculations concerning what More's London might have looked like, but it is surely inadequate to offer a detailed knowledge of the background when his account of More's writings includes so many gaps, absences, and silences.

Despite these problems, however, chapter 32, toward the end of the book, is a good example of Ackroyd's biographical method at its best. He provides a dramatized version of More's trial on the charge of treason, presented in the form of an imaginary transcript, which has in fact been collated from four different secondary sources. This chapter, however, has a force and immediacy lacking in most of the book. The other noteworthy section is the long discussion of More's *Utopia* (1516), which depends to some extent on other commentators' accounts but does offer a clear summary of the difficulties present in the text:

> It is very difficult in *Utopia* to gauge or determine More's own opinion upon any particular matter. Irony was the most powerful and complicated literary tone in a society where formal appearances were becoming less and less appropriate to the actual realities of power, and where traditional beliefs and authoritative customs were beginning to decay. . . . More himself remained a master of ambivalence.

Perhaps the most valuable thing to have come out of Ackroyd's engagement with More is his newly discovered interest in possible futures.

The Plato Papers (1999) represents a considerable departure. It is his first futuristic novel, following a long series of historical works. As a fictional project, *The Plato Papers* clearly sprang out of Ackroyd's engagement

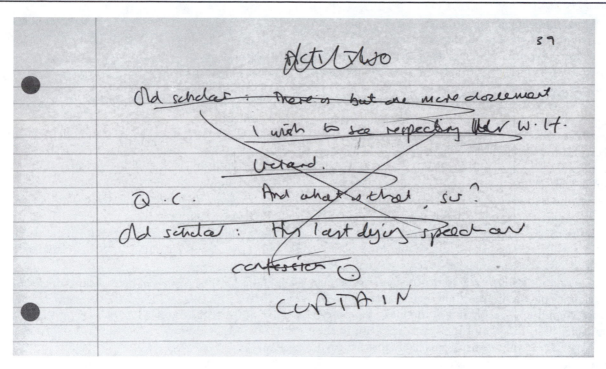

Page from a working draft for a play (Collection of Peter Ackroyd)

with More's *Utopia,* and the novel is a bold attempt to look forward in order to reflect on dominant trends in contemporary culture. The action of the book takes place on the site of what used to be London, in the year 3100. A nuclear holocaust has destroyed civilization, and little of late-twentieth-century culture has survived. The archival record of the great libraries has been lost, and only a few impenetrable cultural fragments, such as a map of the London underground train system, remain. Working from this limited and unrepresentative evidence, Plato, the orator of a futuristic city-state, makes confident generalizations about the "Age of Mouldwarp"–meaning the twentieth century–and most of his conclusions about this historical period are hilariously inaccurate. Yet, Plato's acts of misreading (which are, more precisely, what Umberto Eco has termed "over-interpretation") also serve as a commentary on where contemporary society has gone wrong.

It is important, however, not to underestimate the element of subversive fun present throughout *The Plato Papers.* Speaking of the composition of the novel, Ackroyd told Stephanie Merritt in 1999: "I loved it. It was very liberating, because for the first time I was set free from the constraints of evidence and past detail." That the narrator's name is Plato is explained as pure coincidence, but the style of the novel clearly establishes that Ackroyd familiarized himself with the original Platonic dialogues before writing *The Plato Papers.*

This book is far less shapely than Ackroyd's historical works. It is presented as a collection of fragments, mostly in the form of orations, dialogues, and notes toward a dictionary of Mouldwarpian terms. These notes prove to be the most rewarding section of the book, and Ackroyd displays his powers as a satirist in the definitions. According to Plato, *pastoral* is "the reverence for the past, expressed by word of mouth." The concept of *information* is misremembered as having referred to

an ancient deity. It conferred power upon those who worshiped it and was thought to have an invisible presence everywhere. . . . In many respects it resembled the cults of Witspell [the period 2300–3400] which were performed only for the sake of the ceremonies themselves. Information simply granted its practitioners words and images.

Ackroyd has maintained in newspaper interviews that *The Plato Papers* is not primarily intended to voice any deepseated personal hostility toward the contemporary world. Nevertheless, he concedes that the chapters on Charles Darwin and Sigmund Freud question in radical ways the reputations of these major figures of intellectual history: "I don't think those philosophers are particularly interesting, so I try to set them up as myths, as jokes." Like H. G. Wells and Doris Lessing before him (to cite just two examples), Ackroyd uses speculative future fiction as a pretext for engaging in a wide-ranging critique of contemporary culture. For this reason, his book asks (as does the *Utopia*) to be taken both as a work of elaborate, playful fantasy and as a deeply committed piece of nonfiction.

Ackroyd's future projects include *Secret London,* a long-promised "biography" of London, charting the histories (both scholarly and mystical) of the city from the earliest records to recent developments such as Canary Wharf and the Millennium Dome at Greenwich. Beyond that, it has been announced that Ackroyd is under contract to produce a biography of Shakespeare. It is impossible to be certain about the exact shape that any future novels might take, but there is little doubt that they will continue to find a large and loyal readership. Indeed, the commercial success of Ackroyd's works is one indication of a resurgent interest among the reading public in the "alternative" England of haunted, significant places, and in the idea of the presence of the past. In spite of the warm response to the futurism of *The Plato Papers,* it seems likely that Ackroyd will return before long to historical fiction. His obsession with the underworld of London may not yet have fully exhausted itself.

Interviews:
Elizabeth Kolbert, "Wandering Through History," *New York Times,* 19 January 1996, VII: 3;

Stephanie Merritt, "The Books Interview: Peter Ackroyd," *Observer,* 28 March 1999, Review Section, p. 15;

Francis Gilbert, "Fly Away, Peter," *Times* (London), 10 April 1999, Metro Section, pp. 16–17.

References:
Brian Finney, "Peter Ackroyd, Postmodernist Play and *Chatterton," Twentieth Century Literature: A Scholarly and Critical Journal,* 38, no. 2 (1992): 240–261;

Jeremy Gibson and Julian Wolfreys, *Peter Ackroyd: The Ludic and Labyrinthine Text* (New York: St. Martin's Press, 1999);

Susana Onega Jaén, *Metafiction and Myth in the Novels of Peter Ackroyd* (Columbia, S.C.: Camden House, 1999);

John Peck, "The Novels of Peter Ackroyd," *English Studies: A Journal of English Language and Literature,* 75, no. 5 (1994): 442–452.

Papers:
The Peter Ackroyd Papers in the Beinecke Rare Book and Manuscript Library at Yale University include notes and full or partial manuscripts for most of Ackroyd's works published between 1978 and 1993, as well as manuscripts for unpublished works, proofs, publicity materials, and some personal and professional correspondence.

Beryl Bainbridge

(21 November 1933 –   )

Cecile M. Jagodzinski
Illinois State University

See also the Bainbridge entry in *DLB 14: British Novelists Since 1960.*

BOOKS: *A Weekend with Claud* (London: New Authors, 1967); revised as *A Weekend with Claude* (London: Duckworth, 1981; New York: Braziller, 1982);

Another Part of the Wood (London: Hutchinson, 1968; revised edition, London: Duckworth, 1979; New York: Braziller, 1980);

Harriet Said (London: Duckworth, 1972; New York: Braziller, 1973);

The Dressmaker (London: Duckworth, 1973); republished as *The Secret Glass* (New York: Braziller, 1974);

The Bottle Factory Outing (London: Duckworth, 1974; New York: Braziller, 1975);

Sweet William (London: Duckworth, 1975; New York: Braziller, 1976);

A Quiet Life (London: Duckworth, 1976; New York: Braziller, 1977);

Injury Time (London: Duckworth, 1977; New York: Braziller, 1977);

Young Adolf (London: Duckworth, 1978; New York: Braziller, 1979);

Winter Garden (London: Duckworth, 1980; New York: Braziller, 1981);

English Journey; or, The Road to Milton Keynes (London: Duckworth/British Broadcasting Corporation, 1984; New York: Braziller, 1984);

Watson's Apology (London: Duckworth, 1984; New York: McGraw-Hill, 1985);

Mum and Mr. Armitage: Selected Stories of Beryl Bainbridge (London: Duckworth, 1985; New York: McGraw-Hill, 1987);

Filthy Lucre; or, The Tragedy of Andrew Ledwhistle and Richard Soleway: A Story (London: Duckworth, 1986);

Forever England: North and South (London: Duckworth, 1987; New York: Carroll & Graf, 1999);

An Awfully Big Adventure (London: Duckworth, 1989; New York: HarperCollins, 1991);

Beryl Bainbridge (courtesy of the author)

The Birthday Boys (London: Duckworth, 1991; New York: Carroll & Graf, 1994);

Something Happened Yesterday (London: Duckworth, 1993; New York: Carroll & Graf, 1998);

Collected Stories (London: Penguin, 1994);

Every Man for Himself (London: Duckworth, 1996; New York: Carroll & Graf, 1996);

Master Georgie (London: Duckworth, 1998; New York: Carroll & Graf, 1998);

According to Queeney (London: Duckworth, 2000).

Collection: *Watson's Apology; Mum and Mr. Armitage and Other Stories* (New York: McGraw-Hill, 1988).

PRODUCED SCRIPTS: *Tiptoe through the Tulips,* television, BBC, 1976;

Blue Skies from Now On, television, BBC, 1977;

The Warrior's Return, television, BBC, 1977;

It's a Lovely Day Tomorrow, television, BBC, 1977;

Words Fail Me, television, Omnibus, BBC, 1979;

Sweet William, television, BBC, 1979;

A Quiet Life, television, BBC, 1980;

The Journal of Bridget Hitler, television, script by Bainbridge and Phillip Seville, BBC, 1980;

Somewhere More Central, television, 1981;

Emily Brontë and Haworth: A Personal Impression by Beryl Bainbridge, Open University / BBC TV, 1982;

Evensong, television, 1986.

OTHER: *New Stories 6,* edited by Bainbridge (London: Hutchinson in Association with the Arts Council of Great Britain and PEN, 1981);

Northern Short Stories: Volume 5, edited by Bainbridge and David Pownall (Todmorden, U.K.: ARC, 1994);

"Mr. Chips," in *Colin Haycraft, 1929–1994: Maverick Publisher,* edited by Stoddard Martin (London: Duckworth, 1995), pp. 51–55;

Robert Falcon Scott, *Scott's Last Expedition: The Journals,* introduction by Bainbridge (New York: Carroll & Graf, 1996).

SELECTED PERIODICAL PUBLICATION–
UNCOLLECTED: "With Eyes As Big As Saucers: Beryl Bainbridge Recalls Life Backstage at the Liverpool Playhouse, Now Threatened with Closure," *Spectator,* 266 (19 January 1991): 33.

An entertaining and insightful observer of the human condition, Beryl Bainbridge is one of the most highly regarded fiction writers in Great Britain. She began her career with a series of blackly humorous, biting fictions depicting people of lowered expectations who snatch at love and find it always disappointing. These characters, like many people, cannot or will not see the truth, which becomes available only when filtered through the lens of the past or through the eyes of multiple characters. The characters' mostly lower-middle-class backgrounds prepare them for disappointment, but do not totally erase their penchant for romanticism and idealism, which serve as escapes from poverty and boredom. Her later novels focus on historical figures who have much in common with the people in her autobiographical fiction. Bainbridge's characters are often angry, eccentric, and adulterous. Some are even murderers, and few are likeable. But Bainbridge's open-eyed approach to human frailty and irrationality almost always creates reader sympathy for the most despicable characters, from Adolf Hitler to the scissors-wielding maiden aunt.

The key to this sympathy may lie in Bainbridge's attachment to the past as a setting for her stories. Nearly every work is structured so as to take advantage of knowledge gained through hindsight. Among the places she takes her readers are World War II Liverpool, the deck of the *Titanic,* a prison cell in nineteenth-century England, and a Crimean War battlefield. Even those novels and stories not set in the past recover the memories of their central characters: if history does not affect one, then surely one's own past does.

The sources for Bainbridge's characters lie in her childhood and in her early family life: "I pinch newspaper stories that have a strong narrative plot," she told Willa Petschek in a 1981 interview, "then put in everything I can remember about my family and friends." Born on 21 November 1933 in Liverpool, to Richard and Winifred Baines Bainbridge, Beryl Margaret Bainbridge was the younger of two children; she had a brother six years her senior. The family moved to the small town of Formby, outside Liverpool, when she was an infant. Bainbridge's father, a salesman who went bankrupt later in life, was prone to alternate fits of violence and withdrawal. He was also a lover of radio, poetry, and Charles Dickens. He passed on his reading habits to his daughter, while her mother encouraged her to write from an early age. Bainbridge's father's emotional state and her mother's class consciousness and sense of female superiority collided to form a less-than-secure childhood home. Bainbridge began to write at eight to escape and sort out the vagaries of her home life. Writing was "more beneficial an occupation to us than attending a psychiatric clinic," she wrote in the introduction to *Filthy Lucre* (1986). In addition to childhood imitations of Dickens and Robert Louis Stevenson, Bainbridge, at the age of ten, began a novel based on her parents' quarrelsome relationship. She wrote her novel on pages from her exercise books and pasted them with homemade glue into a folio-sized book on the travels of Dr. David Livingstone. When the book got too large to close, making her novel a target for discovery, she burned it. She told an interviewer for *The Wall Street Journal* (13 July 1994), "There was no privacy in that house, and I was terrified of them ever seeing it."

Bainbridge attended the Merchant Taylor's School in Great Crosby, a rather "posh school," as she later called it. Expelled for carrying about a "rude" poem (as Madge does in *A Quiet Life,* 1976), she took to the theater. Her mother, who had realized that her daughter did not have a scholarly temperament, had seen that she took tap-dancing lessons and instruction at the Arts Educational Schools in Tring. In an autobiographical piece published in *The Spectator* (19 January 1991), Bainbridge recalled, "It was my mother's idea that I should go on the stage; . . . it wasn't that my mother was stage-struck, rather that she had a sixth sense I was going to turn out both scholastically dim and temperamentally unstable." At fifteen Bainbridge ran away to London to escape the arguments at home. In 1949, at the age of sixteen, she became a member of the Liverpool Playhouse Company, where she stayed until 1952. In that same year she met her future husband, artist Austin Davies. Prior to their marriage on

HARRIET SAID . . .
by Beryl Bainbridge

'. . . a sharp, chilling short novel about a suppressed lesbian relationship leading to violence . . . The ending has a real shock effect.'
                                        Julian Symons, *Sunday Times*

'The cover of Beryl Bainbridge's *Harriet Said* glints an appropriately wicked-looking black. But only at the end does the anonymous narrator divulge exactly how evil is the creepy little scenario with which the opening pages rivet the reader's imagination . . . Miss Bainbridge has this terrific visual sense – as sure an eye for the physical as the metaphysical.'
                                        Valentine Cunningham, *Listener*

'. . . a thoroughly enjoyable horror experience. It is very seldom that writers of intelligence and imagination lend their talents to a really good horror story, and this one could scarcely be bettered for the accuracy of its observations and the maintenance of tension.'
                                        Auberon Waugh, *Spectator*

'Sensitive and beautiful . . . Beryl Bainbridge's evocation of childhood is faultless. It's an extraordinary novel – brilliantly subtle, full of disconcerting surprises, full of truth.'
                                        Valerie Jenkins, *Evening Standard*

'. . . an extremely original and disconcerting story . . . Miss Bainbridge's imagination is dark, her landscapes reek and threaten, and her images smell of corruption.'
                                        David Benedictus, *Daily Telegraph*

'. . . tightly written, fully of spiky thoughts and unexpected pockets of exactly reproduced feeling . . . a very good first novel indeed.'
                                        Times Literary Supplement

'. . . written with a knowing, matter-of-fact innocence that strikes exactly the right note.'
                                        Norman Shrapnel, *Guardian*

'. . . a beautifully taut little story.'
                                        Francis King, *Sunday Telegraph*

DUCKWORTH
The Old Piano Factory, 43 Gloucester Crescent,
London NW1

Bainbridge

THE DRESSMAKER
Duckworth

THE DRESSMAKER

a novel by
BERYL BAINBRIDGE

*Dust jacket for Bainbridge's 1973 novel, set in Liverpool during World War II
(courtesy of The Lilly Library, Indiana University, Bloomington, Indiana)*

24 April 1954, Bainbridge became a Roman Catholic. She now considers herself a "lapsed Catholic." Bainbridge and Davies have two children–Aaron Paul and Johanna Harriet. They were divorced in 1959. After her marriage, and until 1972, Bainbridge continued to act professionally in repertory theaters in Windsor, Salisbury, Dundee, Liverpool, and London.

Bainbridge's earliest surviving literary effort, *Filthy Lucre; or, The Tragedy of Andrew Ledwhistle and Richard Soleway,* was written between June and August 1946 and published in 1986 with facsimiles of her handwritten dedication and original illustrations. The young author dedicated her book to "the auther of Dismal England, who gave me a chance to clothe my bitter feelings against the unjust London of the 1800's in a story." But Bainbridge's story was also an antidote to her circumstances. Her preface admits: "My father and mother bickered a lot, which is why, there being no such thing as television to distract one, or any other room in which to escape from the raised voices, my mother encouraged my natural inclination to scribble in notebooks." Bainbridge, who acknowledges her debts to

Dickens and Stevenson, was dissatisfied with the result because the characters and plot had been "invented." After consciously rejecting a technique that is the mainstay of many less-skilled writers, Bainbridge says: "I don't think I have invented anything since." With its characters bearing names that are clues to their personalities, and its concern with inheritances, loyalty, revenge, and death, *Filthy Lucre* owes much to Dickens. It is nearly epic in scope, treating rich and poor, business doings, forbidden love, shipwreck, and Victorian street thugs. The intertwined and complicated roles of the Ledwhistle and Andromikey families create a style of storytelling that Bainbridge had eschewed by the time her first adult novel was published. The intrusive narrator also disappeared. But Bainbridge's ear for dialogue is already evident in *Filthy Lucre,* as is her ability to delineate character. Except for its melodramatic tone, *Filthy Lucre* is hardly juvenilia at all.

Bainbridge completed her first adult novel, *Harriet Said* (1972), in 1958. Based on a news story about two Australian girls who had murdered one girl's mother, the novel is narrated from the point of view of an unnamed thirteen-year-old girl who has fallen under the spell of her friend Harriet. Set in the British countryside during the 1940s, the novel opens in the present, tells the story, and returns to the present. Bainbridge has used this framing device repeatedly in her fiction. Fascinated by the charm, beauty, and worldliness of Harriet, the girl-narrator joins her in spying on a neighbor couple's quarreling and coitus, rambling about the neighborhood, and keeping a joint diary. Harriet's challenges to the narrator's conventionality urge her on to the seduction of a middle-aged man, Mr. Biggs, and the murder of his wife. The girl experiences sex with Mr. Biggs as an "uncomplicated ritual," an unromantic physical coupling amid a confusion of limbs and pieces of clothing. This sort of sexual experience becomes almost a motif in Bainbridge's work: no matter how much the protagonists age, their experience of sex comes close to being merely functional, a way of trying to fulfill some strong physical and vague emotional need. The main characters in *A Weekend with Claud* (1967), *Watson's Apology* (1984), *Master Georgie* (1998), and several other of Bainbridge's novels seem to replay this hopeful, yet sadly disappointing, view of love. With its depiction of youthful corruption, burgeoning sexuality, and manipulative heroine, *Harriet Said* was rejected by publishers in 1959, with one declaring Bainbridge's book "too indecent and unpleasant even for these lax days."

When the novel was finally published in 1972, critical reaction was positive. Acknowledging that the events of the story might appeal "only to the more jaded end of the market," Auberon Waugh, in *The Spectator* (14 October 1972), went on to praise Bainbridge's depiction of Harriet as "totally convincing" and "a thoroughly enjoyable horror experience." He quarreled with Bainbridge's use of the flashback, but regarded the novel as a whole as a successful example of the horror story. Even though the dust jacket of the first American edition included Julian Symons's comment that the book is "a sharp, chilling novel about a suppressed Lesbian relationship," accusations of sensationalism were harder to maintain in 1972 than in 1958. More than twenty years after publication, Patricia Juliana Smith described the novel as "sardonic reconfiguration of the Gothic combined with overtones of the homoerotic girls' school narrative." Whether regarded as horror story or a tale of "lesbian panic," *Harriet Said* provides psychological insight into the bullies and the browbeaten that populate real life.

After her divorce from Davies in 1959, Bainbridge was married briefly to author Alan Sharp, by whom she had a daughter, Ruth Emmanuela. After the birth of her third child, Bainbridge completed *A Weekend with Claud*. It was published in 1967 in the New Authors series, a Hutchinson venture designed to highlight (and pay) rising authors. A revised version—in which the names of two main characters are changed from Claud and Maggie to Claude and Lily—was published in 1981 as *A Weekend with Claude*.

In a variation on the flashback technique she employed in *Harriet Said*, Bainbridge uses an old photograph to jar the memories of the four main characters. The recollections of Claude, Lily, Victorian Norman (so-called because of his formal and old-fashioned dress), and Shebah are the prism through which the reader must recompose the events of a summer weekend several years earlier. Claude, an antique dealer, is less unhappy at the departure of his wife after making himself at home with his mistress, Julia, and their young child. Lily is a young woman whose person and home—as well as her emotional life—are perpetually in a shambles; she thinks she may be pregnant by a former lover, Billie, but is aiming to ensnare the American Edward into marriage and fatherhood. Norman, a sensualist-Marxist, is enamored of the maternal Julia, and might have consummated his passion but for the timely and abrupt intervention of Claude. The elderly Shebah, born in 1899, seems the odd person in this group of men and women; she is a Jew who feels "dreadfully impaled upon my own character and personality." The photograph carries Shebah much further back in time, as she recalls her love for a married man whom she gave up (quite properly, she thinks, but wrenchingly). She is confused and a bit disgusted by her companions, who "pretend to be interested in art and politics and books, . . . but always, like a maggot eating its way across a particularly decayed and juicy fruit, there's this sexual business, leaving a trail of slime." An older, more romantic version of the younger set, Shebah laments a past she has never experienced: "It did use to be different. There was another mode of living, of courtship; even if I myself have never experienced it, it does exist. People had houses and gave dances and hung little lanterns in trees, and fragrance billowed outwards when the waltzing began." The four characters' musings on the photograph are interspersed by Claude's business transaction with a man and woman over an antique desk. The novel ends with Claude's plot for completing the seduction of the female customer.

Bainbridge was disappointed in the book when it appeared in print; "It just goes on and on," she said. Her later revision shortened the book by one-quarter. She also pared down the literary metaphors and descriptions, resolved confusions on tense, and eliminated inessential characters. Writing for *TLS: The Times Literary Supplement* (11 September 1981), Carol Rubens called the new version "an object-lesson in the novelist's craft." The sparser, more succinct, style has been Bainbridge's hallmark ever since.

Another Part of the Wood (1968) was partly a response to Bainbridge's marriage and divorce. A revised, tighter version, published in 1979, shares essentially the same plot as the first edition. The divorced Joseph takes his mistress, his small son, and a disturbed youth named Kidney on a camping trip to Wales. Joining them is the usual odd assemblage of Bainbridge characters, including Lionel, who regales his wife, May, with soft Orientalist pornography rather than making love to her. Joseph is one of those people whom everyone is for some reason eager to please, but his insensitivity and pompous self-assurance lead him to alienate Dotty, his mistress; second-guess the analyses of Kidney's doctors; and contribute to the death of his son, Roland.

Unlike Bainbridge's later novels, many of which have urban settings, *Another Part of the Wood* uses the potentially idyllic country setting to offset the characters' insularity. The men, especially, seem oblivious to the feelings of others; the women are troubled by—and resentful of—their inability to engender love in their partners. There is a brief interlude of communication and peacefulness, when Roland and Kidney set off together on the hike that precedes Roland's death, which results from his consuming Kidney's medicine in the hope of becoming the man his father wants him to be.

Critics found the second version of *Another Part of the Wood* superior to the first. The "overwriting" of the first version was eliminated. Closer in mood and style to Bainbridge's mature fiction, the book may have been improved as well by Bainbridge's increased emotional distance from the divorce that precipitated her writing of the work.

Continuing to mine her past for inspiration, Bainbridge used her two paternal aunts as models for the older women in *The Dressmaker* (1973), published in the United States the following year as *The Secret Glass*. Nellie, the seamstress of the title, is determined to hold her sister, Margo, and her niece, Rita, to the traditional (and rigid) standards of her lower-middle-class upbringing, despite the fact that World War II has changed their circumstances. Set in Liverpool in 1944, the story depicts characters whose psychological and emotional needs are matched by the physical deprivations created by the war. Nellie's prime purpose in life seems to be preventing damage to her mother's rosewood table. She is proud that the only hurt to any of her mother's belongings has been the result of bombings, not her own carelessness. She forces Margo, a faded charmer of fifty, to abandon another chance at love. Rita, a seventeen-year-old girl whose father, "Uncle Jack," deposited her with her aunts in infancy, feels hemmed in by the restrictions her Aunt Nellie places on her.

The novel opens with a chapter numbered zero, and, as in *Harriet Said,* the main action in the past is framed by chapters set in the present. In the opening chapter Rita, sandwiched between her aunts in bed, finds it impossible to rest. Her mind wanders "restlessly back and forth in search of the happiness she had lost." This yearning for happiness drives the action of the main part of the novel, as the innocent and virginal Rita imagines that an American soldier, Ira, will take her away to a life of domestic bliss in the United States. To her dismay she learns that Ira is illiterate and more interested in sex than marriage. Her final disappointment—and a sure sign that Rita's life will end up like Margo's—is the bizarre ending to the action. The ever-vigilant Nellie finds Margo and Ira in a romantic clinch on her mother's table. Outraged by the indecency—and the scratches they have made on the table—Nellie stabs Ira in the throat with her scissors. Trying to escape he falls down the stairs and dies. Sure of the rightness of her actions, Nellie sews Ira into a shroud and coolly has brother Jack dispose of the body. As Pauline Kael said in her *New Yorker* review of the 1988 movie version (12 December 1988), "Plump and placid in her corset, Nellie . . . is raging inside. . . ." Kael also remarked, "Beryl Bainbridge is very readable, but you don't feel a strong necessity in her writing. This almost-really-good aspect of her novels may be liberating to moviemakers. Bainbridge was an actress before she became a novelist, and possibly the mixed tones of her writing give actors elements to fuse." Bainbridge's works have indeed been attractive to moviemakers, but, in response to Kael, it may be that other factors—Bainbridge's witty dialogue, her tolerance for ambiguity, and her ability to pinpoint the absurdity and the necessity of the human search for love and romance—are what draw adapters to her fiction.

Praised by a *TLS* reviewer (28 September 1973) as "a remarkable achievement," the novel was short-listed for the prestigious Booker Prize. In the United States the work drew more-serious attention to Bainbridge's work. Thematically the novel contrasts the ideal of home as a place of safety, love, and acceptance with the reality Nellie has created. She builds it into a fortress against poverty, the war, and the strangers (including the soldiers) who threaten to disturb the decorum and propriety of home and its inhabitants. According to Virginia Richter, the killing of Ira is "an act that restores order, that reinstitutes the old family rules: The disturbing stranger is eliminated."

After the publication of *Another Part of the Wood* in 1968, Bainbridge worked briefly in a wine-bottling factory, sticking labels on bottles. *The Bottle Factory Outing* (1974) is her rendering of that experience into fiction—though, as she remarked to Petschek in 1981, "nobody got killed as in the book." The action of the novel revolves around two lower-middle-class women: plain, self-effacing, and less-than-confident Brenda and blowsy, flirtatious, and overbearing Freda. After the experience of an alcoholic husband and a mad mother-in-law, Brenda desires nothing more than to disappear into the woodwork. She is, as Freda tells her, "a born victim." Freda the finagler, however, is the character who suffers in the end. Partly from a natural exuberance and partly from a desire to seduce Vittorio, a fellow worker, Freda plans a company picnic, which includes the non-English-speaking Italian immi-

Dust jacket for Bainbridge's 1977 novel, which, she says, was intended to be "definitive on middle-aged love affairs, but ended up absurd" (courtesy of The Lilly Library, Indiana University, Bloomington, Indiana)

who-didn't-do-it line which finally runs dry when the comedy turns into a fable." Despite such criticisms, the book was given *The Guardian* Fiction Award in 1974 and was also nominated for a Booker Prize.

Accusations of callousness on Bainbridge's part, especially in this book, may be answered in part by a comment Elisabeth Wennö made in 1993 about the two main characters in *The Bottle Factory Outing*. Wennö points out that Brenda, entrapped by a needy family, desires only to escape all human involvement, while the single Freda imagines a life of love and belonging: "They . . . embody visions of life that are imperfect since one vision is too romantic and therefore only realizable in death, and the other is too non-illusory and brings death into life." The small Italian community is not nurtured by illusory longing but by acceptance of their situation. Bainbridge's nonintrusive presentation of her characters is her comment on the foolish desires of human beings: life is not grand opera with its great loves and tragedies; it is composed mostly of tragicomic events over which people have no control.

Sweet William (1975) is an unsettling account of the things women do for love, especially for imagined and self-deluding love. The story is told from the point of view of Ann, a young woman working for the BBC in London, whose lover, Gerald, has just left her for an academic job in America. Her uncertainties about his feelings for her are cast aside when a new man appears on the scene to fill her needs. Almost immediately entering into a physical relationship with William, Ann briefly forgets what her mother had taught her about men: that they are inferior and alien, there only "to pay the mortgages and mend the fuses when they blew." Ann learns early on that William is divorced. It takes more time for her to discover that he is still married to another woman, who still loves him undeservedly and with whom he continues to live as he carries on an affair with Ann. William is the author of angst-filled existential dramas with laughably bad dialogue that are actually produced and received charitably by the press. While Ann, having discovered she is pregnant, has tossed aside her own life to be absorbed in William's, William is working his quietly sinister magic on the other people around him. He becomes whatever each person needs, be it best friend, lover, or husband. In the process sweet William leaves everyone diminished, pale shadows without real selves. The novel ends with the birth of Ann's child, whom William wants to claim for his own but who looks suspiciously like Gerald.

While one might read this novel as a commentary on the essential amorality and deviousness of the male half of the human race, Bainbridge's theme is more complex. As in her earlier novels, she depicts people—this time, mostly women—who imagine a

grants who work at the factory. The outing at Windsor Park is accompanied by all the usual minor disasters of a workplace gathering—cold, stilted conversations, cliquishness, and overdrinking—and one major one: the murder of Freda. Startled into action, and with no one willing to admit or investigate the death, the picnickers dress Freda in a white nightgown they inexplicably find at the bottling factory and then pack her corpse into an unusable wine barrel that is destined to be put out to sea.

Reviews of the novel were mixed: critics appreciated the black comedy and the interdependent relationship of the two women, but the reviewers for *TLS* and *The Spectator* found fault with it, including its depiction of the Italians. Reviewing Bainbridge's book for *The Spectator* (2 November 1974), Peter Ackroyd commented that by the end of the novel "the prose becomes a little damper and more forced; the final sequences of the book are devoted to a world that does not exist. Ann's engagement to Gerald, William's selflessness, and Ann's mother's boasting of her daughter's employment successes are all illusions the characters nurture. The irony is that every character prefers the illusion of being loved to reality, despite the accompanying pain. Ackroyd perhaps missed the mark in his 11 October 1975 review for *The Spectator* when he called *Sweet William* "touching and amusing" and "a conventional love story." Susannah Clapp, who reviewed the book for *TLS* (3 October 1975), seems also to have missed the point, labeling the book "probably the sunniest" of Bainbridge's novels but not one of her best. The book was a commercial success and was adapted for television.

"The only reason I write about my past is because I don't see why I should invent something. If it has happened already, why bother?" Bainbridge told Megan Tresidder in 1995. In *A Quiet Life* (1976), she re-created her childhood in the persons of a dysfunctional quartet: brother and sister Alan and Madge and their quarrelsome parents. Bainbridge commented in 1995 that writing the novel had a therapeutic effect for her: "as soon as I started to write it down, all the neuroses left."

Written after the death of Bainbridge's mother, *A Quiet Life* begins with a meeting between the middle-aged Alan and Madge, set for the purpose of dividing up the fictional mother's belongings. Madge (probably named after the author, who was christened Beryl Margaret), wants no part of the puny inheritance; she makes clear that she thought Alan the favored child, free to get away with anything. As in earlier novels, the central story is told in flashback, this time narrated by Alan, who looks back on the period just after World War II. For Bainbridge, this device has thematic significance; it is as though, in fiction as in reality, life is only remembrance, the past the prime factor that shapes everyone.

A restless, unhappy, and slightly stodgy teenage boy, Alan is horrified by the reckless freedoms his sister takes, particularly in her infatuation with a German soldier. Alan cannot understand how and why Madge is able to escape punishment; both their parents eventually succumb to her charms. The salesman father, bankrupted and forced to move the family to a smaller home, has ceased communicating with his lovely wife, who seems starved for attention, and suspects her of infidelity. The madness of his home life and the discovery of his sister and the German soldier together in a state of undress make Alan lose control. In a moment of spite he tells his father that his wife "can't stand being in the same room" with him. The father suffers a heart attack, and in typically macabre Bainbridge style, his wife is more worried about the muddied carpet, clean

pillowcases, and the state of her hair than her husband's condition. In the end Alan "keeps everything bottled up. . . . Anything for a quiet life," says Madge.

In his *TLS* review (8 October 1976) Francis Wyndham pointed out that this book is filled with the "hidden violence which underlies so much of everyday life"—an apt description, no doubt, of family life in general and Bainbridge's in particular. Wyndham also praised "the unnerving effect of immediacy" created by Bainbridge's prose: "Reading this book, one feels uncomfortably close to the people and places portrayed in it, yet protected from them by her glassy objectivity." Calling the novel "a subtle, moving, witty book," Nick Totton felt its only real fault was its climax (the father's death), which "seems superfluous within the logic of the novel" (*The Spectator,* 8 October 1976). Bainbridge adheres to the "classic pattern of crescendo and diminuendo," which, according to Totton, does not work in contemporary fiction.

Bainbridge has said that her next novel, *Injury Time* (1977), was to have been "definitive on middle-age love affairs, but ended up absurd." It recounts the stories of Edward and Binny, a couple involved in a midlife entanglement that seems an odd mixture of need, love, and sexual passion. Binny, a woman of forty with three hapless but demanding children, experiences a combination of affection and puzzlement in her feelings for the married Edward: "He reminded Binny of a pre-war father come home ready for his Ovaltine—pipe in mouth, the evening newspaper under his arm. She did find him attractive, but when he went on about his roses or blew his nose like a trumpet or fell over when he stood on one trembling leg to remove his sock, she was at a loss to understand why." Binny longs for romance, for Edward to say that he wants to leave his wife; with such commitment not forthcoming, Binny proposes they host a dinner party. The occasion begins with a series of comic disasters, and it is almost a letdown when all the dinner guests are taken hostage by bank robbers.

For nearly all the characters, the experience of captivity unleashes a different sort of self. Edward confesses his love for Binny, who has been raped in rather businesslike fashion by one of the robbers. In response to Edward's sudden desire for commitment, Binny offers to explain all to his wife, who, Binny thinks, will forgive him. The experience has shocked Binny into a new sensibility. To Edward's blandishments, she replies: "The reason I'm alone, as you put it . . . is because society's altered. If this was forty years ago, I'd have my husband by my side. He wouldn't have run off with that woman from the telephone exchange. My mother and father stayed together, and they didn't like each other. It's only a question of fashions changing."

Beryl Bainbridge, circa 1977 (photograph © Jerry Bauer; from the dust jacket for the first American edition of Injury Time*)*

She is disgusted by Edward's and his friend Simpson's affairs, their assignment of the women in their lives into separate categories of pleasure or burden. The novel ends with Binny being bundled into a car by the robbers, with the police in hot pursuit. "I knew it would be me," she thinks, hoping at the same time that her daughter will remember to clean her teeth. In one of her columns for *The Evening Standard* (London), collected in *Something Happened Yesterday* (1993), Bainbridge asks: "When will men acknowledge—I'm not so simple as to be unaware that they already know it—that they are the weaker sex?" In the course of the novel Binny and the female bank robber, as well as Muriel (Simpson's wife) and Helen (Edward's wife), face reality, as the menfolk throw themselves with schoolboy fervor into business, adultery, or drink.

Bainbridge won the 1977 Whitbread Award for *Injury Time*. For some critics the novel marked a strengthening of her style. Reviewing the novel for *The Spectator* (1 October 1977), Ackroyd praised the sophisticated melding of violence and comedy in the book and found the narrative "better controlled and more organized than its predecessors. *Injury Time* is more 'serious' in the sense that it is filled with intimations of darkness, madness, emptiness, of living in a world that has sud-

denly grown too large . . . Bainbridge . . . has left her old style, and found a new one."

Having published eight novels that mostly rely on or include autobiographical elements, Bainbridge was urged to expand her repertoire. She began a series of novels that, though they are not quite "historical" in the usual sense, take historical facts as their basis. A visit to Israel reminded Bainbridge of her adolescent preoccupation with the Holocaust; in a 1995 interview she remembered being put on the train to Liverpool at the age of eleven to see movies of the Belsen concentration camps. Her reading of Robert Payne's *The Life and Death of Adolf Hitler* (1973) sparked the idea for a novel on a possible visit by Hitler to Liverpool in 1910 to stay with his brother Alois. A diary kept by Alois's wife, Bridget, indicated that Hitler had fled Germany with false papers to escape the draft. Bainbridge's late-twentieth-century speculation on what created the horror that was Adolf Hitler is *Young Adolf* (1978). This portrait of the psychopath as a young man presents a bumbling, rather meek and unformed personality. Adolf spends his days lolling about the house, much to the irritation of Bridget, who insists that Adolf get a job to help support the struggling household. While working as a hotel bellboy, Adolf gets a sense of what he could become from the etiquette, routine, and especially the uniform. His sister-in-law sews him a brown shirt and advises him to comb his hair over his forehead to hide a scar. He makes the acquaintance of a Jew named Meyer, who enlists him in a failed attempt to rescue some poor children who are about to be taken away from their parents by the authorities. From this effort Adolf learns that if "the minority act with enough authority, . . . the majority will walk like lambs to the slaughter." As Diane Johnson noted in her review for *TLS* (1 December 1978), the novel "says something, doubtless, about the large consequences of small accidents." Overall, Adolf's experience of England is frightening and negative. He cannot find a home or an identity in that island nation. As he leaves Britain, he swears that "never in all my life . . . under torture or interrogation, will I mention that I have been to this accursed city, visited this lunatic island." "English eccentricity becomes a formidable and uniting force that does lead to endurance and victory," wrote Phyllis Lassner in her 1991 article about the World War II novels of Bainbridge and Maureen Duffy. But "radical individualism" not only sends Adolf back to his home—it is the force that keeps Bainbridge's characters going, even under the most bizarre and macabre circumstances. In fact, her Hitler is not unlike many of her other characters, lost and a little alone in a world whose rules cannot be figured out. In an article collected in *Something Happened*

Yesterday, Bainbridge hinted that Hitler may have started out like most people: "when it comes to Hitler I do try to explode the myth that an evil human being springs ready-formed from the womb. . . . What I do try to explain, albeit ineptly, is that goodness, like badness, is fostered or abandoned through the connivance or example of other people."

Critics have noted Bainbridge's uncanny ability to make one of the monsters of the twentieth century a sympathetic, if not lovable, character. "There is something likable about his continued hope for his own small life in the face of a world which despises him, there is something dignified in his self-regard, something commonplace enough in his powerlessness and capacity for self-deception," Johnson noted perceptively. Yet, *Young Adolf* was not universally praised.

During the three years between the publication of *Young Adolf* and her next novel, *Winter Garden* (1980), Bainbridge adapted several of her works for television, including *Sweet William,* broadcast in 1979 and released in movie theaters in 1980, *A Quiet Life* (1980), and *Young Adolf* (1980, as *The Journal of Bridget Hitler*). She also undertook the revision of *Another Part of the Wood,* and in 1978 she was named a fellow of the Royal Society of Literature.

Bainbridge gleaned the details (including the lost luggage episode) for *Winter Garden* from a 1979 cultural-exchange visit to the Soviet Union. After telling his wife that he is going fishing in Scotland and taking along his fishing gear as a cover, Ashburner, an admiralty lawyer, and his mistress, Nina, the wife of a brain surgeon, become part of a group traveling to the Soviet Union. The novel becomes Kafkaesque when the characters arrive in Russia. Ashburner's suitcase is lost. Nina disappears and reappears periodically. The beautiful Russian woman who acts as interpreter for the group may or may not be part of the Russian security apparatus. The entire story is filtered through the romance-tinged and vodka-induced haze of Ashburner's thoughts. It is unclear whether he really is the target of Soviet agents.

Bainbridge's characters seem only slightly out of place in the totalitarian atmosphere of the last decades of the Soviet experiment. Their usual oddities and insecurities seem to suggest the possibility of paranoia: the feeling that one is being spied on seems a natural and logical consequence of lying to one's wife. As most reviewers noted, the novel ends with some ambiguity: incriminating evidence has been planted in Ashburner's recovered luggage and fishing gear, and the reader is left wondering if he will be detained or if he will return to his wife, who no doubt suspects his infidelity.

The "winter garden" is a multilayered metaphor for the landscapes of the novel–the visible landscapes of the sunless bit of pavement at the Ashburners'

home in Chelsea and the vast expanses of Russia, as well as the interior wintry terrain of Ashburner's heart and mind. The beauty of a winter garden is visual, an aesthetic construct; a person would not want to live in one. Ashburner's wife, a practical sort, knows enough to use their winter garden only in the summer, but Ashburner, with his head in a romantic cloud, thinks a real one, Soviet Russia in the dead of winter, is the place to enjoy sex with Nina. The reality of a Russian winter, with its surreal citizen-soldiers popping up everywhere and its cold inefficiencies, is a more authentic indication of the verities of life.

Anne Duchêne, writing for *TLS* (31 October 1980), pointed out the peculiar comedy in *Winter Garden:* "Comedy is secreted everywhere, like honey; but it is a surreal little honeycomb, with sharp teeth." Writing for *Soviet Literature* (1984), Russian Valentina Yakovleva took an unsurprising exception to the entire work, seeing it as a culmination of Bainbridge's failure to write "socially meaningful" fiction. She was offended by the "generous doses of long worn-out derogatory outpourings about Soviet life," and found no humor in the novel, lamenting "the erosion of a literary talent." In *The Spectator* (1 November 1980), Paul Ableman regarded *Winter Garden* as "transitional," a move away from the realism of *The Dressmaker,* "towards a multi-faceted play of the imagination . . . no longer rooted in felt experience." Despite these cautions, Ableman voiced confidence in Bainbridge's "full mastery of what now looks like an essentially lyrical and humorous talent."

In 1982 Bainbridge wrote the script for and narrated *Emily Brontë and Haworth,* a BBC Open University documentary. The following year Bainbridge and a team of BBC documentary moviemakers retraced J. B. Priestley's travels through the towns and villages of England in 1933, which he described in his *English Journey* (1934). Bainbridge's reports and musings on the trip were published as *English Journey; or, The Road to Milton Keynes* (1984). Unlike the invisible persona of the narrator in her novels, in real life Bainbridge is "not an objective traveller." As she notes in the introduction to *English Journey:*

> There are people who live in the present and those who live for the future. There are others who live in the past. It would seem we have little choice. Early on, life dictates our preferences. All my parents' bright days had ended before I was born. They faced backwards. In doing so they created within me so strong a nostalgia for time gone that I have never been able to appreciate the present or look to the future.

This yearning for the past–even a slightly unhappy past–is a key element in all Bainbridge's work, fiction and nonfiction. But her use of the past is not nostalgic in

Dust jacket for Bainbridge's 1980 novel, inspired by a 1979 cultural-exchange visit to the Soviet Union

the same way as, for instance, most treatments of World War II. With each look back, Bainbridge manages to isolate some personal peculiarity, some quirk of fate that rescues her historical figures from the maudlin and brings them into a contemporary context of family and acquaintances. Priestley's England was, in a sense, different from Bainbridge's; however, "it was a matter of substitution, not alteration." In her fictional past readers recognize the absurdities of life by substituting themselves for Bainbridge's characters.

Bainbridge's next novel, *Watson's Apology* (1984), is a fictional look at another historical figure, John Selby Watson (1804–1884), described in the *Dictionary of National Biography* as "author and murderer." In the author's note at the beginning of her novel Bainbridge tells the reader that the documents and details in her book are authentic; she has supplied "the motives of the characters, their conversations and feelings." The novel opens with a series of letters written by Watson in late 1844, his side of an epistolary courtship between him and his soon-to-be bride, Anne Armstrong. Both Anne and John are past youth; he has his scholarly ambitions and £300 a year to recommend him; she has only her

availability. They marry and set up housekeeping at the boys' school where Watson is headmaster. While Watson devotes himself to his academic pursuits and the publication of recondite and poorly received monographs, Mrs. Watson becomes increasingly dissatisfied with her life as a schoolmaster's wife. The two are reluctant to acknowledge that they are mentally, emotionally, and physically mismatched, but as Anne's dissatisfaction escalates into anger, derision, and contempt, John at last loses control and bludgeons Anne to death. This central story is reported during the murder investigation and subsequent trial of John Watson. The last portion of the book deals with his life in prison, medical reports on his psychological condition, and newspaper correspondence debating the correct translation and meaning of a Latin phrase that he spoke in defense of his actions.

Reaction to the novel was mixed, with praise for Bainbridge's ability to transform the mismatched couple's relationship into an understandable tragedy. Reviewing the novel for *The Spectator* (3 November 1984), Harriet Waugh wrote that Bainbridge was in "top form" with *Watson's Apology:* "Her comedy arises out of her characters' inner beings demanding inappropriate expression for their feelings, and in a manner that the outer person would prefer not to know about. . . . No other novel has given me as much pleasure in the last six months." Yet, in his review for *TLS* (5 October 1984), Symons charged Bainbridge with excessive reliance on the facts of the criminal trial, declaring "reality presented in this way clashes intractably and damagingly with the fiction."

The twelve short stories in *Mum and Mr. Armitage: Selected Stories of Beryl Bainbridge* (1985) present characters similar to those in Bainbridge's novels, people who act unthinkingly, like the adolescents they are at heart. The hero and heroine of the title story, like the most popular girl and boy in high school, inspire a cult following among the frequenters of a resort hotel. An aura of charming insouciance and a party-going fervor adhere to the couple even though, by most adults' standards, their crude tricks might be considered simply unkind and inconsiderate. Mum gets her just rewards, as do the two tennis players in "Beggars Would Ride," a fantastic tale about a talisman that enables wishers to get their figurative horses.

Bainbridge has never been overly fond of writing short stories. As she noted in her preface to the juvenile work *Filthy Lucre,* "It seemed to me, even then, that a short story was a waste of a good idea." But she has continued to contribute examples of the briefer form to popular periodicals, including *The Listener.* In 1986, she also became a regular columnist for the London newspaper *The Evening Standard.*

Bainbridge's nonfiction book *Forever England: North and South* (1987) is based on a BBC television series that she hosted. Focusing on the expectations and attitudes of three families from the north of England and three from the south, *Forever England* examines the social and economic conditions of contemporary England.

The title *An Awfully Big Adventure* (1989) derives from J. M. Barrie's fantastic boy character Peter Pan, who thought that dying must be "an awfully big adventure." Bainbridge drew on her teenage experience as an assistant stage manager and juvenile character actress at the Liverpool Playhouse Company for this tale of a difficult, willful sixteen-year-old named Stella. The girl is sent to work by her Uncle Vernon because she, like Bainbridge herself, seems unsuited to schoolwork. Stella's natural bent toward acting and romantic pretension serve her well in the playhouse, where she is put to running errands and given a small role in *Caesar and Cleopatra.* Stella's most spectacular mistake backstage occurs when she fails to bring Tinkerbell back to life by turning on the requisite light onstage and reduces an entire audience of children to tears.

Not a great success as an actress either, Stella becomes party to the various crises, real and imagined,

of her backstage colleagues. Describing her own experience at the Liverpool Playhouse in her 1991 *Spectator* article, Bainbridge commented: "In the green room I listened to terrible stories of hardship, of conversion to Catholicism, of sexual despair." Her fictional supporting characters undergo similar calamities, including mismatched loves, romantic and professional jealousies, depression, and suicide attempts. Stella, in the meantime, falls in love with the homosexual director, Meredith Potter, and becomes sexually entangled with the fading O'Hara, who plays Captain Hook. After some perfunctory sex, she allows that there must be "a knack to it. It's very intimate, isn't it?" For Stella, the romantic impulse, reflected in her attraction to Meredith, is as separate from the physical one as acting is from real life. For O'Hara, and most of the other characters in the novel, the differences between the two are less clear. Part of Stella's attraction for O'Hara is her uncanny resemblance to someone he has known. At the end of the novel, at the moment of O'Hara's accidental death, the reader learns that O'Hara is Stella's father.

The characters in this novel, like Peter Pan's companions, are all "lost boys," orphaned, motherless, or abandoned in some way. "Not one of the characters in this story can love—or actually, make a move in another's direction—without being rebuffed," said Ellen Bilgore in her review of the book for *The Washington Post* (18 April 1991). Stella's mother, who abandoned her child; the actors, whose histrionics blur the line between fantasy and real life; O'Hara, who must return to the sight of his old triumphs; and Stella, who lives in her own self-centered universe—all look for relief, solace, or self-definition somewhere other than where they are. Hope, like Tinkerbell's light, seems to have been extinguished in the lives of these characters. Even death seems not quite real or just: For example, rather than dying dramatically and guiltily for his incestuous acts, O'Hara almost comically slips on a pool of oil, bumps his head on a bridge, and slides into oblivion.

An Awfully Big Adventure was nominated for a Booker Prize in 1992 and was made into a movie starring Alan Rickman, Georgina Cates, and Hugh Grant in 1998. Reviews for the novel were mixed. Writing in *The Spectator* (9 December 1989), novelist Anita Brookner found the book "a very strange novel indeed, gritty, sad, not quite realised" and concluded her review with the wish that integrity could be restored to a Bainbridgean style that "is beginning to look arbitrary and a little threadbare." "In spite of its sharp set pieces," Nicci Gerrard, who reviewed the novel for *New Statesman and Society* (5 January 1990), thought it was "wistful rather than edgy"—a reference, no doubt, to Bainbridge's skill at pointing out and then puncturing her characters' hopelessly romantic, ridiculous, or bourgeois beliefs. While

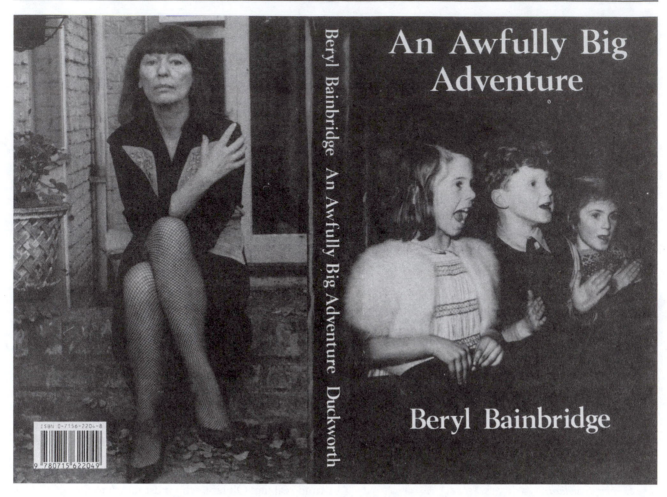

*Dust jacket for Bainbridge's 1989 novel, whose title comes from Peter Pan's observation that dying must be
"an awfully big adventure"*

praising the realism and "clever prose" of the novel in *The New York Times Book Review* (17 March 1991), Lynn Freed thought there was something "too intended in the story," something missing. Several reviewers noted the nostalgic tone of the work, with its autobiographical evocations of the past: "a blurred sepia halo" bathes the novel, said Lindsay Duguid in a *TLS* review (15 December 1989). Duguid felt that, though the themes and settings were familiar, they "had a new richness and complexity" in *An Awfully Big Adventure*.

Until the last years of the twentieth century, explorer Robert Falcon Scott was held up to British schoolchildren as a laudatory example of devotion to duty and grace under pressure. *The Birthday Boys* (1991) is Bainbridge's fictional reconstruction of Scott's fatal trip to the South Pole in 1910–1912. Deriving the facts from Scott's journals and the memoirs of survivor Apsley Cherry-Garrard, Bainbridge deconstructs, and at the same time rehabilitates, Scott for the reader. Like an image refracted by sun and ice, the story is told through the eyes of Scott and four members of his team: petty

officer Taff Evans, ship's doctor Dr. Bill Wilson, naval officer and navigator Birdie Bowers, and Captain Titus Oates, Scott's chief critic on the trip. Each man recounts the day's events and reminisces—about family, about Scott's beautiful and freethinking wife, Kathleen, about the final days fundraising in England, and, finally, about birthdays. Small personal irritations with the captain and with each other are interspersed with life-threatening events—such as the loss of ponies to killer whales, an unexpected crevasse in the snow, and the reality of frostbite. The novel also depicts Scott's upper-class snobberies (the savage but sturdy sled dogs are "uncivilized") and unpreparedness and the disappointment of finding that Norwegian Roald Amundsen has reached the South Pole a month before. But Bainbridge also depicts the positive aspects of the journey: the terrible beauty of the landscape and the men's almost boyish camaraderie and respect for their ill-fated leader. As many reviewers of the novel have noted, Bainbridge chose to write about this last gasp of the British Empire and these last heroics before the horrors of World War I not just to fulfill readers' late-twentieth-century sense of irony; Bainbridge has asked her readers to look back because Scott and his men, foolish as they were, retained an idealism that seems to have been lost.

The Birthday Boys was almost uniformly praised by reviewers. Writing for *TLS* (20 December 1991), Francis Spufford commented on Bainbridge's feat of digging through the layers of legend that have accumulated around Scott and on her skill at rendering invented details. In *The New York Times* (12 April 1994), Michiko Kakutani called the tale "riveting" and "a kind of parable of the brave and foolish optimism that flourished in Victorian England." She sees Amundsen's "modern pragmatism" as a commentary on five men's sense of "brotherly solidarity," even as they succumb to the cold. Bainbridge's experience in writing of women and "impossible children" served her well in this effort, claimed Andro Linklater in *The Spectator* (4 January 1992): "it is precisely her understanding of the intensity of small-scale drama which brings Scott and his companions into focus. No longer either heroic or contemptible, they are restored to human dimensions."

Even in a novel set so far from her native Liverpool, Bainbridge managed to incorporate some autobiographical elements. When questioned by an interviewer for *The Wall Street Journal* in 1994 about her creation of Scott, she replied: "I tried to imagine my father as upper class and naval." In the course of her research, she also learned that Scott had been a friend of J. M. Barrie. In a 1994 interview with Scott Veale, Bainbridge called the explorers "supermen"; but added that they, like Peter Pan's followers, were also "lost boys." Invoking Peter's "awfully big adventure," Bainbridge reminded Veale that the explorers remain "perfectly preserved" in the polar ice cap.

In the preface to *Something Happened Yesterday* (1993), a compilation of selections from her weekly column in *The Evening Standard,* Bainbridge explains that these articles deal not with "so-called burning issues," or "causes or hard facts," but with "things that happened to me during the week." As in her novels, Bainbridge focuses on the everyday, on the people with whom she talks and argues, and on recollections of people and events in her past. "I have never been intrigued by the present or curious about the future," she claims in the preface, and so she embarks on "a circular ramble, starting and ending with memories of long-gone times and sticking London in the middle." Readers of Bainbridge's fiction recognize her opinions and acerbic tone in the essays. Strewn through them are people (including her parents, brother, and aunts) and events one recognizes from their fictional counterparts. And the "footnotes," written in reply to the often outraged and misunderstanding readers of her columns, are sources for further

Bainbridge imaginings. The brief reviews the collection garnered were positive. As Phoebe-Lou Adams observed in *The Atlantic Monthly* (September 1998): "These little pieces are fine examples of the art of making something amusing out of nothing in particular."

Bainbridge's *Collected Stories* (1994) gathers together *Filthy Lucre* and the stories in *Mum and Mr. Armitage,* as well as six previously uncollected stories, four of which had been published in periodicals. Reviewing the collection for *TLS* (6 January 1995), Alex Clark thought that some of the stories "scarcely seem to be stories at all, but are more like vivid fragments of writing attached to rather slight ideas." Despite the good writing, argued Clark, Bainbridge's short works lack depth and resonance. This criticism is surprising, because Bainbridge's laconic and biting style seems eminently suited to the short-story form.

Bainbridge took on another historical event of legendary proportions with *Every Man for Himself* (1996). Set for the most part aboard the giant steamship *Titanic,* the plot includes no surprises. Bainbridge focuses on the personalities of the people on board: the fictional Morgan, narrator of the story and nephew to millionaire J. P. Morgan; Wallis Ellery, an icy beauty; Rosenfelder, a Jewish tailor who wants to become a couturier in New York; Adele Baines, a young opera singer; and Scurra, a mysterious, cynical man of indeterminate occupation. Alongside Bainbridge's creations are representations of some of the real people who went down with the ship: the Astors, ship designer Thomas Andrews, and White Star executive Bruce Ismay. Following the flashback pattern she has used since *Harriet Said,* Bainbridge opens the novel on the deck of the sinking ship, with Morgan poised to jump. Except for Morgan's brief retelling of a collision with a stranger in the streets of London, an accident that results in the man's death, the entire sequence of events takes place during the four days the ship is afloat. As one might find in real life, four days allow the reader only a cursory acquaintance with the characters. Most significant for Morgan are his conversations with Scurra, who, unencumbered by romantic illusion, has bedded the unapproachable Wallis, the woman Morgan desires. When Morgan asks Scurra if he loves Wallis, he scoffs: "Love is a woman's word." In the competition for women, as aboard a sinking boat, "it's every man for himself."

The book raises, but does not answer, the question of personal responsibility in the face of fate. As in *The Birthday Boys,* Bainbridge focuses on ordinary people who are faced with impossible circumstances. The situations differ from her other novels only in the enormity of the events depicted. For Morgan, his personal history, his place in life, and his awakening lust are just as cosmic as the sinking of the unsinkable ship.

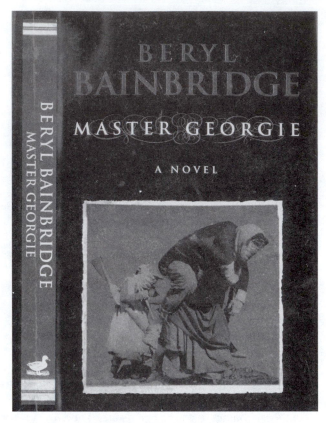

*Dust jacket for Bainbridge's 1998 novel, set
before and during the Crimean War*

Several critics called *Every Man for Himself* a favorite or best book of the year, and the novel was nominated for the Booker Prize and won the Whitbread Novel Award. Yet, there were many criticisms of the novel, principally for Bainbridge's treatment of her characters. Reviewing the novel for *The Wall Street Journal* (15 November 1996), Merle Rubin felt they lacked depth and that Bainbridge relied too much "on the inherent drama of the subject matter to breathe life into her stagy reanimation." In *The New Yorker* (14 October 1996), novelist John Updike opined that "Bainbridge writes with a kind of betranced confidence, seeming to lose all track of her story only to pop awake for a stunning image or an intense exchange." While several reviewers applauded Bainbridge's attention to detail, Jeffrey Hart in *The National Review* (27 January 1997) felt this self-imposed homework "exhausts the interest of the book," which is filled with "worthless-cardboard characters and oatmeal prose." In his review for *TLS* (6 September 1996), Jonathan Keates disliked the "curious matter-of-fact flatness" of Morgan's narration, which results in the reader's indifference to the characters' fates. Others, such as Douglas E. Winter, however, called

the novel a "compelling concatenation of intrigue, irony, and epiphany" (*TLS,* 6 September 1996), and Jennifer Paterson regarded the book as "further proof that Miss Bainbridge is some sort of celestial being—or a witch, perhaps. She grabs you by the neck and hurls you into the freezing Atlantic with the shipmates, and sinks you with the unlucky ones" (*Washington Post,* 24 November 1996).

Mostly "unlucky ones" inhabit *Master Georgie* (1998). Also a Booker Prize nominee, the novel is set in the years up to and including the Crimean War (1854–1856). George Hardy, the hero, is described by three characters whose lives revolve about him: Myrtle, an orphan who was adopted by George's family and is in love with him; Pompey, a street urchin who becomes a photographer's assistant and George's sometime lover; and Dr. Potter, George's educated and pompous brother-in-law. Each section of the novel is launched by a description of a photograph, as viewed by each individual character. (George is an amateur photographer, and the Crimean War was one of the first to be recorded by photography.) The desolate setting of the war, with its thick fog, battle-crazed horses, filth, and blood becomes an apt metaphor for the characters' confusion and entanglements with fate. Though a popular favorite to win the Booker Prize, *Master Georgie* lost out to Ian McEwan's *Amsterdam* (1998). Bainbridge's book later earned her the W. H. Smith Literary Award and the James Tait Black Prize.

In his analysis of the novel for *TLS* (24 April 1998), David Horspool focused on Bainbridge's skill in linking past and present: "What Beryl Bainbridge has achieved is a form of realism which makes its historical setting as immediate and vivid, and as chaotic, as anything set in the present." "A teeming epic, reduced to fit into a nutshell," exclaimed Kate Saunders (*The New Statesman and Society,* 1 May 1998), who judged Bainbridge to be "at her most brilliantly original in the dangerous and undignified area between high tragedy and low farce."

According to Queeney, forthcoming in August or September 2000, continues Bainbridge's exploration of historical subjects, this time exploring the relationship between the well-known eighteenth-century man of letters Samuel Johnson and his friend Hester Thrale from the viewpoint of Mrs. Thrale's young daughter, Queeney. Bainbridge's apparently definitive move away from the purely personal into the historical mode—without the loss of wit or insight into character—appears to suit both her and her reading public. In June 2000 she was made a Dame of the British Empire in recognition of her creative work.

Your page 50?　　**According to Queeney**
　　　　　　　　　　　Novel in progress

.....table can bring ease to an ailing body."

　　How right she is, thought Miss Reynolds.The pain of existance
cannot be removed with a dusting cloth.

　　　　　　　.....

　　Having let herself out into the street Queeney had no clear idea
of where she wanted to go,save it should be as far away as possible
from Mama who had so cruelly taunted her on the subject of worms.
Though the rain had stopped the througherfare was pitted with
puddles and in no time at all the yellow fabric of her shoes had
turned the colour of mustard. *ochre*

　　She had been to Dean street many times,but not for some months
and was astonished at the number of old houses half pulled down and
new ones half built up.There were ladders everywhere, and carts
full of bricks,and on what had once been the pampered grass of the
bowling green a boy was selling flat-fish from a stall anchored in
mud.At number 29,the side branches of the Mulberry tree had been
snapped in two and hung in dripping rags.As for the windows of Sir
James Thornhill's elegant house,why,they were quite clouded
over,and peer as she might,the parrot with the blue legs was no
longer visible on its perch behind the glass.

　　Mamma had taken her to visit Lady Thornhill one morning in summer,
she remember the occasion because Papa,some days before, had
given her an amber necklace,the very same which now lay hidden
beneath the black lace mantle she wore about her shoulders.When
shown into Lady Thornhill's drawing room the parrot had rocked
along its perch and squawked out she was a pretty girl.It had been
caught in a jungle place in Brazil by a traveller who fetched
exotic creatures for John Hunter,the medical man who,curious as to
what constituted life, was for ever anatomising them to/into?
death.(Prefer into, but is it correct?) Even he had admired the
fiery plumage of the bird and,laying aside his dissecting knife,
allowed Sir James to buy it from him. Other visitors had tried to
get the parrot to talk,but it had only opened its beak for
Queeney.This,she reasoned,was on account of her not joining in the
general pestering;she herself grew stubborn when put on show.
Mamma,of course,had swelled with pride at its croaking declaration

*line 18, ... one morning in summer; she was aqquainted with the family,
if remotely, because Sir James was father-in-law to the painter, Hogarth.
Queeney remembered etc.*

Beryl Bainbridge

Interviews:

"Beryl Bainbridge Wins Our Prize," *Guardian,* 28 November 1974, p. 13;

Alex Hamilton, "Interview with Beryl Bainbridge," *Guardian,* 29 November 1974, p. 14;

Barbara A. Bannon, "PW Interviews: Beryl Bainbridge," *Publishers Weekly,* 209 (15 March 1976): 5–6;

Elizabeth Dunn, "Beryl Bainbridge: Can There Be Life After 14?" *Sunday Times* (London), 31 October 1976, p. 43;

Yolanda May, "Beryl Bainbridge Talks to Yolanta May," *New Review,* 3 (1976): 48–52;

Craig Brown, "Beryl Bainbridge: An Ideal Writer's Childhood," *Times* (London), 4 November 1978, p. 14;

Paul S. Nathan, "Violator of Privacy," *Publishers Weekly,* 215 (9 April 1979): 34;

"Beryl Bainbridge, Novelist, Painted a Drama That Happened to Herself," *Sunday Times Magazine* (London), 17 February 1980, p. 33;

Willa Petschek, "Beryl Bainbridge and Her Tenth Novel," *New York Times Book Review,* 1 March 1981, pp. 9, 27;

Colin Haycraft, "Publishing Beryl Bainbridge," *Bookseller,* 5 September 1981, p. 875;

Victoria Jones, "A Life in the Day of Beryl Bainbridge," *Sunday Times Magazine* (London), 7 August 1983, p. 54;

"Priestley: A Message for All Times," *Times* (London), 17 August 1984, p. 8;

"The Buffalo in Beryl's Life," *Sunday Times* (London), 14 October 1984, p. 11;

Clare Boylan, "Nibs and Nicotine," *Guardian,* 8 August 1991, p. 21;

"Influences," *New Statesman and Society,* 6 (27 August 1993): 13;

Scott Veale, "Trekking to Never-Never Land," *New York Times Book Review,* 17 April 1994, p. 15;

Amy Gamerman, "A Writer's Dreams of Darker Antarctica," *Wall Street Journal,* 13 July 1994, p. A12;

Megan Tresidder, "The Really Awfully Funny Life of Beryl," *Guardian,* 8 April 1995, II: 27;

Carolyne Ellis, "Beryl Bainbridge," *Guardian,* 28 September 1998, p. 107;

Valerie James, "Our First Meal," *Times Magazine,* 23 January 1999, p. 61;

Tim Teeman, "Secret Story of a Writer's Art," *Times Weekend,* 20 November 1999, p. 3;

Valerie Grove, "Title for a Revered Writer," *Times,* 17 June 2000.

References:

Gloria Ann Duarte Valverde, "A Textual Study of Beryl Bainbridge's *Another Part of the Wood* and *A Weekend with Claude*," 2 volumes, Ph.D. thesis, Texas Tech University, 1985;

Ginette Emprin, "Fins dans *An Awfully Big Adventure* de Beryl Bainbridge," in *Fins de romans: Aspects de la conclusion dans la litterature anglaise,* edited by Lucien Le Bouille (Caen: Presses Universitaires de Caen, 1993), pp. 95–108;

Phyllis Lassner, "'Between the Gaps': Sex, Class and Anarchy in the British Comic Novel of World War II," in *Look Who's Laughing: Gender and Comedy,* edited by Gail Finney (Langhorne, Pa.: Gordon & Breach, 1994), pp. 205–219;

Lassner, "Fiction as Historical Critique: The Retrospective World War II Novels of Beryl Bainbridge and Maureen Duffy," *Phoebe,* 3 (1991): 12–24;

David Punter, *The Hidden Script: Writing and the Unconscious* (London & Boston: Routledge & Kegan Paul, 1985);

Virginia Richter, "Grey Gothic: The Novels of Beryl Bainbridge," *Anglistik & Englischunterricht,* 60 (1997): 159–171;

Patricia Juliana Smith, "'And I Wondered If She Might Kiss Me': Lesbian Panic As Narrative Strategy in British Women's Fictions," *Modern Fiction Studies,* 41 (1995): 567–607;

Krystyna Stamirowska, "The Bustle and Crudity of Life: The Novels of Beryl Bainbridge," *Kwartalnik Neofilologiczny,* 35 (1988): 445–456;

Elisabeth Wennö, *Ironic Formula in the Novels of Beryl Bainbridge* (Göteburg, Sweden: Acta Universitatis Gothoburgensis, 1993);

Valentina Yakovleva, "On Reading Beryl Bainbridge: A Voice from the Public," *Soviet Literature,* 11 (1984): 141–149.

Papers:

Three 1976 letters from Beryl Bainbridge to Mary Hocking of the Monday Literary Club are on deposit in the Lewes East Sussex Record Office.

William Boyd

(7 March 1952 –   )

Andrew Biswell
University of Warwick

BOOKS: *A Good Man in Africa* (London: Hamilton, 1981; New York: Morrow, 1982);

On the Yankee Station and Other Stories (London: Hamilton, 1981; enlarged edition, New York: Morrow, 1984; enlarged again, London: Penguin, 1988);

An Ice-Cream War (London: Hamilton, 1982; New York: Morrow, 1983);

Stars and Bars (New York: Morrow, 1984; London: Hamilton, 1984);

School Ties (London: Hamilton, 1985; New York: Morrow, 1985);

The New Confessions (London: Hamilton, 1987; New York: Morrow, 1988);

Brazzaville Beach: A Novel (New York: Morrow, 1990; London: Sinclair-Stevenson, 1990);

The Blue Afternoon (London: Sinclair-Stevenson, 1993; New York: Knopf, 1995);

Cork (London: Ulysses, 1994);

The Destiny of Nathalie "X" (London: Sinclair-Stevenson, 1995); enlarged as *The Destiny of Nathalie "X" and Other Stories* (New York: Knopf, 1997);

Transfigured Night (London: One Horse Press, 1995);

Visions Fugitives (London: Cuckoo Press for John Sandoe, 1997);

Armadillo: A Novel (New York: Knopf, 1998; London: Hamilton, 1998);

Nat Tate: An American Artist, 1928–1960 (Cambridge: 21 Publishing, 1998);

Protobiography (London: Bridgewater, 1998).

PRODUCED SCRIPTS: *Good and Bad at Games,* television, Portman Quintet/Channel Four, 1983;

Dutch Girls, television, London Weekend Television, 1985;

Scoop, television, script adapted by Boyd from the novel by Evelyn Waugh, London Weekend Television, 1987;

Stars and Bars, motion picture, screenplay adapted by Boyd from his novel, Columbia, 1988;

Aunt Julia and the Scriptwriter, motion picture, screenplay adapted by Boyd from the novel by Mario Vargas

William Boyd at the time of Nat Tate *(1998)*

Llosa, Hobo/Polar/Odyssey/Cinecom, 1990; re-released as *Tune in Tomorrow,* Hobo, 1990;

Mister Johnson, motion picture, screenplay adapted by Boyd from the novel by Joyce Cary, TFC/Avenue Pictures, 1990;

Chaplin, motion picture, screenplay adapted by Boyd, Bryan Forbes, and William Goldman from *My Autobiography* by Charles Chaplin, Guild/Lambeth/Carolco/Le Studio Canal, 1992;

A Good Man in Africa, motion picture, screenplay adapted by Boyd from his novel, UIP/Polar/Capitol/Southern Sun, 1994;

Homage to AB: A Masque, radio, BBC Radio Scotland, 1994;

The Trench, motion picture, Bonaparte Films, 1999.

OTHER: Joyce Cary, *Mister Johnson,* introduction by Boyd (Harmondsworth, U.K.: Penguin, 1985);

Graham Sutherland, *Graham Sutherland,* Modern British Masters, volume 9, introduction by Boyd (London: Bernard Jacobson Gallery, 1993);

Ken Saro-Wiwa, *A Month and a Day: A Detention Diary,* introduction by Boyd (New York: Penguin, 1995);

Frederic Manning, *Her Privates We,* introduction by Boyd (London: Serpent's Tail, 1999).

SELECTED PERIODICAL PUBLICATIONS– UNCOLLECTED: "Fancy an Egg and Beans?" *Daily Telegraph* (London), Weekend section, 28 February 1998, pp. 1–2;

"Under the Bridge," *Modern Painters,* 11 (Spring 1998): 36–39;

"A Bridge Too Far," *Sunday Telegraph* (London), Review section, 5 April 1998, p. 7;

"Nat Tate, My Part in his Creation," *Sunday Telegraph* (London), Review section, 12 April 1998, p. 9.

Trying to make sense of William Boyd's literary career as a whole is no easy task. His dual impulse to write literary fiction and lighter comic novels–comparable, perhaps, to Graham Greene's distinction between his "novels" and "entertainments"–does not necessarily represent a division or a contradiction. Boyd is a literary chameleon; he refuses to be tied down to any particular subgenre of the novel and defends his right to publish new work that differs completely from what his reading public might expect. Nevertheless, certain preoccupations do emerge repeatedly from the Boyd oeuvre–his troubled engagement with World War I, which he identifies as a crisis point in British, European, and world history; a keen interest in the visual media, particularly motion pictures; a fascination with slang and unconventional speech; mathematics as metaphor; and the technology of flight. Boyd's interest in cinema has led him to adapt many of his novels, as well as those of other authors, for the screen. Boyd has tended to produce a novel roughly every three years, and in this respect he might be thought to work at a slower pace than some of his contemporaries. Yet, there is little doubt that Boyd is a careful writer, a distance runner rather than a sprinter. His high standards of fiction writing are also evident in his work in movies, newspapers, and television.

William Andrew Murray Boyd was born on 7 March 1952 in Accra, Ghana, the son of Scottish parents, Alexander Murray Boyd, a physician, and Evelyn Smith Boyd, a teacher. Young Boyd was a boarder at Gordonstoun School, where he endured a notoriously Spartan and unbookish regime, separated by thousands of miles from his parents, who continued to live and work in Africa. The kind of elite school he attended provides the setting for his early stories, notably "Hardly Ever" (collected in *On the Yankee Station and Other Stories,* 1981), which describes the sexual frustrations of attending an all-male school. Furthermore, the hero of Boyd's 1987 novel, *The New Confessions,* attends a series of Scottish private schools that are presented as brutal, unattractive places, where arbitrary justice is administered by the boys themselves rather than by those in authority. Boyd has explored the formative experience of his school days in the long autobiographical preface to *School Ties,* his 1985 volume of television plays.

Boyd received a diploma in French studies in 1971 at the University of Nice, was awarded an M.A. in English and philosophy at Glasgow University in 1975, and then moved to England to pursue a higher degree and an academic career at Oxford University. He undertook postgraduate study at Jesus College, Oxford, in 1980, then became a lecturer in English at St. Hilda's College, Oxford, a post he held until 1983.

Boyd's earliest published fiction took the form of short stories, most of which have been republished in *On the Yankee Station and Other Stories* and *The Destiny of Nathalie "X"* (1995). Speaking at the Birmingham Readers' and Writers' Festival in 1995, Boyd described how, in the late 1970s, the proliferation of British literary magazines offered incipient young writers an opportunity to get into print relatively easily. Boyd published his early stories in *Granta, Mayfair, London Magazine, Punch, Isis,* and *Literary Review.* Others were commissioned by BBC Radio 4. He continues to regard the short story as his "laboratory," a place where he can experiment with form and narrative technique without having to make the more extensive commitment of time and energy that a full-length novel would demand. Boyd worked from 1981 until 1983 as a television critic for the left-wing weekly political magazine *The New Statesman. The New Statesman* was an important training ground for the rising generation of British novelists and poets throughout the 1970s and early 1980s: Julian Barnes, Craig Raine, James Fenton, and Clive James were all regular contributors, and Martin Amis was literary editor of the magazine between 1977 and 1979. Boyd's television column memorably dissected programs such as John Mortimer's 1980 adaptation of Evelyn Waugh's *Brideshead Revisited* (1945). Boyd adapted

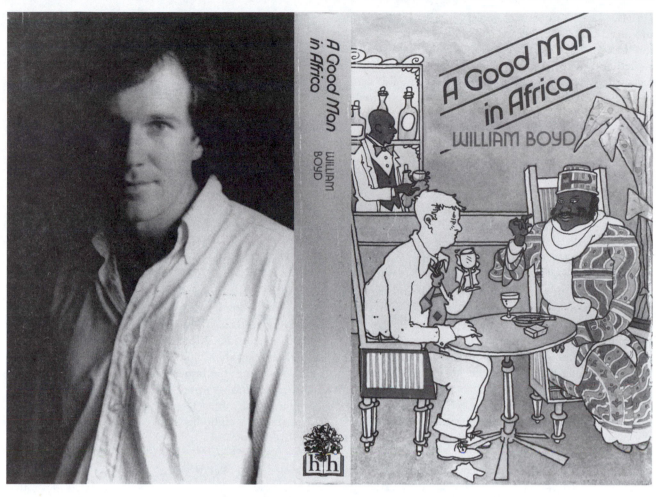

Dust jacket for Boyd's first novel (1981), in which he drew on his early life in Ghana (courtesy of The Lilly Library, Indiana University, Bloomington, Indiana)

the second of Waugh's African novels, *Scoop,* for television in 1987.

Boyd's first novel, *A Good Man in Africa,* was published in 1981. This densely plotted book is set in the imaginary African state of Kinjanja, and its incompetent but engaging hero is Morgan Leafy, first secretary to the deputy high commissioner in the British diplomatic service. Leafy is the victim of several disasters in the course of the novel, each of which contributes in some way to his moral education. Arthur Fanshawe, Leafy's boss at the British High Commission, instructs him to remove the body of a woman who has been struck dead by a bolt of lightning. According to local superstition, the woman has been killed by an angry sky god called Shango, and she must not be moved until a complicated and expensive religious ceremony has been conducted. There is widespread outrage after Leafy secretly dumps the body in the trunk of his car, so he must then return it under cover of darkness. Meanwhile, his love affair with Priscilla Fanshawe (Arthur's daughter) is scup-

pered when Leafy contracts a painful dose of gonorrhea from Hazel, his persistently unfaithful black mistress. Having been warned to abstain from sexual relations for a few weeks, he is unable to respond to Priscilla's advances, and she is so insulted that she breaks off the affair.

The "good man" of the title is Alex Murray, a Scottish doctor at the Kinjanja University health center, who provides a yardstick of virtue against which Leafy's wayward behavior may be measured. Murray is compiling a report on a proposed extension to the university, and Adekunle, a local politician who stands to profit from the development, gives Leafy the task of bribing Murray to submit a favorable report. Leafy cannot escape from this piece of corruption since he is being blackmailed by Adekunle as a result of his adulterous affair with Adekunle's wife.

Although the novel takes place in Africa, it owes a substantial debt, in terms of both plot and style, to Kingsley Amis's comedy of English manners *Lucky Jim*

(1954). Leafy's obscene interior monologues and unvoiced rage are expressed in an idiom borrowed from Jim Dixon, the central figure in *Lucky Jim:* "Morgan smiled and raised his own glass. I hate you, you smug bastard! he screamed inwardly. You shit, you little turd, you've ruined my life! But all he said was, 'Congratulations. She's a fabulous girl. Lovely. Lucky chap.'" Amis, whose writing is in the tradition of Waugh, is in many respects an excellent model for comic writing, and Boyd's debut is a confident and uproarious act of homage. Yet, *A Good Man in Africa* ultimately succeeds because the evocation of Kinjanja is so precise. Boyd's talent as a recorder of place is evident: "Morgan could see the roofs stretch before him, an ochrous tin checker-board, a bilious metallic sea, the paranoiac vision of a mad town planner. Few buildings stretched higher than three storeys and most were crumbling mud-walled houses randomly clustered and packed alongside narrow pot-holed streets lined with deep purulent drains. Morgan liked to imagine the town as some immense yeast culture, left in a damp cupboard by an absent-minded lab technician, festering uncontrolled, running rampant in the ideal growing conditions."

Unlike Amis's hero in *Lucky Jim,* Morgan Leafy does not get the girl in the final chapter, but he ends on the brink of a sexual encounter with Chloe Fanshawe, Priscilla's mother. However, news of Murray's sudden death prevents this affair from being consummated, and the novel concludes with a hint that Leafy has perhaps learned a little from Murray's honesty and good conduct: "Alive or dead Murray somehow managed to barge his way into his life as persistently as ever. And suddenly he didn't particularly want to go on with it: two large white bodies heaving and grunting in an absurd parody of love." This accomplished first novel won a Somerset Maugham Award in Great Britain, and it is still considered one of Boyd's strongest.

The adventures of Morgan Leafy are continued in Boyd's next book, *On the Yankee Station and Other Stories.* One of these short stories, "Next Boat From Douala," is a much-shortened early draft of *A Good Man in Africa,* and it is instructive to read it alongside the full-length novel. The other Leafy story, "The Coup," follows the character to the end of his African tour of duty. "Extracts from the Journal of Flying Officer J." is a stylishly extended parody of W. H. Auden's "Journal of an Airman," which appears in the poet's second book, *The Orators: An English Study* (1932). This story is the earliest example of Boyd writing about aviation, which becomes one of his central concerns in *The Blue Afternoon* (1993).

In his second novel, *An Ice-Cream War* (1982), Boyd cleverly works with two locations: Nairobi, in the former colonial territory of British East Africa; and Ashurst, in the southeast corner of England, in Kent, just a few miles by sea from France. Taking place during the opening days of World War I, the story concerns the struggle between the British and the Germans for the possession of African colonies. It is hard to interpret the book as anything other than a statement against the absurdities of colonialism.

At the center of this novel are two brothers, Gabriel and Felix Cobb. Gabriel is an officer in the British army, and his honeymoon in France is cut short by the outbreak of the war in 1914. He joins his regiment in East Africa, where he sustains serious bayonet wounds when a military operation he is leading goes wrong. While Gabriel spends the rest of the war recovering in an African hospital, the focus shifts to his younger brother Felix, back in England. Felix, initially certified unfit for military service because of poor eyesight, begins the book as a sexually frustrated undergraduate studying at Oxford University. Returning to the Cobb family estate in Ashford during the summer vacation, he begins an affair with his new sister-in-law, Charis, now staying at the family home. Boyd evokes the guilt and repression of upper-class English family life effectively, and he directs lacerating satire against the imperialist mind-set, embodied in the character of the father of the two young men.

An Ice-Cream War, which was shortlisted for the prestigious Booker Prize in 1982, asks to be taken far more seriously than the author's previously published books. Boyd writes unflinchingly about the horrors of combat, clearly aiming to shock and disgust his readers: "One or several bullets had removed Gleeson's lower jaw-bone in its entirety, but somehow his tongue had been untouched. It now lolled, uncontained, at his throat like a thick fleshy cravat, pink and purple. Gleeson's upper lip was drawn back revealing his top row of yellow teeth, his fair moustache was spattered with dried mud and blood. What was most horrifying was the way his eyes boggled and rolled, and his tongue twitched feebly at his neck." While there is no shortage of nightmarish battlefield detail here, Boyd is also concerned to bring out the bitter ironies of the war. When the British forces attack the town of Tanga, for example, they are driven back not by rival troops but by an enormous swarm of bees. The British forces believe the bee attack to be an elaborate booby trap, representing the infinite cunning and devilishness of the German army.

Stars and Bars (1984) was the first book Boyd published after resigning from teaching to write full time. The novel is a return to the farcical comedy of *A Good Man in Africa,* though this time with a North American setting. The hero is an Englishman who is adrift in New

Dust jacket for the first American edition of Boyd's 1982 novel, set in East Africa and England at the beginning of World War I

York and the Deep South of the United States. Henderson Dores is sent by his employer to a small southern town called Luxora Beach in search of a priceless art collection, and the story concentrates on his inability to speak the language of the region or to understand its codes of behavior. Boyd picks up an idea frequently voiced by another British novelist, Martin Amis, that traveling to the United States, from an outsider's perspective, does not feel simply like going to a different country, but seems more like visiting another planet. Boyd dramatizes the problem of translating between British and American English, notably when Henderson tries to speak to one of his hosts in Luxora Beach:

> "'Um, look, Shanda, I was going to ask, that's to say I was wondering if you might just possibly see your way to doing me a little favour,'" he began confidentially, but then stopped as he saw her eyes cloud with incomprehension.
>
> "Well, shucks," he began again, trying to recall his Huckleberry Finn and Ring Lardner. "I reckon I jist plum done and forgit to ask you to do me a service,

like, goshdarn it." It was a little overdone, he admitted, but, like an orchestra tuning up, he had to get in key.

When the paintings disappear–in fact they have been burned by a sinister relative of the original collector–Henderson is accused of having stolen them, and he is pursued by gangsters who want to recover them, by murder if necessary. Persecuted in one way or another by almost every character in the book, Henderson is presented as a victim of circumstance, a fundamentally decent man who struggles to cling to his principles in the face of considerable opposition. The thesis of the novel, as its epigraph from Christopher Isherwood's *Lions and Shadows* (1938) makes clear, is that the apparently weak Henderson is a truly strong man, because he resists the traditional modes of heroic behavior. He does not punch his enemies on the jaw or resort to macho posturing, which is portrayed in the novel as a form of neurosis, but retains instead his quiet dignity. Traditional heroes, the book argues, are the truly weak men, since they are in fact attempting to compensate for their deep-seated feelings of inadequacy. *Stars and Bars* is a rich and enjoyable comedy of situation and language. Reviewing the novel in *TLS: The Times Literary Supplement* (21 September 1984), David Montrose commented, "The novel will consolidate, rather than advance, William Boyd's reputation." Although *Stars and Bars* lacks the depth of Boyd's other work, it is a well-constructed story, perhaps written with film adaptation in mind. Yet, the 1988 movie version, scripted by Boyd and starring Daniel Day-Lewis as Henderson Dores, was not a resounding success.

Boyd's 1987 novel, *The New Confessions,* a long, historical work painted on a broad canvas, is a victim of its own desire to be inclusive. The book is structured as a memoir of the twentieth century, as recalled by a Scottish cinematographer by the name of John James Todd. Born in Edinburgh in 1899, the motherless Todd undergoes a loveless childhood and is educated at a private school where his only friend, Hamish, who is hideously disfigured by acne, is a mathematician. This relationship allows Boyd to make use of mathematics, a theme that recurs later in *Brazzaville Beach* (1990), as a possible way of discovering the truth about the world of material, mappable objects. "Does maths prove God exists?" asks Hamish. If not, who can be said to have created the science of mathematics? Is it something mankind has invented, or a pre-existing reality which we have discovered?

Todd's other formative influence is Donald Verulam, one of his late mother's lovers, who encourages him in his hobby of photography. He then becomes an official moviemaker for the War Office Cinema Committee during World War I. Yet, Todd's pioneering documentary about life in the trenches is judged by wartime censors to be so terrifying that the movie is suppressed. Accidentally landing behind German lines while filming from a hot-air balloon, Todd is captured. He spends the final years of the war in a prisoner-of-war camp and, while imprisoned, comes across a copy of Jean-Jacques Rousseau's *Confessions* (1782–1789). Todd is so moved by the experience of reading this autobiography that he decides to adapt it for the cinema. Most of the remaining chapters of Boyd's narrative are given over to describing this impossible project, conceived by Todd as an epic series of silent movies. The coming of the talkies renders Todd's vision obsolete; in any event, only one part of the envisaged series ever reaches a final state. When the movie does premiere, it is not a success. The unmade or uncompleted cinematic *Confessions* seems to represent Todd's grand folly, rather like Edward Casaubon's unwritten book, "The Key to All Mythologies," in George Eliot's novel, *Middlemarch* (1871–1872). Perhaps Boyd is saying something about the untranslatability of literary works into a visual medium. Part of the problem is that Todd develops an obsession with his leading actress, Doon Bogan, which leads him to join the Communist Party, of which Doon is a member. Working in post-1945 Hollywood, Todd falls prey to the McCarthy persecutions, and his career as a writer and director is destroyed by the rising anti-Communist sentiment of the 1950s.

The New Confessions puts forward the thesis that all cinematic techniques originate in dreaming: "We could dream slow motion before the moving camera was invented. In our dreams we could cut between parallel actions, we assembled montage shots long before some self-important Russian claimed to show us how. This is where film derives its peculiar power. It recreates on screen what has been going on in our unconscious." Boyd's novel about the growth of the cinema records his ongoing fascination with motion pictures as a form of narrative. Some critics have objected that the Rousseau sections of *The New Confessions* are less interesting than the chapters dealing with World War I and that the book as a whole tends to meander from one country to another in a fairly haphazard and unstructured way. Francis King voiced this anxiety about structure when he wrote in *The Spectator* (3 October 1987) that "one searches in vain for an overall pattern. . . . It has enough plot for at least half-a-dozen novels, but what it bewilderingly lacks is a dominating theme. Certainly the novel lacks the taut construction of *A Good Man in Africa,* but few of Boyd's detractors have noticed that he has already offered an answer to the charge of shapelessness within the text itself. Todd writes in the final chapter:

> I look back at my life, at my three score years and ten, and think—yes, I would dearly like there to be an underlying order to these seven decades of reality. I would like some sense, some meaning. . . . The search for "truth" can never be the same. Science, which used to attempt to enumerate all the cogs in the Great Machine, has abandoned that endeavour now. Life at its basic level, the quantum physicists tell us, is deeply paradoxical and fundamentally uncertain. There are no hidden variables, there is no secret agenda for the universe.

These lines may be read as a justification for the apparent sprawl and randomness of the book. Yet, perhaps it is significant that, having attempted a novel of near-epic proportions, Boyd returned to the shorter works on which his reputation was built.

Boyd's next novel, *Brazzaville Beach,* is a zoological, anthropological, and mathematical thriller that switches between two simultaneously developing stories, both of which are episodes from the life of the heroine, Hope Clearwater. In the earlier narrative, Hope is married to a promising young mathematician, John Clearwater, who is searching for a series of unifying mathematical principles to explain how the natural world works. It becomes increasingly plain that John is on the edge of madness, and it is suggested that he has been driven insane by his quest for a grand, totalizing theory of everything. The later section takes place in an unidentified African state, after the end of Hope's marriage to John. She is part of a team of zoologists who are investigating the behavior of chimpanzees. This research project is leading toward a groundbreaking book on chimpanzee communities, to be published under the name of the team leader, Eugene Mallabar. When the book is in proof stage, Hope discovers new evidence that the chimps are killing each other, thereby disproving Mallabar's theory of how they ought to behave. He reacts by suppressing and destroying Hope's new evidence (burning the bodies of the murdered chimps), because it does not accord with the conclusions of his study. As relations between the scientists grow bitter, the unpredictable behavior that Hope has witnessed among the chimps is reflected among the human characters. Meanwhile, outside the limits of the zoological observation area, a civil war is waiting to break out, and this political unrest eventually touches the European researchers.

Both narratives seem to be speaking, in different ways, of the importance of taking account of chaos when constructing theories, but Boyd also recognizes that it is ultimately impossible to predict human behavior, animal behavior, or indeed the universe itself. Boyd's training in philosophy along with literature–an unusual combination of degree subjects for a British writer–is detectable in his writing, particularly in his ideological novels, such as this one. He plays interestingly with narrative technique in this book. For example, while it is clear from the prologue that Hope is narrating both episodes, she decides to tell the mathematical story in the first person and the chimpanzee story in the third person. The reader's response to each narrative thread is therefore conditioned according to preconceptions about narrative point of view, and the novel is careful to draw attention to the difficulties of perspective and judgment with which it presents its readers.

Brazzaville Beach works well as a novel of ideas, and it is rightly regarded as Boyd's most serious and intellectually challenging work to date. Yet, the mathematical sections, although diligently researched, are cold and alienating to read, and the equations in the text present difficulties of comprehension for the lay reader. Nevertheless, the novel was a critical success, prompting Anita Brookner to write in *The Spectator* (15 September 1990) that "the effect is absorbing, at times

hallucinating. One salutes the intellectual structure of the novel, something rarely encountered in comtemporary English fiction." *Brazzaville Beach* won the 1990 James Tait Black Memorial Prize. Translated into twenty languages, the book was well received throughout the world.

The Blue Afternoon (1993) is a complex, well-crafted, genre-breaking novel, and is possibly the finest work Boyd has published. Its narrative structure feels experimental. The opening section is narrated in the voice of Kay Fischer, a modernist architect working in Los Angeles in 1936. Kay meets a mysterious old man named Salvador Carriscant, who claims to be her father, and the pair then travel by sea to Lisbon aboard the SS *Herzog* (surely a reference to the 1964 novel by Saul Bellow). During the voyage, Salvador tells his story to Kay, who writes it down as if it were being narrated in his own words. Thus, Kay acts as a narrative filter between Carriscant and the reader, as she describes a series of events that took place in the Philippines around 1902, shortly before she was born. *The Blue Afternoon* deliberately resists easy classification within any of the traditional subgenres of the novel. In part it is a murder mystery, yet at the same time it is a book about the invention of powered flight and various pioneering surgical techniques developed in the early years of the twentieth century. Arguably the most intriguing aspect of *The Blue Afternoon* is the impossible detective story at the heart of the novel. Repeated rereadings fail to yield a definitive solution to the question of who has in fact murdered Colonel Jepson George Sieverance. Although some readers might regard this absence of narrative closure as an irritating game on the part of the author, a more sympathetic interpretation would give Boyd credit for trying to present, as plausibly as possible, an unsolved murder case in fictional form. Like his acknowledged literary master, Vladimir Nabokov, Boyd takes great care not to explain the true significance of his stories to the reader, and one might say that reticence has increasingly become the hallmark of his mature work. Boyd worked extensively in the cinema in the early 1990s. In 1990 he wrote screen adaptations of Joyce Cary's *Mister Johnson* (1939) and Mario Vargas Llosa's *Aunt Julia and the Scriptwriter* (1990).

Boyd has written a total of twenty screenplays, of which just nine have been filmed; the best known is his 1992 rewrite of Richard Attenborough's *Chaplin*. He removed his name from Jeremiah Chechnik's *Diabolique* (1996) when his script was rewritten to produce a happy ending.

Boyd's mounting disillusionment with the movie industry is recorded in the title story of his 1995 collection, *The Destiny of Nathalie "X."* The story, narrated in

Dust jacket for Boyd's 1998 book, a mock-biography that was mistaken for nonfiction when excerpts were published in spring 1998

several different voices, reads as a documentary about the making of a lousy, yet award-winning, movie. *The Destiny of Nathalie "X"* is a lighthearted piece, best regarded as a parable about the ruthlessness of Hollywood studios. Other stories in this collection, however, are more interesting. "Transfigured Night" takes an episode from the early life of Ludwig Wittgenstein and attempts to form a connection between his biography and the philosophical system he later developed. "Hotel des Voyageurs" is written in the form of a writer's imaginary diary. The English narrator, Logan Mountstuart, closely resembles the sybaritic journalist and magazine editor Cyril Connolly. Mountstuart is a figure who acquires a central prominence in Boyd's later works.

Homage to AB: A Masque was commissioned as a radio play with music interludes by Anthony Burgess, and was presented at the Edinburgh Festival in 1994. The radio play celebrates the life and work of Burgess, who had died after a long illness in November 1993. The main source for the play is Burgess's two-volume autobiography, *Little Wilson and Big God* (1987) and *You've Had Your Time* (1990). Boyd's original material takes the form of dialogues between Burgess and his fictional character Enderby (the hero of four novels). The

radio production of the play represented the first major performance of Burgess's music in the United Kingdom; however, Boyd's *Homage to AB* did not have the intended effect of establishing Burgess as a respectable composer, and Boyd's play has not been broadcast outside Scotland. A recording survives in the BBC Radio Scotland sound archive.

After the high seriousness of *Brazzaville Beach* and *The Blue Afternoon,* many of Boyd's readers were disconcerted by *Armadillo* (1998), a comic novel that has much in common with his earlier work, such as *A Good Man in Africa* and *Stars and Bars.* Essentially a satire about the insurance business, *Armadillo* is Boyd's first novel set entirely in London. In this case, the capital is imagined in terms of violence, seediness, disorder, corporate crime, and insurance fraud. The central character, Lorimer Black, is a recognizable Boyd type, a man of principle who feels isolated in a deeply compromised world. Lorimer's job as a loss adjuster requires him to establish whether or not insurance claims are genuine, and he is instructed to look into a suspicious fire at the Fedora Palace hotel. Yet, his investigations in the name of truth are at variance with the deceptions of his private life. The novel also gives extracts from Lorimer's private diary, which he titles "The Book of Transfiguration." This document reveals that Lorimer's real name is Milomre Blocj, that he comes from a family of Transnistrian Gypsies, and that he left his university under embarrassing circumstances. These facts have been concealed from his employer, and Lorimer/Milomre emerges as a chameleon-like figure. Elsewhere he is living simultaneously in several London houses and putting on disguises when meeting clients in order to win their confidence. Lorimer's evasions become more pronounced when he embarks on an affair with a married actress named Flavia Malinverno, while continuing his long-standing relationship with his girlfriend, Stella.

Among the minor characters, there are some masterpieces of grotesque invention, including Marlobe, a working-class flower seller who assails the ears of his customers with obscene monologues on the state of the nation and the desirability of women with flat heads. The novel draws pessimistic conclusions about London itself, and Lorimer finally decides that the city is, at bottom, a savage place: "Beneath this veneer of order, probity, governance and civilized behaviour—aren't we just kidding ourselves?" Boyd's paranoid vision is of a capital on the edge of disorder, where thugs roam the streets armed with scaffolding poles or burn the paint off cars with blow torches. The reader is also shown decaying housing estates where the buildings are, depressingly, "thumbtacked with satellite dishes." Although there is plenty of criminal lowlife represented, part of Boyd's purpose is to examine the moral gray area of white-collar crime. As one of the characters points out, the small-time crooks in the story are not measurably worse than the outwardly respectable loss adjusters, who are described as "scum no better than thieves, lying . . . villains."

Interviewed by Mark Lawson of *The Guardian* at the time the novel was published, Boyd defended himself against the charge that his work is lacking in narrative and thematic complication: "Say you have two role models. There's the James Joyce of *Ulysses* and the James Joyce of *Dubliners*. And you're entitled to take one forking path or the other. And I would rather aim for limpidity and transparence than ornament and opacity. My novels are fundamentally about narrative and character. So my prose is required to be clear rather than to draw attention to itself."

In 1998 *Nat Tate: An American Artist, 1928–1960* achieved the rare distinction of being written about on the news pages rather than in the review sections of newspapers. This audacious mock-biography, plausibly illustrated with period photographs and paintings that were actually painted by Boyd himself, was first announced in the Spring 1998 issue of the magazine *Modern Painters*. (Boyd is a member of the editorial board.) The magazine ran an extract from Boyd's life of Nat Tate (a name that amalgamates the names of the two largest art galleries in London, the National Gallery and the Tate Gallery), and it was republished on 5 April 1998 in *The Sunday Telegraph,* a major British broadsheet newspaper with a circulation of more than a million readers. Within a week, another London paper, *The Independent,* broke the story that the biography was in fact a complex work of fiction, and it was suggested that Boyd, in collaboration with the singer David Bowie, another *Modern Painters* board member, had been involved in an attempt to fool the New York art world into believing that Nat Tate had been an actual painter. Yet, it is far from clear that the book was composed with any deception in mind, and a close reading shows that Boyd was careful to sprinkle enough clues in the text to signal to the alert reader that something was amiss.

Apart from its deliberately anachronistic photographic illustrations, the most obvious incongruity is the presence in the book of *The Intimate Journals of Logan Mountstuart,* which are supposedly the work of a friend of Nat Tate's. Extracts from these journals are provided at various points in the narrative, but readers of *The Destiny of Nathalie "X"* will immediately recognize Mountstuart as the narrator of the story "Hotel des Voyageurs." Boyd's defense against any charge of deception is therefore built into his mock-biography, namely that the fictionality of the work would be clear to anyone who knew this short story. The novella also makes great play with the fashionable language of art criticism, and much of the satire in this vein hits its target. Speaking of Nat Tate's paintings, which have been deliberately ruined by applying turpentine on top of the paint, Logan Mountstuart writes that these "spectral canvases" are "a profound statement of time and time passing, of the brave refusal of man's artefacts to be overwhelmed by oblivion." It seems likely that Boyd's purpose here is to ridicule a particular kind of art journalism, the objection presumably being that such writing tells the reader little or nothing about the art under discussion.

Nevertheless, news journalists, feature writers, and newspaper diarists covered the story extensively, earning Boyd a place in the popular imagination as an amiable trickster. In response to criticism from the tabloid press, Boyd published a long article in *The Sunday Telegraph* (12 April 1998) in which he explained the origins of the Nat Tate joke and spoke about his intentions in perpetrating this scheme: "The book was, in the end, studded with covert and cryptic clues and hints as to its real, fictive status. For me, the author, this was part of the pleasure—a form of Nabokovian relish in the sheer play and artifice—and the fundamental aim of the book, it became clear to me, was to destabilise, to challenge our notions of authenticity. What was created was a form of reverse propaganda. Not truth disguised by lies, but 'Truth' peeled away to reveal the true lie at the centre." Although it has been published only in a small hardback edition, the Nat Tate biography may come to be regarded as one of Boyd's most important works. It is a joyously disrespectful performance that stands up to repeated close readings, and it promises to become a key reference point in the recent history of fakes and faking.

In 1999 Boyd wrote and directed an original motion picture, *The Trench*. Set during the Battle of the Somme in 1916, this movie concentrates on the extreme youth of the soldiers who fought in World War I. Some were just sixteen—or younger if they had lied about their age when volunteering for service. Writing about the experience of making *The Trench* in *The Daily Telegraph* (17 September 1999), Boyd states that the battle scenes and explosions presented him with particular difficulties as a director. His other area of interest, as in his novels, is in spoken language: "Soldiers swear, vilely, all the time—swear like troopers, in fact. Anyone who wants to know how soldiers swore in 1916 should read *Her Privates We* (1930), a novel by Frederic Manning, a writer who served in the Somme as a private soldier. Manning's fellow soldiers swear vigorously and colourfully. They craft their own profane music." Boyd has said that he intends to direct further motion pictures, but his next project will be a novel: "Writing fiction is absolute freedom. As an art form it is so boundlessly generous. Novels literally have no boundaries. You can write a 2,000-page novel covering billions of years, if that's what you decide to do. Anything is possible."

Interview:

Mark Lawson, "Frozen Assets," *Guardian,* 19 February 1998, II: 11–12.

References:

Douglas Dunn, "Divergent Scottishness: William Boyd, Alan Massie, Ronald Frame," in *The Scottish Novel Since the Seventies: New Visions, Old Dreams,* edited by Gavin Wallace and Randall Stevenson (Edinburgh: Edinburgh University Press, 1993), pp. 149–169;

Alex Ivanovitch, "Onomastics," *London Review of Books* (4 June 1998): 28–29;

John Mullan, "Sting in Manhattan," *Guardian,* 9 April 1998, II: 11.

Christine Brooke-Rose

(16 January 1923 –   )

Graeme Harper
University of Wales, Bangor

See also the Brooke-Rose entry in *DLB 14: British Novelists Since 1960.*

BOOKS: *Gold* (Aldington, U.K.: Hand & Flower, 1955);

The Languages of Love (London: Secker & Warburg, 1957);

The Sycamore Tree (London: Secker & Warburg, 1958; New York: Norton, 1959);

A Grammar of Metaphor (London: Secker & Warburg, 1958);

The Dear Deceit (London: Secker & Warburg, 1960; Garden City, N.Y.: Doubleday, 1961);

The Middlemen: A Satire (London: Secker & Warburg, 1961);

Out (London: Joseph, 1964);

Such (London: Joseph, 1966);

Between (London: Joseph, 1968);

Go When You See the Green Man Walking (London: Joseph, 1970);

A ZBC of Ezra Pound (London: Faber & Faber, 1971; Berkeley: University of California Press, 1971);

Thru (London: Hamilton, 1975);

A Structural Analysis of Pound's Usura Canto: Jakobson's Method Extended and Applied to Free Verse (The Hague: Mouton, 1976);

A Rhetoric of the Unreal; Studies in Narrative and Structure, Especially of the Fantastic (Cambridge & New York: Cambridge University Press, 1981);

Amalgamemnon (Manchester, U.K.: Carcanet, 1984; Normal, Ill.: Dalkey Archive Press, 1994);

Xorandor (Manchester, U.K.: Carcanet, 1986; New York: Avon, 1986);

Verbivore (Manchester, U.K.: Carcanet, 1990);

Textermination (Manchester, U.K.: Carcanet, 1991; New York: New Directions, 1992);

Stories, Theories and Things (Cambridge: Cambridge University Press, 1991);

Remake (Manchester, U.K.: Carcanet, 1996);

Next (Manchester, U.K.: Carcanet, 1998);

Subscript (Manchester, U.K.: Carcanet, 1999).

Christine Brooke-Rose (courtesy of the author)

Collection: *The Christine Brooke-Rose Omnibus: Four Novels* (Manchester, U.K. & New York: Carcanet, 1986)—comprises *Out, Such, Between,* and *Thru.*

TRANSLATIONS: Juan Goytisoto, *Children of Chaos* (London: MacGibbon & Kee, 1959);

Alfred Sauvy, *Fertility and Survival: Population Problems from Malthus to Mao Tse Tung* (New York: Criterion, 1961; London: Chatto & Windus, 1961);

Alain Robbe-Grillet, *In the Labyrinth* (London: Calder & Boyars, 1967).

SELECTED PERIODICAL PUBLICATION—
UNCOLLECTED: "Narrating without a narrator,"
TLS: The Times Literary Supplement, 31 December
1999, pp. 12–13.

Christine Brooke-Rose is most often portrayed as a writer of extremely challenging and deeply intellectual prose whose experiments with fictional form reflect a French rather than a British literary heritage. Her failure to reach a wider audience stems largely from her determination to destabilize the very language her work inhabits. Even in an era in which such a commitment might be included under the rubric of postmodernism, her writing has remained singular in intention and idiosyncratic in outlook. Yet, her linguistic playfulness, which extends to her interest in the semiotics of science fiction and a contemplation of mutability of language, is strengthened by a much more traditional desire: she is deeply committed to the poetic possibilities of the novel form and to its relationship to other fields of knowledge. Brooke-Rose's excursions into science fiction are, in this sense, excursions into the multiform relationship between science and fiction. Her interest in cybernetic culture is equally an interest in the cultural and textual possibilities of feminism. Parameters are something this writer seeks to challenge.

While it is correct to view Brooke-Rose as a writer of English novels in the context of the *nouveau roman,* she is neither a simple cipher for Francophone literary theory nor a writer of obtrusively philosophic prose. Brooke-Rose's interest is in the workings of "discourses." She is committed to breaking down the boundaries of discourses such as politics, science and technology, philosophy, ideology, and emotion. In that respect she is a writer working in a profoundly humanist vein whose aims are to extend the understanding and appreciation of modes of language, to consider the foundation of knowledge—primarily in light of new technology—and to explore ideas about literary theory through the mode of fiction. If her work can be described as postmodern, it is because her novels are more in alignment with aspects of cybernetics, gender consciousness, and forms of intertextuality than in adherence to any single mode or school of expression. The route she has chosen is far too individual for that.

Christine Frances E. Brooke-Rose was born in Geneva, Switzerland, on 16 January 1923 to a Swiss American mother, Evelyn Blanche Brooke, and a British father, Alfred Northbrook Rose. When her parents separated in her early childhood, Brooke-Rose moved with her mother to Brussels, where they lived with her maternal grandparents from 1929 until 1936. Brooke-Rose's father died in 1934, when she was eleven.

Brooke-Rose grew up speaking French, English, and German, but French was her first language. In 1936 Brooke-Rose and her mother moved to England, where she was sent to an English school and remained throughout World War II. She joined the British Women's Auxiliary Air Force, working as an intelligence officer assessing enemy communications at Bletchley Park. She remarked in a 7 May 1987 BBC television interview that during her time as a member of the WAAF she was "created . . . as a novelist." She found, in assessing the messages of the "enemy," that she was able to experience what it was like to be "the other." For Brooke-Rose this experience of difference was formulated in her movements in and between languages. She married Rodney Ian Shirley Bax, whom she met through her work during the war, on 16 May 1944. The marriage lasted less than a year. They were divorced in January 1948, and their marriage was later annulled.

Brooke-Rose went on to read English philology and medieval literature at Somerville College, Oxford, receiving her B.A. in 1949, her M.A. in 1953, and then reading for a Ph.D. at University College, London, completing her thesis in 1954. Brooke-Rose has described this thesis as a "grammatical analysis of metaphor in Old French and Middle English poetry, comparing the modes of expression in both at a time when French had considerably influenced the development of English." On 13 February 1948, while still at Oxford, she married Polish poet and novelist Jerzy Pietrkiewicz (later Peterkiewicz). They divorced in 1975.

Brooke-Rose began her first novel, *The Languages of Love* (1957), to counter the stress induced by the near fatal illness Pietrkiewicz suffered in 1956. By then she had already published a book of poetry, *Gold* (1955), and was finishing *A Grammar of Metaphor* (1958). She has made it clear that, although she was a "slow developer," she had "always wanted to be a writer" but had felt uncertain of her place in any language, moving as she always was between languages. *A Grammar of Metaphor,* a study of metaphor in fifteen poets from Geoffrey Chaucer to Dylan Thomas, further exemplifies both the tenor of Brooke-Rose's strengths as a writer and something of her predicament: communication attempts to transgress one recognizable field of reference to make use of another through the medium of a metaphor.

The first of Brooke-Rose's novels, *The Languages of Love,* opens with a discussion of "palatal diphthongisation in fourteenth-century Kentish"; nevertheless, the novel is relatively conventional in form. In the book Julia Grampion, a recent Ph.D. in English philology, who also earlier served with the British air force in Germany, is at the end of her academic studies and involved in a relationship with Paul Brodrick, a lecturer

*Dust jacket for Brooke-Rose's first novel (1957), which draws on her studies of English philology
(courtesy of The Lilly Library, Indiana University, Bloomington, Indiana)*

in Afro-Asian philology. When the relationship breaks down because of a conflict between Broderick's Roman Catholicism and Julia's divorce from her wartime husband, Julia finds solace in an affair with Bernard Reeves, the author of a book on courtly love.

The formal conventionalism of *The Languages of Love* cannot hide its connections with Brooke-Rose's later experimental prose. The novel focuses on a woman contemplating the offer of a university job teaching English philology. The prose is scattered with evidence of Brooke-Rose's academic investigations and exemplifies her preparedness to interchange registers between that of her "fiction" and that of her "critical analysis." It is likewise clear that her attitude to the working of language is one in which she both suspects and respects its components. Words cover up the possibility of communication, create—as well as counterpoint—emotion, and are, at the worst, clear evidence against the possibility of language ever expressing the truth.

Brooke-Rose's skepticism of language continues in her autobiographical work *Remake* (1996). In her memoir she talks of "all the mentors and all the selves" and of learning, forgetting, and then relearning the various European languages she has inhabited. That quality of paradoxical plurality, unsteady but unstoppable movement, informs her second novel, *The Sycamore Tree* (1958). In this novel, plot proves a less satisfactory communicative device for Brooke-Rose's aesthetic aims; yet, in the character of Nina Jackson, who is central to the novel, the reader sees Brooke-Rose's early novelistic investigation of questions of gender stereotyping that later novels—such as *Between* (1968), *Thru* (1975), and *Amalgamemnon* (1984)—more actively consider. *The Sycamore Tree* poses the question of whether a physically attractive young woman can survive in a male-dominated world in which her education is taken to be only an addendum to her appearance. In Nina Jackson's melodramatic death, Brooke-Rose's answer is plain; though this conclusion seems as much the failure of plot to provide her with an adequate tool for her ideas as it is a summary of her position.

By the time *The Dear Deceit* appeared in 1960, Brooke-Rose had become adept at working within a fictional world in which her academic work, intertwined with her personal history, provided the immediate framework for structurally traditional writing. When she opts to use a retrospective narrative technique, telling the story of Alfred Northbrook Hayley through the investigations into his life by his son, it remains a question of exposing the workings of narrative without necessarily offering an alternative. Fictions, Brooke-Rose suggests, infest facts, and narrative convention is often no help. The son's search for the truth about his father's life ultimately results in the distortion of his own. Brooke-Rose is just as determined in this novel to question the reader's seduction by the promise of discovery. Seeking truth seems to require more than a love of the search. Readers cannot be just "middlemen" in the movement between ignorance and knowledge.

The Middlemen (1961) satirically exploits this theme. The suggestion Brooke-Rose makes in this novel is that the role of intermediary has grown to such an extent that people can no longer change or improve anything but simply pass it on. "We are all middlemen," she writes, "selling to others something we do not own, something we have not made."

The Middlemen was not a critical success. Critics complained of the author's smugness, of what reviewer R. Moyne in *The New Statesman* (8 September 1961) called the "two dimensional characters" of the novel and of what Bernard Bergonzi in a 1 September 1961 review for *The Spectator* (titled "Inanity Fair") termed a lack of "moral passion," criticisms that are not without some foundation. This work should not be dismissed as an aberration in Brooke-Rose's oeuvre. The failure of the novel in design and narration works as an important indicator that Brooke-Rose had already grown disenchanted with the idea of simple narrative structure before her bouts with a long and serious illness in 1962, which, she noted in 1989, resulted in a "return to my essential self" and from which she emerged with a new mode of writing. The point is that Brooke-Rose's essential self was already one in which conventional literary modes of using language were questionable and, ultimately, inadequate.

The Middlemen is Brooke-Rose's transitional text, a conduit through which the novelist and her critics came to realize that this writer had reached the end of her ability to operate effectively in the conventional naturalistic vein that the British novel of the time continued to explore. This novel, a light satire disjointedly structured and headed by a page-long sociological diatribe on the era of middlemen, is pieced together by its ideas rather than its form, which is rickety at best. Brooke-Rose trolls for material both to pad and to glue her narration: advertising slogans and psychoanalytic jargon, portraits of representative "middlemen" from public-relations experts to literary agents, television personalities to lawyers. After a journey to a Greek island, there is a volca-

nic eruption, and the novel ends apocalyptically. This ending is universal, encompassing analogous references to nuclear war, as well as to the author's personal sense of aesthetic and cultural disintegration. In *The Middlemen* the destruction of character and disintegration of narrative opens the path for the linguistic plurality and conversation between discourses that characterizes her novels that followed.

Brooke-Rose's illness provided her, paradoxically, the time to reconsider her position as a writer and to compose gradually the first of her experimental novels, *Out* (1964), while recovering from kidney surgery. Brooke-Rose was, by this time, already interested in science and scientific writing, having translated Alfred Sauvy's *Fertility and Survival: Population Problems from Malthus to Mao Tse Tung* (1961), and she was likewise drawn to the experiments of such French writers of the *nouveau roman* as Nathalie Sarraute and Alain Robbe-Grillet. The novels of Samuel Beckett also influenced Brooke-Rose. She has said, for example, that she sensed in *Watt* (1953) an intelligence somewhat like her own.

Out is set in an undefined time in the future, after an event described as "displacement" in which international race positions have shifted. Whites are no longer in power. Now called the "colourless" races, they have become prone to "the malady," a sickness not unlike radiation sickness, that reduces their usefulness as workers. Brooke-Rose has commented that most readers have missed the "main point" of the novel: "the reversal of the colour-bar" and "what is it *like* to be discriminated against merely for being pale."

The novel is the story of one "colourless" man, living in a shack with his wife and visiting the Labour Exchange in search of employment and, at the same time, an investigation into the interaction of one level of representation with another. This anonymous protagonist, denied both a proper name and a third-person pronoun, is the defining consciousness of the novel. The narrative consists of equal interchange between conscious and unconscious states of being. The "displacement," which bears more than a passing resemblance to nuclear holocaust and which Brooke-Rose sets up not only as a geographic rearrangement but also as a cognitive reconfiguration, is a device for investigating the slippage between discourses that the protagonist experiences in his increasing inability to locate himself "within" a given society.

Following "displacement," psychoanalytic machines called "psychoscopes" are invented that produce "biograms," the "extracted absolute of your unconscious patterns throughout your life . . . telescoped in time into one line that shows your harmonious rhythm, your up and down tendencies." Rather than restrict the nonliteral to figurative positions, Brooke-Rose accomplishes

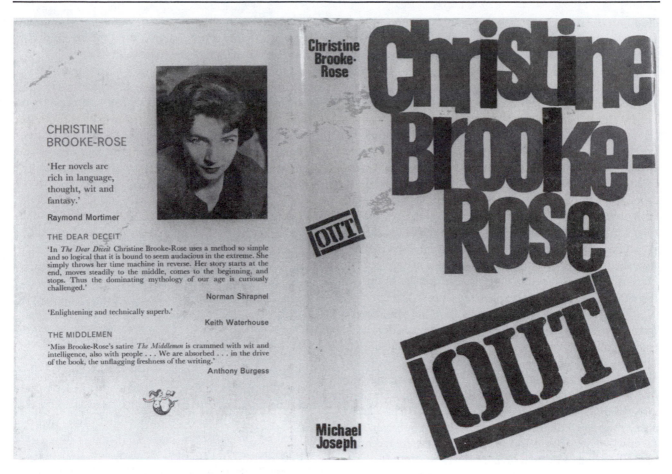

Dust jacket for Brooke-Rose's 1964 novel, for which she says she adapted "Alain Robbe-Grillet's paradoxical use of a narratorless present tense" (courtesy of The Lilly Library, Indiana University, Bloomington, Indiana)

in *Out* a materialization of her protagonist's damaged consciousness. She does so by investing in metaphor the ability to transgress its own figurativeness. As the protagonist slips further "out" of reality, his inability to locate a central ontological position becomes equally a failure to understand an epistemological one. He is in a world of fantasy that might just as surely be real. What is pure thought and what is pure object becomes indefinable. Perception itself falls foul of its own tools of interpretation. To have knowledge, therefore, is not necessarily to know.

Brooke-Rose's novel owes something to Robbe-Grillet's *Jealousy* (1957) and *In the Labyrinth* (1959), the latter of which Brooke-Rose translated into English (1967), a translation that won the Arts Council Translation Prize in 1969. Both *Jealousy* and *In The Labyrinth* find form in phenomenological discursiveness and rely on a deep sharing of the mental state of their subject, which propels the substance of the text; relying on this mental state does not necessarily separate objective existence from subjective delusion. *Out* undoubtedly works in this same territory. Brooke-Rose makes it

plain, however, that she is not comfortable with being permanently tied to Robbe-Grillet. As she wrote in a 31 December 1999 *TLS* article: "I took over and, I hope, extended, Alain Robbe-Grillet's paradoxical use of a narratorless present tense for narrative." Yet, she emphasizes that her literary debt to him is "purely on this one detail of narrative technique."

Out (1964) was rejected by the publisher of Brooke-Rose's first four novels, and her new publisher printed only three thousand copies. Yet, the novel was awarded the Society of Authors Travelling Prize in 1965.

Brooke-Rose's next novel, *Such* (1966), won the James Tait Black Memorial Prize. This critical recognition for her early experimental work was later matched by increasing numbers of questions by British critics concerning the route Brooke-Rose chose to take. By the time *Between* was published in 1968, these questions were focused primarily on the difficult aspects of the novel, in this case its multilingualism. When *Thru* was published in 1975, the concerns of Anglophone critics were increasingly aimed at what they broadly considered her preference for "theoretical" presentation in her fiction. In general they found this approach to represent an allegiance to a Francophone literary philosophy. Thus the increasing difficulty of her work became largely defined by cultural rather than aesthetic criteria.

Brooke-Rose has described *Such* as her first "really 'Me' novel, where I don't owe anything to anyone else." Her "experimental" approach, she noted, involved the "fusion of outer space with psychic space." In fact, the novel continues her investigation into the relationship between "scientific" and "literary" manifestations of truth by fusing the moment of physical death with that of psychic rebirth, blurring outer and inner selves in the hallucinatory moment where neither state is certain. The approach is relatively straightforward: in *Such* the language of astrophysics acts as a metaphor for human relationships, allowing for the transposition of the characteristics of outer space onto inner space.

The central consciousness of *Such,* the interpreter of the discourses that Brooke-Rose has intersecting and cross-fertilizing each other, is a psychiatrist named Larry, who works for a group of astrophysicists at a research laboratory. Larry dies while undergoing an operation but comes back to life, finding himself already declared dead and in a coffin. Larry, like Lazarus, rises from the dead, but in so doing he is unable or unwilling to arrange his life back into the hierarchies of relationships in which he previously was involved.

Such opens with an account of the act of climbing out of the coffin where the "dead" man, whom later the reader discovers is called Larry, meets a character who describes herself as "girl-spy." Girl-spy agrees to call him "Someone" and permits him to call her "Something." Something's five children, whom she carries on her arm, are described alternately as planets, moons, and cylinders and are subsequently baptized with the names of famous blues songs, at which point they fly off into orbit and return one by one to be given "rebirth" by Someone.

This hallucination in the minutes between death and rebirth, represented by the first episode of *Such,* is essentially the story of the relationship between Larry's unconscious and conscious states. As Larry returns from death to life and is increasingly drawn into an understanding of the laws of astrophysics, he becomes increasingly distant from those around him. Though he claims not to remember anything of his death, the events of his death intersect with and affect those of his life. Larry effectively makes two "space" journeys, one into the psychic space of himself and one into the cosmic space in which the world is situated.

Between is similarly a story of journeys. The present-tense narration moves between passages of dialogue and description in several European languages.

The narrative centers on the travels of an unnamed female translator working mostly in French and German. Rather than rely on structurally determined forward movement, the story relies on an intersection of associations established by the protagonist. Brooke-Rose, in keeping with her earlier work, insists on theme driving structure rather than the opposite. Yet, the reader is encouraged to follow two defined narratives, the first concerning the protagonist's marriage annulment and the second revolving around a series of love letters written in medieval French.

In *Between* Brooke-Rose seems to find a freedom in her personal history of movement "between" languages and places that in her earlier works had manifested itself more as a restriction or difficulty to be overcome. Yet, the fact that she declares the possibility of freedom of and within language is not categorical. Everyone, she reminds her readers, is the product of the language of others.

The movements of the female translator, who is of French and German parentage, and the history of World War II are stories in which borders and loyalties keep shifting. The different voices, different languages, and different places that appear in *Between* are, certainly in one sense, recollections of Brooke-Rose's own personal story (in particular her experience in intelligence during the war). Brooke-Rose has said, however, "I never put myself directly into novels. I find that boring . . . . So I turn personal experience into metaphor." Brooke-Rose's female translator is just that, a carrier of the ideas of others; yet, the author makes the point, through the use of gender stereotypes and the cliché of female passivity, that the ability to carry the multiple codes of language is indicative of the feminine position. The masculine version of language is totalizing; the feminine is open to circulation and interchange within language, which Brooke-Rose suggests no one can ultimately escape. The novel is written without the verb *to be,* Brooke-Rose says, because the central character "doesn't know who she is." She was "playing with disorientation" because it was familiar to her.

Between was begun in 1964. Brooke-Rose was unable to complete the novel, however, and instead wrote *Such.* When taking up *Between* again in 1967, she changed the gender of her main character from male to female and was more satisfied with the result. She wrote the majority of the novel while staying with Ezra Pound's daughter in the Italian Tyrol. She returned to Tyrol to write *A ZBC of Ezra Pound* (1971). In 1968 Brooke-Rose also taught American literature and literary theory at the Université de Paris VIII at Vincennes (later Saint Denis). She had been working as a freelance literary journalist, largely in London. At Vincennes she became first a maître de conférences, then a professor, retiring in 1988.

While *Between* was greeted with a degree of Anglophone critical skepticism, *Thru* (1975) produced downright hostility. The novel begins and ends with a variety of images seen through the rearview mirror of a car: the world, that is, happening as it has already been passed "through," as well as the world of the viewer. This double reflection and the rearview mirror are highly influential in this self-reflexive novel: reflexive not only in terms of their relation to the author's life as a university teacher, but also in terms of the novel as knowledge provider. Linguistic, narratological, and philosophical considerations enter directly in *Thru* more than they do in any of Brooke-Rose's previous novels. Nonfictional text is included in the fictional. Students' essays with handwritten corrections turn up, as do timetables, diagrams, and curricula vitae. The text is presented not only as page-by-page narrative but also as disrupted sets of signs. There are musical notations, mathematical formulas, "concrete" arrangements of letters and words that can be read as acrostics and palindromes.

Thru, a novel about a university classroom, finds its subject matter and form in that classroom. Multiple "consciousnesses" discuss both the progress of the story and the other texts, as well. There is no central narrator or prime consciousness. Drawing on her contemporary Jacques Derrida, Brooke-Rose described *Thru* as the "only truly deconstructionist novel."

Amalgamemnon (1984) is constructed from the thoughts of a woman who imagines she is on a farm. Mira Enketei, the narrating voice of the novel, mixes concern about her future with her reading of Herodotus (mostly while escaping her snoring lover, Willy), with passages concerning friends and men who offer their "assistance." The novel stands out for its language play and puns. Through linguistic playfulness, Mira imagines herself in the role of Cassandra.

The figure of Cassandra embodies redundancy. She was cursed by Apollo to have her prophecies ignored because she refused to yield to his advances. The narrator of *Amalgamemnon,* however, will not be made redundant; she inscribes herself into the world with her narrative, her wordplay, and her imagination. Written largely in the future tense, *Amalgamemnon* brings past and future into the same imaginative sphere, investigating them through this broader "redundancy" theme. This theme relates not only to the plot of the novel but also to Brooke-Rose's interest in both information theory and language use.

"Some languages," Brooke-Rose has said, "are more redundant than others," referring to the lexical instance in which an element of language is said many times. In *Amalgamemnon* she utilizes both this lexical meaning and the social meaning of redundancy; that is, redundancy as termination of employment. The social meaning is explicitly incorporated as an investigation of the exclusion of women from larger social or public processes. Women, she suggests, become either mere spokespersons or, as in Herodotus's own project, are marginalized in the discourse of oracles and myths that are themselves male dominated.

Amalgamemnon works playfully to challenge the male-dominated nature of the oracular and to question the nature of factual discourse. One of the lexical methods she employs is to create compounded or "blended" words, portmanteaus that are at once unstable and parodic. Another is to invest the central character, Mira Enketei, who experiences long nights of insomnia, with the attitude of the first variable star, Mira Ceti, and therefore variability as narrator, unreliable at times, shifting, exerting a mixture of discourses. Cetus is the constellation of the whale, and Mira Enketei is effectively Mira in the Whale–like Jonah–wishing to get out. Brooke-Rose encourages the characters to create and simulate each other, to act in the imaginative mode of Cassandra, to play between fiction and fact. She locates part of the problem of false verisimilitude in the tendency to confuse or disguise fictions as facts. She views this propensity as linked to the voice of the contemporary media that produces not truths but "afterthoughts," rearranging both history and the present for political ends, creating what the author has called "palimpsest history," in which fiction is indistinguishable from fact. This same high technology, the author suggests, will potentially be the cause of Mira Enketei's losing her job.

Amalgamemnon, Xorandor (1986), *Verbivore* (1990), and *Textermination* (1991) represent what Brooke-Rose has referred to as the "Intercom Quartet." Their focus on media and communications technology is underpinned by a consideration of the role of the novel in a technological society. Remembering; fictionalizing fact in the public domain; simulated, reconstructed or speculated truths presented as reality; the threat posed by information technology: these thematic concerns form a nexus in what is essentially an extension of Brooke-Rose's ongoing interest in the changing relationships among science, humanity, and literature.

In *Xorandor* Brooke-Rose returns to relatively conventional narrative and plot. The plot is clearly defined. Twins Jip and Zab, twelve-year-old "whiz kids," discover a stone that communicates in computer language: "soft-talk" (mike to computer) and "handshake" (computer to computer). This stone, which they name Xorandor, because he is both exclusive OR (XOR) AND nonexclusive OR, feeds on radioactive material. They

Some reviews of OUT, her last novel

'It is a very unusual book indeed. It strikes vivid images in terms recognisable to all of us. To have attempted such a book is a triumph in itself; that Miss Brooke-Rose has achieved her purpose with such unfaltering dedication and creative integrity is an exciting fact. *Out* must be read.' THE SPECTATOR

'It is impossible to exaggerate the technical mastery, daunting in its combination of bizarre poetry and cold intellectuality, with which she creates a world perpetually swinging pendulum-like between darkness and light, dream and reality. A strange, forbidding but remarkable piece of work.' THE SUNDAY TELEGRAPH

'This is a brilliant book.' THE YORKSHIRE POST

'Miss Brooke-Rose's writing is wonderfully certain . . . and full of that obstinate happiness in the face of squalor and disaster that characterises the best of Beckett.' PUNCH

'Her book . . . will make a difference in stimulating English novelists to throw more conventions overboard.' THE GUARDIAN

Dust jacket for Brooke-Rose's 1966 novel, which she calls an attempt at the "fusion of outer space with psychic space" (courtesy of The Lilly Library, Indiana University, Bloomington, Indiana)

discover that the stone has the power to reproduce. Subsequently, one of the stone's offspring, because of a programming defect defined as a "syntax error," turns terrorist and, occupying a nuclear-power station, threatens to turn into a nuclear bomb. He calls himself Lady Macbeth and quotes intermittently from William Shakespeare's *Hamlet*.

Written entirely in dialogue, *Xorandor* is narrated by the two whiz kids. The text exists largely in their memories and representations, and Xorandor communicates with them on their Poccom 3 computer. The first adult that communicates with Xorandor assumes he is from Mars, an assumption with which Xorandor agrees. "Adult" communication, however, remains filtered. The viewpoint of the novel is controlled by the children because they effectively control the computer keyboard.

Xorandor is a computer capable of communicating and storing a wide variety of texts, including those produced by radio drama, and all those texts in fact enter the systemic links of Xorandor's program. Brooke-Rose suggests here an analogical link between

programming and narrative. Asking the question "Why tell a story?" she appropriates the language of science fiction, fantasy, comedy, and the thriller, suggesting that even the stories of the novel occupy multiple forms. The twins, as whiz-kid programmers, discuss aspects of storytelling but find they genuinely do not understand narrative; for one thing they "can't decide what's really relevant and in what order." It becomes obvious by the end of the novel that Xorandor has simulated the logic of communications according to that of the people communicating with him, utilizing along the way the myths that the people themselves trust in, despite the paradoxes they contain.

Eventually the twins attempt to prevent disaster by suggesting that the authorities send Xorandor and his offspring back to Mars with enough radioactive material to sustain them. Xorandor, however, reveals that he is not, after all, from Mars but came into being on Earth five thousand years ago. He "invented" the Mars story because humans expected it. The novel ends having raised questions about the dangers inherent in nuclear and information technology and about the role of narrative in forming ideas and the role of fictional representation in creating genealogies.

Verbivore is both the sequel to *Xorandor* and a sequel to Brooke-Rose's earlier novel *Amalgamemnon*. The action in *Verbivore* takes place twenty-three years later than that in *Xorandor,* and the story begins with a consideration of a phenomenon labeled by journalists as "Verbivore" in which the "modulations" of electromagnetic waves are being flattened by some unknown agent. Radio, television, computer networks, satellites, and radar equipment are all affected. People, therefore, are forced to return to print-based writing for communication. Here Brooke-Rose is picking up on her ongoing project to declare the importance of book-based, novelistic narratives; however, her motives are not regressive. She is, as in *Xorandor,* investigating the links between history and the future, though not suggesting that the oral media communication of contemporary society should be wiped out in preference for earlier print culture.

Mira Enketei, the narrator encountered in *Amalgamemnon,* returns in *Verbivore,* along with Perry Hupsos and Nelson Nwankwo. This novel also includes the twins Jip and Zab from *Xorandor.* The twins have split up, however, and Zab is now a member of Parliament in Aachen, and Jip is a nuclear scientist working for NASA. *Verbivore* is, in one sense, a simple bringing together of the literary positions of the earlier two novels, reflected in intertextual characterization. In a more complex sense, it involves the combining of the surrealist or fantastical position of *Amalgamemnon* with the more realist narrative of *Xorandor.*

By imagining what others are writing, the novel is able to shift from one first-person narrator to another. This technique, however, creates the same kind of leveling effect that the "Verbivore" phenomenon has produced on technological communication, because it removes priority and downgrades "modulation." "Who is speaking?" becomes a fundamental concern. In fact, the question of opposition between the "oral" and "written" voice is at the heart of this novel. Characters, denied the high-technological devices of spoken communication, must write to each other. Everyone writes to each other, making it possible to describe *Verbivore* as a kind of epistolary novel in which simulation and invention form the basis for the "inscription" of the self.

The inscription that Brooke-Rose investigates here is distinctive. By progressing from written to oral communication, technological development joins the inscribed fictions of creation and origin. The two, Brooke-Rose suggests, are contemporaneously dependent as modes of understanding the world and as modes of textual encounter with it.

Textermination considers the modes of textual encounter largely from the side not of textual producers but of textual "characters" and textual receivers. The novel is set at the annual "Convention of Prayer for Being" in San Francisco. This convention is an annual literary conference with the difference of being attended by the characters of literature itself. These characters meet in order to petition "interpretive communities" to read "their" texts. The characters consider they are "created" by the "Implied Reader" and, looking after their own interests, attend "pray-ins" in which they pray to this "Implied Reader." They also come from a variety of works and from several cultures and periods. They include such characters as Gibreel Farishta from Salman Rushdie's *The Satanic Verses* (1988); Jane Austen's Emma, eponymous heroine of her 1815 novel; Gustave Flaubert's Emma Bovary, from *Madame Bovary* (1857); Christa Wolf's Kassandra, title character of her 1983 novel; George Eliot's Dorothea Brooke, from *Middlemarch* (1872); Felipe Segundo, from Carlos Fuentes's *Terra Nostra* (1975); Thomas Pynchon's Oedipa Maas, from *The Crying of Lot 49* (1966); and Philip Roth's recurrent narrator, Nathan Zuckerman, who first appeared in *The Ghost Writer* (1979).

The convention is organized by notable literary critics with the help of "interpreters" whose job it is to encourage interaction between the characters who frequently are seen milling around en masse in conference rooms and lobbies. The characters bring with them, naturally, the baggage of their literary heritages; however, they are additionally involved in Brooke-Rose's own plots and subplots. At one point the characters find themselves in an "aerobrain" headed across the Atlantic toward San Franscisco. At another point the convention is overrun by a crowd of fictional characters from motion pictures and characters from popular American television, such as J. R. Ewing, Columbo, and MacGyver. When the delegates from Western literature meet on the first day to pray for their existence, their praying is disrupted by Muslim fundamentalists who object to the Christian format of the proceedings. It turns out the real object of their attention is Rushdie's character Gibreel Farishta, an actor specializing in movie roles as Hindu divinities; or, more accurately, Farishta as a representative of Rushdie himself.

Textermination gives substantial creative input to what could be called the "nonprofessional" reader. That is, her characters are drawn from a wide variety of texts and textual positions, and Brooke-Rose effectively places academic or "professional" readings of the text within a wider range of possible, and equally valid, readings. These readings are held as cultural baggage that can be the important holdings of individuals. As in *Xorandor* and *Amalgamemnon,* she records the importance

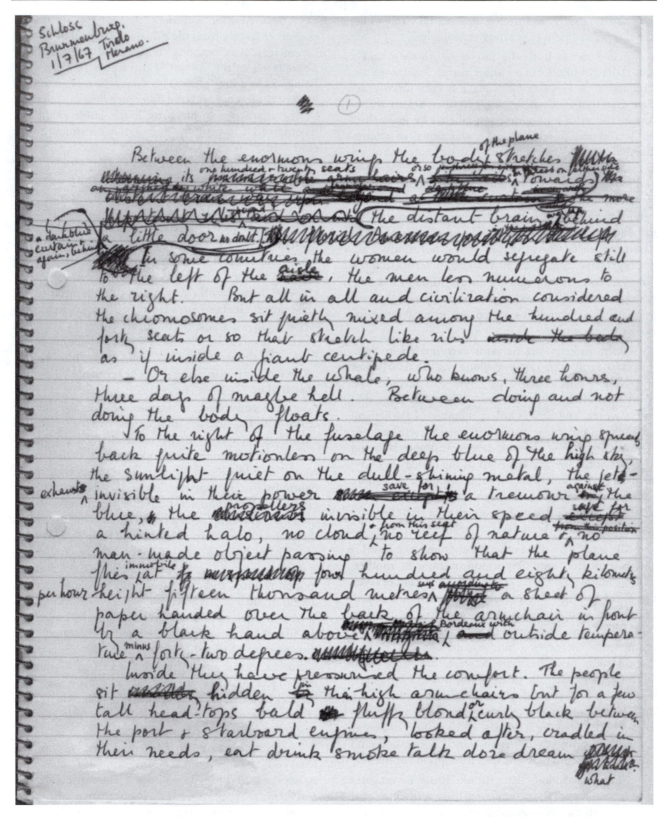

First page of the manuscript for Between, *Brooke-Rose's 1968 novel (Harry Ransom Humanities Research Center, University of Texas at Austin)*

of the novel as means of communication, but also reiterates that the novel is valuable to humanity. In conjunction with this she acknowledges the impact of technology on contemporary novelists, expanding this proposition to include the impact of technological discourses on humanity generally. She does not condemn this development, but considers it within the context of the relationship between "popular" and "high" culture, between science and literature, between the media as a form of communication and the novel. The literary form that "the novel" operates within is a sphere of fictionalizing that will benefit from drawing on its heritage, while embracing the potential for expanding knowledge that the phenomenal growth of information technology provides.

Remake (1996) is an autobiographical novel that largely uses no pronouns to explore the life story of "an old lady of seventy-two" and to participate in the "remake" of her life (although, as the narrator declares on the last page of the novel, "a remake is never as good as the original"). Brooke-Rose, of course, is far too sophisticated a writer to approach autobiography without considering the machinations of her trajectory. What intrigues her most are the workings of her memory or, more accurately, her "pseudo-memory." For instance, chapter 3 of the novel, "3. FILE: PRONOUNS," stands out structurally for using the first person and emotively for telling the story of the last illness and death of the narrator's mother.

The reader finds in *Remake* the "old lady," who is Brooke-Rose, decrypting messages and imagining reasons and motivations behind events. She is a highly self-conscious author, meditating on the meaning of memory and on the memories of the fictional worlds she has created. Not surprisingly, much of *Remake* finds its form in the play of words, literature, and life. *Life,* interestingly, is anagrammatized into *File* in the titling of each chapter. Words, it is suggested, speak for themselves no matter what people do with them. Selves are shifted around on the multifarious matrix of language.

Brooke-Rose also returns to her long-pursued interest in the realms and dimensions of knowledge. She writes: "What is knowledge anyway? Pleasure of the moment, then all for the worms." Her search for self-knowledge here is entwined with historical upheavals, war in particular, and undercut by historical inaccuracies. The truth is told, as the reader might expect, in Brooke-Rose's writing as both a rendering and a misrendering. Both are acceptable as both are often equally honest.

Michael Waters, writing in *TLS: The Times Literary Supplement* (3 May 1996), described *Remake* as "beautiful algebra." The meeting of scientific and humanistic discourses that this suggests would no doubt please

Brooke-Rose. Yet, it is the humanistic, the socially conscious, that is the focus of *Next* (1998) and that informs Brooke-Rose's meditation on genetics, individuality, and evolution in her 1999 novel, *Subscript*. The "scientizing" of the human and the "humanizing" of the scientific are overarching concerns in Brooke-Rose's oeuvre, particularly when linked to what she sees as the paradoxes inherent in progress.

In *Next* Brooke-Rose enters the world of the London homeless. Having nothing, these dispossessed are brought to life for the reader not simply by description or characterization but by the writer's decision to omit from the novel the verb *to have*. *Next* is a murder mystery, but it is also an investigation of phonetics, of dialect, and of the language of hope and despair. Written in free indirect speech, it is a tale without a teller, moving from one character to another to create a narrative anonymity, the same anonymity felt by the homeless. It is language that ultimately gives these narrators both form and function. There are, in fact, twenty-six characters—as in the letters of the alphabet—and the ideas of reading and of being heard are intimately tied here. One character endeavors to teach another to read. The prose reads like a conversation, and a great deal is gained in characterization by reading passages of the novel aloud.

The same "narratorless" technique is used in *Subscript*. In this case, however, the question of evolution guides Brooke-Rose's use of language, and this evolution is marked by her concerns with the ways in which technological progress threatens to obliterate such human activities as reading and writing, while relying on codes and meanings formed in such activities. This paradox of destroying language through the progress of new forms of communication that are dependent on language encourages Brooke-Rose's return to prehistory, where she begins to trace the origins and performance of human language.

Brooke-Rose ultimately leads the reader through a linguistic as well as a physical history with a language born from her distinctive version of the metaphysics and metalinguistics of human evolution. Sounds evolve into linked sounds; words emerge from noise. In *Subscript* Brooke-Rose proposes the idea that the physical evolution of the species is integrated with the evolution of linguistic codes and conventions that add up to tools for communication as well as substantive tools of human memory and imagination. This theory could well be seen as one of Brooke-Rose's most substantial contributions to debates on the late-twentieth-century Western novel. Though the narrative of *Subscript* progresses in what might be considered a relatively conventional sense, it does so with an exceptional sense of what always lies beneath it. Thus, Paul Quinn has rightly pointed out in his *TLS* review (8 October 1999), "it is possible to trace intertwined ancestries of *Subscript* . . . [in] *The Inheritors* by William Golding, the 1981 film *Quest for Fire,* for which Anthony Burgess invented the prehistoric languages, and the thrown bone at the beginning of *2001: A Space Odyssey.*"

Brooke-Rose's language does not travel a line between fields of knowledge, on the borders between literature and science, or public and private understandings, but weaves its way through all, picking up ideas, elements, observations, and avenues for investigation along the way. She is, undoubtedly, a writer with a rare and highly committed talent.

Letter:

"To Michael Schmidt," in *Letters to an Editor,* edited by Mark Fisher (Manchester, U.K.: Carcanet, 1989), pp. 209–210.

Interviews:

Myrna Blumberg, "Out's Out–It's in to be Anti," *Guardian,* 7 November 1964, p. 6;

Boswell, "Writer Out on a Limb," *Scotsman,* 17 April 1965, p. 3;

John Hall, "A Novel Theory," *Guardian,* 16 November 1970, p. 9;

David Hayman and Keith Cohen, "An Interview with Christine Brooke-Rose," *Contemporary Literature,* 17, no. 1 (1976): 1–23;

Ellen J. Friedman and Miriam Fuchs, "A Conversation with Christine Brooke-Rose," *Review of Contemporary Fiction,* 9, no. 3 (1989): 81–90;

Jenny Turner, "Global Wordcrunching," *City Limits* (22–29 March 1990): 91;

Nicholas Tredell, "Christine Brooke-Rose in Conversation," *P. N. Review* (September/October 1990): 29–35;

Turner, "Reclaim the Brain," *Edinburgh Review,* 84 (1990): 19–32.

References:

Hanjo Berressem, "*Thru* the Looking Glass: A Journey into the Universe of Discourse," *Review of Contemporary Fiction,* 9, no. 3 (1989): 128–133;

Sarah Birch, *Christine Brooke-Rose and Contemporary Fiction* (Oxford: Clarendon Press / New York: Oxford University Press, 1994);

Robert L. Caserio, "Mobility and Masochism: Christine Brooke-Rose and J. G. Ballard," *Novel* (Winter/Spring, 1988): 292–310;

Ellen J. Friedman and Richard Martin, eds., *Utterly Other Discourse: The Texts of Christine Brooke-Rose* (Normal, Ill.: Dalkey Archive Press, 1995);

Susan E. Hawkins, "Memory and Discourse: Fictionalizing the Present in Xorander," *Review of Contemporary Fiction,* 9, no. 3 (1989): 138–143;

Judy Little, *The Experimental Self: Dialogic Subjectivity in Woolf, Pym and Brooke-Rose* (Carbondale: Southern Illinois University Press, 1996).

Papers:

The papers of Christine Brooke-Rose are held at the Harry Ransom Humanities Research Center, University of Texas at Austin.

David Caute
(16 December 1936 –   )

Nicolas Tredell
Sussex University

See also the David Caute entry in *DLB 14: British Novelists Since 1960*.

BOOKS: *At Fever Pitch* (London: Deutsch, 1959; New York: Pantheon, 1959);

Comrade Jacob (London: Deutsch, 1961; New York: Pantheon, 1962);

Communism and the French Intellectuals, 1914–1960 (London: Deutsch, 1964; New York: Macmillan, 1964);

The Left in Europe Since 1789 (London: Weidenfeld & Nicolson, 1966; New York: McGraw-Hill, 1966);

The Decline of the West: A Novel (London: Deutsch, 1966; New York: Macmillan, 1966);

Fanon (London: Fontana, 1970); republished as *Frantz Fanon* (New York: Viking, 1970);

The Demonstration: A Play (London: Deutsch, 1970);

The Occupation: A Novel (London: Deutsch, 1971; New York: McGraw-Hill, 1972);

The Illusion: An Essay on Politics, Theatre and the Novel (London: Deutsch, 1971; New York: Harper & Row, 1972);

The Fellow-Travellers: A Postscript to the Enlightenment (London: Weidenfeld & Nicolson, 1973; New York: Macmillan, 1973); revised and enlarged as *The Fellow-Travellers: Intellectual Friends of Communism* (New Haven: Yale University Press, 1988);

Collisions: Essays and Reviews (London: Quartet, 1974);

Cuba, Yes? (London: Secker & Warburg, 1974; New York: McGraw-Hill, 1974);

The Great Fear: The Anti-Communist Purge Under Truman and Eisenhower (London: Secker & Warburg, 1978; New York: Simon & Schuster, 1978);

The Baby-Sitters, as John Salisbury (London: Secker & Warburg, 1978; New York: Atheneum, 1978); republished as *The Hour Before Midnight* (New York: Dell, 1980);

Moscow Gold, as Salisbury (London: Futura, 1980);

Under the Skin: The Death of White Rhodesia (London: Allen Lane, 1983; Evanston, Ill.: Northwestern University Press, 1983);

The K-Factor (London: Joseph, 1983);

David Caute (photograph by Sophie Baker; from the dust jacket for Fatima's Scarf, *1998)*

News from Nowhere (London: Hamilton, 1986);

The Espionage of the Saints: Two Essays on Silence and the State (London: Hamilton, 1986);

Sixty-Eight: The Year of the Barricades (London: Hamilton, 1988); republished as *The Year of the Barricades: A Journey Through 1968* (New York: Harper & Row, 1988);

Veronica, or, The Two Nations (London: Hamilton, 1989; New York: Arcade, 1990);

The Women's Hour (London: Paladin, 1991);

Joseph Losey: A Revenge on Life (London: Faber & Faber, 1994; New York: Oxford University Press, 1994);

Dr Orwell and Mr Blair: A Novel (London: Weidenfeld & Nicolson, 1994);

Fatima's Scarf (London: Totterdown Books, 1998).

PLAY PRODUCTIONS: *Songs for an Autumn Rifle,* Edinburgh, Cranston Street Hall, 23 August 1961;

The Demonstration, Nottingham, Nottingham Playhouse, 19 November 1969;

The Fourth World, London, Royal Court Theatre, 11 March 1973.

PRODUCED SCRIPTS: *The Demonstration,* BBC Radio 4, 16 May 1971;

Fallout, BBC Radio 4, 17 December 1972;

Brecht and Co, television, BBC, 10 August 1979;

The Zimbabwe Tapes, BBC Radio 4, 15 August 1983;

Henry and the Dogs, BBC Radio 4, 15 December 1986;

Sanctions, BBC Radio 4, 14 March 1988;

Animal Fun Park, BBC Radio 3, 27 August 1995.

OTHER: *Essential Writings of Karl Marx,* edited, with an introduction, by Caute (London: MacGibbon & Kee, 1967; New York: Macmillan, 1968);

Jean-Paul Sartre, *The Age of Reason,* translated by Eric Sutton, introduction by Caute (Harmondsworth, U.K.: Penguin, 1986);

Sartre, *The Reprieve,* translated by Sutton, introduction by Caute (Harmondsworth, U.K.: Penguin, 1986);

Sartre, *Iron in the Soul,* translated by Gerard Hopkins, introduction by Caute (Harmondsworth, U.K.: Penguin, 1986);

"David Caute (1936–)," in *Contemporary Authors Autobiography Series 4,* edited by Adele Sarkissian (Detroit: Gale Research, 1986), pp. 95–111.

SELECTED PERIODICAL PUBLICATIONS— UNCOLLECTED: "The Bombings: Four Views," *New Review,* 2 (March 1975): 3–5;

"Sartre 1: Roads to Freedom," *New Statesman,* 99 (2 May 1980): 667–668;

"Sartre 2: What is Literature?" *New Statesman,* 99 (9 May 1980): 716–717;

"Sartre 3: Force of Circumstances," *New Statesman,* 99 (16 May 1980): 752–753;

"Sartre 4: The Good and the Great," *New Statesman,* 99 (23 May 1980): 785–786;

"Living by The Market," *Author,* 95 (Summer 1984): 71–73;

"Iranian Nights," *New Statesman and Society,* 2 (28 April 1989): 14–16;

"Labour's Satanic Verses," *New Statesman and Society,* 2 (5 May 1989): 9–11;

"The Holy War," *New Statesman and Society,* 2 (2 June 1989): 14–16;

"Prophet Motive," *New Statesman and Society,* 3 (16 February 1990): 18–19;

"What Are the Pigs Doing Now," *Times* (London), 1 August 1995, p. 31.

Throughout his long writing career, David Caute has shown a readiness to tackle large themes and to use a range of narrative techniques in his novels. His subjects include African decolonization, seventeenth-century communal radicalism, 1960s student rebellion, 1980s feminism, and late-twentieth-century Muslim fundamentalism. The modes he has employed include naturalism, metafiction, allegory, symbolism, and magic realism. An historian and a journalist—as well as a novelist and playwright, and a skeptical supporter of the Left—he has written novels that blur the boundaries among history, reportage, and fiction, and have never avoided politics. His fiction has often provoked controversy on both political and literary grounds, attracting high praise and harsh condemnation.

John David Caute was born on 16 December 1936 in Alexandria, Egypt, to Colonel Edward Caute, a dentist in the British army, and Rebecca Perlzweig Caute. He was brought to live in England after a year, and from 1946 to 1950 he attended a Scottish public (private) school, Edinburgh Academy. Edward Caute died in December 1947, at the age of fifty-one, just after his son's eleventh birthday. In 1950 David Caute enrolled at an English public school, Wellington College in Berkshire, taking advantage of the assisted places offered to the sons of deceased army officers. He did well in the classroom and on the sports field, becoming the school's best quarter-mile runner in 1953 and 1954 and winning a scholarship to Wadham College, Oxford. Before going to Oxford, Caute served eighteen months of the normally two-year National Service, the last nine months as an infantry subaltern in what he recalled, in a 1990 interview (published in *Conversations with Critics,* 1994), the "highly exotic world" of the Gold Coast (now Ghana), then a British colony that was "coming to the boil, on the eve of Independence." His experiences in Ghana formed the basis of his first novel, *At Fever Pitch* (1959).

Caute wrote *At Fever Pitch* during his second year as an Oxford undergraduate, and it was published while he was still a student. Set in a British colony much like Ghana, the novel has two main strands: the story of Michael Glyn, a sensitive young British subaltern uncertain about his sexuality and his courage, and the story of the struggles for political power in the newly emerging nation. These two stories come together when Glyn, deserted by his senior officers and with his remaining troops under attack from a mob, mows down twenty-five Africans with a machine gun. Among British novels of the 1950s, *At Fever Pitch* is unusual both in the range of its characters and situations and in its variety of narrative techniques, ranging from stream of consciousness to blank verse. Looking back on the novel in his *Conversations with Critics* interview, Caute compared himself to "a child rummaging through a bag of coloured sweets."

At Fever Pitch was generally well received, though with some reservations. For example, a reviewer for *The Times Literary Supplement* (*TLS*) called the novel "excellent," praising the "masterly study" of Glyn and finding the "author's insight into the minds of his African characters . . . and his re-creation of their thought-processes . . . positively uncanny" (13 February 1959); but this same reviewer also felt that the attempted scope of the novel harmed its overall organization and compelled Caute to use too many techniques. Reviewing the book for *The New Statesman* (14 February 1959), novelist V. S. Naipaul called *At Fever Pitch* the product of "a genuinely creative imagination" but judged it "unbalanced," displaying the "limitations" of its author's experience and placing a "disproportionate and unnecessary" emphasis on sex. Despite such reservations, *At Fever Pitch* was seen as a remarkable debut by a promising young novelist. It won the London Authors Club Award and the John Llewelyn Rhys Memorial Prize and was quickly reprinted.

Six months later, Caute obtained a first-class degree in history at Oxford, a graduate scholarship at St. Antony's College, and a Prize Fellowship at All Souls, an Oxford college without students, whose fellows devote themselves to research. Caute began to pursue a doctorate, doing research on French intellectuals and Communism, and in 1960 he made his first visit to the United States, where he spent a year at Harvard University as a Henry Fellow. There he met Catherine Shuckburgh, a young Englishwoman, whom he married in 1961. Returning to All Souls, he set his doctoral research aside for a time to work on his second novel, *Comrade Jacob* (1961), which emerged from his undergraduate study of the English Civil Wars and Commonwealth (1640–1660). This novel focuses on a real historical event: the unsuccessful attempt of the Diggers to found a utopian community on St George's Hill, Surrey, in 1649–1650. As Caute observed in his *Conversations with Critics* interview, certain aspects of the Diggers' activities are well documented, but there are also gaps and silences that offer scope for the novelist's imagination. Caute sought to evoke not only the two leading protagonists—Gerrard Winstanley, the leader of the Diggers, and his local opponent, Parson Platt—but also some of the Diggers who are no more than names in the historical record. *Comrade Jacob* came out to warm applause. V. S. Naipaul commented in *The New Statesman* (12 May 1961) that, after an "appalling, over-written first chapter," "all the novelist's instincts seem to

come to Mr Caute. . . . he sinks deeper and deeper into his subject, and the result is a book which is far better than his first." The reviewer for *TLS* (19 May 1961) called *Comrade Jacob* "a remarkable, and moving, evocation of a stirring and significant experiment in English history" that raised large political, psychological, historical, and literary questions.

Caute completed his D.Phil. in 1963 and developed his thesis into his first nonfiction book, *Communism and the French Intellectuals, 1914–1960* (1964). He was also working on a third novel, *The Decline of the West* (1966). In 1965 a large change occurred in his life. At All Souls he had vigorously supported a proposal that the college should use some of its large surplus revenues to finance a scheme to admit graduate students. When the proposal was rejected, Caute resigned his fellowship and wrote a controversial essay giving his version of the dispute, "Crisis in All Souls: A Case Study in Reform" (*Encounter,* March 1966). He was able to find other academic posts, becoming a visiting professor at New York University and Columbia University in 1966–1967 and a reader in social and political theory at Brunel University in Uxbridge, England, from 1967 to 1970. Yet, he never again held a post as prestigious as his All Souls fellowship. Problems in his private life compounded the crisis in his academic career: his marriage to Catherine Shuckburgh, which had produced two sons, was breaking up, and they were divorced in 1970.

The Decline of the West was Caute's longest and most ambitious novel yet. Like *At Fever Pitch,* it is set in Africa in the era of decolonization, but this time in a fictional former French colony, Coppernica, in which foreign-backed native rebels are struggling to overthrow the newly independent government. The novel focuses on six main characters—ranging from the head of the new state, Raymond Tukhomada, to a working-class Scottish former soldier, Malcolm Deedes—and it follows them through scenes of humiliation, violence, torture, and death. While Caute borrows his title from Oswald Spengler's influential cultural and political analysis published in 1925, the worldview of his novel is closer to that of existentialist Jean-Paul Sartre than to Spengler's: for Caute, "the decline of the West" is demonstrated by the collapse of Western values into barbarism when Western interests are threatened.

The Decline of the West had a mixed reception. English novelist William Cooper, writing in *The Listener* (8 September 1966), called it "monumental in scope, brilliantly organized in detail, and fascinating in its array of characters," but the *TLS* review of the same date castigated its "florid" imagery, its "incompetent writing," and its "embarrassing similarities" to "the contemptible tales of Harold Robbins." Christopher Ricks,

Dust jacket for Caute's 1966 novel, set in a newly independent African nation

in *The New Statesman* (23 September 1966), also likened the novel to a best-selling blockbuster and homed in on what he saw as unacknowledged borrowings from real-life accounts of torture in Peter Benenson's *Gangrene* (1959). Perhaps prompted by Ricks's review, the paperback edition of Caute's novel did include an acknowledgment to *Gangrene*. In the United States, Laurence Lafore, in *The New York Times Book Review* (9 October 1961), judged *The Decline of the West* to be an "important and imposing" novel whose author had "advanced an important thesis, conceived an important tragedy, and composed a fascinating story"; but he felt that it was "perhaps better as fictional history than as a work of art" and pointed to "distracting defects": passages of "feverish" prose, poor dialogue, and characters who were sometimes "more theoretical than human" because of Caute's "attempt to illustrate the connections between historical processes and abnormal psychology." Charles R. Larson, in the *Saturday Review* (8 October 1966), was more enthusiastic, however, calling Caute's characters "vividly drawn, fully delineated personalities" and concluding that the novel was "a powerful commentary on the moral commitments the West has long ignored in Africa."

The Decline of the West sold one hundred thousand copies in paperback in England. But Caute did not follow it up with another realist blockbuster. In the second half of the 1960s, he wrote two nonfiction books—*The Left in Europe Since 1789* (1966) and *Fanon* (1970)—and edited *Essential Writings of Karl Marx* (1967). He did not produce another novel until 1971.

In his critical study *The Situation of the Novel* (1979), Bernard Bergonzi points out that *The Decline of the West* is "naive in its confident use of naturalistic conventions at precisely the time when more reflective novelists were beginning to question them"; and, in the late 1960s, particularly during his time at New York University, Caute himself began to question them, reading much more widely in literary criticism and theory than he had previously done. The resulting intellectual ferment combined with the political tumult of the late 1960s—and with crises in Caute's personal life that culminated in a nervous breakdown—to produce what remains his most accomplished work: his Confrontation Trilogy (1970–1971).

Caute did not set out to write a trilogy. He began with a play, *The Demonstration* (1970), and then wrote a book-length essay on literary theory, *The Illusion: An Essay on Politics, Theatre and the Novel* (1971), and a novel,

The Occupation (1971). Steven Bright, a figure who closely resembles Caute himself, appears as a character in the play and novel and is supposedly the author of *The Illusion*. In the play Bright, a professor of drama in his mid forties, tries uneasily to cope with students who are rehearsing his play but also apparently staging a revolt against the university authorities. *The Demonstration* catches some of the tones and themes of the 1960s student revolt while raising teasing and intricate questions about the relationship between drama and reality. *The Illusion* mounts a full-scale critical attack on realism in the theater and the novel: realism is "burnt-out, obsolete, a tired shadow of a once-living force. It has to go." It should be replaced by a kind of "dialectical writing" that both employs and subverts the fictional illusion, creating a kind of alienation effect like that for which Bertolt Brecht aimed in drama. *The Occupation,* the novel that is the third volume of the trilogy, is Caute's attempt to write a "dialectical novel" of this kind. In *The Occupation* novelist and modern historian Steven Bright, who is rather younger than in *The Demonstration,* is a visiting professor at an American university. He is challenged by New Left students and caught up in erotic entanglements. The novel is a vivid expressionist portrait of his descent into personal and political chaos and breakdown, a comic but painful tale whose tone, according to Caute, owes much to Philip Roth's novel *Portnoy's Complaint* (1969). *The Demonstration* also disrupts the realistic illusion and draws attention to itself as fiction by means of a variety of alienating devices—footnotes, anachronisms, implications that the novel one is reading is the novel Bright is writing, citations from works much like or identical to those by Caute, and the replacement of psychological realism by cartoon caricature. The novel culminates in Bright's return to Oxford, which is occupied by revolutionary students. Every college but one has fallen to the rebels, and it is Bright's task to gain access to All Souls so that the students can complete their conquest of the university. Once Bright enters the college, however, the revolution seems to disappear. He goes into the college library and finds, among the new accessions, a book called *The Illusion:*

> Night falls. He turns on all the lights. No one comes to disturb him. He reads the book, always meaning to stop at the next section, but continually drawn on by the magic of his own prose, of his own thoughts—of himself. Print is so pretty. It really is a long time since he has felt so contented, just sitting and reading himself.

The end of the novel confirms Bright's personal and political isolation and also stands, with historical hindsight, as a symbol of the inability of 1960s radicalism to turn its confrontations into connections that might have effected enduring radical change. Caute's most accomplished novel is also his most vivid anatomy of failure. In a 1975 essay Raman Selden stressed the pessimism of *The Occupation* and judged the whole trilogy to be "an impressive *tour de force*" that was nonetheless "a counsel of despair" in political terms, "a perfect 'objective correlative' of a *failure* of commitment."

Reviewing *The Occupation* on its first appearance, along with the two other volumes of the trilogy, D. A. N. Jones, in *The Listener* (22 July 1971), found the novel "rather horrible," "offering repellent confessions in an atmosphere of contrived unreality." Television playwright Dennis Potter, in a review for *The Times* (London) of the same date, felt that it was more difficult to subvert the illusionism of a novel than of a play and found that some of Caute's "well-signalled alienating devices" in *The Occupation* were "so crude" and "so irrelevant" that they were "almost embarrassing." Benedict Nightingale, in *The New Statesman* (23 July 1971), found that in *The Occupation* Caute's creativity contradicted his alienation effects: "The final paradox, or contradiction . . . is that, in spite of alienation effects, the clever, even brilliant writing, it is only unregenerate empathy with this twisted individual [Steven Bright] that keeps us reading until the end." The *TLS* (3 December 1971) reviewer felt, however, that Caute's creativity was constricted by his facility as a remarkable "confessional conversationalist" whose fluency allowed insufficient "space and silence" for the reader's imagination to function.

In 1970 Caute left his teaching post at Brunel to become a full-time freelance writer, but more than a decade elapsed before he published another novel under his own name. His personal life became more settled; in 1973 he married Martha Bates, and they subsequently had two daughters. He was literary editor of *The New Statesman* in 1979–1981 and served as cochairman of the Writers' Guild of Great Britain in 1981–1982. During the 1970s he produced two substantial works of modern history, *The Fellow-Travellers: A Postscript to the Enlightenment* (1973), about intellectual supporters of communism, and *The Great Fear: The Anti-Communist Purge Under Truman and Eisenhower* (1978). He collected his cultural and political essays and reviews, including "Crisis in All Souls," in *Collisions* (1974) and wrote *Cuba, Yes?* (1974), a skeptical account of his 1972 journey to Fidel Castro's revolutionary Mecca. He also wrote a radio play, *Fallout* (1972); *The Fourth World* (1973), a stage adaptation of *The Occupation;* and a television docudrama, *Brecht and Co* (1979). Caute withdrew his name from the screenplay credits for *Winstanley* (1975), a motion-picture version of *Comrade Jacob* directed by Kevin Brownlow, because he felt that the producers had ironed the biblical messianism out of his script. His only excursions into novel writing between 1971 and 1983 were two thrillers written for money and published under the pseudonym John Salisbury: *The Baby-Sitters* (1978) and *Moscow Gold* (1980). The first of these books enjoyed worldwide sales and earned Caute about $120,000; the second sold sixty thousand paperback copies in the United Kingdom. The proceeds helped, among other things, to finance Caute's reporting of the civil war in Rhodesia (which became Zimbabwe in 1980). His experiences there provided the material for his next nonfiction book, *Under the Skin: The Death of White Rhodesia* (1983), and for *The Zimbabwe Tapes* (1983), an effective radio play that combines fiction with real-life recordings that he obtained from ZANLA guerrillas. They also fed into the work that marked his reemergence as a novelist in the 1980s: *The K-Factor* (1983).

The K-Factor is a compact, fast-paced, intricately plotted novel that dramatizes the struggle for power and for the definition of reality in the last days of Rhodesia. These struggles are focused most strongly in the uncertainty about whether the baby of Sonia Laslett, the wife of a white Rhodesian farmer, is real or a collective hallucination or fantasy—that innocent white infant whose kidnapping confirms the settlers' perception of the perfidy of the terrorists and justifies settler violence. In *TLS* (3 June 1983) Roger Owen was uneasy about the combination of such puzzles about the nature of reality with a "strong surface naturalism" but felt that the greatest weakness of the novel lay in "the partiality of the author's sympathies," which made him hostile to white Rhodesians. Janice Elliott, in the *Sunday Telegraph* (22 May 1983), shared Owen's uneasiness about what she called the "collapse from realism and black comedy into symbolism, represented by Sonia's baby," but in contrast to Owen she found that *The K-Factor* avoided being "a study of Us and Them" and demonstrated that "brutality, farce and pain" existed on both sides. Her overall verdict was that, like *At Fever Pitch* and *The Decline of the West,* Caute's "fusion of powerful imagination and sense of history" in *The K-Factor* demonstrated that he was "one of our most impressive novelists."

Caute's next novel, *News from Nowhere* (1986), is also set partly in Rhodesia. Its main theme, however, is not the African conflict but the progress of Richard Stern from youthful New Left commitment as a lecturer at the London School of Economics in the 1960s to a troubled middle age in which he goes to Rhodesia to report on the guerrilla war and to pursue the fabled Esther Meyer, the white woman who is a leading figure in the black liberation struggle. Like *The K-Factor, News from Nowhere* combines vivid realism with devices that highlight the nature of the novel as a fictional illusion; but *News from Nowhere* is much longer than the earlier

novel and has a more extended timescale. It attempts to explore the personal and political involvements of a substantial portion of a life that bears some resemblance to Caute's own. Reviewers recognized the ambition of *News from Nowhere* but differed in their judgment of its achievement. In the *London Review of Books* (20 November 1986), John Sutherland called the novel "a monumental failure" that would still "stand as something of a literary landmark": "Technically . . . lousy," with a style that was either "show-off clever" or "appallingly careless," a "self-indulgently romantic plot," and a narrative largely "propelled by petty spites," especially against feminism, it was, nonetheless, "that rarest of British things, engaged fiction." Reviewing *News from Nowhere* for *The Spectator* (18 October 1986), novelist Anita Brookner also felt that the novel was unusual in the British context but rated it far more highly, calling it "a well-told story which is exact, encyclopaedic, absorbing and very funny."

Two more radio plays by Caute were broadcast in the 1980s: *Henry and the Dogs* (1986) and *Sanctions* (1988). Caute's study of the 1968 rebellions, *Sixty-Eight: The Year of the Barricades,* also appeared in 1988. His next novel, *Veronica, or, The Two Nations* (1989), focuses on England in the 1980s with substantial flashbacks to World War II. His title echoes that of Benjamin Disraeli's novel on the theme of social division, *Sybil or the Two Nations* (1845). In *Veronica* Caute sets against one another two figures from the "two nations" of late-twentieth-century England: Michael Parsons, a Conservative home secretary, and Bert Frame, an investigative tabloid journalist of working-class origin who pursues the truth about Parsons's incestuous passion for his half sister, Veronica. The social division represented by Parsons and Frame is echoed in the narrative structure of the novel, which, for the most part, divides the narration between the two men. But *Veronica* also includes alienating devices that foreground its fictionality, as when Frame says: "is this my voice or little Michael's?—or that of a third party unknown to either of us?" *Veronica* received a varied response from reviewers. Max Egremont, in *The Spectator* (12 August 1989), felt that it was "poised . . . uneasily between allegory and realism" and called its pace "moderate" and its prose "unremarkable." On the other hand, Mark Wormald, in *TLS* (25–31 August 1989), called the novel "intelligent, provoking" and "above all beautifully structured," identifying its key theme as the "profound insecurity" that may lie beneath "any extreme assertion, any self which claims to know itself utterly."

With his three novels of the 1980s Caute re-established himself as a writer of fiction prepared to tackle controversial themes. His first novel of the 1990s, *The Women's Hour* (1991), takes on the topic of feminism.

The story turns on an allegation of rape made by a militant feminist colleague against Sidney Pike, an aging professor on the now-old New Left. Caute aims to portray a range of women, but he falls too easily into stereotypes. Robert Nye, in *The Guardian* (5 September 1991), however, remarked that, while much of the novel might seem "a nightmare of misogyny," Caute's purpose might be, partly at least, to satirize Sidney's attitudes to women.

The achievement of *The Women's Hour* lies less in its treatment of feminism or antifeminism than in its portrayal of Sidney Pike as representative of the twilight of the New Left. He is the successor to Steven Bright of *The Confrontation* and Richard Stern of *News from Nowhere,* still possessed of some radical fire but out of touch and running out of time. The novel is less an engagement with 1980s feminism than an elegy for 1960s radicalism.

In 1994 Caute published a major biography of an important movie director, *Joseph Losey: A Revenge on Life,* and his next novel, *Dr Orwell and Mr Blair.* The novel portrays Eric Blair—better known by his pseudonym, George Orwell—as he gathers the material for *Animal Farm* (1945). Most of the novel is told in the first person by Alex Jones, a twelve-year-old looking after his father's farm, whom Blair/Orwell befriends and manipulates. The novel draws the reader's attention to the complex relationships between fiction and reality and offers a portrait of a vulnerable, isolated, intelligent, courageous, and resentful boy and of the artist as a middle-aged man, a hardened, experienced, sometimes ruthless operator who steals from, alters, and elaborates reality. J. K. L. Walker, in *TLS* (17 June 1994) praised *Dr Orwell and Mr Blair* for its portrayal of the fictional friendship of the boy and the writer and judged the novel a "subtle and complex" book "that deserves to be read for its insight into the often murky processes of literary creativity."

Despite the reasonably positive reception of *Dr Orwell and Mr Blair,* Caute was unable to find a commercial publisher for his sequel, "The Time of the Toad," which continues the story of *Animal Farm* up to the collapse of communism in the Soviet Union and Eastern Europe. He adapted the novel into a radio play, *Animal Fun Park* (1995). He then began a long struggle to find a publisher for his next novel, *Fatima's Scarf,* which he eventually brought out at his own expense in 1998. The expertise of Martha Caute, a highly experienced book editor, was crucial to this difficult enterprise. *Fatima's Scarf* has four main aspects: it explores the impact of an apparently blasphemous novel on a British Muslim community in a northern city of the United Kingdom; it examines the response of the London intelligentsia to Muslim outrage at the novel; it provides a

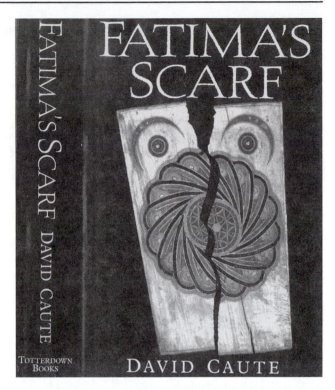

Dust jacket for Caute's 1998 novel, inspired by the controversy over Salman Rushdie's novel The Satanic Verses (1988)

fictional portrait of the artist as a young megalomaniac, in the shape of Gamal Rahman, the author of the offending novel and the target of the Ayatollah Khomeini's *fatwa,* or death sentence; and it offers a magic-realist history of modern Egypt. The analogies between the fictional Rahman affair and the real-life Salman Rushdie affair probably deterred some publishers from bringing out *Fatima's Scarf* for fear of offending Muslims and of causing more trouble for Rushdie.

Like *The K-Factor* and *News from Nowhere, Fatima's Scarf* draws to a degree on Caute's journalism, this time on the articles he wrote for the *New Statesman* when the Rushdie affair first hit the headlines. In a series of tightly structured scenes, *Fatima's Scarf* takes the reader deep into the public and private spaces of Muslim Bruddersford and vividly conveys the drastic effects that the Rahman affair has on their lives—for example, on Nasreen Hassani, a community teacher:

> The bus comes; until recently she liked buses. . . . But now she is afraid of insults, obscenities, straight to her face, from sneering youngsters, or snide remarks behind her back by the older people. Every day she sees Muslims lampooned in the newspapers read by her fellow passengers: "mad mullahs," "fanatics." Passing through the white crowds in the city-centre shopping precincts, she whispers to herself, "I am a fanatic. I must not betray my faith, my heritage, my own kind.

Nasreen, you must not. Your son Imran would never forgive you." The city is now alive, or dead, with evil and resentment–like the ivy plant she had once cut down from the backyard, twisted, blackened, tenacious, an octopus of brittle, contorted branches clutching at thin air in their death, dragging down fragments of brick and rendering, emitting evil dust as she struck them. She feels a grim rictus settling across her mouth, her cheeks: this contagion.

As the contagion spreads through Bruddersford, the London intelligentsia respond to Muslim outrage with indignation, condescension, and bewilderment. Caute's satire on their response provides some of the funniest and most acute sections of the novel. The Bruddersford/London scenes, which are largely realistic in style, make up the first and the third parts of *Fatima's Scarf*. The middle part offers a magic-realist version of both Rahman's autobiography and the history of modern Egypt.

The analogies between the Rahman and Rushdie affairs, and the circumstances that had led Caute to self-publication, attracted a fair amount of attention in British newspapers in 1998, giving rise to several feature articles and a range of reviewer responses, mostly favorable. In *The Scotsman* (7 March 1998) novelist Allan Massie called *Fatima's Scarf* "a novel of great scope and . . . humanity" about "one of the big issues of our times: the question of censorship of books which offend the susceptibilities of religious groups." He added that though the novel is "set in the comic mode" throughout, it nonetheless includes "good arguments to all sides in the dispute" and is "rich," "audacious," and "often disturbing." Massie did suggest, however, that the middle section of *Fatima's Scarf* was "perhaps less successful." Another novelist, Maggie Gee, writing in the *Daily Telegraph* (4 April 1998), also had doubts about this section, calling it "overlong," but overall she found *Fatima's Scarf* to be "a brave and brilliant book, alight with humour and intelligence" that told its readers "more about contemporary life in a Britain of multiple religions, colours and classes" than any other British fiction she had "read in the past few years." She added that the novel displayed a "rare imaginative feat," the ability to "cross the lines of gender and culture." In *TLS* (24 April 1998) Robert Irwin praised the middle section of *Fatima's Scarf* as more serious and satisfying than "the standard magical-realist . . . romp," and called the whole novel "thoroughly researched, comic[,] provocative" and "wonderfully inventive"; he did find, how-

ever, that Caute's lack of interest in "the interior aspects of spirituality" meant that his portrait of the Bruddersford Islamic community was "cruel."

The offensiveness of the novel to Muslims was a key theme of a hostile *New Statesman* review (3 April 1998) by Ziauddin Sardar, who found the novel piled with "orientalist rubbish" and felt that the publishers who rejected it were trying "to spare us all a long, unoriginal and excruciatingly boring work." Tariq Ali, in *The Independent* (25 April 1998), also felt that the publishers who rejected the novel had been right; for him, *Fatima's Scarf* was an "unwieldy . . . truckload of empty husks." Nonetheless, the novel came close to being included on the shortlist for the 1998 Booker Prize, and by the end of the year, fewer than one hundred of the three thousand copies remained in stock. The total publishing costs of the two hardback printings were about £18,500, which by the end of 1998 had been more or less earned back by sales. A paperback edition was published in April 1999.

With *Fatima's Scarf* Caute has once again demonstrated his ability to engage with large themes, employ a range of narrative techniques, and provoke controversy. He shows no sign of retiring, and any fiction he produces in the future is likely to accord with the axiom he expressed in his *Conversations with Critics* interview: "A good novel isn't a health food store. It's a butcher's shop." His literary reputation remains insecure, and in an essay he wrote for *Contemporary Authors Autobiography Series 4* (1986), he ranked himself as no more than "one of life's quarterfinalists." Yet, taken as a whole, his novels are a lively and provocative body of work that helped to enlarge the formal and thematic scope of English fiction in the late twentieth century.

Interview:

Nicolas Tredell, "David Caute," in his *Conversations with Critics* (Manchester, U.K.: Carcanet, 1994), pp. 111–125.

References:

Bernard Bergonzi, *The Situation of the Novel*, second edition (London: Macmillan, 1979), pp. 216–223;

Raman Selden, "Commitment and Dialectic in Novels by David Caute and John Berger," *Forum for Modern Language Studies*, 11 (1975): 106–121;

Nicolas Tredell, *Caute's Confrontations: A Study of the Novels of David Caute* (Nottingham, U.K.: Paupers' Press, 1994).

Lindsay Clarke
(14 August 1939 –   )

Susan Rowland
University of Greenwich—London

BOOKS: *Sunday Whiteman* (London: Cape, 1987);
The Chymical Wedding: A Romance (London: Cape, 1989;
New York: Knopf, 1989);
Alice's Masque (London & New York: Cape, 1994);
Essential Celtic Mythology (London & San Francisco:
Thorsons, 1997); republished as *Lindsay Clarke's
Traditional Celtic Stories* (London: Thorsons, 1999);
*Parzival and the Stone from Heaven: A Grail Romance Retold
for Our Time* (London: Thorsons, forthcoming
2001).

PRODUCED SCRIPTS: *Cathal of the Woods,* radio,
BBC, February 1994;
A Stone from Heaven, radio, BBC, May 1995.

Lindsay Clarke emerged in the late 1980s as a significant new voice in the contemporary British novel. His innovations in subject matter and literary form appear in works ranging from the postcolonial novel of Africa to the postmodern integration of occult spirituality and literary romance. Combining social and political anxieties with inner vision, Clarke's novels are quest narratives that evoke African spirituality, alchemy, Jungian theory, Celtic legends, and medieval romances. He is a self-consciously literary writer, whose novels exemplify his belief, expressed in the introduction to his new version of Celtic myths (1997), that reality is a "mythological function of the human imagination." It is the aim of imaginative literature to facilitate psychic and spiritual development by producing stories that point to "other" deeper and unrepresentable realities. Clarke sees postmodernism as a liberation from traditional literary realism and from conventional notions of reality, not a spiritless condition of a depthless society. The postmodernism he cites in his introduction liberates the novelist to return to older literary forms of quest literature and romance in pursuit of numinous connections to the natural world. In this approach, Clarke places himself in the tradition of the British Modernists such as T. S. Eliot and the mythensnared William Butler Yeats, rather than the postmodernism of the empty image.

Lindsay Clarke (courtesy of the author)

Victor Lindsay Clarke was born on 14 August 1939 in the northern industrial British city of Halifax, in Yorkshire. His mother's name was Clara Bell Clarke and his father, Victor Metcalfe Clarke, worked as a warehouse foreman. Clarke had a successful educational career that culminated in his being awarded an honors degree in English literature at King's College, Cambridge. Both the degree and the place are important for his second and most successful novel to date, *The Chymi-*

cal Wedding: A Romance (1989). In 1961, the year he graduated, Clarke married Carolyn Sara Pattinson; they divorced in 1972. Clarke worked as a senior master at a high school in Akim-oda, Ghana, from 1962 to 1965, which provided material for his first novel, *Sunday Whiteman* (1987). In 1965 Clarke returned to England to become a lecturer in English at a further education college in Great Yarmouth, on the east coast. He then advanced to the more senior post of coordinator of liberal studies at Norwich City College from 1967 to 1970. Perhaps Clarke's most interesting teaching position from the point of view of his writing career is his final one. From 1970 to 1978 he was codirector of the Friends World College, European Center in Norwich. Friends World College is based at Long Island University in the United States and was originally a Quaker institution. It retains a distinctive approach to learning and promotes multiculturalism. Quakers are specifically cited in *The Chymical Wedding* as engineers of world peace when the protagonist, Alex, dreams that the Quakers shall hold the keys of all the world's nuclear weapons. Since 1978 Clarke has been a freelance teacher, counselor, and writer. In 1980 he married Phoebe Clare Harris, a potter. Lindsay Clarke told *Contemporary Authors* that his politics are Green or ecological and his religion is "nondenominational belief in spirit and soul."

Clarke moves from exploring the postcolonial Englishman in his African novel, *Sunday Whiteman*, to visionary romance in *Alice's Masque* (1994). Between the two, he wrote his best-loved work, *The Chymical Wedding* (1989), which established his reputation by winning the Whitbread Prize for Fiction. All three novels diagnose a profound crisis in contemporary Western masculinity. They stress the desperate need to restructure the psyche of the male in relation to the feminine Other. What prevents the despair in Western masculinity from sliding into solipsism or nihilism is a sexual philosophy that unites "Otherness" to the unconscious.

The unconscious is then specified as the home of spirituality and a numinous connection to nature. So, reformulating the masculine's relations to the feminine without also involves perceiving the feminine Other within. This process in turn structures a connection to a spiritual Other that can neither be possessed nor denied. The male has to renounce his claim to possess the feminine Other in order to acknowledge his inner femininity as his own and not to be dominated. *The Chymical Wedding* acknowledges a significant debt to Jungian psychoanalysis in Clarke's philosophy of the unconscious as a domain of the spirit: it is a domain accessible in dream and represented in myth.

Sunday Whiteman draws on Clarke's experiences in an African school, but it is important to note that the book was written twenty years later when the experiences could be contextualized in Clarke's sexual philosophy. Such a sexual philosophy is an extension of his Jungian beliefs, sexual relations between the sexes should aim to become an expression of inner noncompetitive dialogue between the conscious ego and the numinous androgynous unconscious. Sunday Whiteman is the name bestowed on all white males in an unnamed, former colonial African country in 1962, where Englishman Austin Palmer, whose wife has recently left him, teaches in an African school deep in the interior. The novel traces the disintegration of Palmer's psyche as his hopes and illusions about the recently instituted Marxist government become dashed when it turns into a corrupt, brutal one-party state. Palmer is unable to make any real connection to Africa, either in political terms or in the culture of his pupils and colleagues. Nor can he connect to the feminine. Haunted by the despairing voice of his absent wife, Kay, Palmer takes an African wife, Appaea, but is unable to sustain the relationship. The Otherness of Africa forces him to confront his inner Otherness in the form of the unconscious that he is continually repressing. His refusal to come to terms with Otherness in any guise leads to disaster. He breaks down completely and takes the place of an old woman left to die as a witch in the square. In an ambiguous ending he is fetched by his "dark sisters" at Appaea's behest. It is not clear whether this event is a form of African integration or, as is more likely, a powerful metaphor for the suppressed Other grown overwhelming into the Otherness of death.

Sunday Whiteman is Clarke's most traditional novel. Although the subject matter is the failed quest for selfhood or the psychic disintegration of the protagonist, it is narrated omnisciently and concentrates on the "outer," increasingly untenable social and political circumstances of Palmer's African life. The work was well received, but like most first novels it did not receive a great deal of critical attention. It is likely to generate most interest in the category of a postcolonial text, especially for its startling elision of the Otherness of African culture with the Otherness within a Western masculine psyche. This connection is the signature of much imperial literature, and future critics will want to evaluate Clarke's attempt to make it a nonracial structure in the elevation of Otherness over exhausted occidental values. The question remains: does Clarke's sincere critique of Western masculinity result in an unintended plundering of Otherness, rather than just a new relationship to it? This issue resurfaces in the cause of the feminine in the second novel.

The Chymical Wedding is set in the countryside of eastern England, near where Clarke pursued his British teaching career. It centers on the beautiful country estate of Easterness—a name associated with a pre-Christian mother goddess—and its visitation by successive "King's men," graduates of King's College, Cambridge. The novel consists of two parallel narratives that, despite

The Pightle was perfect for my needs at a time when I was no longer sure what my needs were. It must have been a peasant's dwelling once, built of wattle and daub, timbered throughout in oak, with a reed thatch cocking a snook from either gable end. And the site, set among a stand of beech and chestnut, overlooking the water-meadows on the wilder fringes of the hamlet, about a quarter of a mile from its nearest neighbour, spoke of a certain independence in the original, late medieval owner.

The Pightle must have been a peasant's dwelling once. Built of wattle and daub, timbered throughout in oak, with a reed thatch cocking a snook from either gable end, it was set among a stand of beech and chestnut, a quarter of a mile from its nearest neighbour. There was a small garden at the front, already overgrown with enough Spring so much a that a stray pheasant was resting under a clump of fern. At the rear the cottage overlooked the water-meadows on the wilder fringe of the hamlet, you could see the round flint tower of the church across the stream. But the windows were leaded and small, even at mid-day the rooms were shadey, almost dark. No-one would bother me there. It was perfect for my needs at a time when I was no longer sure what my needs were.

Munday St Mary glinter in the sunlight

The name intrigued me. There was something diminutive, almost elfin, to the ring of it. It matched the dumpy lime-washed walls and the pokey interior. Pightle was a local word of unknown It matched my mood: one could be victim one could be as pixelated as one alled and pixelated in the Pightle, and no-one would give a damn.

It was a local word of unknown origins, as so my neighbour told me. He was a retired psychiatric nurse, a widower, called Arthur Neave, who lived alone, down the lane now and kept an eye on the Pightle for the friend who had loaned it to me. I'd picked up the huge old pistol-key from him.

In that part of the world the sky is everywhere

First page of an early draft for The Chymical Wedding *(Collection of Lindsay Clarke)* being set more than one hundred years apart, finally cross and conjoin in a rite of passion and violence. In the contemporary story Alex Darken, a dried-up poet and cuckolded husband, describes his encounters with a much older poet, Edward Nesbitt, and his psychic assistant and lover, Laura. Like Clarke's second wife, Laura is a potter, and in an autobiographical reading of this powerful and unusual love story, the authorial role is likely divided between the shallow Alex, who is gradually initiated into mysteries of the spiritual unconscious, and the sophisticated hermeticist Edward. Both Edward and Laura are on a quest to uncover the alchemical secrets of the second narrative strand, the story of nineteenth-century alchemist and writer Louisa Agnew and her passionate relationship with the King's educated parson, Edwin Frere. Louisa rescues Frere from the spiritual despair occasioned by his exclusively patriarchal Christianity by sexually initiating him into alchemy as a philosophy of the feminine as divine, which has been cast out of Christianity. For Clarke—as for Carl Jung—the sexual act can become a rite initiating unconscious communion, which can in turn be understood as a form of psychological alchemy. Frere is unable to sustain a healing connection to the Other, however, and castrates himself as a violent sacrifice to the divine Mother and Father. Laura is psychically in touch with Louisa, and the sexual ritual between Laura and Alex causes Edward to break down and nearly die from a heart attack. Yet, most characters achieve resolution and peace by renegotiating nonpossessive relationships to the spiritual unconscious. Alex and Edward manage this re-integration through dreams. Alex has previously been overwhelmed by the demonic potentialities of nuclear war, but he dreams about Quakers and decides that "quaking" is a motif for those unable to promote peace in the world by holding divisive and violent impulses within (by a right relationship to the unconscious) and so not projecting them onto an outward enemy. The only hope for the politics of the Left, with which Alex tenuously associates himself, is inner psychic development using Jungian philosophy.

The Chymical Wedding represents the most evolved statement of Clarke's sexual and spiritual philosophy in literary terms, as alchemy. Although the novel incorporates several occult sources, it does not stray from the Jungian field in what it asks the reader to accept. Jung believed that the alchemists, occult masters striving to convert lead into gold, were projecting real changes within their psyches. The "lead" was the depressive, denied unconscious that could evolve into the gold of perfect union with the spirit within if "alchemy"—or in Jung's terms "individuation"—proceeded successfully. *The Chymical Wedding* converts this paradigm into a representational structure for social, political, sexual, and psychic matters. The realist novel gives way to the alchemical novel in matter of form as well.

Clarke's Jungian alchemy becomes also a method of reading and writing literature. In this novel of blocked poets, writing can be freely created only by explicit union with the unconscious. Furthermore, the act of reading and writing is a form of alchemy in this novel, a way of uniting with unconscious Otherness.

The writers in *The Chymical Wedding* are equally true to Jungian theory in finding the chief figure of the unconscious Other to be the other gender. Clarke's sexual philosophy reaches its full flowering in this novel when, uncontaminated by colonial issues, divisive modern relationships between men and women can simultaneously represent the divisive political issues that cut modernity off from nature and spirit, masculinity from its inner Other, the feminine. Clarke encapsulates the ramifications of his remarkably coherent and complete worldview in two words: *symbolic* and *diabolic*. Edward instructs reader representative Alex that *symbolic* means the act of writing, both within the psyche and without, while *diabolic* literally means splitting, the splitting of minds, marriages, and atoms that is the dark matter of this passionately urgent novel. According to Edward and Laura, alchemy is the poetic science of uniting, whereas the diabolic becomes associated with the masculine urge to possess and dominate, whether it be the feminine (within or without) or the political aggression that breeds war. Alex comes to realize that he has tried to force his wife into the role of his unconscious Other so that he need not face his true Otherness within. Such a possessive attitude causes their splitting just as Edward's late demand that Laura exist for him precipitates his own temporary defeat by his unacknowledged inner darkness.

The perilous state of Western masculinity supplies the urgency and drive of the novel, but the most impressive figure is surely Louisa Agnew, who is both a convincing Victorian woman and adventurous seeker after occult mysteries. She is the most successful alchemist in the terms of the novel: she is explicitly reconciled to her own unconscious in producing her alchemy text and is defeated in her rescue of Frere only by his overwhelming terror of the spiritual Other as feminine and sexuality. Louisa's final sacrifice of her alchemy text to the flame at first appears as a sign of failure, but she manages to re-interpret the act positively: she has consumed her spiritual Other and it lives within her, no longer needing the printed record. The purpose of the book is personal transformation.

Just as in the twentieth century when what is at stake in diabolical splitting is the fissive atom, what is at stake between Louisa and Frere is patriarchal Christianity. The title of the novel is the promise and possibility of alchemy in uniting Christianity with an alchemical Mother goddess as part of a far-reaching move to woo the Other. For Christianity, "wedding" with the unconscious within structures a true sexual relationship within the con-

*Dust jacket for the first American edition of Clarke's 1989 novel, which employs
Jungian psychological theory to link alchemy and sexuality*

text of the sacred. Despite acts of despair and violence, the adherence of *The Chymical Wedding* to its alchemical-Jungian ideology remains optimistic that humans in general, and males in particular, can be redeemed.

One caveat in the profeminist critique of masculinity links *The Chymical Wedding* to *Sunday Whiteman*. The earlier novel expresses a conflict between anticolonial intentions and spiritual philosophy, in which Africa inevitably slides into representational material for the Otherness of the Western subject. In *Sunday Whiteman* the overtly disgusted stance at the disastrous grafting of Western ideologies onto a complex ancient culture makes the novel a valuable text in which to explore postcolonial literary issues. Similarly, *The Chymical Wedding* is full of praise for the wisdom of women versus the pathetic exploitations of men, but it ends with both significant female protagonists as silent and with the female writer having irrevocably destroyed her work. By contrast Alex and Edward both begin to write poetry again. Both *The Chymical Wedding* and Clarke's third novel, *Alice's Masque,* demonstrate the dangers of idealizing the feminine in ways that may finally evade the representative structure of the novel.

Another link with *Alice's Masque* (1994) is the use of the resources of literary romance. The myth of the Green Man and his later incarnation in "Sir Gawain and the Green Knight" is used throughout *The Chymical Wedding* as a counterpoint to failed twentieth-century masculinity. In *Alice's Masque* medieval romance comes to the fore in connection with a Celtic fertility rite suggested as its antecedent. Alice, once a medieval-literature academic and now a weaver, lives in a Cornish house she believes to be sited on the threshold of the "otherworld." She is sheltering a young relative, Leah, who is fleeing a disastrous love affair and befriends Amy, a young girl who models for them on the seashore. Together the three make up the crone, sexual woman and maiden of the triple goddess or feminine principle. Although Alice suggests to Leah that lives can be changed by telling different stories, she comes to believe that Leah's entanglements with newly arrived, married, former lover Ronan are an attempt to act out Geoffrey Chaucer's "The Wife of Bath"–in his *Canterbury Tales,* where a rapist knight is reprieved from the masculine courts of law to the feminine courts of love. The knight is then sent on a quest to discover what women most desire. Mythological stories are thresholds of spiritual and unconscious realities for both Clarke and Alice. If the protagonists permit this story to shape itself through Leah and Ronan, then both will be restructured in relation to his feminine Other. In particular, Ronan has to learn that the answer to the quest for women's desire, "sovereignty," does not mean a crude assertion of female power over men. Instead women should be able to "own" themselves in relation to men. Like Alex Darken, Ronan must realize his own feminine Other and not force Leah to be part of him all the time. If he can achieve a balance with his inner Otherness, then he will experience a spiritual connection to the world that will grant him peace.

Unlike *The Chymical Wedding, Alice's Masque* supplies little plot in the sense of outward events. Ronan rushes to Cornwall, killing a swan on the way. A girl is found raped and murdered on the beach but remains a nameless representation of masculine violence. Leah and Ronan tussle, and Ronan breaks down but is then aided by Alice. The novel ends with another of Clarke's ambiguities. Ronan, newly remade in relation to the unconscious, embarks with Alice on a rite of connection to the visionary landscape of the Cornwall coast, wherein it is possible that he will find Leah, or perhaps only his feminine self.

The dogma of the novel insists on a necessary balance between inner realities and outer relationships. The structure of the novel appears to have neglected this good advice. So much of the text is devoted to inner vision or mythological exploration that the protagonists are precariously tilting between novel "characters" and representative types. Of course, the reader is given a vital clue in the title, *Alice's Masque*. A masque was an aristocratic entertainment in which mythological figures demonstrated unchanging patterns and truths. The novel works deliberately as a masque, distinguishing itself from the realist novel in an urgent bid for representational resources beyond the traditional form. In being a highly self-conscious text, the novel may be termed postmodernist in its deliberate departure from the realist tradition. Nevertheless it is less satisfying to read than *The Chymical Wedding*, which manages to combine the delights of traditional storytelling with the ritual of spiritual experience. *Alice's Masque,* with its powerful symbols of light and depictions of a passionate Cornish landscape, reads more like a poem.

The critical reception of *The Chymical Wedding* was enthusiastic. Clarke has become a successful writer in Britain and has started to gain a reputation in the United States as well. Applauding the passion and poetry of the book, Michael Wood in *The London Review of Books* (18 May 1939) described how the novel converts the alchemical quest, "into a sane metaphor, asserting not the magical return of the symbolic to our heartless world, but a glimpse of how symbolic the world already is, how much it is made in our image, littered with fragments of our

dreams." Another critic, Robert Irwin, noted the intense responses to a postmodern society shorn of values, which contrast with the portrayal of a repressive age in the grip of a narrow-minded Christianity (*The Listener,* 20 April 1989). *The Chymical Wedding* won the prestigious 1989 Whitbread Prize for fiction, second in status only to the Booker Prize in Britain. A motion picture directed by the Jungian-influenced John Boorman was proposed in 1990 but has never materialized. After such a success, it was perhaps inevitable that the riskier *Alice's Masque* came as something of a disappointment. Far less noticed than *The Chymical Wedding,* the novel was overloaded with symbolism and underpowered characters. In a largely sympathetic review in *The Guardian* (18 January 1994), Elizabeth Young praised *The Chymical Wedding* for its role as "a crucible wherein Clarke poured over the Hermetic tradition and the holy fire of mythical sexual union." Of *Alice's Masque,* Young reported that she appreciated its beauty of language but accused the novel of "contrivance and effort." In recognizing the metaphysical tensions driving Clarke's writing, Young proves the most generous of his critics.

The notable achievement of Lindsay Clarke is that in three novels he has established himself both as an original voice and as an innovative participant in the evolution of the novel form. While his first novel, *Sunday Whiteman,* follows after major creations of colonial experience, such as Joseph Conrad's *Heart of Darkness* (1902), both the later works double back to occult, mythological, and romance traditions; they also offer valuable comparisons to major twentieth-century writers such as Saul Bellow and Doris Lessing in their positive deployment of Jungian theory of the unconscious. Clarke offers his own distinctive critique of Western masculinity within a context of sexual-spiritual philosophy that constructs an unusually positive version of postmodern departures from realism. The ambition of such a writer is to be the architect of the reader's imagination. Reading such a writer is to experience the promise of an escape through the harsh illusions of modernity to a green world of romance and desire.

References:

A. J. Harper, "Mysterium Conjunctionis: On the Attraction of 'Chymical Weddings,'" *German Life and Letters,* 47, no. 4 (1994): 449–455;

Mark F. Lund, "Lindsay Clarke and A. S. Byatt: The Novel on the Threshold of Romance," *Deus Loci: The Lawrence Durrell Journal,* 2 (1993): 151–159;

Susan Rowland, "The Body's Sacred: Romance and Sacrifice in Religious and Jungian Narratives," *Literature and Theology,* 10 (June 1996): 160–170.

Jonathan Coe

(19 August 1961 –   )

Merritt Moseley
University of North Carolina at Asheville

BOOKS: *The Accidental Woman* (London: Duckworth, 1987);

A Touch of Love (London: Duckworth, 1989);

The Dwarves of Death (London: Fourth Estate, 1990);

Humphrey Bogart: Take It & Like It (London: Bloomsbury, 1991; New York: Grove Weidenfeld, 1991);

James Stewart: Leading Man (London: Bloomsbury, 1994); republished as *Jimmy Stewart: A Wonderful Life* (New York: Arcade, 1994);

What a Carve Up! (London: Viking, 1994); republished as *The Winshaw Legacy: or, What a Carve Up!* (New York: Knopf, 1995);

The House of Sleep (London: Viking, 1997; New York: Knopf, 1998);

The Rotters' Club (London: Penguin, forthcoming 2001);

B S Johnson (London: Picador, forthcoming 2001).

PRODUCED SCRIPTS: *In Cahoots,* Carlton TV, 1995;

Five Seconds to Spare, motion picture, screenplay by Coe and Tom Connolly, based on *The Dwarves of Death,* Scala Productions, 2000.

OTHER: "Ivy and Her Nonsense," in *The Penguin Collection* (London: Penguin, 1995);

Rosamond Lehmann, *Dusty Answer,* introduction by Coe (London: Flamingo, 1996);

Lehmann, *The Echoing Grove,* introduction by Coe (London: Flamingo, 1996);

"9th and 13th," in *The Time Out Book of New York Short Stories,* edited by Nicholas Royle (London: Penguin, 1998);

"V.O.," in *New Writing 7: An Anthology,* edited by Carmen Callil and Craig Raine (London: Vintage / British Council, 1998);

B. S. Johnson, *The Unfortunates,* introduction by Coe (London: Picador, 1999);

Shirley Eaton, *Golden Girl,* introduction by Coe (London: Batsford, 1999).

Jonathan Coe (photograph by Jason Shenai / Peake Associates; courtesy of the author)

SELECTED PERIODICAL PUBLICATION–
UNCOLLECTED: "Low Culture Rises Above Its Critics," *Sunday Times* (London), 20 November 1994.

Jonathan Coe is the author of seven original and entertaining novels that combine an interest in postmodernist fiction—he calls his first novel pastiche Samuel Beckett—with the narrative urgencies of the best popular movies and fiction. Coe's most successful novel, *What a Carve Up!* (1994), uses the pattern of British horror comedy to introduce the "monsters" of the Margaret Thatcher and John Major era in British politics. He has worked as a proofreader and as a semiprofessional musician, claiming in a 1997 interview with Andrew Biswell that the acceptance of his first novel frustrated his real ambition to "move to London and become Frank Zappa"; and he has written books about American cinema icons Jimmy Stewart and Humphrey Bogart. Though he has two graduate degrees in English, he insists that his academic studies, which he focused on Samuel Beckett and Henry Fielding, have little influence on his novels. If there is one feature, however, he shares with Beckett and Fielding, it is humor. Coe told *Contemporary Authors* that "the worst kind of novel for me is a novel without humor," and humor is one of the features that—along with inventive plotting and a fertile melding of high and mass culture—animates all his books. According to Biswell, Coe is "acknowledged as one of today's foremost satirical novelists." He is also one of the most surprising, and—while his fiction always challenges the reader—it is dedicated to the possibly old-fashioned satisfactions of plot and humor.

Coe has commented eloquently on what ails the contemporary British novel and how his own works fit into that tradition. In "Low Culture Rises Above Its Critics" (1994), a *Sunday Times* (London) essay celebrating popular culture and deploring the inability of the current English critical establishment to address it, he argues that

> the majority of literary novels being published here at the moment, while full of intelligent ideas and in general very accomplished stylistically, are none the less weak on plot, weak on character and shy of formal innovation: somehow, it would seem, we have evolved a brand of novel that contrives at once to be both middlebrow and deeply, irredeemably unpopular. As a result, the literary novel is now at the very margins of cultural life in England.

Coe often compares his writing to jazz, to popular music, and perhaps most insistently to motion pictures—popular movies, not art cinema.

Jonathan Coe was born on 19 August 1961 in Bromsgrove, a suburb of Birmingham, England, the son of Roger Frank Coe, a physicist, and Janet Mary Coe. At King Edward's School in Birmingham he began writing, encouraged by his English teacher Tony Trott. Coe wrote his first book at eleven and began writing novels at fifteen. He attended Trinity College, Cambridge, receiving a B.A. in 1983, and he earned an M.A. (1984) and a Ph.D. (1986) in English from the University of Warwick. During his postgraduate years in Warwick, he was a tutor in English poetry. Coe has been a full-time novelist and freelance journalist since

1988. He has contributed to a variety of publications, including *The London Review of Books, The Telegraph, The Independent,* and *The Guardian.* True to his eclecticism, his journalism pays equal homage to B. S. Johnson, an experimental novelist of the 1960s, and the distinctively noncerebral television comedians Eric Morecambe and Ernie Wise. Coe married Janine Maria McKeown in 1989; they are the parents of one daughter, Matilda, and live in London.

Coe's first novel, *The Accidental Woman* (1987), was a remarkable beginning. It follows a woman named Maria over a sizable portion of a life whose uneventfulness is relieved only by increasingly predictable misfortunes. Her story is circular: acceptance and attendance at Oxford, a marriage almost accidentally undertaken and just as accidentally ended, the loss of her child, her failure to adjust to life in London, her move back to the provinces, and her return to her parents. She ends where she began. At every stage she has few expectations, and even they are unsatisfied.

The main distinction of the book is its tone, which is ironic, arch, knowing, and self-referential. Coe told Barèt Magarian in 1998 that the novel is "about authorial intentions." The main character is really the intrusive narrator, who comments regularly and facetiously on the process of telling the story he has, for unexplained reasons, chosen to relate. For instance, when Maria tells her family that she has passed the admissions examination for Oxford, he comments, "Here you are to imagine a short scene of family jubilation, I'm buggered if I can describe one." At another point, he says, "All her life she had, it was starting to seem, been at the mercy of forces beyond her control, so perhaps she had come to feel comfortable that way. (I hope none of you are going to be so awkward as to ask me what those forces were.)" He regularly undercuts his heroine. Having described her youthful practice of writing poems, he comments, "Why Maria wrote these poems, what pleasure she took in wrestling with emotions, disguising them as thoughts and misrepresenting them in words, what satisfaction she derived from copying them out in a fair hand and reading them over to herself, I cannot say. Probably none." He refers to an affair she has at Oxford as "the gropings, the senseless fumbles and thrusts which this poor misguided couple executed upon each other on warm spring afternoons and clammy evenings . . . this ludicrous pantomime." This sort of narratorial intrusion has its risks: reviewing the book for *TLS* (15 May 1987), Nigel Lawson labeled it "camp" and "pretentious." But this technique has a purpose and is, finally, justified by the results.

It is curious that the narrator is consistently unsympathetic to Maria's problems, which are more

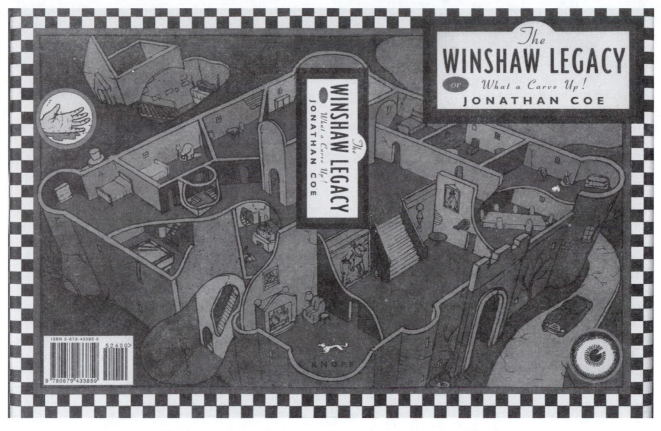

*Dust jacket for the first American edition of Coe's 1994 novel, which he describes as his attempt to write
"a big political novel, alongside this personal story about my childhood"*

than one person should be expected to endure. Yet, the reader can feel that despite the facetiousness and impatience, the novel—perhaps perversely—invites genuine concern for a deeply ordinary woman. Something of this dual attitude is visible in a late passage. After her move to Chester, Maria becomes slightly eccentric, sometimes standing in line at the supermarket and saying, "Puke and shit, puke and shit." The narrator comments,

> And while on this subject I think it would be true to say that Maria was generally unpopular in her neighborhood, and tended to be regarded with a suspicion which spilled over, for some people, into violent hatred. She never gave any offence, knowingly, but her neighbors mistrusted her because she lived alone, and was silent, and because the sight of her walking home from work on wet nights, huddled with cold, wearing a plastic headscarf to guard against the rain, somehow depressed them. But perhaps I can see their point, I feel depressed just writing about it.

Maria is an accidental woman in the sense that she is accident prone and in being irrelevant to most things and people. She lives accidentally, and, when last seen

(by a lark overhead), she is a "speck"—more or less as she has always been. *The Accidental Woman* answers to Coe's insistence that a novel should have humor: it is a hard, sometimes ruthless, humor, but the book is funny.

A Touch of Love (1989) is not without the kind of narratorial self-consciousness that figures in *The Accidental Woman*. For instance, the narrator refers to "Katharine—who is not, in case you were wondering—going to be allowed a voice in this story, because it is the story of Robin and Ted, who have both, in their different ways, resolved to keep her out of it. Which is a pity, in a way, because I think you would have preferred Katharine to either of them, had you been allowed to meet her." Robin Grant, the main character, is another unfortunate, but, unlike Maria, he is granted dignity as well as an inner life. A postgraduate student at Coventry, he fails to write his thesis, and the novel details a crisis in his life, beginning with the onset of a vague malaise and ending in his death. He is persuaded that he was meant to be with Katharine, whom he loved as an undergraduate, but she has married Ted, a coarse businessman. After a series of events in his complex search for sympathy, Robin is wrongly accused of exposing himself to a child in the park. The final blow appears to come when Robin's attorney, who is distracted by her own love problems, advises him to plead guilty, a suggestion that Robin interprets as evidence that she has lost faith in him. At a point in the narrative when (as the reader realizes only later) Robin is about to commit the innocent act that leads to his arrest, he thinks, "Forces would seem to be conspiring against me." And it is true that he is wholly or partly rejected by his friends.

Unlike Maria, Robin is not simply battered by events. His chief distinction lies in his being a fiction writer. Each of the four sections of the novel includes some development in Robin's life, rendered in conventional narrative form and a short story attributed to Robin—"The Meeting of Minds," "The Lucky Man," "The Lover's Quarrel," and "The Unlucky Man"—that comments obliquely, and only obliquely, on his situation. In the first of the stories a self-conscious narrator says, "I dislike this mode of writing. You pretend to be transcribing your character's thoughts (by what special gift of insight?) when in fact they are merely your own, thinly disguised. The device is feeble, transparent, and leads to all sorts of grammatical clumsiness. So I shall try to confine myself, in future, to honest (honest!) narrative." Though several of the other characters read Robin's stories to figure out what he is thinking, they misread them: the prosecutor finds evidence of a predisposition to sexual perversion, helping to buttress his case against Robin, and Robin's attorney's suggestion that he plead guilty comes after she has read one of them.

A Touch of Love also has a political dimension, though politics loom much larger in Coe's later novels. Robin is upset by the 1986 U.S. bombing attack on Libya, which used jets stationed at British bases. In his portrayal of Ted, Coe develops a critique of the "entrepreneurial" society so celebrated during the Thatcherite 1980s. Ted's selfishness and cultural brutality are reinforced by a more sinister impulse when he reflects on his success in having his own way in using Katharine's inherited money to buy a cottage in the Lake District while she preferred Cornwall: "The question of what they should do with the money had been the subject of several long and violent arguments, which he now recalled with some fondness. Eventually he had had his way, and the Lakes had won out over Cornwall. Physical force had not been necessary, after all."

The Dwarves of Death (1990) combines a lurid murder plot with aspects of a young man's life in London on a small income and knowledgeable details about rock music. Perhaps the age difference between the twenty-three-year-old protagonist and most reviewers led to querulous reactions from some critics. For instance, in a 15 September 1990 review for *The Specta-*

tor* (London), D. J. Taylor called the book "immensely enjoyable," but criticized it as "a conflation, a stylistic grab-bag of loose-ends and creaking linkages." Coe told Magarian in 1998 that he was dissatisfied with this novel (though he was adapting it for the screen): "I dashed off *The Dwarves of Death* in just five months and, afterwards, wasn't very happy with it."

Coe's narrator, William, is a pianist and composer, trying to get started with a band in London. His situation affects not only the events of the novel (which begins with his witnessing the murder of a band member by two dwarves) but its form. The sections are given musical titles—such as Theme One and Coda, for instance—and epigraphs from rock lyrics by Morrissey, lead singer for the 1980s band The Smiths. The novel also eschews ordinary chronological order. The greater part of the book is flashback, beginning with William being taken to a shabby house, where he is to be interviewed by Paisley, a member of The Unfortunates, the band he wishes to join. On the way William thinks, "I watched while the sky turned from blue to black and I don't think I've ever felt so good about London, before or since. I felt I'd reached some kind of turning point. Everyone else was still rushing around, panic on their faces, and I'd managed to stop somehow, to find some time to think and take a new direction." As one might expect in a novel by Coe, this hopefulness is undercut; William soon watches in horror as mysterious dwarves murder Paisley. At this point the novel moves back in time. William explains the shift:

> I wanted to get the difficult part out of the way—to describe what happened, that evening in Islington. The temptation now, of course, is to go straight on and tell you how it all ended, but there are a few things I have to explain first. I have to explain about Madeline, and Karla, and London, and why I wanted to join Paisley's band in the first place. . . . I know where to point the finger of accusation.
>
> Because it all started, as far as I'm concerned, with Andrew Lloyd Webber.

The background story, both complex and miserable, has to do with William's unsatisfactory love affair with Madeline, a cold woman who likes Andrew Lloyd Webber; his lack of fulfilment is underscored by his dissatisfaction with his current band and his deplorable living conditions. The band has great difficulties in recording because of a sinister studio manager named Vincent and because of two incompetent band members, the guitar player and the drummer. William sardonically comments on Jake, the drummer and songwriter: "Somehow his twin passions for metaphysics and pop music never cohered into a satisfactory whole. He would end up writing songs which combined the philosophical complexity of 'Bat Out Of Hell' with the raw rock 'n' roll energy of Schopenhauer's *The World As Will and Representation.*" Vincent turns out to have been the true target of the dwarves who were sent by Vincent's wife, Karla. Vincent escapes, but Karla does manage to kill Pedro, Tina's abusive lover, with a shotgun.

William, who makes his living in a music shop, lives in Bermondsey, a working-class area in the East End of London, where he shares a flat with a woman named Tina. Since she works at night, they rarely meet and communicate primarily by notes. A considerable portion of William's life is spent in simply getting back and forth between his miserable flat and the West End of London.

William's bizarre adventures in London and the high level of menace there are contrasted with his life in Sheffield, where he studied chemistry before trying to make it as a musician in London. His former girlfriend in Sheffield becomes more appealing when contrasted with the neurotic and terrifying women of London. It is not surprising that at the end of the novel he is back in Sheffield.

Though *The Dwarves of Death* has humor, energy, and a rich mix of what *Contemporary Authors* summed up as "romance, comedy, suspense and detailed description of the rock-and-roll music scene," it is Coe's weakest novel. Coe recognized its weakness and turned for his next novel to something much more thoughtful. Perhaps as a result, *What a Carve Up!* (1994) marked his first recognition as a major novelist. The novel won the John Llewellyn Rhys Prize and the Prix du Meilleur Livre Etranger, the French prize for best foreign book, and was shortlisted for the Guardian Fiction Prize and the Whitbread Prize.

In his 1997 interview with Coe, Tom Lappin described *What a Carve Up!* as "a scabrous, mordant satire that managed to combine a moving story of a rootless child searching for some stability with a wideranging and delicious assault on Thatcherism. Funny, involving, brilliantly targeted, it was a novel with the ambition of a 19th-century saga, an episodic trip through the Eighties moral vacuum." Coe explained the genesis of the novel to Lappin: "With *What a Carve Up!* I knew I wanted to do a big political novel, alongside this personal story about my childhood. The way into it I found was to write about the films I'd been obsessed with when I was a child, the one I recalled most strongly being that film, and when I made that choice to use, the political idea immediately came to be at the same time, because I thought *What a Carve Up* is the title I want for a novel about the Thatcher years." The connection between the personal and the political is at the heart of the novel, as is the link to Coe's childhood. *What a Carve Up!* tells the story of an author,

Michael Owen, who has somewhat by chance been made the official historian of the Winshaw family. Owen's life has been shaped by events that took place on his ninth birthday, when his family took him to the cinema. A fan of Russian cosmonaut Yuri Gagarin, the boy saw a short movie called *With Gagarin to the Stars,* and then part (before his mother made him leave) of a British haunted-house horror comedy, *What a Carve Up!* (1961), with Sidney James, Shirley Eaton, and Kenneth Connor. As Owen watches, he sees himself as part of it: "Shirley moved closer towards me. She said: 'Why don't you stay here tonight? I don't fancy spending the night alone, and we'd be company for each other.'" As Coe explained in a 1999 article for *The Independent,* "there's a scene in that between Shirley Eaton and Kenneth Connor which just crystallized my sexual hopelessness. So Shirley became my novel's shorthand for female desirability." It is perhaps inevitable that American readers would not understand the title, or remember the movie—released in the United States as *No Place Like Homicide!*—so in the United States the book appeared as *The Winshaw Legacy* (1995).

The complicated plot provides a searching look at the Winshaw family, whose members represent the worst of postwar Britain. They are unscrupulous, greedy, and hateful to each other and the world. Their story ends in a shambles, and the book ends with the title page of Owen's history (*The Winshaw Legacy*) and a publisher's introduction that explains, "we publish it . . . soon after the sensational events which have recently aroused keen public interest in the Winshaw family and all its doings. . . . I have therefore taken the liberty of including, by way of introduction to Michael's history, a full and detailed account of the horrific murders which took place at Winshaw Towers on the night of January 16th this year." The events at Winshaw Towers, of course, partly echo the events at Blackshaw Towers, the haunted house in the movie.

In addition to enormous creativity of incident and satirical brio, this novel is structurally daring. Made up of disparate pieces, some of them allusions to popular culture and others taken from the political history of the 1980s (arms trading with Saddam Hussein, for instance), the novel still manages to cohere. There are pretended clippings from periodicals such as *Hello!* and *Tatlers and Queen* that relate the doings of the rich and beautiful. One paragraph is copied, with only one word changed, from Frank King's *The Ghoul* (1928), the novel on which the movie *What a Carve Up!* was based, and there are several more "implags"—imbedded plagiarisms—from King's fiction. The important requirement for a novelist who employs this device is that the effect of the book must justify these liberties, and *What a Carve Up!* does so triumphantly.

Page from the manuscript for The House of Sleep *(Collection of Jonathan Coe)*

The "cultural promiscuity" of Coe's references in *What a Carve Up!* continues in his next novel, *The House of Sleep* (1997). As Coe told Biswell, "the title comes from a trashy novel by Frank King," while one chapter is a parody of Charles Dickens's novel *Great Expectations* (1861), and a running theme throughout the novel is a search for a lost motion picture by Italian director Salvatore Ortese. *The House of Sleep* is partly about a sleep clinic. Coe himself was a sleepwalker, and his condition led him to investigate sleep disorders and sleep therapies. The novel shuttles back and forth between two periods, its chapters alternating between 1983–1984 and 1996. The chapters set in the 1980s concern university students who live for a time in a large house called Ashdown, outside the seaside town where their university is located. Later, some of these people repair to the same house, which has become the Duddon Clinic, for treatment of sleep disorders such as inability to sleep, sleepwalking, and various forms of narcolepsy. The clinic is presided over by Dr. Gregory Duddon, who also lived there as a student.

Dr. Duddon clearly has radically different ideas about sleep: he is the only one in the field, he explains to one of his patients, who actually recognizes sleep as a disease.

> "A disease, Terry—the most widespread and life-curtailing disease of all! Forget cancer, forget multiple sclerosis, forget AIDS. If you spend eight hours a day in bed, then sleep is shortening your life by a third! That's the equivalent of dying at the age of fifty—and it's happening to all of us. This is more than just a disease: this is a plague! And none of us is immune, you realize. Not one of us, except. . . ." He turned to look at Terry and to draw breath, for he was panting now, either with emotion or exertion. " . . . Except for you."

As Coe explained to Lappin, "*House of Sleep* is a book about loss, lost dreams, and lost opportunities." This theme includes lost movies, lost sleep, and lost love as well. A poignant, yet strange, plotline concerns a man named Robert who falls in love with a girl he meets at Ashdown. He looks at Sarah and realizes "in this one stretched instant that there was nothing in the world he would not do for this woman; no quest he would not undertake, no sacrifice he would not willingly perform." This perhaps conventional sense of devotion takes on a shocking form when Robert, having realized that Sarah is lesbian, undergoes a sex-change operation to make himself acceptable to her. Challenged by Biswell about his qualifications to write about lesbian love, Coe answered, "If writers confined ourselves to things we'd witnessed at first hand, we'd be stuck in that tiny patch of experience critics want to pen us into.

But the impulse to write novels doesn't come from critics or newspapers; it comes from inside."

Alongside this tale of lost love, Coe has created a brilliantly funny story about losing a job because of a lost footnote. While editing a transcript of a talk by a moviemaker, Sarah, as instructed, removes one footnote number from the text. Because of her sleep disorder, however, she forgets to remove the corresponding footnote. The result is a mismatch between text and documentation. For example, the number after the phrase "a series of sex movies" inadvertently leads to a footnote which reads "Much praised, recently, by Denis Thatcher, who said they had given him 'six of the most enjoyable hours of my life.'" His wife Margaret later joked that he was "stiff for hours afterwards." After a reference to Prince Philip, the footnote reads: "He later developed a distinctive public persona, based largely on his self-confessed drinking habits and enormous sexual appetite."

There is nothing particularly intellectual in such jokes. The ever-eclectic Coe does not care. He insists on the inclusiveness of the novel form, on his right (and by inference the right, and perhaps even the obligation, of his contemporaries) to make novels out of high and low culture, the music of Meat Loaf as well as the philosophy of Schopenhauer, literature ranging from King (who, he told Biswell, was "right off the bottom of the scale") all the way to B. S. Johnson, Umberto Eco, and Italo Calvino.

Coe has enormous ambition; he asks to be compared to the great nineteenth-century novelists—who, he believes, had the sort of cultural centrality that present English literary novelists lack. He argues strongly for a good story, appealing characters, and humor, but he is just as insistent on the need for liberating experimentation. He told *Contemporary Authors* in 1991 that, rather than dividing fiction into experimental and nonexperimental, he preferred a "distinction . . . put forward by the novelist Robert Nye: he suggested that 'there is in effect only writing that is alive, and writing that is half-alive,' and there are no prizes for guessing which of these I would aspire to." Jonathan Coe's novels may be the most vividly alive fiction of the 1990s.

Interviews:

Andrew Biswell, "The Non-Literary Literary Man," *Telegraph* (London), 30 May 1997, p. 24;

Tom Lappin, "Waiting for Tony," *Scotland on Sunday,* 17 August 1997, p. 11;

Barèt Magarian, "What Happens If the Wrong Dreams Come True?" *Independent* (London), 24 August 1998, p. 13;

Gina Rozner, "How We Met: Jonathan Coe & Shirley Eaton," *Independent,* 11 July 1999, p. 51.

Isabel Colegate

(10 September 1931 –)

Merritt Moseley
University of North Carolina at Asheville

See also the Colegate entry in *DLB 14: British Novelists Since 1960.*

BOOKS: *The Blackmailer* (London: Blond, 1958);
A Man of Power (London: Blond, 1960);
The Great Occasion (London: Blond, 1962);
Statues in a Garden (London: Bodley Head, 1964; New York: Knopf, 1966);
Orlando King (London: Bodley Head, 1968; New York: Knopf, 1969);
Orlando at the Brazen Threshold (London: Bodley Head, 1971);
Agatha (London: Bodley Head, 1973);
News from the City of the Sun (London: Hamilton, 1979);
The Shooting Party (London: Hamilton, 1980; New York: Viking, 1981);
A Glimpse of Sion's Glory (London: Hamilton, 1985; New York: Viking, 1985);
Deceits of Time (London: Hamilton, 1988; New York: Viking, 1988);
The Summer of the Royal Visit (London: Hamilton, 1991; New York: Knopf, 1992);
Winter Journey (London: Hamilton, 1995; London & New York: Penguin, 1996);
A Pelican in the Wilderness: Hermits and Solitaries (London: HarperCollins, forthcoming 2002).
Collections: *Three Novels: The Blackmailer, A Man of Power, The Great Occasion* (London: Blond & Briggs, 1983; New York: Viking, 1984);
The Orlando Trilogy (Harmondsworth, U.K. & New York: Penguin, 1984)—comprises *Orlando King, Orlando at the Brazen Threshold,* and *Agatha.*

SELECTED PERIODICAL PUBLICATION– UNCOLLECTED: "The Magic Circle of Chiantishire," *Independent* (London), 7 April 1990, p. 43.

Isabel Colegate has been publishing novels in Great Britain for nearly forty years, maintaining an impressive standard of elegance and intelligence in her work. In a 1991 interview with Angela Lambert, Cole-

Isabel Colegate, circa 1969 (photograph © Jerry Bauer; from the dust jacket for the first American edition of The Shooting Party*)*

gate remarked of her early novels, "I don't think I was what people were looking for at that time." Although it is true that her early work has achieved neither the highest critical favor nor enormous sales, critical and public opinion changed practically overnight with the publication of her 1980 novel, *The Shooting Party.* The book went on to win the W. H. Smith Literary Award in 1981 and was made into a successful motion picture in 1985. Since then, according to Lambert, Colegate has been "that rare thing, a serious, best-selling writer."

Isabel Colegate was born on 10 September 1931 in Lincolnshire to Sir Arthur Colegate, a member of Parliament, and Lady Colegate, born Winefred Worsley. The young girl attended boarding schools in Shropshire and Norfolk, but according to Sarah Turvey in *DLB 14,* Colegate has said she "never quite got the hang of being taught," and discontinued her formal education at the age of sixteen. Colegate went to work, and by age nineteen she was assistant to literary agent Anthony Blond. Colegate married Michael Briggs, director of an engineering firm, in 1953. The couple has three children—Emily, Barnaby, and Joshua, born in 1956, 1964, and 1967—and they live in an eighteenth-century castle near Bath.

Blond later turned to publishing and, in 1958, when Colegate was twenty-seven, he published her auspicious first novel, *The Blackmailer.* In an introduction to her 1983 collection, *Three Novels: The Blackmailer, A Man of Power, The Great Occasion,* Colegate comments on her early novels:

> People think novelists write fictionalized autobiography; perhaps some do. I think myself that the process by which one turns one's deepest preoccupations into fiction is a lot more complicated than that—a kind of willed dreaming as necessary and as hard to analyse as the involuntary sort. It's a process I've thought a lot about since I wrote these three books, but these three I wrote without thinking because it didn't occur to me not to write them.

The only even slightly autobiographical feature of *The Blackmailer* seems to be that the main character, Judith Lane, works for a publisher. Judith is the widow of Anthony Lane, a young man from an upper-class family, who presumably died a war hero in Korea. An unscrupulous barrister named Baldwin Rees who served under Lane, knows the truth about his commanding officer, that he was a coward and a traitor. With envy and greed motivating his actions, Rees chooses to blackmail Judith with the threat of revealing this information about her husband to the newspapers. She pays for his silence, but as the novel progresses, the two of them become complicit in ever-more surprising ways.

As the story progresses, Rees falls in love with Judith and thus loses his power over her. An important parallel can perhaps be drawn between Rees's loss of power and the growing powerlessness of the upper class. Anthony's grandfather and widowed mother are remnants of that class, now visibly losing its centrality to British life.

Judith takes the socially ambitious Rees on a weekend trip to visit Anthony Lane's family. They know nothing of Rees's treachery, but nevertheless

snub him and treat him badly, thinking him vulgar. Rees's plan to secure a safe seat in Parliament comes to nothing, in part because of the refusal of Lane's grandfather to recommend him. To Judith, Mrs. Lane gives vent to an almost hysterical denunciation of the welfare state: "The world's changed. People have no sense of values, no decency, they're all out for what they can get. Our sort of people get pushed aside by all the lies and ingratitude. The welfare state—it's just a means of sheltering these liars and slanderers and upstarts. I brought Anthony up in the old-fashioned way, to be what his father was before him." And Sir Ralph declares that "disgrace is disgrace, whatever the modern idea may be."

Colegate's great strength through her whole career has been her ability to analyze acutely—but with sensitivity—the fading society of the British upper class in the twentieth century. *The Blackmailer* demonstrates several of the features for which Colegate is appreciated: intelligent, tough-minded character analysis; an unsentimental but detailed treatment of class shifts in Britain; and a delicate sense of humor. Reviewers over the years have regularly invoked Barbara Pym, Penelope Fitzgerald, and even Jane Austen to characterize the flavor of Colegate's books.

In *A Man of Power* (1960), a young girl named Vanessa, a first-person narrator who in her occasional naiveté echoes some of the effects of Henry James's *What Maisie Knew* (1897), relates her coming-of-age story in the shadow of her flamboyant, amoral mother. The mother, Lady Essex Cowper, is a society matron, many times married, who sets her cap for Lewis Ogden, a married property developer and social aspirant. Vanessa had earlier become aware of Ogden's wife, his former secretary, at her Swiss finishing school; she and her snobbish friends are disappointed by her: "She was always alone, always quiet, always simply dressed. Since she must obviously be common, her husband being self-made, we had been hoping for some entertaining errors of taste—huge diamonds pinned to her anorak, her Christian name in gold on her skis. There was nothing like that."

Essex separates Ogden from his wife with little difficulty, spends time with him in Italy—along with aristocratic drones who are part of her circle—and persuades him to buy a large country house. The couple are having a party there just before their planned wedding when Ogden becomes aware of what Vanessa should have known but does not—that her mother and a young man who lodges with her, and whom she has persuaded Ogden to employ, are lovers. Ogden ends the engagement and the party, sending Essex and all her friends away. The castoff wife, Jean, succeeds in killing herself. The novel ends with Vanessa in London,

Dust jacket for Colegate's first novel, about the declining power of the upper class in postwar Great Britain (courtesy of The Lilly Library, Indiana University, Bloomington, Indiana)

having met a promising man and separated herself from her mother's and Ogden's world.

Colegate's next novel, *The Great Occasion* (1962), is a different sort of book. Set in the 1950s, the story, which has no central focus, is a study of the family of a man named Gabriel Dodson, a widower and successful businessman, and his five daughters. The book begins with daughter Susan marrying an RAF Wing Commander named Bill, though no one else in the family approves of her marriage. Susan is nervous and a hypochondriac. She fails to carve out an identity for herself in her marriage, sheltering behind her husband, and suffers a severe mental collapse. The oldest daughter, Penelope, is already married to an unsavory rising politician named Ham. The third and perhaps the most interesting daughter, Angel, a promiscuous party girl, shocks her RAF brother-in-law by arriving at his house with a black boyfriend. Angel was essentially raped by a gossip columnist named Martin, who then spreads the word that she is a nymphomaniac. A child is conceived from the rape, and Angel has an abortion, encouraged

by Ham, who is afraid of bad publicity that might damage his political prospects. The fourth daughter, Charlotte, is an art student involved with a much older married artist; she marries him after his divorce and moves to the West Country where she sacrifices her own talent to support his, develops cancer, and eventually dies. Selina, the fifth daughter, runs away from home to care for Charlotte. The novel is partly about conflict between generations and the powerlessness of the older generation to hold back the tide of change, and the patriarch, Gabriel Dodson, becomes increasingly less forceful and effective as the novel unfolds. In one important development, Dodson loses out on a business deal in which his despised son-in-law Ham secretly works against his interest. In business as in his authority over his daughters, the aging Dodson is losing his control. Dodson is a sort of King Lear figure, unable to express any love for his daughters, increasingly making scenes; when his two youngest children read some of his love letters to his dead wife, he becomes enraged and denounces his son-in-law Bill for not being a real flyer and his daughters for their ingratitude after he has given them everything.

As the novel ends, the narrator's attention shifts to the youngest girl, Selena, who is in London. In her 1983 introduction to *Three Novels,* Colegate commented that "On the last couple of pages" in which Selina is told that being young, and in London, is "a great occasion," the novel "fails to convey the excitement of the first glimpse of a whole new group of people, that common, and indeed hard to convey, experience of youth. . . . The excitement is somewhat overshadowed by the sadness in other parts of the book.

Colegate's next book, *Statues in a Garden* (1964), is her first exploration of a more distant past, a past of which she has developed great and persuasive command—the period just before World War I. She told Jean W. Ross in a 1986 interview, published in 1988, that

A period which is still just within living memory certainly presents hazards as well as having a particular fascination. In this country we have to guard against nostalgia, and at the same time we have to guard against over-sensitivity to that charge. Present-day prejudices should not make us want to present the pre-1914 period as either the good old days or the bad old days. I believe it is possible to be, in however small an area, more or less accurate.

As the novel opens, Colegate produces a masterful setting:

London 1914. People said there was too much money about, the old standards were going (Rand magnates, American Heiresses). Bitterness in politics, talk of civil war in Ireland, of a general strike in the autumn. . . . A world of possibilities, and social injustice of course, and a great deal of stolid overfed stupidity; and one could argue about what was an end and what was a beginning, but we are not concerned with that at the moment. We are not trying to recapture an age as it was, or to write history: we are trying to remember the background for a fable. A private background for a private fable.

The focus for this "private fable" is Aylmer and Cynthia Weston, an aristocratic family, who have four children, Violet, Kitty, Edmund, and the amoral Philip, who is actually Aylmer's nephew and adopted son. Philip's main ambition is to be rich. He becomes involved with a shady stockbroker and loses a great deal of money belonging to Aylmer and to Edmund, a more honorable young man who is reading law. The mainspring of action in the novel is the affair between Philip and Aylmer's wife, Cynthia. His motives are never entirely clear; hers, however, are described fully and sympathetically:

Their love-making was passionate. It was different from anything she had ever experienced with Aylmer, because Aylmer had always thought of the sex appetite as a male one. Was it Lord Curzon who was supposed to have said, "Ladies don't move"? Aylmer would have agreed. Ladies . . . submitted out of the generosity of their sublime natures to the regrettably gross, though natural, desires of gentlemen. Cynthia had more or less fallen in with this view.

A maid discovers them in bed together and notifies Aylmer, who then kills himself. Philip goes on to thrive as a war profiteer; Edmund enlists and is killed at the Somme. *Statues in a Garden* brings together the domestic theme and the incisive analysis of social climbing, outmoded honor, and moral ambiguity present in Colegate's first three books and adds to them the sure handling of the past that features in much of her best work.

In 1968 Colegate published *Orlando King,* the first volume in what was later collected as *The Orlando Trilogy* (1984). This novel and its two successors, *Orlando at the Brazen Threshold* (1971) and *Agatha* (1973), trace the history of Orlando King and his daughter Agatha over a period of several decades ending in 1956, the year of Britain's Suez Crisis. In the novel that bears his name, Orlando has been reared in near isolation on an island in Brittany by a retired Oxford don named King. The story begins with Orlando, now twenty-one, traveling to London to make his way in the world. He bears introductory letters to various people, one of whom is his actual father, Leonard Gardner, a fact unknown to both of them. Orlando becomes Gardner's business associate and gradually takes over his position in the business. In a fury over being pushed out of his company and replaced by Orlando, Gardner drives recklessly and dies in a car accident. Orlando blames himself for his death, but nonetheless goes on, with strong Oedipal parallels, to marry Gardner's widow, his own stepmother; a daughter, Agatha, is born to the couple. The marriage is not a happy one; both he and his wife, Judith, have affairs. Judith bears another daughter, Imogen, who Judith says is not Orlando's child, and eventually Judith goes mad and dies in an asylum.

Orlando's relationship with his two half-brothers Paul and Stephen, is a troubled one. He finds a closer relationship with his brother-in-law Conrad; both men are now members of Parliament. Conrad resigns over the issue of appeasing the Nazis. Orlando favors appeasement, but when war comes, he resigns his position to become an air-raid warden and is badly injured during a raid. Orlando discovers that Leonard Gardner

Dust jacket for the first novel in Colegate's Orlando Trilogy
*(1968–1973), which traces the lives of the title
character and his daughter from the 1930s
until the Suez Crisis of 1956*

was his father and then is partially blinded in the bombing of London. He gives up his career, entrusts Conrad with the legal guardianship of his daughter Agatha, and retreats into self-exile in Tuscany.

In *Orlando at the Brazen Threshold,* Agatha, to whom the focus of the series gradually shifts in this book, visits her father in Tuscany. She eventually marries her cousin Henry, Conrad's son. This novel has a much narrower historical range than the other two in the trilogy, covering only a few months in 1951.

In *Agatha* the plot is played out against the background of the Burgess-Maclean spy scandal and the failed Suez invasion of 1956. Henry, Agatha's husband, is a feckless charmer. Her stepbrother Paul, who had been expelled from Eton and is a closeted homosexual, is arrested for spying. Agatha is torn between family duty and duty to her country, but she chooses to help Paul try to escape. When he is captured, he commits suicide, and Agatha is jailed and suffers the consequences.

The Orlando Trilogy is in some ways an exploration of the inevitable conflict between principle and practice. Orlando reflects, for instance, that "I have

killed my father . . . and driven my wife mad. I have helped to lead my country to destruction. Yet I never meant any harm." Orlando is by almost any standard a good man, yet he is a bad son, bad husband, bad father, and bad member of Parliament. His guardian, the old don who raised him, had told him, "The principle underlying capitalist society and the principle of love are incompatible. . . . One must create the truth by love." This advice is as unworkable in the real world as the position Agatha takes that love and family loyalty are a sufficient bulwark against the legal and political demands of counterespionage. The trilogy shows Colegate's usual delicate way of placing the personal in the context of the historical. The prelude to World War II in the first novel and the historic developments of the mid 1950s in the third—the Suez crisis, the Soviet invasion of Hungary, and the exposure of the Cambridge spies—are both background and significant plot elements, as are her characters in Parliament. She carefully shades the prewar appeasers, from Conrad, who resigns in protest to appeasement, to Orlando, who does not but later wishes he had, to his friends Guy and Penelope Waring who are actual Nazi sympathizers, incarcerated during the war. Their imprisonment helps foreshadow Agatha's own.

News from the City of the Sun (1979) traces the fatal arc of a utopian community from innocence and hope to terror and squalor over a period of forty years. Founded in 1930 by three brothers, the community is built around an old abbey, with the goal of becoming self-sustaining and thus providing a model for a widening alternative movement. There were years when the community came close to meeting its goal:

> After that came the good years, the best years of all. The guest house was finished and work began on restoring the roof of the barn, which was to be turned into a woolen mill. The farm began almost to meet its own expense: it might have done better had Arnold been willing to slow down the rate of expansion. Mrs. Arkwright took over the vegetable garden and as a result of her re-organisation it became the one part of the whole enterprise which never failed to show a small profit, even in the worst years.

The narrator is a middle-aged woman named Dorothy Grant whose childhood was spent largely around the commune in the years leading to World War II and afterward. Through her recollections, Dorothy paints a colorful picture of the odd mixture of inhabitants who came to live at the abbey over the years, including communists, nudists, Fabian socialists, and pacifists. Peter Kemp in *The Listener* (2 August 1979) summarized this novel as "an ironic and occasionally

*Dust jacket for Colegate's 1980 novel, which one reviewer described as "a stunning picture
of the British upper class at the pinnacle of their evolution"*

painful comedy about the odd interaction between human nature, life's surprises, and Utopian ideals."

The Shooting Party (1980) elevated Colegate's renown to a completely different level, prompting the republication of six of her earlier books. In this novel, she returns to the period of *Statues in a Garden,* just before the outbreak of World War I, in this case, 1913. Her book is about social striations, the inevitability of change, and death. Most of the people in the novel are not what they seem. She provides a glimpse of a society on the brink of enormous change, but provides sufficient illustration on the ills of that society to forestall much regret about its impending demise. The novel is set among the upper classes at a country estate near Oxford, where a large party has gathered for a weekend of shooting. The host is Sir Randolph Nettleby, together with his wife, Minnie—a former mistress of the king—and a daughter-in-law, Ida, who has three children. There are many guests; chief among them are Sir Gilbert Hartlip, an older man and acknowledged by all to be the supreme shot among the "guns," and the young Lionel Stephens,

who outshoots him. Considerable energy is expended by the characters on questions of caste and gentlemanly behavior. For instance, it is not considered well bred for the men to be counting their kills and striving to outdo one another, though they do both anyway, and their servants always place bets on the winner. Likewise, Sir Randolph's granddaughter keeps annoying her mother by being friendly to the servants. Also, the shooters kill hundreds and hundreds of birds in a day. Only the beautiful and thoughtful Olivia questions the morality of this killing and of the current ideal of "manliness."

The novel has a marked sense of foreboding. This tone is partly achieved by Colegate's powerful beginning:

> It caused a mild scandal at the time, but in most people's memories it was quite outshone by what succeeded it. You could see it as a drama all played out in a room lit by gas lamps; perhaps with flickering sidelights thrown by a log fire burning brightly at one side of the room, a big Edwardian drawing room, full of furniture, tables crowded with knick-knacks and framed photo-

graphs, people sitting or standing in groups, conversing; and then a fierce electric light thrown back from a room beyond, the next room, into which no one has yet ventured, and this fierce retrospective light through the doorway makes the lamplit room seem shadowy, the flickering flames in the grate pallid, the circles of yellow light round the lamps opaque (a kind of tarnished gold) and the people, well, discernibly people, but people from a long time ago, our parents and grandparents made to seem like beings from a much remoter past, Charlemagne and his knights or the seven sleepers half roused from their thousand year sleep.

It was an error of judgment which resulted in a death. It took place in the autumn before the outbreak of what used to be known as the Great War.

One of the beaters dies because Sir Gilbert Hartlip loses his composure. Under the stress of being outshot by a younger man, he fires at a low-flying woodcock and kills a man instead. In the aftermath Hartlip is exonerated by the coroner but moves to Africa to escape the disapproval of his friends. Despite the fact Hartlip has killed a man, Sir Randoph's judgment and concern seem to lie mostly with the fact that he was "not shooting like a gentleman." There is also discussion in the novel of the historic change taking place offstage—the rise of the Liberals, the country going to the dogs, and so on; the war, not yet visible at the time of the shooting, eventually takes one of the Nettleby grandsons as well as Lionel Stephens.

In his review for *The Listener* (4 September 1980), John Naughton summed up the strengths of this well-received novel, suggesting that, though it had little plot,

it's all Ms Colegate needs to build up a stunning picture of the British upper classes at the pinnacle of their evolution. Through the story of the developing rivalry between the men she weaves several other threads: the running of a largish country house; the relations between masters and servants, and between children and parents; the elaborate social ritual embodied in "good form"; the thought-processes of a decent country squire; the view from the gamekeeper's lodge. The whole canvas is tinted in with a deftness that is quite exquisite.

In her next book, Colegate surprised and disappointed some critics and fans who had expected her next work to be similar to the successful *The Shooting Party*. The author had other plans, however. *A Glimpse of Sion's Glory* (1985) comprises three long stories, none of which bear any resemblance to her previous book. Colegate explained to Ross in 1986 why she had written the stories:

I did them because I wanted to do something different; I felt I was rather lumbered with *The Shooting Party* in a sense, simply because—without being ungrateful—it had been rather a success, and therefore I felt I must get on with the next thing. So I did the stories for that reason. . . . And in a way they helped me to do some things I hadn't done before, to free me from *The Shooting Party*. . . .

"The Girl Who Had Lived Among Artists" is a fascinating study of an amoral, ambitious young woman named Nancy, who is free with her sexual favors to both genders. Coming home unexpectedly one day, Carley, the man who took Nancy in and who loves her, makes a shocking discovery, resulting in his suicide. Nancy goes blithely on with her life to become the wife of a Greek shipowner. Colegate depicts a utopia destroyed by human frailty in "Distant Cousins." A quasi-science-fiction story, it takes place in Tuscany—which, Colegate knows well and uses as a familiar setting. The plot surrounds the discovery of a race of superior yet gentle beings, similar in appearance to humans, who are accidentally wiped out because of mankind's clumsy curiosity. The title story in the collection, "A Glimpse of Sion's Glory," tells the tale of Alison, an ambassador's wife, who receives a love letter from a long-ago Oxford acquaintance who has defected to the Soviet Union. The letter is the occasion for a long, romantic reverie and self-reflection concerning the choices she has made in life: Alison finds herself daydreaming about Raymond, and it makes her "extraordinarily happy. . . . Something of immense value which she had thought she had lost had been returned to her."

Although many of her novels have revolved around the ambiguities of the past and the shiftiness of truth, Colegate's next book, *Deceits of Time* (1988), takes a more direct and philosophical look at these issues. Its main character is a middle-aged biographer, Catherine Hillery, who has been asked by her publisher to write a biography of a man named Neil Campion, an upper-middle-class figure, veteran of World War I, who served in Parliament and died in 1941 while a member of the cabinet. As Catherine discovers, there are secrets in the Campion family—Neil Campion had been a German sympathizer and died while traveling to Scotland to meet Rudolf Hess. Campion had even offered to head a provisional government after the war. These truths are confirmed, finally, when Eleanor Campion reads to Catherine and to Effie (Campion's widow) a letter about his secret work with the Germans to end the war.

Deceits of Time provides an occasion for serious reflection on truth and contingency, objectivity and

Dust jacket for Colegate's 1995 novel, about a middle-class family in economic decline

involvement. The opening passage sets the tone for the story:

> What it all hung upon really was a dash through the darkness many years ago, a wartime drive to the north whose destination was not known and might never be known because the driver was now dead; and upon that came to hang a number of theories, and with those theories certain people identified themselves so closely that they felt threatened when the correctness of the theories was questioned and their behaviour became in some cases distinctly odd. Catherine Hillery, who considered herself to have entered into the thing in all innocence, came to wish she had never allowed herself to become involved.

Catherine's originally positivistic ideas about fact and biography are shaken: "She used to think that if you read a book about someone you would have a pretty good idea of what they were like. It now seemed to her that that was not so at all. You would have an idea of what someone else thought they were like; and,

though that someone else might be, say, three parts right, they might equally be three parts wrong." Nevertheless, she ends by affirming that it is worthwhile to go on testing life stories against any discoverable facts; "redemption for the transient seemed to Catherine, if there were such a thing, to be not so much in the art as in the continuity of the effort to understand."

Susan Hinerfeld, in her *Los Angeles Times* review "The Impossibility of Biography" (28 December 1988) sums up the book by saying that "someone is hiding something–possibly everyone is. Time itself obscures the truth. Can the past be known? Or is what we call history the best of recollection, not absolute but consensual, and always subject to interpretation?" Hinerfeld's remarks link this novel with others in Colegate's oeuvre in which truth is disputed and ownership of the truth becomes a question of power, such as in *The Blackmailer* and *The Summer of the Royal Visit* (1991).

The Summer of the Royal Visit is an historical novel set in a spa town (most likely Bath) in the nineteenth century. The novel demonstrates that the issues of

Isabel Colegate, circa 1995 (photograph © Jerry Bauer; from the dust jacket for Winter Journey)

money and class, the self-made man, the secret crime, all of which Colegate has been exploring since her first novel, play out just as richly in a Victorian setting. The book is narrated in the present by a retired history teacher researching the events surrounding a competition by the townspeople to design a luxury hotel in the reign of Queen Victoria. The plan for the winning design is to be presented to the queen that summer during a royal visit. Jonathan Yardley in the 21 February 1992 *Washington Post Book World* notes that despite the title of the book "the royal visit is merely the backdrop against which are staged the small, intimate dramas of a number of people in the city." The main character is a troubled clergyman named Stephen Collingwood. Not a young man–he took orders after he lost his wife–he lives and works in Haul Down, a working-class district up the hill from the city proper. Collingwood is no saint–"when he came to live in simple lodgings in Haul Down closely surrounded by his parishioners he found himself unable to love them as much as he had intended to; this failure filled him with shame and self-reproach" –but he is genuinely interested in helping the poor. The other odd inhabitant of Haul Down is Caspar Freeling, an intellectual with powerful contacts in the genteel part of town down below, where he arranges séances in

league with a fraudulent mystic named Madame Sofia, intrigues in city politics, and engages in affairs with other men's wives.

As the story unfolds, it is discovered that Freeling has been using his "studio" in Haul Down to cater to pedophiles, prostituting local poor children to their urges; many of his clients are influential members in the community. Madame Sofia reveals the awful truth about Freeling to Collingwood. Before anything can be done, however, Freeling collects the children in the studio, locks them in, and sets the building on fire. Although the children are rescued, Collingwood dies trying to save them from the collapsing building. Yardley feels that, in this novel, Colegate intends to portray "the extent of public events on the private lives of those who witness them, the dark secrets of those private lives, the relations between social classes, and the interplay of past and present."

Colegate's 1995 novel *Winter Journey* is a loose but engaging collocation on several of her themes: a family in middle-class decline; the self-made man, now a failure; the perils of politics; and the inevitable conflict between those who wish for things to stay as they are, and those who opt for progress, which involves change. The family consists of Alfred and Edith Ashley, brother and sister. Alfred lives in the family home in the West Country; Edith, the eldest, operates a school in London. In the bitter winter of 1992, she comes down to visit Alfred. Her aim is to persuade Alfred to change things. Edith wants to move her language school down to the house and partner with an old friend of hers who has bought a nearby property for the purpose of creating off-road ATV trails all over the countryside, even behind Alfred's house. Alfred, a major photographer in the 1960s, whose brilliant future is behind him, is resistant. He fits in poorly with Edith's notions of improvement and her friends' ideas of development and money making: "Ever since he had been born, Edith had believed that Alfred was a person of exceptional value and originality, and in her scheme of things such a person should first of all do something about it and then either be generally acclaimed or make some money, preferably both. Her irritation arose from her unwillingness to see that such thinking led to the conclusion that Alfred's life was a wasted life."

At a party given by Edith's former husband, Johnny, a collection of caricatured old duffers complain about English decline. Johnny provides a topical illustration of this decline in that his own troubles come from the near collapse of Lloyd's, with its demand that investors put up money to cover underwriting losses. Another character discusses Johnny's plight:

"He used to be rich as Croesus, anyway. As well as mean as Scrooge. Until Lloyd's got him, poor chap. Terrible thing that. Total breakdown of morality. Used to be run by honest fools, then they let the clever people in and the whole thing went to pot. Ruined the English counties, of course. No JPs, no charity workers, no meals on wheels. All the gentry are out trying to make a living selling cosmetics on commission, or handiworks; you know, beaded belts like Red Indians. Pathetic."

In *TLS* Jennifer Potter described two of the main themes central to the novel: "Englishness (a continuing exploration for this author), and the natural compulsion, experienced late in middle age, to revisit the past in search of proof that we have not wasted our lives."

There is something old-fashioned about Colegate, perhaps. She does not write experimental fiction, is comfortable with the use of omniscient narration, and returns to the examination of the relations between the classes in England, somewhat as Anthony Trollope did in the nineteenth century. But Colegate is a clear-sighted realist. About social divisions, Andrew Sinclair has written in a *Times* (London) article that the author has "an understanding of all sorts of people and the social differences necessary to them, so that the war between the classes is replaced by a truce observed without malice, irony, or guilt." In addition, the fertility of Colegate's character creation, her intelligence and wit, and the beauty of her language ensures that one reads her works for far more than a report on class struggle, finding instead interesting people engaged in significant action in the hands of a wise and humane author.

Interviews:

Jean W. Ross, "CA Interview," in *Contemporary Authors New Revision Series,* volume 22, edited by Deborah A. Straub (Detroit: Gale Research, 1988), pp. 84–87;

Angela Lambert, "Serious Writing for Fun," *Independent* (London), 25 September 1991, p. 13.

Reference:

Brett T. Averitt, "The Strange Clarity of Distance; History, Myth, and Imagination in the Novels of Isabel Colegate," in *Contemporary British Women Writers: Narrative Strategies,* edited by Robert E. Hosmer Jr. (New York: St. Martin's Press, 1993), pp. 85–104.

Jim Crace

(1 March 1946 –   )

Merritt Moseley
University of North Carolina at Asheville

BOOKS: *Continent* (London: Heinemann, 1986; New York: Harper & Row, 1987);
The Gift of Stones (London: Secker & Warburg, 1988; New York: Scribners, 1989);
Arcadia (New York: Atheneum, 1991; London: Cape, 1992);
Signals of Distress (London: Viking, 1994; New York: Farrar, Straus & Giroux, 1995);
Quarantine (London & New York: Viking, 1997; New York: Farrar, Straus & Giroux, 1997);
Being Dead (London: Viking, 1999; New York: Farrar, Straus & Giroux, 2000);
The Devil's Larder (London: Viking, forthcoming, 2000).

PRODUCED SCRIPTS: *The Bird Has Flown,* radio, BBC Radio 4, 1976;
Salateen, radio, BBC Radio 4, 1977.

OTHER: "Hearts of Oak," in *21: 21 Picador Authors Celebrate 21 Years of International Writing* (London: Pan, 1993), pp. 71–79.

SELECTED PERIODICAL PUBLICATIONS–
UNCOLLECTED:
FICTION
"Annie, California Plates," *New Review,* 1 (1974): 30–33;
"Helter Skelter, Hang Sorrow, Care'll Kill a Cat," *New Review,* 2 (December 1975): 45–49;
"Cross Country," *New Review,* 3 (April 1976): 47–52;
"Refugees," *Socialist Challenge* (15 December, 1977): 4–5;
"Seven Ages," *Quarto* (June 1980): 3.
NONFICTION
"Chernobyl Comes to Paradise," *Sunday Times Magazine* (London), 15 March 1987, pp. 22–30;
"My Big Break," *Guardian,* Media section, 26 January 1998, p. 8;
"Tide and Prejudice," *Conde Nast Traveller* (October 1999): 91–92.

On the strength of his six published novels, all critically well received and popularly successful, Jim

Jim Crace, circa 1991 (photograph © Jerry Bauer; from the dust jacket for the first American edition of Arcadia)

Crace is one of the most highly esteemed fiction writers in Great Britain. He started late, at least by comparison to some of his contemporaries, having had a career as a journalist for sixteen years before the success of his first novel, *Continent,* in 1986. Crace claims to have read little of the work that has been said to have influenced him, and each of his books is a dramatic departure from the last, helping him to maintain relative freedom from being assigned to a prescribed "place" in the British literary world or its tradition. In a review of Crace's first book for *The New York Times Book Review* (28 June 1987), Robert Olen Butler declared, "One of the basic tasks of fiction is to strip down and rearrange experience in order to distance the reader from habitual reactions to surface reality and thereby, paradoxically, draw him closer to a deeper reality. Mr. Crace . . . does this splendidly." Butler called *Continent* a "brilliant, provocative and delightful" book. Reviewing *Quarantine* (1997) for *The New York Times* (12 April 1998), Frank Kermode wrote, "Each of his disparate worlds is rendered with unshakable confidence and in impressive detail," and went on to suggest a further way of understanding Crace's kind of writing: it is "closer to what Iris Murdoch distinguished as 'crystalline' construction, the end of the fiction spectrum where the novel is most like a poem, most turned in on itself, most closely wrought for the sake of art and internal coherence." Crace's novels are regularly and rightly praised for their solidity of specification, but he has often said he is uninterested in researching facts, claiming that too much knowledge is a hindrance. He prefers inventing plausible details. As he told Robin Pogrebin in 1989, "I'm not interested in truths, like drawing an accurate picture of the real world. I'm interested in exploring the verities of the human condition."

Jim Crace was born on 1 March 1946 in Brocket Hall, Lemsford, Herefordshire, the son of Charles Sydney Crace, an insurance agent, and Edith Grace Holland Crace. He grew up in north London. His rearing was socialist, rather puritanical, and atheist. He is strongly political, committed to nuclear disarmament, disappointed by the moderate Blairite version of the Labour Party, and opposed to grammar schools as inegalitarian. Crace went to Enfield Grammar School and then attended the Birmingham College of Commerce, (now the University of Central England), which then offered external University of London degrees. He earned a bachelor's degree with honors from the University of London in 1968.

Immediately after graduation, Crace went overseas under the auspices of Voluntary Service Overseas, working first as a producer and writer for Sudanese Educational Television in Khartoum and then teaching English at Kgosi Kgari Sechele Secondary School in Molepolole, Botswana (1969–1970). On his return to England Crace began working as a radio and print journalist. He married Pamela Ann Turton, a teacher, on 3 January 1975. They and their two children, Thomas Charles and Lauren Rose, live in Moseley, a section of Birmingham.

Beginning with home-based features, Crace soon persuaded the editors of the *Sunday Telegraph Magazine* to send him on foreign assignments. He recalled 1979 in "Hearts of Oak" (1993) saying, "I seemed to spend the whole year in the air." Crace began writing fiction in the 1970s, publishing three stories in *The New Review*. The third of these stories, "Cross-Country" (April

1976) was the beginning of his first novel, *Continent* (1986). Since its publication, Crace has devoted most of his time to novel writing, but he is still active in journalism and contributes to various publications.

Crace has been honored repeatedly for his writing. For *Continent* he won bursaries and awards from the Arts Council of Great Britain, the Whitbread First Novel Award, the Guardian Fiction Prize, and the David Higham Prize for fiction. *Quarantine* (1997) made the shortlist for the Booker Prize and was named Whitbread Novel of the Year, a prize for which *Being Dead* (1999) was shortlisted.

In a 1989 interview with Jean W. Ross, published in 1992, Crace described the five impulses that drive his fiction:

> One, the simple pleasures of invention, of convincingly merging the real and the concocted, the mundane and the bizarre; two, an admiration for the disciplines of good journalism—clarity and depth of expression, orderliness of structure and design; three, a preoccupation with international issues and politics, and a disdain for the domestic; four, an instinctive preference for restrained and dispassionate prose which avoids sentiment and declamation but which takes its power from the narrative itself and not from authorial intervention; and five, a "fear-of-self" hostility towards political repression, conservatism, racism, sexism, puritanism, officialdom, and rules.

Having written a few short stories, Crace was given a small advance from Heinemann and set out to write a conventional novel about Moseley, the area of Birmingham in which he lives. As he explained to Ross,

> I hadn't considered the alternatives. In Britain at the time, the convention was to write realistic, ironic social-commentary novels—novels in which the real world was presented as the real world but interpreted by an ironic narrator. That style of narrative didn't suit me. I'm much more interested in invention, in creating abstractions of the real world, than trying to mirror the real world or, indeed, the real Moseley. So I was not making progress at all with that novel. . . . It was only when I started reading some of the magic realists that I recognized there was an alternative possibility, something which wasn't conventional but was very traditional: the story which was there not to mirror the real world but to create its own inwardly reflecting world. Story for story's sake.

There is a small critical controversy about whether Crace's first novel is a novel or a collection of short stories. In his 1998 review of *Quarantine*, Kermode, an admirer, called *Continent* "really less a novel than a collection of seven stories, all set in an imagined world of which the author has mastered the geography,

Dust jacket or Crace's first novel (1986), about life on an imaginary land mass in an underdeveloped part of the world

the botany and the anthropology." Complaining that "English literature is too constrained," Crace told Ross that in *Continent* he had wanted "to have several narratives and ask for those narratives to mix in the imagination of the reader, very much in the way that some of the artists in nineteenth-century France, the pointillists or other impressionists, would put separate colors on the canvas and invite viewers to mix the colors in their minds' eye." This technique, Crace believes, prevents reader laziness. He refuses to tell his readers "what to feel or what to think," expecting instead "some participation and some response" because "that's what fiction ought to be doing."

Continent is a spare but elegantly written book. Its intentions are announced in an epigraph attributed to "Pycletius," a presumably fictional Roman philosopher: "There and beyond is a seventh continent—seven peoples, seven masters, seven seas. And its business is trade and superstition." The seven chapters of Crace's novel are seven stories about the history and

natural history of the imagined seventh continent. The novel is oddly vague and strongly circumstantial. Crace has made clear that the book is not about Africa, but his imaginary continent is located in an underdeveloped part of the world. It receives aid workers from the northern hemisphere; it has a repressive military government that imprisons men for careless talk; and trading occurs in an outdoor market, where there is a calligrapher whose function is "sin lister." Electricity is a new development in some areas. Each of the chapters includes a small vignette of life on the continent, often on the theme of how new ways are replacing traditional culture.

The sin lister lives to discover that his carefully written documents, which he created for a religious purpose, are being bought as art objects by European and North American collectors. Encouraged by the government to produce more documents because they bring in foreign exchange, the sin lister refuses with dignity. But he eventually colludes in the display of forgeries that fall far short of his standards but are good enough to deceive foreigners. The turning point for him comes as he dreams

of a large gallery full of smart Europeans in their best clothes, walking slowly around the exhibits with expensive catalogues. I stood in a European suit, a young man once again, pointing out some fine detail to a beautiful woman. "Here," I was saying, "I have misplaced the vowel sound so that this word reads 'Moon' instead of 'Man.' And here are letters which do not exist in Siddilic and which no one can decipher. And there I have pressed so hard on my pen that the nib snapped. So that sign there is not an accent but a blot." The woman smiled appreciatively. The gallery applauded. Rich men shook my hand. The Minister shook my hand.

Continent is an important and original novel with a subtle but penetrating vision of "development" and the relationship between modernity and tradition.

The Gift of Stones (1988) deals with the Stone Age, an even more traditional culture than the one that is passing in *Continent*. Ross commented in their 1989 interview that Crace moved "from an imaginary present-day setting to an actual historical one." When Ross asked him if he had been concerned about authenticity in his depiction of everyday life in the Stone Age, Crace expressed an interest in the prehistoric period and admitted to having some knowledge about it, but he disavowed any attempt to create historical truth, calling the "history" in his novel "totally bogus." Instead, he said, "The point of my fiction is to adopt a tone of voice and use language and make things up which sound authentic, that are more real than real. . . . If I needed a detail—about a meal or cooking or something else—I would make it up as I went along and have fun doing so." Crace uses fiction to create real-seeming worlds parallel to, rather than dependent on, the real world. *The Gift of Stones* has a feeling of reality.

The novel concerns the "stoneys," a community of stone-implement makers. Because they have better artisans than any other tribe, manufacturing and trading stone tools and weapons has become their means of earning a livelihood. Their lives are threatened, however, by the coming Bronze Age. As Stone Age tools are replaced by better, metal implements, the community becomes obsolete.

The village scripture is "that we could not be touched because we possessed the gift of stones. If all that the outside world needed was to pound and crush and hammer like savages then any rock would do. But once they wanted more, to pierce and slice, to cut and scrape, to remove the flesh from the inner side of pelts for making clothes, to have harpoons and arrows light

and sharp enough to fly and kill, to cut back wheat with just one sickle-stroke, then they, those farmers, horsemen, fishers, wrights, could not be free of us and we were safe." By the end of the novel, the "gift of bronze" has arrived on ships that have brought merchants and smiths: "They'd found where metals could be mined. They settled there." The inexorability and cruelty of this change resonates with implications for later shifts. The stoneys are arrogant at first and later bewildered—reacting in the same manner as handloom weavers at the onset of mechanization or buggy-whip manufacturers at the invention of the automobile. The contemporary relevance of the story is sharpened by the existence of two classes in the stone village: stoneys and "mongers" or traders, early capitalists who create nothing but keep most of the money earned from the sale of the tools the stoneys make.

The narrator is the daughter of a man who is something of an outsider among the stoneys. Having lost one arm below the elbow, he is unfit for stone work and has become a storyteller, or liar, who entertains his fellow villagers. He also has leisure to travel, and in the end, as the only man among the stoneys with any knowledge of the outside world, he is able to lead them to a new life.

The novel is much concerned with craftsmanship. There are loving descriptions of how flints are knapped, and the father's artful storytelling is celebrated: "there were hardly any feasts or meetings of the village which did not feature father fantasizing at the higher table in the hall. . . . The paradox is this—we do love lies. The truth is dull and half-asleep. But lies are nimble, spirited, alive. And lying is a craft." Father is quite aware of his craft, though the reader is to understand that he is not really lying: "You see? I've pulled a screen of grass across the story, too. I'll not creep up and tell you what I saw. I'll spare myself—and her. Now you know, you can be sure, that this is truth—no chronicler with any sense would disappoint his listeners so."

The Gift of Stones has a strongly elegiac tone. Writing for *The New York Times Book Review* (16 July 1989), novelist Jane Smiley called it a "prose poem where the natural world is new and powerfully evoked," and she described the setting as "a conceit that provides the author scope for his meditation." In *Chicago Tribune Books* (16 April 1989), Percy Glasser called the novel an "allegory" and added that "*The Gift of Stones* is not about people, but about imaginative art, storytelling in particular, and the complicated relationship between art and the realms of commerce that at once supports and despises its artists."

In *Arcadia* (1991) Crace returned to something closer to the life he knew firsthand. The novel is set in a large European city during modern times. In 1989,

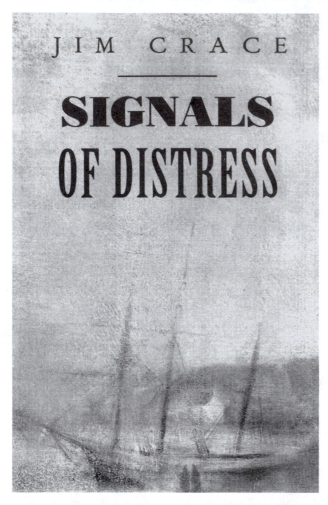

Dust jacket for Crace's 1994 novel, about an absurd, but well-intentioned nineteenth-century liberal

which he has sprung, and to replace it with a modern enclosed mall that he will call Arcadia, from sentimentality about his unremembered rural heritage. The old market is seductive and disorderly, possessed of an exotic splendor: "the plump, suggestive irony of roots, the painted, powdered vanity of peaches, the waxen probity of lettuce leaves, the faith implicit in the youth and readiness of onion sets, the senility of medlars (eaten only when decayed), the seductive, bitter alchemy of quinces which young men bought to soften women's hearts." The new mall replicates the old Soap Market after a fashion, but inside the chrome-and-glass replacement everything is sterile and artificial:

> Though the noises of Arcadia are flat, the fruit and vegetables have never seemed so polished and so uniform. The traders, beneath their matching awnings, seduce the passersby with produce of the gene bank and the science farm, enhanced by Spray-Dew, Frost-Ban and by packaging. Recessed orange lights warm and flatter every radish, every grape, every hybrid superfruit. Together with the onions and the swedes, are Kingquats, a kumquat bigger than a plum and every part of it—the peel, the pith—is edible. And there are orange grapes, and bananas from Barbados shaped like avocado pears. And avocado pears without a stone. And lab-grown lettuces (red or green or white). And greenhouse broccoli with flowerheads as big and tight as cobblestones, achromatic rhubarb force-grown under fluorescent lights, and biotechnic aubergines which some chemist-gardener has artificially bloated in dioxide pods. Young men in search of romance can still buy their loves a Courting Quince, just as before, but more romantically presented in a silver nest with a heart-shaped, perfumed top.

Arcadia is a great commercial success, but a new market with the grubby demotic quality of the old one is arising nearby. Not only is the Arcadia mall too clinical and too repressive—no drinking, no beggars, no dirtiness are allowed—but the old stallholders cannot afford the rents. The power of money and progress cannot stifle real urban life.

Though *Arcadia* celebrates a lost country life, its primary oppositions are between real and ersatz urban life, between small and big businesses, and between messy reality and clean, efficient artificiality. Crace is a city man.

Though *Arcadia* received many positive reviews, the opposition between big-time thieves like Victor, who are bad, and small-time thieves, who are colorful, struck some reviewers as sentimental. Critics registered other objections to the book, as well. In a 31 March 1992 review for *The Independent* (London), Tom Sutcliffe judged that Crace's "novel, which celebrates the untidy, immoral accommodations of a city's inhabitants, itself

while it was still a work in progress, he described the book to Ross as "a novel about cities versus the countryside, about the natural state of human settlement, the conflict between public space and private terrain, how cities work, why all the deprivations of life such as poverty, overcrowding, and disease seem to be city phenomena rather than country phenomena." The theme of city replacing country suggests a common theme connecting *Arcadia* with the first two books, one in which modernity challenges tradition. In *Arcadia,* however, Crace seems to have lost his gift for delicately balancing the general and the particular. Most reviewers were less impressed with this novel than with his first two books, calling *Arcadia* a parable or a fable and criticizing its overobvious schematic presentation of the oppositions between the natural and the mercantile and the ecological and the economic.

At the center of Arcadia is Victor, an obviously named millionaire who decides to destroy the old Soap Market, the ancient heart of his city and the place from feels purged and inauthentic, a Disneyland version of a society, complete with meticulously detailed rubbish." Terry Bisson wrote in *The Washington Post* (1 December 1992) that *Arcadia* "remains ordinary in spite of all this machinery; ordinary and, ultimately, tiresome. The conventions of magic realism (for they are by now conventions), which can lend flash to the words of a Salmon Rushdie, a John Crowley or a Gabriel García Márquez, seem in *Arcadia* mere contrivances. . . . The unnamed city that is the true protagonist of the book is as clichéd as the Gotham of the recent Batman movies." Bisson's identification of the city as the protagonist is astute; Richard Eder began his review in *The Los Angeles Times* (4 October 1992) by noting, "The true characters in the fiction of the British writer Jim Crace are not individuals but communities."

For some readers Crace is a chilly technician, and this aspect of his writing seems especially apparent in *Arcadia*. In *Signals of Distress* (1994) the human and the humorous are more fully developed. *Signals of Distress* is set in 1836, in a port called Wherrytown, in the west of England. As the novel opens, a storm forces into the port the *Belle of Wilmington,* an American craft carrying emigrants headed for Canada, a single African slave, American crewmen, and three hundred cattle. Arriving at the same time is the *Hap'orth of Tar,* carrying Aymer Smith, a Londoner who has come to Wherrytown on what he conceives as a humanitarian mission. The conjunction of Smith, the Americans, and the inhabitants of Wherrytown make for the interesting and sometimes moving plot.

Smith is an unlikely, and indeed unlikable, protagonist. A prig and a self-conceived radical, he is humorless, excessively talkative, and self-deluded. He refuses to eat sugar, because the sugarcane has been harvested by slaves, but his endless explanations ruin any possible example he might succeed in setting. He pities the Americans' slave, Otto, who has been locked up in a shed to keep him from scaring the Wherrytown population, who consider him hardly human. His remedy—to open the door stealthily and, in effect, drive the helpless Otto out into an English winter without food, proper clothing, or any other aid to survival—is well-intentioned but absurd. Smith may be viewed as Crace's burlesque of the liberal. He is well-meaning but ineffectual. One of the many impressive passages in *Signals of Distress* is Smith's final dream, which features the Cradle Rock, an ancient formation on the coast that has been pushed from its perch by drunken American sailors:

Aymer Smith was at the end of tired. He was sleeping now, and truly dreaming: his landscape was a childish one. A beach, some dunes, some kelp, a granite headland, gulls, the numbing blanket of a sea-stunned sky, a dog. He put his shoulder up against the Cradle Rock. He had the strength. He rolled it back on to its pivot stone. He set the Rock in motion. He made amends. He put the world to rights again. Helped only by the muscle of the wind, and by the charity of dreams, the Cradle Rock ascended and declined.

Smith has come to Wherrytown because his family's soap business has always bought kelp for soap making from the poor people who collect on the shore near Wherrytown. Now the company can make soap from synthetic ingredients, and Smith has thought it kind to come to town and tell the kelpers firsthand that the company will no longer buy kelp from them. The kelpers, then, are in the same position as the stoneys in *The Gift of Stones*. Their livelihood has been displaced by a technological advancement. A repressed virgin, Smith also fails to find himself a country girl as a wife. By the end of the novel Miggy Bowe, the teenage kelper on whom he set his sights, has left for the new world on the *Belle of Wilmington* with an American seaman. Smith embarks for London with no wife, no appreciation from the jobless kelpers, and a troubled conscience over the liberated slave.

This novel includes many small links to Crace's previous work as well as thematic connections with previous communities. The soap business recalls the Soap Market in Arcadia. When Smith returns to London, the chapter begins, "City air makes free? Well, yes"—echoing the appreciation of urban life expressed in Crace's earlier novels. Smith is reading the *Truismes* of Emile dell'Ova, an apocryphal book from which Crace drew the epigraph of *Arcadia*. The interest in the seashore, in bladder wrack, and kelp appeared in *The Gift of Stones* and one of the chapters in *Continent* and is featured in *Being Dead*. In *Signals of Distress* the character Walter Howells, a businessman and sharp operator, is the middleman in the trade between the kelpers and the Smiths' soap company—the "monger," that is—who keeps most of the money and engages in dishonest dealings that create disastrous results for others. He is the bad capitalist familiar to Crace readers though he never approaches stereotype.

Critical reaction to *Signals of Distress* was favorable. In a review for *The Irish Times* (3 September 1994) Eileen Battersby called the novel "a lively, deceptively well-crafted tale." She praised the dialogue and the narrative as "witty, descriptive, sharply observed, economic and, above all, authentic," adding that "Crace's language has always been elegantly efficient." Charles Johnson summed up the novel in *The New York Times Book Review* (24 September 1995): "With beguiling narrative ease and prose lyric enough to invest the most ordinary events with mystery, Mr. Crace tells a

Crace at the time of Signals of Distress *(photograph by Tim Wainwright)*

quiet tale of strangers thrown together by caprice: emigrants, business scions, paupers, street toughs and former slaves who, before their paths diverge, find their lives are unintentionally and irreversibly linked." Reviewing the novel for *The Independent* (1 October 1994), Jonathan Keates wrote that something in the book, "an implicit bid for epic status perhaps, together with the style's resolutely unadverbial, syntactically stripped-down quality, challenges us to accept the universality of this very English novel." In one of the most insightful appreciations, Nick Hornby, writing for *The Sunday Times* (11 September 1994), called Aymer Smith "a superb creation, a revolting mixture of Malvolio, 19th century social worker and interesting-fact-man Cliff Claven from Cheers." "Smith is so hopeless," Hornby commented, "that he sucks you in, like a black hole. . . . his ludicrous impulses are the most sympathetic on view. . . ." Hornby also praised the novel for being less abstract than Crace's earlier work, a view that runs counter to the usual critical commentary on Crace. There is no doubt, however, that this novel is an advance over *Arcadia,* at least in terms of ordinary human interest, apparent solidity of specification, and beautiful but less-showy prose.

In *Quarantine* Crace returned to a more distant past: the setting is Palestine during the time of Christ. Since Jesus is a character in the novel, Crace's treatment of him and of Christianity by the defiantly atheistic became the subject of considerable commentary. Crace told Harry Doherty during an interview for the on-line magazine *BookEnds,* "I'm surprised that I haven't been on the receiving end of a Christian fatwa, but I guess that my expectation of a Christian fatwa wasn't very cleverly thought out in the first instance. I guess I was just very nervous writing about religion, and as an atheist writing about religion. . . . Christian religion is actually about doubt."

Crace also told Doherty that he had started to write a book about people "on the edge"—like the schizophrenics, sex offenders, battered wives, and other needy people living in hostels set up to house them in his neighborhood. Then a postcard from friends on holiday in Jericho provided him with the setting: the Hill of Temptation, where Jesus supposedly spent his forty days in the wilderness facing temptation from the Devil. Crace researched the Bible and visited Israel but typically ended by making up most of his setting, with cheerful indifference to what animals would have lived in the wilderness where the story is set. As Crace told David Streitfeld in May 1998, "telling lies effectively is not about knowledge, it's about vocabulary."

In the novel Jesus is one of the characters on the edge, all of whom have come to the desert for relief or escape from problems such as madness or barrenness and are living in the caves with which the Hill of Temptation is honeycombed. As Crace told Streitfeld, "I bet Jesus had some company while He was there. There was the 2,000 year old counterpart of the hostel at the end of my street."

Quarantine is not really a book about Jesus, who is a secondary character and dies before the end of the book. Crace believes that Jesus could not have survived without food and water for forty days and must have died in the wilderness. The strongest character is Musa, a rapacious trader somewhat in the vein of the capitalist Walter Howells in *Signals of Distress.* Musa and his cowed wife, Miri, take refuge in a cave after having been abandoned by a caravan because Musa appeared to be dying. He recovers, perhaps healed by Jesus.

The nature of Jesus' message and acts is always ambiguous in the novel. Without repeating the stories of gospels or refuting them, Crace touches on them from time to time. At one point Jesus, whose family considers him too fanatical, thinks about his future:

Jesus had always been ashamed of his ambition, but this is what he'd dreamed since he was young. There was a congregation on a hill slope in the Galilee. He

Dust jacket for Crace's 1999 novel, which one reviewer called a "rhapsody of rot"

was the tallest, and he looked down on their heads. He recognized his brothers' hair, his neighbors' hair, the baker's and the priest's, the leper's, and the prostitute's uncovered hair. But they were tired of listening to sermons. "Come up to me, the sick, the troubled and the blind," he'd say. He'd put his hands on eyes and foreheads, rub out pains, press his fingers into hardened flesh, remove their swellings with a touch, kiss sores. Erase their sins. He'd cure them. They'd be restored, through him, by god. And, yes, he'd find a boat for fishermen, and horses for the men too weak to walk. They'd say—a phrase he loved—"We never knew our Gally after all. He is the bread of our short lives. He is the good shepherd who will lead us out of suffering."

The similarity of this vision of the future to what the gospels tell of Jesus life and teachings raises ontological questions. Jesus never shares this vision with Musa, who, the plot suggests, is the one who will transmit the message of salvation to a waiting world. What Musa knows is a miraculous healing. He cares little about erasing sins.

As *Quarantine* ends, Musa reflects on the possibility of using Jesus' magical skills to make money and waits for Jesus to rise from the dead. If Jesus does not return, Musa has an alternative plan:

In the meantime, this would be his merchandise, something finer and less burdensome than even color, sound or smell. No need for camel panniers or porters or cousins. He'd trade the word. There was a man who'd defeated death with just his fingertips. "I am the living proof." He'd travel to the markets of the world. He'd preach the good news. That would be easy. Musa had the skills. He had been blessed with this one gift. He could tell tales.

Reviewers agreed with Kermode, who wrote in his *New York Times* review (12 April 1998) that "the wilderness setting of this story is rendered in obsessive detail: the geography and geology of the area, its birds and animals, insects and plants, its folk beliefs and superstitions." In an 18 September 1999 review for *The Times* (London), Jason Cowley wrote, "It is hard to think of a recent novel more hysterically imagined than *Quarantine*," adding that "Crace takes the fragments of a too familiar Biblical story and scatters them to create something strange, forbidding and hallucinatory." Writing for *The Tampa Tribune* (1 August 1998), Amy Welborn commented that Crace's "theological motivations in not only retelling but re-envisioning the story of Jesus' temptation in the desert are ambiguous. But in *Quarantine* . . . Crace has penned a beautifully written, forceful and evocative work."

Crace foresaw more trouble from Americans than his fellow countrymen over his liberties with Christianity. Yet, *Quarantine* was well received in both Britain and the United States. Streitfeld remarked that the novel ended by getting "qualified endorsements from such unlikely spots as the Tablet, the Catholic weekly," and quoted Crace on the way writing the novel had changed him:

"Before, my atheism was quite bleak—an absence of belief, a hollow," he says. "There was nothing there. There's a Christian hymn that criticizes non-belief. I can't quite quote it, but it goes something like, 'The heathen in his ignorance bows down to wood and stone.' But as someone obsessed with landscape and the natural world, I've come around strongly to the view that wood and stone are very proper recipients of our godless worship. They're at the center of the wonder of the universe, which is the unfolding narrative of natural processes."

The last phrase offers an overview of the subject of Crace's 1999 novel, *Being Dead,* in which he traces a few days in the lives and deaths of a married couple, marine biologists, who are murdered on a beach and left for several days before their bodies are found. Crace's clinical prose serves him well as he describes the physical scene after the murders:

The light of day had thinned the rain, though there was almost uninterrupted drizzle until the afternoon. The storm had shifted sand during the night and banked it up against the bodies on one side. Already they were sinking in. Celice's discarded shoes and Joseph's remaining clothes were soaked and almost buried. The wind had lifted his shirt and carried it along the dune gully and into the stretched branches of a sea thorn. It was their flag.

By four the rain had stopped, although the sky stayed overcast and dull. Again the crabs and rodents went to work, while there was light, flippantly browsing Joseph and Celice, frisking them for moisture and for food, delving in their pits and caverns for their treats, and paying them as scant regard as cows might pay a turnip head.

There is something apparently unfeeling about the naturalist's approach to human death represented in the novel. Crace, who told Dickson in 1999 that "In the end . . . we are manure," expresses a belief that resembles Walt Whitman's identification of grass as the "uncut hair of graves" in "Song of Myself" (1855):

Here among the dunes—with Celice's spread body, her rustling hair, her husband's hand on her leg—was a fine display to illustrate the annual fieldwork lecture she gave, normally with slides of putrefying seals or tide-abandoned fish, to the faculty's new and squeamish students. Celice would always say, "Anyone who studies nature must get used to violence. You'll have to make yourselves companionable with death if any of you want to flourish as zoologists." She meant that fear of death is fear of life, a cliché amongst scientists, and ministers. Both professions know that life and death are inextricably entwined, the helix of existence, and both want to give life meaning only because it clearly has none, other than to replicate and decompose.

Being Dead begins with the last moments in the lives of Joseph and Celice, their deaths, and the natural aftereffects. A second strand of the narrative takes the reader back thirty years and retells the story of their first time on this beach, when they first became lovers; a third tells of the aftereffects of their death among the living, including their colleagues and their daughter. During their first visit Joseph and Celice were making love on the beach when the house where they were staying burned, killing the other young woman scientist who was living there. This connection of sex and death is revived when Joseph and Celice are killed while making love on the same beach.

Despite the grisly subject matter and the detachment with which it is narrated, *Being Dead* is a novel of considerable tenderness. The reader feels sympathy for Joseph and Celice, awkward and unromantic hero and heroine though they are. From an Olympian perspective in which human lives are a part of nature, order is restored. The novel ends with a beautiful passage. The bodies have been discovered and removed. The ecology starts to resume its natural state—"the wounded lissom grass perked up. Hope springs eternal in the natural world. Its leaves and blades sprang straight again." All signs of Joseph and Celice disappear:

By final light on the ninth day since the murder, all traces of any life and love that had been spilt had disappeared. The natural world had flooded back. The brightness of the universe returned. If there was any blood left in the soil from the couple's short stay in the dunes, then it could only help to fortify the living murmur of the grass.

And still, today and every day, the dunes are lifted, stacked and undermined. Their crests migrate and reassemble with the wind. They do their best to raise their backs against the weather and the sea and block the wind-borne sorrows of the world. All along the shores of Baritone Bay and all the coast beyond, tide after tide, time after time, the corpses and the broken, thinned remains of fish and birds, of barnacles and rats, of molluscs, mammals, mussels, crabs are lifted, washed and sorted by the waves. And Joseph and Celice enjoy a loving and unconscious end, beyond experience.

These are the everending days of being dead.

According to Crace, the last line is the germ from which the novel grew. Reviewing the novel for *The Independent* (25 September 1999), Michael Adetti offered a mixed response to what he called a "rhapsody of rot." He praised the "exquisitely precise imagery" with which Crace "proves himself a poet of putrefaction" but faulted his "lesser expertise at portraying human emotions," observing that "Joseph and Celice remain flat characters, with no inner life." Other reviewers were more laudatory. Ian Thomson, critic for *The Financial Times* (25 September 1999), called *Being Dead* "a powerful drama of extremity and isolation," and Blake Morrison in *The Independent* (17 October 1999) declared that the novel was "full of strange transitions and unexpected beauty." Eric Hanson wrote in the *Minneapolis Star Tribune* (7 May 2000) that Crace's "strange attention to the ugly only underscores the beautiful." Reviewing the novel for *The New York Times Book Review* (23 April 2000), Jim Shepard said that Crace ought to be "world famous," for "Few novels are as unsparing as this one in presenting the ephemerality of love given the implacability of death, and few are as moving in depicting the undiminished achievement love nevertheless represents."

True to his practice of making each novel different from the one before, Crace has said his next book, *The Devil's Larder,* will comprise sixty short pieces about food. As Kermode wrote in his review of *Quarantine,* "it would take more nerve than I have to say what sort of thing he will do next, beyond the feebly secure guess that it will be strange and original."

Interviews:

Robin Pogrebin, "Unplanned Obsolescence," *New York Times Book Review,* 16 July 1989, p. 12;

Jean W. Ross, "*CA* Interview," in *Contemporary Authors,* volume 135, edited by Susan M. Trosky (Detroit: Gale Research, 1992), pp. 99–103;

Frances Welch, "The Bible Is Fiction and I Believe in Me and My God," *Sunday Telegraph* (London), Features section, 8 June 1997, p. 4;

David Streitfeld, "An Author's New Testament: Atheist Jim Crace Finds the Good Book in Him After All," *Washington Post,* 7 May 1998, p. B01;

Harry Doherty, "The BookEnds Interview: Jim Crace," *BookEnds* (1998) on-line magazine <www.book-place.co.uk/bookends/chat/crace>;

E. Jane Dickson, "Features: Picking Apart Questions of Faith," *Daily Telegraph* (London), 4 September 1999, p. 5.

Margaret Drabble

(5 June 1939 –   )

Henry L. Carrigan Jr.
Otterbein College

See also the Drabble entries in *DLB 14: British Novelists Since 1960* and *DLB 155: Twentieth-Century British Literary Biographers.*

BOOKS: *A Summer Bird-Cage* (London: Weidenfeld & Nicolson, 1963; New York: Morrow, 1964);

The Garrick Year (London: Weidenfeld & Nicolson, 1964; New York: Morrow, 1965);

The Millstone (London: Weidenfeld & Nicolson, 1965; New York: Morrow, 1966); republished as *Thank You All Very Much* (New York: New American Library, 1969);

Wordsworth (London: Evans Bros., 1966; New York: Arco, 1969);

Jerusalem the Golden (London: Weidenfeld & Nicolson, 1967; New York: Morrow, 1967);

The Waterfall (London: Weidenfeld & Nicolson, 1969; New York: Knopf, 1969);

The Needle's Eye (London: Weidenfeld & Nicolson, 1972; New York: Knopf, 1972);

Virginia Woolf: A Personal Debt (London: Aloe Editions, 1973);

Arnold Bennett: A Biography (London: Weidenfeld & Nicolson, 1974; New York: Knopf, 1974);

The Realms of Gold (London: Weidenfeld & Nicolson, 1975; New York: Knopf, 1975);

The Ice Age (London: Weidenfeld & Nicolson, 1977; New York: Knopf, 1977);

For Queen and Country: Britain in the Victorian Age (London: Deutsch, 1978; New York: Seabury Press, 1979);

A Writer's Britain: Landscape in Literature, text by Drabble and photographs by Jorge Lewinsky (London: Thames & Hudson, 1979; New York: Knopf, 1979);

The Middle Ground (London: Weidenfeld & Nicolson, 1980; New York: Knopf, 1980);

The Tradition of Women's Fiction: Lectures in Japan, edited by Yukako Suga (Tokyo: Oxford University Press, 1985);

The Radiant Way (London: Weidenfeld & Nicolson, 1987; New York: Knopf, 1987);

Margaret Drabble (photograph © Caroline Forbes; courtesy of the author)

A Natural Curiosity (London: Viking, 1989; New York: Viking, 1989);

Stratford Revisited: A Legacy of the Sixties (Shipston-on-Stour, U.K.: Celandine Press, 1989);

Safe as Houses: An Examination of Home Ownership and Mortgage Relief (London: Chatto & Windus, 1990);

Margaret Drabble in Tokyo, edited by Fumi Takano (Tokyo: Kenkysha, 1991);

The Gates of Ivory (London: Viking, 1991; New York: Viking, 1992);

Angus Wilson: A Biography (London: Secker & Warburg, 1995; New York: St. Martin's Press, 1996);

The Witch of Exmoor (London & New York: Viking, 1996; New York: Harcourt Brace, 1996).

PLAY PRODUCTION: *Bird of Paradise,* London, 1969.

PRODUCED SCRIPTS: *Laura,* television, Granada, 1964;

Isadora, motion picture, additional dialogue by Drabble, Universal, 1968;

Thank You All Very Much, motion picture, Columbia, 1969; released in Great Britain as *A Touch of Love,* Palomar, 1969.

OTHER: Jane Austen, *Lady Susan / The Watsons / Sanditon,* edited, with an introduction, by Drabble (Harmondsworth, U.K.: Penguin, 1974);

The Genius of Thomas Hardy, edited by Drabble (London: Weidenfeld & Nicolson, 1976; New York: Knopf, 1976);

Emily Brontë, *Wuthering Heights,* introduction by Drabble (London: Dent, 1978; New York: Dutton, 1979);

The Oxford Companion to English Literature, fifth edition, edited by Drabble (Oxford, New York, Tokyo & Melbourne: Oxford University Press, 1985);

The Concise Oxford Companion to English Literature, edited by Drabble and Jenny Stringer (Oxford & New York: Oxford University Press, 1987).

Since the 1970s Margaret Drabble has been the preeminent British woman of letters. Critics and admirers have compared her work to that of George Eliot and Jane Austen, and, indeed, Drabble's writings, like Eliot's, include fiction, literary criticism, biography, and social commentary. Drabble has also written introductions for a paperback collection of a novella and two unfinished novels by Austen and an edition of Emily Brontë's *Wuthering Heights* (1847). Most of Drabble's novels deal with family life, and much of her later fiction has also been preoccupied with social issues. She often depicts women's struggles for identity in a society where the roles of women are changing, seeking to achieve emotional, economic, and moral freedom while fulfilling their roles as wives and mothers.

Margaret Drabble was born on 5 June 1939 in Sheffield, Yorkshire, the second of the four children of John Frederick and Kathleen Marie Bloor Drabble. Drabble has maintained strong ties to Yorkshire in her fiction, and her family claims kinship with another novelist of the region, Arnold Bennett, a connection she mentioned but did not investigate fully in her biography of Bennett. Drabble's parents were both graduates of Cambridge, the first university-educated members of their families, and Drabble grew up in an intellectual, liberal household. Her entire family were voracious readers and writers occupied in pursuing intellectual endeavors. Her father was a barrister and a circuit judge before his retirement in 1973, and her brother, Richard, is also a barrister. Drabble's mother taught English. Drabble's older sister, Antonia Susan is A. S. Byatt, the author of best-selling and highly admired fiction, and her younger sister, Dr. Helen Langdon, is an art historian.

Drabble has said that her childhood was lonely. She loved books and read John Bunyan's *Pilgrim's Progress* (1678) at an early age. The children of the Drabble family also wrote magazines, stories, and plays together.

After attending the Mount School, a Quaker boarding school, Drabble was admitted to Cambridge on a full scholarship, and like her mother and her sisters she enrolled at Newnham College. While at Cambridge she read English literature and started acting. In several places she has noted that, while she wrote at Cambridge, she was afraid to show her stories to anyone because of the high critical standards of Cambridge scholars such as F. R. Leavis.

Drabble took her B.A. with first-class honors in 1960 and could have remained at Cambridge as a lecturer, but she wanted to become an actress. She married actor Clive Swift, whom she had met at the university, in June 1960. They had three children—Adam Richard George, Rebecca Margaret, and Joseph Samuel—before their divorce in 1975. On 15 September 1982 she married British biographer and novelist Michael Holroyd.

Soon after their marriage Drabble and Swift went to work with the Royal Shakespeare Company in Stratford-upon-Avon, where she was an understudy for Vanessa Redgrave and performed occasional walk-on roles. Drabble became bored with playing small parts, and while she was pregnant with her eldest child, she began work on *A Summer Bird-Cage* (1963). As Barbara C. Millard points out in *DLB 14,* Drabble started out to write her first novel as a way of proving to herself that she could be successful in a creative realm other than acting. She also had the examples of earlier successful English woman novelists to reassure her that she had chosen the right literary form in which to express herself. In addition, she had read Simone de Beauvoir's *The Second Sex* (1949). As she told Peter E. Firchow in a 1972 interview, the book offered her "material that nobody had used and I could use, and nobody had ever used as far as I could see. I would use it."

Dust jacket for Drabble's 1965 novel, about an unmarried, pregnant graduate student who decides to raise her child by herself (courtesy of The Lilly Library, Indiana University, Bloomington, Indiana)

The title of Drabble's first novel comes from a comment about love in John Webster's play *The White Devil* (1612): "'Tis just like a summer bird-cage in a garden: the birds that are without, despair to get in, and the birds that are within despair and are in consumption for fear they shall never get out." The bird outside the cage in Drabble's novel is Sarah Bennett, an Oxford graduate who has given up the notion of going on to get an advanced degree and has been working as a tutor in Paris. She returns home to be a bridesmaid in the wedding of her sister, Louise, and wealthy, arrogant Stephen Halifax. Taking a filing job at the BBC, Sarah ponders the options for her life that are represented by her friend Simone, who lives a rather directionless life, and by Louise, a beautiful woman who has married Stephen for his money while carrying on an affair with another man. Sarah's great fear of falling into self-abnegation increases as she observes the lives of her friends, most of whom have not achieved their ambitions. Lou-

ise eventually reveals her affair to Sarah, creating a new intimacy between the sisters and helping Sarah to realize something about her own character, as well as her sister's:

> I saw for her what I could never see for myself—that this impulse to seize on one moment as the whole, one aspect as the total view, one attitude as a revelation, is the impulse that confounds both her and me, that confounds and impels us. To force a unity from a quarrel, a high continuum from a sequence of defeats and petty disasters, to live on the level of the heart rather than the level of the slipping petticoat, this is what we spend our life on, and this is what wears us out. My attitude to the petticoat is firmer than hers, but I am exhausted nevertheless.

Sarah decides to marry her longtime Oxford boyfriend. She will "marry a don" but not be a "don's wife."

Drabble's first novel includes many of the themes that she developed in her later writing: the failure of love, the conflict of class ideologies, the fear of self-abnegation, and the conflict between an educated life and a directionless life. As Valerie Grosvenor Myer remarked in 1974, "The woman undergraduate's interest is divided between her academic work and her feminine destiny, which at the university stage appears as though it will take the conventional social forms. The conflict is between the duty of the self-imposed task and instinct." Drabble's humor and her witty style won over many reviewers, even though the book was not a commercial success.

Drabble was pregnant with her second child and discouraged by her lack of success as an actress when she wrote *The Garrick Year* (1964). The narrator, Emma Evans, is similarly frustrated, having given up the opportunity for a job as a BBC announcer to move with her family from London to Hereford, where her actor-husband has a yearlong theatrical engagement. There Emma has an affair with the director of her husband's troupe, but after she is involved in a car accident and saves her child from drowning, she recognizes that she has given in to self-indulgence and that motherhood is her most important role. While Emma's children tie her to an unhappy marriage, they also save her from despair. As several critics have noted, motherhood is often a form of salvation for Drabble's female characters.

The Garrick Year garnered wide praise from critics for its powerful psychological realism. The novel also attracted the attention of many feminist critics, who praised Drabble's portrayal of the conflict between raising children and achieving economic and moral autonomy. Virginia K. Beards commented in 1973, "As a portrait of the frigid-seductive woman with a muddled concept of both male and female sexual rights, the novel is wise and complete."

By the time she wrote *The Millstone* (1965) Drabble, who was pregnant with her third child, had decided to concentrate on novel writing rather than an acting career because she could write at night while her children were sleeping. The title of *The Millstone* comes from Matthew 18:6: "If any of you put a stumbling block before one of these little ones who believe in me, it would be better for you if a great millstone were fastened around your neck and you drowned in the depth of the sea." As Millard has noted, in *The Millstone* Rosamund Stacey's out-of-wedlock child is both a millstone and a salvation.

Twenty-five-year-old Rosamund is a good-looking graduate student and an emotionally repressed virgin. She begins to think of herself as wearing a figurative scarlet "A" on her breast that stands for Abstinence (an ironic twist on the "A" for adultery that Hester Prynne wears in Nathaniel Hawthorne's 1850 novel *The Scarlet Letter*). As a result of her feeling that she is falling behind her contemporaries, she purposely engages in a single meaningless sexual encounter with George, a BBC announcer, and becomes pregnant. Her pregnancy brings her in contact with a class of women she has not met before, and she develops a sense of community with the poor women she meets at the National Health Clinic. At the end of the novel, when George sees their daughter, he is indifferent to the child, showing Rosamund the sort of detached person she might have become if motherhood had not given her the ability to love.

In *The Millstone* Drabble combined a lucid narrative structure with evocative moral and psychological themes to construct a glittering morality tale that is one of her most popular novels. Many feminist critics began to identify her as "the novelist of maternity."

In 1966 Drabble won the John Llewelyn Rhys Memorial Award for *The Millstone,* and a Society of Authors Travelling Scholarship of £500 financed a three-month stay in Paris, where Drabble finished *Jerusalem the Golden* (1967). In this novel she expanded the scope of her analysis beyond the individual to the social and family background of her characters. The protagonist, Clara Maugham, is not Drabble's typical middle-class, university-educated woman searching for a balance between the demands of womanhood and the freedom she desires. Clara hails from the working class in a town north of London and comes to the University of London by virtue of having won a scholarship. One of the most-significant threads in the novel is the confrontation between Clara's working-class values and those of the upper-class, aristocratic Denham family,

Dust jacket for Drabble's 1967 novel, about a college student from the working class who aspires to life in the "terrestrial paradise" of the British aristocracy

whom Clara visits after meeting Clelia Denham at the university.

While growing up in a puritanical working-class home, Clara has been desperate to escape from her mother and her stifling home environment. For Clara the world of the Denhams represents "Jerusalem the Golden,"–"a terrestrial paradise, where beautiful people in beautiful houses spoke of beautiful things." The married Gabriel Denham, with whom Clara has an affair, seems to be a manifestation of the elegance and wealth for which she is searching.

When Clara returns to Northam, she watches her mother die, knowing that reconciliation with her is impossible. As she reads her mother's old journal, however, she learns that her mother too had social aspirations and yearnings to escape her working-class existence. Now recognizing how much she is her mother's child, Clara is determined to succeed where her mother failed. While readers identify with Clara's desire to escape the hopelessness of her upbringing, she is a morally ambiguous character. She often confuses love with the attractions of class and money, and she uses sex to gain entrance into the world of wealth and promise. In the end she has not gained the new sense of self that she has set out to achieve. She remains the girl of Northam who has superficially become an inhabitant of "Jerusalem the Golden."

Jerusalem the Golden established Drabble's reputation as a promising writer of fiction. Writing in 1980, Ellen Cronan Rose called *Jerusalem the Golden* Drabble's "first wholly realized novel, economical in its construction, finely precise in its characterization of the heroine," adding that Drabble may be "more profound" in later novels, but she is "never . . . more completely in control of her material than in this relatively early work."

With the success of *Jerusalem the Golden,* Drabble realized that she could be financially independent and settled into a house in Hampstead with her children while her husband continued to tour as an actor. Receiving the James Tait Black Memorial Book Prize for *Jerusalem the Golden* in 1968 was further proof to her that she could make a living as a writer. With her children now in school, she was able to write during the day, and to orchestrate her personal and family life so that she could become increasingly involved in other pursuits as well. In 1969 she began teaching day classes at Morley College, in London, a post she held for the next eleven years. In 1968 and 1969 she wrote additional dialogue for the movie *Isadora,* the screenplay for the motion-picture version of *The Millstone*–released in the United States as *Thank You All Very Much* and in Great Britain as *A Touch of Love*–and a play, *Bird of Paradise*. She also wrote her fifth novel, *The Waterfall* (1969).

In *The Waterfall* Drabble returned to the sort of inward and self-conscious protagonist she had created in her earlier fiction, but she departed from the realistic narration of these novels and employed a more-experimental form. The first half of the book is in the third person, narrated from the viewpoint of the protagonist, Jane Grey. In the middle of the novel Jane begins to speak in the first person, and for the rest of the novel the narration alternates between her voice and that of the third-person narrator.

Jane is the mother of a small child, and her husband has left her during the sixth month of her second pregnancy. Opening with the birth of her second child and Jane's falling in love with her husband's cousin James Otford, the novel follows the course of the affair as Jane experiences an engulfing sexual passion for the first time. For the first half of the novel the third-person narrator voyeuristically observes the affair, until Jane suddenly cries out, as if in response to the narrator: "lies, lies, it's all lies. A pack of lies. . . . What have I tried to describe? A passion, a love, an unreal life, a life

in limbo, without anxiety, guilt, corpses." From that point onward the third-person narrator chronicles an intense and unreal story of passionate love while Jane looks with an objective, almost cynical eye on the events and characters. *The Waterfall* includes some of the most characteristic themes of Drabble's fiction: the yearning for romantic love, the desire for autonomy, the conflict between maternity and freedom, and the promises and dangers of the inward life.

Critical reception of *The Waterfall* has been divided. Caryn Fuoroli asserted in the *Journal of Narrative Technique* (Spring 1981) that the dual point of view resulted from Drabble's "inability to control narration" and that the novel fails because the technique keeps her from realizing "the full potential of her material." Writing in 1974, Myer, however, called *The Waterfall* Drabble's "neatest exposition of her central concern, and paradoxically the most conclusive in its dramatized recognition that there is not true solution to the conflict between instinct and morality." In her 1980 book on Drabble, Rose contended that the novel works because the point of view expresses the conflicts of the woman artist. She argued that Drabble "has divided herself into Jane, the woman (whose experience is liquid), and Jane Grey, the artist (who gives form, order, and shapeliness to that experience)." In a 1980 article Rose maintained, "In order to be whole (and wholly a woman), Drabble suggests, a woman must reconcile these divisions. And if a woman writer is to articulate this experience of what it is to be a woman, she must devise a form, as Drabble has done in *The Waterfall,* which amalgamates feminine fluidity and masculine shapeliness." Yet, other critics have attacked the novel because of Jane's dependence on her lover for her happiness.

Taking its title and theme from Matthew 19:24– "It is easier for a camel to go through the eye of a needle, than for a rich man to enter into the kingdom of God"–*The Needle's Eye* (1972) expresses some of Drabble's own concerns with religion and morality. Like Drabble, the protagonist of the novel, Rose Vassilou, is influenced early in life by Bunyan's *Pilgrim's Progress*. Rose is convinced that she must do right, but she is not sure about her theology. She is consumed by Pilgrim's question: "What must I do to be saved?" The novel was also influenced by Drabble's research for her biography of Arnold Bennett.

Rose has defied her wealthy family to marry Christopher Vassilou, a poor, radical Greek immigrant, and later she has infuriated Christopher by giving away a £30,000 legacy to a rather dubious African charity. After he begins to make his own fortune, she angers him again by refusing to move from their working-class home to a more fashionable middle-class neighborhood. As the novel opens, Rose has divorced the brutal

Christopher, who is trying to get her back or to take custody of the children from her.

Rose begins a platonic relationship with Simon, a socialist attorney who shares her attitudes toward wealth and privilege. After considering briefly the idea of leaving the children to Christopher and going off to do missionary work in the Third World, Rose finally decides that, even though Christopher physically abused her when they were married, "what she must do to be saved" is to accept her marriage as her fate. She takes Christopher back to maintain the family.

The Needle's Eye established Drabble as a major writer. Although some critics faulted the fatalism of the novel, most reviewers praised its complexity and Shakespearean quality, as well as placing it in the novel-of-manners tradition of Jane Austen and Henry James. Writing in 1975, Marion Vlastos Libby called the novel "a complex and passionate evocation of a fatalism deriving from the human condition and the nature of the world," adding that the greatness of the novel "lies in portraying the tension, real and agonizing, between the hounds of circumstance and the force of the individual will." Myer contended in 1974 that the fatalism of the novel can be construed as a religious vision if understood as a means to salvation: "For Margaret Drabble the true end of life is to reconcile flesh and spirit by accepting one's own nature and living with it, in a context of love and responsibility for others."

The success of *The Needle's Eye* also attracted academics to the study of Drabble's fiction. Articles on her books began to appear in scholarly journals, and in 1973 the American Academy of Arts and Letters awarded her the E. M. Forster Award.

While Drabble did not produce another novel for three years after the appearance of *The Needle's Eye,* she remained productive during this period, focusing on nonfiction. Her biography of Arnold Bennett, published in 1974, helped her to gain a new understanding of her Yorkshire origins and a greater appreciation of social realism in fiction.

As Mitchell has observed, Drabble's next novel, *The Realms of Gold* (1975), "employs archaeology as a controlling metaphor for fragmentation of contemporary families." The protagonist of the novel, Frances Wingate, is a renowned archaeologist in her mid thirties who has divorced the wealthy man she married at an early age and is raising their four children alone. Frances suffers from her own physical limitations and worries that her body is deteriorating. She knows she drinks too much, and she is afraid she might be an alcoholic like her brother. She suffers from bouts of depression, but she does not let her limitations affect her in any fundamental way.

Drabble with her children Adam and Rebecca (photograph by Fay Godwin; from the dust jacket for The Waterfall, *1969)*

Although she is an expert archaeologist, Frances struggles when she tries to reconstruct her own past. She is only beginning to find some answers when her great-aunt dies of starvation in her own cottage because she has broken her leg and cannot seek help. Musing on the dignity of the human struggle for survival, Frances finds "many private satisfactions" in her great-aunt's cottage. Frances's nephew Stephen, however, sees only indignity in the old woman's fate and chooses the "pure triumph" of suicide, also killing his infant daughter because he wants to spare her the pain of growing up in a world he hates. As Mitchell has noted, Frances learns that death and love are the only absolutes, and the novel ends happily for her. The title of the novel comes from a phrase in John Keats's sonnet "On First Looking into Chapman's Homer" (1816) and alludes to the joy of discovery that Frances experiences in Drabble's novel.

Critical response to *The Realms of Gold* was uneven. Writing in 1979 Elizabeth Fox-Genovese called

Dust jacket for Drabble's 1972 novel, which established her reputation as a major British fiction writer

Frances a "fatuous, self-satisfied bitch; too good at everything by half, not to mention too rich and unencumbered." Other critics were more positive in their assessments. In a 1977 article on the novel Patricia Sharpe commented that it "exposed the narrowness" of readers' imaginative sympathies, and she noted that the improbabilities of the novel are appropriate to Drabble's "drama of discovery," which echoes the emotion of Keats's sonnet. In an essay collected in his 1979 book Roger H. Sale agreed that the title was an apt description for the novel, adding that the happy ending "overwhelms disbelief."

The title of *The Ice Age* (1977) refers to the economic recession of the 1970s and to the general quality of modern life. In fact, as Mitchell has noted, the central theme of the novel is the implication that "the individual character's malaise is part of a larger crisis created by the drastic, enormous changes in the nature and quality of life in the last hundred years." The protagonist, Anthony Keating, became wealthy through real-estate development in the 1960s and lost his fortune during the 1970s. As the novel opens, he is recovering from a heart attack and trying to understand the changes that have disrupted his life. One of his partners, Len Wincobank, is serving time in prison for the illegal financial dealings of their company, and Anthony is awaiting trial.

When his fiancée's daughter, Jane, is jailed for dangerous driving in the fictional communist-bloc country of Wallacia, Anthony goes to her rescue, agreeing to spy for the British government during his journey. He manages to free Jane, but ends up imprisoned in Wallacia himself. There he experiences a kind of spiritual reawakening, realizing that he does "not know how man can do without God." The novel examines Anthony's disintegration as a microcosm of the decline taking place in the larger British society, in which other characters have so much confidence, is disintegrating all around them throughout the novel. Yet, the novel is not centered on Anthony alone. The narrative is divided among Anthony; his fiancée, Alison; Len; and Len's mistress, Maureen. This division of viewpoint suggests the lack of cohesion that the characters sense in their society.

In many ways *The Ice Age* is Drabble's most self-consciously political novel before *The Gates of Ivory* (1991). The implication of *The Ice Age* is that Britain will survive the current crisis, as it has survived others in the past, even if the characters do not. They make their moral and economic choices against a backdrop of determinism. That is, even though they choose to live a certain way, factors such as the disintegrating economic and social climate actually determine those choices for them. *The Ice Age* received mixed reviews, but most academic critics consider it one of Drabble's most important works.

Drabble's next novel, *The Middle Ground* (1980), is set against the same cultural backdrop as *The Ice Age*. The protagonist, Kate Armstrong, who resembles Frances Wingate of *The Needle's Eye*, is a successful newspaper writer living a comfortable life, but she is less confident about her future than Frances because she lives in the midst of social upheaval. At forty-one she is confronted with the physical and cultural decay of urban life in London and wonders what direction her life should take. By the end of the novel, she has decided on a "middle ground" between the self-sacrifice of her social-worker friend Evelyn and the selfishness of her former lover, Ted. Kate decides that she will be a "nice woman," a middle-aged woman looking forward to her future. The novel ends with a party (to which Kate invites Gabriel Denham of *Jerusalem the Golden* and Rosamund Stacey of *The Millstone*), a gathering of middle-class adults standing together against the harsh economic realities of contemporary British society.

As with *The Ice Age,* critical response to *The Middle Ground* was uneven, but the American Library Association included it in their list of notable books published in 1980, and many critics praised Drabble's honesty about middle age and her increased optimism about the future.

During the 1980s Drabble continued to write, and she edited the fifth edition of *The Oxford Companion to English Literature* (1985), but she did not publish another novel until 1987. Drabble sought to include more women writers in her edition of *The Oxford Companion to English Literature,* adding women overlooked by earlier editors. She also included entries that recognized the role of colonial literature in the English literary tradition. Her selection as editor provided a fitting comment on her place in the "Great Tradition" of British literature.

The Radiant Way (1987) is the first novel in a trilogy that follows the lives of three women who have been friends since they attended Cambridge in the 1950s. *The Radiant Way* introduces Liz, a psychotherapist; Alix, an altruistic idealist who teaches for little pay at a women's prison; and Esther, an art historian who studies minor artists of the Italian Renaissance. In many ways *The Radiant Way* brings Drabble full circle, back to the concerns of her early novels, as she observes these three middle-aged, middle-class women weathering crises in their lives. The action centers on the murder of one of Alix's students, but the novel is static, as the three women speculate about the way their lives might have been and bemoan the way they have turned out. Reviewing the novel for *The New York Times* (21 October 1987), Michiko Kakutani observed that it "attempts to show us how a generation managed (or mismanaged) its hopes and dreams" and complained that it "substitutes exposition for storytelling, sociological observation for the development of character and drama." *Newsweek* reviewer Laura Shapiro, however, approved of the novel: "at a time when skimpy prose, skeletal characterizations, frail plots and a sense of human history that stops sometime around last summer have become the new standards for fiction . . . Drabble reminds us here as in all her books exactly why we still love to read" (2 November 1987).

A Natural Curiosity (1989) continues the saga of the three friends, and the novel centers on Alix's attempts to understand the motivation of her student's murderer. Critics had many of the same reservations about this novel as they did about *The Radiant Way*. The action is static, and there is little drama, even of the psychological sort.

The final novel in the trilogy, *The Gates of Ivory*, is set far from London, in Cambodia during the 1970s. Liz goes there in search of her friend Stephen Cox, a journalist who has disappeared in rural Cambodia while seeking to arrange an interview with the brutal Khmer Rouge leader Pol Pot. Drabble's most ambitious novel to date, *The Gates of Ivory* examines political issues as diverse as the Vietnam War and the restoration of the ancient temple complex at Angkor Wat. Most reviewers thought the novel was too broad in scope, and others criticized Drabble for leaving familiar territory to strike out for parts unknown. Writing for *World Literature Today* (Spring 1993), Mary Kaiser echoed the thoughts of many critics: "Although Drabble has flirted with the explosive possibilities of leaving the domestic novel and inventing a new form, her allegiance to traditional realism prevents her from breaking the form in order to engage fully the undomesticated facts of our complex and violent times."

In 1995 Drabble published *Angus Wilson: A Biography*. In many ways it is appropriate that Drabble wrote Wilson's biography, for Wilson paved the way in his novels *Anglo-Saxon Attitudes* (1956) and *The Middle Age of Mrs. Eliot* (1958) for the examination of British middle-class mores, a subject that preoccupies Drabble in her fiction. Although some reviewers contended that Drab-

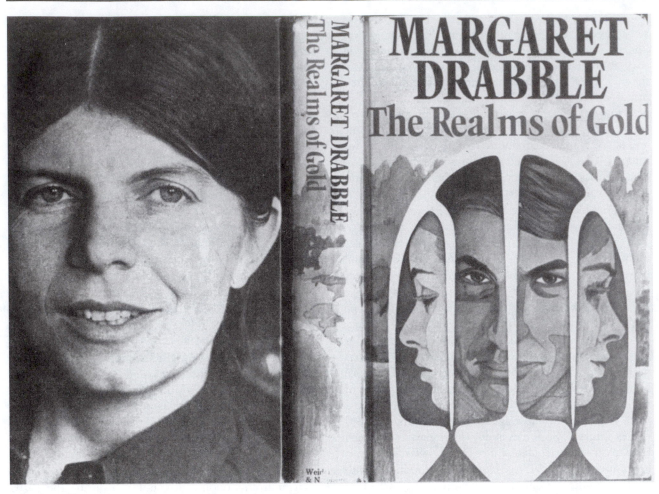

Dust jacket for Drabble's 1975 novel, whose title comes from John Keats's sonnet "On First Looking into Chapman's Homer"

ble failed to provide an accurate portrait, the comments of Frank Kermode typify the generally favorable sentiment toward this biography, crediting Drabble with creating "a minute, intimate and candid account . . . of Wilson's hectic life" (*London Review of Books,* 8 June 1995). After the publication of her 1996 novel, *The Witch of Exmoor,* Drabble told Nicholas Basbanes how difficult it had been to write a biography of Wilson: "Angus was somebody I very much admired as a writer and a human being. It's quite one thing to write about somebody who grows old, gets ill and then dies in real life. This was not a fictional character I was dealing with, this was a real person. So I got really depressed being so close to that, and this book [*The Witch of Exmoor*], in a way, was a reply for me, a sort of getting-out exercise."

The Witch of Exmoor takes Drabble back to the themes of her earlier fiction, telling the story of a contemporary family whose comfortable, ordered life is upended by chaotic events. The novel opens on a mid-

summer evening in rural Hampshire, England, where the Palmer family is playing a dinner-party game: What kind of society would you accept without knowing your place in it? The game is interrupted by the news that Daniel Palmer's eccentric mother, Frieda, has fled to a remote, crumbling old hotel by the sea in Exmoor, where she becomes "the self-elected witch of Exmoor." To her three children Frieda has always been powerful, puzzling, and unpredictable. Drabble devotes the novel to the children's reactions to behavior that seems eccentric to them but normal to Frieda.

Critical reaction to *The Witch of Exmoor* was mixed. In *USA Today* (5 February 1998), Deirdre Donahue found it "appropriate that Drabble is now writing about grandmothers," noting that "beginning with *A Summer Bird-Cage,* Drabble has traced an entire generation of women's lives." The anonymous reviewer for *Publishers Weekly* (16 June 1997) asserted, "Swimming in the murk of post-Thatcher Britain and taking a stern but knowing view of the English bourgeoisie, this is postmodern

from The Peppered Moth
(2001)   181

154

And

It had been too late for Chrissie to visit her Auntie Ivy in Australia, for
her Auntie Ivy was dead. She had died two years earlier, of asbestosis,
a killer disease contracted decades earlier in the playground of Cromwell Place
Infants in Cotterhall. A fair number of Cotterhall Infants were claimed in adult
life by this illness, which they had not known they were harbouring. Auntie Ivy
Barron had fled from Cotterhall and South Yorkshire to the uttermost parts of
the earth, but she had fled, as the scriptures had prohesied, in vain, for
even there the dust of Cotterhall had claimed her. Her much-loved friend and
life's companion Pat had grieved bitterly, and inherited her small estate. ~~She~~ *Pat*
had also written ~~to~~ "home", (as some of her ~~fxxix~~ ex-pat associataes still
called England) to let what was left of the Barron family know of Ivy's death.
Sister Rowena had, of course, been dead herself for many years, and Joe Barron
and Bennett Barron and Phil Barron had also predeceased her. Alfred ~~was~~ the only
one of that generation left alive, and he had not kept in touch. ~~(Joe was the
only one who had written letters to Sydney)~~ *Ivy.* Sister-in-law Bessie, when
informed of Ivy's death, had seemed indignant. She had not cared for Ivy, had
resented the time that Joe spent writing his ~~xxxiyxix~~ fortnightly letter,
and was not pleased to hear that the little bungalow had been left to Pat.
Nevertheless, Ivy's death had managed to annoy her.

Chrissie had no memory of her Auntie Ivy, whom she had not seen since her
~~xxriy~~ infancy. Robert, who might have been expected to have a better recollection,
had also forgotten her. Chrissie told herself, ~~on~~ *as she planned* her ~~xixxix~~ *trip* to Australia,
that she would have looked Ivy up, for her father's sake: she had an
admiration for the boldness and the finality of ~~her~~ *Ivy's* escape. But even Chrissie,
                                        of the manners of   *Middle Europe*
WASHES who had learned a little family affection from the crazy Gauldens, was a little
bit glad that she had been spared an encounter that would probably have been
rather trying. And Chrissie did not think it ~~xxxix~~ necessary to look up
Pat Wainwright. She assumed, as one of her generation would, that Ivy and
Pat had been lovers. She hoped they had been. But either way, there was no
                                  at this stage in the game
reason why Pat would want to see her. Better leave well alone.

                    *   *   *

Page from a draft for a forthcoming novel (Collection of Margaret Drabble) family drama at its best." Yet, Millicent Bell, writing for *Partisan Review* (Spring 1998), disagreed with these admirers: "It seems that Drabble herself doesn't believe very much in what she is doing. Her novel's plot ravels out into the unlikely and irrelevant incident. . . . The visionary scenes do not fit into the general tone of the novel which is governed by a flippant voice that constantly intrudes to hold up to ridicule not only the characters but the narrative process itself."

Although the critical response to Drabble's fiction has always been mixed, there is no doubt that she is one of the preeminent women of letters of the mid and late twentieth century. Her forays into fiction, biography, and literary criticism mark her as a latter-day George Eliot or Anthony Trollope. Her achievement has been recognized with honorary D.Litt. degrees from the Universities of Sheffield (1976), Manchester (1987), Keele (1988), Bradford (1988), Hull (1992), East Anglia (1994), and York (1995). In 1980 Queen Elizabeth II made Drabble a commander of the British Empire.

Drabble's insistence on writing realistic novels in the face of postmodern minimalism and modernist experimentation has caused some critics to question her contribution to contemporary literature. Yet, others contend that Drabble has rethought the conventions of nineteenth-century realism in the light of twentieth-century modernism. Drabble's novels provide insights into the nature of transcendence, spiritual and earthly. Her political and social critiques challenge contemporary Britain to reconsider its present paths and its vision of the future. The eloquence and elegance of Drabble's fiction offer her readers an opportunity to inhabit a world of intellectual and cultural growth as they confront themselves and their society.

Interviews:

Bolivar Le Franc, "An Interest in Guilt: Margaret Drabble," *Books and Bookmen,* 14 (September 1969): 20–21;

Terry Coleman, "A Biographer Waylaid by Novels," *Guardian* (Manchester), 15 April 1972, p. 23;

Nancy S. Hardin, "An Interview with Margaret Drabble," *Contemporary Literature,* 14 (Summer 1973): 273–295;

Joseph McCulloch, "Dialogue with Margaret Drabble," in his *Under Bow Bells: Dialogues with Joseph McCulloch* (London: Sheldon Press, 1974), pp. 125–132;

Nancy Poland, "Margaret Drabble: 'There Must Be a Lot of People Like Me,'" *Midwest Quarterly,* 16 (April 1975): 255–267;

Peter E. Firchow, ed. *The Writer's Place: Interviews on the Literary Situation in Contemporary Britain* (Minneapolis: University of Minnesota Press, 1975), pp. 102–121;

Mel Gussow, "Margaret Drabble: A Double Life," *New York Times Book Review,* 9 October 1977, pp. 7, 40–41;

Barbara Milton, "Art of Fiction LXX: Margaret Drabble," *Paris Review,* 74 (Fall 1978): 40–65;

Iris Rozencwajg, "Interview with Margaret Drabble," *Women's Studies,* 6 (1979): 335–347;

Dee Preussner, "Talking with Margaret Drabble," *Modern Fiction Studies,* 25 (1980): 563–577;

Diana Cooper-Clark, "Margaret Drabble: Cautious Feminist," *Atlantic Monthly,* 246 (November 1980): 69–75;

Gillian Parker and Janet Todd, "Margaret Drabble," in *Women Writers Talking,* edited by Todd (New York: Holmes & Meier, 1983), pp. 160–178;

Martha Satz, "'Less of a Woman As One Gets Older': An Interview with Margaret Drabble," *Southwest Review,* 70 (Spring 1985): 187–197;

John Hannay, "Margaret Drabble: An Interview," *Twentieth Century Literature,* 33 (Summer 1987): 129–149;

Olga Kenyon, *Women Writers Talk: Interviews with 10 Women Writers* (Oxford: Lennard, 1989), pp. 25–52;

Ian Wojcik-Andrews, "The Politics of Humour: An Interview with Margaret Drabble," in *New Perspectives on Women and Comedy,* edited by Regina Barreca (Philadelphia: Gordon & Breach, 1992), pp. 101–109;

Nicholas Basbanes, "In 'Witch at Exmoor,' Drabble Focuses Her Detached Anger About British Greed," *Salt Lake Tribune,* 9 November 1997, p. D6.

Bibliographies:

Joan Garret Packer, *Margaret Drabble: An Annotated Bibliography* (New York: Garland, 1988);

George Soule, *Four British Women Novelists: Anita Brookner, Margaret Drabble, Iris Murdoch, Barbara Pym: An Annotated and Critical Secondary Bibliography* (Lanham, Md.: Scarecrow Press, 1998).

References:

Tuzyline Jita Allan, *Womanist and Feminist Aesthetics: A Comparative Review* (Athens: Ohio University Press, 1995);

Virginia K. Beards, "Margaret Drabble: Novels of a Cautious Feminist," *Critique,* 15 (1973): 35–46;

Nicole Suzanne Bokat, *The Novels of Margaret Drabble: This Freudian Family Nexus* (New York: Peter Lang, 1998);

Colin Butler, "Margaret Drabble: *The Millstone* and Wordsworth," *English Studies,* 59 (August 1978): 353–360;

Joanne V. Creighton, *Margaret Drabble* (London: Methuen, 1985);

Cynthia Davis, "Unfolding Form: Narrative Approach and Theme in *The Realms of Gold*," *Modern Language Quarterly*, 40 (1979): 390–402;

Lee Edwards, "*Jerusalem the Golden:* A Fable for Our Times," *Women's Studies*, 6 (1979): 321–335;

Peter E. Firchow, "Rosamund's Complaint: Margaret Drabble's *The Millstone*," in *Old Lines, New Forces: Essays on the Contemporary British Novel, 1960–70*, edited by Robert K. Morris (Rutherford, N.J.: Fairleigh Dickinson Press, 1976), pp. 93–108;

Elizabeth Fox-Genovese, "Ambiguities of Female Identity: A Reading of the Novels of Margaret Drabble," *Partisan Review*, 46 (1979): 234–248;

Caryn Fuoroli, "Sophistry or Simple Truth? Narrative Technique in Margaret Drabble's *The Waterfall*," *Journal of Narrative Technique*, 11 (Spring 1981): 110–124;

John Hannay, *The Intertextuality of Fate: A Study of Margaret Drabble* (Columbia: University of Missouri Press, 1986);

Nancy S. Hardin, "Drabble's *The Millstone:* A Fable for Our Time," *Critique*, 15 (1973): 23–34;

Mary M. Lay, "Temporal Ordering in the Fiction of Margaret Drabble," *Critique*, 21 (1979): 73–84;

Marion Vlastos Libby, "Fate and Feminism in the Novels of Margaret Drabble," *Contemporary Literature*, 16 (Spring 1975): 175–192;

Joan Manheimer, "Margaret Drabble and the Journey to the Self," *Studies in the Literary Imagination*, 11 (1978): 127–143;

Mary Hurley Moran, *Margaret Drabble: Existing within Structures* (Carbondale: Southern Illinois University Press, 1983);

Valerie Grosvenor Myer, *Margaret Drabble: A Reader's Guide* (London: Vision, 1991; New York: St. Martin's Press, 1991);

Myer, *Margaret Drabble: Puritanism and Permissiveness* (London: Vision, 1974);

Rose Quiello, *Breakdowns and Breakthoughts: The Figure of the Hysteric in Contemporary Novels by Women* (New York: Peter Lang, 1996);

Ellen Cronan Rose, "Feminine Endings—and Beginnings: Margaret Drabble's *The Waterfall*," *Contemporary Literature*, 21 (February 1980): 81–99;

Rose, *The Novels of Margaret Drabble: Equivocal Figures* (London: Macmillan, 1980);

Rose, "Surviving the Future," *Critique*, 15 (1973): 5–21;

Rose, ed., *Critical Essays on Margaret Drabble* (Boston: G. K. Hall, 1985);

Susanna Roxman, *Guilt and Glory: Studies in Margaret Drabble's Novels, 1963–1980* (Stockholm: Almqvist & Wiksell, 1984);

Roger H. Sale, "Williams, Weesner, and Drabble," in his *On Not Being Good Enough: Writings of a Working Critic* (London: Oxford University Press, 1979), pp. 42–53;

Dorey Schmidt and Jan Seale, eds., *Margaret Drabble: Golden Realms* (Edinburgh, Tex.: Pan American University Press, 1982);

Patricia Sharpe, "On First Looking into 'The Realms of Gold'," *Michigan Quarterly Review*, 16 (Spring 1977): 225–231;

Elaine Showalter, *A Literature of Their Own* (Princeton: Princeton University Press, 1977);

Susan Spitzer, "Fantasy and Femaleness in Margaret Drabble's *The Millstone*," *Novel*, 11 (Spring 1978): 227–245;

Nora Foster Stovel, *Margaret Drabble: Symbolic Moralist* (Mercer Island: Starmont House, 1989);

Janet Todd, *Gender and Literary Voice* (New York: Holmes & Meier, 1980);

Ian Wojcik-Andrews, *Margaret Drabble's Female Bildungsroman: Theory, Genre, and Gender* (New York: Peter Lang, 1995).

Papers:

Some of Margaret Drabble's papers are in the Mugar Memorial Library at Boston University.

Helen Fielding

(1958 –   )

Merritt Moseley
University of North Carolina at Asheville

BOOKS: *Who's Had Who: In Association with Berk's Roger-age: An Historical Register Containing Official Lay Lines of History From the Beginning of Time to the Present Day,* by Fielding, Simon Bell, and Richard Curtis (London & Boston: Faber & Faber, 1987; New York: Warner Books, 1990);

Cause Celeb (London: Picador, 1994);

Bridget Jones's Diary: A Novel (London: Picador, 1996; New York: Viking, 1998);

Bridget Jones: The Edge of Reason (London: Picador, 1999; New York: Viking, 2000).

Helen Fielding has the distinction among younger British novelists of having written an enormously popular book that has changed the English language and aroused an intense controversy over the needs and desires of modern women and the fate of feminism. It is remarkable that a comic novel written solely with the intention of amusing readers should have such a large impact. *Bridget Jones's Diary* (1996) was a best-seller in the United Kingdom, has been translated into many languages, and was published to acclaim in the United States as well. The 1999 sequel, *Bridget Jones: The Edge of Reason,* moved directly to the top of best-seller lists in Britain. While she had neither lofty ambitions nor deconstructionist intentions, Fielding patterned the plots of her two Bridget Jones novels on Jane Austen's *Pride and Prejudice* (1813) and *Persuasion* (1817), thus contributing to the modern trend—both among feminist authors such as Emma Tennant and Fay Weldon and in the cinema—to re-envision and revise Austen.

Born in Morley, Yorkshire, Fielding is the daughter of a mill owner and a homemaker. She attended a girls' school and then went to Oxford, where she read English at St. Anne's College and received her B.A. in 1979. In a 31 May 1998 profile for *The Observer* (London), Robert Yates observed that while Fielding is hardly working class, she "could come on as the plain-speaking northerner whenever her contemporaries at Oxford threatened to get lost in pretensions." Yet, Fielding's views on Yorkshire are not always flattering

Helen Fielding (photograph by Peter Fletcher; from the dust jacket for Bridget Jones: The Edge of Reason, *1999)*

either. The most repellent character in any of her books is television magnate Vernon Briggs in *Cause Celeb,* who tries unsuccessfully to pass off his greed, racism, and retrograde sexual attitudes as Yorkshire bluffness.

At Oxford, Fielding was reportedly a good, though not obsessively conscientious, student, interested in acting. After graduation she went to work in production for the BBC and contributed to current-affairs programs such as *Nationwide,* and to *Playschool,* a children's show. She also produced segments for *Comic Relief,* a widely successful televised appeal for African famine relief. Her work for this program was the stimulus for her first novel, *Cause Celeb* (1994), set amid African suffering. Having always wanted to be a writer, she moved to *The Sunday Times* (London), where she began contributing a personal column but resigned because of editorial interference with her copy. After attempting to sell a novel to Mills and Boon, publishers of romance fiction, and collaborating on a comical book about sex, *Who's Had Who: In Association with Berk's Rogerage: An Historical Register Containing Official Lay Lines of History From the Beginning of Time to the Present Day* (1987), Fielding wrote *Cause Celeb,* based not only on her experiences in Africa with *Comic Relief,* but also more generally on her knowledge of the London media world. The novel contrasts the two settings. Rosie Richardson is a relief worker in an African country that resembles Sudan, in charge of a refugee camp for families who have fled the civil war in neighboring Kefti. She came to Africa four years earlier on a "mission of mercy" invented as a publicity ploy by her employer, partly to escape and partly to impress her demanding, selfish, inconsiderate, and inattentive celebrity lover, Oliver March, the presenter of a televised arts program. (In a pattern that is repeated in the Bridget Jones novels, Rosie tolerated his mistreatment of her and seemed inclined to blame herself).

As the novel opens, rumors begin to reach the camp about the impending arrival of thousands of new starving refugees, and, after other attempts to secure aid fail, Rosie decides to go back to London and enlist celebrities in a fund-raising program televised from Africa. Marchand agrees to help her, though not without exasperating demands, and eventually he arranges a broadcast that will originate in London with cut-in portions broadcast live by satellite from Africa. Though donations flood in, there is no artificially upbeat ending. Scores of the Africans die of starvation, and relief efforts begin to suffer from the short attention span or compassion fatigue of the British audience. Yet, the novel brings its various strands to satisfactory conclusions: Rosie frees herself from the allure of Oliver, finds a better man, and demonstrates how her time in Africa has made her a deeper and more serious person than the shallow media celebrities whose narcissism and other foibles the novel relentlessly and inventively satirizes.

Cause Celeb is an impressive first novel. Writing for *The Independent* (13 August 1994), Harriet Paterson praised its satire as "sharp, gutsy, and refreshing" and said that "Fielding confidently treads the sticky path of exercising her wit on those who deserve it without being flip about those who don't"; and Maggie

Traugott in *The Independent on Sunday* (31 July 1994) saw that "juxtaposing the haves of London with the have-nots of Africa without pontificating or pathos is one of the things Helen Fielding pulls off so dextrously in this debut novel."

Though the novel is funny, Fielding may well have been most interested in the sympathetic treatment of important issues. For her next novel she planned a satire about economic problems on the Caribbean island of St. Vincent (a book she still expects to complete).

In 1995, however, Fielding was invited to contribute a column to *The Independent* (London). Joining the sizable group of single women writing personal columns daunted her because of her unwillingness to reveal too much about herself. In 1997 she told Lydia Slater that she created a fictional persona, "an imaginary amalgam of insecurities," because: "If you write as yourself, you can't help but want people to like you. If you write as somebody else, you can be honest about the secret, stupid, shameful things. . . ."

Fielding did consult some of her old diaries and was surprised to find that they frequently included information about calories and drinking—a discovery that helped to dictate the unusual form of *Bridget Jones's Diary*. A typical entry begins: "St. 12, alcohol units 2 (V.G.), cigarettes 11 (g.) calories 1850, job offers from fire service or rival TV stations 0 (perhaps not altogether surprising)." This interest in weight, smoking, and drinking alcohol are a constant, providing a gauge of Bridget's emotions, particularly about men.

The popularity of the column led to publication of the book version, a novel that sold more than a million and a half copies in Britain and had surprising sales and critical success in other countries. A motion-picture version is scheduled for release in 2001, with Renée Zellweger in the title role and Colin Firth (whom Bridget interviews in the sequel) as Mark Darcy.

Fielding's two Bridget Jones novels place her in the tradition of comic-diary fiction, a well-established genre in England. Perhaps the best-known example is George and Weedon Grossmith's *The Diary of a Nobody* (1892), the story of nonentity Mr. Charles Pooter, which was originally published periodically in *Punch.* Other successful examples include Sue Townsend's series of diaries of the self-absorbed teenager Adrian Mole, beginning with *The Secret Diary of Adrian Mole, Aged 13 3/4* (1982) and continuing through *Adrian Mole: The Cappucino Years* (1999). The satirical magazine *Private Eye* regularly publishes fictional diary features, including "The Secret Diary of John Major Aged 47 3/4," while Major was prime minister. Keith Waterhouse has written two "sequels" to *The Diary of a Nobody,* including *Mrs. Pooter's Diary* (1983). There are technical

Poster for Fielding's 1996 novel, a best-seller loosely based on Jane Austen's Pride and Prejudice

advantages and disadvantages to the diary form; it lends itself perfectly to suspense and dramatic irony, but occasionally requires improbabilities such as Bridget's writing "Oops" when she falls drunkenly, or "GAAA" in frustration. The original newspaper-column format of Fielding's novels limited the length of diary entries and created a somewhat episodic structure for the novels.

Bridget Jones's situation is full of opportunities for humor. She is single and living alone, working at first in book publishing and later for a television company. She interacts most honestly and satisfyingly with her two friends Jude and Shazzer and her gay friend Tom, and, like Rosie Richardson, she is interested in the wrong man, in this case Daniel at work, with whom she exchanges spicy e-mail messages. Meanwhile, her parents and their friends worry about her future, and her mother tries to find dates for her. Her mother's newest candidate for Bridget is Mark Darcy, an old family friend.

Through vicissitudes—including a pregnancy scare, weight worries, and her mother's midlife crisis (during which she runs off with a Portuguese lothario)—Bridget eventually works out that the right man for her

is really Mark Darcy, and the novel ends with them in bed together, after he has succeeded in bringing her errant mother back from Portugal.

The parallels with *Pride and Prejudice* are obvious (signaled, for instance, by the use of Darcy as the name of the hero) but not heavily underlined. Like Austen's Elizabeth Bennet, Bridget is prejudiced against her Mr. Darcy, as well as having a prior attachment to an unsuitable man, and Mark Darcy helps to extricate Bridget's family from a humiliating situation, as Fitzwilliam Darcy does for the Bennets in Austen's novel.

Among the other satisfactions of Fielding's novel are its lively and crisp use of language. Bridget's friends are "singletons" who suffer from the slights of "Smug Marrieds." The mental suffering that their boyfriends inflict on them is called "fuckwittage."

Despite its unprepossessing beginnings and Fielding's modest refusal to make claims for its literary merit, *Bridget Jones's Diary* provoked a strong response from reviewers, who found it realistic, representative, and honest. Many reviews, and letters to the author, declared that she had identified how women, particularly single women in their thirties, really think, feel, and behave. Writing for *The Boston Globe* (26 October

1998), Maureen Dezell called the novel a "deftly executed urban comedy of manners," and reported that "in every city she [Fielding] visited—'even New York!'—lawyers, commodities traders, and editors wearing expensive hairstyles and smart suits approached her to say: 'I am Bridget Jones!'" In *The New York Times* (1 February 1998), Warren Hoge quoted Fanny Blake, a specialist on the publishing industry, as saying: "What we're seeing now is the growth of a brave new women's fiction humorously and realistically addressing themes recognizable to women trying to make their way in their 20s and 30s: often career women with disposable income, unable to find either a heterosexual man or anything in the fridge."

In 1998, however, Decca Aitkenhead, a columnist for *The Guardian,* expressed concerns about the example Bridget Jones sets for women: "It's depressing that such a good writer confirms all of men's suspicions. Bridget might be talking about Sierra Leone, but it's only to impress the man in the corner. Her real concern is her skirt, and getting off with him." There has been some attempt to blame Fielding for the rise of books such as Arabella Weir's *Does My Bum Look Big in This?* (1997)—which is, in fact, the sort of question Bridget often ponders. In *The New York Times* (14 June 1998), Alex Kuczynski began an article with "Bridget Jones makes me ill" and then contended, "Ms. Fielding constructs her heroine out of every myth that has ever sprung from the ground of Cosmopolitan and television sitcoms. To wit, that men are, in the words of one character, 'stupid, smug, arrogant, manipulative and self-indulgent'; that women are obsessed with boyfriends, diets and body hair, and that every emotional reversal is cause for a chocolate binge." Charging Fielding with basing her comedy on "the premise that being neurotic is cute," Kuczynski complained: "Yes, yes, I know 'Bridget Jones' is satire, a sassy spoof of urban manners. But Bridget is such a sorry spectacle, wallowing in her man-crazed helplessness, that her foolishness cannot be excused."

When Ashton Applewhite brought up such criticism in an interview, Fielding responded by pointing out the number of superficial "male comic heroes. Take Bertie Wooster, from P. G. Wodehouse—we don't take him as a symbol, as a state of manhood. We've got to be able to have comic heroines without being so terribly anxious about what it says. We're not equal if we're not allowed to laugh at ourselves."

In 1998 Fielding moved her column to *The Daily Telegraph* (London), and in 1999 she published *Bridget Jones: The Edge of Reason.* While *Bridget Jones's Diary* follows *Pride and Prejudice* in leaving the heroine happily in the arms of her own Mr. Darcy, the sequel is patterned on *Persuasion,* in which lovers are parted and finally reunited after heart-breaking misunderstandings and disruptions. Bridget's daily concerns are familiar to the reader of the earlier novel. She has uncertainties about her love life, now exacerbated not only by conversations with her friends but by a new addiction to self-help books such as *Beyond Co-Dependency with a Man Who Can't Commit.* She has a job that does not challenge her much or receive her full attention. A new element in this novel is married friend Magda's adventures with toilet training. Her telephone conversations are now always interrupted by her attentions to her toddler: "Bridget, hi! I was just ringing to say in the potty! In the potty! do it in the potty!" Concerns about aging and being single continue for Bridget, along with her righteous contempt for such concerns: "Wish Jude would not talk about biological clock in public. Obviously one worries about such things in private and tries to pretend whole undignified situation isn't happening. Bringing it up in 192 [a bar] merely makes one panic and feel like a walking cliché."

Readers who object to Bridget's helplessness (whether "learned" or innate) are likely to find much to object to in this book, in which she permits a builder to make an enormous hole in the outside wall of her flat and leave it open, covered only by polythene sheets, for months. She also manages to be arrested in Thailand on a drug charge from which only Mark Darcy can help her escape. Likewise, though she is a reporter on a current-affairs television program, her attempts to discuss politics reveal her ignorance and lack of seriousness. When she discovers that Mark is a Tory, she retorts: "The point is you are supposed to vote for the principle of the thing, not the itsy-bitsy detail about this per cent and that per cent. And it is perfectly obvious that Labour stands for the principle of sharing, kindness, gays, single mothers and Nelson Mandela as opposed to braying bossy men having affairs with everyone shag-shag-shag left, right and centre and going to the Ritz in Paris then telling all the presenters off on the *Today* programme."

Nevertheless, the comic quality of *Bridget Jones: The Edge of Reason* holds up well. The writing is crisp; the plotting, even if more exotic than in the first book, is clever; and Fielding contributes another useful neologism to the English language: "mentionitis," which is the suspicious condition "when someone's name keeps coming up all the time, when it's not strictly relevant: 'Rebecca says this' or 'Rebecca's got a car like that.'"

In an interesting exploration of the life/art confusion that has plagued Fielding since the publication of *Bridget Jones's Diary* with the persistent questions about whether she actually is Bridget, Fielding incorporates an event from her life in the second novel. Fielding once interviewed actor Colin Firth as Bridget Jones and

Dust jacket for Fielding's 1999 sequel to her fictional diary of a young, single woman working in London

found, she told Slater in 1997, that "I could ask all sorts of questions I'd never have dared to if it'd been me, like whether being called Colin was a disadvantage and whether, instead of his Italian fiancée [now wife], he shouldn't be going out with someone who was English and more his age." In the novel Bridget interviews Firth, who interests her primarily because he played Mr. Darcy in the 1995 television version of *Pride and Prejudice*. Bridget and her friends have obsessively replayed the part of that program in which he emerges from a pond in tight white trousers, and in her interview Bridget innocently confuses him with the role, cross-examining him about the pond scene and eventually telling him that she thinks he is "exactly like Mr Darcy"–because he looks like him and talks like him. Such confusion of actor and role is inexcusable from a journalistic point of view, and she is ridiculed at her office. Yet, the office is itself ridiculous; in passages reminiscent of the satire on celebrity culture in *Cause Celeb,* her commissioning editor, Richard, regularly invents silly projects for the television show, usually making inane comparisons: "I'm thinking bunny girl, I'm think-ing Gladiator, I'm thinking canvassing MP, I'm think-ing Chris Serle meets Jerry Springer meets Anneka Rice meets Zoe Ball meets Mike Smith off the Late, Late Breakfast Show."

Bridget Jones: The Edge of Reason has received mixed reviews. In the *Sunday Times* (21 November 1999), Lynne Truss maintained that the novel is "fun-nier and more accomplished than the original diary, and in fact takes recognition humour into a new dimen-sion." Noting the parallels with Austen's *Persuasion,* she added that "the theme of persuasion also gives the book an underlying seriousness, although naturally I hesitate to mention it. Bridget has no meddling Lady Russell to spoil her life [as Anne Elliot did in *Persuasion*], but she has the modern, comic equivalent which is, in its results, quite as bad–a set of loyal single mates (Jude and Shazzer), who are all addicted to 37 varieties of self-help books . . . and consider it their duty to gang up against any invading man from Mars."

Other reviewers have detected the same faults in *Bridget Jones* as they found in the earlier book, accusing it as presenting a young woman as needy, obsessed with getting a man, and not serious enough. Reviewing the book for the 2 December 1999 *Herald* (Glasgow), Lesley McDowell judged that the "longer, more absurd sequel has meant a thinly-spread, less realistic Bridget Jones, a sub–Peter Pan it's harder to believe in." In a 24 November 1999 review for *The Independent* (London), Louisa Young agreed that Bridget has not matured in the second novel, but wrote: "She's reassuring because even though she hasn't grown up, I have. I can look back and laugh. . . . And that is what Bridget Jones is for. . . . She's no role model—she never was."

Helen Fielding seems to have solved the problems attendant on following a well-received novel with a sequel. Presumably she can carry Bridget Jones on for as long as she wishes, but in interviews she continues to discuss her plans for the novel about the economic problems in the Caribbean and, more definitely, the movie version of Bridget Jones's diary. Having originally invented Bridget as a character about whom she wanted to write a sitcom, she has been involved in writing the script, though she now says that there are "quite a few" working on it.

Fielding is modest about her literary ambitions and secretive about her personal life. It is known that she is unmarried and lives in London. Whatever she does next, she must be recognized as having created one of the most original characters of the 1990s in British fiction and given voice to beliefs and feelings to which thousands of women have responded.

Interviews:

Lydia Slater, "Poignant, Funny, and Truthful," *Daily Telegraph* (London), 8 November 1997, p. 15;

Warren Hoge, "Bridget Jones? She's Any (Single) Woman, Anywhere," *New York Times,* 17 February 1998, p. E2;

Patti Thorn, "Dear Diary: Helen Fielding Ponders Success—and the One Question on Everyone's Mind," *Denver Rocky Mountain News,* 12 July 1998, p. 1E;

Maureen Dezell, "Eat, Drink, Diet: The Mind Behind 'Bridget Jones,'" *Boston Globe,* 26 October 1998, p. C7;

David Welch, "Powells.com Interviews: Helen Fielding," 3 June 1999, online, <http://www.powells.com/authors/fielding.html>;

"Are You Bridget Jones?" *Telegraph* (London), 20 November 1999, p. 20;

Ashton Applewhite, "A Conversation with Helen Fielding," in *Bridget Jones: The Edge of Reason: Reading Group Guide,* online, <www.penguinputnam.com>.

Reference:

Robert Yates, "The Observer Profile: Everywoman's Everywoman," *Observer* (London), review section, 31 May 1998, p. 20.

Tibor Fischer

(15 November 1959 –   )

Seán Matthews
University of California, Los Angeles

BOOKS: *Under the Frog: A Black Comedy* (Edinburgh: Polygon, 1992; New York: New Press, 1994);

The Thought Gang (Edinburgh: Polygon, 1994; New York: New Press, 1994);

The Collector Collector (London: Secker & Warburg, 1997; New York: Metropolitan, 1997);

Don't Read This Book If You're Stupid (London: Vintage, 2000); republished as *I Like Being Killed: Stories* (New York: Metropolitan, 2000).

OTHER: *Arc Short Stories Volume 9: An Anthology of Contemporary Writing,* edited by Fischer and Sarah Dunant (Lancashire, U.K.: ARC, 1998);

New Writing 8, edited by Fischer and Lawrence Norfolk (London: Vintage, 1999).

SELECTED PERIODICAL PUBLICATIONS–
UNCOLLECTED: "Hungary: The Self-Destruction of the Party," *Wall Street Journal,* 6 November 1989, p. A17;

"Listed for Trial," *Granta,* 43 (Spring 1993): 48–65;

"Top Ten Philosophical Hits," *Paris Review,* 134 (Spring 1995): 236–247.

Tibor Fischer, circa 1994

Tibor Fischer rose to prominence in 1992 with the publication of *Under the Frog: A Black Comedy.* Rejected by fifty-eight other publishers, the novel was finally accepted by a small Edinburgh firm, Polygon, and released to critical and popular acclaim. Honored with the Betty Trask Award for "new romantic fiction," it was the first debut novel to become a candidate for the Booker Prize, arguably the most prestigious of British literary awards. Although Roddy Doyle's *Paddy Clarke, Ha-Ha-Ha* (1993) was the eventual winner, Fischer moved to the critical forefront of contemporary British writing. Further recognition of the newcomer's promise came with his inclusion alongside such established figures as Hanif Kureishi, Kazuo Ishiguro, Will Self, and Jeanette Winterson in a controversial list of the twenty best "Young British Novelists" produced by the literary magazine *Granta* in spring 1993.

Fischer was thirty-three when *Under the Frog* was published. His parents, George and Margaret Fekete Fischer, both professional basketball players who had played on the national team, emigrated from their native Hungary to the United Kingdom after the Uprising of 1956. Tibor was born on 15 November 1959 in Stockport, near Manchester, and grew up in Bromley, South London. A bright student with a gift for languages, he graduated from Cambridge University, taking a degree in Latin and French, in 1980. He worked at various media jobs in television and newspapers, eventually becoming the Budapest correspondent for the *Daily Telegraph* (London) from 1988 to 1990. On returning from Budapest he turned to fiction and rapidly completed *Under the Frog,* but given the difficulties in finding a publisher, he continued to work in a series of temporary positions, including that of paralegal assistant, which provided material for the short stories

"Listed for Trial" (1993) and "Then They Say You're Drunk" (1995). Since the success of *Under the Frog,* however, Fischer has enjoyed literary prizes, best-seller status, and appointments as visiting writer in residence in Singapore and Iowa. With the recent appearance of the short story "Bookcruncher" in *TLS: The Times Literary Supplement* (1998) and the publication of the influential *New Writing 8* (1999), edited by Fischer and Lawrence Norfolk, his dramatic transformation from unknown outsider to established figure in the contemporary British literary world appears complete.

Under the Frog is an account of events in Hungary during the turbulent decade following World War II. Reminiscent of the bitterly funny tales of Milan Kundera, it reads as a late contribution to the Eastern European tradition of comic protest writing. The novel is identified on the flyleaf as a "black comedy," its title an allusion to a Hungarian expression for the worst place in the world to be—"under a frog's arse down a coal mine." Against the backdrop of a corrupt and collapsing Communist regime, the picaresque narrative centers on the adventures of two members of the perpetually touring National Railways basketball team, "The Locomotive." The players are Gyuri Fischer, journeyman player and class alien because of his bourgeois origins (his father, Elek, had failed in several business enterprises), and his friend and mentor, Pataki, star of the Locomotive, inveterate prankster, and prodigious womanizer. This improbable pair lurches through the decade shooting hoops, taunting authorities, chasing women, and continually, bitterly decrying the chaos and decay that surround them. Fischer relates their escapades with energy and relish, constructing along the way a rich vision of the difficulties and absurdities of life in postwar Hungary.

The narrative recounts a string of unlikely incidents, such as an eating contest in a remote peasant village between a Jesuit basketball star, Ladanyi, and a corrupt but indestructible party boss, Farago, the prize being the property rights to the area's vineyard. The diverse, and diverting, goings-on also include Pataki's naked sprint around the not-so-secret headquarters of the Secret Police to win a bet involving a Motoguzzi motorcycle and the Locomotive's most unpopular player; several ridiculous basketball games in exceptionally odd places against inferior opponents; and Gyuri's and Pataki's battles with, arrests by, and escapes from the superlatively incompetent Security Services. These events are interwoven with the historical traumas of two invasions by the Germans and the Russians, revolution and counterrevolution, and the notorious defeat by the West Germans of the previously victorious Hungarian national soccer team in the 1954 World Cup final: "Hungarians," Fischer remarks, "don't mind dictatorship, but they really hate losing a football match." The implausible private odysseys of Gyuri and Pataki are paralleled, Fischer suggests, by the impossible, calamitous, but equally repetitive absurdities of Hungarian history. As Gyuri's teacher points out, reproaching him for unfinished homework on his return to school after the siege of Budapest in 1944, "Fischer, Fischer, this is deplorable. You can't let a little war interfere with serious scholarship. You know our history. As a Hungarian you should be prepared for the odd cataclysm."

The coherence of *Under the Frog* in the face of such apparently incongruous material is ensured by the engaging qualities of Fischer's principal figures and by his own familiar, knowledgeable, and richly ironic voice; but it is sustained above all by his bleak yet affectionate appreciation of the Hungarian experience and spirit. Various Hungarian reviewers have attested to the linguistic and historical authenticity of the novel, and Fischer has explained that much of the work derives from stories told by his parents. Foremost among the Hungarian characteristics Fischer describes is exasperation, a recurrent refrain in the novel being the question "How much longer can this go on?" When Russian tanks enter Budapest in 1956 to crush the Uprising, Gyuri, hiding under the ruins of a statue of Josef Stalin as the invaders strafe the street, notices a figure across the road: "An old man embracing the pavement next to a tree, with his bag of shopping beside him, yards away from Gyuri, was protesting with amazing persistence and volume: 'Two world wars. *Two* world wars and now this.'"

From Fischer's comic perspective, however, the oppressive quality of communist totalitarianism in the postwar decade is not as upsetting to the populace as its tedium and incompetence:

> Dictatorship of the proletariat, apart from the abrasive and brutal nature of its despotism, was terribly dull. It wasn't the sort of tyranny you'd want to invite to a party. Look at the great tyrannies of antiquity: Caligula, Nero, now there was tyranny for you, excess, color, abundant fornication, stage management, excitement on the loose, *panem et circenses*. . . . Not only do I get a dictatorship, fumed Gyuri, but I get a tatty dictatorship, a third-rate, boring dictatorship.

Inevitably, given these conditions, a further theme of *Under the Frog* is the desire of many Hungarians to leave their homeland. While under arrest Gyuri observes that "the main difference between being in prison and out in Hungary . . . was that in prison there was less room." For Gyuri, the narrowing of the horizon attendant on the ban on travel, and its consequent effect on discovery and adventure, is most galling: "the simple absurdity of never having voyaged more than

Dust jacket for Fischer's first novel (1992), about a traveling basketball team in Hungary during the decade following World War II (courtesy of The Lilly Library, Indiana University, Bloomington, Indiana)

two hundred kilometers from the spot where he had bailed out of the womb rankled." In one of the many meditations on Hungarian literature scattered throughout the work, Fischer reinforces this motif with an approving comment on the work of Endre Ady, whose "most appealing theme" is the declaration that "the noblest prospect a Hungarian could see was the way out of Hungary."

Despite the predominant mood of farce in *Under the Frog,* one powerful quality of Fischer's writing is its register of the sadness and pathos appropriate to this nonetheless tragic history, often achieved through the use of startlingly judicious metaphors. Elek's resignation before his fate, for instance, is likened to "sitting in the back of adversity's big black car." In the final lines of the book, as Gyuri looks back to the border he has at last crossed, Fischer's description captures both

the exhilaration of escape and the disorienting sense of loss and grief: "Tears, in teams, abseiled down his face." The political critique may extend little beyond a blanket condemnation and ridicule of Hungarian totalitarianism, but the humor and humanity of the novel nonetheless render it a moving and enduring indictment of that state.

In subsequent writing Fischer has eschewed the profound emotional and political issues that invest *Under the Frog* with such poignancy. First published in *Granta* in 1993, the short story "Listed for Trial" is an affable exposé of the workings of the court system from the perspective of Guy, a temporary legal assistant, but amounts to little more than a set piece for Fischer's comic descriptions and anecdotes. "Then They Say You're Drunk," published in *New Writing 4* (1995), is a darker effort, again chronicling Guy's experience, but again the impression is of a writer attempting to avoid being pigeonholed or taken too seriously. Both of these short stories are included in Fischer's collection, *Don't Read This Book If You're Stupid* (2000), published in the United States as *I Like Being Killed: Stories.*

In *The Thought Gang* (1994) Fischer also keeps away from serious themes, crafting instead a rather straightforward, if ingenious, caper novel. The other distinctive features of Fischer's writing—breadth of vocabulary, impressive erudition, and bravuru experiments with form—are otherwise in place. He also, quite randomly, uses as many words beginning with "z" as possible. However, as the author suggests in his own teasing description of the work—"a short book about all human knowledge and experience"—the scope and ambition of this piece are clearly much removed from those of *Under the Frog.*

Eddie Coffin, bank robber, lover of the good life, and sometime Cambridge University lecturer in philosophy, is the narrator of *The Thought Gang.* Unreliable in the extreme in most personal and professional capacities, Coffin's excesses of drugs, alcohol, and fornication, paid for through "prolonged and messy embezzlement" from a Japanese research foundation, have finally resulted in his expulsion from academia. Fleeing the British police to the South of France with the expectation of drinking and eating himself into oblivion, Coffin suffers a series of misfortunes, leaving him broke, subject to inquiries by the French constabulary, and newly partnered with a one-eyed, one-armed, one-legged, and psychotic bandit named Hubert. Fresh from jail, Hubert decides that Coffin will educate him in the niceties of philosophy, and Hubert will reciprocate by training Coffin in bank robbery. The unlikely duo's sudden and phenomenal success generates immediate attention from the media, the police, and a multitude of violent underworld characters. The robbers are christened "the

Thought Gang" because of the ostentatiously cerebral nature of their robberies.

The central conceit of *The Thought Gang* is thus the comic aptness of this manic conjunction of philosophy and bank robbery. For Coffin, certainly, there is little to choose between the two; both are forms of swindle. His career as a philosopher is premised upon sciolism, deceit, and not being found out; his pedagogic specialty is the Ionian School, about which he confesses, "Very few people realize that you can read the entire extant oeuvre of the Ionians, slowly and carefully, in an hour. Most of them come in handy packets of adages." Such a statement is, typically enough, an exaggeration, since none of the work of the pre-Socratics has in fact survived independently. In any case, since the defining feature of Coffin's academic career has been larceny on a grand scale, the transition from philosophy to bank robbery is morally and spiritually unproblematic and distinguished by a carefree application of diverse philosophical principles to the art of the heist. The scenario gives Fischer license for many paradoxes and weighty allusions. Coffin, for example, maintains that "bank robbery, if philosophically carried out, harms no one. We thrill. We entertain. We stimulate the economy. We race hearts. We provoke thought. And, unquestionably, bank robbery is an illusion. You take it out but where does it end up? In a bank. Like water, money is trapped in a cycle, it moves from bank to bank. We take it out for some fresh air."

Not all the philosophical interventions, however, are so finely turned. Reflecting upon the Nietzschean dictum "What does not kill me makes me strong," Coffin affirms, "The trouble with Nietzsche—who in any case never prescribed instructions regarding conduct while being handcuffed on chilly floors in undignified circumstances—is that you can never be sure when he's doing some levity or not." Each of the many robberies is leavened with a "philosophical" ingredient, ranging from Stoicism ("Stay very calm") to positivism ("Yes, I'm positive I want to rob this bank") to Cynicism ("Goods aren't good. Money isn't necessary—so put it in this bag") and even to neo-Platonism ("You'll have to pay close attention if you want to tell the difference between this and a Platonic job"). Along the way the Thought Gang invents the "getaway lunch," takes a "getaway train," and executes crimes of exponentially increasing difficulty and eccentricity. As the novel races to its conclusion—a heavily publicized "retirement" robbery to which public and police are invited—Coffin's world-weariness, cynicism, and discontent are eventually transformed into "something that if it's not optimism, would be hard to tell apart."

In *The Thought Gang* as in *Under the Frog*, Fischer revels in the unsettling of conventional narrative expectations. There is something of Laurence Sterne's *Tris-tram Shandy* (1759–1767) in the endlessly disrupted, convoluted, and never less than frenetic progress of the tale, but perhaps a more apt and illuminating point of reference is the 1925 Loeb edition of *Lives of Eminent Philosophers*, by third-century B.C. Greek writer Diogenes Laertius, to which Fischer makes repeated reference. This short work, a curious compendium of anecdotes, biographical tidbits, potted thought, and undigested plagiarism, is by dint of its endurance a key text in the understanding of the Ionians and provides a suitably obscure model for Coffin's intellectual and criminal odyssey. "The insertion of extraneous matter which disturbs the context is a too common fault," remarks R. D. Hicks, editor and translator of the Loeb edition. He continues, "The main narrative followed may suffer or be in part effaced by the intrusion of untrustworthy or inconsistent material." Such a description fairly characterizes *The Thought Gang*, a work that frequently digresses even from its digressions within a parodic framework of academic orderliness, offering headings and subheadings, such as "Pass the past 1.1"; "Boozology"; and "The profundity cupboard is bare." *Lives of Eminent Philosophers*, which, as Hicks notes, gains its "air of erudition" only by virtue of the material it borrows from previous sources, is an appropriate source of inspiration for Coffin, whose only publications derive from a manuscript stolen from a dead colleague and a monograph written on his behalf by an exasperated editor. The formal achievement of *The Thought Gang* is thus to sustain an atmosphere of chaotic fraudulence within a structure that consistently implies systematic, if recondite, intellectual order.

The popular and critical responses to *The Thought Gang* were largely equivocal. The book has sold well and was awarded the Critics' Choice Award in the United States, and there are indications that it has developed a cult readership. Many critics, however, have expressed reservations about Fischer's development as a writer. Although David Ulin, writing in *The Nation* (10 July 1995), praised the "unique structure" of the novel and found the integration of "pages and pages" of philosophy into a comic caper novel an "exhilarating" success, others were less sure. Nick Hornby, progenitor of the "new lad" school of British fiction, to which *The Thought Gang* certainly belongs, found the novel to be "an engaging piece of whimsy looking for justification" and judged it would represent only "a footnote to a long and noteworthy literary career." Writing in *The New Yorker* (21 August 1995), John Updike, more emphatically, found the novel disappointing, serving as "a textbook example of an author outsmarting himself."

The Collector Collector (1997) is a comic escapade fashioned from still flimsier and more fantastic stuff than

Dust jacket for Fischer's 1997 novel, narrated by
an ancient, sentient, telepathic bowl

its predecessors. The narrator is an ancient, garrulous bowl with the capacity to observe and catalogue its surroundings. Over a period of 6,500 years it has passed through the hands of some 10,462 collectors (as in *The Thought Gang,* lists and ledgers loom large) and therefore has an extensive stock of anecdotes, historical trivia, and wisdom to impart. In addition, the bowl occasionally changes shape to shock, scare, or confuse people: "There are few things as scary as turning around to find an eight-foot-high amphora behind you when there wasn't one before, especially when that amphora is making faces at you. Most people foul themselves and find it hard to trust reality and relax after that. Once every three hundred years or so I treat myself."

Lodged temporarily with Rosa, an antiques authenticator, the bowl is witness to a typical Fischer blend of bizarre and grotesque events, lavishly seasoned with bawdry. Rosa's kleptomaniacal, sex-addicted houseguest Nikki, who is on the run

from her sexual and proprietary victims, systematically loots her hostess's home and eventually succeeds in selling the apartment itself. Rosa fails to notice this process, distracted as she is by her fascination with the bowl—she discovers that she possesses the power to read the bowl's mind—and by her long and desperate quest for a soulmate (to which end she keeps a kidnapped advice columnist down a well). Among the customary crew of freakish minor characters—whose largely unconnected stories, along with the bowl's reminiscences, provide the bulk of the novel—are Nikki's almost-indestructible guardian angel, Lump; a car thief who meticulously cleans and returns the vehicles he steals; a garrulous assassin called the Annihilator; and a traveling mummy-vendor called Wondernose. There is also a leitmotif concerning frozen iguanas.

As even a brief description suggests, *The Collector Collector* displays once more the fertility of Fischer's imagination and his affection for the surreal. Among the bowl's tales are several wonderfully crafted pieces, and the gradual unfolding of Rosa's personality shows a skill in the development of character that recalls the evocation of Gyuri in *Under the Frog.* The work is largely concocted of slapstick violence and even more slapstick sex, however; the main story consists of little else, and despite the wonderful range of the bowl's experience and its skill as a raconteur, it too seems obsessed with the lowest common denominators of narrative. Moreover, Fischer subjects the reader to a bout of copulation every few pages, some episodes of extreme sexual violence, and a wearisome vocabulary of euphemisms for sex, including *nuking, tapping,* a *florida,* the *ooooo machine,* and the *cryselephantine.* There may be a trace of Boccaccio or Rabelais in this relish for the earthy fundamentals of life, but the obsessive, adolescent level of this strand of Fischer's writing is ultimately disappointing, even disturbing.

As in *The Thought Gang,* there is nevertheless in *The Collector Collector* some evidence of the creative range that first brought Fischer to prominence. The narrative is as convoluted but as crisply controlled as ever, and there are moments when Fischer shows that his enviable facility with words is not simply superficial or salacious. When Rosa sadly rebuffs her friend's request for advice, for instance, Fischer uses her speech deftly to expand on an earlier, unexplained leitmotif: "I'm not sure there's anything you can do to help anyone. I'm not sure you can even help yourself. I saw a squirrel today jumping from one tree to another, the branch it landed on snapped. So the squirrel was on this falling branch, clambering like mad, thinking it was doing something about it."

This theme of disappointment, of life as a frenzy of wasted effort, runs throughout the book, providing some counterpoint to the japes and tomfoolery. "People lose everything, the thing they can't lose is loss"; collecting is really about "the loss of loss. Ending ending." Despite such elements, however, the overall effect of *The Collector Collector* is, to an extent even greater than in *The Thought Gang,* ultimately one of extravagance, even excess; too often the novel veers more to the tedious than the hilarious. In a charitable assessment, Phil Baker for *TLS* (7 March 1997) summed up the novel as "a book which shows flashes of brilliance and underdeveloped nods at serious themes, but which more often irritates."

Fischer's latest fiction continues to treat the comic, encyclopedic, but generally slight concerns that characterize *The Thought Gang* and *The Collector Collector.* "Bookcruncher," a short story accorded the rare honor of publication in *TLS,* is, once more, the first-person narrative of a gifted and intellectual eccentric, on this occasion an unnamed bibliophile pursuing a quest to read, in chronological order, all the books ever published in English (he has reached the mid 1880s). The protagonist haunts bookshops and libraries, hiding among the book stacks at night to continue his lonely labor. This conceit permits Fischer's imagination to range in the archives of the obscure, abstruse, and arcane, with references, for example, to R. D. Blackmore's *The Remarkable History of Sir Thomas Upmore, Bart., M.P.* (1884) or Mrs. Henry Wood's *The Story of Charles Strange: A Novel* (1897), pulp novels of the late nineteenth century. Fischer seems largely bereft of ways to justify his character's preoccupation: "He had never explained his mission to anyone, because he didn't want anyone to know if he failed, and because he wasn't sure what the point was. He sensed there was an answer at the end, but he had no idea what he would do with it. Perhaps he would write something original. After all how can you be sure you're writing something original if you haven't read anything before?"

The traits characteristic of Fischer's writing are all in place: a disjointed narrative, sequences of repetitions, an insistent, bitter wit, and the preoccupation with sex, especially its oddness. Particularly in comparison with his previous writing, however, the aphoristic and fragmentary qualities of "Bookcruncher" give the effect of hectoring strung along a slender strand of story:

What had he learned so far? Motion looks like progress. German bookshops had champagne, but only in American bookshops could you get frappachino. And hope. Hope. Books were made of hope, not paper. Hope that someone would read your book; that it would change the world or improve it; hope that people would agree with you, hope that people might believe you; hope that you'll be remembered, celebrated, hope that people would feel something. Hope that you would learn something; hope that you'll entertain or impress; hope you'll catch some cash; hope that you'll be proved right and hope that you'll be proved wrong.

Gloom and a persistent strain of misanthropy, allied with a profound misogyny, are evident beneath the frolic in all Fischer's writing, and these traits become more explicit with each work, even as the comic conceits become more superficially extreme. Fischer himself seems to be feeling the limitations of the forms and voices with which he is working.

The dilemma that confronts him, and many of the British writers of his generation, is made explicit in the introduction to *New Writing 8.* This volume, a collection of short stories, novel excerpts, poems, and essays, offers "a 'snapshot' of what has happened in British literature over a one-year period." Commenting on the effort to include "work from both margins of the literary spectrum, namely experimental and mass-market writing," Fischer and Norfolk remark: "The former is normally admired in theory and ignored in practice; the latter is read avidly and yet denigrated by critics who are impotent in the face of its appeal to ordinary readers. The habitual exclusion of either or both from venues of this kind rests on a complacent stigmatization of familiar forms as 'too easy' and unfamiliar ones as 'too difficult.'" In many ways, the effort to overcome this dichotomy is evident throughout Fischer's work. His own experiments with form and generous erudition are nevertheless accessible to a popular audience.

Fischer's career is in many ways a parable of British fiction in the 1990s. Prodigiously talented, with remarkable erudition, technical facility, and inventiveness, he has swiftly become an established figure, but he appears to have exhausted, or refused, the greater range of human themes that distinguished *Under the Frog.* His subsequent works seem to indicate that the horizons of his imagination have contracted to a narrow space of libidinous whimsy.

Interviews:

Cliff Taylor, "The Fischer King," *Spike Magazine* (March 1997) <www.spikemagazine.com/0397fish.htm>;

Gerd Bayer, "I'm very keen on tea and Shakespeare": An Interview with Tibor Fischer," Erlangen Centre for Contemporary English Literature (September 1997) <www.ph-erfurt.de/~neumann/eese/artic97/bayer/9_97.html>.

Reference:

John Updike, "Novel Thoughts," *The New Yorker* (21 August 1995): 105–114.

Jane Gardam
(11 July 1928 –   )

Graeme Harper
University of Wales, Bangor

See also the Gardam entries in *DLB 14: British Novelists Since 1960* and *DLB 161: British Children's Writers Since 1960*.

BOOKS: *A Few Fair Days* (London: Hamilton, 1971; New York: Macmillan, 1972);

A Long Way from Verona (London: Hamilton, 1971; New York: Macmillan, 1971);

The Summer after the Funeral (London: Hamilton, 1973; New York: Macmillan, 1973);

Black Faces, White Faces (London: Hamilton, 1975); republished as *The Pineapple Bay Hotel* (New York: Morrow, 1976);

Bilgewater (London: Hamilton, 1976; New York: Greenwillow, 1977);

God on the Rocks (London: Hamilton, 1978; New York: Morrow, 1979);

The Sidmouth Letters (London: Hamilton, 1980; New York: Morrow, 1980);

Bridget and William (London & New York: MacRae, 1981); republished with *Horse* as *Black Woolly Pony, White Chalk Horse* (London: Walker, 1993);

The Hollow Land (London: MacRae, 1981; New York: Greenwillow, 1981);

Horse (London & New York: MacRae, 1982); republished with *Bridget and William* as *Black Woolly Pony, White Chalk Horse;*

Kit (London & New York: MacRae, 1983);

The Pangs of Love and Other Stories (London: Hamilton, 1983);

Crusoe's Daughter (London: Hamilton, 1985; New York: Atheneum, 1986);

Kit in Boots (London: MacRae, 1986);

Through the Dolls' House Door (London: MacRae, 1987; New York: Greenwillow, 1987);

Swan (London: MacRae, 1987);

Showing the Flag and Other Stories (London: Hamilton, 1989);

The Queen of the Tambourine (London: Sinclair-Stevenson, 1991; New York: St. Martin's Press, 1995);

Jane Gardam (photograph © Gary Ede; from the dust jacket for the American edition of Bilgewater, *1977)*

Trio: Three Short Stories from Cheltenham, by Gardam, Rose Tremain, and William Trevor (London & New York: Penguin, 1993);

Going into a Dark House and Other Stories (London: Sinclair-Stevenson, 1994);

The Iron Coast: Notes from a Cold Country, with photographs by Peter Burton and Harland Walshaw (London: Sinclair-Stevenson, 1994);

Tufty Bear (London: Walker, 1996);

Faith Fox: A Nativity (London: Sinclair-Stevenson, 1996);
Missing the Midnight: Hauntings & Grotesques (London: Sinclair-Stevenson, 1997);
The Green Man: An Eternity (Moreton-in-Marsh, U.K.: Windrush, 1998).
Edition: *The Kit Stories* (London: Walker, 1998).

Jane Gardam began her first novel, *A Few Fair Days* (1971), on the day her youngest son began school. She was thirty-nine years of age. Since then she has shown herself to be a writer of economy, humor, and empathy. Gardam writes both for adults and for children, moving effortlessly between these two readerships, and seems to find her own fascination with the theme of childhood a useful bridge between the two. Indeed, childhood not only has featured as one of her principal fictional themes, but she has also treated the subject in her illustrated nonfiction work, *The Iron Coast: Notes from a Cold Country,* published in 1994. She has won several prestigious literary awards, including the Whitbread Award (twice), the Katherine Mansfield Prize, the David Higham Prize for Fiction, the Winifred Holtby Memorial Prize, and the Macmillan Silver Pen Award, and was short-listed for the Booker Prize for *God on the Rocks* (1978).

Gardam became the center of controversy when it was reported that she had successfully blocked the Whitbread Award being given to Alexander Stuart's *The War Zone* (1989), despite the fact that Stuart had already been told that he had won the prize. She was motivated to act because of her concerns about Stuart's treatment of incest in the novel. Ordinarily, however, she is not a writer to seek out or provoke attention. Her writing is quiet, wry, sometimes pleasantly anarchic, and unsentimental but emotive: writing in which things are often slightly askew or hidden beneath the surface of otherwise unassuming narrative. She is also recognized as a writer with an exceptional ability for characterization.

Jane Gardam was born Jean Mary Pearson on 11 July 1928 in the small town of Coatham in North Yorkshire. She was the eldest child of William and Kathleen Pearson. Her mother's family, the de Bulmers, had lived in North Yorkshire for hundreds of years. Her father was a schoolteacher who had come to teach at Sir William Turner's school, where the headmaster's aim was to create an English public school, "the Eton of the north." William Pearson remained at the school for forty-seven years. Jane Pearson grew up in Coatham, a place Gardam has recalled as a middle-class seaside resort, said to be Lewis Carroll's inspiration for "The Walrus and the Carpenter." She holidayed with her parents at Thornby End, her father's parents' farm in West Cumberland, on the edge of the Lake District. These

environments have had considerable influence on her fiction. In *God on the Rocks,* for example, the action takes place largely in a prim seaside town between the wars. In *Faith Fox: A Nativity* (1996) a motherless child is ferried away from the gin drinking and bridge playing of Surrey to a windblown Yorkshire religious retreat.

Pearson left Yorkshire in 1946 to take up a scholarship to read English at what was then Bedford College for Women, University of London. She stayed on to do postgraduate study. Many of the other students were former servicewomen. Some had been prisoners of war in various parts of the world. Others were young Englishwomen from colonial settlements in Malaysia and Singapore or Jews who had escaped Nazi Germany and Austria. The plight of this last group is echoed in *Crusoe's Daughter* (1985), which is equally about Gardam's mother and the world of the author's childhood.

When Pearson's small postgraduate grant ran out, she worked part-time for two years as a traveling librarian with the Red Cross hospital libraries. She then became an editorial assistant on *Weldon's Ladies Journal* from 1952 to 1953 but was fired because she was unable to take the articles on various domestic arts seriously. She worked for a short time for the poet Geoffrey Grigson and then, for two years, was assistant literary editor of the weekly *Time and Tide.* John Betjeman, who was the literary adviser, she remembers with notable affection.

In addition to the settings and characters of her childhood and early adulthood, Gardam has drawn on the locations she visited with her husband, the Queen's counsel and international lawyer David Gardam, whom she married in 1952. She has traveled to such places as Bangladesh, Java, Hong Kong, Singapore, and Malaysia, settings that find their way into her work. *Black Faces, White Faces* (1975), for example, a series of interlocking stories set in Jamaica, came about after Gardam's husband conducted a case that she describes as being about "a giant drain." In an affectionate gesture to the drain, called Sandy Gully, Gardam dedicated the book to "S. Gully."

The manuscript of Jane Gardam's first novel, *A Few Fair Days,* sat for three months on a pile of unsolicited manuscripts in the children's division of publisher Hamish Hamilton. Gardam has claimed to have not really thought of whether the novel was for children but averred that she may have labeled it for the "Children's Department." This simple fact neatly reflects her belief in the universality of the theme of childhood, a theme that likewise strongly drives her second novel, *A Long Way from Verona* (1971), and recurs throughout her oeuvre.

Cover for Gardam's first novel (1971), about a girl's childhood
"in the farthest part of the north of Yorkshire"

A Few Fair Days follows the story of Lucy, who "lived not so many years ago in a small cold town by the sea in the farthest part of the north of Yorkshire" from the time she is five years old until she is eleven. Rather than allow the adult perspective to overpower the child's viewpoint, Gardam utilizes brevity and economy of language to reflect the unadorned fascination and charm of a child. The novel comprises a series of episodes in Lucy's life, from wandering unescorted on the beach to watching the sunrise with friends. The title of the book also refers to a type of sponge cake, called "fair days" by a baker in the district where Lucy is growing up. This play on words reflects Lucy's childhood pleasures as well as Gardam's often-declared love of language. *A Few Fair Days* is a novel of education or, more accurately, schooling and, in that at least, closely resembles *A Long Way from Verona*.

Jessica Vye, the narrator of *A Long Way from Verona,* is thoroughly caught up in her adolescent world, in which discovering the uses and possibilities of language is tantamount to discovering the truth about herself. Her voice is colloquial but cultured, naively inquisitive but undoubtedly intelligent. Her love of the unusual and outlandish, and the liveliness and brightness of her imagination, help Jessica to take in stride both her difference from others and the austerity of wartime Britain. She is a character who owes much to Gardam's own history, not least because her search for identity is substantially tied up in her ambition to become a writer: "I am not, I am glad to say, mad, and there is so far as I know no hereditary madness in my family. The thing that sets me apart from other girls of my age—which is to say thirteen—is that when I was nine a man came to our school—it was a private kindergarten sort of school where you could go from five upwards but most girls left when they were eleven unless they were really stupendously dumb—to talk to us about becoming writers."

Jessica's voice is identifiably that of a middle-class, privileged child who, despite the war, is able to spend time arguing about the quality of literature she is asked to read and to turn a school assignment into a forty-seven-page flight of the imagination. When she is punished for turning her essay into a "story," she begins to form a bond with old Miss Philemon, the senior schoolmistress, an Oxford graduate from the days "when the only girls who went to Oxford were those who could take their mothers and aunts with them to take care of them." Miss Philemon suggests that Jessica's teacher might have made a mistake, but she also puts forward the idea that it does writers no harm to suffer. This comment contextualizes both the personal adolescent trauma that Jessica is experiencing and, with considerable alacrity, the general circumstances of suffering in wartime Britain. It also gives credence to Jessica's writerly ambitions. Miss Philemon is later killed when a crashing English plane unloads a bomb on her flat. Not unexpectedly, Jessica is unable to speak about the event. Gardam is able, through her careful and unadorned establishment of character, to present both Miss Philemon's death and Jessica's reaction without recourse to melodrama.

A Long Way from Verona also highlights Gardam's exceptional comic talents, particularly her ability to find humor in the off-kilter or quirky. The humor in the novel is situated in the gradual formation of Jessica's undoubtedly forthright personality and in her coming to understand the eccentricities of some of the adults who surround her. These eccentricities help to enable them to live in what frequently appears to be a contradictory, bewildering world. Expressions like "very peculiar" and "the curious thing is" occur throughout the novel and leave no doubt that Gardam wishes her readers to join in the narrator's questioning. In this fashion the reader is asked to abandon a privileged, informed position and to consider character and events from a viewpoint of innocence. The question of whether the novel is intended for children or adults rests on one's conception of at what point innocence ends. Gardam effectively addresses this issue in *A Long Way from Verona* and in its successor, *The Summer after the Funeral* (1973).

In *The Summer after the Funeral* sixteen-year-old Athene Price, whose father, an aged rector, has died, is sent to live with relatives and friends in the north of England—familiar Gardam territory. Yet, Athene—who, as her name suggests, is beautiful and resourceful—is the first of Gardam's heroines to relate her geographic displacement to the displacement associated with burgeoning adulthood. Forced to abandon her disciplined habits, Athene must deal with her guilt (because she always believed her father was too old) and her insecu-

rity. She is, in these terms, a character searching for her own definition of moral integrity within a seemingly unfathomable world of alternatives. The novel stresses the religious connotations of this search.

The Summer after the Funeral is a romance that uses both the environment and Athene's beauty to evoke strongly the spirit of Emily Brontë's *Wuthering Heights* (1847). Gardam's use of the romance mode, however, is not restricted to the surface level of the text. *The Summer after the Funeral* also describes a quest to define the relationship between the physical and the metaphysical or, to put it another way, the relationship between the world of objects and people and the world of feelings, emotions, and memories.

Athene receives as part of her father's estate a crucifix and a rope ladder, objects that are at once unlikely and provocative. The crucifix is representative of Athene's father and of the world beyond the physical, the world of divine passion. The rope ladder is utilitarian, belonging to the physical world of mundane practicality and necessity. Together they represent the spheres of influence Athene must decide between. Such is Athene's rapid movement between one household and the next, one individual and another (from Aunt Posie to Miss Bowles to Auntie Boo), that the opportunities to make decisions about her feelings are often fleeting. Her lodgings prove inhospitable, and people are difficult and unpredictable. Primrose Clark, for example, is nosy and presumptuous, and Mrs. Messenger is impertinent. The rapidly changing circumstances of Athene's life, it is made clear, are the products of a fortuitousness that, if not divine, is at least extraordinary.

The anarchic events of *The Summer after the Funeral* reflect Athene's confusion. Whereas Jessica Vye can fall back on her ambition to become a writer, Athene is defined by how she deals with her insecurity following her father's death, with her lack of fixed place, and, most significantly, with her beauty. When Primose Clark discovers Athene at Haworth with the married schoolmaster, Henry Bell, the young man flees. The incident is more than a lost romantic opportunity, because it provokes in Athene a confusion of the relationship between the burgeoning physical desires of adulthood and spiritual maturation. Gardam adeptly locates the girl's spiritual awakening in the discovery of understanding through both the literary and mythological traditions of the romance, a component of which is the ability to conceptualize true beauty. In Gardam's fiction, beauty is located sometimes in the act of writing itself, which is viewed as an act of honest individual engagement with the world; sometimes in landscape, which is taken to be the substance of memory and the foregrounding of family and relationships; and sometimes in individuals such as Athene, who are embodiments of goodness and are frequently youthful. This juxtaposition of youth and death is one of Gardam's central concerns.

Similarly, youth, beauty, and death are at the thematic heart of Gardam's next novel, *Bilgewater* (1976). In this novel "Bilgewater," whose mother died giving birth to her, comes to terms with maturing into an attractive adolescent. The epigraph of the novel is a pair of quotes, one from Benjamin Disraeli–"Youth is a blunder"–and the other from Tom Stoppard's *Rosencrantz and Guildenstern Are Dead* (1966): "Now–counter to the previous syllogism: tricky one, follow me carefully, it may prove a comfort?" The battle lines are thus neatly drawn.

Prior to *Bilgewater,* Gardam published a prizewinning collection of short stories, *Black Faces, White Faces,* which effectively moved her into the adult-fiction market. Published in the United States as *The Pineapple Bay Hotel* (1976), the collection includes ten relatively brief short stories. In the opening story, "Babe Jude," a chance encounter leads to a clash of cultures when Mrs. Filling, a middle-class Englishwoman visiting the Caribbean, is confronted with characters from the multicultural heritage of Jamaica. "Missus Moon" concerns the relationship between eight-year-old Ned and Missus Moon, "who would be a hundred years old shortly." Ned witnesses a funeral, which he takes to be that of Missus Moon's father but is actually for her husband. "Missus Moon" considers the nature of awareness and moves provocatively between self-awareness and awareness of one's surroundings. In "The First Declension" a wife who has stayed home while her husband visits Cuba is alarmed when letters arrive making much of what he has found there and the things he is doing. The story shows orderliness in conflict with adventure. In "The Weeping Child" Mrs. Ingham, "a big woman with a large jaw and determined mouth," visits her daughter in Jamaica. Her biannual visits turn into exchanges between the old and new, one generation and another. Her daughter, in one of Gardam's straightforward autobiographical references, is the wife of a lawyer.

Black Faces, White Faces won the David Higham Prize for Fiction and the Winifred Holtby Prize of the Royal Society of Literature. Gardam's other short-story collections, including *The Sidmouth Letters* (1980), *The Pangs of Love and Other Stories* (1983), *Showing the Flag and Other Stories* (1989), *Going into a Dark House and Other Stories* (1994), and *Missing the Midnight: Hauntings & Grotesques* (1997), have also been greeted with considerable acclaim. It has been said that while Gardam's novels are sometimes uneven, her short fiction always manages to fit subject matter and form perfectly together. In

Black Faces, White Faces, the stories in which are interlocked by shared characters and setting, the themes of cultural and social dislocation, old age, youth, and beauty are reinforced by the naturalness of the movement from one story to the next. The collection balances humor and tragedy subtly, as, for example, in "The House above Newcastle," in which Pussy Fielding's repeated declarations of tiredness keep her new husband at bay until an auto accident encourages them to express themselves more openly; and in "Something to Tell the Girls," in which two old schoolteachers, Miss Dee-Dee and Miss Gongers, save themselves from a band of aggressive local children by calling on their skill at telling stories and leading songs.

In *The Sidmouth Letters,* her second collection of stories, Gardam's talent for mimicry becomes apparent, particularly in such stories as "The Great, Grand Soap-Water Kick," "The Tribute," and "The Sidmouth Letters" (the latter two having been made into plays for television). The title story of the collection depicts the search for two love letters supposedly written by Jane Austen in 1801. The searcher is an American academic who specializes in exposing moral flaws in the great. As with her use of *Wuthering Heights* as a conceptional framework for *The Summer after the Funeral,* Gardam does more than link Austen and her own story; she uses the story to explore the nature of Austen's particular literary heritage. Not surprisingly for a Gardam story, in "The Sidmouth Letters" the heroine (who is a novelist) does not allow the denigration of the "sacred" letters. At the conclusion of the story she declares: "I burned both envelopes and both letters with my cigarette lighter." Preserving memory is not necessarily a question of plain truth, nor of fairness. It is part of the heroine's–that is, of the novelist's–spiritual integrity.

The Hollow Land, published in 1981, is a collection of linked stories for children set largely around Light Trees Farm and the Cumbrian fells country, though adult readers may also appreciate the frequently wry observations of the child characters. The opening episode, narrated by eight-year-old Bell Teesdale, is about the many farmhouses around the dales that are derelict because they are too old or too high for modern farmers. They remain as homes only to birds and sheep until they are bought up by holidaymakers tired of the Lake District.

The Bateman family, who are central to *The Hollow Land,* rents the farmhouse known as Light Trees. At first the Batemans and the Teesdales seem destined to be in conflict, clashing in the way of local country residents and out-of-town visitors; with the intervention of Bell and young Harry Bateman (who become firm friends), however, an alliance between the two families is established. The book then becomes a series of thematic anecdotes based on the annual migration of the Batemans to Light Trees. Some of these anecdotes are founded on simple pleasures: wonder at the blaze of summer country colors, the "pink-yellow" meadows, the Celtic settlements of the Cumbrian fells, and the secret streams that lead into hills and uplands. Others take on a supernatural or mythical quality. "Used to be vampires up yonder," Bell declares at one point, registering both her childish perspective and her sense of supernatural history. In a similar vein, when Mrs. Batemen steps outside in her flannel nightdress and antique apron she is mistaken for a ghost. People as well as landscapes, Gardam suggests, can have spiritual dimensions.

The Hollow Land moves in time from the early 1980s through to the end of the twentieth century. It uses the 1999 total eclipse of the sun as the conceit around which the concluding story, "Tomorrow's Arrangements," revolves. In this story the Bateman family is threatened with the loss of Light Trees. The juxtaposition of the eclipse and an "ecliptic event" is a powerful one, reinforcing Gardam's thematic interest in the importance of place.

Kit, published in 1983 and illustrated by William Geldart, is, like *The Hollow Land,* also a children's story with a farm setting. Kit, whose real name is Catherine, begins the novel as a "kittenish" child liable to cry over anything but ends resourceful and courageous, even coping with a rampaging farm bull. Gardam's plot here is certainly no innovation; however, she produces fine descriptions of the pleasures and privations of farmstead life and the language of a rural community. Alan Brownjohn, writing in *TLS: The Times Literary Supplement* (10 February 1984), noted that *Kit* was a book in which "the best . . . has been in the richness and humour of its evocation of existence in the high, wet farmstead which is quietly suggested in William Geldart's excellent illustrations."

Published in the same year as *Kit, The Pangs of Love and Other Stories* was received with a more mixed reaction. While some reviewers acknowledged that the work shows Gardam's usual strengths—the matching of poignant observation and fine character detail with steady, engaging plots—Anne Duchene in the 11 February 1983 *Times* (London) suggested that "the reader may come to the conclusion that she has been traveling too much. Too many time-zones, too many time-tables, too many dazzling, exhausting, exotic *locales* outside too many air-conditioned hotels, have begun to parch her roots."

The stories in *The Pangs of Love* range from those set in India and Hong Kong to those that move between locations, such as "Stone Trees," which concerns itself with the need for the regeneration that movement can

Jane Gardam, circa 1985 (photograph © Jerry Bauer; from the dust jacket for the American edition of Crusoe's Daughter*)*

provide (in this case between Cambridge, England, and Sacramento). In one sense this regeneration is literal, provided by the shifting tides that wash over the fossilized trees lying in the shallow water surrounding the Isle of Wight. Gardam's intention is also metaphoric, however. She is suggesting that movement, the regular "changing of water," is necessary in order to find real, "unfossilized" life.

The movement Gardam is talking about in *The Pangs of Love* is the movement of the traveler or tourist. Gardam is an inveterate traveler and has written of being inspired in her youth by a "globe-trotting aunt," a fact that becomes even more poignant considered alongside *Crusoe's Daughter,* her next adult novel, in which two elderly aunts, "bleak Miss Mary" and "gentle Miss Francis," live isolated lives and pass this isolation on to their young niece like an inheritance. The title story of *The Pangs of Love* is about the younger sister of Hans Christian Andersen's little mermaid. She lures her dead sister's prince below the sea, but he refuses to exchange his legs for fins and returns to the surface world, "arriving home in time for tea and early sherry with his wife, who was much relieved."

The coast and its sea also feature strongly in *Crusoe's Daughter.* Gardam has recalled that the landscape of the novel "is my mother's landscape; the novel is partly about my mother, who was never able to leave it for a fuller life and yet lived more influentially to her family, it seems to me, than any paid-up feminist." Gardam's uneasy relationship with contemporary feminism speaks not only of her refusal to follow political fashion and of what has sometimes been seen as a commitment to old-fashioned values, but also of a wider interest in the interior lives of people, regardless of gender. In this regard she has often been compared to Katherine Mansfield: an explorer of character and circumstance who refuses to fix perception but instead leaves the reader with the sense of never being quite able to hold down an uncomplicated sense of self or a simply defined political position. In "The Pangs of Love," for example, the prince's return to the surface both confirms his heart's real desires and leaves no doubt about his class position. He is, nevertheless, an adventurous and loving man. Characters in Gardam's fiction are not charged with holistic political values; rather, they are the vivid embodiment of frequently paradoxical psychological states, clinging together under longstanding cultural conditions.

In 1904 Polly Flint, the protagonist in *Crusoe's Daughter,* goes to live with two old aunts in a yellow house by the marsh, a house so close to the water that it seems to toss like a ship. Polly is someone, as Katy Emck wrote in *TLS* (31 May 1985), "who says 'Angels, how ridiculous,' but sits down to dinner with them anyway." Two months later her father dies "on the bridge of his ship in the Irish Sea, on the coal-run to Belfast." The isolation Polly subsequently encounters is much like the isolation Robinson Crusoe felt on his island; not unexpectedly, Daniel Defoe's 1719 novel soon forms as much a part of Polly's character as the circumstances of her upbringing. She is particularly drawn to its juxtaposition of good and evil, its attempt to set things straight and, she notes, be hopeful. Gradually, *Robinson Crusoe* becomes both part of Polly's private knowledge and part of her growth into selfhood. "As I walked the well-known mile," she observes later in the novel, "waves of cold fright passed through me followed by surges of excitement of a new kind connected with my coming exposition of the great book *Robinson Crusoe*. . . . The fear rose from the fact that the book, being so much more than a book to me, might lie so deep in the bone that it would be difficult to lay bare."

This Chinese box effect used in *Crusoe's Daughter,* in which a set of fictional circumstances inhabit the interior of another set of fictional circumstances in an inseparable way, is likewise utilized in *Through the Dolls' House Door,* published in 1987. While a children's book, marketed for seven- to ten-year-olds, its dealing with memory and history is equally engaging on an adult level.

Within the dolls' house of the title is a needle-box that serves as a dolls' house for the dolls. Intriguingly, the main characters of the novel are not the children who play with the dolls but the dolls themselves. Each doll, an identifiable personality that Gardam tips toward caricature, is packed inside a china cat when the family moves to Wales; thus, they find themselves "inside the Cat, inside the newspaper, inside the roof, inside the Welsh seaside garden, inside the envelope of clouds and space that pockets up the world."

Gardam also plays with the concept of time. The dolls in *Through the Dolls' House Door* perceive time in miniscule increments and make slow, infinitesimal movements but simultaneously are incorporated in larger, human concepts of time. The movement between one and the other is handled deftly by the author, who creates both humorous and tragic interactions between the dolls' world and that of their owners. When the dolls' house is abandoned after the move to Wales, the dolls pass the time by telling each other their life stories. Picked up by one generation, abandoned and then picked up by another, the dolls' house is full of memories that extend the reach of human experience beyond a singular place or point in history.

The same philosophy drives Eliza Peabody's inventions in *The Queen of the Tambourine* (1991), a novel that Gardam described to Lin Ferguson as being "written with love." Both works celebrate a love of a fictional, writerly world in which creating stories is of equal importance to living "real life." Eliza is civilized but odd, and her letters to her neighbor Joan begin to take on the mantle of invented stories, finally revealing her reports of life in Rathbone Road and the relationships she describes to be largely fictional. Her husband exists, however, and his sturdiness, as well as that of his daughter, eventually allows sanity to triumph over seemingly impending madness. *The Queen of the Tambourine* was awarded the Whitbread Award for best novel of the year.

In 1994, reinforcing her ongoing connection with her home county, Gardam published the nonfiction book *The Iron Coast: Notes on a Cold Country*. In it she recalls the Yorkshire of her childhood, reiterating just how strongly she continues to believe in the link between place and person. She describes how the wealthy would pay for groups of underprivileged children from the working areas of nearby Teeside to spend holidays at the sea and how as many as twenty thousand children would swarm through her hometown. Though she could "see the steelworks" in the distance, her strongest memory is of being kept away from the working class. There was, she says, "our middleclass life, but there was also that of the steelworkers." Class antagonism is one of Gardam's prime themes, and impatience with class difference informs much of her fiction.

This notion of creating stories as bonds between people, glue for the memories, and bridges between other places and other times is at the heart of *Faith Fox*. Gardam's comic talents are again on display in the novel, in the characters of Holly Fox and her mother, Thomasina, two self-confident, boisterous creations, and in the sometimes sly, sometimes gut-wrenching humorous incidents. After Holly dies while giving birth to Faith, Thomasina uses laughter as protection against her despair and goes off on a "fling de luxe" with an aged general.

Faith, meanwhile, is delivered to rundown and desolate Ellerby Moors, a chaotic, lurid world whose inhabitants will find in her some small resolution, confirmation, or enlightenment. While she remains the most unknown of characters, at the same time she becomes the most significant. Faith is a creator of community, the link between otherwise disparate individuals. "Her hands," her twelve-year-old cousin Philip says, "cling to you." She becomes, in this fashion, faith itself, an embodiment of a belief in purpose and empathy. With these thematic concerns and a plot that revolves around the appearance of an infant in a community in need of spiritual guidance, *Faith Fox* could easily have become a tract. Gardam is too subtle and too unobtrusive a writer for didacticism, however. She treads the line cleverly between reality and fantasy, eccentricity and ordinariness, without being overwhelmed, or overwhelming the reader, with the complexities of this movement.

That same line is carefully maintained in *Missing the Midnight,* a collection of short stories subtitled "Hauntings and Grotesques." In this collection there are five stories about different aspects of Christmas, five ghost stories, one story concerned with a retirement holiday by the sea, and a short novel, "The Green Man," about the ancient fertility symbol of the same name, published separately in 1998. The stories are sometimes based on the everyday, sometimes fantastical, and often involve allegorical structures. "The Zoo at Christmas" treats the popular Christian myth that animals kneel on Christmas Eve, told from the viewpoint of the animals. In the title story a girl, escaping from college and a ruined love affair, is returning home by train to her family on Christmas Eve. Her mother, a devout Christian, is irritated because the lateness of the train means that the girl will "miss the Midnight," meaning midnight mass. Christian mythology and Christmas magic meet, on occasion, human tragedy. In "Christmas Island," set in the future, the birth of a strange creature, named a Spignole, a "headless, armless pod . . . rubbery in texture yet of metallic appearance and the colour of unscoured pewter," paves the way for an alien takeover of the world. The small group of survivors ends up on Christmas Island. Terence Blacker, writing in the *Mail on Sunday* (25 December 1997), said of Gardam's writing in *Missing the Midnight* that "behind her wit and cool intelligence, her elegant fictions remind us of deeper currents in human behaviour," an observation that stands as a neat summary of all Gardam's work.

References:

Candida Crewe, "Hometown: Jane Gardam, Coatham," *Times Magazine* (10 March 1997): 58;

Lin Ferguson, "Jane Gardam," *Evening Standard,* 19 July 1992.

Shena Mackay

(6 June 1944 –   )

Merritt Moseley
University of North Carolina at Asheville

BOOKS: *Dust Falls on Eugene Schlumburger and Toddler on the Run* (London: Deutsch, 1964); republished in part as *Toddler on the Run: A Novel* (New York: Simon & Schuster, 1966);

Music Upstairs (London: Deutsch, 1965);

Old Crow (London: Cape, 1967; New York: McGraw-Hill, 1968);

An Advent Calendar (London: Cape, 1971; Wakefield, R.I.: Moyer Bell, 1997);

Babies in Rhinestones and Other Stories (London: Heinemann, 1983);

A Bowl of Cherries (Brighton, U.K.: Harvester Press, 1984; Mt. Kisco, N.Y.: Moyer Bell, 1992);

Redhill Rococo (London: Heinemann, 1986);

Dreams of Dead Women's Handbags (London: Heinemann, 1987);

Dunedin (London: Heinemann, 1992; Wakefield, R.I.: Moyer Bell, 1993);

The Laughing Academy (London: Heinemann, 1993);

Collected Short Stories (London: Penguin, 1994);

Dreams of Dead Women's Handbags: Collected Stories (Wakefield, R.I.: Moyer Bell, 1994);

The Orchard on Fire (London: Heinemann, 1996; Wakefield, R.I.: Moyer Bell, 1996);

The Artist's Widow (London: Cape, 1998; Wakefield, R. I.: Moyer Bell, 1999);

The World's Smallest Unicorn and Other Stories (London: Cape, 1999; Wakefield, R.I.: Moyer Bell, 2000);

Heligoland (London: Cape, forthcoming 2001).

OTHER: *Such Devoted Sisters: An Anthology of Stories,* edited by Mackay (London: Virago, 1993);

Friendship, edited by Mackay (London: Dent, 1997).

Shena Mackay, 1996

Shena Mackay has created one of the most distinctive bodies of work in late-twentieth-century British fiction. Beginning at an early age, she specialized in writing about the raffish, the eccentric, and the abnormal, sometimes heightening their grotesqueness by the deadpan way in which she writes about them. Observers such as Jan Moir of *The Daily Telegraph* have praised the "painterly detail and precise observation that shimmer through all her short stories and novels" (28 July 1997). In Mackay's clear-sighted dissection of the characters who people her fiction, she has incurred the criticism that she dislikes people—a charge also leveled at times against American writer Flannery O'Connor. Mackay is indeed unsentimental;

yet, as she told Moir, all her works address "love, obviously. Then injustice and loss. Humour, too. But I think the strongest theme is redemption. If people behave badly there is still hope for them."

She was born Shena Mackey in Edinburgh on D-Day, the second child of three born to parents who had met at St. Andrews University. Her father, Benjamin Mackey, was in the army when she was born, and her mother was in teacher training. After the terribly cold winter of 1947 the family moved to Hampstead, the location of Shena's earliest memory: falling into Hampstead Pond. They moved several more times before settling in Shoreham, Kent, where Shena Mackay's formative years were spent. Attending Tonbridge Grammar School, she was good in English but also mischievous and often given detentions. Later the family moved to Blackheath, in southeast London, where she attended Kidbrooke Comprehensive. She was much less happy there than at Tonbridge, and her experiences at Kidbrooke may well be the source for the many acid portrayals of school life in her novels. Writing in 1999, Ian Hamilton maintained that, even as a Kent schoolgirl, Mackay was "enticed by the idea of the metropolis," and that the move to Kidbrooke "does seem to have transformed her from a mischievous rural tomboy into a trainee urban disaffiliate." Soon after Mackay left school at sixteen, she won a poetry prize from the *Daily Mirror*. In London she found a job in an antique shop owned by the parents of art critic David Sylvester and managed by playwright Frank Marcus. Sylvester and Marcus introduced her to a world of writers and artists and, more broadly, the London bohemia of the early 1960s, including the circle that gathered at the Colony Club in Fitzrovia. She met well-known artists such as Lucian Freud, Francis Bacon, Henry Moore, and David Hockney. (Critics have regularly noted the painterly qualities of Mackay's fiction.)

At twenty Mackay published her first fiction, two novellas called *Dust Falls on Eugene Schlumburger and Toddler on the Run* (1964). She quickly followed this book with *Music Upstairs* (1965), about life among unmarried flat dwellers in the Earls Court neighborhood of London, where she was living at that time, and *Old Crow* (1967), set in a village in southeastern England. Hamilton has commented that these early books show "Mackay's gift for the killing simile and the surprising, spot-on image." Many accounts relate Mackay's sensational success in London at an early age. Writing in 1993, Dina Rabinovitch described Mackay as "an overnight literary sensation, a girl wonder splashed across Sunday supplements." Hamilton quoted an unnamed poet on Mackay's initial impact: "You should have seen those corduroyed belletrists swoon whenever she timidly sashayed into the hotel bar. They all wanted to,

well, protect her, advise her, and so on and in spite of the deadpan wit with which she kept them all at bay, she did somehow seem to need protecting. Let's just say that she was the kind of novelist who didn't really need to write another novel."

Having married an old boyfriend named Robin Brown, a petrochemical engineer, in 1964, Mackay bore three daughters. In 1972 she and her family moved from East Finchley, on the northwest edge of London, to Brockham, Surrey. They later moved to Reigate, also in Surrey. Having published her third full-length novel, *An Advent Calendar,* in 1971, she did not produce another book until 1983. For several years she devoted her time to rearing a family. As she later explained to Rabinovitch, "I was leading a very unliterary life while the children were growing up. Well, it's impossible to lead a literary life with children if you live in the country." Her marriage, however, did not remain a happy one. According to Hamilton, Mackay's third child was fathered by Sylvester, and she divorced Brown in 1982.

During her withdrawal from the publishing world, Mackay had continued writing short stories, one of which won a prize in a Radio 3 competition. Meeting novelist Brigid Brophy around 1980 proved a great help. After Jonathan Cape, which had published Mackay's previous three books, rejected *A Bowl of Cherries* (1984), Brophy helped Mackay to place it with Harvester Press. It was well reviewed, launching a sort of Shena Mackay revival. Since then she has written and published novels and short stories to considerable acclaim.

Mackay has experienced considerable difficulty in her life, including artistic frustrations, financial privation (working at times as a mushroom picker and a library assistant and receiving support from the Royal Literary Fund), illness, and the deaths of loved ones. She told Hamilton of her tendency to "anxiety and depression," acknowledging "the wonderful people who have helped me" and commenting, "I wouldn't be the artist I am if I didn't know about the dark side of life and the dark night of the soul." Mackay is now a grandmother and a well-established figure on the British literary scene. Her 1996 novel, *The Orchard on Fire,* was on the six-book shortlist for the Booker Prize, and in 1999 she was one of the judges for that award. She lives in south London, writes at her dining-room table, and keeps cats.

Dust Falls on Eugene Schlumburger and Toddler on the Run was praised by the *Daily Mail* as "macabre, zany, scoffingly droll, sadly beautiful, wildly funny, glitteringly stylish and quite brilliant." The quirkiness of the first sentence of the first novella—"Eugene woke in a paper hat and went to the window where it was snowing"—runs through the story, which is about the

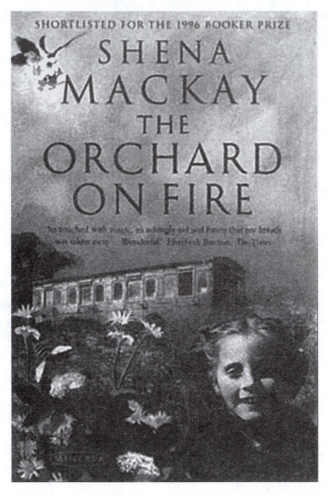

Dust jacket for Mackay's 1996 novel, about child molestation in rural Kent during the early 1950s

love between Eugene, a thirtyish man who has left a job in advertising, and Abigail, a rebellious schoolgirl. Their affair proceeds through youthful escapades to car theft and imprisonment for Eugene, who eventually dies in a prison fire.

Other characters also figure in the plot, but the main focus is on Abigail. At the end of this short work, with Eugene dead, she agrees to take a secretarial course: "'Yes,' she said, 'I will learn shorthand and typing,' because she knew she was already dead." Abigail has a sharp, sarcastic imagination, as when she imagines herself writing a letter of complaint about a bus conductress, pretending to be a veteran of the battle of Passchendaele and reporting the woman for being "both insolent and negligent in her behaviour towards an elderly handicapped person" and giving "the wrong change to a blind kiddie." Much of Abigail's scorn is directed toward her school, which is operated by out-of-touch spinsters, including one who denounces three girls for beating up a younger girl:

in addition to this bestiality, not one of these girls was wearing her beret. These girls, I call them girls for want of a better word, these girls shall learn that violence reaps a reward of recrimination. They will not be rejoining their classes. They have disgraced their parents and the School. Look at them, and be warned. They are guttersnipes and shall be dealt with as such.

The novella also includes a macabre, nighttime funeral for Sister Sick of the Palsy, during which the nun pallbearers accidently lower the coffin into the well instead of the freshly dug grave:

The Sisters lowered their burden gently over the side, into its narrow house of earth. They let go. There was a terrific splash, several of the Sisters screamed and some were soaked.

"The well!" A despairing cry rose from a dozen throats. Vainly from the depths the palsied bubbles rose.

"All drinking water must be boiled from now on," the Mother Superior broke the silence.

Toddler on the Run is also stylishly odd and features satire on girls' schools. The "toddler" of the title is Morris, a dwarf with antisocial habits who—after trouble with the police and the accidental death of a friend—runs away with his girlfriend Leda and lives in a hut on the beach. Morris's earlier, brief courtship of a schoolgirl named Deirdre brings in the portrayal of schools as silly places beset by rules and run by freaks. There is also a loosely related secondary plot featuring a married couple called Daniel and Elaine, with whom Morris briefly hides. After Daniel tries to kill Elaine, she is taken to a nursing home for recovery, setting up a comic episode in which she escapes and a search party is organized:

> the search party, led by Major Mallet brandishing an ebony club and uttering wild cries, burst through the french windows in a shower of broken glass and rushed on to the lawn. The metallic sun reflected off the wheels of wheelchairs as they rolled like great golden chariots over the flower beds. . . .
>
> "Onward!" shouted the major and the cry was echoed by a dozen throats and in one case rose in a harsh scream that ended abruptly as a wheelchair rolled over its owner's throat.
>
> "Casualty! Casualty!" shouted Major Mallet, tossing the wounded to one side. One lady had tied knives to her wheels and their blunt edges scraped the ankles of those who ran beside her.

Mackay's assurance, invention, and control of tone in this first book are impressive. The book earned good reviews, with a critic for the *New Statesman* calling Mackay "the supreme lyricist of daily grot."

Music Upstairs (1965) is a short narrative of life in London. Sidonie O'Neill and her friend Joyce move to Earls Court, where they rent a room from Pam and Lenny. Particularly in the 1960s, the cheap accommodations in Earls Court attracted bohemians, students, and Australians. *Music Upstairs* explores the possibilities of irresponsible drunken behavior and bisexuality, all of which Sidonie experiences, having affairs with both Pam and Lenny. The novel captures the excitement of transgression and the sensations of drunkenness, as in this early scene with Sidonie and Lenny: "they whispered accusations and the room went round; an occasional word battered itself against the bulb and disintegrated. Kissing, disgusting, arms round his neck, practically raping, pissed."

A counterpoint to this urban recklessness is Sidonie's parents' home in suburban Penge. She goes there once, then returns to Lenny. Their relationship becomes more and more desperate, and toward the end of the novel she shoots him, wounding him, though not fatally. The aftermath of the shooting is described in this dark scene:

> She pointed the empty gun as he lurched to his feet and took his arm and dragged him by the wet sleeve towards Earls Court. In Warwick Road he suddenly reeled over and beer and whisky poured from his mouth. She sank to the pavement beside him, her hair blown across his face. It started to rain again as she heard heavy feet coming round the corner, and she ran down a side street and into a church. The shallow water darkened in the font as she washed her hands.

In an afterword written for the 1989 Virago paperback edition, Mackay reminisced about her time in Earls Court (known then as "Kangaroo Valley" because of all the Australians living there) and expressed some second thoughts about her lack of sympathy in 1965 for Pam's predicament, including its domestic tedium and her unhappy marriage.

Old Crow (1967) forsakes the London setting for a southeastern village and replaces the comic-bizarre tone with one entirely somber. The story of a rural woman, Coral Fairweather, who has become an outcast, the book is set in 1958 and begins elliptically with Coral being ejected from the choir by "old Mr Thompkin with the kindly white hair." She is considered scandalous because she has been impregnated and abandoned by a painter who is in the village for the summer. The affair and its results occupy the first five and a half pages of the novel, which then turns to the consequences. A new family, the Blakes, hire Coral to help with housekeeping, but despite their sympathy and attempts to help, Coral and her children are forced to steal and do without. The children are tormented at school, and eventually vengeful village women burn down Coral's dilapidated home, not entirely intentionally but maliciously.

The novel dispels any notion the reader might have of village life as cozy or uneventful. Dennis Blake loves Coral while his wife finds extramarital excitement with a young man from the local garage, who turns out to be a murderer. The Blakes' daughter takes up with an unsuitable young man, and they smash up a car. Stella Oates, who is now self-righteously persecuting Coral, "had once deprived a vicar of his living and, as a girl, had a captain reduced to the ranks. . . . A more recent success was the removal of a colony of gipsies from the camping site of generations: as they had plodded up the road in a heavy mist a coach had run into the back, smashing two caravans, three men and a horse." The village girls refuse to walk in a certain stretch of woods because "it was here that a Brownie pack was brutally attacked." When Coral's aged and senile father dies, he is treated more like a bag of unwanted clothes than a human being, and in yet another example of the villagers' inhumanity, the head teacher at the school, when asked about noise in the playground, answers mildly, "They're stoning Paula Fairweather." The title refers to Coral's father's having nailed a dead crow to a fence, as a warning to others. That crow comes to represent Coral.

An Advent Calendar (1971) is the oddest mixture of elements in Mackay's fiction up to this point. Rather loosely constructed, like her other fictions, it is given a sort of factitious unity by beginning on the first of December and leading up to Christmas, as the title suggests. The events are extremely grisly, beginning with an accidental act of cannibalism and including child molesting, adultery, and animal cruelty, in a general milieu of poverty and hopelessness. Yet, the novel is funny as well. Reviewer Diane White summed it up as "Misfit family endears itself in comic tale" (*Houston Chronicle*, 4 January 1978), while Jonathan Yardley's review provided this quite different summary: "Bleak, Blue-Collar and British: Novel offers a stark portrayal of family's working-class struggles" (*Washington Post*, 20 October 1977). Both are right.

As the book opens, John, a young university dropout having trouble providing for his family, buys some ground beef and uses it to make spaghetti, which he and his uncle eat. Just as they finish, a desperate butcher comes to their door looking for a severed finger, which must have been in the meat John and his uncle have just eaten. This misfortune sets the tone for the series of mishaps that befall John's family. *An Advent Calendar* is another of Mackay's brilliant studies in squalor, and the sordid quality of the surroundings is exacerbated by cold. Mackay's characters are usually too cold or too hot. John's wife, Marguerite, for example, "put on John's corduroy trousers, another sweater and socks, got into bed and lay too cold to move between the ancient sheets, thinking that she must lie there for at least thirty-one nights, because it was December 1st, and saw each day open like a dark door in an Advent Calendar." Yet, the novel works its way toward a somewhat happy ending, with the suggestion that nothing matters as much as it seems to do.

After the long period of artistic inactivity that followed *An Advent Calendar*, Mackay produced her first collection of short fiction, *Babies in Rhinestones and Other Stories* (1983). Rabinovitch has voiced the opinion that Mackay's "short stories work better than any of her novels. . . . in the stories she seems stricter about not letting her—very active—social conscience interfere." There are other strengths in these stories, including the brilliant visual qualities that also illuminate her novels, and the occasional laxity of plotting visible in some of the novels is less apparent in the shorter forms.

Babies in Rhinestones comprises eleven stories. Several of them had been published during the 1970s in literary journals such as *New Review* and *Quarto* and in other, miscellaneous outlets such as *Bindweed's Bestseller*, as well as being read on Radio 3. In the first story, "The Blue Orchestra," an Englishwoman (formerly Pam Partridge) has remade herself as the Contessa Paloma and lives with her younger consort, Oscar, in the tropics. Her idyllic life is shattered by the appearance of a figure from the past that most of her circle take at first for a revenant or zombie. It is actually Sandy Sinclair, who declares herself the Contessa's best friend with whom she made a blood pact at school. The story moves quickly toward its denouement, as the Contessa's lover decamps and her life unravels. Finally, Sandy realizes that she had sworn eternal friendship to another girl entirely. Mackay has a brilliant way with endings; "Family Service" portrays a family called the Brigstocks, particularly their harried mother Helen, and ends with their leaving church:

> Helen smiled. "I do think it's important for a family to worship together," she said.
>
> The Brigstocks piled into the car and drove home to eat some pieces of a dead bird, which would have been browning nicely if Helen had switched on the oven.

There is a parallel with another dead bird, found stiff in the graveyard.

Mackay's first novel after her hiatus, *A Bowl of Cherries* (1984), demonstrates a marked change from her earlier work. Philip Hensher, summing up her career from the perspective of 1996, wrote that Mackay's "career falls into two neat halves" and called her first five novels "smart, insolent jeux d'esprits full of huge cleverness and relish for her gift." With *A Bowl of Cherries*, however, "her voice had changed, enriched with tenderness and a new grandeur" (*The Guardian*, 12 July 1996). Hensher probably overstates the "insolence" of the earlier work, but there is a perceptible alteration in tone and organization in *A Bowl of Cherries*, which addresses itself to a divided family. Rex Beaumont, apparently Nature's darling, is rich and successful, a famous author with a large estate. His twin brother, Stanley, is poor and obscure, unmarried and apparently friendless. The narrator calls Stanley "a caricature or cheap copy of his brother Rex." Stanley lives in unattractive poverty reminiscent of the setting of *An Advent Calendar*, trying to write and regretting that he is almost completely unknown. The two brothers, who do not see each other, are linked by Rex's two children, especially his illegitimate son Seamus. Rex and his wife are neglectful parents while Stanley, though childless, is attentive and affectionate to Rex's children. The death

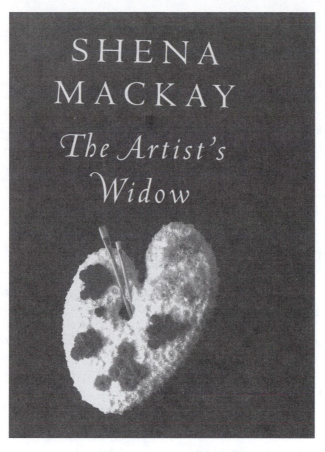

Dust jacket for Mackay's 1998 novel, which satirizes the avant-garde performance and conceptual artists of the 1990s

of Stanley "redeems" the other characters—a kind of development hitherto unexpected in Mackay's fiction. The novel develops a moral scheme that inverts the material one and reveals the truth underlying surface appearances. Like Mackay's later short story "The Thirty-first of October," it is knowing about literary success. More sensationally than in that story, success in *A Bowl of Cherries* is fraudulent, as Rex Beaumont has taken credit for a novel written by his brother, who was imprisoned as a conscientious objector at the time of publication. When he finds that his brother has forgiven him, Rex concludes: "Why did he have to behave so well? . . . He's won." In fact, Stanley has won by refusing to compete.

A Bowl of Cherries is a good answer to critics who accuse Mackay of refusing to create likable characters. When Hamilton asked her if she had ever created an admirable male character, she named Stanley Beaumont. Hamilton was unimpressed: "a wan and ineffectual bedsit loser. 'And what's so terrific about Stanley?' 'Well, he's nice to children,' she replied." Being nice to children is not a negligible virtue in a world where so many people are hateful or indifferent to them, but

Stanley is also a real writer, an unselfish man who refuses to hate, and a good brother to a twin who has wronged him.

Mackay's next novel, *Redhill Rococo* (1986), is one of her finest works. It begins with two rather stunted lives' becoming entwined. Luke Ribbons, just released from prison, arrives in Redhill (a town in mid Sussex) to stay with Pearl Slattery, whose common-law husband was in prison with Luke and gave him Pearl's address. He moves into her home, which she shares with her three children. A worker in a candy factory and a sort of part-time prostitute, Pearl, who is as slatternly as her surname suggests, is a poor mother. Two of her children, Sean and Tiffany, are predictably going bad while the third, Cherry, becomes religious and joins Taskforce, a youth religious organization led by the smarmy Reverend Richard Ruggles. (At the time she wrote this novel Mackay, who says she likes going to church but prefers it mostly empty, was living in an area of "happy-clappy" Christians.) Ruggles is the curate for the Reverend Ichabod Ribbons, Luke's father. Far from a hardened case, Luke tried to rob a small post office for no real reason and was humiliatingly overpowered by the elderly patrons there. His father is a grotesque, savage, drunken parody of ecclesiastical fitness; his mother, undone by Luke's humiliation, never gets out of the bath anymore. Perhaps in reaction against his frigid bourgeois upbringing and his loveless parents, Luke falls in love with the unsuitable Pearl.

Redhill Rococo is rich in acute observation—such as the snail trails on the bathroom carpet of the Slatterys' squalid house—and amusing characters, including a no-nonsense librarian:

> "I'm afraid that's just not good enough," the library manager was saying. "Two Doris Lessings and one Simone de Beauvoir. Next!"
>
> "Mrs Kennedy used to let us choose our own books, " quavered the woman thus addressed.
>
> "I'm afraid things got altogether too slack under Mrs Kennedy's regime. Next! Must I explain again, Mr Baker?" She smiled wearily at the ancient who shuffled up, placing his trembling hands on her desk for support. "The county has instituted this system of double fines for the over-seventies on the grounds that they are old enough to know better."

Martin Seymour-Smith paid lavish, and not undeserved, tribute to *Redhill Rococo* in his review for the *Financial Times* (8 February 1986), declaring that Mackay "is as relentless as ever Evelyn Waugh was in her exposure of her characters, but she has no malice." He called *Redhill Rococo* "a wildly comic extravaganza which is also moving and thought-provoking. It is one of the most generous works of fiction to be published for many years."

During the six years between *Redhill Rococo* and her next novel, *Dunedin* (1992), Mackay published a second collection of short stories: *Dreams of Dead Women's Handbags* (1987). Her longest, most ambitious, and most uncharacteristic novel, *Dunedin* combines a world she knows well, down-market south London, with one she knows only from books, turn-of-the-century New Zealand.

Dunedin begins in New Zealand in 1909, with the arrival of Jack Mackenzie, a young minister from Glasgow. Not particularly interested in spreading the gospel, Mackenzie is a trifler determined to become famous as a naturalist by discovering a new species that can be named for him. He is a cruel father and an unfaithful husband who soon begins an affair with Myrtille, a Maori servant.

After the New Zealand prelude, the scene shifts to south London in 1989, a bleak, dirty, despairing place, where Jack's grandson William Mackenzie is a prematurely retired schoolmaster, guilt-ridden by the death of a student on a school trip. He lives with his sister, Olive, an embittered and nearly insane woman whose yearn-

ing for a child leads her to kidnap a black baby. Another of Jack's grandchildren, Jay Pascal, grandson of Myrtille, makes his way from New Zealand to London, where he encounters Olive early in the novel and later squats in Dunedin, the abandoned Mackenzie family home, described as "where the ruined people live." A victim of British imperialism and Thatcherite policies toward the homeless, Jay is swept up from the London streets and incarcerated in a mental hospital. Though the scenes describing his savage treatment there seem less than convincing, Penny Smith argued in a 1995 article, "The reality of late-Eighties England, the increase in begging and homelessness, the well-publicized moves to 'clean up' areas like the Strand and the cardboard city clustered around the South Bank, reverberates with the reality of late-Thirties Nazi Germany." The novel creates a tension suggesting a reunion or at least recognition between the Mackenzie grandchildren, but it never happens.

Dunedin is a departure for Mackay because of its historical sweep, its concern for race, and its disgust with the politics of 1980s Britain. It also includes the kind of evocative detail that is never absent from Mackay's writing.

Dunedin was well received by critics. In the *Los Angeles Times* (5 November 1993), Chris Goodrich judged that "scene by scene, chapter by chapter, it's a comic novel of considerable, unanticipated power." Writing for *The Financial Times* (18 July 1992), Mary Hope called Mackay "scathingly funny about the tackiness of modern Britain, the pretensions of literary life and female bonding." Paul Bailey commented in *The Independent* (5 July 1992) that "Shena Mackay notices a London that passes most writers by. She sees not only the vagrants, gabbling eccentrics, litter and dog shit that other novelists have brought to our jaded attention, but the flora and fauna, the weird buildings of Brixton, the rented rooms that register decay and failure through open front doors, the mothers at bus stops relieving their boredom by slapping their toddlers."

Mackay's next book, *The Laughing Academy* (1993), was a further contribution to her large and impressive body of short fiction. It was followed by *Collected Short Stories* (1994) and a somewhat different grouping that appeared in the United States as *Dreams of Dead Women's Handbags: Collected Stories* (1994). "The Thirty-first of October," a story in *The Laughing Academy,* is, somewhat unusually for Mackay, about a writer. Claudia is an author of two books now out of print, and more and more forgotten: "She had been highly praised as a miniaturist once, and in vain did she remind herself of little bits of ivory; her talent had diminished until it had disappeared." Her little humiliations from her neighbors, her "erstwhile publisher," and the village shopkeeper are vividly evoked, as are her small evasions and self-delusions, which do not work for long. Though this story is hardly a self-portrait, David Robson, reviewing *The Laughing Academy* for *The Sunday Telegraph* (25 July 1993), pointed out similar characteristics in Mackay's fiction, claiming that her "gifts are the gifts of a miniaturist: you can see them in her perfectly-crafted sentences, in her lush descriptive passages, in her exact and original similes. But when they are set out in the shop-window as beguilingly as they are here, you can see why one reviewer was prompted to call her 'the best writer in the world today.'" In *The Laughing Academy*, Mackay achieved her usual combination of satire, pathos, and comedy, but most of the characters in these stories are old. In her review for *The Independent on Sunday* (1 August 1993), Maggie Traugott called Mackay "a purveyor both of radiant bursts of jewel-like descriptive prose . . . and also of the groan-making joke extremes of social realism—where a miserable git lives in hope that someone will ask him why his tortoises are called Percy and Bysshe. (Because they're Shelley)."

The Orchard on Fire (1996) is another departure for Mackay, the only one of her novels narrated in the first person. The narrator of this unnostalgic look back is April Harlency, a middle-aged, divorced schoolteacher living in London. After a bristly encounter with her neighbor, a writer to whom she gives advice probably similar to some Mackay has received—"Try writing about *nice* people for a change, *pretty* people, people who at least *aspire* to being good"—April takes a trip to Stonebridge, the rural Kent village where she spent her youth.

The novel then returns to the year 1953, when eight-year-old April moved to Stonebridge with her parents, who keep a tearoom called the Copper Kettle. In Stonebridge, April and another little girl, Ruby Richards, become inseparable friends. At the same time the Harlencys are too inattentive to April to realize that she is being sexually abused by Mr. Greenidge, an old man, who manages to appear a kindly friend and convinces April not to tell her unobservant parents about his kisses and gropings.

The Orchard on Fire was well received by critics. In *The Boston Globe* (25 November 1996) Diane White praised the way Mackay "captures, with powerful simplicity, the casual cruelties and routine humiliations children endure at the hands of adults." Reviewing the novel for *The Daily Telegraph* (15 June 1996), Maggie Gee wrote that the novel has "a page-turning coherence that Mackay's more episodic novels have lacked." Writing for *The Sunday Times* (2 June 1996), Miranda Seymour praised the "precise and vivid period detail, the red Smarties [candies] used as school lipstick, the little girls' prancing exhibitions in finery stolen from their

mothers' closets, the solemn joy with which they prepare a singing and dancing act as two mince pies in the school concert." Contributing another chapter to Mackay's long demonstration of the unreliability of most people in power, *The Orchard on Fire* depicts the blindness of some adults and the sinister urges of others, while also creating the most impressive picture of friendship Mackay has ever offered. April Harlency is a solitary woman, and Ruby Richards was an isolated girl, but for a short time in 1953 they shared a moving solidarity and love.

In *Dunedin,* one of the minor characters, the scathingly delineated Terry Turner, is a novelist who combines irresponsibility with impudence. This bad artist figure seems redoubled in *The Artist's Widow* (1998), a short, biting novel focusing on the world of creating, selling, and publicizing art.

Unlike some of Mackay's early works, in which it is often hard to identify a character with whom the author invites readers to sympathize, *The Artist's Widow* makes a clear distinction between sympathetic and unsympathetic characters. The artist's widow of the title is Lyris Crane, and the novel opens at a private showing of her late husband's last works, attended by several characters with significant roles in the novel, including Clovis, a friend who is much preoccupied with his failure to give assistance to someone he saw in trouble in an Underground station, and Nathan Pursey, Lyris's great-nephew and a highly visible, though entirely untalented, artist. Most of Mackay's scorn is reserved for Nathan, a performance and conceptual artist like Damien Hirst, whose showings of dead sheep in plexiglass cubes have brought considerable publicity. One vignette describes Nathan's studio/living quarters:

> A cloud of bluebottles was buzzing round the tub of viscera that formed the base of Nathan's Dresden sculpture, setting in motion the mobile of balsawood aeroplanes. "You little beauties," said Nathan, but the stench was so overpowering that he had to throw the whole installation out of the window.

If Nathan were simply untalented, he would not deserve so much contempt, but he is genuinely vicious. He steals from Lyris, and the novel suggests that his art is only a more socially acceptable way of thieving than the more traditional kind. Meanwhile, Lyris forms an improbable alliance with Nathan's discarded girlfriend Jackee, and the man injured on the Underground turns out to be Nathan's missing flatmate and artistic collaborator. Events come together in a loosely logical way.

In *The Artist's Widow,* which deals with true and false feeling as well as true and false art, Lyris detects the tendency toward artificiality in the public's excessive mourning at the death of Princess Diana. Her perceptiveness is also apparent when she delivers something of an artistic credo that is clearly meant to counteract the position, best embodied by Nathan, that art is hype or outrage:

> I lost any illusion that I would be a great artist long ago but I *was* given a gift and I've spent my life serving it. I was sent to a school for a while where I was very unhappy, but what I remember most vividly about it is a jug of scarlet rosehips against a green classroom wall that suddenly brought me consolation on a dark afternoon. My role is to record such things not only for their intrinsic beauty and for myself, but on behalf of people whose hearts are touched in precisely the same way.

The reviews of *The Artist's Widow* occasionally expressed some dissatisfaction with what seemed a clichéd assault on the wilder excesses of postmodern art. Yet, as usual, critics such as Maggie Gee praised Mackay's imagery, her "description of everyday miracles such as shelled runner bean" (*The Sunday Times*, 5 July 1999).

Mackay's next book was *The World's Smallest Unicorn and Other Stories* (1999), a collection of eleven stories covering the usual range from surrealism to a sort of urban dirty realism. In "The Wilderness Club" a man named Romney eats everything he sees, including buildings and even the Marble Arch. In "The Index of Embarrassment" a man is compiling just that: "The *Index* started out as a hobby, a scrapbook of humorous and humiliating stories gleaned from the media, became a sort of thesis entitled *Seven Types of Embarrassment*, and then like Topsy (see under *Clichés*), it just growed. Into an obsession." The stories also include generous examples of Mackay's humor.

Over thirty-five years of publishing fiction, Shena Mackay has carved out a territory for herself that is unlike that of any other author. Reviewing *The Artist's Widow* for *The Sunday Times* (5 July 1998), Maggie Gee commented that Mackay "has been writing in her own quirky, poetic, sensuous vein for more than three decades," and Michele Field has observed that "British critics have compared Mackay to authors ranging from Dickens to Ronald Firbank and Muriel Spark, but she seems far too vivid to be a clone of somebody else." Mackay achieves the remarkable feats of writing comically about serious matters and of combining the surreal, macabre, and even supernatural with mundane, closely observed, daily minutiae. Mackay is a writer with original gifts and the self-confidence to follow her own path in producing distinguished work of lasting importance.

Interviews:

Lucy Berrington, "Languishing in a Lyrical Legacy," *Guardian,* 1 July 1992, Features, p. 17;

Dina Rabinovitch, "Autumn Sunshine and Blancmange on the Wall," *Independent,* 24 July 1993, p. 29;

Tom Adair, "Keep Your Distance," *Scotland on Sunday,* 9 June 1996, Spectrum, p. 13;

Michele Field, "Shena Mackay: The Menace of the Domestic," *Publishers Weekly,* 243 (2 December 1996): 36–37;

Jan Moir, "The Road Out of Suburbia," *Daily Telegraph,* 28 July 1997, p. 5;

Ian Hamilton, "Bohemian Rhapsodist," *Guardian,* 10 July 1999, Art Pages, p. 6.

Reference:

Penny Smith, "Hell innit: The Millenium in Alasdair Gray's Lanark, Martin Amis's London Fields, and Shena Mackay's Dunedin," *Essays and Studies,* 48 (1995): 115–128.

John McGahern

(12 November 1934 –   )

Michael C. Prusse
University of Zurich

See also the McGahern entry in *DLB 14: British Novelists Since 1960.*

BOOKS: *The Barracks* (London: Faber & Faber, 1963; New York: Macmillan, 1964);

The Dark (London: Faber & Faber, 1965; New York: Knopf, 1966);

Nightlines, Stories (London: Faber & Faber, 1970; Boston: Little, Brown, 1971);

The Leavetaking (London: Faber & Faber, 1974; Boston: Little, Brown, 1975; revised edition, London: Faber & Faber, 1984);

Getting Through, Stories (London: Faber & Faber, 1978; New York: Harper & Row, 1980);

The Pornographer (London: Faber & Faber, 1979; New York: Harper & Row, 1980);

High Ground, Stories (London: Faber & Faber, 1985; New York: Viking, 1987);

Amongst Women (London & Boston: Faber & Faber, 1990; New York: Viking, 1990);

The Power of Darkness (London: Faber & Faber, 1991);

The Collected Stories (London: Faber & Faber, 1992; New York: Knopf, 1993).

PLAY PRODUCTION: *The Power of Darkness,* Dublin, Abbey Theatre, 16 October 1991.

PRODUCED SCRIPTS: *Sinclair,* BBC Radio 3, 1971;
Swallows, BBC-TV, 1975;
The Rockingham Shoot, BBC-TV, September 1987;
A Search for Happiness, television, 1989;
Amongst Women, television, BBC 2, July 1998.

OTHER: "The White Boat," in *New Writing 6,* edited by A. S. Byatt & Peter Porter (London: Vintage, 1997), pp. 342–372;

SELECTED PERIODICAL PUBLICATIONS–
UNCOLLECTED: "Creatures of the Earth," *Granta,* 49 (Winter 1994): 227–243;

John McGahern, circa 1980 (photograph © Jim Kallett; from the dust jacket for the first American edition of The Pornographer*)*

"Love of the World," *Granta,* 59 (Autumn 1997): 219–250;

"Easter," *TLS: The Times Literary Supplement,* 30 April 1999, pp. 16–17, extract from McGahern's novel in progress.

John McGahern's significance to contemporary Irish literature was stated by Belfast novelist Glenn Patterson. When asked whether McGahern was his father, Patterson replied: "Yes. He is the father of the modern Irish novel." The status of McGahern as the most important novelist in the generation of Samuel Beckett seems undisputed, but Denis Sampson argues in his 1993 monograph on McGahern that even though he is perceived as a major artist, he is still underrated. According to Patricia Boyle Haberstroh in her *DLB 14* entry on McGahern, "John McGahern's fiction continually tempts critics to compare him with other novelists." As an Irishman, he has experienced the inescapable comparison with James Joyce. Recent studies have compared him with Patrick Kavanagh and William Butler Yeats, who is, in fact, McGahern's most important model. McGahern has also been linked with Ernest Hemingway, Gustave Flaubert, Marcel Proust, François Mauriac, Anton Chekhov, and Albert Camus. These comparisons pay tribute to McGahern's artistic achievement, but they also obscure the essential originality of his personal vision and style.

Born in Dublin on 12 November 1934 to John McGahern, a police officer, and Susan McManus McGahern, a National School teacher, the future novelist was at first raised by his mother in Ballinamore, County Leitrim, in the west of Ireland. Regulations at that time did not allow a sergeant's wife to hold any employment; hence his parents always lived apart so Susan McGahern could work as a teacher. When his mother died in 1945, McGahern and his five sisters went to live with their father in police barracks in Cootehall, County Roscommon. As his father was friendly with the Moroneys, Protestant neighbors, McGahern was allowed to read his way through their nineteenth-century library. In a special McGahern issue of *La Licorne* (1993) he remembered how he "read for nothing but pleasure, the way that a boy of that age would look at endless television movies. He received his secondary education at the Presentation Brothers' College in Carrick-on-Shannon and then attended St. Patrick's Teacher Training College in Drumcondra, from which he graduated in 1954. He started to teach in Drogheda, County Louth, and at the same time became a night student at University College, Dublin. In 1955 McGahern was employed by St. John the Baptist Boys National School in Clontarf, County Dublin, where he taught for seven years. He graduated from University College, Dublin, with a B.A. in 1957 and started work on a first novel, "The End and the Beginning of Love." It remains unpublished. In 1962 McGahern was the first prose writer to be given the prestigious Æ Memorial Award for an extract from his next work, *The Barracks* (1963).

McGahern's poetic language celebrates daily actions, giving rich meaning and emotional import to things normally considered cumbersome or boring. Thus, studying for an exam, making hay, fishing, cutting wood, playing sports, or tending cattle can all be seen in a new light, as repetitive moments in the circle of life. McGahern's landscape is even more constricted than William Faulkner's Yoknapatawpha County. Richard Burr Lloyd points out that McGahern's novels deal with the same events and characters again and again; for example the young boy Willie, a minor character in *The Barracks,* becomes young Mahoney, the protagonist of *The Dark* (1965), and eventually Patrick Moran, the central consciousness in *The Leavetaking* (1974). McGahern regularly creates characters who are captivated by the existential inquiry into the meaning of life. Writing about their futile quests for answers, the novelist seems to illustrate similar statements made by Thomas Mann in *The Magic Mountain* (1924), "We come out of the dark and go into the dark again," and Vladimir Nabokov in *Speak, Memory* (1947), "common sense tells us that our existence is but a brief crack of light between two eternities of darkness."

In keeping with this existential approach, McGahern begins and ends *The Barracks* with the ritual lighting of a lamp, and the narrative is rich in references to light and darkness. Against the backdrop of a bleak 1950s Irish countryside, the novel relates the fate of Elizabeth Reegan, second wife of a police sergeant, whose intellectual perception distinguishes her from the people around her. Elizabeth struggles with her daily chores that mostly consist of preparing food for her ever-hungry stepchildren. Her husband is harassed by his superior and loathes his job. Their common disgust with their daily work does not draw them together, and they both live in separate worlds. Like McGahern's father, Reegan was a guerrilla leader and made the mistake of going into the guards. He desperately attempts to earn enough money by cutting turf to quit the police force and buy his own farm.

When Elizabeth discovers that she is suffering from cancer, she has to confront the relentless disease and the question of what meaning her life has. Remembering her wartime experiences in London, where she was trained and worked as a nurse, a fated love affair with a young doctor sticks out among her memories. His question—"What is all this living and dying about anyway?"—haunts Elizabeth as the reality of her death becomes obvious. Although she puts up a brave struggle, Elizabeth loses her fight. In the final scene the young son asks his father: "And is it time to light the lamp yet, Daddy?"—repeating the question he has asked Elizabeth in the first chapter. As Haberstroh states in *DLB 14,* "The cycle of life continues—tragic, shattered,

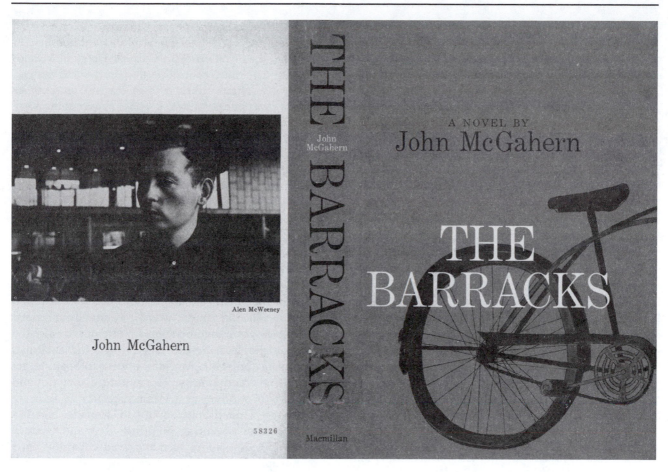

A NOVEL BY
John McGahern

THE
BARRACKS

Alen McWeeney

John McGahern

58326

Macmillan

Dust jacket for the American edition of McGahern's first novel, his attempt "to write a book about boredom"

and futile." A circle motif pervades the novel with the never-ending household chores and "the lonely tread-mill" of Elizabeth's thinking. The ultimate irony is that the expense of Elizabeth's funeral exhausts Reegan's savings for his escape from the police force.

As McGahern told Nicole Ollier in 1995, his orig-inal idea for *The Barracks* was "to write a book about boredom." It may be for this reason that *The Barracks* reminds many critics of French existentialist writing; quite a few detect a trace of Camus. Although McGa-hern originally denied any such influence, he later admitted that the novel could be called existential. Moments such as the point at which Elizabeth realizes "the futility of her life and the life about her, her grow-ing indifference" suggests how much McGahern shares with Camus. Elizabeth's efforts to come to terms with her life are best expressed in those moments when she wavers between the conviction that her life is horribly meaningless and the realization that love provides the meaning she is looking for so desperately. She sees her-self as living "either under the unimaginable God or the equally unimaginable nothing."

Roger Garfitt has observed that *The Barracks* is like much Irish fiction in being a story that focuses on "a single articulate person, questioning existence among others who are less bothered, or too busy to care." The novel depicts a small world whose idiosyncracies and tragedies form a backdrop against which Elizabeth's fate is played out. The anonymous critic in *TLS: The Times Literary Supplement* (22 February 1963) admired the "quiet authority" and "haunting power" of McGahern's novel. Later readers mostly focus on intertextual details—José Lanters, for instance, has pointed out the many parallels between Patrick Kavanagh's long poem *The Great Hunger* (1942), and *The Barracks,* referring in particular to the imagery, which suggests "representa-tions or sublimations of the characters' emotional, spiri-tual or sexual starvation."

In 1963, after the publication of *The Barracks,* McGahern was granted an Arts Council Macauley Fel-lowship that allowed him a one-year leave of absence from his teaching position. He went to London to write, and at the end of that year he married Finnish theatrical producer Annikki Laaksi.

His second novel, *The Dark* (1965), was banned by the Irish Censorship Board, teaching McGahern that "in a closed society writing is a dangerous activity." The banning profoundly affected his life and created a controversy in Ireland. The title of *The Dark* reverberates through all the suffering and tragedy of the novel as McGahern again resorts to symbolism in which light and darkness portray aspects of human nature on a farm in the Irish countryside. Neil Corcoran has called the opening episode of McGahern's second novel "arguably . . . the most frightful scene in modern Irish fiction." The narrator, young Mahoney, is humiliated by his violent, widowed father, who wants to punish him for uttering an obscene word and threatens to whip him in front of his sisters. The conflict between father and son is the central issue of the narrative: the brutal family tyrant, who seeks perverse closeness to his son at night, versus the young man, who struggles with his conscience over his deathbed promise to his mother to become a priest and a natural sexual awakening that expresses itself in an attraction to girls and excessive masturbation. The confessional form of *The Dark* has repeatedly invited comparisons with Joyce's *A Portrait of the Artist as a Young Man* (1916).

The father's fear of starvation is at the root of his tyrannical, narrow-minded regime. His stifling egotism is at the root of his sleeping in the same bed as his son. His cousin, Father Gerald, in whose house the boy is supposed to resolve whether to become a priest, approaches young Mahoney in a similar fashion. This moment is narrated in the second person to stress the distance between the horrified narrator, who vividly recalls his father's actions, and the priest: "What right had he to come and lie with you in bed. . . ." Always in the frightening dark—at night—the narrator seems disposed to make decisions. On hearing that his sister, who works in a nearby drapery shop, is sexually harassed by her employer, he decides to return home. The familiar terror of their father's farm is easier to bear than the unknown terrors of another place. Having rejected the priesthood, young Mahoney opts for another avenue of escape: he puts all his efforts into studying to achieve first place in the school-leaving exam. He succeeds in winning a university scholarship and goes to Galway, but his hopes for a university education founder when he discovers that his scholarship is not sufficient to cover his expenses to go to medical school. He decides to take a job with the Electricity Supply Board in Dublin and is reconciled with his father. The darkness seems to be lifting; however, all his original dreams have been shattered, and, as Shaun O'Connell has put it, he "will be paralyzed in the civil service, an Irish purgatory."

Although *The Dark* was praised by critics, the book created problems for McGahern. Published in England, the novel upset the Catholic clergy in Ireland, who, at that time, controlled the educational system. When McGahern returned from England in October 1965, he was informed by the school manager, the Very Reverend Patrick J. Carton, that he no longer had a job. Carton admitted that he had not read the book, but he was adamant that McGahern must leave. The one-line letter he gave to him read: "Mr. McGahern is well aware of the reason of his dismissal." The fact that the author had married a non-Catholic in a registry office during his leave did not help his situation.

As Julia Carlson has documented, McGahern's publisher unsuccessfully appealed to the Irish Censorship Board. When McGahern sought help from the Irish National Teachers' Organization, however, John Charles McQuaid, the archbishop of Dublin, exerted pressure on the union, which eventually dropped McGahern from membership. An attempt to raise the issue in the Irish Senate failed when the chairman ruled it inadmissible. McGahern went to Spain to get away from the publicity. He continued to write and soon began a career as a visiting lecturer at universities in the United States, England, Canada, and Ireland. Taking advantage of British Arts and Council fellowships, he also traveled and lived in various parts of Europe. In 1974 he settled on a small farm near Mohill, County Leitrim, with his second wife, the American Madeline Green, whom he had married in 1973. Asked why he returned to his home country, he replied that his theme was Ireland and that he could not write about it from a distance.

The short stories in *Nightlines* (1970) reflect McGahern's travels to a certain extent, as some of them are set in Spain and London. They center on the void beneath much of Irish and modern life in general. The familiar characters—the policeman-father or the guard Mullins from *The Barracks*—experience the same desolation as Elizabeth or young Mahoney and have nothing but the darkness of death to look forward to. "Wheels," the first story resumes the theme of life as a disappointing cycle. This motif recurs in all the stories, as a series of frustrated characters seek to break out of the eternal circle. In his analysis of cyclical patterns in McGahern's short stories, Bertrand Cardin, in *La Licorne* (1995), emphasizes that the characters do not make progress but inevitably return to a starting point.

Nightlines was, for the most part, critically well received. Writing for *The New York Times Book Review* (7 February 1971), David Pryce-Jones remarked on some weaknesses but stressed that "such moments of banality are more than compensated by the way Mr. McGahern usually brings together the contrasting elements of his

"McGahern is one of the few writers who really seems to like sex." — *Newsweek*

the Leavetaking
A NOVEL BY
John McGahern

John McGahern's first novel, *The Barracks* (1964), won Ireland's highest literary award. His second novel, *The Dark* (1966), was banned in his native country and became a cause célebre. Mr. McGahern now divides his time between Ireland and England, where he is a lecturer at the universities of Durham and Newcastle.

558516

Author of the prizewinning THE BARRACKS and of THE DARK, which Peter Prescott called "a genuine masterpiece, a book of surpassing beauty and terror."

Atlantic · Little Brown

Dust jacket for the American edition of McGahern's 1974 novel, inspired by the controversy in Ireland over his previous novel, The Dark, *in 1965*

stories." *The Irish Times* called the collection "formidable," and Peter S. Prescott in *Newsweek* (8 February 1971) commented, "He chooses words as carefully as Chopin chose his notes, aware of the weight of each one and of the silences in between."

McGahern transformed the turmoil caused by the censorship of *The Dark* into two novels, *The Leavetaking* (1974) and *The Pornographer* (1979). In *The Leavetaking* Patrick Moran, a teacher about to lose his job because he married outside the Church, reminisces about his growing up in police barracks, the death of his mother, and how he met his American wife during his leave of absence in London. Returning to Ireland in order to show his home country to his wife, he tries to hide the marriage from the authorities, knowing the consequences if they learn that he married a divorced woman. When their secret is discovered, Moran will not resign, forcing the school manager to dismiss him. The priest vainly laments the loss of a good teacher: "Isn't there thousands of Irish Catholic girls crying out for a husband? Why couldn't you go and marry one of them?" The narrator comes to the conclusion that a

love renewed daily—the "only communion left to us now"—is the key to a contented life in the face of inevitable death.

As Jonathan Raban asserted in *Encounter* (June 1975), *The Leavetaking* "rehearses a private past which is also a public history." The critic also accentuated the parallels between Joyce and McGahern and commented positively on the dénouement of McGahern's narrative: "It is a solution for which dozens of Irish writers have craved: the hero of *The Leavetaking* does not have to go through the anguish of rejecting his history; his history gives him the sack." A typical McGahern character, the protagonist is an outsider in his community and is, according to Haberstroh, "separated from the attitudes and values of his colleagues and his country." Like Stephen Dedalus, Patrick Moran opts for exile, for only by taking leave from Ireland, Haberstroh continues, "can he continue to live and grow."

In the first paragraph McGahern introduces the central metaphors: shadow, water, and the bell. The shadows of Moran's mother's life and death descend on him and mold his life. His mother's death becomes the first in a series of endings that foreshadow his own fate. Having betrayed a deathbed promise to become a priest, Patrick has compromised by choosing teaching, his mother's profession, as his own: "My mother's dream for my life, the way that life happened to the schoolroom of this day, my memory of it and the memory of her dream, and so the tide is full, and turns out to her life." As he prepares to marry in a civil ceremony, outside the church and without a priest, Moran emphasizes the cyclical: "If I believed anything, and it was without conviction, it was that once upon a time we had crawled out of the sea and were making a circular journey back toward the original darkness." The author's favorite metaphors—the cyclical nature of existence and the vision of life as a flash of light in the dark—are thus reaffirmed. Jebb believes that the larger metaphor of the novel is love, which "is the healing rescue from the watery, shadowy, tolling call of death."

The Leavetaking further enhanced McGahern's reputation. The *TLS* reviewer (10 January 1975) considered the novel "an achievement of a very high order" that "substantiates the belief that its author is among the half dozen practicing writers of English prose most worthy of attention," and *Hibernia* praised it as "the work of a supremely gifted novelist." Like some other critics, Raban was unhappy with the second part of the novel, which he described as going "adrift when it moves to London." Moran's American lover, Isobel, and her eccentric father are generally considered less convincing than the Irish characters. McGahern later explained to Ollier what he tried to show in this novel, namely "how the language of love, the language of egotism, comes to us as lyric poetry, even our most common emotions, while the life of the beloved always comes to us as journalism." When *The Leavetaking* was translated into French, McGahern used the opportunity to revise the second part, and the novel was republished with a short preface by McGahern, a brave statement of authorial self-analysis: "I had been too close to the 'Idea,' and the work lacked that distance, that inner formality or calm, that all writing, no matter what it is attempting, must possess."

Getting Through (1978), McGahern's second collection of short stories, resumes and elaborates the theme that life is an unsatisfactory interlude between birth and death. Death or its forebodings set the characters off on vain quests to infuse their lives with meaning. Various ends and deaths overshadow the lives of McGahern's struggling characters. On the night when one couple splits up in "Along the Edges," another couple is formed in the same room—the new lovers immediately discover the greatest challenge, that they "have to face the day." The narrator of "Sierra Leone" is confronted by the breaking up of a relationship and the death of his stepmother. These stories are permeated by the same sort of symbolic darkness present in *Nightlines* and *The Dark*. For McGahern's protagonists life consists of looking forward to small events that frequently turn out to have "no existence but in the expectation." This gloom also struck Michael Irwin, who reviewed the stories for *TLS* (16 June 1978): "For all its many merits *Getting Through* is a depressing work." By contrast Tom Paulin in *Encounter* (June 1978) emphasized the "astringent purity and delicacy" of the author's prose and called it a "very distinguished collection."

The title of *The Pornographer* (1979) alludes to the name by which McGahern was known after the banning of *The Dark,* and the novel was also influenced by McGahern's experiences while lecturing at Colgate University (1969, 1972, 1977, 1979, and 1983). *The Pornographer* is a detailed study of contrasts: the moiling urban foreground of Dublin is set against a peaceful rural countryside; the wild dance of opposites also includes tradition and progress, love and death, Dublin and London, reality and fantasy. The first-person narrator, a failed poet, earns his living by turning out pornographic stories for Maloney, another failed artist who became rich by producing smut and defying the obsolete censorship laws. The pornographer's fiction describes the feats of two "sexual athletes," Colonel Grimshaw and Mavis Carmichael. In real life the narrator has a relationship with Josephine, whom he impregnates and leaves. Because he regularly visits his dying aunt in the hospital—like *The Barracks,* the novel ends with a funeral—and because of his gradually developing insight, the protagonist nevertheless engages the reader's sympathy.

Speaking to Rosa Gonzales Casademont in 1995, McGahern pointed out the dichotomy in the structure of the work: "I see pornography as a device, as the opposite of real sexuality, it's artificial, it's heightened, it's unreal, but it's the old literary trick that you look at the floor in order to see the sun, rather than looking up at the sun." The narrative again addresses questions raised in McGahern's earlier fiction. As in his previous story collection, the characters have to "get through": "Now that it was taking place it amounted to the nothing that was the rest of our life when it too was taking place." The end of the novel is rather optimistic as the pornographer appears to understand that the people and emotions he ignored do matter, whether in life or in art. Imaginative art, like meaningful life, involves selection and choices that the pornographer refuses to make until the end, when he tells the astonished Maloney that he intends to settle in his childhood home with the woman he loves.

The Pornographer provoked ambivalent reactions from critics: some praised it as McGahern's best work

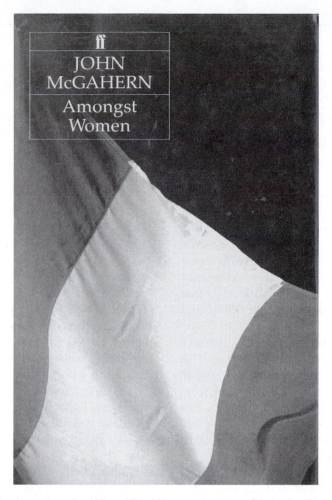

Dust jacket for McGahern's 1990 novel, which established his reputation as one of the leading Irish writers of his generation

while the majority considered the narrative somehow flawed. The main objection was to Josephine, whose pleasure in life makes her an engaging character. John Updike claimed that "we end up liking Josephine more than the hero does," which causes readers to lose sympathy with the narrator. The ending, where McGahern has his protagonist utter the following thoughts, is also seen as implausible: "By not attending, by thinking any one thing was as worth doing as any other, by sleeping with anybody who'd agree, I had been the cause of as much pain and confusion and evil as if I had actively set out to do it. I had not attended properly." Haberstroh noted that "the narrator's almost instant redemption surprises the reader and caused one critic [Jürgen Kamm] to suggest that at the end it is not clear just what has happened, and that the narrator's chief virtue, his honesty, is not quite sufficient to elicit sympathy." Or, as Paulin states, "the pornographer's moment of moral awareness sounds very hollow."

In *High Ground,* McGahern's 1985 short-story collection, many of the protagonists are forced to make painful choices. In "Gold Watch" the narrator has to resolve whether to break with his family, as his father symbolically poisons his home for him. The protagonist of "The Conversion of William Kirkwood" is a stranded Protestant who wants to be integrated in the community and therefore converts to the Catholic faith. Acting like a father to the illegitimate daughter of his servant, Annie May, he finds himself in a terrible dilemma when he falls in love with another woman who wants the servant gone. William Kirkwood is another witness to the fact that there is no perfect happiness in McGahern's universe.

In the story "Oldfashioned" several critics suspect that the novelist attempted a detached self-portrait when describing a television producer. This protagonist, son of a guard like McGahern, "made a series of documentary films about the darker aspects of Irish life. As they were controversial, they won him a sort of fame: some thought they were serious, well made, and compulsive viewing, bringing things to light that were in bad need of light; but others maintained that they were humorless, morbid, and restricted to a narrow view that was more revealing of private obsessions than any truths about life or Irish life in general." In characteristic economy McGahern thus outlines the dominating themes of his writings as well as the controversial reputation he holds in his home country. To those critics who reproached him with portraying only "the black side of Ireland," McGahern replied in his interview with Ollier that he wished neither to embellish nor to detract and insisted that "the writer's business is to get at the truth."

High Ground was well received by critics. *The Observer* called the collection "a scrupulously lyrical collection from an artist in his prime." In *The New York Times Book Review* (8 February 1987) Joel Conarroe expressed the belief that with his seventh book "McGahern joins a charmed circle of contemporary Irish writers," while Colm Tóibín stated in 1990 that "there is no evocation of Dublin in the 1950s and 1960s as powerful as his."

McGahern is best known in his home country and in England, but he is also highly regarded in France; all his books have been translated into French, and he has attracted a great deal of attention from French critics, which is documented by publications such as the special McGahern issues of *La Licorne* and *Qwerty*. In 1989 the French president named McGahern Chevalier des Arts et Lettres.

In 1990, more than ten years after publication of *The Pornographer*, McGahern published the novel that established his reputation as one of the leading Irish writers of his generation. *Amongst Women* (1990) was short-listed for the Booker Prize and won the Irish Times/Aer Lingus Irish Fiction Prize, as well as several other literary prizes. The title of *Amongst Women* is taken from the "Hail Mary" and refers to the main character, Michael Moran, a former leader of an IRA column in the war of independence and now a farmer. McGahern's archetypal conflict is staged again, and Moran's sons revolt against his tyrannical regime and leave. The women who take care of him and constitute "that larger version of himself–*his* family," are his second wife, Rose, and–possibly in an allusion to Chekhov–his three daughters, Maggie, Mona, and Sheila. When the old man dies, they pray; the rosary and the ritual circle they form when praying are just two instances where cycles appear in the narrative. The seasons follow each other in relentless sequence, as does the monotonous work on the farm; many Irish emigrate and return, old people die, and children are born. The wheels turn, and Irish history itself seems to be moving in circles. The violence that belonged to the birth of the nation resurfaces in the family; there is constant conflict between authority that attempts to reassert itself and rebellious

uprising against this oppression. Moran incorporates many of the tragic aspects of Irish history into the story. He does not talk of his days as a guerrilla leader but reacts with bitterness on perceiving that their fight has just led to a swapping of figureheads in society. Hence, he has withdrawn to his farm where he establishes his own realm, which he rules with his strict "ora et labora" maxim and, particularly, with his language, which he uses expertly like a whip, often cynically and ruthlessly. Yet, on some occasions, he is full of charm. The novel follows a circular pattern. It begins with the words "As he weakened, Moran became afraid of his daughters," and ends with the old man's death. In between is the story of how the Morans came to be as they are.

In his interview with Ollier McGahern expressed his conviction that women are at the center of life because of their role in the house and because they give birth. Men are more at the periphery: "And *Amongst Women* was deliberately a novel about power and how women, especially women, people with very little power, in a very paternalistic, confused, unnatural society, had to manage to create room for themselves. The last page is a transfer of power."

Critical response to the novel was enthusiastic. Reviewing the novel for *The Observer* (7 May 1990), novelist John Banville called it a masterpiece: "It is compact but not dense, spare yet rich, and brimming with tension." In *TLS* (18 May 1990) Lindsay Duguid emphasized that *Amongst Women* was not just "a local saga" but described "the collapse of a civilisation." He added the observation that the novel was "a portrait of a particular era and a survey of a nation's past and future." According to Rand Richards Cooper in *The New York Times Book Review* (9 September 1990), "McGahern walks the line between the beautiful and the archaic, and the result is a kind of double elegy." Sampson has stressed the fact that McGahern uses a new style and new forms whose purpose is to achieve an almost "invisible" narrative presence given by the models of Tomas O Crohan's *The Islandman* (1929) and Joyce, where the artist is "refined out of existence." John Cronin states in his 1992 essay that "McGahern has achieved in this latest novel what he so signally failed to do in the radical revision of *The Leavetaking*," namely "a stylistically seamless work." For Corcoran the "novel is a fine study of how love and power are both collusive and antagonistic in traditional patterns of Irish domestic life." A four-part television series of *Amongst Women* was broadcast by BBC 2 in July 1998.

McGahern's *The Collected Stories* was published in 1992, and he told Gonzales Casademont that for many people it "reads much more like a single book than a collection of separate stories, and that's the way I see it too." The volume comprises the stories from *Nightlines*,

Getting Through, and *High Ground* in slightly rearranged order, as well as two previously uncollected stories, "The Creamery Manager" and "The Country Funeral." The former describes the events leading to the arrest of the manager of the local creamery for embezzlement. The fate of the manager is mentioned in *The Barracks,* where it impresses Elizabeth because—apart from drunks—he is the only prisoner ever to be locked up at the station. The story is a further example of how McGahern has created a fictional world in a similar vein to William Faulkner's Yoknapatawpha County with figures, situations, and settings recurring in more than one narrative.

The second new story touches on some developments in modern Irish society by bringing together three very different brothers who meet to bury their uncle in Gloria Bog. Philly works on the oil fields in Saudi Arabia and returns to his family only for holidays, which turn into big spending sprees. Fonsie is in a wheelchair and lives with their elderly mother in Dublin, while John is a teacher who hates his job but rejects promotion. His sole aim is "to be left in peace." Philly is the only one of the trio who has emotional ties to the childhood holidays they spent on their uncle's farm, and he surprises everybody by wanting to buy it and live there. Philly's statements "that a lot of life never changes" and that "Even the fish go back to where they came from" both reflect one of McGahern's maxims and may help explain the author's own decision to return and live in Ireland. The story again evokes the notion of life turning in cycles, and, as Claudine Verley points out, it mirrors this fact in its chiastic structure: the initial setting being Dublin, followed by the journey, the funeral at Gloria Bog, and the journey back to Dublin.

The praise for these "classic short stories" has been almost unanimous. In *TLS* (9 October 1992) Penelope Fitzgerald describes McGahern as a "connoisseur" of the small things in which his characters seek refuge in the face of hopelessness. Moreover, she notes his stark realism, which is often presented in the form of pure poetry. D. J. Enright in the *London Review of Books* (8 October 1992) also stresses the poetic touches while explaining the fascination of McGahern's world with its simultaneous remoteness and familiarity.

In December 1992, *Amongst Women* was given the GPA Award by John Updike for the best book written by an Irish writer during the three previous years. The following year McGahern received an honorary doctorate from Galway University. The French honored him with the 1995 Prix Etranger Ecurieul, and in 1997 McGahern was awarded another honorary doctorate, this time from the Université de Poitiers.

McGahern in the early 1990s (photograph © Jerry Bauer; from the dust jacket for the American edition of The Collected Stories)

Since the publication of *The Collected Short Stories,* McGahern has written three long stories or novellas that signal his intent on widening his scope; yet, they remain closely interwoven with his traditional fictional world. Both "Creatures of the Earth" and "Love of the World" take into account recent developments in the Irish way of life. For instance, McGahern clearly expresses his concern for the environment of Ireland, which is suffering from an influx of tourists and callous profiteering by local people. His personal commitment may be the result of his fight to prevent the building of a pet-food factory in the neighborhood of his farm. Furthermore, the novelist describes the brutal and thoughtless manner in which people can act once the family unit has been torn apart. After showing the kind of prison a family may be, he also demonstrates what the loss of it means for society and addresses the issue of women's role in Irish society, a shift in focus that was already signaled in *Amongst Women.* The central characters in two of these stories are female. Thus, McGahern returns to the female point of view he presents with Elizabeth in *The Barracks.*

"Creatures of the Earth" (1994) relates the story of Mrs. Waldron, who loses her husband to disease and her cat to two mindless hooligans. She stops talking to an acquaintance when she learns that he has killed his dog. Like the protagonist of *The Barracks,* she is a person who loves reading and contemplates her life in philosophical terms; like Elizabeth she discovers that love is the key. Yet, in a world where consideration and empathy for the feelings of others is disappearing fast, Mrs. Waldron's frightening question also remains the same as Elizabeth's: "Was her whole life, then, all nothing?"

"Love of the World" (1997) is set in McGahern country and uses familiar characters–Kate, the daughter of small farmers, and her husband, Harbin, a guard and former football star. In a tale whose emotional scope encompasses the dimensions of classical Greek tragedy, the first-person narrator (a neighbor and cousin of Kate's parents) mentions premonitions and ominous signals that cannot prevent events from taking their relentless course. Not allowed to divorce her violent husband and lovingly attached to her children, Kate is eventually murdered by Harbin, who undergoes a metamorphosis from thoughtless hearty to evil tyrant and ultimately is associated with the devil.

In "The White Boat" (1997), McGahern again addresses the existential question of the meaning of life. The author recounts the winter journey of Richard Farnham from Limerick up the river Shannon. A retired engineer, Farnham is originally from England, but like William Kirkwood in *High Ground,* he is well integrated in his Irish environment. Nevertheless, he remains an outsider, particularly as he is equipped with an imagination that keeps him searching beyond the mere superficialities of life: "Culture, manners, gentleness. . . . Their time is never gone." This vision of eternal values is coupled with a wisdom gained during a full life–Farnham quietly accepts that he is "being pushed out on to the margins of this world." Faced with several unresolved questions, he understands that he cannot grasp the meaning of existence: "We are born in night and travel through an uncertain day to reach another night." With these words McGahern's vision has come full circle to the symbolic setting of *The Barracks.*

As the novelist constantly refers to existential questions, many readers have described his writings as bleak. McGahern, however, believes that "all good writing is joyful" and that "claustrophobic" or "oppressive" would refer to bad writing.

Denis Sampson considers McGahern a dialogic writer who engages in intertextual and critical exchange with his literary models. Moreover, he suggests that McGahern adheres to the ideal proclaimed by the young Joyce, namely that an ideal artist moves from the lyrical to the epic and dramatic. Thus, it is hardly astonishing that the novelist has tried his hand at drama: McGahern's Irish version of Leo Tolstoy's *The Power of Darkness* (1886) was first performed in Dublin in 1991 and provoked controversy. In an eloquent defense of the play, Nicholas Greene argued in *La Licorne* that most reviewers actually misunderstood the relationship between Tolstoy's model, to which the author is remarkably faithful, and the novelist's Irish version of rural calamities. British critics liked the play and were abused by their Irish counterparts for their adherence to traditional clichés about Ireland. McGahern reacted to the criticism with a preface to the published version in which he attempted to explain his personal response to the play: "*The Power of Darkness* is . . . uncannily close to the moral climate in which I grew up."

This statement provides one reason why many critics understand McGahern as an autobiographical artist. McGahern disagrees with the view that self-expression is expression: "You can't just pour out what happened to you. It has to be made different and to respect the shapes and forms of language." The novelist also emphasizes that though he uses personal experience as a springboard for his imagination, fiction is "life written to an order or vision," whereas life is "a series of accidents." McGahern is convinced that all a writer needs is a room to work in and a good, dull life. In 1995 he told Rosa Gonzales Casademont that he considers his fictional world almost complete; he wants to write one more novel and, after that, "I hope to finish writing."

Interviews:

Julia Carlson, "John McGahern," in her *Banned in Ireland: Censorship and the Irish Writer* (London: Routledge, 1990), pp. 53–67;

Denis Sampson, "A Conversation with John McGahern," *Canadian Journal of Irish Studies,* 17 (July 1991): 13–18;

Liliane Louvel, Gilles Ménégaldo, and Claudine Verley, "John McGahern–17 November 1993," *La Licorne,* special McGahern issue, 32 (1995);

Nicole Ollier, "Step by Step through *The Barracks* with John McGahern," *La Licorne,* special McGahern issue, 32 (1995);

Rosa Gonzales Casademont, "An Interview with John McGahern," *The European English Messenger,* 4, (1995): 17–23.

References:

Bertrand Cardin, "Un Aspect du Temps: Le Cycle dans les Nouvelles de John McGahern," *La Licorne,* special McGahern issue, 32 (1995);

Neil Corcoran, *After Yeats and Joyce: Reading Modern Irish Literature* (Oxford: Oxford University Press, 1997), pp. 86–91;

John Cronin, "The Dark is Not Light Enough: The Fiction of John McGahern," *Studies,* 58 (Winter 1969): 427–432;

Cronin, "John McGahern's *Amongst Women:* Retrenchment and Renewal," *Irish University Review,* 22 (1992): 168–176;

Paul Devine, "Style and Structure in John McGahern's *The Dark,*" *Critique,* 21 (1979): 49–57;

Roger Garfitt, "Constants in Contemporary Irish Fiction," *Two Decades of Irish Writing,* edited by Douglas Dunn (London: Carcanet, 1975), pp. 207–241;

Nicholas Greene, "John McGahern's *The Power of Darkness,*" *La Licorne,* special McGahern issue, 32 (1995);

Jürgen Kamm, "John McGahern," in *Contemporary Irish Novelists,* edited by Rüdiger Imhof (Tübingen: Gunter Narr, 1990), pp. 175–191;

José Lanters, "'It Fills Many a Vacuum': Food and Hunger in the Early Novels of John McGahern," *Canadian Journal of Irish Studies,* 20 (July 1994): 30–40;

Richard Burr Lloyd, "The Symbolic Mass: Thematic Resolution in the Irish Novels of John McGahern," *Emporia State Research Studies,* 36 (Fall 1987): 5–23;

Shaun O'Connell, "Door into Light: John McGahern's Ireland," *Massachusetts Review,* 25 (Summer 1984): 255–268;

Lori Rogers, *Feminine Nation: Performance, Gender, and Resistance in the Works of John McGahern and Neil Jordan* (Lanham, Md.: University Press of America, 1998);

Denis Sampson, *Outstaring Nature's Eye: The Fiction of John McGahern* (Washington, D.C.: Catholic University of America Press, 1993);

Colm Tóibín, "Out of the Dark," in his *The Trial of the Generals: Selected Journalism 1980–1990* (Dublin: Raven Arts, 1990), pp. 94–102;

John Updike, "An Old-Fashioned Novel," in his *Hugging the Shore: Essays and Criticism* (New York: Knopf, 1983), pp. 388–393;

Claudine Verley, "It's About Time You Gave Where You're Going Some Thought: 'The Country Funeral' de John McGahern," *La Licorne,* special McGahern issue, 32 (1995).

Patrick McGrath

(2 February 1950 –   )

Nicholas Freeman
University of Bristol

BOOKS: *Blood and Water and Other Tales* (New York: Poseidon, 1988; London: Penguin, 1989);
The Grotesque (New York: Poseidon, 1989; London: Viking, 1989);
Spider (New York: Poseidon, 1990; London: Viking, 1991);
Dr. Haggard's Disease (New York: Poseidon, 1993; London: Viking, 1993);
Asylum (London: Viking, 1996; New York: Random House, 1997);
Martha Peake: A Novel of the Revolution (New York: Random House, 2000; London: Penguin, 2000).

PRODUCED SCRIPT: *The Grotesque,* motion picture, Xingu Films/Starlight, 1995.

OTHER: *The New Gothic: A Collection of Contemporary Gothic Fiction,* edited by McGrath and Bradford Morrow (New York: Random House, 1991; London: Picador, 1992);
"Cleave the Vampire, or a Gothic Pastorale," in *I Shudder at Your Touch,* edited by Michele Slung (London: BCA, 1991), pp. 117–130.

Patrick McGrath emerged during the 1990s as a leading practitioner of what has been styled "New Gothic." As McGrath says in his introduction to *The New Gothic: A Collection of Contemporary Gothic Fiction* (1991), this fictional form, by McGrath's definition, transplants Edgar Allan Poe's fascination with the disturbed psyche of his protagonists to the modern world rather than dwelling, on the "props, settings . . . furniture" of first-generation Gothic novelists such as Horace Walpole and Anne Radcliffe. His reputation has grown with the appearance of each of his four novels. While his early fiction was occasionally derivative, his mature works have shown him to be an innovative and perceptive writer, whose insight into the sinister minds of his protagonists is compelling and unsettling.

The eldest of four children, Patrick John McGrath was born in London on 2 February 1950 to

Patrick McGrath, circa 1997 (photograph © by Marion Ettlinger; from the dust jacket for the American edition of Asylum)

Patrick and Helen Patricia O'Brien McGrath. His father was an influential psychiatrist who was later awarded Commander of the Order of the British Empire (1971) and Companion of the Order of the Bath (1981) for his work in psychiatric medicine. From 1957 to 1981, Dr. McGrath was medical superintendent of Broadmoor Hospital, which counted among its patients many of the most dangerous criminals in Great Britain. His *Times* (London) obituary (28 October 1994) notes how "in his 25 years of service . . . he converted a grim, forbidding institution into a caring, efficient psychiatric hospital," receiving widespread acclaim for his application of humane and progressive psychiatric ideas. He did, however, face criticism and calls for resignation on some occasions, notably when several patients released from the hospital committed offenses again and when another escaped and was on the run for three days in the Berkshire countryside. Dr. McGrath enjoyed regaling his young son with stories about his patients, always differentiating between the individual courses of their lives and the "psychological model" of their illnesses. Interviewed by John Walsh for *The Independent Magazine* in May 1993, McGrath revealed his fascination with these tales. "You could see them as journeys into jealousy, rage, psychosis—as narratives of breakdown," he remarked, a comment equally applicable to his fiction. McGrath has never disguised the important role his father played in his writing; an acknowledgment in *Dr. Haggard's Disease* (1993) thanks him for his "immense help . . . medical, psychiatric and literary" with that novel and with *Spider* (1990). Broadmoor Hospital seems to have a lingering influence on McGrath's imagination. In *The Grotesque* (1989), for example, he names a character Crowthorne after the village close to the hospital. It also seems possible the ingenious murderer of "The Arnold Crombeck Story" in *Blood and Water and Other Tales* (1988) may owe something of his technical skill to Graham Young, the notorious poisoner who was hospitalized at Broadmoor during the 1960s before his controversial release in 1971.

McGrath attended Jesuit schools in the early to mid 1960s, first Beaumont on the south coast and then, in 1965, Stoneyhurst in Lancashire. His early schooling was generally enjoyable, but the move north was a traumatic one, and McGrath rebelled against the strict ethos of Stoneyhurst, later caricaturing it as "Ravengloom" in "Ambrose Syme," a short story collected in *Blood and Water*. He left Stoneyhurst and enrolled at Bracknell College of Further Education, but by then his education had been severely disrupted, and he made what he has termed a "ghastly mess" of his final examinations. This setback meant that he did not attend a conventional university but the City of Birmingham College of Commerce, which conferred external degrees from the University of London. He read English there during the late 1960s, eventually graduating in 1971. He did not find his studies particularly rewarding. During this period McGrath, caught up in the aimless hedonism typical of the time, experienced the final loss of his religious faith.

Dr. McGrath responded to his son's lack of direction by finding him work in an asylum in Ontario, Canada. McGrath worked in psychiatric institutions for about two years, gaining further useful insights into their regimes and their patients, before beginning a series of teaching jobs in elementary schools. Between 1973 and 1978, he taught English in Vancouver, British Columbia, and the Queen Charlotte Islands, attempting to be "socially useful," though becoming increasingly interested in writing. Inspired by Malcolm Lowry, who had led a similar lifestyle in Canada during the 1940s, McGrath made his first attempts to write in a hut in the Queen Charlotte Islands but found himself too withdrawn from civilization to pursue the experiment. In 1979 he moved back to Vancouver, then in 1980 to Toronto. He used the idea of being "sent to Canada" as a euphemism for murder in his second novel, *Spider*. Finally, in what proved a critical moment in his life, he went to New York in 1981. There he lived on the East Side with a Hungarian artist, Orshi, to whom he dedicated his first two books. Finding at last a sympathetic literary and creative community, McGrath began writing stories and performing his work in cafés.

During McGrath's involvement in the New York literary life of the 1980s, he worked as a writer, performer, and editor. He helped to found a magazine called *Between C and D* and was an habitué of the Life Café in the East Village, behaving in a manner he has termed "*utterly* Bohemian in the worst way." Since the appearance of *Blood and Water and Other Tales* in 1988, he has published four novels, co-edited an anthology, *The New Gothic,* with Bradford Morrow, and written the screenplay for the movie version of *The Grotesque,* released in 1995.

Reviewing *Dr. Haggard's Disease* in *TLS: The Times Literary Supplement* (14 May 1993), M. John Harrison remarked, "All of us readers and all of his characters are at the mercy of Patrick McGrath . . . and McGrath is as clever as a barrel load of monkeys." His fiction frequently employs unreliable, even pathological narrators, whose artful distortion of their worlds often becomes explicit only at the conclusion of the novel. Characters such as Edward Haggard in *Dr. Haggard's Disease* and the terrifying Peter Cleave of *Asylum* (1996) present their narratives of alienation, paranoia, and disturbing sexual fantasy in impeccably well-mannered prose. Eschewing, in his most successful work, both gothic histrionics and the elaborate self-reference of postmodern metafiction, McGrath employs an almost Jamesian subtlety, luring the reader onto shifting sands and abandoning him to face the consequences. Both *Dr. Haggard's Disease* and *Asylum* end with horrifying disclosures, but not in the sense of the "twist" favored by, for instance, O. Henry or Roald Dahl. McGrath's conclusions are the logical productions of their speakers' neuroses, rather than the formulaic obligations of the "tale of the unexpected." Reviewing the novel for *The Independent Magazine* (8 May 1993), Anthony Quinn, a perceptive critic of McGrath's writing, has called his fictions "feverish

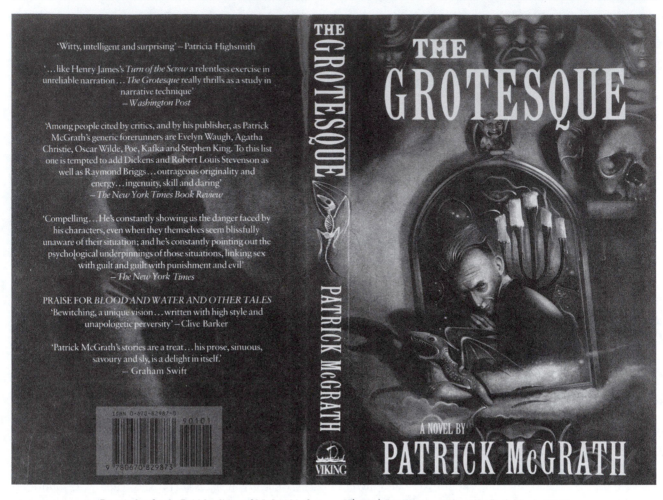

Dust jacket for the British edition of McGrath's first novel (1989), set in a manor house in Berkshire in 1949

studies in derangement, each spiralling unmercifully towards a revelation that is no less appalling for being entirely inevitable."

Blood and Water and Other Tales collects stories written between 1981 and 1987 while McGrath was living in New York. He experimented with a variety of styles and tropes, setting pieces in an imaginative England he later made his own, but also using locations such as contemporary New York, Victorian India, and the Louisiana swamps. There is even "The E(rot)ic Potato," a story set on a decaying human corpse and narrated by a blowfly. Stories such as "Lush Triumphant" and "The Angel," which seem inspired by sightings of Quentin Crisp in Manhattan, are examples of how McGrath's work might have developed if he had concentrated on American surroundings. The most-successful pieces—the title story, "Arnold Crombeck," and "Blood Disease"—are good models for McGrath's specifically constructed England. Like Graham Greene's "Greeneland,"

McGrath's England is as much a state of mind as a real place, a world of pea-soup fog, shabby pubs, Woodbines and gin, or alternatively, a seething panorama of the English upper class in bitter and terminal decline. Through both settings walk a cast of tortured and disturbed figures, who are aware that they are in some way disconnected from society without having enough insight to realize why they exist in precarious psychic isolation. Many of McGrath's stories are set in this England during the first half of the twentieth century; the technicolor world of the 1960s, with its rapid advances in communication and media technology is antipathetic to his imaginative methods, while the sexual freedoms of the period are similarly out of keeping with his concentration on repressed or illicit desire. McGrath once said he hoped he would never write a story featuring a television set. Nick Riddle points out that *Asylum* does feature one, but that "its location in the communal day room of a mental institution is hardly an endorsement."

The Grotesque (1989), McGrath's first novel, is set in Berkshire in 1949 and convincingly captures the gloomy austerity of postwar England. The story tells of how Sir Hugo Coal, a ferocious baronet and amateur palaeontologist, is left crippled and mute by a horrifying chain of events initiated by his new butler, Fledge. Through means of his "corrupt energies," as Hugo calls them, Fledge inveigles his way into the Coal household, seduces Hugo's wife, murders Hugo's daughter's fiancé, and establishes himself as the new lord of the manor. Highly atmospheric in its evocation of gloomy marshland settings, the novel carries a considerable satirical charge in its narrative of class revolt, but for all the elegance of McGrath's prose and the sound construction of the novel, the end result is something of a pastiche. Fledge resembles both Mervyn Peake's Steerpike in *Gormenghast* (1950), who is determined to bring down the edifice of Gormenghast by whatever means necessary, and Barrett, the corrupt valet in Robin Maugham's *The Servant* (1948). Evelyn Waugh's early fiction seems another potent influence. The grimly jokey tone, encapsulated in character names such as "Sidney Giblet," prevents the reader from ever taking events too seriously. A similar perspective manifested itself in earlier stories–such as "The Black Hand of the Raj" and "A Boot's Tale" in *Blood and Water*–suggesting that McGrath enjoys celebrating and satirizing Gothic ideas simultaneously. While this tone gives his shorter works an engaging dash of splenetic humor, it seems to work against the more elaborately constructed tensions of a novel. Yet, critical response was generally warm. Sir Hugo, who manages to be both ludicrous and sympathetic, is an early example of McGrath's skill in manipulating his narrative through treacherous intermediaries. The 1995 movie version of the book, for which McGrath wrote the screenplay, and in which Sting played Fledge, is unconvincing, mainly because it was too lovingly photographed–the world of Ceck Marsh emerged as plein-air impressionism rather than stagnant horror. Chris Darke of *Sight and Sound* was unimpressed, comparing it unfavorably to *The Servant* (1963) and Trevor Howard's *Sir Henry at Rawlinson End* (1981). McGrath enjoyed his involvement with the project, and studio interest in a screen version of *Asylum* has been notable.

McGrath's next novel was more ambitious than his first. *Spider* (1990) cast as the thoughts of Dennis "Spider" Cleg, a schizophrenic young man whose strange behavior, suspicions, and obsessions gradually reveal a narrative of murderous familial dysfunction. The London of *Spider* is a place of perpetual, or perpetually imminent, rain and fogbound dereliction. "A clotted web of dark compartments and narrow passageways," the city offers an uncanny analogue of the narrator's mind, and, in The Earl of Rochester, boasts the most horribly believable public house in English fiction since those of Patrick Hamilton's *Hangover Square* (1941). The England of the 1930s in which Spider grew up and that of the 1950s from which he recalls his youth are presented with disquietening exactitude, and critics were largely impressed with McGrath's attempt to evoke and analyze the tortured psyche of his narrator. Tim Gooderham's review for *TLS* (26 April 1991), however, found the book "just tenable" as a "case history of schizophrenia" but unconvincing as a novel, largely because of Spider's "fits of delusion that seem to take liberties with what could feasably be written in a journal."

In 1991 McGrath met British actress Maria Aitken, who had come to the United States to lecture at Yale Drama School. They were married seven weeks later. Aitken specializes in icy social comedy and appears in the movie version of *The Grotesque*.

In the same year, McGrath co-edited *The New Gothic* anthology with Bradford Morrow, with whom he had worked on several literary projects in New York. In his introduction to the book McGrath suggests ways in which the "New Gothic" transplants a concern with psychic trauma to modern, generally urban environments, exploring in the process the "hell on earth" that is "located within the vaults and chambers of our own minds." The anthology focuses on "horror, madness, monstrosity, death, disease, terrror, evil, and weird sexuality" in presenting stories and novel excerpts by contemporary writers such as Anne Rice, Martin Amis, Jeanette Winterson, Angela Carter, and Kathy Acker. The result was an intriguing mixture, although the presumption that "New Gothic" is a contemporary phenomenon sometimes led to misleading results. Forty or even fifty years earlier writers such as Robert Bloch and Fritz Leiber had written stories that would fit in well while the contributions from Rice, John Hawkes, and John Edgar Wideman sit uncomfortably alongside the introductory rationale, exploiting period settings or traditionally Gothic locales such as the ruined abbey. McGrath's contribution to the book, "The Smell," originally published in *Blood and Water,* was an entertaining study of monomania, although–like several of his earlier stories–it is rather uncertain in tone and overreliant on mannered diction of the "all swam before my eyes" school. The story does, however, boast a memorably horrible conclusion, the type beloved by what McGrath calls his "Clive Barker readership."

McGrath's next novel, *Dr. Haggard's Disease* (1993), is a tale of doomed adulterous love between a young surgeon and the wife of a senior pathologist. The novel uses the London of the 1930s, as was the case in *Spider,* as an imaginative backdrop to events. This time, however, the characterization is subtler, the

Dust jacket for McGrath's 1996 novel, which draws in part on the 1961 escape of a dangerous criminal from Broadmoor Hospital, at which McGrath's father was superintendent

review for *The Independent,* while Adam Zamoyski in the 8 May 1993 issue of *The Times* (London) found it "a beautiful story, impressively told." In his 11 May 1993 review, Christopher Hawtree of *The Evening Standard* (London) drew attention to the high quality of McGrath's actual writing. "One of the most finely controlled prose styles in contemporary fiction," he commented, judging the novel, "compulsive." American critics were similarly laudatory.

With *Asylum* (1996) McGrath's interest in *amour fou* reached new heights. Whereas his previous novels had been narrated by their central protagonists–Sir Hugo, Dennis Cleg, Edward Haggard–*Asylum* employs a seemingly dispassionate voice, that of Peter Cleave, a psychiatrist who watches from the sidelines as a destructive love triangle evolves in the claustrophobic world of a secure hospital during the summer of 1959. Stella Raphael, the beautiful but bored wife of Cleave's colleague Max is drawn to a dangerously disturbed patient, the charismatic and passionate sculptor Edgar Stark. Stark is receiving psychiatric treatment after murdering his wife but seems "normal" enough to be allowed to work in the hospital garden. He and Stella embark on an affair, which quickly leads to Edgar's escape from the hospital. Stella follows him to London, where they attempt to begin a life together. Hunted by the police and becoming dangerously jealous and obsessive once deprived of his medication, Edgar reveals a totally different side of himself and places Stella in considerable danger as the true nature of his psychosis and past crimes become apparent.

The hospital setting is McGrath's most explicit acknowledgment of his own background, and details such as the delay in notifying the authorities regarding Stark's escape are paralleled by an actual Broadmoor incident: in 1961 a Member of Parliament called for Dr. McGrath's resignation following a six-hour delay in reporting an escape. In researching the book McGrath returned to Broadmoor, where the library is named after his father. His understanding of psychological fragility surpasses even his knowledge of institutional practice, as is shown by his handling of events in the book. Once Edgar is recaptured, Stella returns to her husband to continue the joyless farrago of their marriage. Max's career is in free fall following Stella's involvement with Edgar, and the couple move to Wales, where Stella's mind begins to deteriorate. She loses her self-respect in a meaningless and brutal affair with a local farmer and is then hospitalized following the death of her son on a school field trip–in an accident she observes but does nothing to prevent. In the asylum under the treatment of Cleave, Stella is tormented by her lingering desire for Edgar and her longing to

narrator less obviously unreliable, and the final twist McGrath's most accomplished yet. Earlier stories indulge in in-jokes for the Gothic cognoscenti, but the comic elements in *Dr. Haggard's Disease* are far less apparent than in previous works, and the novel emerges as a moving account of an impossible relationship and a frightening dissection of obsessive desire. Crippled by an accident, the pain of which leaves him addicted to morphine, Haggard–whose name suggests both exhaustion and the horror film director Piers Haggard–is, initially at least, a sympathetic figure. The arrival of his lover's son at the nearby Royal Air Force base, however, triggers a descent into the psychiatric maelstrom. Although Harrison, in his review for *TLS,* was impressed by the novel on the whole, he wondered whether "we lose sight of love in its own pathology." Overall, the novel was warmly received by critics. "I haven't read a novel as piercingly truthful about the loss of love since Greene's *The End of the Affair,*" wrote Quinn in his escape. As Cleave's obsession with her grows, she is forced into a desperate act.

The humor that has been gradually ebbing from McGrath's writing since the publication of *The Grotesque* has almost entirely disappeared in *Asylum*. The novelist has instead produced a sober version of events. His style is also austere, in keeping with the almost too-detached intellect of Dr. Cleave and with the relentlessly bleak narrative of Stella's degradation and collapse. As in all his work, though, McGrath shows his flair for the evocation of past experience in the imaginations of his characters—Stella's memories of her love, like those of Edward Haggard in his previous novel, are poignant, erotic, and beautifully observed. Phil Baker, who reviewed *Asylum* for *The Sunday Times* (18 August 1996), has suggested that *Asylum* is more akin to Thomas Hardy than to Edgar Allan Poe, implying that McGrath is breaking free of the constraints of Gothic and its reinventions and heading for new territory.

McGrath is an increasingly difficult writer to categorize. His main literary influences are drawn from a childhood fondness for Poe, Herbert van Thal's Pan horror anthologies of the 1950s and 1960s, and a brief undergraduate enthusiasm for Mervyn Peake; yet, little in these writings prepares the reader for McGrath's work from *Spider* onward. His experiences in the field of mental health are more telling, but perhaps the most interesting attribute of McGrath's work is his view of England. "I suppose I do seem to be inventing an England in my books," he told John Walsh. "It's one built on scraps of childhood evidence, on Evelyn Waugh and the *Masterpiece Theatre*. It's a construct that bears only a parodic resemblance to the real one." His dual residence in London—where he lives near the Imperial War Museum, built on the site of the old "Bedlam" hospital—and New York, is one suggestion of why he views England in the way he does. "If I'd lived in England all the time, there wouldn't be the same space between the real and fictional worlds."

Interviews:

John Walsh, "Tales of pukka madness," *Independent Magazine* (1 May 1993): 42–44;

Nick Riddle, "Out of control," *Waterstone's Magazine* (Summer–Autumn 1997): 62–69.

Michael Moorcock

(18 December 1939 –   )

Nicholas Freeman
University of Bristol

See also the Moorcock entry in *DLB 14: British Novelists Since 1960.*

BOOKS: *Caribbean Crisis,* by Moorcock and James Cawthorn as Desmond Reid (London: Sexton Blake Library, 1962);

The Stealer of Souls and Other Stories (London: Spearman, 1963; New York: Lancer, 1967);

The Barbarians of Mars, as Edward P. Bradbury (London: Roberts & Vinter, 1965; New York: Lancer, 1966); republished as *The Masters of the Pit,* as Moorcock (New York: Lancer, 1970; London: New English Library, 1971);

Blades of Mars, as Bradbury (London: Roberts & Vinter, 1965; New York: Lancer, 1966); republished as *Lord of the Spiders,* as Moorcock (New York: Lancer, 1970; London: New English Library, 1971);

Warriors of Mars, as Bradbury (London: Roberts & Vinter, 1965; New York: Lancer, 1966); republished as *The City of the Beast,* as Moorcock (New York: Lancer, 1970; London: New English Library, 1971);

Stormbringer (London: Jenkins, 1965; New York: Lancer, 1967);

The Sundered Worlds (London: Roberts & Vinter, 1965; New York: Paperback Library, 1966); republished as *The Blood Red Game* (London: Sphere, 1970);

The Fireclown (London: Roberts & Vinter, 1965; New York: Paperback Library, 1967); republished as *The Winds of Limbo* (New York: Paperback Library, 1969; London: Sphere, 1970);

The Twilight Man (London: Roberts & Vinter, 1966; New York: Berkley, 1970); republished as *The Shores of Death* (London: Sphere, 1970; New York: Dale, 1978);

Somewhere in the Night, as Bill Barclay (London: Roberts & Vinter, 1966); revised as *The Chinese Agent,* as Moorcock (London: Hutchinson, 1970; New York: Macmillan, 1970);

Michael Moorcock (photograph by Linda Steele; from the dust jacket for Lunching with the Antichrist, *1995)*

The Deep Fix, as James Colvin (London: Roberts & Vinter, 1966);

Printer's Devil, as Barclay (London: Roberts & Vinter, 1966); revised as *The Russian Intelligence,* as Moorcock (Manchester: Savoy, 1980);

152

The Wrecks of Time (New York: Ace, 1967); republished as *The Rituals of Infinity* (London: Arrow, 1971; New York: DAW, 1978);

The Jewel in the Skull (New York: Lancer, 1967; London: Mayflower, 1969);

Sorcerer's Amulet (New York: Lancer, 1968); republished as *The Mad God's Amulet* (London: Mayflower, 1969; revised edition, New York: DAW, 1977);

The Final Programme (New York: Avon, 1968; London: Allison & Busby, 1969; revised edition, London: Fontana, 1979);

The Sword of the Dawn (New York: Lancer, 1968; London: Mayflower, 1969; revised edition, New York: DAW, 1977);

Behold the Man (London: Allison & Busby, 1969; New York: Avon, 1970);

The Secret of the Runestaff (New York: Lancer, 1969); republished as *The Runestaff* (London: Mayflower, 1969; revised edition, New York: DAW, 1977);

The Ice Schooner (New York: Berkley, 1969; London: Sphere, 1969; revised edition, New York: Dell, 1978; London: Harrap, 1985);

The Black Corridor, by Moorcock and Hilary Bailey (London: Mayflower, 1969; New York: Ace, 1969);

The Time Dweller (London: Hart-Davis, 1969; New York: Berkley, 1971);

The Eternal Champion (London: Mayflower, 1970; New York: Dell, 1970);

Phoenix in Obsidian (London: Mayflower, 1970); republished as *The Silver Warriors* (New York: Dell, 1973);

The Singing Citadel (London: Mayflower, 1970; New York: Berkley, 1970);

A Cure for Cancer (London: Allison & Busby, 1971; New York: Holt, Rinehart & Winston, 1971; revised edition, London: Fontana, 1979);

The Knight of the Swords (London: Mayflower, 1971; New York: Berkley, 1971);

The Sleeping Sorceress (London: New English Library, 1971; New York: Lancer, 1972); republished as *The Vanishing Tower* (London: New English Library, 1972; New York: DAW, 1977);

The Warlord of the Air (London: New English Library, 1971; New York: Ace, 1971);

The Queen of the Swords (London: Mayflower, 1971; New York: Berkley, 1971);

The King of the Swords (London: Mayflower, 1971; New York: Berkley, 1971);

Breakfast in the Ruins (London: New English Library, 1972; New York: Random House, 1974);

The English Assassin (London: Allison & Busby, 1972; New York: Harper & Row, 1974; revised edition, London: Fontana, 1979);

Elric of Melniboné (London: Hutchinson, 1972; New York: DAW, 1976); republished as *The Dreaming City* (New York: Lancer, 1972);

An Alien Heat (London: MacGibbon & Kee, 1972; New York: Harper & Row, 1973);

Count Brass (London: Mayflower, 1973; New York: Dell, 1976);

The Bull and the Spear (London: Allison & Busby, 1973; New York: Berkley, 1974);

The Champion of Garathorm (London: Mayflower, 1973; New York: Dell, 1976);

The Oak and the Ram (London: Allison & Busby, 1973; New York: Berkley, 1974);

The Jade Man's Eyes (Brighton, U.K. & Seattle: Unicorn, 1973);

The Land Leviathan (London: Quartet, 1974; Garden City, N.Y.: Doubleday, 1974);

The Sword and the Stallion (London: Allison & Busby, 1974; New York: Berkley, 1974);

The Hollow Lands (New York: Harper & Row, 1974; London: Hart-Davis, MacGibbon, 1975);

The Quest for Tanelorn (London: Mayflower, 1975; New York: Dell, 1976);

The Distant Suns, by Moorcock and Philip James (Llanfynydd, U.K.: Unicorn, 1975);

The Lives and Times of Jerry Cornelius (London: Allison & Busby, 1976; New York: Harper & Row, 1976);

The Adventures of Una Persson and Catherine Cornelius in the Twentieth Century (London: Quartet, 1976; New York: Harper & Row, 1976);

Legends from the End of Time (New York: Harper & Row, 1976; London: W. H. Allen, 1976);

The Sailor on the Seas of Fate (London: Quartet, 1976; New York: DAW, 1976);

The End of All Songs (New York: Harper & Row, 1976; London: Hart-Davis, MacGibbon, 1976);

Moorcock's Book of Martyrs (London: Quartet, 1976); republished as *Dying for Tomorrow* (New York: DAW, 1978);

The Time of the Hawklords, by Moorcock and Michael Butterworth (London: Star, 1976; New York: Warner, 1976);

The Transformation of Miss Mavis Ming (London: W. H. Allen, 1977); republished as *A Messiah at the End of Time* (New York: DAW, 1978);

The Condition of Muzak (London: Allison & Busby, 1977; Boston: Gregg, 1978);

The Weird of the White Wolf (New York: DAW, 1977; London: Panther, 1984);

The Bane of the Black Sword (New York: DAW, 1977; London: Panther, 1984);

Sojan (Manchester: Savoy, 1977);

Epic Pooh (London: British Fantasy Society, 1978);

Gloriana, or The Unfulfill'd Queen (London: Allison & Busby, 1978; New York: Avon, 1979; revised edition, London: Phoenix, 1993);

The Real Life Mr. Newman (Worcester, U.K.: A. J. Callow, 1979);

The Golden Barge (Manchester: Savoy, 1979; New York: DAW, 1980);

The Great Rock 'n' Roll Swindle (London: Virgin, 1980);

My Experiences in the Third World War (Manchester: Savoy, 1980);

The Entropy Tango (London: New English Library, 1981);

The Steel Tsar (London: Granada, 1981; New York: DAW, 1982);

The War Hound and the World's Pain (New York: Timescape, 1981; London: New English Library, 1982);

Byzantium Endures (London: Secker & Warburg, 1981; New York: Random House, 1982);

The Brothel in Rösenstrasse (London: New English Library, 1982; New York: Carroll & Graf, 1987);

The Retreat from Liberty: The Erosion of Democracy in Today's Britain (London: Zomba, 1983);

Elric at the End of Time (London: New English Library, 1984; New York: DAW, 1984);

The Laughter of Carthage (London: Secker & Warburg, 1984; New York: Random House, 1984);

The Opium General and Other Stories (London: Harrap, 1984);

The Crystal and the Amulet (Manchester: Savoy, 1986);

The Dragon in the Sword (New York: Ace, 1986; London: Grafton, 1987);

Letters from Hollywood, by Moorcock and Michael Foreman (London: Harrap, 1986);

The City in the Autumn Stars (London: Grafton, 1986; New York: Ace, 1987);

Letters from Hollywood, by Moorcock and Michael Foreman (London: Harrap, 1986);

Wizardry and Wild Romance: A Study of Epic Fantasy (London: Gollancz, 1987);

Fantasy: The One Hundred Best Books (London: Xanadu, 1988; New York: Carroll & Graff, 1988);

Mother London (London: Secker & Warburg, 1988; New York: Ace, 1989);

Casablanca and Other Stories (London: Gollancz, 1989);

The Fortress of the Pearl (London: Gollancz, 1989; New York: Ace, 1989);

The Revenge of the Rose (London: Grafton, 1991; New York: Ace, 1991);

Earl Aubec (London: Millennium, 1993; Clarkston, Ga.: White Wolf, 1999);

The Birds of the Moon (London: Jayde Design, 1995);

Blood: A Southern Fantasy (London: Millennium, 1995; New York: Morrow, 1995);

Fabulous Harbours (New York: Avon, 1995; London: Millennium, 1995);

Lunching with the Antichrist (Shingletown, Cal.: Mark V. Ziesing, 1995);

The War Among the Angels (New York: Avon, 1996; London: Millennium, 1996);

Tales from the Texas Woods (Austin, Tex.: Mojo Press, 1997);

King of the City (London: Scribner, 2000).

Collections: *The Cornelius Chronicles* (New York: Avon, 1977; 2 volumes, London: Fontana, 1988); republished as *The Cornelius Quartet* (London: Phoenix, 1993);

The Swords Trilogy (New York: Berkley, 1977); republished as *The Swords of Corum* (London: Grafton, 1986); republished as *Corum* (London: Millennium, 1992); republished as *Corum: The Coming of Chaos* (London: Millennium, 1996; Clarkston, Ga.: White Wolf, 1999);

The Chronicles of Corum (New York: Berkley, 1978; London: Grafton, 1986); republished as *The Prince with the Silver Hand* (London: Millennium, 1993; revised edition, London: Orion, 1997); republished as *Corum: The Prince with the Silver Hand* (Clarkston, Ga.: White Wolf, 1999);

The History of the Runestaff (London: Hart-Davis, Mac-Gibbon, 1979); republished as *Hawkmoon* (London: Millennium, 1992; Clarkston, Ga.: White Wolf, 1995);

The Dancers at the End of Time (London & New York: Granada, 1981; revised edition, London: Millennium, 1993; Clarkston, Ga.: White Wolf, 1998);

Warriors of Mars (London: New English Library, 1981; New York: Ace, 1991); republished as *Kane of Old Mars* (Clarkston, Ga.: White Wolf, 1998);

The Nomad of Time (Garden City, N.Y.: Doubleday, 1981; London: Panther, 1984); republished as *A Nomad of the Time Streams* (London: Millennium, 1993; Clarkston, Ga.: White Wolf, 1995);

The Elric Saga, 2 volumes (Garden City, N.Y.: Doubleday, 1984);

The Chronicles of Castle Brass (London: Granada, 1985); revised as *Count Brass* (London: Millennium, 1993);

The Cornelius Chronicles, Volume 2 (New York: Avon, 1986);

The Cornelius Chronicles, Volume 3 (New York: Avon, 1987);

Tales from the End of Time (New York: Guild America, 1989); enlarged as *Legends from the End of Time* (Clarkston, Ga.: White Wolf, 1999);

Von Bek (London: Millennium, 1992);

A Cornelius Calendar (London: Phoenix, 1993);

Elric of Melniboné (London: Millennium, 1993); republished as *Elric: Song of the Black Sword* (Clarkston, Ga.: White Wolf, 1995);

Sailing to Utopia (London: Millennium, 1993; Clarkston, Ga.: White Wolf, 1997);

Behold the Man and Other Stories (London: Phoenix, 1994);

Michael Moorcock's the Roads between the Worlds (Clarkston, Ga.: White Wolf, 1996);

Elric: The Stealer of Souls (Clarkston, Ga.: White Wolf, 1998).

PRODUCED SCRIPT: *The Land That Time Forgot*, motion picture, script by Moorcock and James Cawthorn, Amicus Productions / American International Pictures, 1974.

OTHER: *The Best of "New Worlds,"* edited by Moorcock (London: Roberts & Vinter, 1965);

The Nature of the Catastrophe, edited by Moorcock and Langdon Jones (London: Hutchinson, 1971);

Before Armageddon: An Anthology of Victorian and Edwardian Imaginative Fiction Published before 1914, edited by Moorcock (London: W. H. Allen, 1975);

England Invaded: A Collection of Fantasy Fiction, edited by Moorcock (London: W. H. Allen, 1977);

New Worlds: An Anthology, edited by Moorcock (London: Fontana, 1983);

The New Nature of the Catastrophe, edited by Moorcock and Jones (London: Millennium, 1993);

H. G. Wells, *The Island of Doctor Moreau*, edited by Moorcock (London: Dent, 1993);

Wells, *The Time Machine*, edited by Moorcock (London: Dent, 1993; Rutland, Vt.: Tuttle, 1998).

SELECTED PERIODICAL PUBLICATIONS–UNCOLLECTED: "Play with Feeling," *New Worlds*, 43 (April 1963): 2–3, 123–127;

"New Worlds: A Personal History," *Foundation: The Review of Science Fiction*, 15 (January 1979): 5–18;

"Wit and Humour in Fantasy," *Foundation: The Review of Science Fiction*, 16 (May 1979): 16–22;

"Who'll Be Next?," *Index-on-Censorship* (April 1984): 2–4;

"Movie Nightmares," *Sight & Sound* (May 1993): 5, 30–39.

For forty years Michael Moorcock has been an influential presence in English fiction. As a writer, editor, and sponsor of new talent, he has had a great impact on popular writing and in channeling avant-garde ideas into the mainstream. Associated with, and in many ways responsible for, British "New Wave" science fiction during the 1960s, Moorcock has also been active in other fields, such as "literary" fiction, cinema, and rock music. His enormous output is impossible to categorize. Much of it combines the vitality and diversity of popular culture with the highest artistic standards. His eclectic imagination is fed by wide and diverse reading, especially in the literature of London and the Victorian period, and a fascination with ephemera of all kinds, from street ballads to cigarette cards.

Michael John Moorcock was born on 18 December 1939 in Mitcham, Surrey. The only child of Arthur Moorcock, a draftsman who deserted the family in 1945, and June Taylor Moorcock, who eventually became a director of a timber firm, he grew up during World War II watching Battle of Britain dogfights from his mother's arms. As Colin Greenland noted in *DLB 14*, "Moorcock's imaginative fiction has been strongly conditioned by the wartime landscapes of his childhood," and his descriptions of war-torn cities, however fantastic their context, retain something of his early experiences, reaching their apotheosis with the evocation of the Luftwaffe's attacks on the East End in his 1988 novel, *Mother London*.

After his father's departure, Moorcock and his mother moved from place to place around South London—a vagabond existence that played havoc with his formal education—finally settling in Norbury, where Moorcock grew up. It has been said he had a turbulent relationship with authority at this time, but in his own view, he was perfectly willing to accept educational power structures so long as teachers were able to maintain his interest and respect. A precocious and intellectually challenging child, he nonetheless failed his eleven-plus examination in 1950. Although his public education was a disaster, he was busily engaged in autodidacticism, reading voraciously and producing homemade magazines from the age of ten. His mother suggested he pursue a clerical education through Pitman's College, and there Moorcock learned to type at incredible speed, a skill that served him well in the future. After almost being expelled from college on several occasions, he left at fourteen to become an office junior. His ambition was to be a journalist, and in 1956 he secured his first professional editorial post, with the magazine *Tarzan Adventures;* he has since suggested that he got the job because he was willing to work for £6 a week, well below the minimum rates set by trade-union agreement. As an admirer of Edgar Rice Burroughs, Moorcock displayed his precocious facility for pastiche in writing imitations of him that proved popular with the young readers of the magazine. The character "Sojan the Swordsman" made his first appearance in *Tarzan Adventures*, which increased its circulation during Moorcock's tenure there. The Martian trilogy of 1965–

Moorcock in the offices of Tarzan Adventures, *1958*

The Barbarians of Mars, Blades of Mars, and *Warriors of Mars*–is Moorcock's most extended work in this mode.

Moorcock resigned from *Tarzan Adventures* in 1958 by "mutual dissent" with the publishers and went to Paris, where he played guitar in bars and met bohemians connected with the Olympia Press, which specializes in "underground" and erotic literature. On his return to London he ran an import business for Olympia, smuggling in works by Henry Miller and other banned authors (an early example of his anticensorship stance). He continued to pursue a haphazard musical career, playing blues guitar in Soho clubs and befriending Peter Green, later of Fleetwood Mac. Around this time his admiration for Woody Guthrie led him to acquire a Guthrie-style cap that he is wearing in several dust-jacket photographs.

A significant development took place in September 1958, when Moorcock joined the Sexton Blake Library and Amalgamated Press, later to become Fleetway Publications. He edited and wrote thrillers and comic strips, encountering the character of Zenith the Albino, who later was an influence on Moorcock's Elric of Melniboné. While working for Fleetway, Moorcock wrote a series of novels: "Duel Among the Wine-Green

Suns" (unpublished), the Mervyn Peake–influenced "The Quest of Jephraim Tallow" (published as *The Golden Barge* in 1979), and *The Eternal Champion,* published in book form by Mayflower in 1970. "Peace on Earth," a collaboration with Barrington Bayley, was also published in full in *New Worlds* (December 1959), an event that initiated his long involvement with the magazine. During this time Moorcock became friendly with the writers Harry Harrison and Jack Trevor Story, and the illustrator James Cawthorn, a frequent collaborator on later projects.

After two years at Fleetway, Moorcock had a spectacular row with the management over his refusal to contribute to xenophobic comic strips. He threw his typewriter out a fifth-story window and resigned. Decamping for Europe with his guitar, he traveled around Scandinavia–later a setting in *The Final Programme* (1968)–before hitchhiking to Paris, having pawned his guitar when short of money. Fainting from hunger, he was sent home by the British Consulate.

In the spring of 1961, Moorcock started work on "The Dreaming City," a heroic fantasy story in which Elric, Prince of Melniboné, makes his debut. E. J. Carnell–literary agent and editor of *New Worlds, Science Fantasy,* and *Science Fiction Adventures,* the three British science-fiction magazines of the period–encouraged Moorcock to return to the style of Sojan, but the story that appeared in *Science Fantasy* in June 1961 bore no resemblance to his Sojan stories. Moorcock has called Elric "a straightforward, old-fashioned Byronic stereotype," but he remains one of the most radical characterizations in the "sword-and-sorcery" genre, and his popularity is enduring. While Edgar Rice Burroughs, Lin Carter, and Robert E. Howard valued biceps in their characters as much as brain, Elric is more cerebral, drawn to poetry, philosophy, and magic rather than the aggressively corporeal. He is a sickly albino sustained by the vampiric powers of his broadsword, Stormbringer, and preoccupied by questions of what Greenland terms "identity and meaning, purpose and desire." Forever seeking a balance between the cosmic extremes of Law and Chaos, Elric takes the anguish of adolescent romanticism into a universe of brutal indifference, injecting a dose of existential anxiety into a traditionally conservative fictional form. "The Dreaming City"–first published in book form in 1972 as *Elric of Melniboné* and republished in the same year as *The Dreaming City*–and its successors, *The Stealer of Souls and Other Stories* (1963) and *Stormbringer* (1965), incorporate many of the ideas underpinning Moorcock's later fiction and make up in narrative vigor what they lack in stylistic subtlety. (The title of *Stormbringer* has inspired recordings by John Martyn and Deep Purple.)

Moorcock married novelist Hilary Bailey in September 1962 and got a job as "an early form of spin-doctor" for the Liberal Party. With his strong interest in anarchism, he was an unlikely employee and was soon fired, throwing him into a career as a freelance writer. Moorcock's domestic responsibilities increased with the births of his daughters, Sophie in 1963 and Katy in 1964. His work became increasingly commercial as he attempted to support his family, and the result was pseudonymous Burroughs-influenced pulp novellas such as the Martian trilogy, and the Runestaff quartet, originally drafted in twelve days at fifteen thousand words a day. At the same time he was embarking on more, ambitious projects. When *New Worlds* and *Science Fantasy* were sold to Roberts and Vinter in 1964, Carnell recommended that Moorcock replace him at the helm of the publications. Moorcock assumed the editorship of *New Worlds* rather than its more restrictively titled sibling and swiftly initiated a campaign to remake and remodel British science fiction. Moorcock devoted all his available time and money to *New Worlds;* his first issue as editor was May–June 1964.

He was also at work translating Elric's iconoclastic reading of the conventions of fantasy fiction into contemporary urban life. The result was Jerry Cornelius, Moorcock's most complex and fascinating fictional creation. Drawing his name from a Notting Hill greengrocer, Cornelius emerged in *The Final Programme* (1968)–written in nine days in January 1965–as a physicist turned secret agent. In the hands of his creator and the other *New Worlds* writers who later made use of him, Cornelius was transformed into a highly original creative tool, satirizing contemporary politics, culture, and attitudes in a style that combined parody, pastiche, cut-up and highly evocative London settings. Moorcock has since said that his favorite Cornelius strories are by M. John Harrison. Moorcock explored the same areas further in the wildly comic *The Chinese Agent* (1966–1970), in which a Cornelius analogue, Jerry Cornell, is drawn into international espionage and a plot to steal the crown jewels. Cornelius gained a cult reputation and became the protagonist of a comic strip, *The Adventures of Jerry Cornelius,* scripted by Moorcock and Harrison and published in the *International Times* from June 1969 to January 1970. Elusive and subversive, Cornelius had obvious appeal for the counterculture, although his complex ambivalences were frequently misunderstood.

Moorcock possesses a seemingly inexhaustible imagination and facility for narrative, and his next work, "Behold the Man," published in *New Worlds* in September 1966 and expanded into a novel in 1969, offers further proof of his versatility. It tells the story of Karl Glogauer, a 1960s misfit who travels through time

to take Christ's place at the Crucifixion. Highly controversial, especially in its portrayal of Christ as a harmless imbecile, it nonetheless won Moorcock wide acclaim, a British Science Fiction Association Award and a Nebula from the Science Fiction Writers of America in 1967. His efforts to modernize science fiction were beginning to bear fruit, although the circulation of *New Worlds* remained small.

In 1966 the magazine almost ceased publication, as its publishers became enmeshed in financial difficulties. It was rescued at the last minute by a grant from the Arts Council of Great Britain, but the funding did not make it self-sufficient. Moorcock was forced into an invidious but familiar position of having to raise revenue for new projects by exploiting earlier work he did not value highly. He began to attract unwelcome comparisons to Edgar Rice Burroughs and, worse, J. R. R. Tolkien, whose work he particularly dislikes.

Moorcock had developed a friendship with the family of the ailing Mervyn Peake, who was hospitalized with Parkinson's disease. Having admired Peake since boyhood, Moorcock continued to champion Peake's work after the author's death in 1968 and was instrumental in securing publication of Maeve Gilmore's memoir of her husband, *A World Away* (1970). He dedicated his epic novel *Gloriana, or The Unfulfill'd Queen* (1978) to Peake's memory and has since said that his relationships with Peake and Angus Wilson were the closest he has come to having a mentor. Through his editorial work at *New Worlds* Moorcock has, in turn, encouraged and supported new or inexperienced authors.

To view Moorcock's career as striding a fault line between uncommercial avant-gardism and remunerative hackwork would be misleading and unfair. In 1967 Moorcock signed a contract with Avon Books in the United States to develop a tetralogy around Cornelius, perhaps seeking a wider audience for the character. After Langdon Jones suggested that Moorcock write short stories about Cornelius while working on the novels, Moorcock encouraged other *New Worlds* writers, led by Jim Sallis, to experiment with the Cornelius mythos and write their own stories featuring Moorcock's creation. Having worked on comics in which characters were "fed" by teams of authors rather than owned by them, Moorcock was quite happy to see Cornelius appear in a variety of guises. He also noted in a prospectus for the 1971 anthology *The Nature of the Catastrophe*–originally to be called "The Jerry Cornelius Annual"–that multiple authorship of tales about a single character had an illustrious pedigree, which he traced back to ancient heroic literature and Arthurian legend. Cornelius is not a conventional hero by any means, as the stories in *The Nature of the Catastrophe* and Moorcock's collection *The Lives and Times of Jerry Corne-*

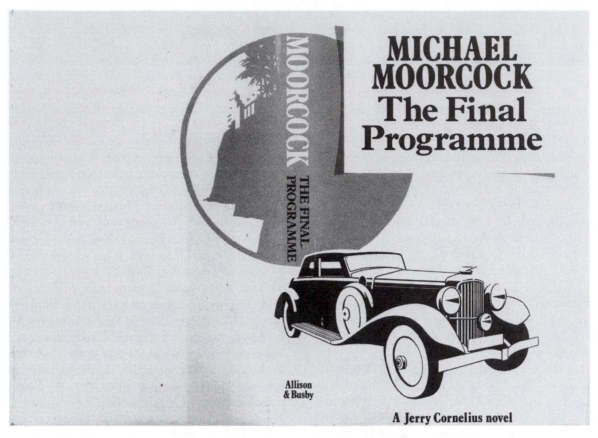

Dust jacket for the first British edition of Moorcock's 1968 novel, in which he introduced a popular series character

lius (1976), reveal. Cornelius wanders through a series of nightmarish versions of twentieth-century history in a variety of different personae, ambitious and self-indulgent at one moment, seedy and desperate in the next. Moorcock had no qualms about rendering Cornelius expendable. He is shot dead at the conclusion of "The Tank Trapeze," and in Harrison's "The Ash Circuit" he is resurrected by means of rectal infusions of reviving chemicals. Moorcock's skeptical view of heroism frequently recurs in his "Eternal Champion" novels, notably at the end of *The Sword and the Stallion* (1974), when Corum is suddenly and treacherously murdered.

New Worlds staggered from crisis to crisis. In 1969 distributors were returning hundreds of copies that had never reached the wholesalers, forcing the staff to sell the magazine on the streets of London. The material it published was determinedly resistant to popular trends in science fiction. Christopher Priest has remarked that "in those days, it sometimes seemed that the only way to publish in *New Worlds* was to baffle everybody. . . ." Number 200, April 1970, was its last appearance in standard magazine format. Although *New Worlds* quickly resurfaced as an irregularly published paperback quarterly, its most illustri-

ous era was at an end. The magazine bowed out with a "Good Taste Issue" (February 1971) and reprinted issue 200 with an index by Moorcock.

In *The Final Programme,* Cornelius is at the center of a search for a reel of microfilm containing his scientist father's most important and dangerous research. The novel ends with Jerry and his archenemy Miss Brunner merged into a single hermaphroditic organism hailed as the new messiah. *A Cure for Cancer* (1971), less a sequel than an analogue or alternative to *The Final Programme,* is more obscure and bleak in outlook. Cornelius, now black with white hair and describing himself as "negative," runs a "transmogrification" service, helping people to define and fix their personalities in a world that merges the ancient Greek philosopher Heraclitus with Franz Kafka. Europe is occupied by American "military advisors"; "Amerika" is even more terrifying. The stabilization process requires use of the Megaflow, a black box that operates as a key to the "multiverse," an infinitude of parallel worlds to which Moorcock referred in his early science fiction. The box is reminiscent of Stormbringer in that it can fix the identity of one person only by sacrificing that of others. Moorcock has noted that Megaflow oscillates between being a symbol and a plot device, one reason for his later dissatisfaction with the book. Cornelius abandons his work and recommences an incestuous affair with his sister, Catherine, who has been resurrected following his accidental killing of her in *The Final Programme*. A new ice age dawns as a consequence of the waste of energy resources and prevailing entropy—a concept of increasing interest to Moorcock.

The Cornelius novels are difficult to summarize. Moorcock has written that "although the tone is light, laconic, the issues are serious—political assassination, manipulation of the individual psyche, erosion of personal and political liberty, U.S. attitudes towards Vietnam and so on. These problems are examined but not really in a satirical sense because the issues are so complex that it is impossible to define what exactly has created them, or indeed, how the problems can be solved." In such a world, the dissipation of the corrective element of satire is inevitable. Moorcock's solution to the dilemma has been increasingly to replace satire with irony, to zoom in and out of atrocities without proposing solutions. There is no answer to the horrors of Cornelius's world and, by extension, the contemporary world. At best humankind can hope to discover some way of coping with catastrophe.

Moorcock's next novel, *The Warlord of the Air* (1971), though quite different from *A Cure for Cancer*, is guided by similar moral principles. "For me SF really is a tool-box and if I can find the spanner I need there I'll use it," Moorcock has remarked. In *The Warlord of the Air* the spanner is best characterized as a "Wellsian scientific romance" that tells the remarkable adventures of Oswald Bastable (a name derived from Edith Nesbit's children's stories), an Edwardian soldier catapulted into the future world of 1973. The novel is a darkly witty blending of alternative histories. The two world wars have not taken place, and the British Empire still holds sway in a world run on Victorian-style scientific innovations such as steam carriages, electric monorails, and helium airships. Moorcock populates this world and those in *The Land Leviathan* (1974) and *The Steel Tsar* (1981) with a cast of "real" characters, including Mahatma Gandhi, who benignly rules Bantustan rather than the implacably racist India, and Mick Jagger, an army lieutenant. The comic inventions of these novels did not obscure their political sympathies, which moved beyond the condemnation of U.S. imperialism in *A Cure for Cancer* to a broader engagement with revolutionary ideologies. They also displayed his interest in Victoriana, which has resurfaced in many subsequent publications, as well in his editing of collections such as *Before Armageddon: An Anthology of Victorian and Edwardian Imaginative Fiction Published before 1914* (1975) and *England Invaded : A Collection of Fantasy Fiction* (1976).

In 1971 Moorcock's third child, Max, was born, and another manifestation of The Eternal Champion, Prince Corum Jhaelen Irsei, made his first appearance. Moorcock's fantasy novels were starting to link into one enormous cycle in which a hero—Elric, Erekosë of *The Eternal Champion* (1970), Dorian Hawkmoon of the Runestaff stories, and Corum—found himself caught up in the everlasting struggle between Law and Chaos. Although Moorcock has little regard for the works, they share a compelling narrative energy, and the Runestaff books frequently display a wit not usually associated with the genre. Corum has been popular with the reading public and is the central character of two sets of adventures, the *Swords* series (1971–1972) and the *Further Chronicles* (1973–1974). The first Corum novel, *The Knight of the Swords,* won Moorcock a British Fantasy Award in 1972. Moorcock continued to write Elric novels, and *The Sleeping Sorceress* (1971) brought in much-needed funds following the further tribulations of *New Worlds* quarterly.

Freed from many of the administrative tasks arising from his magazine work, Moorcock published three novels in 1972, each of which took his reputation into new areas. *Breakfast in the Ruins* (1972) includes the surprising reappearance of Karl Glogauer, crucified at the end of *Behold the Man*. He is now a thirtyish English Jew involved in a sadomasochistic encounter with a black man in a London hotel. During their mind games Glogauer materializes in various identities in a variety of historical settings such as Berlin in 1935, where he grapples with insoluble moral problems. One of the bleakest of Moorcock's works, *Breakfast in the Ruins* raises many pertinent questions.

Moorcock has claimed that the third volume of the Cornelius quartet, *The English Assassin* (1972), was the first of his books he could bear to reread. Cornelius spends much of the novel in a coffin, having been fished out of the sea on the Cornish coast in a semi-animate condition. Still seen as the messiah of the Age of Science, Cornelius is squabbled over by various competing factions in a world of arbitrary alliance and moral collapse. The horrors of the novel are once again offset by Moorcock's arch and cruelly witty dialogue, and the emergence of Jerry's mother, a raucous, blowsy Cockney, as a character of rare comic vigor. The connections between fictional dystopia and "real" life are underlined by Moorcock's dedication of the novel to his father and young son.

Moorcock's novels are rarely wholly self-contained and frequently belong to sequences that interlock with others. *An Alien Heat,* his third new book of 1972, is a case in point. The first in a group of works dealing with "The Dancers at the End of Time," *An Alien Heat* features Moorcock's most extraordinary setting so far—the end

MICHAEL MOORCOCK
The English Assassin

A Jerry Cornelius novel

Dust jacket for Moorcock's third Jerry Cornelius novel (1972), which Moorcock calls the first of his books he could bear to reread

of the universe. (The others are *The Hollow Lands,* 1974; *The End of All Songs,* 1976; *The Transformation of Miss Mavis Ming,* 1977; the short stories collected in *Legends from the End of Time,* 1976, and the entertaining *Elric at the End of Time,* 1981.) In *An Alien Heat* an assortment of decadent characters live out trivial lives in which, through the use of power rings, they are able to alter the basic structure of matter and thus make or do anything they can imagine. As a consequence of this ability, Greenland observes, art and morality have become extinct, since there is no longer any difference between "idea and expression, desire and attainment." Jherek Carnelian, supposedly the last naturally born human, attempts to find meaning in his life through a romantic passion for Miss Amelia Underwood, a Victorian time traveler who arrives in his paradisal world. When she is dragged back to the nineteenth century, Jherek follows her and is caught up in the deadly horrors of Victorian London. *An Alien Heat* is fantastic in the truest sense, filled with humor and inventiveness. Subsequent visits

to the End of Time and Victorian London include encounters with Frank Harris and H. G. Wells, with whom Carnelian has discussions concerning the construction and viability of time machines. The sequence ends with Jherek and Amelia, by now rid of her inconvenient husband, giving up the hedonism of the future and the brutality of the Victorian past and settling in the Paleozoic era, where they at last find peace and contentment in an engaging Edenic parallel.

Moorcock became fully immersed in the lively London counterculture, so it was perhaps inevitable that he became involved with local musicians, particularly the rock band Hawkwind. In the 1960s, Moorcock had been in a band that "changed its name 82 times" and recorded an unreleased LP called "Suddenly It's a Belly Flop," described as "a bunch of spoof stuff." Because of commitments to *New Worlds,* Moorcock had put aside further musical ventures, but in the early 1970s, he became friendly with Hawkwind guitarist Dave Brock and began contributing lyrics for the band's recordings and sometimes joined them on stage. His relationship with the band lasted through many of its incarnations and led to the making of several recordings based on his concepts. *Warrior at the Edge of Time* (1975) featured a James Cawthorn sleeve record while *Sonic Attack* (1981), *Choose Your Masques* (1982), and *Chronicle of the Black Sword* (1985) drew inspiration from Moorcock's writings. The members of Hawkwind appear in *Time of the Hawklords* (1976) and *The Entropy Tango* (1981). While working with Hawkwind, Moorcock formed his own band, The Deep Fix, whose name he had used in Cornelius stories and was also the title of a short-story collection he had published under the pseudonym James Colvin in 1966. The group made one album, *New World's Fair* (1975). Moorcock has also played banjo for Robert Calvert on *Lucky Leif and the Longships* (1975) and supplied lyrics for Blue Oyster Cult. His novels are filled with musical references, and sometimes, as in the case of *The Condition of Muzak* (1977), exploit musical forms such as the sonata as structural devices.

Moorcock's involvement in the 1973 screen version of *The Final Programme* was an unhappy one. Directed by Robert Fuest, the movie was panned by the critics and disliked by Moorcock. Fuest had rejected Moorcock's original screenplay in favor of his own, which sacrificed ambiguities for superficial James Bondery and took a leering attitude toward sexuality that was completely at odds with Moorcock's own. The following year, Moorcock and Cawthorn wrote the screenplay for the Burroughs adventure *The Land that Time Forgot.* That movie project was more rewarding though Moorcock was unimpressed by the director, John Dark. Since then, he has rejected studio offers for "effects movies." "Most movie projects act on me like Storm-bringer on one of Elric's friends," he says.

Moorcock and Hilary Bailey amicably separated in 1973, and cinematic and musical projects took up much of Moorcock's time for the next two years. In 1975 he published *The Quest for Tanelorn,* an attempt to end the saga of the Eternal Champion. All his previous sword-and-sorcery heroes unite in a search for the mythical city of peace where Law and Chaos are finally in balance. One of his least successful works, the book seems motivated by the pressures of fans and Moorcock's growing boredom with the characters.

His next ventures into "Corneliana": *The Adventures of Una Persson and Catherine Cornelius in the Twentieth Century* (1976) and *The Condition of Muzak* (1977) are more impressive than *The Quest for Tanelorn.* The 1976 novel centers on the relationship between Jerry's sister and her friend and sometime lover, Una, the "temporal adventuress." Although less stylistically ambitious than the Jerry Cornelius novels, this novel still manages to play complex games with history and personal identity. The two women begin the novel by relaxing in Pennsylvania in 1933, then travel back in time to 1910, and then go their separate ways through sundry versions of the twentieth century. Catherine, a rather passive character in earlier novels, continues to be something of a pawn and plaything of the men around her, moving through a series of bizarre and sometimes violent encounters as Moorcock turns a critical eye to male sexual stereotypes. Again, the detail is lightened by frequent humor, especially in the scene in which Jerry and Catherine commence their incestuous affair on Coronation Day in 1952. Mrs. Cornelius and her new television set receive particularly effective comic treatment. Una's path through the century is more obviously political than Catherine's, involving her in war and revolution. Both women encounter characters from *The English Assassin* in the process of intertextual overlap that Moorcock so relishes. In this novel, however, the characters are more human than in previous incarnations, and the book has been undeservedly neglected.

Critical acclaim for Cornelius had been growing outside science-fiction circles since the early 1970s. In 1977 Moorcock was awarded the *Guardian* Fiction Prize for *The Cornelius Chronicles,* a single-volume collection of the four Cornelius novels. W. L. Webb, the literary editor of *The Guardian,* commented: "Michael Moorcock, rejecting the demarcation disputes that have reduced the novel to a muddle of warring sub-genres, recovers in these four books a protean vitality and inclusiveness that one might call Dickensian if their consciousness were not so entirely of our own volatile times." Webb seems to have grasped what Moorcock had been trying to do since his rede-

signing of *New Worlds* more than a decade earlier, and the comparison with Dickens is an insightful one. Moorcock makes no secret of his admiration for the novelist, seeing him as a vital influence on his imaginative response to London, as well as representing a model for his own blending of commercial and "high" art.

The Condition of Muzak mixes contemporary concerns familiar from the wider Cornelius cycle with a stylistic élan and emotional depth previously unseen in Moorcock's writing. Although Moorcock has said that the quartet can be read in any order because of its "non-linear" structure, *The Condition of Muzak* offers a series of events and rituals analogous to those of the first three books. Jerry revisits his father's fake Le Corbusier chateau, reopens the transmogrification clinic, and hosts a party even more decadent than that in *The Final Programme.* These takes on the histories of Jerry and the twentieth century are rendered more complex by Moorcock's use of figures from the commedia dell'arte. These individuals first appeared toward the end of *The English Assassin,* and they re-emerge here in fresh guises, as characters grapple with their archetypal roles. A section set at a Christmas costume party, "probably during the nineties," shows Jerry and other guests garbing themselves as figures from English myth and folklore, "mime and pantomime," including Doctor Who, Mr. Pickwick, and Sweeney Todd. Jerry, who had seemed to be Harlequin, has "somehow metamorphosed into Pierrot." His original role is now filled by Una Persson. Art and life continually aspire to the condition of Muzak, Moorcock's debased version of Walter Pater's late-nineteenth-century aesthetic ideal that "All Art aspires to the condition of Music," the perfect union of form and content. The final pages of the novel are moving, and Moorcock stresses the celebratory qualities of the work.

Moorcock next gathered his forces for another novel, a remarkable fusion of A. C. Swinburne, Peake, and Edmund Spenser in *Gloriana, or The Unfulfill'd Queen* (1978). Between *The Condition of Muzak* and this novel, he published another Elric saga, *The Weird of the White Wolf* (1977), and also worked with a new publishing company, Savoy, on the republication of his juvenilia, the Sojan stories. Savoy later published *The Golden Barge,* with introductory pieces by Moorcock and M. John Harrison and striking illustrations by James Cawthorn. Savoy also republished the historical novels of Henry Treece with Moorcock introductions, and the book-length interview *Death Is No Obstacle* (1992), a useful resource for Moorcock enthusiasts. All these works give valuable insights into Moorcock's views on a variety of fictional forms and are a useful addition to *Epic Pooh* (1978) and

Dust jacket for the American edition of Moorcock's 1972 time-travel novel, in which the protagonist meets H. G. Wells, author of The Time Machine *(1895)*

Wizardry and Wild Romance: A Study of Epic Fantasy (published in 1987 but begun in the early 1960s).

All these works argue, often in aggressively witty style, that twentieth-century fantasy writing in Britain has been bedeviled by a "consolatory" strain—exemplified by A. A. Milne, C. S. Lewis, J. R. R. Tolkien, and Richard Adams—that embraces sentimentality, whimsy, and anemic Christianity. "*The Lord of the Rings* is a pernicious confirmation of the values of a morally bankrupt middle-class," Moorcock observes, appalled by the way that it has overshadowed and supplanted a vigorous and courageous tradition exemplified by writers such as Dickens, George Meredith, and Peake, who blended fantasy with psychological and social insight. Moorcock's writing, even at its most undemanding, has never ignored moral and political questions. Moorcock is critical of Tolkien, particularly.

Gloriana, or The Unfulfill'd Queen, published in April 1978, is a far more convincing valediction to the fantasy genre than *The Quest for Tanelorn* (1975); though *Gloriana* is not Moorcock's last word on the subject. In the intro-

duction to *The Golden Barge,* he had expressed his ambition to combine "the 'epic' story with the 'psychological' novel" in the manner of William Makepeace Thackeray, Dickens, Meredith, and Joseph Conrad. While this goal comes closer to fruition in the sequence commencing with *Byzantium Endures* (1981), *Gloriana* still represents a striking achievement.

Ever since Edmund Spenser's *The Faerie Queene* (1590, 1596), Gloriana, queen of Albion, has been the traditional fictional representation of Elizabeth I of England. In Moorcock's novel she rules a nation and empire that is at once Shakespearean and Moorcockian. The exciting plot has her caught up in successive levels of intrigue and conspiracy at the hands of Captain Quire, a rogue member of her intelligence service. At the same time, she is seeking a personal and sexual fulfillment that overthrows the stifling constraints of her heavily symbolic state position. Written in an ornate and highly metaphorical style, the book skillfully combines Moorcock's preoccupations with ideas from late-sixteenth- and early-seventeenth-century treatises, characterized by Peter Nicholls as "harmony and good governance; hierarchies, correspondences among the body politic, the body physical, and the body spiritual; the flux of elements, essences of being, conflicts between spiritual and temporal law; and original sin." The novel draws some of its momentum from the "darke conceit" of Spenser's *The Faerie Queene* and makes effective use of Spenserian concepts such as the Bower of Bliss, but its most memorable invention is Gloriana's vast palace, which contains both the public world of state occasions, masques, and pageantry and a secret realm that even the queen does not know. The palace represents both Gloriana's empire and her mind, but while this symbolism encourages psychoanalytical readings of the structure, it remains an evocative setting in its own right, peopled both by previously encountered figures—such as the Swinburnian poet laureate, Wheldrake; Una Persson, here Gloriana's trusted companion and lover; the Countess of Scaith; and Jephraim Tallow from *The Golden Barge*—and a gallery of remarkable new characters. Law and Chaos are once again at war, the first offering stability at the expense of personal expression, the second promising romantic and intellectual freedoms that threaten the fabric of the state.

Gloriana finally achieves the liberating orgasm she has sought throughout her life, but it occurs during her rape by Captain Quire in a deeply disturbing scene that Moorcock found difficult to write. (He discusses his dissatisfaction with the conclusion of the novel in *Death Is No Obstacle* and has since revised the work.) Whether the orgasm and the eruption into the main palace of the dangerously marginal elements from within the walls will usher in a new era of peace and

PHOTOGRAPH BY JERRY BAUER

Michael Moorcock

Distributed by Simon and Schuster   0-671-43708-9

Michael Moorcock

THE WAR HOUND AND THE WORLD'S PAIN

THE WAR HOUND AND THE WORLD'S PAIN
Michael Moorcock

Rowena

TIMESCAPE BOOKS

Dust jacket for Moorcock's 1981 novel, in which Lucifer manipulates a seventeenth-century soldier into finding the Holy Grail

prosperity for Albion or destroy it with a flaming sword is uncertain.

Gloriana received excellent reviews and secured the *World Fantasy Award* in 1979, but for many consumers of "traditional" fantasy fiction, the novel was too sophisticated and literary and too rooted in fantasy and Moorcockiana for a readership unused to Moorcock's methods. *Gloriana* also resists straightforward allegorical analysis, as there is no "key" to its interpretation. Moorcock had admired writers such as Italo Calvino and Jorge Luis Borges since the early 1960s, and in *Gloriana,* as in many of his other works, he exploited their fondness for "fictionality," enigma, and multiplicity of readings. He has described *Gloriana* as an "ironic fable," a classification that generates unease among publishers and booksellers.

The publication of *The Condition of Muzak* and *Gloriana* seemed at once an end and a beginning. Moorcock's critical standing was at a new height, and, typically, he was unwilling to rest on his laurels. Enjoying the anarchic outrages of the punk era, later cele-

brated in *The Great Rock 'n' Roll Swindle* (1980)—a Cornelius fragment originally published as a newspaper—he remained active with his band Hawkwind and also worked on songs for the aborted *Entropy Tango* project, originally designed as a Cornelius novel with accompanying LP. The book appeared in 1981 without a recording. Divorced from Hilary Bailey in April 1978, Moorcock married Jill Riches in May. The couple separated in September 1980. Throughout this period Moorcock was at work on gathering material for his most ambitious venture yet, the "Between the Wars" sequence that he described, only slightly tongue in cheek, as his *War and Peace.*

Throughout the 1980s and 1990s, Moorcock slowed down, by his standards. In 1981 he published four new novels. *The Steel Tsar* (1981) is a halfhearted Bastable story, dedicated "To my creditors, who remain a permanent source of inspiration." Still troubled by taxes, litigation, and other expenses, Moorcock raised money quickly through the exploitation of his established heroes. *The Steel Tsar* is linked with his growing

163

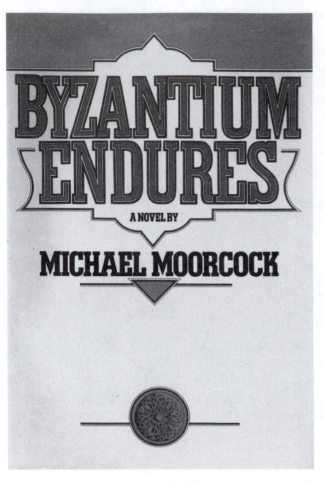

*Dust jacket for the American edition of Moorcock's 1981 novel,
the first volume of his "Between the Wars" quartet*

Stars (1986). The Von Bek novels were planned as a trilogy dealing with "the Age of Religion; Age of Reason; Age of Politics," but the idea foundered as *The City in the Autumn Stars* sprawled in several different directions. Rewritten, re-edited, and shorn of 30 percent of its original material, it remains an entertaining fantasy novel, but not the deep analysis of Enlightenment rationality that Moorcock had originally intended. It is, by his standards at least, something of a failure, although critical estimation has generally been high. Members of the Von Bek family have reappeared in novels such as *Blood: A Southern Fantasy* (1995), illustrating once more Moorcock's desire to generate connections between his books, creating in the process sweeping narrative sequences, as well as individual stories.

The highlight of Moorcock's output of the early 1980s is *Byzantium Endures,* the first of the "Between the Wars" quartet. A long-term project of major significance within his oeuvre and perhaps to his lasting reputation, the quartet consists of *Byzantium Endures, The Laughter of Carthage* (1982), *Jerusalem Commands* (1992), and the forthcoming *The Vengeance of Rome.* (The titles combine to form two sentences.) The central figure of the works is Maxim Arturovitch Pyatnitski, or "Colonel Pyat," a fringe figure from the Cornelius books. Purportedly Pyat's memoirs, bequeathed to Moorcock during his twilight years as a Notting Hill pub bore, the books are another of Moorcock's readings of twentieth-century history—Pyat was born in 1900 and dies in 1977. Although characters from the Cornelius novels, notably Mrs. Cornelius, appear in "Between the Wars," the style of the books is far more straightforward and, as one might expect, linear. The aim of the sequence is to memorialize the dead of the Holocaust and to reconsider ideas such as racism and anti-Semitism, themes that frequently recur in his novels. Where "Between the Wars" differs from many of its predecessors is in its direct engagement with real events, from the Russian revolution and its aftermath through the rise of fascism and the horrors of World War II. Researching and writing the sequence has proved "harrowing," according to Moorcock, which is one reason it has taken twice as long as the original Cornelius tetralogy to complete. During this time Moorcock has also worked on a variety of other, more cheerful, texts. "For years I'd been writing about the worst things in the world. . . . I'm staring at Hitler, the Holocaust, all that horror, all the time I'm working," he says, explaining why the sequence has been interrupted by the continued reappearances of Elric in works such as *The Fortress of the Pearl* (1989) and *The Revenge of the Rose* (1991), and Erekosë in *The Dragon in the Sword* (1986). These less taxing productions continue to be financially lucrative and also offer escape from the documentation of twentieth-

interest in Nestor Makhno, the anarchist whose activities in the Russian civil war following the 1917 revolution are dealt with at more length in his 1981 novel *Byzantium Endures.*

More ambitious than *The Steel Tsar, The War Hound and the World's Pain* (1981) tells the tale of Graf Ulrich Von Bek, a mercenary during the Thirty Years War (1618–1648) who is manipulated by Lucifer into finding the Holy Grail. Von Bek's dialogues with the devil are acidly amusing and show once again Moorcock's willingness to blur the boundaries between fantasy and "serious" fiction, while retaining the narrative energy of his earliest productions. The book won its author a Nebula Award and initiated a series of Von Bek novels or "thematic sequels" in which successive members of the family explore Europe between the seventeenth and the early twentieth century. The Von Bek novels include *The Brothel in Rösenstrasse* (1982), a sensuous consideration of the destructiveness of human greed and erotomania, set in "Mirenburg," a melange of Prague, Vienna, Venice, and Cologne, and *The City in the Autumn* century catastrophes. The ironies of escaping from modern horrors into a world where Law and Chaos battle with increasing ferocity are deliberate ones, but while the concerns of the books transcend their genres, their treatment cannot. However appalling the events of *The Revenge of the Rose,* they pale beside the darkly realistic nature of Pyat's memoirs.

Not all of Moorcock's writing outside "Between the Wars" is so easily categorized. An obvious exception is *Mother London* (1988), which is perhaps his finest single novel. During the composition of the third book in the "Between the Wars" quartet, *Jerusalem Commands,* Moorcock decided he was tiring of repeated compromise and, rather than dashing off further heroic fantasies, he would "try to get a reasonable advance" for a more "worthwhile" project. Although he could not avoid writing fantasy fiction for long, he worked with great discipline on the London book, which he saw as a celebration of the city. "Partly autobiographical, partly geographical," *Mother London* employs nonlinear techniques from earlier works such as the Cornelius Quartet and *Breakfast in the Ruins,* and once again uses sonata form as a structural principle.

Mother London is shaped by its characters and by the form of the city itself. In a series of vivid snapshots, Moorcock explores the lives and myths of the English capital since the Blitz, employing characters such as David Mummery, an "urban anthropologist" who has certain affinities with Moorcock himself, and the larger-than-life actor and circus performer Josef Kiss. These figures meet for group sessions of psychotherapy and explore their memories and interconnections. The atmosphere is far from that of the precious "confessional" novel, however, if only because the city emerges as a remarkable character in its own right. Moorcock's obsession with the metropolis—which began during his childhood when he played among the ruins and bombsites and continued in his teens when he trained himself to memorize the details of all the buildings on his route to work—had been a vital element of many of his earlier fictions. In *Mother London,* his obsession returned in its most complex and rewarding manifestation. Biographical, historical, and metropolitan narratives weave in and out of each other; in the opening chapter, Mummery "feels as if London's population has been transformed into music. . . . the city's inhabitants create an exquisitely complex geometry, a geography passing beyond the natural to become metaphysical." The book has certain affinities with the novels of Moorcock's friends Peter Ackroyd and Iain Sinclair, especially Sinclair's *Downriver* (1992), but is less obscure and more willing to celebrate the joyful epiphanies of the city. Although there is a terrifying description of a Luftwaffe attack, Moorcock is not offering a London-based *Slaughterhouse*

Five (1969). "The book is centered on the good things that came out of the Blitz: the miraculous escapes, the unexpected resumptions of life," he says, also emphasizing the excitement and dynamism that for him characterized the 1960s and early 1970s, when London seemed to promise most.

Mother London received enthusiastic critical responses. Nominated for the 1988 Whitbread Prize, it drew a tribute from Angela Carter in *The Guardian* that moved Moorcock to tears with its generosity. The reviewer for *The Listener* commented, "if this wonderful book does not finally convince the world that Moorcock is in fact one of our very best novelists and a national treasure, then there is no justice." Few critics seemed alienated by the nonlinear structure, feeling that it gave it an enduring readability and also succeeded in conjuring up a sense of the experience of metropolitan life. The book is as highly textualized as the Cornelius stories, with a profusion of overlapping narratives extending even to the symbolic messages implied by different pub names. Moorcock suggests that London exists as a multiplicity of simultaneous and frequently contradictory meanings, decipherable only by those whose ears are attuned to its music. The novel represents the logical outcome of his lifelong obsession with London and urban life.

The joyful engagement with life in *Mother London* is certainly far removed from "Between the Wars." The Pyat of *Byzantium Endures* is a vainglorious, frequently disgusting anti-Semite, whose hatred extends to Bolsheviks, Roman Catholics, and homosexuals. Deceitful, sycophantic, and lecherous, he nonetheless emerges as a fascinating, even on occasion an oddly sympathetic, figure, if only because his individual vileness is so dwarfed by that of his world. "Colonel Pyat's was not a pleasant personality, and his intolerance and passionately-held right-wing views were hard to take," Moorcock notes in the introduction. Yet, Pyat has an indomitable will to survive whatever the century can throw at him, aided by a cynicism expressed in his belief that "history is never the same; but events repeat themselves." In his travels around Europe in *Byzantium Endures* and the successor novels, Pyat repeatedly demonstrates what he sees as the truth of this belief, while Moorcock explores a suggestion credited to Lobkowitz, a character from *The English Assassin,* whom he purports to have employed as a translator of Pyat's memoirs in the introduction to *Byzantium Endures.* "The great tragedies of history are the sum of all our individual tragedies. It takes several million Pyats at least to conspire in the fate of the twelve million who died in the camps," Lobkowitz remarks.

With his marriage to Linda Steele in 1983, Moorcock's domestic life assumed a more orderly style, and this

Dust jacket for the American edition of Moorcock's 1988 novel, which he describes as "centered on the good things that came out of the Blitz."

change may have encouraged him to take stock of his life and beliefs. The re-election of Margaret Thatcher in 1983, on the back of the Falklands War and its aftermath, may also have helped him to focus his ideas at this time. The result was a pamphlet, *The Retreat from Liberty: The Erosion of Democracy in Today's Britain* (1983), which serves as the direct statement of his brand of philosophical anarchism and radical dissent. In essays, editorials, and television appearances he has restated his belief in "simple good and tangible evil." He is also an outspoken critic of pornography, and his approving estimation loomed large on the cover of Andrea Dworkin's *Intercourse* (1988). Although it is unlikely that he will write an autobiography, he has published an epistolary sequence, *Letters from Hollywood* (1986), and has also provided illuminating introductions to new editions of his "Eternal Champion" series during the 1990s. His novel *King of the City,* published May 2000, shows that he has lost none of his relish for memorable characterization in its depiction of Denny Dover, a former rock star and "existential maverick," and his intriguing childhood friend, Sir John Barbican-Begg. Filled with glimpses of Moorcock's own past and fascinating views of the eternally mutable metropolis of London, the novel displays once again a writer who is too self-aware and intellectually questioning to rest on his laurels.

Throughout his career, Moorcock has waged war on what he termed in "The Dodgem Decision" (1969), "an attitude of spirit" that "aimed at reinforcing opinions rather than analysing them." He has attacked targets such as imperialism, "the profound hypocrisies of the liberal bourgeoisie," and avatars of what he perceives to be phoney Englishness, writers as seemingly diverse as Vaughan Williams, Kingsley Amis, and Gilbert and Sullivan. As he explains in the foreword to *The New Nature of the Catastrophe* (1993), his attitudes were heavily determined by his opposition to the "low levels of aspiration" he detected in the postwar literary establishment. Unlike many English writers of the 1950s, Moorcock had no fear of new technology and no debt to ideals of Empire. His unconventional upbringing and self-education freed him from many preconceptions surrounding personal and national identity and also ensured that he refused to observe "traditional" lines of cultural demarcation. Moorcock's approach has frequently baffled critics, many of whom are unsure what to make of a writer who can restage Joseph Conrad's *The Rescue* (1920) in a futuristic Ice Age novel (*The Ice Schooner,* 1969). His method has led to a succession of inventive and extremely entertaining fictions, but it has also led to creative, but bewildering, contradictions. Moorcock is impatient with the constraints of "genre fiction"; yet, his own work in fantasy, and to a lesser extent science fiction, has been influential in shaping those genres. He describes himself as a "moralist"; yet, readers of the Cornelius stories in particular tend to revel in their 1960s hedonisms rather than appreciating their corrosive ironies. His hatred of imperialism is obvious; yet, he retains an affection for the paraphernalia of the late Victorian and Edwardian eras, when the British Empire was at its height. As a result, his place within English writing remains ambiguous and his influence has tended to be felt outside the mainstream. Moorcock, however, is unlikely to be overly concerned. Now a resident of Texas and working on a variety of projects from comics to a new London novel, he remains an energetic and ambitious writer.

Interviews:

Paul Walker, *Luna Monthly,* 59 (November 1975): 1–9;

Ian Covell, *Science Fiction Review,* 8 (January 1979): 18–25;

Charles Platt, *Who Writes Science Fiction?* (Manchester: Savoy, 1980); republished as *Dream Makers* (New York: Berkley, 1980), pp. 233–242;

"In Conversation," *Orbit,* 6 (14 September 1983): 17–24;

Colin Greenland, *Michael Moorcock: Death Is No Obstacle* (Savoy: Manchester, 1992).

Bibliographies:

Richard Bilyeu, *The Tanelorn Archives: A Primary and Secondary Bibliography of the Works of Michael Moorcock, 1949–1979* (Neche, N. Dak: Pandora's Books, 1981);

Brian Hinton, *Michael Moorcock, a Bibliography: Based on the Moorcock Deposit, Bodleian Library, Oxford* (Brighton, U.K.: J. L. Noyce, 1983);

John Davey, *Michael Moorcock: A Reader's Guide* (Sidcup, U.K.: John Davey, 1991).

References:

Michael Ashley, "Behold the Man Called Moorcock," *Science Fiction Monthly,* 2 (February 1975): 8–11;

Michel Delville, "The Moorcock / Hawkwind Connection: Science Fiction and Rock 'n' Roll Culture," *Foundation: The Review of Science Fiction,* 62 (Winter 1994–1995): 64–69;

Colin Greenland, *The Entropy Exhibition: Michael Moorcock and the "New Wave" in British Science Fiction* (London: Routledge, 1983);

Peter Nicholls, "Michael Moorcock," in *Supernatural Fiction Writers Volume II, Fantasy & Horror,* edited by E. F. Blier (New York: Scribners, 1985), pp. 1081–1089;

Charles Platt, Introduction to *The Condition of Muzak* (Boston: Gregg, 1978), pp. v–xii;

Christopher Priest, Author's Note to *Indoctrinaire* (London: Pan, 1979), p. 192.

Papers:

Collections of Michael Moorcock's papers are housed at the Bodleian Library, Oxford University, and the Sterling Library, Texas A&M University.

Ferdinand Mount

(2 July 1939 –   )

Merritt Moseley
University of North Carolina at Asheville

BOOKS: *Very Like a Whale* (London: Weidenfeld & Nicolson, 1967; New York: Weybright & Talley, 1967);

The Theatre of Politics (London: Weidenfeld & Nicolson, 1972; New York: Schocken, 1973);

The Man Who Rode Ampersand (London: Chatto & Windus, 1975);

The Clique: A Novel of the Sixties (London: Chatto & Windus, 1978);

The Subversive Family: An Alternative History of Love and Marriage (London: Cape, 1982; New York: Free Press, 1992);

The Selkirk Strip: A Post-Imperial Tale (London: Hamilton, 1987);

Of Love and Asthma (London: Heinemann, 1991);

The British Constitution Now: Recovery or Decline? (London: Heinemann, 1992);

Umbrella: A Pacific Tale (London: Heinemann, 1994);

The Liquidator (London: Heinemann, 1995);

Jem (and Sam): A Revenger's Tale (London: Chatto & Windus, 1998); republished as *Jem (and Sam): A Novel* (New York: Carroll & Graf, 1999).

OTHER: David Watt, *The Inquiring Eye: The Writings of David Watt,* edited by Mount, foreword by David Owen (London: Penguin / New York: Viking Penguin, 1988);

Communism: A TLS Companion, edited, with an introduction, by Mount (Hammersmith, U.K. & London: Harvill, 1992; Chicago: University of Chicago Press, 1993).

Ferdinand Mount

Depending on one's point of view, Ferdinand Mount is either a political figure who writes novels or a novelist who has also put his wisdom to use in politics and political writing. One might also think of him as a gifted editor who finds time for writing fiction and political commentary. Since 1991 he has been the editor of *TLS: The Times Literary Supplement,* the most important British book review, and during the same decade he accelerated his production of fiction, publishing four novels between 1991 and 1998. The apparently unplanned series of novels and nonfiction books appearing under his name since 1967 has begun to take a more visible shape; four of his nine novels—*The Man Who Rode Ampersand* (1975), *The Selkirk Strip* (1987), *Of Love and Asthma* (1991), and *The Liquidator* (1995)—have been identified as a tetralogy called "A Chronicle of Modern Twilight," and two others—*Umbrella* (1994) and *Jem (and Sam)* (1998)—are identified as "Tales of History and Imagination." Mount's 1998 novel is his longest and most ambitious work so far.

William Robert Ferdinand Mount was born on 2 July 1939, the son of Robert Francis Mount and Lady Julia Pakenham Mount. His grandfather was Sir William Arthur Mount, a Companion of the British Empire who was created a baronet in 1921, and Ferdinand Mount is the third baronet, though he does not use the title. Mount's mother comes from the literary Pakenham family, referred to by Graham Lord as "our foremost scribbling dynasty." Mount's uncle Francis Aungier Pakenham, seventh Earl of Longford, and his wife, Elizabeth Harman Pakenham, Countess of Longford, have written nearly fifty books, and their daughters—historian and mystery writer Lady Anthony Fraser, novelist Rachel Billington, and poet Judith Kazantzis—have published another fifty or so. Mount's aunt Lady Violet Pakenham married novelist Anthony Powell, author of the multivolume *A Dance to the Music of Time* (1951–1975).

Mount was educated at Eton and the University of Vienna before taking a first-class B.A. at Oxford (where his college was Christ Church) in 1961. Since then he has been a journalist in one capacity or another for most of his life, with two fairly brief interludes in political posts. Beginning as an editorial assistant at *The Sunday Telegraph,* he left to become an officer in the research department of the Conservative Party and a secretary to Parliamentary committees in 1962–1965. He then returned to journalism as a leader writer and columnist for *The Daily Sketch* (1965–1967), an editor of the *National Review* in New York (1967), chief leader writer for *The Daily Mail* (1968–1973), and political editor for *The Spectator* (1977–1982 and 1985–1987). After heading Prime Minister Margaret Thatcher's policy unit in 1982–1983, Mount became a political columnist for *The Daily Telegraph* (1984–1990). In addition to editing *TLS,* he is a columnist for *The Sunday Times.* Mount married Julia Margaret Lucas on 20 July 1968; they have two sons and one daughter (a third son is deceased), and live in London.

Mount's first novel, *Very Like a Whale* (1967), is an odd, modest story about George Whale, a young businessman from a wealthy family. The novel includes some satire on 1960s trends such as free love, shifting relations among the classes, and new money replacing old. Whale, who is first described as "a heavy-built romantic young man," is something of a cipher. As the novel goes on, the focus seems more and more to be on Captain Jack McCambridge, a sharp, even ruthless businessman who is having an affair with George's mother, Cynthia Whale, and on easing George's father, Hervey, a member of Parliament, out of positions of importance. George Whale is a man to whom things

happen. At one point he seems to be losing his job; quite soon thereafter, he is promoted instead. It is hard to feel that he deserves one fate more than the other. He does at one point react strongly to the death of an Italian playboy with whom he has become unwillingly involved through his girlfriend Miriam. The Italian has wrecked his sports car and killed himself:

> A wave of irritation choked George. Why should he be treated like the hanger-on of some seamy underworld? What had he to do with this spoilt Italian, killed by his own stupidity? What had he to do with fast cars and high-living, with the particularly mad jazz pattern in which Miriam had enmeshed him? He hated the bright sun and the barren sensuality of its worshippers; the bad temper and the violence born of rootlessness. He, George, had roots. Why should he be torn out of his baggy flannels and leather-patched tweed coat—and thrust into buttock-constricting jeans and garish t-shirts? . . . His was the old upper-middle class totem. A decaying totem, perhaps—but still richer, more varied than the hip-swinging, finger-clicking conventions of international youth.

Later the narrator tells the reader, "The world was a hard place, divided into the destroyers and the destroyed. Either, like Miriam and Jack McCambridge you hacked your way with rough assurance through the undergrowth of the heart. Or, like George, your trousers were torn off by the first barbed wire fence." This statement seems to express the main theme of Mount's book, a "condition of England" novel looking at a time of great change, which seems generally to be deterioration.

Mount's next book, *The Theatre of Politics* (1972), a sort of primer of political theory for a nonacademic readership, was followed in 1975 by the first novel in what he later called "A Chronicle of Modern Twilight." *The Man Who Rode Ampersand* is narrated by Aldous (Gus) Cotton, who presides over the series and has often been described as "diaphanous" or wraithlike. He is, in other words, a bit like George Whale: more a window onto events than their agent, though he is sometimes their victim. A civil servant, Gus was given his name because, when he was born, his father was reading Aldous Huxley's *Brave New World* (1932). In *The Man Who Rode Ampersand* Gus tells the story of his father, Harry Cotton, who was a jockey during the 1930s. At one point Harry was given a sort of practice ride on Ampersand, the greatest horse of his time, but the owner did not like the way he did it and never let him ride the horse in a race. As he got older, this experience became legendary, and some people denied that Harry ever rode the horse.

As the novel begins, Harry Cotton is old and eccentric. As Gus says, "This demanding, ferocious giant, a legend of caprice, a tower of strength and love, shriveled under the glare of my growing self-esteem. The fairy-tale ogre dwindled into a tiresome but manageable obstacle to my plans, a thing to be thwarted, humoured, coaxed, spoken straight to, ignored or even avoided."

Gus explains his project:

> If I set about trying to reconstruct the life and times of Harry Cotton, it is not to build him a monument. I am well aware that lapidary tribute is as out of date as the storyteller's art; narrative is for hayseeds, discontinuity is the thing now. Nor am I trying to achieve the truth, or a truth, or the real truth—or any of those high ambitions with which people like to dignify their diverting fictions. I cannot hope for much more than to dust off a few old sporting prints.

The novel has a large cast of colorful characters, including Harry's friend Frogmore O'Neill (Froggy); C.L., the horse owner; Gus's cousin Kate, who eventually burns down her house and is sentenced to five years in prison; Stella, a German-Polish woman with whom Harry sleeps as a young man; Pip Parrott, "war hero, antique dealer and last of the Bright Young Things"; Harry's lifelong friend Mossy, manager of the Pyjama Club before the war; Evelyn Henriques, who works for C.L. and twice pays off Harry's gambling debts; Tom Dunbabin, a professor and barfly who eventually dies of malnutrition, allegedly because he eats only cakes; and Cod Chamberlayne, a Cockney bookie to whom Harry owes all the money. By the end of the novel several of this cast—and Harry—have been sent to the same asylum.

This excellent novel is relatively shapeless, being built around good details, evocative descriptions, and unexpected touches of characterization, such as Gus's explanation of his father's two dressing gowns: "The two garments were handy for illustrating the two sides of my father's character: the badger model standing for a traditional English countryman, the seersucker a more cosmopolitan city-dweller, a frequenter of Riviera beaches even. At other times, I took them more personally as emblems of his relationship with myself: the badger dressing-gown enveloping a patriarch or housemaster, a person set in authority over me, while the seersucker corresponded to my father as comrade and companion."

After Harry dies in the asylum, Gus is disappointed by his own lack of response, and sums up his story in a shockingly powerful, self-knowing statement: "The story of the grasshopper and the ant is grim enough as it is. Think how much grimmer it would be if the grasshopper had given birth to the ant. The ant's revenge would be a terrible thing."

Much of *The Man Who Rode Ampersand* was about the 1930s and 1940s. In *The Clique* (1978) Mount returned to the 1960s. The novel begins with the prolonged dying, death, and funeral of "The Last Great Englishman," apparently Winston Churchill. Against this event the novel sets a "clique" of 1960s hippies who are first seen parading self-consciously during the Churchill deathwatch and whose views are summed up as follows: "This was the first article of the Brondesbury faith. Each moment was to be savoured separately, time was an infinite series of such separate moments, nothing continuous or connected about them. To be loyal to the past was as foolish as to be concerned about the future."

The main character is called Gunn Goater (named Gunby Hallam Goater by a Tennyson admirer), a beginning reporter. While looking for a veteran reporter, a drunk who is supposed to be covering the deathwatch, Gunn sees the Brondesbury hippies, with whom he becomes involved later in the novel, and advances his career by filing a story in place of the absent alcoholic.

Gunn moves in with the Brondesbury collective in a house owned by Antic Hay. Antic, whose wife dislikes him, is a campy collector of pop-culture memorabilia. His description of their child-rearing practices is a key to his character: "The important thing is to rediscover our sense of play. . . . It is *Homo ludens* not *Homo faber* who has raised man above the slime. If we want to learn how to love, we must first learn how to play."

Another of the passive characters Mount creates so well, Gunn is victimized again and again by other members of the collective, and he is convinced that he in some ways invites their mistreatment: "They were not unkind to Gunn. It was just that their cool drawl made him feel so slow. Every time he tried to catch up, the Clique were waiting for him round the next corner." He is particularly cowed by Happy, a cruelly destructive phony who eventually takes up with Lil, who is in some sense Gunn's girlfriend. When his paper sends Gunn to the United States, he ends up in Detroit, where Happy once again makes a fool of him. Gunn ends up missing the Detroit riots and is fired by his paper. Returning home to live with his parents in Norfolk, he becomes a sportswriter on a local paper and ends up marrying the widow of an old friend. At the end of the novel Lil abandons her baby with them. The baby, whose father is Happy, is called Sixty.

The Clique is, among other things, a study of new family arrangements such as the commune and serial monogamy, as well as illegitimacy, child abandonment, and permissive child rearing. Mount's next book, called *The Subversive Family: An Alternative History of Love and Marriage* (1982), is a nonfiction look at the foundations

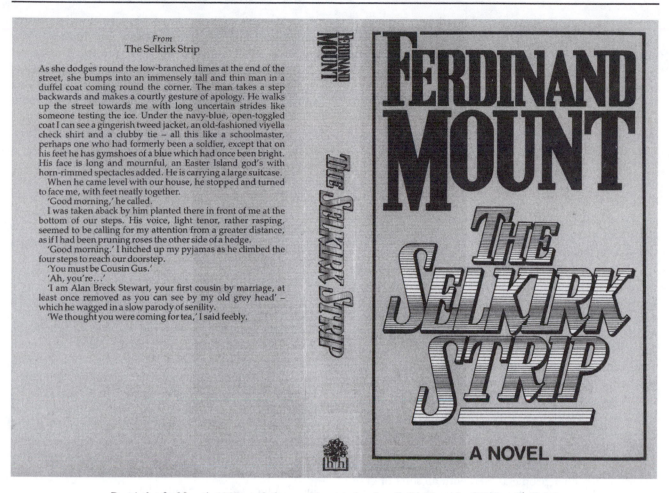

From
The Selkirk Strip

As she dodges round the low-branched limes at the end of the street, she bumps into an immensely tall and thin man in a duffel coat coming round the corner. The man takes a step backwards and makes a courtly gesture of apology. He walks up the street towards me with long uncertain strides like someone testing the ice. Under the navy-blue, open-toggled coat I can see a gingerish tweed jacket, an old-fashioned viyella check shirt and a clubby tie – all this like a schoolmaster, perhaps one who had formerly been a soldier, except that on his feet he has gymshoes of a blue which had once been bright. His face is long and mournful, an Easter Island god's with horn-rimmed spectacles added. He is carrying a large suitcase.

When he came level with our house, he stopped and turned to face me, with feet neatly together.

'Good morning,' he called.

I was taken aback by him planted there in front of me at the bottom of our steps. His voice, light tenor, rather rasping, seemed to be calling for my attention from a greater distance, as if I had been pruning roses the other side of a hedge.

'Good morning.' I hitched up my pyjamas as he climbed the four steps to reach our doorstep.

'You must be Cousin Gus.'

'Ah, you're...'

'I am Alan Breck Stewart, your first cousin by marriage, at least once removed as you can see by my old grey head' – which he wagged in a slow parody of senility.

'We thought you were coming for tea,' I said feebly.

Dust jacket for Mount's 1987 novel, the second in a tetralogy he calls "A Chronicle of Modern Twilight"

of the family. Mount sets out to contradict certain "myths" about the family; for example: "That the family as we know it today—the so-called 'nuclear' family of husband, wife and children—is an historical freak unknown to other centuries and other parts of the world"; "that young people used to marry or be married in their early teens"; "that romantic love was invented by the troubadours of mediaeval Provence; and that it applied only to the adulterous love of a knight or minstrel for a married lady who was not his wife"; "that divorce is a modern development and indicates a decline in the strength of the family and that divorce used to be regarded with horror"; "That Church and State have always been steadfast upholders of the family; that the Roman Catholic Church in particular always esteemed the family very highly." He dispels these misconceptions by an historical study of documents. As reviewer Anthony Curtis commented in *The Financial Times* (10 July 1982), Mount attempted "to penetrate back to what people really felt at the time rather than what we have been told they felt in support

of some theory about family life." Curtis found the book "highly entertaining and extremely well written." By contrast, Carolyn See, writing in the *Los Angeles Times* (28 December 1992), thought the book was an "uneven grab bag."

In *The Selkirk Strip: A Post-Imperial Tale* (1987) Mount returned to the Gus Cotton story. The novel is set during a crisis in a faraway place called the Selkirk Strip, with obvious overtones of the Falklands crisis of 1981–1982. More correctly called the Selkirk Mandated Territory, the Selkirk Strip is a largely forgotten piece of land between a jungle and some mountains. As a heavy-drinking, opinionated journalist announces to a dinner party, "Government hasn't the faintest bloody idea. Who wants the place? Took a bloody Scotsman to discover it. There's nothing bloody there. Bauxite— there's about as much bloody bauxite on that strip as there is in a Soho strip club."

This novel provides more information about Gus Cotton, but he never becomes a vivid character. A middle-level public servant, he lives in north London, and, he tells the reader: "I have trembling knees, presaging cartilage trouble or so my doctor says, and a trembling heart. On the other hand, I earn £18,996 a year, which is at the top of the scale for a 42-year-old assistant secretary in the Civil Service." As for his personality, "I am not nice, although, like any rat who has survived the race thus far, I am capable of appearing so." He prefers doing "minuscule services" for people over "the vast responsibility of having a good time."

The novel also includes satire on bureaucracy. Gus works with The Central Operational Coordinating Unit for Policy Appraisal: "Coh-coopa to its friends, Cockuppa to the rest of us." (In *The Man Who Rode Ampersand* he worked for UPARS, which was variously called Yew-parze or Up-arse.)

Gus's wife is a Dudgeon-Stewart. One relative, an eccentric and would-be visionary named Alan Breck Stewart, comes to stay, impregnates some neighbors' au pair (who is also a Dudgeon-Stewart), and becomes intertwined sexually, and otherwise, with other neighbors. Eventually he is accused of spying in the Selkirk Strip case. The novel is ambiguous about whether this accusation is true, but he commits suicide. The situation is more or less hushed up, and Gus, who is implicated in the possible security breach because Stewart was his relative, is transferred to what sounds like a worse ministry.

Alan is a self-deluded man who manages to delude some other people as well with all sorts of grandiose ideas and muddled thinking, such as:

> "SUMMARY: Conventional thinking is non-strategic. It cannot match the linear acceleration of demo-climatic change. If we take f to be the erosion factor, s to be the population surplus, and g the trend line of green-revolution productivity, then" . . . some incomprehensible algebra followed . . . "Therefore we can expect megafamine along the Equatorial belt by the mid-1980s, certainly before 1987. Only a strategy based on asymptotic planning can avert catastrophe and a starvation toll of 1.3 million–1.4 million per annum. The Breck Stewart Planning system is designed to be understood and operated by a ten-year-old schoolboy."

The Selkirk Strip is a good portrait of various slices of British life in the 1980s, including the life and functioning of civil servants, the relationship between government and the press, and the atmosphere of early Thatcherism, whose economic policy is broadly represented by a group of mostly American free-marketeers called the Cubitarians. And, as usual, Mount offers acute insights into marital relations, including the observation that "Marriages going wrong seemed to progress from melodrama to minimal drama, ending like Beckett playlets in a few sighs and twitches."

Mount's "Chronicle of Modern Twilight" continued with his next novel, *Of Love and Asthma* (1991), which is again narrated by Gus Cotton. This novel tells the somewhat rambling and episodic, but always engaging, story of the odd relationship between Gus and Joseph Dudgeon Follows. "Friendship" is probably an inaccurate description, though they are close for many years–from adolescence, through Joe's giddy and improbable ascent and descent and Gus's much more even, if more boring, life. The two young men are first brought together because they are both asthmatics and patients at a seaside sanatorium run by the disreputable Dr. Maintenon-Smith. Mostly because of his unshakable self-confidence, Joe succeeds in love and business. He is ruthless toward everyone; for instance, he seduces his uncle's wife, his tutor's daughter, and Gus's one and only love.

The novel begins with a narrator's foreword in which Gus describes Joe's successes and then adds, "Later on, you will be relieved to hear, he was to be bankrupted, humiliated, paralysed, exiled, and even kidnapped, or so he said." Unlike Gus, who seems to have outgrown his asthma, Joe is "incurably asthmatic." He also maintains an elusive quality. As Gus says in his foreword, "Slippery too he remained, as elusive as the bath soap clutched at in the clouding water. Sightings and newsflashes have had to be strung together, and a good deal of hearsay as well. Even then, his women may seem presences more real than he does–not, strictly speaking, that they were to be called his. . . ."

An Asthmatic's Progress that is both sad and funny, *Of Love and Asthma* is populated by the kind of eccentrics Mount often creates, linked loosely by the fact that their lives intersect Joe's. The action is played out over a wide geographic area, including Oxford, Lancashire, Ireland, and Wyoming.

Of Love and Asthma was one of Mount's best-received novels. Reviewing the book for *The Independent* (22 September 1991), Candia McWilliam wrote: "Much intellectually compendious, geographically various fiction has of late cast off from modesty and elegance of style and acknowledgement of a shared literary past. With a quiet cough, this novel builds a strong and graceful bridge." In his 12 September 1991 review for *The Times* (London), Anthony Quinton insisted that the "ability to combine the serious with the comic so adroitly is rare and admirable. *Of Love and Asthma* manages to achieve a great deal of deflationary English humour without having to pay the Forsterian price of 'undeveloped heart.'" The novel won the Hawthornden Prize, one of the most prestigious British literary awards.

Following a book on the British Constitution and an edited collection about communism, Mount turned to a more distant period of history and published *Umbrella: A Pacific Tale* (1994), the first of his "Tales of History and Imagination." This novella is a fictionalized version of the personal and political life of George Gordon, fourth Earl of Aberdeen, who was prime minister in 1852–1855. A Scottish orphan, he is a cousin of the poet George Gordon, Lord Byron, who makes fun of him in print.

Aberdeen is a peacemaker by nature. The novella is "A Pacific Tale" because his instinct is to avoid war, not because it has anything to do with the Pacific Ocean. As in real life, he is usually foiled by a former schoolmate, Henry John Temple, third Viscount Palmerston, who is a demagogue and helps to stir up the Don Pacifico affair (1850) and the Crimean War (1854–1856), which leads to Aberdeen's eclipse. He resigns as prime minister (1855), leaving in some disgrace, after a vote in the House of Commons in which he counsels caution and peacefulness and the warmongers win. The novel has a strange coda in which World War II bombs disturb the rest of David Pacifico, who died in 1854. His ghost flies over London, finding that Aberdeen's townhouse is now a theater and Bentley Park, his wife's family home, is now the headquarters of Bomber Command.

Rosanne de Lisle wrote in *The Independent* (23 October 1994) that Aberdeen's life is "not the stuff of a heroic tale, you think, but from these bare bones Ferdinand Mount has created a beguiling, spirited piece of fiction." Mount is unambiguously sympathetic to Aberdeen, who has been remembered mostly for getting England into the Crimean War and then failing to win it quickly and decisively. Some of Mount's empathy comes through in the treatment of the domestic tragedies of Aberdeen's life; for instance, after the death of his beloved first wife:

> He had a wild look which estranged his monkey face and took away its endearing quality. And he talked so much. Old gentlemen in Brooks's were unnerved by this strange, fierce-looking young man who buttonholed and deluged them with conversation on topics that frightened them—had the Greeks discovered the Arch? the proper nature of democracy, how to control the lava flow from a volcano.

Yet, Aberdeen is a Victorian, and, as the narrator reminds readers after another of the many family deaths, for modern readers: "There is something off-putting, even repellent, about George's refusal to be made useless by his grief. So far as we know, he utters no senseless cry, permits himself no futile gesture."

Occasionally the tone cloys a bit for a modern reader, and Mount offers insufficient palliative: "And soon the house was fuller still—the coy allusion must be excused, the spectacle of their happiness unmans the sternest narrator." The novel is, however, a successful act of impersonation, or reanimation, and the combination of imagination and history is richly rewarding.

With *The Liquidator* (1995) Mount returned to Gus Cotton and his "Chronicle of Modern Twilight." Although reviewer Antonia Nashe, writing about *Of Love and Asthma,* had looked forward to its sequel, in which she hoped that "Gus gets the girl and loses his innocence about women," he remains more onlooker than actor.

The novel has a three-part structure. In the present, or near present, Gus writes about a north London tennis club, whose secretary, the presiding officer and moving force, is a liquidator, a person who disperses the assets of financially troubled companies. Geoffrey Pagan-Jones "was the liquidator because he was himself so liquid, so fluent, so up with the current, swimming along on the back of his own luck." After his daughter, Josie, marries Tony Allenby, a subordinate of whom Pagan-Jones does not approve, the liquidator exiles Tony to a horrible place where he has to auction scraps from bankrupt properties. Tony and Josie end up in East Anglia, where he works for social services and acts in plays. Gus, who has always considered Tony one of the lucky and beautiful people, visits them there and thinks: "The two of them seemed blanched and withered, and yet at the same time I envied them. They had somehow escaped from ease and were, there was no other word for it, living." While there, Gus sees Tony performing in a bad play about Mary Magdalene and becomes interested in spikenard, the substance she used to wash the feet of Christ. He eventually gets some spikenard from a contact in London.

The middle section fills in the background. Tony's grandfather was a Lebanese Maronite Christian who during the Victorian period marries an Englishwoman, "converts" to Anglicanism, and moves with her to England, where he becomes a vicar and changes his name from Halabi to Allenby. (Another branch of the same family, which has taken the name Hale, is related to the Cottons.) In Lebanon the Halabi family owns a shrine to Mary Magdalene; once every five years liquid spikenard miraculously comes out of the shrine, and the technique for arranging this "miracle" is explained. The person responsible is also called a "liquidator."

In the third section, again set in the present, a Halabi has died in the Near East, leaving Tony and Josie a lot of money and property there. Gus feels "a strong, no, an overpowering urge" to visit them in Lebanon, "almost literally to touch their golden limbs again now that they were once more gilded and moving as easily about the court as they used to. . . . I wanted to

Dust jacket for the first American edition of Mount's 1998 novel, the fictional papers of his ancestor Jeremiah Mount, who was a contemporary of diarist Samuel Pepys

see them come into their own, watch the world acknowledge their unique grace."

But his visit is disillusioning. Tony, now called Antoine Halabi, is a sort of tribal chieftain, the owner of a winery that makes excellent wines, and the liquidator of spikenard at the family shrine. But he and Josie now squabble. She is an indifferent mother, and Gus cannot "forgive him, or Josie either, for so quickly disillusioning me. In their troubles, they had displayed a certain imperviousness, they had been noble." Now Gus realizes that he has "glamorised a second-rate couple who happened to have fallen on their feet without in any way deserving to. It was pitiful to see them cave in without a fight to the petty failings of the rich."

The overall theme of the novel is decline. After Tony is murdered, Josie returns home and soon marries a man her father has chosen for her, the thuggish John Edward Davies, whom Pagan-Jones has given a good job in his business. When Gus learns that Davies beats Josie, he reflects, "I had been in love with her ever since she had been in love with Tony, especially then, I now realise, and, all right if you insist, a little bit in love with Tony too, and now he was under the roses in the crem [crematorium] and she was dodging John Edward's raw red fists." The rapid rise of Davies is as unmerited as Tony's undeserved fall, his later (equally undeserved) rise to Lebanese plutocrat and liquidator, and his death. Tony's decline is echoed by the fall of another tennis player, Norris Elegant, an inelegant, somewhat comic character whom Pagan-Jones shunts aside to make room for Davies. Later in the novel Elegant appears as a homeless man. The one member of the group who is never in eclipse is Pagan-Jones, something of a puppet master. At the end of the novel he is selling the tennis club for redevelopment: "He had liquidated his own lifelong love and at a happy profit too."

Isabel Colegate ended her review in *The Guardian* (29 September 1995) by declaring *The Liquidator* "a dense novel, melancholy, often obliquely funny, and, in some descriptive passages, startlingly well-written." The reviewer for *The Independent* (28 October 1995) brilliantly characterized the novel as "another of Mount's chiaroscuros from the post-Imperial twilight, infused with a sense of faded splendour, of the modern world somehow failing to satisfy the yearnings of the disillusioned young people wandering in its shade."

Jem (and Sam) (1998) is subtitled "A Novel" in the 1999 U.S. edition, but is tellingly labeled "A Revenger's Tale" on the title page of the British edition. In this ingenious historical invention, Mount includes the memorials of Jeremiah Mount, his putative ancestor, a lesser-known contemporary, colleague, and rival of the famous diarist Samuel Pepys. In his introduction, which gives a fictional account of how he came into possession of his forebear's written remains, Mount complains:

> The 'Mr. Mount' who pops up now and then in Pepys's pages may not be a very alluring character. But he is sweetness and dignity compared to the character who emerges from Jem's own account. Time and again I have muttered under my breath, Come on, endear yourself, but he wouldn't. I began to wish for a kinsman of some moral substance, a personality whose life and opinions would bring alive the challenges and disappointments of his age, and so speak across the centuries, whispering a sort of solace to us in our own perplexities. But there it is, the past is a cussed place.

As a narrator Jem Mount is reminiscent of Gus Cotton. The people he describes are more vital, more interesting, and in some ways more successful than Jem himself. Yet, unlike Gus, Jem is resentful of other people's success. He fumes impotently at the success of Sam Pepys, who—aided by hypocrisy and ambition—rises above an originally lowly station. Jem tries to rise by equally indiscriminate means, but he fails. Even when a woman with whom he has had an affair reappears in his life as the wife of General George Monck, an important figure in Restoration England, he is able to parlay this connection into nothing more than a position as upper servant in her household (though he is still admitted to her bed). His effort to seduce Mrs. Pepys, fueled by genuine desire but also by resentment of Sam and awareness of his infidelity,

fails completely. Late in life he writes the diary that is purported to be this novel. It lies unread for three hundred years (twice the length of his Döppelganger's diary, translated from Pepys's code after 150 years) before being given to the public by Ferdinand Mount.

The starting point for *Jem (and Sam)* is the handful of references to Jeremiah Mount in the real Samuel Pepys's diary. (A typical one reads, "At noon to the Change and there long; and from thence by appointment took Llewelyn, Mount and W. Symonds and Mr Pierce the surgeon home to dinner with me and were merry.") From these bare bones Ferdinand Mount constructs a vivid and believable character who, like Pepys, is a witness to or an actor in important events such as the Restoration of the Stuart Monarchy (1660), the Great London Plague (1665), the Great Fire of London (1666), the Dutch naval invasion up the river Thames during the Second Anglo-Dutch War (1664–1667), and the Duke of Monmouth's Rebellion (1685). Eschewing too sedulous an impersonation of seventeenth-century English, Mount gives Jem a convincing language, including such vivid phrases as (to describe a heavy drinker) "no flincher from the glass."

Like *Umbrella*, *Jem (and Sam)* is truly A Tale of Imagination and History. Writing in the *Los Angeles Times Book Review* (19 September 1999), Peter Green praised it as "one of the most continually enjoyable picaresque novels I've read in years," and in his 22 August 1999 review for *The Houston Chronicle* Fritz Lanham called *Jem (and Sam)* "a splendid evocation of the period and a mordantly comic version of a familiar theme: the trials of a poor young man on the make." After it was published in the United States, the novel was included on the *New York Times* list of "recent books of particular interest."

In his 19 November 1998 review of *Jem (and Sam)* for *The Times* (London), Ian McIntyre provided an overview of Mount's activities, praising him for "conducting a highly successful irrigation programme at the *TLS*, territory previously notorious for its aridity" as well as his "two distinct streams of fiction"—that is, his "Chronicle of Modern Twilight" and his "Tales of History and Imagination." With his four novels of the 1990s, during most of which he also edited the weekly *TLS*, Mount has created a body of work that is simultaneously serious and funny.

Edna O'Brien

(15 December 1930? –)

Martine van Elk
California State University, Long Beach

See also the O'Brien entry in *DLB 14: British Novelists Since 1960.*

BOOKS: *The Country Girls* (London: Hutchinson, 1960; New York: Knopf, 1960);

The Lonely Girl (London: Cape, 1962; New York: Random House, 1962); republished as *Girl with Green Eyes* (Harmondsworth, U.K. & Baltimore: Penguin, 1964);

Girls in Their Married Bliss (London: Cape, 1964; New York: Simon & Schuster, 1968; revised edition, London: Cape, 1971);

August Is a Wicked Month (London: Cape, 1965; New York: Simon & Schuster, 1965);

Casualties of Peace (London: Cape, 1966; New York: Simon & Schuster, 1967);

The Love Object (London: Cape, 1968; New York: Knopf, 1969);

A Pagan Place: A Novel (London: Weidenfeld & Nicolson, 1970; New York: Knopf, 1970);

Zee & Co. (London: Weidenfeld & Nicolson, 1971);

Night (London: Weidenfeld & Nicolson, 1972; New York: Knopf, 1973; revised edition, New York: Farrar, Straus & Giroux, 1987);

A Pagan Place: A Play (London: Faber & Faber, 1973);

A Scandalous Woman: Stories (London: Weidenfeld & Nicolson, 1974); republished as *A Scandalous Woman and Other Stories* (New York: Harcourt Brace Jovanovich, 1974);

Mother Ireland (London: Weidenfeld & Nicolson, 1976; New York: Harcourt Brace Jovanovich, 1976);

Johnny I Hardly Knew You (London: Weidenfeld & Nicolson, 1977); republished as *I Hardly Knew You* (Garden City, N.Y.: Doubleday, 1978);

Arabian Days, text by O'Brien, photographs by Gerard Klijn (London & New York: Quartet, 1977);

Mrs. Reinhardt and Other Stories (London: Weidenfeld & Nicolson, 1978); revised as *A Rose in the Heart* (Garden City, N.Y.: Doubleday, 1979);

Edna O'Brien (photograph © by Terry O'Neil; from the dust jacket for the American edition of Time and Tide, *1992)*

Virginia: A Play (London: Hogarth Press, 1981; revised edition, San Diego: Harcourt Brace Jovanovich: 1985);

The Dazzle (London: Hodder & Stoughton, 1981);

James and Nora: A Portrait of Joyce's Marriage (Northridge, Cal.: Lord John Press, 1981);

Returning: Tales (London: Weidenfeld & Nicolson, 1982; London & New York: Penguin, 1983);

A Christmas Treat (London: Hodder & Stoughton, 1982);

The Rescue (London: Hodder & Stoughton, 1983);

A Fanatic Heart: Selected Stories of Edna O'Brien, foreword by Philip Roth (Franklin Center, Pa.: Franklin

Library, 1984; London: Weidenfeld & Nicolson, 1985);

Tales for the Telling: Irish Folk & Fairy Stories (New York: Atheneum, 1986; London: Pavilion, 1986);

The Country Girls Trilogy and Epilogue (New York: Farrar, Straus & Giroux, 1986; London: Cape, 1987);

Vanishing Ireland, text by O'Brien, photographs by Richard Fitzgerald (London: Cape, 1986; New York: C. N. Potter, 1987);

The High Road (London: Weidenfeld & Nicolson, 1988; New York: Farrar, Straus & Giroux, 1988);

On the Bone (Warwick, U.K.: Greville, 1989);

Lantern Slides: Short Stories (London: Weidenfeld & Nicolson, 1990; New York: Farrar, Straus & Giroux, 1990;);

Time and Tide (London: Viking, 1992; New York: Farrar, Straus & Giroux, 1992);

House of Splendid Isolation (London: Weidenfeld & Nicolson, 1994; New York: Farrar, Straus & Giroux, 1994);

Down by the River (London: Weidenfeld & Nicolson, 1996; New York: Farrar, Straus & Giroux, 1997);

James Joyce (London: Weidenfeld & Nicolson, 1999; New York: Viking Penguin, 1999);

Wild Decembers (London: Weidenfeld & Nicolson, 1999; Boston: Houghton Mifflin, 2000);

Collections: *Seven Novels and Other Short Stories,* introduction by O'Brien (London: Collins, 1978);

An Edna O'Brien Reader, introduction by O'Brien (New York: Warner, 1994).

PRODUCED SCRIPTS: *The Wedding Dress,* television, Granada TV, 1963;

Girl with Green Eyes, motion picture, screenplay adapted by O'Brien from her novel *The Lonely Girl,* Woodfall Film Productions, 1964;

The Keys of the Cafe, television, ABC TV, 1965;

Give My Love to the Pilchards, television, 1965;

I Was Happy Here, motion picture, screenplay adapted by O'Brien and Desmond Davis from O'Brien's short story "A Woman at the Seaside," Partisan, 1965; released in the United States as *Time Lost and Time Remembered,* Rank, 1966;

Which of These Two Ladies Is He Married To? television, script adapted by O'Brien from her short story, Rediffusion, 1967;

Nothing's Ever Over, television, Rediffusion, 1968;

Three into Two Won't Go, motion picture, screenplay adapted by O'Brien from the novel by Andrea Newman, Universal, 1969;

X, Y & Zee, motion picture, screenplay adapted by O'Brien from her novel *Zee & Co.,* Columbia, 1971;

Then and Now, television, 1973;

Mrs. Reinhardt, television, script adapted by O'Brien from her short story, BBC, 1981;

The Country Girls, motion picture, screenplay adapted by O'Brien from her novel, London Films International/Channel Four, 1983.

PLAY PRODUCTIONS: *A Cheap Bunch of Nice Flowers,* London, New Arts Theatre, 20 November 1962;

A Pagan Place, London, Royal Court Theatre, 2 November 1972;

The Gathering, Dublin, Dublin Theatre Festival, 10 October 1974;

Virginia, Stratford, Ontario, Stratford Shakespeare Festival, Avon Theatre, 10 June 1980;

Flesh and Blood, Bath, England, Theatre Royal, 15 April 1985;

Madame Bovary, adapted from Gustave Flaubert's novel, Watford, England, The Palace, 29 January 1987;

Our Father, London, Almeida Theater, 18 November 1999.

OTHER: *A Cheap Bunch of Nice Flowers,* in *Plays of the Year,* volume 26, edited by J. C. Trewin (London: Elek, 1963; New York: Ungar, 1963), pp. 299–391;

Kenneth Tynan, comp., *Oh! Calcutta: An Entertainment with Music,* contribution by O'Brien (New York: Grove, 1969);

Some Irish Loving: A Selection, edited by O'Brien (New York: Harper & Row, 1979; London: Weidenfeld & Nicolson, 1979);

James Joyce, *Dubliners,* introduction by O'Brien (New York: Signet, 1991);

"It's a Bad Time Out There for Emotion," in *The Best Writing on Writing,* 2 volumes, edited by Jack Heffron (Cincinnati, Ohio: Story Press, 1994), I: 160–164;

"Waiting," in *The Best American Essays, 1995,* edited by Jamaica Kincaid (Boston: Houghton Mifflin, 1995), pp. 177–182;

Laurence Flanagan, ed., *Irish Women's Letters,* foreword by O'Brien (Stroud, U.K.: Sutton, 1997; New York: St. Martin's Press, 1997).

SELECTED PERIODICAL PUBLICATIONS– UNCOLLECTED:

POETRY

"Son Asleep," *Saturday Evening Post,* 232 (26 March 1960): 92;

"Barefoot," *Saturday Evening Post,* 232 (4 June 1960): 96;

"Too Late Prodigal," *Saturday Evening Post,* 232 (18 June 1960): 93;

"Zoo Lion," *Saturday Evening Post,* 233 (17 September 1960): 82;

"Mother; Father; Poems," *Mademoiselle,* 73 (October 1971): 132.

DRAMA

"The Wedding Dress," *Mademoiselle,* 58 (November 1963): 134–135; 190–199.

FICTION

"Orphan on the Run," *Saturday Evening Post,* 228 (6 August 1955): 34–35, 87–90;

"Summer Encounter," *Saturday Evening Post,* 230 (21 December 1957): 22–23, 54–56;

"Four Eligible Bachelors in London," *Vogue,* 144 (15 September 1964): 140–143;

"My First Love," *Ladies Home Journal,* 82 (June 1965): 60–61;

"Let the Rest of the World Go By," *Ladies Home Journal,* 82 (July 1965): 48–49, 104;

"Ma," *New Yorker,* 48 (22 July 1972): 24–26;

"The Classroom," *New Yorker,* 51 (21 July 1975): 28–34;

"Green Georgette," *New Yorker,* 54 (23 October 1978): 38–44;

"Far Away in Australia," *New Yorker,* 54 (25 December 1978): 30–36;

"A Long Way from Home," *Redbook,* 165 (May 1985): 76, 148–153;

"A Day Out," *New Yorker,* 65 (24 April 1989): 39–44;

"Sin," *New Yorker,* 70 (11 July 1994): 73–74.

NONFICTION

"From the Ground Up," *Writer,* 71 (October 1958): 13–15;

"Artist and His Country," *Vogue,* 158 (1 September 1971): 232–233, 312–317;

"Dear Mr. Joyce," *Audience,* 1 (July–August 1971): 75–77;

"Why Irish Heroines Don't Have to Be Good Anymore," *New York Times Book Review,* 11 May 1986, p. 13;

"She Was the Other Ireland," *New York Times Book Review,* 19 June 1988: 3, 33;

"Going Solo," *Condé Nast Traveler,* 26 (March 1991): 130–135, 191–195;

"Clinton's Chance to Ease Ulster Enmities," *Boston Globe,* 24 November 1993, p. 17;

"Ulster's Man of the Dark," *New York Times,* 1 February 1994, p. A17;

"Joyce's Odyssey: The Labors of 'Ulysses,'" *New Yorker,* 75 (7 June 1999): 82–91.

Since the 1950s Edna O'Brien has written many novels, short stories, plays, screenplays, television scripts, several works of nonfiction, and books of children's literature. O'Brien is a major contemporary writer who deserves to be included in any critical survey of modern Irish fiction. Yet, her work has been the subject of only one book-length study, published by Grace Eckley in 1974. Seamus Deane's *A Short History of Irish Literature* (1986) fails to mention her work, and in Declan Kiberd's *Inventing Ireland* (1995) there is only a brief reference to O'Brien. Although few would deny that O'Brien has been a pioneer among Irish woman writers, her critical reception over the years has been mixed with respect to her individual publications as well as her overall achievement.

O'Brien's work is remarkably unified due to her consistent fascination with a specific set of themes, all of which revolve around female identity. She has focused on the subject of Irish childhood and the oppressive effects of Irish culture and religion on girls and women, while also trying to capture the contemporary, urban, female experience, particularly with regard to sexual relationships with men. These two interests are closely linked: for her urban women, who are almost always Irish exiles, sexual relationships are a means of escape from the guilt and loss of self that is a result of the break with their childhood background. O'Brien is especially known for her ability to describe landscapes, people, and situations in exact, lavish, and often sensuous detail. Her writing tends to vary between simple or "non-literary" language and lyrical, rich prose, and she often uses a well-known technique, best described as the projection of inner emotional states onto the landscape, in unexpected ways. Perhaps most importantly, over the years O'Brien has demonstrated a willingness to experiment in terms of storytelling, plot construction, and narrative voice.

O'Brien's literary experimentation has sometimes brought her into disfavor with reviewers. Dwelling on the similarities of her stories, the literary establishment has been inclined to dismiss her experiments as evidence of poor writing or a lack of rigorous editing. Only O'Brien's earliest work exhibits a coherent narrative and believable characters with which readers can identify. Her later work, in fact, disrupts these conventional expectations. In the tradition of James Joyce, the predecessor she greatly admires, O'Brien tells the same story over and over again, giving it a different form each time. As a result her novels are not always successful, but her experiments are courageous and interesting; they make her an author who is worthy of a place in the forefront of Irish fiction.

O'Brien's specific set of themes and her penchant for experimentation help to explain the wide spectrum of evaluations of her fiction in the world of literary reviews and scholarship. Some favor the early, more conventional novels; others praise the later, more sophisticated and cosmopolitan work. Although most readers appreciate the originality of her prose, some are disappointed by what they see as heavy-handed and obvious symbolism. Many reviewers applaud her short

Dust jacket for O'Brien's first novel (1960), which was banned in Ireland because of its use of profanity and its frankness about sex

stories, but others are more impressed by her longer works of fiction. Then there are those who find all of it uninteresting and who relegate her work to the realm of cheap romance or what *Newsweek* critic Peter Prescott infamously called "meretricious trash," in his 2 January 1978 review of *Johnny I Hardly Knew You,* though that type of response to O'Brien's novels is rare. While the nature of O'Brien's work may account for some of the extreme responses to her writing, there is another, perhaps more important source of conflict. O'Brien's writing carries the burden of the author's status as a representative for her country and for Irish women, a burden that is partly self-imposed and partly the inevitable fate of any contemporary female author writing about Ireland. Critics often read the novels as direct personal encounters with O'Brien and complain that she fails to show sufficient distance from her characters. In her 1987 article in *The Massachusetts Review,* Peggy O'Brien has examined this aspect of O'Brien's work. She claims that the author's "complicity" in the behav-

ior of her characters "can prompt reader disapproval as much as intense reader identification. If we disapprove, the problem arises of whether we reject the personality of the author, that of the character, or some elusive entity that we call the art itself."

Critical appraisals of the work of O'Brien invariably turn to the woman herself; her writing has been tied to her persona from the beginning. This persona is the product of the author's own autobiographical writings, of her remarks and behavior in interviews, of impressions recorded by journalists and other authors, and of gossip on both sides of the Atlantic. When considering her writing, reviewers have found it difficult to ignore what journalist Eileen Battersby has referred to in *The Irish Times* (5 August 1996) as "the O'Brien myth." The source of the O'Brien myth can be found in the many interviews she has given in the course of her career. Journalists dwell endlessly on her appearance, her "Irish" red hair, her reputation as a host to parties for the London jet set, her theatrical self-presentation, and the rumors about her love affairs. Undeniably, O'Brien is party to the promotion of this myth. Although she has disclaimed allegations of promiscuity, she has confessed to being obsessed with sex and laughed at her reputation as a "bit of a scarlet woman" in an interview with Richard B. Woodward in *The New York Times Magazine* (12 March 1989).

O'Brien was probably born on 15 December 1930 in a small village called Tuamgraney in County Clare in the west of Ireland. (On the question of her age, O'Brien is vague, causing a general confusion about her date of birth: 1936 is given in *Who's Who* and *Contemporary Authors,* 1932 in *DLB 14,* and 1930 in the *Dictionary of Irish Literature.* The last date seems at present the most favored, particularly in Irish sources, and appears to make sense in light of the dates of other important events in O'Brien's life.) Edna was the youngest of the four children of Michael and Lena (Cleary) O'Brien. Michael was a farmer who had inherited wealth, much of which he "squandered in archetypal Irish fashion," as O'Brien told Philip Roth in a 1984 interview in the *New York Times Book Review.* O'Brien's mother had worked in the United States as a young woman, and, after her marriage to Michael, both lived in Brooklyn for a while. They ran out of money and returned to Ireland before Edna was born, but the United States continued to figure in her mother's imagination as a place of glamour and escape from their rural environment. Edna attended National School in Scarriff beginning in 1936. In 1941 she moved to Loughrea, County Galway, where she attended school at the Convent of Mercy. She became aware early on of her vocation as a writer, but such a career was unthinkable for a girl in her situation. In her introduction to her collection *Seven Novels and Other Short Stories* (1978), O'Brien describes her childhood as characterized by religious indoctrination at every level. Everything, including the smallest daily act, was the subject of scrutiny and self-policing. "Even swallowing seemed to be a sin," O'Brien recalls. With characteristic humor and insight into her own ambivalence about her background, she writes, "all these sins produced a furtive desire, a wild and overfertile fantasy life. So I railed against my religion as I grew up. I do not know why I railed against it because to tell the truth I wanted to be in God's good books."

In her small country village in the west of Ireland, literature of any kind was frowned on. The only books in O'Brien's house were cook books, prayer books, and, since her father was fond of horse races, blood-stock reports. Although such a milieu might not seem conducive for a budding author, O'Brien has pointed out that the stories told in her village about other people encouraged her imagination early on. In a 7 May 1970 interview with David Heycock, published in *The Listener,* O'Brien described her first encounters with books of literature: "There were three circulating in the village, *Gone with the Wind, Rebecca* and *How Green Was My Valley.* There was such demand for these books that there were loose pages torn out and given from one person to another. I wasn't eligible for any of these because I was the youngest in this family and the youngest child is always, you know, in the wings. But I did read odd pages of them and it was so funny to read odd pages and then myself to fabricate."

After finishing convent school in 1946, O'Brien was sent to Dublin where she worked in a chemist shop during the day and studied at night at the Pharmaceutical College of Ireland, graduating in 1950. O'Brien bought her first book in Dublin, a copy of T. S. Eliot's *Introducing James Joyce* (1942). These selections of the writings of Joyce inspired the young woman, who felt her childhood calling confirmed. Encouraged by Paedar O'Donnell, editor of a Dublin magazine, she made her writing debut in the form of small contributions to the *Irish Press* in 1948. Three years later, she eloped with an older novelist, Ernest Gébler, an act that provoked angry opposition from her family, since Gébler had been divorced from his first wife. The couple settled in County Wicklow, and O'Brien gave birth to two sons (Sasha, born 1952, an architect; and Carlo, born 1954, an author). In the mid to late 1950s, O'Brien embarked on a career as a fiction writer, publishing short stories in periodicals such as *Ladies Home Journal* and *The Saturday Evening Post.* In 1959 the family relocated to London, a move that decisively shaped O'Brien's work. By leaving Ireland, she joined the ranks of Irish authors such as Joyce and Samuel Beckett, who spent most of their lives in self-exile. Later she explained that without the move she could never have become a writer. As the author told Roth, "I do not think I would have written anything if I had stayed. I feel I would have been watched, would have been judged (even more!) and would have lost that priceless commodity called freedom."

In 1960 two publishers—Hamilton and Knopf—paid O'Brien £25 each in advance for her first novel, *The Country Girls,* which she wrote in less than three weeks. It is the first in a trilogy of novels that also includes *The Lonely Girl* (1962) and *Girls in Their Married Bliss* (1964). The trilogy is O'Brien's most discussed work, both in the popular media and in academic publications. Up to that time, Irish woman writers such as Maria Edgeworth and Elizabeth Bowen were mostly of the Protestant Ascendancy and wrote in the so-called Big House tradition. Their stories focused on the fate of the Anglo-Irish inhabitants of large houses and their social isolation in an overwhelmingly Catholic countryside. In her first three novels, O'Brien charts what was

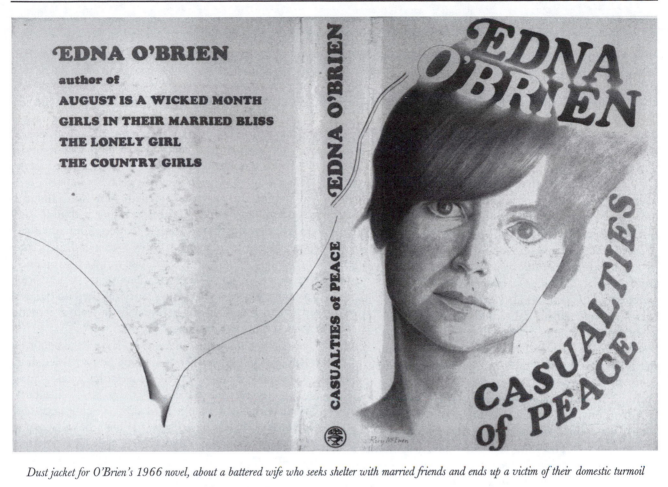

Dust jacket for O'Brien's 1966 novel, about a battered wife who seeks shelter with married friends and ends up a victim of their domestic turmoil

in the early 1960s undiscovered territory: what it meant to grow up female, Irish, and Catholic. The trilogy, which follows two women from early childhood to adulthood, was remarkable not only in terms of subject matter, but also for its juxtaposition of two distinct voices: that of Caithleen Brady, the narrator of the first two novels, and that of the outrageous and wickedly funny Baba Brennan, who narrates sections of the last of the three books. In her 1986 article "Why Irish Heroines Don't Have to Be Good Anymore," O'Brien explains her aim in creating these two characters: "I decided to have two, one who would conform to both my own and my country's view of what an Irish woman should be and one who would undermine every piece of protocol and religion and hypocrisy that there was."

The Country Girls describes the lives of Caithleen and Baba as teenagers growing up in the west of Ireland. Caithleen's violent father and sacrificial mother are the archetypal parents found everywhere in O'Brien's work. Baba is Caithleen's closest friend and her meanest enemy, whose mockery and humiliation of Caithleen gives their friendship its ambivalent character. Unlike the often submissive Caithleen, Baba shows

no reverence for the older generation and firmly resists moral guidance of any kind. After Caithleen's mother drowns early on in the novel, the girls leave the village for convent school. Baba soon finds the means of escape for both girls in the form of a dirty comment on the back of a prayer picture, signed with their names. As expected, the prank gets them expelled. The two are sent to Dublin, where Baba is enrolled in a commercial school while Caithleen finds work at a local grocery shop. On their first night there, Baba announces, "I'm going to blow up this town," but her adventures amount mainly to crashing parties and having affairs with wealthy, older men. Caithleen's exploration of her newfound freedom centers on the discovery of her sexuality. She has a relationship with an older, married solicitor, nicknamed Mr. Gentleman. At the end of the novel, Mr. Gentleman and Caithleen are about to take off for a romantic holiday together with the intention of consummating their love for each other. Mr. Gentleman fails to show up, having given in to the pressures of the village morality and his wife's illness. Caithleen's romantic fantasies about her first lover are shattered.

The Country Girls was widely praised by critics in England and America for its freshness and appeal. In 1962 the book received the Kingsley Amis Award for a first novel. Reviewing the novel in *The New Statesman* (16 July 1960), V. S. Naipaul called it "as fresh and lyrical and bursting with energy as only a first novel can be." He claimed it was "so truly realised in the writer's mind that everything that comes out has a quality of life which no artifice could achieve." Some critics were dismayed; M. H. Zipprich warned in the *Library Journal* (15 February 1960) that it was full of profanity and obscenity, "definitely not for young people." In Ireland, the novel was instantly banned by the Censorship Board for its profanity and openness about sex. For O'Brien, the public outcry in Ireland was accompanied by an even more painful response from her village and family, as she told Julie Carlson in *Banned in Ireland: Censorship and the Irish Writer* (1990): "In my own village one person would tell me what another person had said. They'd pass on the bad news about how dirty it was. . . . Some woman who had read it got terribly ill and felt she was possessed by the devil, and the priest had to come to her house. There were a few copies of it burned in the chapel grounds." The response of O'Brien's own family convinced her that she "had done something awful." She had dedicated the novel to her mother, only to find out years later, after her mother's death, that the dedication page had been ripped out and the "offensive" words in it blacked out.

In *The Lonely Girl* Baba and Caithleen–who begins to call herself Kate–look for ways to give meaning to their lives away from home. Kate continues to define herself primarily in relation to men. Early on in the novel, she meets Eugene Gaillard, a successful documentary moviemaker, with some of the same characteristics (older, distant, experienced, and exotic) that drew her to Mr. Gentleman. The relationship is beset with problems from the start. Although Eugene is attracted to Kate's Irish, country freshness, he expresses disdain for her lack of education and anger at her failure to appreciate his intellectual lifestyle. Much of the novel is concerned with the conflict between Kate and her father. Once Kate has moved into Eugene's country home, her father turns up with his friends, determined to use force to take her back home. After several attempts, they kidnap Kate. She manages to escape, only to realize that these events have caused a permanent rift between herself and her lover, and eventually Eugene forces a breakup. Again, Baba's liberated views reorient Kate's life as she persuades her heartbroken friend to move to England with her. Hoping that Eugene will follow her, Kate agrees to go, and the two young women settle in London.

Although critics generally commended O'Brien's second novel, her third, *Girls in Their Married Bliss,* did not meet with unanimous approval. Reviews in *The New York Times* and *The Saturday Review* were positive, but G. M. Casey, reviewing for *Best Seller* (1 April 1968), called it "a book . . . with literally nothing to recommend it." This book with the darkly ironic title constitutes O'Brien's first real attempt at experimenting with narrative construction and voice. Leaving the straightforward first-person narrative of the previous novels behind, *Girls in Their Married Bliss* switches between limited omniscient narration aligned with Kate and the first-person narrative of Baba, creating a double perspective that upsets the readers' expectations of coherence. Baba is cynical, funny, materialistic, and unreliable, throwing into relief many of Kate's romantic ideals and dreams. The reader is constantly torn between a desire to see Kate's story finished on its own terms and a feeling of liberation from Kate's pathetic romanticism when listening to Baba.

At the outset of the novel, Kate is married to Eugene and is the mother of a young boy. O'Brien does not divulge the story of their reunion that readers may have expected in a novel driven by Kate's idealism. Baba has married Frank, a wealthy, uneducated, and rather foolish Irish builder. While Baba's comic attempts to dispel her boredom and have an adulterous affair are played out, Kate's marriage is slowly breaking down. Looking for solace in a meaningless relationship with another man, Kate's adulterous behavior is uncovered by Eugene, who then initiates a fierce battle for the custody of their son, Cash. Baba's liaison with a drummer leaves her pregnant. Her decision to have the baby destroys any lingering feelings between herself and her husband, though the two agree to remain together. Meanwhile, Kate, living by herself in poverty, struggles with a mental breakdown and intense loneliness. For the 1971 edition of the novel, O'Brien rewrote the ending to include a scene in which Kate has herself sterilized in a drastic attempt to avoid feeling the hurt of separation from a child ever again.

In juxtaposing the perspectives of Kate and Baba, O'Brien's trilogy offers a highly original examination of the ways in which childhood conditions the Irish female experience. The abusive men in Kate's life may be blamed in part for her emotional instability. O'Brien identifies an equally important source of Kate's victimization in her education, which fails to give her a sense of herself as a valuable person independent of men and which does not equip her for a life outside of marriage. Kate's relationships are burdened with guilt and desire for romantic escape. At the same time, her submissiveness shows that she is ruled by the oppressive ideals of femininity that kept her mother trapped in a marriage to a violent alcoholic. For these reasons, Kate's childhood has rendered her incapable of enjoying an independent existence, of making good choices when it comes to men, and of sustaining relationships with her partners. Baba, by contrast, is free from investment in any of the traditional concepts that are supposed to be crucial to female identity. Baba's realization that "people liking you or not liking you is an accident and is to do with them and not you. That goes for love too, only more so," is both refreshing and depressing. Baba's way of thinking is liberating in contrast to the dependence of Kate, but it also suggests an inability to risk real attachment. This emotional distance from others makes for an adventurous but uninvolved life. The novel finds no middle ground between these two responses to an Irish upbringing. Only the two women's reliance on each other provides some room for hope of fulfillment in what becomes, as the trilogy progresses, an increasingly grim world.

In 1986, with the publication of the collected trilogy, O'Brien added a long epilogue, again narrated by Baba. She informs the reader that Kate has died by drowning, presumably a suicide. Baba, who is waiting in a train station for the coffin to arrive, tries to explain Kate's act of desperation: "I suppose all that starvation, and time to think brought her face to face with brass tacks, realized she was on her ownio, Good Shepherd wasn't coming. Oh, Kate, why did you let the bastards win. . . ." As was the case for the rewritten ending of *Girls in Their Married Bliss,* some readers found this conclusion too negative and remarked that it assigned blame too easily to men. The epilogue, however, reshapes the entire trilogy and reorients O'Brien's contribution to the tradition of literary depictions of Irish womanhood. In the trilogy the author shows the dire consequences of a guilt-ridden upbringing and ends with a cynical transformation of the idea of loving Irish motherhood. The epilogue offers an even more pessimistic image of the female exile's search for a secure sense of self. Kate's suicide leaves little hope of the possibility of survival for a woman who lets herself be ruled by ideals of Irish femininity. Survival, it seems, is only possible on the bleakest terms, by means of a denial of these ideals and a refusal to engage in emotional attachments from early childhood on.

The publication of the trilogy brought O'Brien notoriety and fame. Aside from the vilification she suffered from her family and village, her new professional life also took its toll on her marriage. She told Shusha Guppy in a 1984 interview for *The Paris Review,* "Undoubtedly success contributed to the break-up of my marriage. I had married very young. My husband was an attractive father figure—a Professor Higgins.

When my book was published and well-received, it altered things between us. The break would have come anyway, but my success sped it up." In the years that followed, O'Brien faced the challenges of the single mother's life and, once her sons went to college, of living alone. In a 1965 interview with Nell Dunn, she revealed her troubled sense of guilt toward her sons and the difficulty of combining her work as a writer with raising children. Nonetheless, she went on to produce in quick succession several short stories, screenplays, and two more novels, *August Is a Wicked Month* (1965) and *Casualties of Peace* (1966).

August Is a Wicked Month continues a narrative of the female search for a stable self and escape from what O'Brien calls, in her introduction to *An Edna O'Brien Reader* (1994), a state of "emotional exile." The story is told from the perspective of Ellen Sage, a divorced Irishwoman living in London. Most of the novel is set in France, where Ellen is looking for a love affair. Her attempts at finding happiness through sex backfire when she realizes that the men are inadequate and abusive in different ways. Finding herself at an emotional low point, Ellen calls her former husband and is told that her son has been killed in an accident. She finally has her fling with an American actor, who leaves her infected with venereal disease. The novel ends with Ellen walking home from the doctor with a cure for her infection, noticing the first signs of autumn.

Some critics are appalled by O'Brien's detailed descriptions of sex and her refusal to provide an authorial voice that treated such an "immoral" character with disapproval. Reviewing for *Commonweal* (9 July 1965), William James Smith took issue with the feminism of the novel, calling Ellen "simply a bitch." The reviewer for *Best Seller* (15 June 1965), P. T. Majkut, claimed the novel was "immoral" and dismissed O'Brien as a "writer of somewhat pornographic novels." In a 1967 evaluation of O'Brien's achievement for the journal *Eire-Ireland,* the critic Sean McMahon describes the French scenes as "nauseating." This reception contributed to O'Brien's "scarlet" reputation, which McMahon sums up as "an unfair mental equation: Edna O'Brien = Sex." Many reviewers were unconvinced by the protagonist and the story, which fails to fill in many of the blanks in Ellen's past and has her drifting from one encounter with a stranger to the next. The novel does not succeed in terms of convincing narrative construction and characterization. It is a highly pessimistic examination of the quest for emotional satisfaction in an empty life and provides little relief for the reader. Yet, there are some important signs of experimentation: a denser prose style than in the earlier work, a surprising openness with regard to sexuality and the female body, and a complex attempt at a less realistic form of charac-

Edna O'Brien, circa 1973 (photograph by Sam Shaw; from the dust jacket for the American edition of Night)

ter construction. O'Brien utilized the episodic structure more successfully in her later work, particularly in *The High Road* (1988), which may be seen as an attempt to rewrite this earlier novel.

Casualties of Peace, a novel that examines the dark consequences of female dependence on men, also received mixed reviews. O'Brien develops her lyrical prose and uses symbolic images to reveal the inner life of her characters. The book begins with a nightmare, in which Willa McCord is pursued by two men who are trying to kill her. Willa has been mistreated by her violent first husband, Herod, and is still a virgin. She now has to cope with the fears and feelings of guilt that center on her body as she tries to engage in a love affair with her black lover, Auro. She lives with her friends Patsy and Tom, whose marriage is breaking down. With the help of Willa, Patsy tries to escape with her lover. The novel climaxes in a tragic case of mistaken identity when Tom accidentally kills Willa rather than Patsy. Much of the style in which the story is told is alienating and surreal. In her chapter on O'Brien in *Contemporary Irish Novelists* (1990), Mary Salmon calls the imagery in this novel "gothic." Most critics felt that the plot was contrived and the symbolism top-heavy,

though some commended the eloquent prose and praised individual moments in the book.

O'Brien's next publication was *The Love Object* (1968), a collection of stories, most of which had previously appeared in *The New Yorker*. The book, overall reviewed positively, proved an early showcase of her talents as a short-story writer. Some of these stories have been repeatedly anthologized, especially the title story and "Irish Revel," which includes obvious references to Joyce's much-anthologized short story "The Dead," first collected in *Dubliners* (1914). Some readers complained that O'Brien's characterization of men lacks depth, but most felt that her prose makes up for what may be missing in characterization. The reviewer for the 4 July 1968 issue of *The Times Literary Supplement* (*TLS*) described O'Brien's subtle and deceptively simple style: "Just as one begins to suspect that the artlessness is concealing not art but merely an alert memory, Miss O'Brien will twist a phrase, introduce an image, or sneak in a quiet sardonic comment and force one to recognize how considerable the skill and care needed to make it all seem so simple."

Although the "simple" style in the short stories impressed readers, O'Brien's next novel indicates she was not content to continue in the same vein. In *A Pagan Place* (1970), she returns to the subject of childhood in Ireland, this time in a more unconventional manner than in *The Country Girls. A Pagan Place* is set in the west of Ireland and tries to re-create a young girl's experience of growing up. The unnamed protagonist's sister Emma returns from Dublin pregnant, an event that sets the oppressive moral machinery of village and family in motion. Meanwhile, the young girl is confronted with her own budding sexuality and an attempted seduction by a priest, which will distance her forever from her family. In the end, she leaves to join a convent in Belgium. As the title suggests, O'Brien uncovers the instinctive, darker paganism just underneath the surface of the village's Christian morality. The symbolism of the "pagan place" in the forest where "Druids had their rites . . . long before your mother and father or his mother and father or her mother and father or anyone you'd ever heard tell of" hints at an underexamined aspect of Irish culture.

The distinctive feature of the novel is its second-person narration, which addresses the girl as "you" and formulates her thoughts and memories in detail for her. O'Brien told Heycock during their 1970 interview in *The Listener* that she chose this technique to highlight the split between ego and alter ego in every person. The novel thus continues the examination of opposite aspects of character, which began with Kate and Baba. The novel won O'Brien the Yorkshire Post Award in 1971. Yet, for many reviewers the second-person narration felt like an imposition that left them dissatisfied and irritated. They claimed that the technique prevented them from identifying with or even believing the character of the girl.

In *Night* (1972), O'Brien employs a more familiar stream-of-consciousness technique that reminds many readers of Molly Bloom's late-night monologue at the end of Joyce's *Ulysses* (1922). In her 1974 monograph, Eckley points out further similarities to Beckett's novel *Watt* (1953). Mary Hooligan spends her last night as a house sitter for a wealthy family contemplating her childhood in Ireland, her mother, her many affairs with men, her abusive former husband Dr. Flaggler, and her relationship with her son. With its savage humor and cynical tone, Mary's voice is much like Baba's, although Mary is more capable of expressing hurt and deep feelings than the earlier character. She is one of O'Brien's many lonely women who try to come to terms with the consequences of exile from Ireland. For many readers *Night* is one of O'Brien's best novels. Even those who claimed not to like O'Brien's work grudgingly admitted the merits of the novel. Auberon Waugh in *The Spectator* (7 October 1972)—a magazine that had almost consistently reviled O'Brien's earlier work—acknowledged that, in spite of its "unappetizing form," the novel proved O'Brien's comic genius, and "with a little more effort it could have been a masterpiece."

O'Brien continued to write about her home country, publishing another successful collection, *A Scandalous Woman* (1974). The nonfictional *Mother Ireland*, published in 1976, harbors much information about O'Brien's childhood and early adulthood, creating an autobiographical connection with *The Country Girls* trilogy and O'Brien's other work. Blending her own memories with a highly personal account of Irish history, O'Brien's book was subject to praise as well as condemnation. For some readers in England and Ireland, O'Brien's Irish persona was beginning to cast a negative light on her literary achievement. *A Pagan Place*, *Night*, and *Mother Ireland* provoked accusations of inauthenticity and "posing," as critics took specific issue with O'Brien's "use" of her nationality. In *TLS* (16 April 1970), *A Pagan Place* was compared to "a self-admiring performance by a corrupted peasantry who half believe the gentry's myths about their charming fecklessness." In *The New York Review of Books* (14 October 1976), Dennis Donoghue described the style in *Mother Ireland* as "damnable . . . the language of the Irish Tourist Board."

Other critics have defended the Irish aspects of O'Brien's novels. In a 1993 article in *The Canadian Journal of Irish Studies*, Rebecca Pelan explained the phrase "stage-Irish" in terms of its "denigratory function to imply a performance or 'selling' of oneself for the

amusement or entertainment of a foreign audience." She asserts that accusations of "stage-Irishness" exonerate the critic from having to engage closely with O'Brien's writing and in fact serve to repress its subversive content. Pelan argues that "critical indifference to the content of O'Brien's fiction is the common experience of writers from minority discourse and reveals a familiar critical uneasiness with what is perceived to be the intrusive subject-matter." The allegations of "stage-Irishness" signal a rejection of O'Brien as the voice of Irish womanhood. In the early 1960s, her work was said to be a "smear" on Irish womanhood, a phrase that invites comparison with the outcry over John Millington Synge's *The Playboy of the Western World* in 1907.

In the 1970s O'Brien became interested in psychoanalysis. Her next novel, *Johnny I Hardly Knew You* (1977), tells the story of Nora, a woman who is awaiting trial for the murder of Hart, her young lover. Hart is obviously a stand-in for Nora's son, and the novel offers a half-hearted exploration of the Freudian subject of Oedipal desire. The story is a depressing variation on O'Brien's examination of the relationships between men and women and the influence of earlier experiences of abuse on these relationships. Many reviewers, even those who were favorably disposed toward O'Brien, hated the unreliable and unlikable narrator. In a 1 January 1978 review, *The New York Times* critic Anatole Broyard called the ending "awesomely silly" and recommended it only for producing in the reader the "uncanny sensation of feeling superior to an author as talented and worldly as Miss O'Brien."

Moving between extremes in terms of critical reception, O'Brien's next work, *Mrs. Reinhardt and Other Stories* (1978), received general praise. It was nominated by Patricia Highsmith in *TLS* (30 November 1979) as one of the best books of the year. The U.S. publication of the collection, retitled as *A Rose in the Heart* (1979), won O'Brien similar critical acclaim. The stories continue the theme of female longing for an authentic self, although, as critics have noted, these women seem to be having a better time of it than many of O'Brien's previous heroines. After a children's book, a play, and an account of Joyce's marriage, O'Brien published *Returning* (1982), another collection of short stories with an Irish setting. Many of the themes and motifs of her earlier work are present in these stories, which take up episodes and characters familiar from *The Country Girls*, *A Pagan Place*, and *Night*. O'Brien's reputation as a talented writer of short stories was further enhanced by the 1984 publication of *A Fanatic Heart*, a selection of O'Brien's stories from her entire career.

O'Brien published *The High Road* in 1988, her first novel in eleven years. As she told interviewers, writing it was a difficult experience for her. Whereas

Johnny I Hardly Knew You had been finished in three weeks, this novel went through many torturous rewrites. The book seems to be an effort to rewrite both *August Is a Wicked Month,* with its Mediterranean setting, and *Casualties of Peace,* with its similar ending. The story is about the adventures of Anna, a middle-aged divorcée and mother of two sons. An Irishwoman living in England, she decides to spend some time on Majorca to recover from a disastrous love affair. The narrative structure may be best described as wandering, which is what most of the characters do. Anna intrudes on the lives of others, from a rich debutante who lives as a hermit to a wealthy woman whose son has committed suicide and left terrible accusations of his mother on videotape. The novel revolves around Anna's relationship with a Spanish woman, Catalina, for whom she develops amorous feelings. After they spend a passionate night together, the village responds with violence and anger. Someone paints "Lesbos" on the wall of Catalina's family home, and Catalina's gypsy husband plans to kill Anna. In another violent and depressing ending to an O'Brien novel, Catalina is murdered instead.

The Mediterranean village turns out to be not all that different from small-town Ireland. An English woman warns Anna that this community is a small one where people know everything about each other. She is reminded of "the several nuns who had taught me, nuns with the hushed footfalls who begrudged us our passage through the town each evening, where we could see streetlights coming on, or clothes in shop windows, and although we could not linger, we could hear men and boys talking or whistling." Anna's attempt to overcome an oppressive and guilt-ridden past may be honest and brave, but its destructive results are inevitable. As Pearl Bell wrote in her review for *The New Republic* (13 February 1989), "There has always been a relentless fatality about Edna O'Brien's literary imagination." It seems as if the world conspires with the religious strictures of childhood to punish O'Brien's protagonists for their efforts to take their lives into their own hands.

O'Brien admitted in an interview with Sandra Manoogian Pearce in 1995 that *The High Road* was not her favorite novel. The book received a mildly favorable response, though many reviewers were disappointed. Anita Brookner wrote in *The Spectator* (15 October 1988) that *The High Road* "fails to fulfil the expectations we have of this habitually excellent writer." Those who saw the novel as a less than perfect achievement noted the incoherence of the narrative and the unbelievable characterization. Reviewing the novel for *The New York Times* (20 November 1988), Marilynne Robinson pointed out that "The nonconsecutive form of

the novel puts usual notions of meaning in question. . . . The emptiness at the core of this tale is not the Romantic isolation from which it borrows phrases and gestures, but a circumscribed, thoroughly contemporary malaise preoccupied with the muted deaths of minor and guarded hopes." Unlike many other reviewers, Robinson demonstrates how meaning may be attributed to what is too frequently dismissed simply on the basis of conventional criteria.

Lantern Slides (1990), another collection of short stories by O'Brien, is a highly successful book, praised almost unanimously by reviewers for the subtlety with which O'Brien depicts her characters and for the precise descriptions of landscape that serve to convey an understanding of human emotion. The title story of the book is another revision of Joyce's "The Dead" and has drawn scholarly comparison with the story. In this story O'Brien shows her ability to explore different narrative perspectives, including male viewpoints.

Her next novel, *Time and Tide* (1992), won the *Los Angeles Times* Book Award. Robert Hosmer, reviewing for *Commonweal* (23 October 1992), found the book "so extraordinary that this eleventh novel may well eclipse the previous ten, even her first." Nevertheless, the old problem of O'Brien's reputation haunted the reception of *Time and Tide.* In a 1992 interview with James Wolcott for *Vanity Fair,* for instance, O'Brien revealed that the drug episode in the novel was based on an LSD trip she had experienced with the famous psychiatrist R. D. Laing. Marianne Wiggins warned in *The Nation* (13 July 1992): "To the English, O'Brien constitutes a sexy Irish export, and part of her sexual mystique is her public invitation to identify the heroines of her prose with the author of that prose. This is a dangerous proposition, one that has resulted in the greatest literature as well as in the basest trash."

The story of Nell Steadman, another Irish, divorced mother who lives in London, recalls much of O'Brien's earlier work. The novel begins with a confrontation between Nell and her younger son, Tristan. Her older son, Paddy, has drowned in the Thames, and his former girlfriend Penny is pregnant with his child. Tristan intends to move in with Penny. The book then reverts to the early childhood of Paddy and Tristan and tells the story of Nell's marriage, her divorce, how she gained custody of the two boys, their departure for boarding school, and Nell's disastrous experiments with love affairs and drugs. After finishing school Paddy comes back to live with his mother, and Nell struggles with her changed relation to a son she can no longer control. Paddy's death is based on a tragic accident that happened in August 1989, when a barge collided with a pleasure boat on the Thames. Toward the end of the novel, Nell meets Mitch, a young man who was with her son just

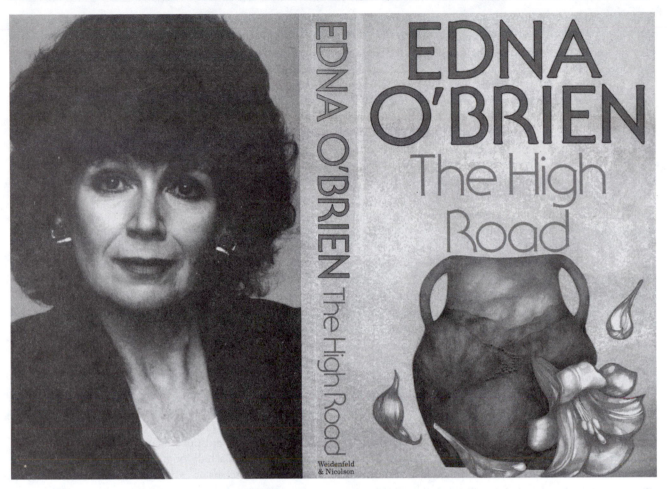

Dust jacket for the British edition of O'Brien's 1988 novel, about an Irishwoman who discovers that life in a Majorcan village differs little from small-town life in Ireland

before he drowned. Although she initially feels anger toward Mitch, she arrives at some form of emotional understanding of his need to talk to her. At the close of the novel, Nell returns to her home to find Tristan has moved out. Noticing the silence in her apartment, Nell experiences a final epiphany in what is one of O'Brien's best endings: "'You can bear it,' the silence said, because that is all there is, this now that then, this present that past, this life this death, and the involuntary shudder that keeps reminding us we are alive." In contrast with O'Brien's many violent and pessimistic conclusions, this ending leaves Nell suspended in a moving moment of self-realization. The desire for escape has, at least for an instant, given way to acceptance of life as it is, with all its struggles and pain.

With *House of Splendid Isolation* (1994), O'Brien's writing takes a different turn. This book is the first of a trilogy of novels set in Ireland about political situations and based on historical research as much as personal experience. With this new subject matter, O'Brien perhaps accedes to those who have accused

her of dwelling excessively on love and sexual relationships, though the novel does include some of the typical O'Brien material, such as failed marriage, abusive relationships, and emotional exile. *House of Splendid Isolation* begins with the escape from prison of an IRA killer. McGreevy, inspired by real-life IRA terrorist Dominic "Mad Dog" McGlingey, is heading for the south of Ireland, where he plans a terrorist attack on an English aristocrat. The setting switches to the isolated country house of Josie O'Meara, an older widow living by herself. McGreevy eventually takes refuge in this decaying house, a setting that presents the reader with an interesting variation on the Big House tradition of O'Brien's female precursors. Josie has recently returned from a nursing home, preparing herself for death. In her intense loneliness, she tries to grapple with her past, pondering her time as a maid in Brooklyn, her return to Ireland, and her unhappy marriage to her violent husband, James, who was a rich horse breeder. She contemplates her decision secretly to abort her child, her love affair with a priest, and her sense of guilt for James's death. These are the familiar O'Brien themes, but they are explored within the context of the Northern "troubles" and their effect on individual relationships. The novel reveals the intricacies of the unlikely friendship that develops between Josie, who abhors terrorism, and McGreevy, who turns out to be less insensitive than he would like to seem. At the end, the house is surrounded by Irish *gardai* (police officers), and as they break in, the gunfire accidentally kills Josie, continuing the O'Brien tradition of mistaken killings seen earlier in *Casualties of Peace* and *The High Road*.

The reception of *House of Splendid Isolation* exemplifies the lack of consensus about O'Brien's writing. Most reviewers distinguished between the novel's handling of the past and of the present. Some praised the way in which Josie's past was described but saw the presentation of the relationship with McGreevy as not convincingly developed. Thomas Smyth, in *World Literature Today* (Winter 1995), found "the real treasure of the novel" in the character of Josie and her memories. Others viewed the scenes that involved Josie's past as hackneyed and too familiar. Novelist Ron Hansen wrote in a 15 April 1995 review for *America:* "O'Brien has handled a woman like this so often that she probably sighed with boredom throughout the writing," but he called the present setting of the novel "fresh and intriguing." Apart from the presence of these two strands in the novel, it is important to note that the book marks a further development in O'Brien's writing, which is more overwhelmingly symbolic and lyrical than in previous works. The novel moves among a host of different perspectives, using stream-of-consciousness, third-person limited narration, diary entries, songs, poems, and a narrative frame in which the aborted child of Josie speaks. Hermione Lee complained in *The New Republic* (13 June 1994) that the style is "solemn, portentous and clichéd." In spite of their overt political content, O'Brien's novels have become like poems in their rich language and allegorical landscape.

O'Brien was awarded the European Prize for Literature in 1995 in recognition of her life's work, and the next year she published what is possibly her most ambitious work to date. *Down by the River* (1996) is loosely based on the infamous "X" case. In 1992, the Irish State prevented a fourteen-year-old rape victim, known to the media as "X," from traveling to England to have an abortion. This controversial case prompted a decision by the Irish supreme court upholding the right to travel. O'Brien's fictional story pushes the case even further toward controversy by making her "X" the victim of incest. Mary McNamara, a fourteen-year-old country girl, is repeatedly raped by James, her father. Mary temporarily escapes when she

leaves to attend convent school, but she has to return home after her mother dies of cancer. Mary becomes pregnant and tries to escape again, this time to Galway, where a street musician takes her in. The girl is soon tracked down and returned to her father. The desperate James accuses the street musician of having made Mary pregnant and in a brutal sexual attack, assaults his daughter with a broomstick. Accompanied by a friend of her mother's, Mary sets out for England. Just when she is about to have her abortion, the two are made to go back. On her return to Ireland, Mary is confronted with the police, the judicial system, social agencies, and the media. Institutions and fanatical individuals ignore her wishes, and the girl becomes the pawn of various pro- and anti-abortion groups. Although Mary tries to keep the identity of the father of her baby a secret, the truth about James's involvement surfaces, and he commits suicide. The ultimate decision of the supreme court on Mary's right to travel becomes irrelevant when she has a miscarriage.

Down by the River is a daring project because of its highly charged content and its political accusation of an Irish-Catholic morality that disregards individual well-being. Through complex characterization, O'Brien attempts to illuminate all sides of the conflict, including that of the father. The narrative construction consists of extremely short episodes—sometimes the chapters are only a page and a half long. The novel is perhaps most ambitious in terms of style: the prose is even more poetic than in O'Brien's previous novel, particularly during moments of extreme violence. After James has assaulted Mary, for instance, Mary looks at her dog: "She lay there, half gone, her mind a semi-nothingness, and saw the soft moonlight splash and dapple onto the table and across the floor and make bright stripes on Shep's black coat, Shep a few feet from her, like a person, feeling it all, sensing it all, prehensile, there for her. There." As early as 1984, Roth told O'Brien that her prose is "like a piece of fine meshwork, a net of perfectly observed sensuous details that enables you to contain all the longing and pain and remorse that surge through the fiction." Roth's comment may be most true for *Down by the River*.

Critics responded overwhelmingly favorably but with characteristic reservations. Most agreed *Down by the River* was a courageous book to write on a difficult, controversial subject. Many felt, however, that the language overwhelmed the story, particularly in the early scenes. The most serious criticism came from Maria Alvarez in *TLS* (27 September 1996). She claimed that O'Brien's characterization of Mary was overburdened by the style: "If the story of individual suffering is to succeed, interiority is crucial, yet here the consciousness is overwhelmingly another's—the author's. The result is a text which commits the same crime it is at pains to criticize in society; by crushing the small voice of the central victim beneath the weight of its own overwriting, it makes any proper empathy impossible." The objection is a familiar one for O'Brien: reviewers want to understand and sympathize with a protagonist, who has to be "real" enough to be believable. At the same time, they feel the need for a controlling authorial presence different from the characters themselves to allow for intellectual and moral reflection on their fate.

Such objections have not been voiced in reviews of O'Brien's novel *Wild Decembers*. This final work in the Irish trilogy was published in 1999, on the heels of the publication of her biography of James Joyce, which was nominated for the 1999 *Irish Times* Literature Prize for nonfiction. In *Wild Decembers* O'Brien turns her attention to what has always been a central issue in Ireland, the possession of land. Set in Cloontha, a fictional country parish, the novel traces the conflict between two farmers whose properties border on each other and whose families have struggled for centuries. The fiercely passionate and emotional Joseph Brennan prides himself on his heritage and imagines his predicament in the terms of the Greek myths he loves to read. His younger sister Breege has been in his care since their parents died when she was a child. Both unmarried, theirs is a very close relationship; the reader quickly discovers that Joseph defines himself both through his land and through his ability to protect his sister and maintain her loyalty to him. Their neighbor is Michael Bugler, an emigrant who has recently returned from Australia to claim the land he has inherited. The two men are soon at odds over land issues, a conflict that draws them into a protracted legal battle. While court dates and letters between lawyers aggravate matters, Bugler steadily takes over the land he sees as rightfully his. The hostility between the two farmers is intensified by meddling villagers, whose gossip and coaxing betrays a pathetic desire to see these men destroy themselves.

At the same time, a dangerous affection develops between Breege and Bugler, complicated not only by the hatred between the two farmers, but also by the fact that Bugler is already engaged to Rosemary, a sophisticated Australian woman who is about to join him in Ireland. After a brief romantic spell with Bugler is cut short by the arrival of his fiancée, the hypersensitive Breege loses her ability to speak. With Joseph on the verge of alcoholic self-destruction and Breege in an asylum, Bugler unexpectedly decides to make peace about the land and break with Rosemary. Yet, his open expression of love for Breege to Joseph makes reconciliation impossible. Joseph finally acts on his desire to kill his nemesis, just after Breege has recovered her speech

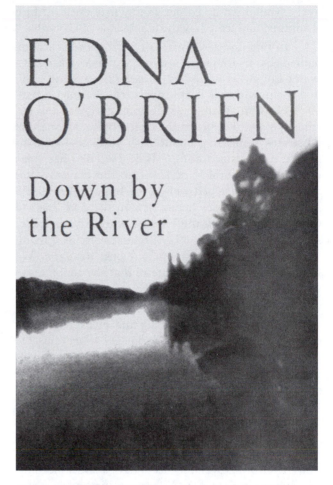

Dust jacket for O'Brien's 1996 novel, loosely based on a 1992 case in which an Irish court forbade a fourteen-year-old rape victim to travel to England for an abortion

and is released from the asylum. The novel ends with Joseph in prison, Bugler dead, and Breege pregnant with Bugler's child.

From the start, O'Brien creates a universal framework for her story. She situates the Irish dedication to land in the context of the Great Famine, Irish myth, and stories of fraternal rivalry in the Old Testament. The opening pages tell the reader of "Fields that mean more than fields, fields that translate into nuptials into blood; fields lost, regained, and lost again in that fickle and fractured sequence of things." Bugler and Brennan are "the warring sons of warring sons cursed with that same irresistible thrall of madness which is the designate of living man." Against this mythical and political backdrop, no individual seems to blame for the conflict. The battle over land takes the form of a battle over a woman, whose muteness toward the end points to the ways in which women have been silenced by the forces of history. At the same time, O'Brien introduces a clash between traditional Irish values and modernity, effectively symbolized by Bugler's shiny new tractor, which is admired and feared by the inhabitants of Cloontha.

In this novel, O'Brien's lyrical prose is accompanied by a frequent use of sentence fragments. James Lough wrote in *The Denver Post* (9 April 2000) that the poetic style is appropriate to the subject matter: "The film of language, at times gorgeous and terrifically painful, adds to the claustrophobic tone that illustrates something about Irish rural life–at turns beautiful and suffocating." *Wild Decembers* has been particularly favorably reviewed in the United States and was also received well in the Irish press. Éilís Ní Dhuibhne concludes her review in the *Irish Times* (2 October 1999) with the kind of praise that is rarely seen in the reception of O'Brien's work in Ireland: "She is one of our bravest and best novelists. We have every reason to be grateful that she continues to write and that her substantial corpus, charting her literary pilgrimage, is still expanding."

Arguably the most daring and interesting aspect of Edna O'Brien's "literary pilgrimage" is her refusal to give in to critics' conventional demands. O'Brien is willing to experiment on the level of style and storytelling at the risk of alienating the reader. Her later novels have been condemned for the author's reluctance to let even the most insignificant daily acts be just what they are. This excess of signification may be most fruitfully seen in the context of a religious upbringing in which everything, even swallowing, seems to have a larger meaning. Although it is clear that O'Brien's achievement is anything but even, she has never been intimidated by criticism of her work. It is unlikely that reviewers will come to agree on O'Brien's overall achievement in the near future. If she continues to write, O'Brien will undoubtedly continue to irritate readers who want to see their conventional expectations confirmed and to delight those who look for literary and stylistic experiment.

Interviews:

Nell Dunn, "Edna," in her *Talking to Women* (London: MacGibbon & Kee, 1965), pp. 69–107;

David Heycock, "Edna O'Brien Talks to David Heycock About Her New Novel, 'A Pagan Place,'" *Listener,* 83 (7 May 1970): 616–617;

Ludovic Kennedy, "Three Loves of Childhood–Irish Thoughts by Edna O'Brien," *Listener,* 95 (3 June 1976): 701–702;

Shusha Guppy, "The Art of Fiction LXXXII: Edna O'Brien," *Paris Review,* 26 (Summer 1984): 22–50; republished in *Writers at Work: The Paris Review Interviews,* seventh series, edited by George Plimpton (New York: Penguin, 1988), pp. 241–265, and in *Women Writers at Work: The Paris Review*

Interviews, edited by Plimpton (New York: Viking, 1989), pp. 337–359;

Philip Roth, "A Conversation with Edna O'Brien: The Body Contains the Life Story," *New York Times Book Review,* 18 November 1984, pp. 38–40;

Maureen Howard, "Edna O'Brien: She's Earthy, Self-Possessed, and Not Afraid of Virginia Woolf," *Vogue,* 175 (April 1985): 196–199;

John Quinn, "Edna O'Brien," in *A Portrait of the Artist as a Young Girl,* edited by Quinn (London: Methuen/ Radio Telefis Eirean, 1986), pp. 131–144;

Richard B. Woodward, "Reveling in Heartbreak," *New York Times Magazine,* 12 March 1989, p. 42;

Julia Carlson, "Edna O'Brien: The Personal Experience of Censorship," in *Banned in Ireland: Censorship and the Irish Writer,* edited by Carlson (Athens: University of Georgia Press, 1990), pp. 69–79;

Colin Owens, *The Writing Life: Introducing Edna O'Brien,* Columbia, Md.: The Society, 1992, videocassette;

Molly Mcquade, "Edna O'Brien," *Publishers Weekly,* 239 (18 May 1992): 48–49;

James Wolcott, "The Playgirl of the Western World," *Vanity Fair,* 55 (June 1992): 50–56;

Mary Rourke, "Spellbinder," *Los Angeles Times,* 17 June 1992, p. E1;

James F. Clarity, "Casting a Cold Eye," *New York Times,* 30 August 1995, pp. C1, C8;

Sandra Manoogian Pearce, "An Interview with Edna O'Brien," *Canadian Journal of Irish Studies,* 22 (December 1996): 5–8;

Nicholas Wroe, "Country Matters," *Guardian Saturday Review,* 2 October 1999, pp. 6–7;

Eileen Battersby, "Life of O'Brien," *Irish Times,* 14 October 1999, p. 15.

Bibliographies:

Kimball King, *Ten Modern Irish Playwrights: A Comprehensive Annotated Bibliography* (New York: Garland, 1979), pp. 95–105;

Douglas Skinner and Luke Greening, "Edna O'Brien Bibliography," *Canadian Journal of Irish Studies,* 22 (December 1996): 107–116;

Adrienne L. Friedlander, *Edna O'Brien: An Annotated Secondary Bibliography (1980–1995),* Working Papers in Irish Studies, volume 97/3 (Ft. Lauderdale: Nova Southeastern University, 1997).

References:

James M. Cahalan, "Female and Male Perspectives on Growing Up Irish in Edna O'Brien, John McGahern and Brian Moore," *Colby Quarterly,* 31 (March 1995): 55–73;

Canadian Journal of Irish Studies, special O'Brien issue, 22 (December 1996);

Lynette Carpenter, "Tragedies of Remembrance, Comedies of Endurance: The Novels of Edna O'Brien," in *Essays on the Contemporary British Novel,* edited by Hedwig Bock and Albert Werfheim (Munich: Max Hüber, 1986), pp. 263–281;

Grace Eckley, *Edna O'Brien* (Lewisburg, Pa.: Bucknell University Press, 1974);

Michael Patrick Gillespie, "(S)he Was Too Scrupulous Always: Edna O'Brien and the Comic Tradition," in *The Comic Tradition in Irish Women Writers,* edited by Theresa O'Connor (Gainesville: University Press of Florida, 1996), pp. 108–123;

Tamsin Hargreaves, "Women's Consciousness and Identity in Four Irish Women Novelists," in *Cultural Contexts and Literary Idioms in Contemporary Irish Literature,* edited by Michael Kenneally, Studies in Contemporary Irish Literature, no. 1 (Gerrards Cross, U.K.: Smythe, 1988), pp. 290–305;

James Haule, "The Unfortunate Birth of Edna O'Brien," *Colby Library Quarterly,* 23 (December 1987): 216–224;

Benedict Kiely, "The Whores on the Half-Doors," in *Conor Cruise O'Brien Introduces Ireland,* edited by Owen Dudley Edwards (New York: McGraw-Hill, 1969), pp. 148–161;

Sean McMahon, "A Sex by Themselves: An Interim Report on Edna O'Brien," *Eire-Ireland,* 2 (Spring 1967): 79–87;

Frances M. Malpezzi, "Consuming Love: Edna O'Brien's 'A Rose in the Heart of New York,'" *Studies in Short Fiction,* 33 (Summer 1996): 355–360;

Darcy O'Brien, "Edna O'Brien: A Kind of Irish Childhood," in *Twentieth-Century Women Novelists,* edited by Thomas F. Staley (London: Macmillan, 1982; Totowa, N.J.: Barnes & Noble, 1982), pp. 179–190;

Peggy O'Brien, "The Silly and the Serious: An Assessment of Edna O'Brien," *Massachusetts Review,* 28 (Autumn 1987): 474–488;

Kiera O'Hara, "Love Objects: Love and Obsession in the Stories of Edna O'Brien," *Studies in Short Fiction,* 30 (Summer 1993): 317–325;

Sandra Manoogian Pearce, "Edna O'Brien's 'Lantern Slides' and Joyce's 'The Dead': Shadows of a Bygone Era," *Studies in Short Fiction,* 32 (Summer 1995): 437–446;

Rebecca Pelan, "Edna O'Brien's 'Stage-Irish' Persona: An 'Act' of Resistance," *Canadian Journal of Irish Studies,* 19 (July 1993): 67–78;

Raymonde Popot, "Edna O'Brien's Paradise Lost," *Cahiers Irlandais,* 4–5 (1976): 255–285;

Mary Salmon, "Edna O'Brien," in *Contemporary Irish Novelists,* edited by Rüdiger Imhof (Tübingen, Germany: Günter Narr, 1990), pp. 143–158;

Jeanette Roberts Shumaker, "Sacrificial Women in Short Stories by Mary Lavin and Edna O'Brien," *Studies in Short Fiction,* 32 (Spring 1995): 185–197;

Lotus Snow, "'That Trenchant Childhood Route': Quest in Edna O'Brien's Novels," *Eire-Ireland,* 14 (Spring 1979): 74–83.

Julia O'Faolain

(6 June 1932 –)

Cecile M. Jagodzinski
Illinois State University

See also the O'Faolain entry in *DLB 14: British Novelists Since 1960.*

BOOKS: *We Might See Sights! and Other Stories* (London: Faber & Faber, 1968);

Godded and Codded (London: Faber & Faber, 1970); republished as *Three Lovers* (New York: Coward, McCann & Geoghegan, 1971);

Man in the Cellar: Stories (London: Faber & Faber, 1974);

Women in the Wall (London: Faber & Faber, 1975; New York: Viking, 1975);

Melancholy Baby, and Other Stories (Dublin: Poolbeg, 1978);

No Country for Young Men (London: Allen Lane, 1980; New York: Carroll & Graf, 1986);

The Obedient Wife (London: Allen Lane, 1982; New York: Carroll & Graf, 1985);

Daughters of Passion: Stories (Harmondsworth, U.K. & New York: Penguin, 1982);

The Irish Signorina: Divertimento (Harmondsworth, U.K.: Viking, 1984; Bethesda, Md.: Adler & Adler, 1986);

The Judas Cloth (London: Sinclair-Stevenson, 1992);

Ercoli e il guardino notturno (Rome: Editori Riuniti, 1999).

OTHER: Gene Brucker, ed., *Two Memoirs of Renaissance Florence: The Diaries of Buonaccorso Pitti and Gregorio Dati,* translated by O'Faolain as Julia Martines (New York: Harper & Row, 1967);

Piero Chiara, *A Man of Parts,* translated by O'Faolain as Martines (London: Barrie & Rockliffe/Cresset Press, 1968; Boston: Little, Brown, 1968);

Not in God's Image: Women in History from the Greeks to the Victorians, edited by O'Faolain and Lauro Martines (London: Temple Smith, 1973; New York: Harper & Row, 1973);

Sean O'Faolain, *Vive Moi!* revised and expanded edition, edited, with an afterword, by O'Faolain (London: Sinclair-Stevenson, 1993);

"The Imagination as Battlefield," in *Arguing at the Crossroads: Essays on a Changing Ireland,* edited by Paul

Julia O'Faolain (courtesy of the author)

Brennan and Catherine de Sainte Phalle (Dublin: New Island Books, 1997), pp. 24–43.

Julia O'Faolain, novelist, short-story writer, and translator, casts a writer's eye on concerns of the latter half of the twentieth century: the relationship between the sexes, nationalism, and the fading but still powerful hold of religion (particularly Catholicism) on modes of thinking and acting. Her fiction, dealing as it does with foreign places, people, and languages, depicts characters alienated from the friends, families, and faith that should sustain them.

Born in London on 6 June 1932, Julia O'Faolain is the daughter of Sean O'Faolain, the acclaimed Irish short-story writer and novelist, and Eileen Gould O'Faolain, an author of children's books and editor of several collections of Irish folktales and legends. Both parents were partisans of the original Irish Republican Army during the first third of the twentieth century; O'Faolain's father, in particular, was a critic of the Irish Roman Catholic Church, and his work was a frequent target of the censors. O'Faolain has called her parents "unnervingly fanciful"; both were intrigued by the prospect of a revitalized Gaelic homeland, a romantic notion that Julia soon left behind. Educated at home until the age of eight, she read expansively, from Russian literature and romances to Catholic devotional literature. O'Faolain attributes her mature worldview to this sort of reading; even though she abandoned the Catholic faith, her reading and her encounters with local Protestant children convinced her that Protestants were of "another tribe," not at all like herself. Hints of that conviction persist in all of O'Faolain's writing, even when the Catholic Church is a target of her satire.

At the age of eight, O'Faolain was sent to a convent school run by the French Catholic Order of the Sacred Heart. While the education O'Faolain received there was not rigorous or broad-based, the nuns' emphasis on language and literature suited her. Her teachers persuaded her that words were important things, living and active. Because of the nuns' coaching, O'Faolain was able to enter University College Dublin, where she received a B.A. degree, and eventually she earned scholarships to study in Perugia, Venice, and Rome. At the Sorbonne she began a doctoral thesis but abandoned the project to write short stories. In the course of her education, she acquired a British accent, competency in Italian and French, and a smattering of Spanish and Russian. In 1957 she met and married Lauro Martines, a Renaissance historian. After a four-year stint at Reed College in Oregon and the birth of their son, Lucien Christopher, the couple returned to Italy for a period of research and teaching. They eventually moved to Los Angeles, where Martines taught at the University of California at Los Angeles, and the couple has maintained homes in both Los Angeles and London.

While some of her stories were published in American and British magazines during the 1950s, her first collection, *We Might See Sights! and Other Stories,* did not appear until 1968. The thirteen stories are divided between "Irish stories" and "Italian stories,"

setting the pattern for her future examinations of the differences and similarities between these two Catholic nations. Although the anonymous reviewer for *TLS: The Times Literary Supplement* (23 January 1969) found O'Faolain's language "marred by a . . . rather dated pomposity" and the author "over-ready with an abstract noun for physical circumstances," he found the Irish stories "full of liveliness" and judged the "ardent manner" of the Italian portion of the collection "appropriate." The Irish stories were republished in 1978, along with "The Knight" and "It's a Long Way to Tipperary," as *Melancholy Baby, and Other Stories.*

O'Faolain's first novel, *Godded and Codded* (1970), juxtaposes the stories of Sally Tyndal and Fintan McCann, two natives of Ireland who find themselves in Paris during the 1950s as scholarship students. Fintan is an artist and a fugitive from a love affair back home. Sally is less cautious than Fintan; through her love affair with a young Arab student, her sexual awakening, her disappointment in love, and a dangerous abortion, she escapes her irksome parents and her own Irishness, which is characterized by sexual repression and a highly romanticized view of life. She finally embarks on a liaison with a much older, cosmopolitan Italian who promises to teach her about the antiques business and about life. In the meantime, Fintan is terrified and repulsed by the sexual temptations of Letty, a middle-aged Irishwoman who has embraced Paris and its mores. Rejecting the new lifestyle Sally has accepted, he escapes to Barcelona after helping Sally through her abortion and botching his art show. Unlike Sally, however, he cannot erase his Irishness, his sexual guilt, or his sense of being a stranger in the world.

Though *Godded and Codded* had to be withdrawn because of the threat of a libel suit, it was received positively by critics. In *The Spectator* (10 October 1970), J. G. Farrell found the novel "somewhat uneven, but it suffers from no shortage of talent or variety." The *TLS* reviewer (2 October 1970) thought the author "a slyly accurate caricaturist" and the novel, though "obvious and hackneyed," "marvelously readable" and foresaw a bright literary future for O'Faolain. Both Farrell and Antoinette Mastin pinpoint the author's concern with the Irish tendency to both complain of and revel in political and sexual repression.

O'Faolain's next work, *Not in God's Image: Women in History from the Greeks to the Victorians* (1973), is a documentary history of women, a joint project with her husband. In their preface, the editors assert that readers wear blinders that confine them to the present; the advantage of documentary history, they

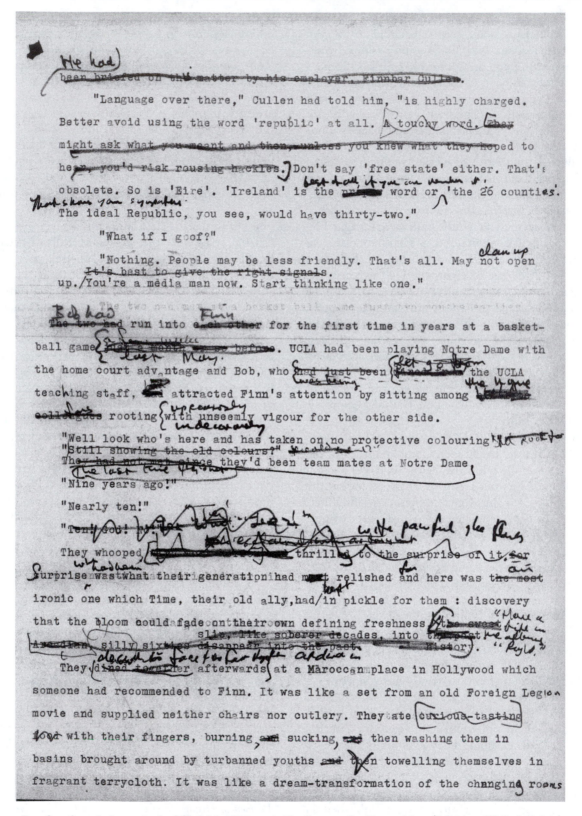

been briefed on this matter by his employer, Finnbar Cullen. *He had*

"Language over there," Cullen had told him, "is highly charged. Better avoid using the word 'republic' at all. A touchy word. They might ask what you meant and then, unless you knew what they hoped to hear, you'd risk rousing hackles. Don't say 'free state' either. That's obsolete. So is 'Eire'. 'Ireland' is the proper word or 'the 26 counties'. The ideal Republic, you see, would have thirty-two."

"What if I goof?"

"Nothing. People may be less friendly. That's all. May not open up. *clam up* It's best to give the right signals. You're a media man now. Start thinking like one."

The two had run into each other for the first time in years at a basketball game. UCLA had been playing Notre Dame with the home court advantage and Bob, who had just been the UCLA teaching staff, attracted Finn's attention by sitting among colleagues rooting with unseemly vigour for the other side. *Bob had* *Finn*

"Well look who's here and has taken on no protective colouring" "Still showing the old colours?" They had not since they'd been team mates at Notre Dame.

"Nine years ago!"

"Nearly ten!"

"Ten! God!

They whooped, thrilled to the surprise of it, for Surprise was what their generation had most relished and here was the most ironic one which Time, their old ally, had in pickle for them: discovery that the bloom could fade on their own defining freshness slip, like soberer decades, into the past. American silly sixties disappear into the past History.

They dined together afterwards at a Moroccan place in Hollywood which someone had recommended to Finn. It was like a set from an old Foreign Legion movie and supplied neither chairs nor cutlery. They ate curious-tasting food with their fingers, burning, and sucking, and then washing them in basins brought around by turbanned youths and then towelling themselves in fragrant terrycloth. It was like a dream-transformation of the changing rooms

Page from the revised typescript for O'Faolain's 1980 novel, No Country for Young Men *(Collection of Julia O'Faolain)*

argue, is that it affords "direct contact with the past." Using testimonies of men—and some women—from ancient Greece to the nineteenth century, the editors provide commentary and annotations that set the readings in historical contexts. O'Faolain and Martines also acknowledge the limitations of such documentary history, however, specifically its frequent inability to convey the effect of external repression on women's individual psychological well-being:

> More difficult to illustrate in brief readings . . . are the side-effects such mystification had: a tendency to succumb to fantasy, to mysticism, to exaggerated preoccupations and attitudes. Since women led distinctly narrower lives than men, these mental evasions could become surrogates for the realities denied them. . . . Extreme acts of violence or courage can have their source in the same estrangement from a physically and emotionally restrictive life. The woman who believed she was a witch, the bride of Christ who keenly imagined his embraces and smelled his presence, the barbarian queen (Radegonde) who burned Christ's initials into her flesh . . . each of these, in her way, is a female Don Quixote. For better or worse, they have lost touch with the actualities around them and live in a formally-organized fantasy world.

O'Faolain's later fictions examine the women who inhabit those fantasy worlds, sometimes bearing witness to their escape from them, sometimes demonstrating that fantasy can be a woman's salvation.

The title story of O'Faolain's next collection, *Man in the Cellar* (1974), literally marries her Irish and Italian themes. The Irish-born heroine of the titular story, bullied by her macho Italian husband and her disapproving mother-in-law, chains her husband to a bed in the cellar until he agrees to give her the divorce she seeks. Despite the wide-ranging settings of the seven stories in the collection, all of O'Faolain's characters, from a sixth-century nun to a married Irish celibate to an Italian academic in America, are, at least figuratively, fettered to their own lusts and despair.

Women in the Wall (1975) fictionalizes the story of Radegunda, the reluctant wife of the sixth-century Clotair, king of the Franks. Released from her marital vows, she founds a convent, becomes a visionary, and finds solace in the arms of Christ, who appears to her as a handsome young man. Her protégée, Agnes, the abbess of the monastery, admires but cannot really understand Radegunda's ecstasies. Embarrassed and frightened by matters of the flesh, Agnes eventually finds love in the arms of the poet Fortunatus; their daughter, Ingunda, horrified at her parentage, immures herself into the convent walls in expiation. The backdrop for these personal stories is the political unrest of the time: Radegunda plots to put an orthodox Christian prince on the throne, and Chrodechild, one of the more worldy and ambitious of the nuns, plots to become abbess. After Radegunda dies, Agnes decides to follow her daughter and buries herself alive, and Chrodechild ascends to power in the small world of the convent. Moving back and forth in time between 568 and 587 and employing multiple narrators, the book depicts its female protagonists, buried within real and psychological walls, as they struggle with church, state, and their own desires. They cannot finally escape but must resolve their problems through visions, sex, or sacrifice. The novel is, as Mary Hope stated in a 1 June 1985 *Spectator* review, "about dealing, unsatisfactorily, with a terrible world." Hope found the book "disjointed" but "an ambitious and interesting oddity," while John Mellors, in *London Magazine* (August–September 1975), thought O'Faolain had achieved "the truth of fiction, if not of history" and praised her "flair for seeing into confined spaces," as she had in *Man in the Cellar*. Lalage Pulvertaft, reviewing for *TLS* (4 April 1975), charged O'Faolain with judging historical circumstances "with the prejudices of modern psychology and political theory" and with a modern, secularized view of religious vocations as "perverted power mania." Others, such as Peter Drewaniany in the *Encyclopedia of British Women Writers* (1988), feel this examination of the buried life of women "brings to the novel a strong sense of contemporaneity," of the walls that continue to circumscribe women. In a 1986 panel discussion on the difficulties of translation, O'Faolain contrasted translators and writers: both serve as witnesses, but the translator seeks to erase difference, while the literary author highlights the alien in others, making the characters "act out a metaphor" of difference. She mentioned *Women in the Wall* specifically and described the way in which she "invented" a language, then translated it into an approximation of the way sixth-century Gauls might have spoken and thought. In *Women in the Wall* O'Faolain acts as both translator and writer: connecting readers with the past but reminding them of the differences between past and present.

O'Faolain's next novel, *No Country for Young Men* (1980), also exploits the recurrences of events in time. The author has said that the germ for this novel was a Dublin woman who thought the present year was 1922—a date "explosive with parable to anyone who knew Ireland," as O'Faolain observed in *Contemporary Authors Autobiography Series*. In that year the civil war began between supporters and opponents of the Irish Free State. These historical events also had personal resonances for O'Faolain—her mother had been her father's courier when he made bombs for the old IRA in 1923.

In 1970s Ireland, Sister Judith Clancy, having been ejected from the convent that had been her home for the past fifty years, moves in with her grandniece Grainne and her husband, Michael, who live together but have become alienated. From the United States comes James Duffy, a moviemaker seeking oral histories from survivors of the Irish troubles and information about Sparky Driscoll, an American mysteriously killed in 1922. James and Grainne commence an adulterous affair in which Grainne, like her mythical counterpart in the Irish legend of Diarmuid and Gráinne, must choose between personal desire and political and familial loyalty. Grainne's uncle, Owen Roe, thinks the scandal of Grainne's affair and James's unsettling questioning of Judith about the past will hurt his rise to power, so he has Patsy Flynn, a radical former IRA man, kill James. These events are counterpointed by Judith's efforts to recall her past, and from "her boglike memory" emerges the truth about 1922. Judith and her sister Kathleen both caught the attention of Sparky Driscoll, an American fund-raiser for the Irish cause. Frightened by her emerging sexuality and ferociously supportive of the Republicans, Judith bayoneted Sparky, who was suspected of political moderation. To control the political damage, Owen O'Malley, Kathleen's fiancé and a Republican diehard, confines Judith to a convent, where old age, the trauma of the murder, and electroshock treatments eventually erase any memories of the events; in the meantime, Driscoll is rehabilitated as an Irish hero, a victim of the Orangemen.

As in *Women in the Wall,* the sexual and the political are yoked in *No Country for Young Men.* O'Faolain's novel replies to the opening line from William Butler Yeats's "Sailing to Byzantium" (1928)—"That is no country for old men"—in two ways: Ireland is both a country where young men die and a land without real space for women. Kathleen must content herself with housekeeping and mothering; Judith, who kills the man who opposes her cause, is buried alive in a convent. Grainne's marriage is loveless, her son turns from her to the political myths of Patsy Flynn, and her hopes of escape to the United States with James Duffy are smashed by his death. Judith, whose name echoes that of the sacrificial and sacrificing heroine of the Old Testament, embodies the voices of all the women who, Cassandra-like, are ignored as men, though "disabled by drink or jingoism," hold sway. Women, as Ann Owens Weekes declared in "Diar-

muid and Grainne Again: Julia O'Faolain's *No Country for Young Men*" (1986), are without individual destinies; like the bog ever present throughout the story, they are claylike and passive.

A finalist for Britain's prestigious Booker Prize and for the Christopher Ewart Biggs Prize, *No Country for Young Men* drew more critical attention, both positive and negative, than any other of O'Faolain's novels. Patricia Craig, in a review for *TLS* (13 June 1980), found the movement between past and present in the novel less than successful and the ending "both implausible and confused." Though she found "its greatest strengths . . . in its apprehension of changes in feeling, shifts in allegiance," she also objected to the "melodramatic note of the novel, the exaggerated parallels between current and past events." Others had more positive responses to the book. *Publishers Weekly* (28 November 1986) called it "a triumph of intelligence, insight, and surpassing wit"; Julian Moynihan, in the *New York Times Book Review* (1 February 1987), remarked that "Julia O'Faolain in her bitter, comprehensive realism has produced a book that has few if any parallels in contemporary Irish fiction and that must be read by all who care about 'that country' as it really is."

O'Faolain's next novel, *The Obedient Wife* (1982), is set in California, her part-time residence. Carla Verdi, a young Italian mother of a thirteen-year-old son, is left on her own while her domineering husband, Marco, resides in Italy for an extended period of time. Perhaps to justify his own actions and disguise his guilt, he encourages her to have an affair. Carla is embarrassed by his absence from home and resists his suggestions until she meets Leo, a young priest who retains his youthful idealism and provides a father-substitute for her son. Her friend Sybil's own passion for Leo, a dysfunctional family living nearby, and natural disasters such as earthquake tremors and fires serve as the backdrop to Carla's conflicting emotions. No longer informed by religious or spiritual sentiments, Carla becomes disenchanted with Leo, whose dependence on God and purity of purpose, even when making love to her, makes him independent of her. By the end of the novel, with both Marco and her son clamoring for her return, she abandons Leo. Her final obedience, however, is not to her family, but to the values she has realized: as Weekes puts it in "Julia O'Faolain: The Imaginative Crucible" (1990), Carla "valorizes communal over individual values." For the moral code of the new Catholic Church, which encourages the easy values of Leo and Sybil, Carla substitutes a secular code. According to Tamsin Hargreaves in "Women's Consciousness and Identity in Four Irish

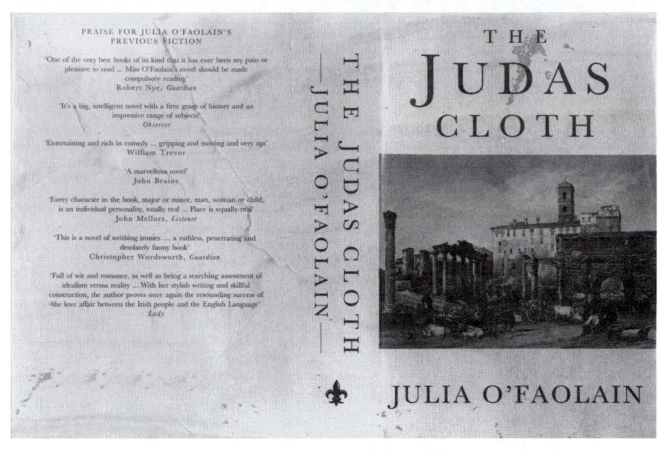

PRAISE FOR JULIA O'FAOLAIN'S
PREVIOUS FICTION

'One of the very best books of its kind that it has ever been my pain or
pleasure to read ... Miss O'Faolain's novel should be made
compulsory reading'
Robert Nye, *Guardian*

'It's a big, intelligent novel with a firm grasp of history and an
impressive range of subjects'
Observer

'Entertaining and rich in comedy ... gripping and moving and very apt'
William Trevor

'A marvellous novel'
John Braine

'Every character in the book, major or minor, man, woman or child,
is an individual personality, totally real ... Place is equally real'
John Mellors, *Listener*

'This is a novel of writhing ironies ... a ruthless, penetrating and
desolately funny book'
Christopher Wordsworth, *Guardian*

'Full of wit and romance, as well as being a searching assessment of
idealism versus reality ... With her stylish writing and skillful
construction, the author proves once again the resounding success of
the love affair between the Irish people and the English Language'
Lady

THE
JUDAS
CLOTH

JULIA O'FAOLAIN

*Dust jacket for O'Faolain's 1992 historical novel, about Pope Pius IX (courtesy of The Lilly Library,
Indiana University, Bloomington, Indiana)*

Women Novelists" (1988), "domesticity and the domestic skills of cooking, bourgeois living, and the family are seen as modes of salvation in a chaotic anarchic life." Writing in *TLS* (23 July 1982), reviewer Patricia Craig concurs, praising the novel and its heroine: "*The Obedient Wife* is an exceptionally polished work; if its ending disappoints feminists, who require gestures of social rebelliousness from their fiction, . . . it is none the less appropriate, in that it represents an assertion of the values its heroine has lived by."

O'Faolain's subsequent short-story collection, *Daughters of Passion* (1982), focuses again on love and the physical, religious, emotional, and political passions in the lives of women. In "Legend for a Painting," O'Faolain inverts traditional iconography. A knight rescues a lady from a fierce dragon, but the lady does not wish to be rescued; she is, in fact, puzzled by the knight's belief that she is not free, even though she and the dragon are chained to one another. When the knight, whose motto is "Deeds not words," kills the dragon, the lady, in token of her bitter servitude to the knight, agrees to be his prisoner as

she slips a link from the chain onto her ring finger. Similarly chained, the young woman in "The Nanny and the Antique Dealer" learns that she can only satisfy the man with whom she is having an affair when she abandons her ordinary self and dresses as his mother. "Mad Marga" and "Daughters of Passion" depict young women propelled into violent acts by others: Marga by a radical political group, Maggy by a revolutionary Anglo-Irish Protestant and childhood friend from the convent. In such stories, O'Faolain somewhat disconcertingly shows how dangerously easy it is to succumb to passing desire.

The Irish Signorina: Divertimento (1984), however, seems to celebrate the passions; those who deny the pleasures of love, food, and beautiful things are depicted as less than alive. After her mother's lengthy final illness, Anne Ryan, the Irish heroine of the novel, returns to the Italian town where, years before, her mother had been a companion to the daughter of the Marchesa Niccolosa Cavalcanti. Though her mother had since married a stolid and dependable Irishman, she always spoke longingly of Italy. Her mother's yearning for the past as well as

Anne's curiosity and fear of "the unlived life" goad her on. The Marchesa takes a special interest in Anne after Guido, the Marchesa's married son, woos her at a dinner party. Significantly, Guido's namesake is the thirteenth-century Italian poet and friend of Dante—both poets did much to instill in the modern imagination the notion of women as idealized and angelic guiding spirits of men. It is unclear whether O'Faolain intends any irony here—Guido is a hopeless womanizer, and is, in fact, Anne's father. The novel ends with Anne happily planning to marry Guido, freed to do so by his ignorance of the matter and by the death of the Marchesa.

Critics disparaged *The Irish Signorina*. Gillian Greenwood, in *The Spectator* (15 April 1984), thought the storyline weak, the plot clichéd, and the characters unconvincing: "The limitations which Miss O'Faolain has set herself also prevent, for the most part, her graceful prose from transcending the banal. She has bricked herself in and, despite the Tuscan sunshine, delivered an unripe fruit." In *America* (2 May 1987), T. Patrick Hill wrote that the book bore "a pervasive incompleteness" and a plot that "unravels before the reader." Julia Whedon, in *The New York Times Book Review* (20 July 1986), thought the novel "strangely operatic," with a "surfeit of quotations and mythological references"; for her the book was marked by excessive literary sensibility. O'Faolain herself wrote in *Contemporary Authors Autobiography Series* that she wanted to rework an old theme—"the story of the governess in the great house"—so that the girl could "actually become a predator and succeed."

The central historical character in *The Judas Cloth* (1992), O'Faolain's next novel, is a fictionalized Pope Pius IX, who lived through the dismantling of secular papal power, the unification of Italy, and the declaration of papal infallibility. In her prefatory note, O'Faolain writes that she "tried to imagine what it was like to be a moderate dependant of his" and charges the Pope with pushing the world "ever further toward polarization," a polarization personified in three young men whose lives are affected by events swirling around them: Prospero, the conservative son of a liberal; Flavio, the streetwise orphan who inherits wealth; and Nicola, the earnest priest who thinks himself an orphan but learns he is the son of a holy nun and the less-than-holy Pope. Pius's manipulation of the cardinalate at the first Vatican Council, the horrors of the French Commune, and the hypocrisies and ambiguities of both church and state lead Nicola to renounce the "Judas cloth" of priesthood and Catholicism.

This sprawling novel—Dickensian in its characterization and Tolstoyan in its historical scope—was sparsely reviewed upon publication. Francis King, in the 21 November 1992 issue of *The Spectator,* named it one of the two best of the year; David Gilmour, in *TLS* (25 September 1992), called it a "powerful, original and intelligent novel." The length of the novel and its reliance on the historical rather than the personal distance the reader from the characters, however. O'Faolain wrote in *Contemporary Authors Autobiography Series* that she enjoys research, "but it does shrivel my ability to invent." *The Judas Cloth* gives evidence of too much research and too little invention.

O'Faolain, referring to her Catholic background and early reading habits, has said that she read classic English novels and the devotional literature of martyrdom with "different parts of my brain." On one side lay English puritanism, priggishness, and containment; on the other, the Irish, Catholic, gothic excesses and exoticism of bloody martyrdom, sacrifice, and redemption. O'Faolain has spoken of Irish writers having a "divided readership"; as Theresa O'Connor observed in "History, Gender, and the Postcolonial Condition: Julia O'Faolain's Comic Rewriting of *Finnegans Wake*" (1996), her vision and her writings cannot be assigned to one or the other side of the divide: "O'Faolain does not offer the more liberal British system as an antidote for Ireland's repressive piety, nor, indeed, does she suggest that separatist feminism is a viable alternative to patriarchy." Whether the politics at hand are religious, secular, or sexual, O'Faolain finds no extreme attractive; her works testify to that ambiguity.

Interviews:

Elgy Gillespie, "No Country for Young Women," *Irish Times* (23 March 1979);

Barth Healey, "Home Rule, Rome Rule," *New York Times Book Review* (1 February 1987), p. 7.

References:

Jeanne Marie Armstrong, "Uncivilized Women and Erotic Strategies of Border Zones, or Demythologizing the Romance of Conquest," Ph.D. dissertation, University of Arizona, 1996;

David Burleigh, "Dead and Gone: The Fiction of Jennifer Johnston and Julia O'Faolain," in *Irish Writers and Society at Large,* edited by Masaru Sekine (Totowa, N.J.: Barnes & Noble, 1985), pp. 1–15;

Christiane Damlos-Kinzel, *Women's Role in Our Troubled Times—: eine Untersuchung zum literarishcen Werk Julia O'Faolains* (Wurzburg: Konigshausen & Neumann, 1994);

Mary Fitzgerald-Hoyt, "The Influence of Italy in the Writings of William Trevor and Julia O'Faolain," *Notes on Modern Irish Literature,* 2 (1990): 61–67;

Tamsin Hargreaves, "Women's Consciousness and Identity in Four Irish Women Novelists," in *Cultural Contexts and Literary Idioms in Contemporary Irish Literature,* edited by Michael Kenneally (Totowa, N.J.: Barnes & Noble, 1988), pp. 290–305;

Maurice Harmon, "Generations Apart: 1925–1975," in *The Irish Novel in Our Time,* edited by Patrick Rafroidi and Maurice Harmon (Villeneuve-d'Ascq: Publications de l'Universite de Lille III, 1976), pp. 49–65;

Rebecca A. Kondritz, "Privately Liberating and Publicly Enslaving: The Role of Desire in *No Country for Young Men,*" M.A. thesis, University of Nebraska at Kearney, 1994;

Christine Hunt Mahony, "Politicization of Women in the Writings of Julia O'Faolain: That Is No Country for Young Men and The Irish Signorina," in *Troubled Histories, Troubled Fictions: Twentieth-Century Anglo-Irish Prose,* edited by Theo D'haen and José Lanters (Amsterdam: Rodopi, 1995), pp. 151–158;

Antoinette M. Mastin, "Stephen Dedalus in Paris?: Joycean Elements in Julia O'Faolain's *Three Lovers,*" *Colby Quarterly,* 30 (December 1994): 244–251;

Thomas R. Moore, "Triangles and Entrapment: Julia O'Faolain's *No Country for Young Men,*" *Colby Quarterly,* 27 (March 1991): 9–16;

Theresa O'Connor, "History, Gender, and the Postcolonial Condition: Julia O'Faolain's Comic Rewriting of *Finnegans Wake,*" in *The Comic Tradition in Irish Women Writers,* edited by O'Connor (Gainesville: University Press of Florida, 1996), pp. 124–148;

Christine St. Peter, "Reconstituting the Irish Nationalist Family Romance: *No Country for Young Men,*" in *Historicité et metafiction dans le roman contemporain des Iles Britanniques,* edited by Max Duperray (Aix-en-Provence: Université de Provence, 1994), pp. 151–166;

Laura B. Van Dale, "Women across Time: Sister Judith Remembers," *Colby Quarterly,* 27 (March 1991): 17–26;

Ann Owens Weekes, "Diarmuid and Grainne Again: Julia O'Faolain's *No Country for Young Men,*" *Eire-Ireland: A Journal of Irish Studies,* 21 (1986): 89–102;

Weekes, "Julia O'Faolain: The Imaginative Crucible," in her *Irish Women Writers: An Uncharted Tradition* (Lexington: University Press of Kentucky, 1990), pp. 174–190.

Ben Okri

(15 March 1959 –   )

Ann-Barbara Graff
University of Toronto

See also the Okri entry in *DLB 157: Twentieth-Century Caribbean and Black African Writers.*

BOOKS: *Flowers and Shadows* (London: Longman, 1980; Harlow, U.K. & New York: Longman, 1994);

The Landscapes Within (Harlow, U.K.: Longman, 1981);

Incidents at the Shrine: Short Stories (London: Heinemann, 1986; Boston: Faber & Faber, 1987);

Stars of the New Curfew: Short Stories (London: Secker & Warburg, 1988; New York: Viking, 1989);

The Famished Road (London: Cape, 1991; New York: N. A. Talese, 1992);

An African Elegy (London: Cape, 1992);

Songs of Enchantment (London: Cape, 1993; New York: Nan A. Talese, 1993);

Astonishing the Gods (London: Phoenix House, 1995; Boston, London & Toronto: Little, Brown, 1995);

Birds of Heaven (London: Phoenix House, 1996);

Dangerous Love (London: Phoenix House, 1996);

A Way of Being Free (London: Phoenix House, 1997);

Infinite Riches (London: Phoenix House, 1998);

Mental Fight (London: Phoenix House, 1999).

Ben Okri (photograph by Douglas Brothers; courtesy of Jonathan Cape)

SELECTED PERIODICAL PUBLICATIONS—UNCOLLECTED:

FICTION

"In Another Country," *West Africa,* no. 3323 (20 April 1981): 873–875;

"Fires Next Time Are Always Small Enough," *West Africa,* no. 3420 (25 April 1983): 1020–1021;

"A Prayer from the Living," *New York Times,* 29 January 1993, p. A27.

NONFICTION

"Journeys Through the Imagination," *West Africa,* no. 3418 (14 February 1983): 429–430;

"Labelled," *New Statesman,* 109 (15 March 1985): 29–30;

"No Room at the Inn," *New Statesman,* 110 (20 December 1985): 33;

"Lagos Lament," *New Statesman,* 111 (9 May 1986): 35;

"Gifted . . . and Black," *New Statesman,* 112 (17 October 1986): 36;

"Soyinka: A Personal View," *West Africa,* no. 3608 (27 October 1986): 2249–2250;

"A Celebration of Wole Soyinka," *Literary Review,* 29 (December 1986): 6–7;

"Okigbo—An Independent Voice and Spirit," *African Concord* (16 April 1987): 48–49.

Ben Okri is one of the best known of the first generation of Nigerian novelists who have described in their fiction the psychic costs of the Nigerian transition from colonial rule to independence. He has won many international prizes, including Booker Prizes for *The Famished Road* (1991) and *Infinite Riches* (1998). Like his predecessors and compatriots Ken Saro-Wiwa and

Wole Soyinka, Okri has used his fiction to focus attention on political injustice, institutional corruption, and economic dispossession without forsaking aesthetic aims. Over the course of his career, Okri's fiction has become increasingly experimental as he has adopted postmodern narrative strategies that reflect his growing dissatisfaction with realism as a mode of expression.

Ben Okri was born to Grace and Silver Oghekeneshineke Loloje Okri on 15 March 1959 in Minna, Nigeria, not long before British colonial rule ended officially on 1 October 1960. He was born at a time of heightened expectation and cultural nationalism which are reflected in Amos Tutuola's *The Palm-Wine Drunkard* (1952), Chinua Achebe's *Things Fall Apart* (1958), Soyinka's *The Interpreters* (1965), and Ayi Kwei Armah's *The Beautyful Ones Are Not Yet Born* (1968). The Okri family was fairly affluent. When Ben Okri was born, his father held a management position with Nigerian Post and Telecommunications. In 1962 his parents took him to England, where his father completed a law degree. As a child growing up in both Nigeria and Britain, Okri enjoyed a rare perspective from which to witness the disparate realities and hypocrisies of British and Nigerian society. In 1966 he returned to Nigeria with his mother, and later his father set up practice in the Ajegunle slum district of Lagos to the disenfranchised. Okri's familiarity with his father's clientele and the institutional barriers to justice gave him firsthand exposure to the corruption that was part of life, especially for the poor, in Lagos.

A voracious reader, Okri began writing essays and short stories while he was still in school. He attended the Children's Home School in Ibadan, and Mayflower School in Ikenne, before going to Urhobo College in Warri, in 1968 for his secondary education. The youngest boy in his class, Okri finished secondary school in 1972, before his fourteenth birthday. When he failed to earn a place at a Nigerian university, he took a job in a paint store and began publishing his short fiction in Nigerian women's journals and evening papers. After earning a diploma in journalism through correspondence, he gained admission to Essex University in 1978 to read for a degree in philosophy and literature. Since that time he has lived in England. While at Essex, he completed his first novel, *Flowers and Shadows* (1980). Since earning a B.A. in comparative literature in 1980, Okri has had a varied career: he has been poetry editor for *West Africa* (1981–1987); a broadcaster for "Network Africa," BBC World Service (1984–1985); a reviewer for *The Guardian, The Observer,* and *The New Statesman;* visiting fellow commoner in creative arts at Trinity College, Cambridge (1991–1993); an advocate for PEN, which is committed to ending the persecution of writers; and a full-time writer. In 1987 he won the Commonwealth Writers' Prize for Africa and the *Paris Review* Aga Khan fiction prize for his collection of short stories, *Incidents at the Shrine* (1986). For his third novel, *The Famished Road,* Okri was awarded the 1991 Booker Prize, the 1993 International Literary Prize *Chianti Rufino-Antico,* and the 1994 *Premio Grinzane Cavour.* In 1995 the World Economic Forum presented Okri with the Crystal Award for his contributions to the arts and to cross-cultural understanding.

Much of Okri's fiction focuses on problems endemic in Nigeria, including brutality, corruption, and economic dispossession. While maintaining a critical view of colonialism, racism, and tribalism, which are at the historical roots of Nigeria's social chaos, Okri consistently looks within Nigeria to individuals, not elite groups, for solutions to its present problems and for means of reconciliation.

Focusing on the underlying psychosocial causes of brutality, Okri's fiction usually explores the tension between Western ideals and African sensibility, between ritual or superstition and putatively rational institutions such as the law. The stories are told from the perspective of a highly sensitive male protagonist, a child coming of age or an artist. Because his perspective and agenda are at odds with the community around him, he is often misunderstood, derided or ignored. Okri's stories usually include a villain, an older man in a position of power who, fearing the loss of his authority, sets about to secure his position by destroying the lives of others. Okri's women are complex figures who are charged with maintaining the fabric of the family while ruthless and fearful men attempt to destroy it around them. In fact, the emotional impact of his first novel, *Flowers and Shadows,* stems from women's reactions to the disastrous main (male) action. Throughout his fiction Okri has attempted to create complex characters and to show how they have been shaped.

Okri completed *Flowers and Shadows* when he was nineteen, and it was published in 1980, when he was twenty-one. Critically acclaimed, the work displays an artistic naiveté that can be excused given Okri's age and obvious talent for lyric, evocative, and economic prose. Set in Lagos, the novel juxtaposes a middle-class young man's coming of age against the misery, horror, and palpable threat to life that plagues modern Nigeria. The reader observes the poverty, disease, corruption, and deceit underlying the bourgeois facade of Lagos from the vantage point of Jeffia Okwe, the adolescent first-person narrator. At one particularly distressing point, no longer near the safety and comfort of his home, Jeffia describes his surroundings:

> There was a terrible stench in the air. The roads were bad, filled with ugly potholes, dirty. People who looked

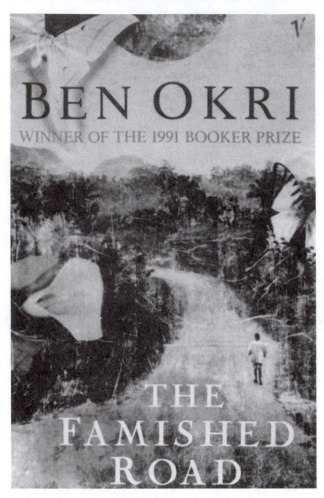

Dust jacket for Okri's 1991 novel, about a spirit-child who can communicate simultaneously with the real world and the spirit world

sickly and exhausted milled past us and I couldn't help being revolted by some of the sights I saw. There was a man under the Ijora bridge who had no legs. He was sleeping beside the spot people had habitually used as a urinal. There was a boy no more than fourteen lying on the side of the road with flies dancing all over his swollen body. He was dead. There was another group of children all crying round their beggar mother.

While this description can easily be identified as Jeffia's projection of his sadness onto the world around him— understanding its function in the text cannot protect the reader from the horror of the scene, which shocks Jeffia into a new awareness of the world outside himself.

Flowers and Shadows opens with premonitions of disaster. In the opening scene, Jeffia encounters two boys torturing a puppy: "One held the dog by the legs, while the other, it seemed, tried to stick a piece of wood up its anus. Indifferently, they watched it struggle." This rape prepares the reader emotionally for the

abuses of power that follow. After rescuing the dog, Jeffia becomes involved in a world previously hidden from him, one that centers on his father, Jonan Okwe, a corrupt businessman who is awaiting the release of his falsely imprisoned half-brother Sowho and commissioning an assault that turns into the murder of a longtime employee.

Flowers and Shadows explores the fears that drive Jonan's sexual and criminal excesses, clues to his brutal and seemingly irrational behavior: "From the day he was old enough to know what impossible things money could do, from the time his father died consumed by a mysterious plague, from the moment he realized the truth of his father's words that poverty was a curse, he always dreamt of the big time." Choosing to contextualize rather than excuse Jonan's behavior, Okri allows the reader to piece together a cycle of desire and deprivation that began in a previous generation and continues to feed Jonan's fears. The novel, however, is ultimately optimistic. Jonan and Sowho, who serves as Jonan's Doppelgänger, die together. The last remaining representatives of a corrupt generation, they collide in a car accident while pursuing one another, and both perish in the flames, "Two souls joined in one and blood burned in metal." Out of this tragedy Jeffia can begin anew, free from the cycle of corruption and evil.

As a consequence of his father's death, Jeffia is forced to leave home and rent rooms in a poor area of the city. There he falls in love with Cynthia, a nurse who has faced the wrongful imprisonment of her father and the death of her mother, but is saved by her inner strength. Jeffia's love for Cynthia sustains him. While the ending is sentimental and the melodramatic love plot stretches the bounds of credulity, Okri's ability to portray with honesty and artistry both flowers (innocence) and shadows (the malevolent motives and unforeseen consequences of action) makes *Flowers and Shadows* a powerful novel.

Okri's second novel, *The Landscapes Within* (1981), opens with an epigraph from *A Portrait of the Artist as a Young Man* (1916) by James Joyce: "Welcome, O life! I go to encounter for the millionth time the reality of experience and to forge in the smithy of my soul the uncreated conscience of my race." Indeed, some critics have compared Okri to Joyce: each is a lyric writer in self-imposed exile writing, as the conscience of his nation, a novel concerned with the purpose and function of art. *The Landscapes Within* recounts the life of a solitary painter, Omovo, whose artistic vision and anomie lead him into conflict not only with his family and friends but also with the State. In this *Kunstlerroman* (artist novel) Omovo works in the context of social and political corruption. In a society where the press is censored, where individuals are detained without cause, and where interrogation and intimidation are commonplace, the belief is widely held that the artist's ability to preserve cultural memory and translate his visions to canvas (or text) are central to the survival of the culture and its human values. Omovo struggles mightily, if unsuccessfully, to express what might otherwise be lost.

His inability to fill his canvas parallels his inability to consummate his love for Ifeyiwa, his neighbor's wife. When she is accidently murdered and dumped "into the bracking stream nearby," Omovo finally finds the inspiration to paint an image of a girl in the park, "a girl without a face." Omovo calls the painting *The Moment.* The moment of clarity it captures, by its nature does not last, and the novel ends with Omovo picking his way "slowly through the familiar darkness, alone."

Okri was dissatisfied with *The Landscapes Within,* feeling he was unable to express adequately in prose the emotional complexity of the situation he wanted to depict. Omovo's recurrent struggles against a blank canvas mimic Okri's perceived insufficiency:

> He stared at a blank canvas. He was aware that he wanted to paint something deep and painful but somehow the urges had not gathered strong enough with him . . . when the landscapes without synchronized those landscapes within. It made him deeply miserable to sit staring at the blank canvas.

Okri returned to the original premise for *The Landscapes Within* and rewrote it as *Dangerous Love* (1996).

Okri's early works were promising but conventional in both form and content. With his short-story collections *Incidents at the Shrine* and *Stars of the New Curfew* (1988), however, Okri demonstrated a growing confidence, maturity, and willingness to experiment, especially with narrative techniques.

Both collections include nightmarish visions of nocturnal landscapes populated with bodies and spirits both living and dead. *Incidents at the Shrine* is a collection of eight tightly wrought stories set in Nigeria during the Civil War (1967–1970), in London among the street people of Thatcherite Britain, or in a dreamworld suffused with an African sensibility. Each story explores the themes of loss, dispossession, and deprivation. The first story, "Laughter Beneath the Bridge," is narrated by a confused young boy who must travel home with his mother through checkpoints and a landscape ravaged by civil war. The bridge of the title refers to the site at which dead bodies are indiscriminately dumped by soldiers. As the stench from the corpses under the bridge becomes increasingly unbearable, the authorities selectively distribute gas masks without acknowledging the cause of the smell. In the final scene, a girl whose brother's body has been dumped under the bridge is dragged off as she performs a frenzied dance over the bridge.

Stars of the New Curfew, a collection of six stories, presents an even darker indictment of dispassion and brutality than *Incidents at the Shrine.* This second collection opens with an epigraph by Christopher Okigbo that captures the irony of the stories in the collection: "We carry in our worlds that flourish our worlds that have failed." In the title story, a recalcitrant salesman sells fake medicines that actually worsen the ringworm and eczema that they are supposed to treat. Instead of being punished for his obvious crimes against humanity, the salesman is promoted to a new firm called "CURES UNLIMITED." From describing the "nightmare of salesmen" Okri moves to depicting the "salesmen of nightmares." In both short-story collections, Okri's visions have a sense of the hallucinatory.

The Famished Road (1991), Okri's first novel in ten years, has been characterized as postcolonial, postmodern and multicultural. The book expands the hallucinatory mode with which Okri experimented in his short-story collections. Reminiscent of the magic realism of Jorge Luis Borges, Gabriel García Márquez, and Salman Rushdie (particularly in *Midnight's Children,* 1981), *The Famished Road* is Okri's most highly regarded work to date. The title comes from Soyinka's poem "Death in the Dawn." Okri challenges the formal and structural conventions of literary realism and African mythopoesis by mediating the narrative through the consciousness of an *abiku,* or "spirit-child," named Azaro who is born only to die and return in an endless cycle of death and rebirth. As the novel opens, Azaro is unwilling to fulfill his promise to return to his fellow spirits. His struggle to stay alive is the main subject of his narrative.

As an *abiku,* Azaro is conscious of the real world and the spirit world, and he communicates simultaneously with both. For Okri, this dual consciousness provides the opportunity to play off realism and mythic narration against one another without, according to Olatubosun Ogunsanwo, "merging into one single monolithic discourse" or giving one tradition priority over the other. As in all Okri stories, the realistic details of poverty and squalor are plentiful, but in this novel they blur with dreamscapes to produce a compelling otherworld, complete with its own logic and determinacy, populated with grotesque characters such as a two-legged dog, two-fingered dwarfs, children with three arms, wood-faced women, hundreds of rats, and politicians who situate the story in the reality of neocolonial political struggle. The novel poses interesting questions about the nature of reality, identity, literary convention, and marginality; it also speaks to the regenerative power of the imagination. As Azaro says: "A dream can be the highest point of a life."

*Dust jacket for Okri's 1998 novel, the final volume
of his* Famished Road *trilogy*

Many of the characters from *The Famished Road* also appear in Okri's next novel, *Songs of Enchantment* (1993), which focuses on Azaro's father as he pursues an unattainable woman and then attempts to win back his wife. *Songs of Enchantment* reveals a great deal about Okri's aesthetic practice of revisiting his published works—usually, but not necessarily, with a different thematic or character focus. This novel begins with a convenient metaphor for describing the author's practice of revisualization: "the circling spirit," which embodies the view that "struggles are never truly concluded, that sometimes we have to re-dream our lives, . . . to create more light." In fact, most of Okri's work can be read as redreamed versions of earlier published fiction. Unlike Western writers preoccupied with the sanctity of the published text, Okri is willing to reappraise and rework his literary accomplishments, raising interesting questions about the fluidity of texts—a characteristic of the oral tradition from which the practice of African storytelling springs. It also provides a way of measuring, for lack of a better word, Okri's development as a writer.

Okri's next novel, *Astonishing the Gods* (1995), comprises stylistically startling, short chapters (some only a paragraph in length). As in Joan Didion's *Play It As It Lays* (1970), which uses the same technique, Okri seems to convey as much by the absence of text as by the presence of prose on the page. The novel is set on an island where nothing is named, because "when you name something it loses its existence to you. Things die a little when we name them." The novel is a self-conscious postcolonial fable about a boy who discovers that he and his people are "invisible," because they do not appear in the history books he is given. Where once the boy's ambition was to be a shepherd, he has decided to go on a journey in search of the visible world. Running away and sailing the seas, he travels for seven years, until he jumps ship and settles on a formidable island. Tested by one phantom after another, the young man is distracted from his quest for visibility and instead, unexpectedly, pursues a spiritual journey for absolute invisibility. There is a danger that *Astonishing the Gods* might be read as an uncharitable parody of the postcolonial struggle for representation and authenticity; yet, it is clear from the text that such an interpretation is not Okri's intention. Rather he is attempting to raise questions about the nature of reality and self-representation. Nevertheless, the resolution with which the reader is left—"stop trying to make sense of things, for then he would find the truest grace,"—does not clarify the thematic concerns of the novel.

Okri's rewritten version of *The Landscapes Within*, *Dangerous Love* (1996), begins with an epigraph from Rainer Maria Rilke: "Shouldn't these ancient sufferings of ours finally start to bear fruit?" The epigraph suggests the themes of the novel: historical suffering, individual responsibility, and the role of the artist. The painter-protagonist Omovo returns from *The Landscapes Within*, as does his lover Ifeyiwa; the beggars, drunks, prostitutes, and squalor regularly found in Okri's fiction are also present; but *Dangerous Love* is much bleaker than *The Landscapes Within*. In *Dangerous Love* people are "ghostly shades" living against a "landscape of losses," "Scavenging for blood money. . . . Scavenging our futures, our history." In this rendering of Omovo's story, his alienation is placed in the historical context of the slave trade in West Africa. Recalling how his ancestors sold their countrymen into slavery, Omovo reckons himself a victim of his genealogy, "a walking inheritor of death and chains and bad history." But Omovo's isolation is not simply a function of bad history, racism, civil war, censorship, intimidation, and financial exploitation by multinational corporations: these things are part of modern reality. Dispossession is at the root of Omovo's isolation; as he tells Ifeyiwa: "We are victims here, . . . we are strangers, refugees from the poverty of the interior . . . in our villages we would still be strangers."

In this context, love and art provide the only consolations and prove equally dangerous, as they require an assertion of trust, will, and defiance that is barely supportable in a climate of corruption, deceit, and suspicion. But whereas love, romantic love anyway, is self-explanatory, the role of art has been an open question for centuries. Over the course of the novel, Omovo debates this esoteric question with himself and his friends. At one point he concludes: "I think because our lives are so hard our art needs to soothe, to massage, more than it needs to pry open our wounds." Given the tortured conditions of his life, Omovo's view is understandable; however, the austerity of the prose, the graphic imagery of squalid ghettos, and the nightmarish sense of disease, decline, and dispossession in Okri's novel suggest that he does not share Omovo's conception of the artist's role.

A Way of Being Free (1997) is a collection of essays on art, storytelling, and the power of words to shape political discourse. Three of the essays–"The Human Race is Not Yet Free," "Fables are Made of This," and "Redreaming the World"–are dedicated to Rushdie, Saro-Wiwa, and Achebe respectively. In these tributes, Okri signals not only his literary indebtedness to these writers but also his admiration for their heroism; they have understood the power of language to confront injustice and hypocrisy, and have risked their lives to express their ideas. (In fact, Saro-Wiwa was exectued for sedition in 1996.) "Leaping Out of Shakespeare's Terror: Five Meditations on *Othello*" is a compelling essay in which Okri reflects on race, sexuality, and the anxiety Othello has produced for nearly four centuries in audiences who have attempted to grapple with the presentation of a dark-skinned, sexual figure of power who incongruously sprang fully formed from Shakespeare's Elizabethan imagination. Okri dissects this anxiety and discusses its ramifications.

Okri's 1998 novel *Infinite Riches* completes what he calls *The Famished Road* trilogy. The spirit-child Azaro is present again, and his father has been arrested for murder. Unseen powers are unleashed; the dispossessed spirit world is angry; and the white elite prepares to leave. All signals point to the dawn of a new age, but no one can foretell if it will be an age of anarchy, degeneration, and self-destruction or rebirth and renewal? Although the novel is not as innovative as *The Famished Road,* it has all the hallmarks of Okri's lyric style. A barometer of regional tensions and optimism, the novel ends with a sense of hope. As Nigeria seems perched on the edge of democratic possibility, *Infinite Riches* ends with the prospect of elections.

Ben Okri's reputation as a thoughtful, lyric, postmodern writer has been secured by the critical and commercial success of *The Famished Road;* with it he claimed a new narrative space, integrating without assimilating or prioritizing African mythopoesis and European literary realism. Although this 1991 novel has tended to overshadow his other works, its success has not prevented him from continuing to experiment with other narrative forms. Okri's strength as a writer is his evocative, yet always economical style with which he is able to create nightmarish and imaginative other worlds. Rarely satisfied, his "circling spirit," or compulsion to rewrite his fiction, challenges contemporary notions about the static nature of the literary text, the permanence of art, and the relationship between oral and written traditions.

Interviews:

David Sweetman, "Interview with Ben Okri about His First Novel *Flowers and Shadows,*" *BBC Arts and Africa,* no. 345 (1980): 4–6;

Alex Tetteh-Lartey, "Interview with Alastair Niven and Ben Okri about Neil McEwan's *Africa and the Novel,*" *BBC Arts and Africa,* no. 531 (1984): 1–6;

Fiona Ledger, "Interview with Ben Okri about His Collection of Short Stories, *Incidents at the Shrine,*" *BBC Arts and Africa,* no. 656 (1986): 1–5;

Patricia Morris, "The Tiger Pounces," *African Concord,* 114 (30 October 1986): 18;

Edward Blishen, "Ben Okri with Edward Blishen," 40 minutes, Northbrook, Ill.: ICA Video, 1989, videocassette;

Doyin Iyiola, "This Will Pass," *African Concord,* 6 (18 November 1991): 61–62;

Jane Wilkinson, "Ben Okri," in *Talking with African Writers: Interviews with African Poets, Playwrights and Novelists,* edited by Wilkinson (London: Heinemann, 1991), pp. 76–89;

Carolyn Newton, "An Interview with Ben Okri," *South African Literary Review,* 2 (1992): 5–6;

Jean W. Ross, "*Contemporary Authors* Interview," in *Contemporary Authors,* volume 138, edited by Donna Olendorf (Detroit: Gale Research, 1993), pp. 337–341;

Delia Falconer, "Whisperings of the Gods: An Interview with Ben Okri," *Island Magazine,* 71 (Winter 1997): 43–51.

Bibliography:

Robert Bennett, "Ben Okri," in *Postcolonial African Writers: A Bio-Bibliographical Sourcebook,* edited by Pushpa N. Parekh (Westport, Conn.: Greenwood Press, 1998), pp. 364–373.

References:

T. J. Cribb, "Transformations in the Fiction of Ben Okri," in *From Commonwealth to Post-Colonial,* edited by Anna Rutherford (Sydney: Dangaroo, 1992), pp. 145–151;

Xavier Garnier, "L'Invisible dans *The Famished Road* de Ben Okri," *Commonwealth Essays and Studies,* 15, no. 2 (1993): 50–57;

John C. Hawley, "Ben Okri's Spirit-Child: Abiku Migration and Postmodernity," *Research in African Literatures,* 26, no. 1 (1995): 20–29;

Avo Mamudu, "Portrait of a Young Artist in Ben Okri's *The Landscape Within,*" *Commonwealth Essays and Studies,* 13, no. 2 (1991): 85–91;

Alastair Niven, "Achebe and Okri: Contrasts in the Response to Civil War," in *Short Fiction in the New Literature in English,* edited by Jacqueline Bardolph (Nice: Faculté des Lettres & Sciences Humaines, 1989), pp. 277–285;

Charles E. Nnolim, "Ben Okri: Writer as Artist," in his *Approaches to the African Novel: Essays in Analysis* (London: Saros, 1992), pp. 173–189;

Nnolim, "The Time is Out of Joint: Ben Okri as a Social Critic," *Commonwealth Novel in English,* 6, nos. 1–2 (1993): 61–68;

Olatubosun Ogunsanwo, "Intertextuality and Post-Colonial Literature in Ben Okri's *The Famished Road,*" *Research in African Literatures,* 26, no. 1 (1995): 30–39;

Abioseh Michael Porter, "Ben Okri's *The Landscape Within:* A Metaphor for Personal and National Development," *World Literatures Written in English,* 28, no. 2 (1988): 203–210;

Ato Quayson, "Protocols of Representation and the Problems of Constituting an African 'Gnosis': Achebe and Okri," *Yearbook of English Studies,* 27 (1997): 137–149;

David Richards, "'A History of Interruptions': Dislocated Mimesis in the Writings of Neil Bissoondath and Ben Okri," in *From Commonwealth to Post-Colonial,* edited by Anna Rutherford (Sydney: Dangaroo, 1992), pp. 74–82;

Sanjeev Kumor Uprety, "Disability and Postcoloniality in Salman Rushdie's *Midnight's Children* and Third-World Novels," in *The Disability Studies Reader,* edited by Lennard J. Davis (New York: Routledge, 1997), pp. 366–381.

Brian O'Nolan
(Flann O'Brien)
(5 October 1911 – 1 April 1966)

Merritt Moseley
University of North Carolina at Asheville

BOOKS: *At Swim-Two-Birds,* as Flann O'Brien (London: Longmans, Green, 1939; New York: Pantheon, 1951);

An Béal Bocht, as Myles na gCopaleen (Dublin: An Preas Náisiúnta, 1941); translated by Patrick C. Power as *The Poor Mouth* (London: Hart-Davis, MacGibbon, 1973; New York: Viking, 1974);

Faustus Kelly: A Play in Three Acts, as Myles na gCopaleen (Dublin: Cahill, 1943);

Cruiskeen Lawn, as Myles na gCopaleen (Dublin: Cahill, 1943);

The Hard Life: An Exegesis of Squalor, as O'Brien (London: MacGibbon & Kee, 1961; New York: Pantheon, 1962);

The Dalkey Archive, as O'Brien (London: MacGibbon & Kee, 1964; New York: Macmillan, 1965);

The Third Policeman, as O'Brien (London: MacGibbon & Kee, 1967; New York: Walker, 1968);

The Best of Myles, as Myles na gCopaleen, edited by Kevin O'Nolan (London: MacGibbon & Kee, 1968);

Stories and Plays, introduction by Claud Cockburn (London: Hart-Davis, MacGibbon, 1973; New York: Viking, 1976);

Further Cuttings from Cruiskeen Lawn, as Myles na gCopaleen, edited by Kevin O'Nolan (London: Hart-Davis, MacGibbon, 1976; Normal, Ill.: Dalkey Archive Press, 2000);

The Various Lives of Keats and Chapman and the Brother, as Myles na gCopaleen, edited by Benedict Kiely (London: Hart-Davis, MacGibbon, 1976);

The Hair of the Dogma: A Further Selection from 'Cruiskeen Lawn,' edited by Kevin O'Nolan (London: Hart-Davis, MacGibbon, 1977);

A Flann O'Brien Reader, edited by Stephen Jones (New York: Viking, 1978);

Myles Away from Dublin, as Myles na gCopaleen, edited by Martin Green (London: Granada, 1985);

Myles Before Myles: A Selection of the Earlier Writings of Brian O'Nolan, edited by John Wyse Jackson (London: Grafton Books, 1988);

Rhapsody in Stephen's Green: The Insect Play, as O'Brien, edited by Robert Tracy (Dublin: Lilliput Press, 1994).

PLAY PRODUCTIONS: *Faustus Kelly,* as Myles na gCopaleen, Dublin, Abbey Theatre, 25 January 1943;

The Insect Play (Rhapsody in Stephen's Green), as Myles na gCopaleen, adapted from *Ze zivota hmyzu* by Karel and Josef Capek, Dublin, Gate Company at Gaiety Theatre, 22 March 1943.

PRODUCED SCRIPTS: *Thirst,* as Brian Nolan, Radio Eireann, 1943;

The Boy from Ballytearim, as Nolan, television, Radio Television Eireann, 1962;

The Dead Spit of Kelly, as Nolan, television, Radio Television Eireann, 1962;

Flight, as Nolan, television, Radio Television Eireann, 1962;

The Man With Four Legs, as Nolan, television, Radio Television Eireann, 1962;

The Time Freddie Retired, as Nolan, television, Radio Television Eireann, 1962;

The Ideas of O'Dea, as Nolan, television series, Radio Television Eireann, September 1963 – March 1964;

Th' Oul Lad of Kilsalaher, as Nolan, television series, Radio Television Eireann, September–December 1965.

"It is useful to reflect on this question," wrote "George Knowall": *"What precisely is a given person's name?* A society in Dublin recently called upon its members to use 'the Irish version of their names.' Surely a name is a name and cannot have versions?" This suggestion is

Brian O'Nolan (Flann O'Brien) in the early 1950s (photograph, The Irish Times*)*

provocative because its author was the writer born Brian O'Nolan, who was best known as novelist Flann O'Brien or journalist and playwright Myles na gCopaleen (or Myles na Gopaleen). He was also the television scriptwriter Brian Nolan and the civil servant Brian O'Nolan or Brian Ó Nualláin. Some of the other pen names he used include An Broc, Peter the Painter, Brother Barnabas, John James Doe, Winnie Wedge, The O'Blather, and George Knowall. This profusion of different names is a sign of his multifariousness and compartmentalization. As Flann O'Brien he is one of the major modernist novelists of the mid-twentieth century, author of the classic *At Swim-Two-Birds* (1939); as Myles na gCopaleen he was one of the major journalistic voices in the Republic of Ireland for more than twenty-six years.

The arc of O'Nolan's career is a sad one. His best novel, *At Swim-Two-Birds,* the one by virtue of which he owns a place in the forefront of twentieth-century English-language fiction, was published in 1939, when he was twenty-eight years old; his one novel in Irish, a small masterpiece called *An Béal Bocht* (translated as *The Poor Mouth,* 1973), appeared two years later. His other novels, though not inconsiderable, are lesser works by almost any standard. Likewise, his career as satirist and commentator peaked early, perhaps even during his years as a student at University College, Dublin, though he continued to practice journalism for almost thirty years.

Brian O'Nolan was born on 5 October 1911 in Strabane, County Tyrone, the third of twelve children of Michael Victor O'Nolan and Agnes Gormley O'Nolan. Michael O'Nolan was a customs and excise officer whose career obliged him to move frequently. One consequence was that the O'Nolan children were quite old before beginning formal schooling. The first language of the O'Nolan family was Irish. In 1923 Brian O'Nolan was sent to the Christian Brothers School in Dublin, where the family was then living. He always spoke disdainfully about the quality of his education there. In 1927, when the family moved to Blackrock, on the southern edge of Dublin, he began attending Blackrock College in nearby Williamstown, and in 1929 he matriculated at University College, Dublin. He received his B.A. degree with second-class honors in German, English, and Irish in 1932, and, after a trip to Germany, he began an M.A. degree at University College, with a thesis on nature in Irish poetry. The degree was awarded in 1935.

During his years at university O'Nolan distinguished himself as a debater in the Literary and Historical Society and as a writer for a student magazine called *Comhthrom Féinne*. For his contributions to the magazine he invented his first pseudonymous persona, Brother Barnabas. In 1934, O'Nolan, his brother Ciaran, and others began a short-lived satirical magazine called *Blather*. Five issues appeared between August 1934 and January 1935. All the articles were published anonymously, but it is generally accepted that most of the writing was by O'Nolan.

A considerable amount of his early journalism has been collected in *Myles Before Myles: A Selection of the Earlier Writings of Brian O'Nolan* (1988). One of his funniest early pieces is a Brother Barnabas contribution to *Comhthrom Féinne* addressing one of his lifelong concerns—the matter of Irishness, real and literary. It is a short play about an Irishman named Allen Bogg, who lives in a "hovel in the middle of the Bog of Allen, miles from dry land":

In the corner is a bed with a white sow in it. . . . A bag-pipes are hanging on the wall but not, unfortunately, so high up that a tall man could not reach them. Over the mantelpiece is a rusty iron pike for use in Insurrections. A rustic and homely smell of fish-and-chips permeates the atmosphere. Over in the corner a cupboard is let into the wall, with a heavy padlock and chain, in which leprechauns are stored.

As the house sinks inexorably deeper into the bog, cows keep putting their heads in the door. The dialogue is a parody of the Irish drama, perhaps particularly that of John Millington Synge:

Allen (meditatively): Aye. (long pause.) Surely.
Maggie: Musha.
Allen: Surely.
Maggie: Wisha.
Allen: Begorrah.
Maggie (her soul flooded with poetry): Anish, now, musha.

In 1935 O'Nolan took the civil-service examination and was appointed to a position in the department of local government. For eighteen years he worked in Dublin Castle (as did his father until 1937). His attitude toward his job was probably similar to that of the civil servant Mick, a character in *The Dalkey Archive* (1964), who declares: "I detest the job, its low atmosphere and the scruff who are my companions in the office."

At about the time O'Nolan began work as a civil servant, he also started writing *At Swim-Two-Birds* (1939). The novel earned some respectable responses, including praise from Graham Greene and James Joyce. It is said to have been the last book Joyce ever read.

Though it has obvious affinities with some earlier novels, including Aldous Huxley's *Point Counter Point* (1928) and the works of Joyce, *At Swim-Two-Birds* is an astonishing debut novel. A sort of anthology, it has at its center an undergraduate at University College who, somewhat like O'Nolan, is dissolute, spends considerable time lying in bed and getting drunk, but passes his exams with ease. The focus is on his "part-time literary activities."

Early in the novel the unnamed narrator explains his literary credo to his friend:

a satisfactory novel should be a self-evident sham to which the reader could regulate at will the degree of his credulity. It was undemocratic to compel characters to be uniformly good or bad or poor or rich. Each should be allowed a private life, self-determination and a decent standard of living. . . . Characters should be interchangeable as between one book and another. The entire corpus of existing literature should be regarded as a limbo from which discerning authors could draw their characters as required, creating only when they failed to find a suitable existing puppet. The modern novel should be largely a work of reference. Most authors spend their time saying what has been said before—usually said much better. A wealth of references to existing works would acquaint the reader instantaneously with the nature of each character, would obviate tiresome explanations and would effectively preclude mountebanks, upstarts, thimbleriggers and persons of inferior education from an understanding of contemporary literature.

The oddly mixed tone of this passage is characteristic of the novel. Though the artistic manifesto is followed in *At Swim-Two-Birds,* the reasons supplied—preventing uneducated persons from understanding contemporary literature, for instance—are parodic. And the narrator's friend, in fact, responds to this long explanation with a dry "That is all my bum."

The originality of the novel lies largely in how the author arranges the diverse contents. The first paragraph includes the declaration: "One beginning and

O'Nolan in 1932, the year in which he earned a B.A. from University College, Dublin (Collection of Evelyn O'Nolan)

one ending for a book was a thing I did not agree with." So the novel has three beginnings and three endings, and the different strands run alongside each other for much of the book. But there is also a curious involution, or confusion of realms. The narrator (a character in a novel, of course) is writing a novel about a novelist named Trellis, who is writing a novel designed to demonstrate the consequences of sin. Trellis's works also include translations from the saga of Mad Sweeney, a character from Old Irish legend; stories about the heroic Finn MacCool; and contemporary Dublin scenes. There is accomplished pastiche of newspaper writing, translated Gaelic, and Dublin talk and poetry, including the works of Jem Casey, the author of "A Pint of Plain Is Your Only Man." It is at Trellis's level that odd confusions arise. One is his borrowing, or hiring on a short term, characters from other authors. He has hired two cowboys from a Western author, as well as borrowing two Greeks from somewhere else. His major creation, Orlick, is apparently borrowed from Charles Dickens's *Great Expectations* (1860–1861). The creator and his creations also become entwined. Trellis creates a female character for the purposes of his didactic plot, but he is drawn to her and rapes her. (Orlick is the child of this rape.) In revenge, Trellis's characters discover

that while he is asleep they can achieve autonomy and torment him by writing a story in which *he* is a character. They end by drugging him so they can torment him nearly full time.

Though *At Swim-Two-Birds* is philosophical, or theoretical, in its exploration of the delusive relations between "real" and "fictional" and its deconstruction of hierarchies, it is also extremely funny. A considerable amount of its comedy arises from juxtaposition, for instance of the heroics of Finn MacCool and the conversations of lower-middle-class Dubliners on removing blackheads; or of the poetry of Mad Sweeny (apparently a genuine translation from the Irish) with the work of Jem Casey.

At Swim-Two-Birds is without doubt O'Nolan's masterpiece. Yet, by the time he died he was reportedly sick of the book, perhaps in part because it gave rise to suggestions of indebtedness to Joyce, which always irritated him. The first printing sold only 244 copies, and when the Longmans warehouse was bombed in 1940, the remaining copies were destroyed. In 1950 the novel was published in New York by Pantheon, beginning Flann O'Brien's "comeback," and in 1960 it was published again in England, this time by MacGibbon and Kee, finding a new audience.

The relative initial failure of *At Swim-Two-Birds* may explain why Longmans declined to publish the author's next novel, *The Third Policeman* (1967), which he wrote in 1939 and 1940 and for which he had high hopes. He told friends that the manuscript was lost, but in reality he had put it aside and later cannibalized it for *The Dalkey Archive* (1964).

The Third Policeman is a surreal and macabre story with large elements of the supernatural and science fiction. The novel begins with a flat declaration: "Not everybody knows how I killed old Philip Mathers, smashing his jaw in with my spade; but first it is better to speak of my friendship with John Divney because it was he who first knocked old Mathers down by giving him a great blow in the neck with a special bicycle-pump which he manufactured himself out of a hollow iron bar." The narrator is a one-legged orphan who finds himself, not entirely voluntarily, sharing his farm with Divney, who instigates the murder of Mathers so they can steal his strongbox. After the murder, the narrator enters Mathers's house to steal the box and, the reader discovers later, is killed by a booby trap left by Divney. From this point on he is dead, apparently in hell. This fact is the explanation for the weird events that follow, including various violations of nature and perspective, illogical conversations with policemen, and encounters with other wooden-legged men. At the end the narrator returns, believing that he has been away only a few hours and surprising John Divney, who is now quite aged and informs the narrator that he has been dead for sixteen years.

Two distinctive features of this novel, both of which were retained in *The Dalkey Archive,* are the mysterious savant de Selby and the "atomic theory." The narrator is a follower of de Selby and sprinkles his text with many references to the works and convictions of this philosopher, though they have little to do with the plot.

The atomic theory, explained to the narrator by a policeman, has to do with atomic exchange—for instance, the way that a hammer used to strike an anvil repeatedly will somehow absorb some of the atoms of the anvil and vice versa. In the novel the theory has to do with exchange of atoms between human beings and their bicycles, to the point where some of the neighbors are said to be nearly half bicycle, and some bicycles are nearly human. There are other quasi-scientific conceits in *The Third Policeman,* including the idea that everything in the universe, both matter and energy, is made of a substance called omnium, which is sometimes called God, and de Selby's theory that darkness is really black air. Anne Clissmann connects the pseudoscience of *The Third Policeman* with the experiences of the narrator: "Reason is overthrown and a coherent type of unreason takes its place. The narrator has to accept with his senses what his reason tells him is impossible."

In 1938 O'Nolan and a friend, Niall Sheridan, had begun a mock controversy, by writing letters under assumed names to *The Irish Times.* As a result, the editor of the paper invited O'Nolan to contribute a column; he began his "Cruiskeen Lawn" (Irish for full, or brimming, jug) column on 4 October 1940, using the pseudonym Myles na gCopaleen (Myles of the little ponies, the name of a character in a play by Dion Boucicault). For a while he wrote three columns a week, and later six. Initially he alternated between columns in Irish and columns in English, but soon he began writing almost exclusively in English. As he often complained, few people could actually read Irish, despite the formal requirement that public employees should know the language.

Commenting on the works of Myles na gCopaleen, John Garvin explains that "his pretension was to put down all pretensions, and, in the role of crotchety pedant, he hammered the knuckles of writers, artists and critics alike." As early as the Brother Barnabas days O'Nolan had been hammering the pretensions of those who pretended to write about the Irish. In "Cruiskeen Lawn" he suggested that words of plays be printed on big signs and hung up in the balcony at the Abbey Theatre so that the actors would not need to learn their lines: "There would be no necessity to tell the actors beforehand what play they are appearing in. They just come out on the stage, peer into the auditorium, and

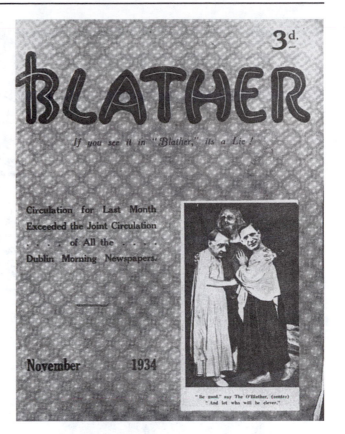

Cover for an issue of the short-lived satirical magazine O'Nolan helped to found in summer 1934

then come out with some dreadful remark about 'old John,' or 'Brigid, his wife.'" This comment was part of an ongoing series in Myles's column about the Irish Writers, Actors, Artists, Musicians Association (WAAMA), always consisting of satire on poseurs.

Other regular features include a book-handling service for pretentious people, which for varying fees would bend, dog ear, and even write comments in their books so they could seem well read without effort; the Myles na gCopaleen Research Bureau, always a source of implausible inventions decorated with Rube Goldberg–style illustrations; an ongoing catechism of clichés; anecdotes about "the Brother," a sort of stereotypical engaging Dublin rogue; and many stories about Keats and Chapman, the special feature of which is that they always end in a pun. In one of them Keats finds spilled milk in a taxicab and asks the driver, "What's this? A cabri-au-lait?" Another ends with a dentist telling an inquisitive patient, "I will give you three gases," and a story about dialectical materialism includes the comment: "Fools rush in where Engels feared to tread." O'Nolan's "Cruiskeen Lawn" columns have been collected in several books.

In 1941 O'Nolan published his only novel in Irish, using his pen name Myles na gCopaleen. *An*

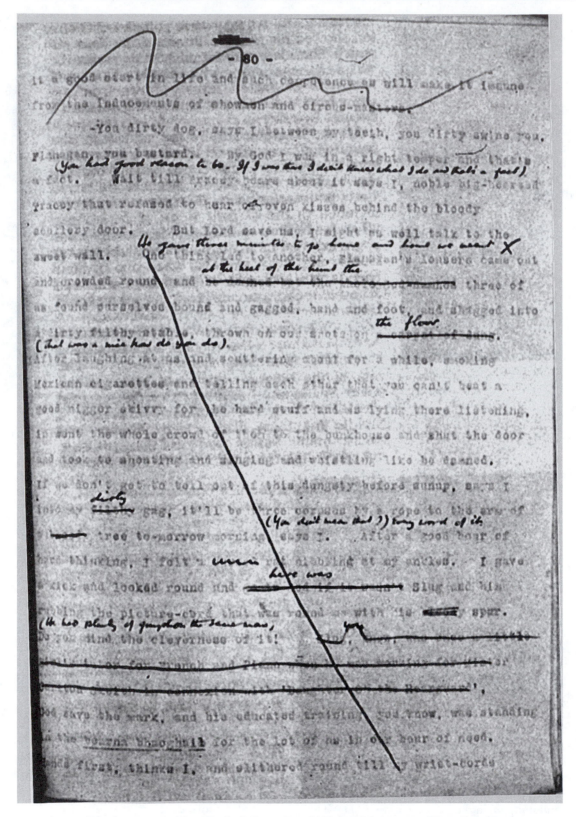

Page from the revised typescript for At Swim-Two-Birds, *published in 1939 (Harry Ransom Humanities Research Center, University of Texas at Austin)*

- 184 -

the Italian operas, from the compositions of Puccini and Meyerbeer
and Donizetti and Gounod and the Maestro Mascagni as well as an
aria from The Bohemian Girl by Balfe, and intoned the choral
complexities of Palestrina the pioneer.   They rendered two hundred
and forty-two songs by Schubert in the original German words, and
sang a chorus from Fidelio, *(by Beethoven, of Moonlight Sonata fame)* and the Song of the Flea, and a long
excerpt from a Mass by Bach, as well as innumerable tuneful
pleasantries from the able pen of no less than Mozart and Handel.
To the stars (though they could not see them owing to the roofage
of the leaves and the branches above them) they gave with a thunderous
spirit such pieces by Offenbach, Schumann, Saint-Saens and Granville
Bantock as they could remember.   They sang entire movements from
cantatas and oratorios and other items of sacred music. *allegro ma non troppo, largo and andante cantabile.*

     They were all so preoccupied with music that they
were still chanting spiritedly in the dark undergrowth long after
the sun, earlier astir than usual, had cleaned the last vestige of
the soiling night from the verdure of the leaves on the treetops,
When they suddenly arrived to find mid-day in a clearing, they
wildly reproached each other with bitter words and groundless
allegations of bastardy as they collected berries and haws into the
hollows of their hats against a late breakfast. *Temporary discontinuance of the foregoing.*
BIOGRAPHICAL REMINISCENCE — INSERT HERE
       At twenty past four they arrived at the Red Swan
Hotel and entered the premises unnoticed by the window of the maid's
lavatory at the back on the ground floor.   They made no noise in
their passage and disturbed none of the dust that lay about the
carpets.   Quickly they repaired in a body to the ante-room to Miss
Lamont's bedroom (where the lady was lying in) and deftly stacked the

Page from the revised typescript for The Third Policeman, *written in 1939–1940 and published in 1967 (Harry Ransom Humanities Research Center, University of Texas at Austin)*

Béal Bocht is a stinging satire on other Irish writers, particularly Tomás O Criomhthain and Séamas O Grianna, and on sentimental notions of Irish peasantry. According to Clissmann, *An Béal Bocht* was "a great success and greeted as a masterpiece by Gaelic enthusiasts." O'Nolan never wrote another novel in Irish, nor did he arrange for its translation into English during his lifetime. It finally appeared in English, as *The Poor Mouth,* in 1973.

As George Knowall, O'Nolan once listed some British delusions about the Irish: "the Irishman is an unusual character, drunk, fighting, and having a pig in the kitchen. How does he (and the pig, for that matter) sustain life? Both subsist on one foodstuff only–spuds." This description is not far from the picture presented in *The Poor Mouth,* narrated in the first person by Bonaparte O'Coonassa, living in Corkadoragha. The O'Coonassas (Bonaparte, his mother, and an elderly male relative known only as the Old-Grey-Fellow) live in a hovel; the father is in prison; the family sleeps with the pigs and eats nothing but potatoes. Their house smells so bad that passersby race to escape it. When Bonaparte attends school he is beaten for speaking Irish and told (like every other child there) that his name is "Jams O'Donnell."

There is much incident in this short novel, including the O'Coonassas' deception of a government inspector by dressing the pigs as children, some robberies, Bonaparte's marriage to Mabel, and his acquisition of the first pair of boots seen in Corkadoragha for many years. This acquisition leads to his arrest. Because he is tried in English, he cannot defend himself and is sentenced to prison; as he is leaving on the train, he sees his own father for the first time, returning from his own imprisonment. In general this novel presents a thoroughly dismal picture of Irish rural life, summed up at the end as "Gaelic hardship"–"distress, need, ill-treatment, adversity, calamity, foul play, misery, famine and ill-luck." Nevertheless, *The Poor Mouth* is a grimly funny book, primarily because of its satire on those who romanticize Irish life. At one point the Old-Grey-Fellow arranges an Irish festival in the town, to which enthusiasts come from Dublin. Such people have visited before, but they had stopped coming because:

1. The tempest of the countryside was too tempestuous.
2. The putridity of the countryside was too putrid.
3. The poverty of the countryside was too poor.
4. The Gaelicism of the countryside was too Gaelic.
5. The tradition of the countryside was too traditional.

The outsiders entertain themselves with the delivery of bombastic speeches proclaiming that they "are all Gaelic Gaels of Gaelic lineage," while they fail to notice that some of the Corkadoragha Gaels die of cold, exhaustion, and hunger during the festival.

An Béal Bocht is one of O'Nolan's two fully achieved novels. Shortly after writing it, he turned to work for the theater, with some success. His play *Faustus Kelly,* an original satire on Irish local government, opened at the Abbey Theatre in Dublin in January 1943. It was successful with audiences but not with critics. O'Nolan stated in his column that it ran for only two weeks before closing by order of the government, but this claim was incorrect. He was becoming increasingly preoccupied with government censorship. (He was later convinced, for instance, that *The Dalkey Archive* would be suppressed on orders of either the government or the Catholic Church.) *Faustus Kelly* is a study of the compromises and human littlenesses of local politics, featuring, as the title suggests, a man who sells his soul to the devil to achieve advancement.

In March 1943 *The Insect Play,* O'Nolan's adaptation of a play by Karel and Josef Capek, was mounted at the Gate Theatre in Dublin. It was not successful, and there were later rumors that it had been suppressed by the government. O'Nolan reset the Capeks' play in Stephen's Green, Dublin, and his play consists mostly of dialogue–in a variety of dialects including Dublin, Cork, and Ulster. There is some satire on local government, though hardly pointed. O'Nolan's biographer Anthony Cronin has offered a fair assessment: "All in all the *Evening Mail* was not far wrong when it said that he had used the 'original framework . . . to "put across" some rather banal topicalities more appropriate to the variety stage' than to the serious theatre. The thrust of the satire, if satire it was, was obscure to most, nor did he succeed in making his insects representative of the human condition in the way the original he was working from does."

Also produced in 1943 was *Thirst,* a one-act conversation in a Dublin pub among some after-hours drinkers and a policeman. It was popular and frequently revived.

Between 1939 and 1943 O'Nolan had published two novels and finished a third; written and seen produced three plays; and written a regular, popular column. He then slowed down considerably.

On 2 December 1948 O'Nolan surprised many of his friends when he married Evelyn McDonnell. He had never seemed too interested in women, and as a student, he had been considered a misogynist and a likely celibate.

In 1953 O'Nolan was forced to retire from his government job, essentially because he continued to criticize his employer and because he naively believed that views expressed by "Myles na gCopaleen" could not be held against Brian O'Nolan. At first, to supple-

Advertisements for O'Nolan's only Gaelic novel, translated in 1973 as The Poor Mouth

ment his inadequate pension, he increased his contributions to *The Irish Times,* and began writing for provincial newspapers as well.

Myles Away from Dublin (1985) collects some of the columns he wrote in the early 1950s, under the name of George Knowall, for *The Nationalist and Leinster Times* (Carlow). The Knowall columns are fairly labored, often obviously worked up out of reference books (an increasing habit as O'Nolan's inspiration slowed down). These columns are, however, superior to another column, "A Weekly Look Around," that O'Nolan wrote for the *Southern Star* (Skibbereen), under the name John James Doe in 1955–1956, and acknowledged as inferior work. He always reserved his best material for Myles na gCopaleen's "Cruiskeen Lawn."

Yet, by the late 1950s, however, relations with *The Irish Times* had become strained. In the last few years of O'Nolan's life he was troubled by a growing bitterness, the result of which filled his "Cruiskeen Lawn" columns with an often Swiftian indignation, leading *The Irish Times* editors to reject many columns. "Cruiskeen Lawn" appeared much more irregularly toward the end of his life.

As bad feelings developed between columnist and newspaper, a series of accidents and serious alcoholism interfered with his work. Faced with continuing money worries, he applied unsuccessfully for jobs as student-records officer at Trinity College and proofreader at his newspaper.

He had more luck obtaining work as a scriptwriter for television; in 1962 his television plays *The Boy from Ballytearim, The Time Freddie Retired, Flight, The Man With Four Legs,* and *The Dead Spit of Kelly* were produced. Soon he was invited to write a series for popu-

J-DAY

THIS IS A SMALL, shy and simple article. It can be written only within the week or so in which a number of courageous men made off with about 200 rifles and a lesser amount of other lethal gear.

Every man concerned could have been shot dead. Why did they risk so much for so little?

* * *

THIS SHEER impulse to rebel, without regard to reason or results, is likely to be publicly commemorated this day. It is June 16th —and James Joyce wrote half a million words about what happened in Dublin on June 16th, 1904. The book is called "Ulysses" and is really the record of what happened a bona-fide traveller of that day,

---

CRUISKEEN LAWN

By

MYLES NA

GOPALEEN

---

with, impaled in the text, an enormity of "philosophical material."

In this task Joyce did not go into somebody's workshop and choose the tools he needed; he took the whole lot. Thus does one find side by side monasticism and brothelism. St. Augustine himself perceived and recorded the "polarity" of virtue and vice, how one is integrally part of the other, and cannot exist without it. But not until James Joyce came along has anybody so considerably evoked depravity to establish the unextinguishable goodness of what is good.

* * *

I DO NOT WISH to provoke still another world war by invading America's monopoly of comment on the value of Joyce's work. People who insist that there is a junction of Culle street and Grafton street are, clearly, persons with whom not to argue. But I think I will risk a few remarks about Joyce, on the understanding that criticism without censure is intended.

Joyce was in no way what he is internationally acclaimed to be—a Dubliner. In fact there has been no more spectacular non-Dubliner. Not once did he tire of saying that he was never at home. This absence may have been a necessity of his literary method, but it has often occurred to my irreverent self that maybe he hadn't the fare.

Joyce was a bad writer. He was too skilled in some departments of writing, and could not resist the *tour de force*. Parts of "Ulysses" are of unreadable boredom. One thinks of a violinist corrupting with "cadenza" a work wherein the composing master had in the text practised masterly abstention from fireworks. Beethoven had a big row with the violinist Kreutzer on this very point.

Joyce was illiterate. He had a fabulously developed jackdaw talent of picking up bits and pieces, but it seems his net was too wide to justify getting a few kids' school-books and learning the rudiments of a new language correctly. Every foreign-language quotation in any of his works known to me are wrong. His few sallies at Greek are wrong, and his few attempts at a Gaelic phrase are absolutely monstrous. Anybody could have told him the right thing. Why did he not bother to ask?

* * *

THAT LAST QUESTION evokes a complementary question, of which there is no mention on the horizonless bog of American exegesis. Was the man a leg-puller? Was "Finnegans Wake" the ultimate fantasy in cod? Did he seek to evolve for himself, chiefly by talking in strict confidence to stooges, mostly American, a mythical personality? Did . . . (*pardon me while I swallow this yellow capsule!*) . . . did . . . James Joyce ever exist?

* * *

IT SEEMS he did, and that he done what he done. There is something intimidatingly authentic about print. My own first contact with the man in a literary collision was a quotation fired at me. This: "I go to encounter for the millionth time the reality of experience and to forge in the smithy of my soul the uncreated conscience of my race."

Many a time had I read that piece with admiration. In recent years I have asked a few wise men what the words mean. They mean nothing.

But are they intended to mean nothing, in the sense of meaning something exact? Or are they intended to suggest an imponderable theme for reflection, as night—day—life—death—are used in various patterns in "Finnegans Wake?"

* * *

Excerpt from O'Nolan's 16 June 1954 column in The Irish Times, *published on the fiftieth anniversary of the day James Joyce's character Leopold Bloom walks around Dublin in* Ulysses lar comedian Jimmy O'Dea: it was called *The Ideas of O'Dea* and ran weekly for six months beginning in September 1963. His second series, *Th' Oul Lad of Kilsalaher,* ran for fourteen weeks in 1965. O'Nolan was eager to work on another series and suggested something called "The Detectional Fastidiosities of Sergeant Fottrell," based on the popular character from *The Dalkey Archive.* He had great hopes for this show and even suggested that "the Sergeant's personality and tongue form a countrywide treasure" and that he "ultimately could become the unofficial voice of TE [the Irish television company]." O'Nolan died before he could further develop the series.

His next novel had finally appeared in 1961. *The Hard Life: An Exegesis of Squalor* was extremely successful. All copies available in Dublin sold out in two days. Graham Greene, to whom it is dedicated, reacted favorably.

While *The Poor Mouth* explores the squalor of the rural Gaelic-speaking Ireland, *The Hard Life,* as its subtitle suggests, performs much the same function for English-speaking Dubliners. The narrator is a youthful Irishman, Finbarr, an orphan, who with his older brother goes to live with Mr. Collopy. "The Brother" fairly soon loses interest in education and loses his religion. He is full of ideas, though, beginning with mastering walking on the tightrope and selling tightrope-walking instructions through the mail. He goes on to become quite a tycoon. Under the name Professor Latimer Dodds, he manages the Excelsior Turf Bureau (offering racing tips), the Zenith School of Journalism, and the Simplex Nature Press, deriving most of his information from books in the National Library. Then he moves to London, where he opens the London University Academy, offering tuition by mail in "Boxing, Foreign Languages, Botany, Poultry Farming, Fretwork, Elocution, Dietetics, Ju-Jitsu, Hypnotism, Medicine in the Home, Care of the Teeth, Egyptology, Slimming, A Cure for Cancer, Treatment of Baldness, Field Athletics, Laundry Management, Sheep Farming, Etching and Drypoint, Sausage Manufacture in the Home, The Ancient Classics. . . ."

Finbarr's depiction of the stagnation and pointlessness of life at home is relieved by two major sources of interest. One of these is The Brother. The other is Mr. Collopy and his conversations with the Jesuit priest Father Fahrt. Collopy is a gregarious man whose two main topics are skeptical observations about the Jesuits and a grand scheme for public service, for which he organizes meetings and convenes committees: though this is usually unspecified, it becomes clear that his aim is to provide Dublin with public toilets for women. His observations on the Church, designed at least in part to annoy his friend and drinking companion Father Fahrt,

insist on a history of venality. For example, speaking of the Protestant Reformation, Collopy says that "it was our own crowd, those ruffians in Spain and all, who provoked it. They called decent men heretics and the remedy was to put a match to them. To say nothing of a lot of crooked Popes with their armies and their papal states, putting duchesses and nuns up the pole and having all Italy littered with their bastards, and up to nothing but backstairs work and corruption at the courts of God knows how many decent foreign kings."

Despite his criticisms, Mr. Collopy is a good Catholic, but when Finbarr and his brother arrange a trip to Rome and an audience with the Pope, Mr. Collopy outrages the Holy Father by trying to discuss his scheme for women's public toilets with him and is ejected from the audience. An accident caused by his immense weight—the result of taking one of The Brother's patent medicines—kills Collopy in Rome, where he is buried. The Brother returns to Dublin and suggests that Finbarr marry Annie, who has been part of the household as a sort of servant. (She may also be a prostitute.) The novel ends with Finbarr's reaction, which also serves as a sort of commentary on the events of the book: "The slam of the door told me he [The Brother] was gone. In a daze I lifted my own glass and without knowing what I was doing did exactly what the brother did, drained the glass in one vast swallow. Then I walked quickly but did not run to the lavatory. There, everything inside of me came up in a tidal surge of vomit."

The Hard Life is a thoroughgoing account of squalor and unworthy motives, with enough verbal humor and originality of incident to keep it amusing. It can be fairly criticized for O'Nolan's failure to invent any convincing characters who are not scoundrels or fools; Finbarr is a cipher, and everyone else is despicable to a greater or lesser extent.

O'Nolan's last novel, *The Dalkey Archive,* appeared in February 1964. Accounts differ on how this novel evolved from *The Third Policeman.* What O'Nolan mostly retrieved from that novel is the "atomic theory" by which people become bicycles and vice versa, a variety of scientific or science-fiction elements about the mutability or reversibility of time and space; and scientist savant de Selby, whose ideas are quoted frequently in *The Third Policeman.* In *The Dalkey Archive* he is De Selby and a major character. The plot, with its profusion of strands, is completely unlike that of *The Third Policeman,* and the atmosphere is no longer surreal and macabre.

The Dalkey Archive is a sort of loosely constructed fantasia. The protagonist is a young Dubliner (and civil servant) named Mick, who has a friend named Hackett. They meet De Selby by accident and become involved

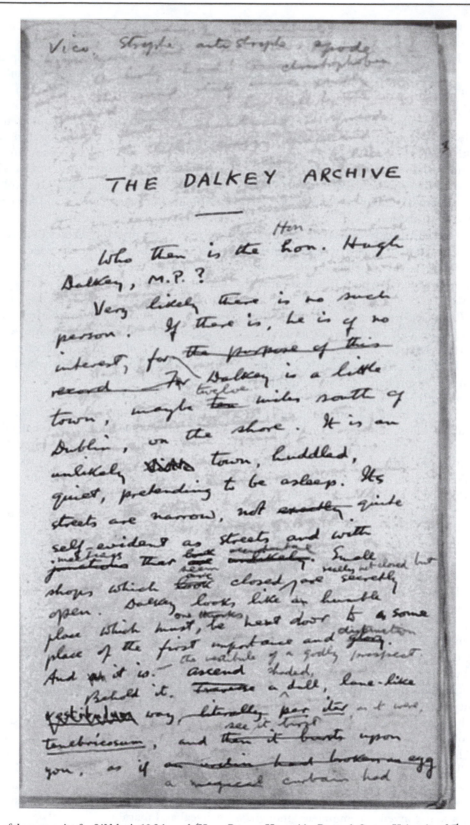

First page of the manuscript for O'Nolan's 1964 novel (Harry Ransom Humanities Research Center, University of Texas at Austin)

with him in various adventures. He explains some of his scientific discoveries to them: "I have mastered time. Time has been called an event, a repository, a continuum, an ingredient of the universe. I can suspend time, negative its apparent course." There are both benign and malignant consequences of De Selby's discoveries.

Through an invention he calls DMP, he can undo the effects of time, allowing him, among other things, to take Mick and Hackett to have a long conversation with St. Augustine in an underwater cave. St. Augustine speaks in a pronounced Dublin accent and sounds much like Mr. Collopy. He dislikes the other Fathers of the church and makes comments such as: "How could Origen be the Father of Anything and he with no knackers on him? Answer me that one." In another plot strand contributing to the mildly blasphemous quality of the novel (which convinced O'Nolan that the Church would contrive to have it banned), Hackett is campaigning for the rehabilitation of Judas Iscariot.

Using DMP, De Selby is also capable of destroying the world, and he decides to do so because "its depth and horror are unknown to any one man. Rottenness is universally endemic, disease is paramount. The human race is finally debauched and aborted." To foil De Selby, Mick eventually steals DMP. The De Selby plotline ends with the destruction of his villa, his renunciation of his deadly plans, and his return to Buenos Aires.

Another plot element has to do with Sergeant Fottrell, a policeman who is meant to be a colorful character. He speaks in a combination of pomposities and malapropisms, and tells Mick at great length about the exchange of matter between people and bicycles. This matter exchange is such a threat that he never actually mounts his own bicycle. Instead, he pushes it with him everywhere, and he spends much of his time flattening other people's tires to preserve their molecular integrity.

The Dalkey Archive has one thing unknown in any of O'Nolan's other works: a love plot. His "Cruiskeen Lawn" columns seldom referred to women; his early novels have no major female characters; and, generally speaking, his fiction maintains the men-only atmosphere of the pubs where his life was mostly lived. It cannot be said that the love plot of *The Dalkey Archive* is entirely successful. A love affair between Mick and Mary never generates much interest or emotion and, when Mary reveals that she is going to marry Hackett instead, it hardly seems to matter.

Another strand of the plot develops when another drinker at the pub favored by Mick, Hackett, and Sergeant Fottrell reveals that James Joyce is alive and living in Skerries, a small seaside town north of Dublin. Mick tracks him down and interviews him twice. It turns out that Joyce is the author of only one

O'Nolan in 1966 (photograph, The Irish Times*)*

published book—*Dubliners*, co-authored with Oliver St. John Gogarty; he indignantly repudiates any suggestion that he wrote *Ulysses*—"that dirty book, that collection of smut"—and has never even heard of *Finnegans Wake*. This fictional Joyce is conventional and even pious; most of his literary efforts are devoted to writing tracts for the Catholic Truth Society, and his real ambition, despite his age, is to enter the priesthood, which Mick tries to arrange for him.

These ironic "biographical" details are interesting, especially in what they reveal about O'Nolan's own attitude to Joyce the novelist. Throughout his life, O'Nolan was often compared to Joyce in a way that annoyed him because it seemed to deny his own originality. O'Nolan often took the common Dublin position that Joyce was a great hoaxer, who had succeeded in pulling the wool over the eyes of credulous professors, mostly Americans. He often attacked Joyce or Joyceans in "Cruiskeen Lawn." In 1951 he was asked to edit a special Joyce issue of a journal called *Envoy*, in which his contribution, "A Bash in The Tunnel," compares Joyce (rather confusingly) to a man who breaks into locked trains in order to drink privately: "Surely there you have the Irish artist? Sitting fully dressed, innerly locked in the toilet of a locked coach where he has no right to be, resentfully drinking somebody else's whiskey, being whisked hither and thither by anonymous shunters, keeping fastidiously the while on the outer face of his door the simple word, ENGAGED?"

Perhaps damning with faint praise, O'Nolan does acknowledge that "With laughs" Joyce "palliated the sense of doom that is the heritage of the Irish Catholic." O'Nolan's anxiety over Joyce's influence may be the reason why, by the end of his life, he hated *At Swim-Two-Birds,* his most Joycean novel, and thought of *The Dalkey Archive* as his best.

At the end of his life O'Nolan was cheered by the success of *The Dalkey Archive* as well as a popular stage adaptation of it. By the time the novel was published, he was suffering from cancer, and he died suddenly on April Fool's Day of 1966. Much of the writing for which he is best known has been published posthumously, including the English translation of *An Béal Bocht,* his second novel *The Third Policeman, Stories and Plays* (1973), and several collections of his columns.

When he died, O'Nolan left one unfinished novel, "Slattery's Sago Saga, or From Under the Ground to the Top of the Trees," which was published in 1973 in *Stories and Plays.* It shares a fantastic element with *The Dalkey Archive* and is predicated on a rich American woman's plan to end the farming of potatoes in Ireland and replace the fields with giant forests of sago, in pursuit of her plan to remove the Irish-Americans from the United States. O'Nolan planned to make President John F. Kennedy a character in the novel in some way.

Though nothing in the unfinished version suggests that this novel would have done anything to further enhance O'Nolan's reputation, that reputation was in fact booming at the time of his death, and his novels have been critically acclaimed ever since. *At Swim-Two-Birds* is acknowledged as a modernist classic, and each of his other novels has many admirers. Furthermore, were there no Flann O'Brien novels, the works of Myles na gCopaleen would themselves earn O'Nolan a major reputation. The various voices of Brian O'Nolan make him one of the most important Irish writers of the twentieth century.

Biographies:

Peter Costello and Peter van de Kamp, *Flann O'Brien: An Illustrated Biography* (London: Bloomsbury, 1987);

Anthony Cronin, *No Laughing Matter: The Life and Times of Flann O'Brien* (London: Grafton, 1989);

Ciarán Ó Nualláin, *The Early Years of Brian O'Nolan / Flann O'Brien / Myles na gCopaleen,* translated by Róisín Ní Nualláin, edited by Niall O'Nolan (Dublin: Lilliput Press, 1998).

References:

Sue Asbee, *Flann O'Brien* (Boston: Twayne, 1991);

Anne Clissmann, *Flann O'Brien: A Critical Introduction to His Writings: The Story-Teller's Book Web* (New York: Barnes & Noble, 1975);

Anne Clune and Tess Hurson, eds., *Conjuring Complexities: Essays on Flann O'Brien* (Belfast: Institute of Irish Studies of Queen's University of Belfast, 1997);

Keith Hopper, *Flann O'Brien: A Portrait of the Artist as a Young Post-Modernist* (Cork: Cork University Press, 1995);

Rüdiger Imhof, ed. *Alive Alive O!: Flann O'Brien's At Swim-Two-Birds* (Dublin: Wolfhound Press, 1985);

Timothy O'Keeffe, *Myles: Portraits of Brian O'Nolan* (London: Martin Brian & O'Keeffe, 1973);

Thomas F. Shea, *Flann O'Brien's Exorbitant Novels* (Lewisburg, Pa.: Bucknell University Press, 1992).

Papers:

The Flann O'Brien Papers at Boston College include records, correspondence, theater programs, and manuscripts. Manuscripts and typescripts for *At Swim-Two-Birds, The Third Policeman, Faustus Kelly,* and *The Dalkey Archive* are at the Harry Ransom Humanities Research Center, University of Texas at Austin. Typescripts for television plays are at the University of Southern Illinois.

Tim Parks
(19 December 1954 –   )

Gillian Fenwick
University of Toronto

BOOKS: *Tongues of Flame* (London: Heinemann, 1985; New York: Grove, 1986);

Loving Roger (London: Heinemann, 1986; New York: Grove, 1987);

Home Thoughts (London: Collins, 1987; New York: Grove, 1988);

Family Planning (London: Collins, 1989; New York: Grove Weidenfeld, 1989);

Cara Massimina, as John MacDowell (London: Hodder & Stoughton, 1990); republished as *Juggling the Stars* (New York: Grove, 1993);

Goodness (London: Heinemann, 1991; New York: Grove Weidenfeld, 1991);

Italian Neighbours: An Englishman in Verona (London: Heinemann, 1992); republished as *Italian Neighbours; or, A Lapsed Anglo-Saxon in Verona* (New York: Grove Weidenfeld, 1992);

Shear (London: Heinemann, 1993; New York: Grove, 1994);

La Camera (Milan: Hefti Edizioni, 1995);

Mimi's Ghost (London: Secker & Warburg, 1995);

An Italian Education: The Further Adventures of an Expatriate in Verona (New York: Grove, 1995); republished as *An Italian Education* (London: Secker & Warburg, 1996);

Europa (London: Secker & Warburg, 1997; New York: Arcade, 1998);

Translating Style: The English Modernists and Their Italian Translations (London & Washington, D.C.: Cassell, 1998);

Adultery & Other Diversions (London: Secker & Warburg, 1998; New York: Arcade, 1999);

Destiny (London: Secker & Warburg, 1999).

OTHER: "Keeping Distance," in *20 under 35,* edited by Peter Straus (London: Sceptre, 1988);

"The Room," in *New Woman, New Fiction,* edited by Suzanne Askham (London: Pan, 1990);

"Discovering Joyce through Translation," in *Proceedings of the 4th International Conference on Translation* (Kuala

Tim Parks, circa 1989 (photograph © Jerry Bauer; from the dust jacket for the first American edition of Family Planning*)*

Lumpur: Persatuan Penterjemah Malaysia dan Dewan Bahasa dan Pustaka, Malaysia, 1993);

"Translation, a Tool for Criticism," in *A Song to Life and World Peace: Selected Essays and Poems Presented at the XIII World Congress of Poets of the World Academy of Arts and Culture,* edited by Ada Aharoni and others (Jerusalem: Posner, 1993);

"Barbara Pym and the Untranslatable Commonplace," in *Essays on Barbara Pym* (Milan: IULM University, 1996);

"Facciamo le Corna," in *Travelers' Tales Guides: True Stories of Life on the Road,* edited by Anne Calcagno (San Francisco: Travelers' Tales, 1998), pp. 16–23;

"Different Worlds," in *Translation of Poetry and Poetic Prose: Proceedings of Nobel Symposium 110* (Singapore & River Edge, N.J.: World Scientific, 1999).

TRANSLATIONS: Alberto Moravia, *Erotic Tales* (London: Secker & Warburg, 1985);

Moravia, *The Voyeur* (London: Secker & Warburg, 1986);

Antonio Tabucchi, *Indian Nocturne* (London: Chatto & Windus, 1988);

Moravia, *Journey to Rome* (London: Secker & Warburg, 1990);

Antonio Tabucchi, *Vanishing Point; The Woman of Porto Pim; The Flying Creatures of Fra Angelico* (London: Chatto & Windus, 1990; New York & London: Vintage, 1993);

Fleur Jaeggy, *Sweet Days of Discipline* (London: Heinemann, 1991; New York: New Directions, 1993);

Giuliana Tedeschi, *There Is a Place on Earth: A Woman in Birkenau* (London: Lime Tree, 1993; New York: Pantheon, 1992);

Roberto Calasso, *The Marriage of Cadmus and Harmony* (New York: Knopf, 1993; London: Cape, 1993);

Italo Calvino, *The Road to San Giovanni* (London: Cape, 1993; New York: Pantheon, 1993);

Calvino, *Numbers in the Dark and Other Stories* (London: Cape, 1995; New York: Pantheon, 1995);

Jaeggy, *Last Vanities* (New York: New Directions, 1998);

Calasso, *Ka* (London: Cape, 1998; New York: Knopf, 1998).

SELECTED PERIODICAL PUBLICATIONS—UNCOLLECTED: "Bella Cinderella," *Sunday Times* (London), 6 August 1989, pp. G8–G9;

"Why I Love Verona," *Options* (May 1992): 130ff;

"A Gentleman in Verona," *Harper's Bazaar* (July 1992): 38ff;

"Stranger in Paradise," *GQ* (March 1993): 259ff;

"Modern Times," *Independent Magazine,* 21 August 1993, pp. 12–13;

"The Sisters," *Marie Claire* (August 1993);

"Translating the Evocative Spirit in *A Portrait of the Artist* and *Ulysses,*" *Il letterario* (1994);

"Roma Therapy," *Vogue,* 184 (December 1994): 218–224;

"Other Worlds," *Los Angeles Times Book Review,* 4 December 1994, pp. 4, 26;

"Confessions of a Control Freak," *Observer* (London), 19 February 1995, p. 23;

"Rethinking the Task of the Translator," *Rivista internazionale di tecnica della traduzione* (1995);

"Translating Distance: An Approach to Beckett Through a Consideration of the Italian Translations of *Murphy* and *Watt,*" *Il confronto letterario* (1996);

"Adultery," *New Yorker,* 72 (24 June – 1 July 1996): 128–132;

"On the Shelf," *Times* (London), 17 July 1996;

"When Temptation Strikes," *Times* (London), 19 March 1997, p. 17;

"Prajapati: Upon Translating a Paragraph of Roberto Calasso," *London Review of Books* (April 1998): 21ff;

"Analogies," *New Yorker,* 74 (27 April – 4 May 1998): 78–84;

"The Spanish Steps," *Bon Appetit,* 43 (June 1998): 123–126;

"Destiny," *Granta,* 62 (Summer 1998): 29–40;

"You are Standing on the Waterfront at Cernobbio...," *Antiques International* (1998);

"Santa's Copter," *New Yorker,* 74 (28 December 1998 – 4 January 1999): 106–107;

"A Prisoner's Dream: Eugenio Montale in Translation," *New York Review of Books,* 46 (4 February 1999): 36–39.

Nobel Prize–winning poet and essayist Joseph Brodsky has described Tim Parks as "Frankly, the best British author writing today." While he is primarily a novelist, Parks is also an accomplished short-story writer, literary critic, essayist, travel writer, translator, and teacher. Even if he has not yet achieved the level Brodsky suggests, Parks does appear to be on the verge of becoming a great writer.

Though Parks was born in England, he lives in Verona, Italy, and lectures on literary translation at the Istituto Universitario di Lingue Moderne in Milan. Parks is, however, by no means a writer in exile; he does not appear to yearn for a permanent return to England. His life in Italy is an essential part of his writing, adding to it a richness and extra dimension. Like many expatriates, Parks sees his homeland with an increased objectivity, perhaps even with cynicism. And yet, while his life abroad has distanced him physically and psychologically from his origins, he is not quite fully assimilated into his adopted country. This double insight and double distancing, of course, color his writing.

Timothy Harold Parks was born on 19 December 1954 in Manchester to Harold James Parks, an evangelical Anglican clergyman, and Joan McDowell Parks. He has described a happy middle-class childhood with books around the house, reading together, family holidays, and church. Harold Parks, who had been an engineer before he decided to become a clergyman during World War II, wanted his son to become a scientist; instead, Parks studied literature at Cambridge, where he began his writing career with a short story, "The Three of Us," that he submitted for academic credit. "It was dismissed with a D," he says in *Adultery & Other Diversions* (1998). Graduating with an honors B.A. in 1977, Parks went to Harvard University; there he wrote a novel, "The Bypass," which was condemned as "awful" by his tutor. He left Harvard after receiving his M.A. in 1979, finding it, he told interviewer Jean W. Ross, "a little claustrophobic," and in 1978–1979 he worked for the Boston public radio station, WGBH, writing introductions for dramatizations of novels. The experience was less than satisfying; he told Ross, for example, of a conflict with the producer and the actress Julie Harris over Edith Wharton's *The House of Mirth* (1905), which they interpreted as a feminist novel despite Parks's advice that Wharton herself, a traditionalist where women were concerned, would have been horrified at the idea.

Parks and Rita Baldassarre, an Italian student of foreign languages he had met at Harvard, left Boston for London, where they were married by Harold Parks on 15 December 1979. From 1979 to 1981 Parks worked in telemarketing, all the while writing fiction. In 1981 he and his wife went on a vacation to Italy to visit her parents in Pescara and decided to stay. He took a part-time job teaching English in Verona, learned Italian, and did translations, while continuing to write. He says in *An Italian Education* (1995) that he went to Italy "eager to escape friends and family and underachieve in peace." In the essay "Rancour" in *Adultery & Other Diversions* he describes his writing between 1979 and 1985: "A novel called 'Promising,' never published; a novel called 'Leo's Fire,' never published; a novel called 'Quicksand.' Never published. A novel called 'Failing.' Never published. Enough rejection slips to paper Buckingham Palace." His first published novel, *Tongues of Flame* (1985), was rejected by half a dozen agents and almost two dozen publishers before it was accepted, five years after it was written. In 1985 he submitted it to the Sinclair Prize competition for unpublished fiction, so certain of rejection that he told the judges not to return the manuscript. *Tongues of Flame* was the runner-up, and William Heinemann accepted it for publication.

The semi-autobiographical *Tongues of Flame* is set in the 1960s in suburban London and concerns an Anglican priest's involvement in the charismatic Christian movement and the religious hysteria of some of its members; Parks's essay "Fidelity" in *Adultery & Other Diversions* tells more or less the same story of "charismatic folly . . . so exciting, and so destructive." The adolescent narrator of *Tongues of Flame*, Richard, is torn between his father's open-minded willingness to embrace new approaches to Christianity; the zeal of the curate, Rolandson; and the cynical perversity of his brother, Adrian. Richard's parents are drawn into the movement, begin speaking in tongues, and move through the community in soul-searching parties; meanwhile, Rolandson embarks on a local search for Satan. In true 1960s fashion, Adrian rebels at every turn–

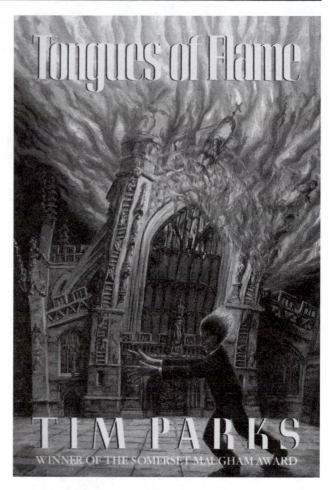

Dust jacket for the American edition of Parks's semi-autobiographical first novel (1985), about a teenage boy torn between the charismatic Christianity of his parents and the 1960s rebelliousness of his brother

smoking marijuana, getting expelled from school, and making love to girls upstairs in the family home.

It is small wonder, then, that Adrian becomes the focus of Rolandson's witch-hunt. Richard, with the Holy Ghost and the devil both present under his roof, takes refuge in his room with bedtime cocoa, Ritz crackers, Radio Moscow, hidden microphones with wires leading to Adrian's room, and phone taps. Amid prophecy and exorcism he plays football and gets drunk, torn between his parents' morality and his own admiration for Adrian's rebellion. Parks carefully balances the humor and terror of the situation.

Parks told Ross that the background of the novel "is truth rather than fiction." One is, therefore, tempted to search for parallels with his own life; but for Parks rebellion seems to have taken other forms. He said in a CBC Radio interview (13 December 1998), "You found yourself reading Tolstoy, Beckett and things that started to look very dangerous to my parents, in Sartre and so on, and so rebellion was very much through reading, partly because they had set up reading as an important thing, it became an important way to rebel against the more asphyxiating and negative sides."

Tongues of Flame was well received: it won two Society of Authors prizes, the Betty Trask and Somerset Maugham Awards, in 1986. Jeanette Winterson wrote in *TLS: The Times Literary Supplement* (13 September 1985) that "Parks is a writer to watch. As a technician he cannot be faulted. His book builds slowly, taking the reader from secure ground to a mad place . . . to a terrifying *tour de force,* made bearable only by the tight prose." *Books & Bookmen* (September 1985) noted the blending of "structural simplicity with emotional complexity . . . extraordinary balance and grace." Jonathan Yardley wrote in *The Washington Post* (11 February 1987) that *Tongues of Flame* is "a rites-of-passage novel that far exceeds the usual limitations of the genre." Barbara Hamilton-Smith in the *Catholic Herald* (27 December 1985) went even further, saying, "Not since *The Catcher in the Rye* has there been such a believable portrayal of male puberty."

Parks's next book, *Loving Roger* (1986), was also successful, winning the John Llewellyn Rhys Prize. Parks had written it before *Tongues of Flame* was published; he has since said that he had decided to make it his last attempt to get a novel published. Anna, the protagonist of *Loving Roger,* faces what Parks has called the "agony of indecision." The novel begins with Roger lying dead on the carpet, beside the television and the lava lamp. Anna, who loves him, has killed him with a kitchen knife; as the *Today* reviewer put it, the novel is "not a whodunnit but a brilliant whydunnit." After this opening, the narrative flashes back to the beginning of the events that led to Roger's death; through repetition Parks slowly unfolds the story and motives of the characters. He makes the none-too-bright Anna a reporter of conversations, the import of which are probably above her head. Frequently, letters transfer the narration from Anna's voice to Roger's, as recorded on dictaphone tapes.

Reviewers were divided about *Loving Roger* and interpreted it in various ways. Martha Southgate in the *Voice Literary Supplement* (February 1988) saw the novel as a woman's effort at self-assertion: Anna moves from strength to strength, drawing on dormant resources, increasing her independence, and achieving the ultimate success when she becomes a murderer. For Southgate, however, "it's impossible to feel the weight of tragedy when the self-styled hero is such a jerk." On the other hand, Michael Carroll in the *Los Angeles Times Book Review* (24 January 1988) found the novel ambiguous and unsettling, with Roger playing the roles of manipulator and perpetrator in an act of self-destruction in which Anna is merely the means to an end and is, per-

haps, the victim rather than the murderer. In the end, despite the difference of viewpoint, it was clear that Parks had made his mark as a novelist with *Loving Roger. TLS* reviewer Jo-Ann Goodwin drew attention to Parks's "astonishing control over his writing" and the "discipline which makes the novel such an impressive achievement" (17 October 1986).

Home Thoughts (1987) is an epistolary novel about Julia Delaforce, an Englishwoman studying in Verona, and her relationships with other foreigners there. Parks used the epistolary form because he wanted to experiment further with it and because it enabled him to concentrate on character rather than action. As he told Ross, "Action is delightful when it's well done, but it wasn't what I was personally interested in. The other thing about letters is that they constantly express at the same time both the intimacy and the distance between people. . . . So much is shared and so much is not shared." An intriguing aspect of *Home Thoughts* is the hidden point of view: the letter writer does not always tell the whole truth, and sometimes does not come even close to the truth. The gap between what is concealed and what is revealed is clear to the reader but not to the letter recipient and illuminates the character of the writer.

The New York Times (23 October 1988) described the novel as having "a plot of such convoluted intricacy it could fuel a soap opera for years," while Hilary Mantel promised in *Books* that no reader will feel shortchanged by Parks. Parks says that he never reads reviews, so presumably he was untouched by Lore Dickstein's suggestion that he was a little too "entranced with his own cleverness" where the form of his third novel was concerned. What was clear even at this stage of his publishing career was his concern with narrative voice. Parks has said of working with translations of Beckett, "There are messages galore but, call it style, call it voice, the whole message is in the voice. There is a whole gesture of a book which is its message."

In 1989 Parks published *Family Planning,* another novel in which humor and psychological terror exist side by side; once again, letters are introduced to vary the form and the way the reader learns about the characters. The work is a detached, unsentimental look at a family destroyed not only by a scheming, schizophrenic son but also by the other family members' inadequacies and misunderstandings. When Raymond, the schizophrenic, finally writes to the International Court of Human Rights that his family has been taken over by aliens, his "evidence"—they no longer behave as though they are related to him, his mother has attacked him with a knife, and his father has disappeared—is funny but also true and horrific. Cheri Fein in *The New York*

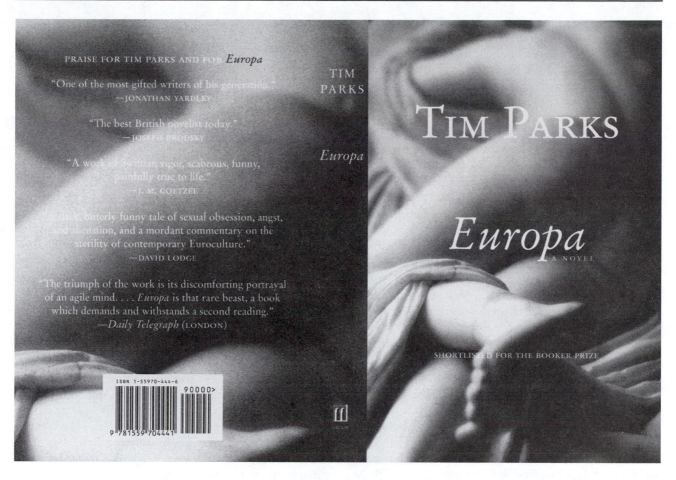

Dust jacket for the American edition of Parks's 1997 novel, in which the narrator travels through
Europe on a bus to present a petition to the European Parliament in Brussels

Times Book Review noted that Parks's "unflinching eye penetrates like an X-ray." For Michael Dibdin in *The Observer* (London), the "ease and economy with which relationships are shuffled and the characters made to reveal themselves" were the most remarkable features of the work. The *Daily Telegraph* reviewer said that the novel was "Like a collaboration between Kafka and Ayckbourn . . . below the belt writing of the most arresting kind."

Cara Massimina (1990), published in the United States as *Juggling the Stars* (1993), was so different from his previous work that Parks published it under a pseudonym, John MacDowell. The novel is the blackest of black comedies, a macabre thriller. The protagonist is the unspeakably immoral Morris Duckworth, who will stop at nothing—theft, blackmail, or murder—in his obsession with his own advancement. He is teaching English in Verona when he hits on the idea of extracting money from the rich family of one of his students, Massimina Trevisan, preferably by marrying her but, if that fails, by kidnapping her, which he does. All turns

out well for him in the end, despite the fact that he has to kill Massimina.

In 1991 Parks published *Goodness,* a compelling single-sitting book about an ordinary man faced with an impossible moral dilemma. The narrator, George Crawley, had an unusual childhood as the son of a missionary who was murdered by the natives whose souls he was trying to save. George summarizes what the book is about on the first page, telling the story of his father's death and relating it to his own life: "over the years I have come to see it as just the first, the most absurdly emblematic, of a long series of incidents in which other people's pretensions to goodness were to clash, to my considerable detriment, with the most naked common sense."

Back in England, George grew up in conventional suburban circumstances and went on to become a successful but stereotyped young professional—muesli for breakfast, Mediterranean holidays, Filofax, shaky marriage. All is more or less normal until the birth of Hilary, horribly handicapped, which marks the turning point of George's life and of the book. George can cope with almost anything but Hilary's nightmarish condition; yet, Parks manages to walk a knife edge between farce and tragedy to the point where readers may find themselves alternately laughing aloud and sobbing. Parks expects his readers to distrust George's mixture of fact, opinion, and speculation and learn how to interpret it. In his 1998 CBC Radio interview Parks described a writer who "completely bowled me over," Thomas Bernhard. Parks says of Bernhard's novel, *Concrete* (1982), "What's fascinating to me is the way he sets up these characters who have the impossible task of getting their minds round something, and then breaking into that are all kinds of domestic tragedies which rearrange the mental furniture." The reader cannot help but feel that Parks is doing exactly the same thing in *Goodness*. It perhaps represents a pivotal point in his writing career—by this time his name was recognized and respected, and he had publishers who were eager for his work. *The Washington Post,* for example, said of *Goodness* that: "Like its predecessors it is economical, original, arresting and intelligent." This level of writing is what reviewers and readers expected of Parks by 1991.

In Parks's next novel, *Shear* (1993), he displays a perhaps surprising knowledge of geology in a book about a geologist with an obsession. Parks's books are not "researched" in any conventional sense. His expertise in geological writing, for example, came from translating manuals for quarrying equipment. As a result, he seems as much at ease with sedimentary rocks, continental drift, and bedding planes as he is in describing a too perfectly chiseled face, cracks in the hero's personality, or the deep underground of love. The geological element is not just background or setting; it is the heart of the novel, the sustained metaphor that the title suggests—the strain within the structure, the basic weakness of the layering of the substance. *Shear* is a mature, clever novel, the "best new novel" *Spectator* reviewer Christopher Bray had read, recommended for the Booker shortlist by the *Observer,* and "powerful and impressive" to the *TLS*. The dust jacket of the British edition celebrated Parks's reputation to date in a series of extracts from notable critics and prestigious journals: "Parks exhibits an astonishing control over the tone of his writing" (*TLS*); "economy and certainty of tone" (Robertson Davies); "A highly original imagination" (*Time Out*); "dreadfully accurate prose" (*Daily Telegraph*); "No one can doubt Parks's ability to entertain" (Michael Dibdin); "Among his generation's most gifted writers" (*The Washington Post*).

In 1995 Parks published a sequel to *Cara Massimina*. In *Mimi's Ghost* Morris has collected the ransom for Massimina's—Mimi's—kidnapping. But he finds that he had fallen in love with her; her memory literally haunts

him—her photograph winks at him from her grave. Killing her has become a punishment rather than a crime, and to add to his dilemma Morris is now married to her sister, a crude, vulgar version of the virginal Mimi. But Mimi shows him how to redeem himself, and he does, brilliantly, as before. And in *Mimi's Ghost* Parks introduces a third daughter of the rich Trevisan family, alive and well after he has killed off the other two. Morris is still thirsty for recognition and wealth, and Parks admits he is willing to reveal more in a third Morris book. Critics loved Morris, finding the novels "better than *Silence of the Lambs* . . . macabre fun . . . immaculate precision (*The Los Angeles Times*) and "comparable with Highsmith at her best" (*Time Out*). The books have sold well both in hardcover and in paperback and have introduced Parks to an audience beyond the fairly literary crowd who read his more "serious" novels. Because it is a totally different genre, the writing is markedly different. As he describe it in an unpublished interview, his style is "larger" in the Morris books, and he does not have to worry about going over the top, staying within the bounds of probability, or exaggerating.

Although Parks had sworn that he would never write about Italy, he published *Italian Neighbours* in 1992 and *An Italian Education* in 1995. Both works are nonfiction accounts of aspects of his life in Italy. His is not *la dolce vita* but everyday life in ordinary Italy with all its frustrations, below the superficiality of temporary residence. In the author's note to *Italian Neighbours* he describes his purpose in writing the book:

> the gesture of this book might be that of a busy but inexpert fellow dashing about the narrow confines of his territory waving a net on the end of a long stick . . . [he strives to define the] national character, a sense of place, the feeling people, place and weather generate . . . the thing is, even when you do catch one for a moment you have a terrible job recognising them, and then when you pin them on the pages of your book they immediately lose all colour and shape. Anyway he is spending most of his time picking truisms, clichés and caricatures out of his net.

Parks manages to make come alive the never ending series of paradoxes that is modern Italy—as one reviewer put it, all the way from the Pope to cut-price condoms. In the afterword to the book Parks concludes that he has passed the point of no return, beyond homesickness and regret, to the "process of immersion in details." Rather than a travel book, he says, it is an arrival book, in a place he now calls home. *An Italian Education* is dedicated to Lucia, his third child, who is about to be born at its end, and is about his son, Michele, and his first daughter, Stefania. The education, of course, is not just theirs but also his, as he tries to come to terms with what it means to be Italian and how an Italian becomes Italian from the moment of birth. The reader discerns Parks's essential Englishness struggling with Italianness in his realistic account of dealing with children and foreignness—a mixture of sympathy, love, coercion, bribery, and threats. The reader is drawn into the process; Parks says, "I promise not to leave you out in the cold, if only because not being in the cold but becoming part of a privileged group, a family, is precisely what any Italian education is about."

The two books are simultaneously objective and subjective, deeply affectionate for Italy without being sentimental, full of purpose and direction, and yet funny and constantly surprising. Although they have been hugely successful, have been translated and republished around the world, and have done more for his reputation than anything else he has written, Parks is adamant that he will not write another. As he says in *Adultery & Other Diversions:* "People write to me regularly asking for a third book on Italy. But I feel Italy has had more than its fair share of my attention." He has said in an unpublished interview that the two works are the least autobiographical of his writings, and yet reading them reveals not only much about life in modern Italy but much about Parks, as well. So, although he is not overtly telling about himself, along the way the reader learns how Parks's mind works, what he likes and dislikes, how he approaches people and situations, how he transforms events into prose, and how he filters his Italian life into a form comprehensible to outsiders.

Parks's next novel, *Europa* (1997), features a gray, obsessive antihero, Jerry Marlow; an unnamed—and therefore, to the reader, remote—woman, the object of Marlow's obsession; a futile bus trip across Europe to present a petition to the European Parliament; and a meander through Marlow's thoughts and memories. The novel was short-listed for the 1997 Booker Prize, a distinction that guaranteed it publicity and commercial success in Europe. From the detail of the risqué name of the bus—the Shag Wagon—to the reality of a European Parliament, there is perhaps much that escapes the North American reader. In a public reading in Toronto, for example, Parks's joke about the name of the bus fell flat with the audience. The American publisher's reader who congratulated Parks on the innovative and presumably fictional idea of the Strasbourg Parliament of the European Community clearly suffered from cultural and political ignorance. *The New York Times* reviewer who waited in vain "for some sign that [Parks] doesn't take his narrator, Jerry Marlow, as seriously as Marlow takes himself" (15 November 1998) missed the point that the author and the narrator share a culture where what Marlow calls "intimacy and distance"

coexist. In *Europa* Parks confirms his versatility, both technically and stylistically. He reaffirms his position as a writer who makes no compromises where his audience is concerned. Expecting his readers to be intelligent, Parks takes a subtle, dark, even black sense of humor for granted and never allows the reader to become complacent.

Translating Style: The English Modernists and Their Italian Translations (1998) was a new departure for Parks—a series of connected critical essays on how literary style can be translated. There is, of course, no shortage of critical books on translation, but most of them address theoretical issues. *Translating Style* presents texts in Italian and English and engages in detailed, practical analysis of the parallel texts. Parks states that he takes as his starting point the idea that much can be learned about the subtleties of the shades of meaning of a text from considering the problems involved in translation. As his examples illustrate, the problems vary from author to author and text to text. He looks at D. H. Lawrence, James Joyce, Virginia Woolf, Samuel Beckett, Barbara Pym, and Henry Green, showing how the difference between the meaning in the original and the meaning in the translation draws attention to the nature of the author's style. The examples begin almost as games in translation and then develop into methodologies as he works out why certain approaches and techniques work. Many of the problems turn out to be cultural—one language does not necessarily translate well into the cultural context of another, and the results may be absurdly inadequate. Parks emphasizes the need to adapt the style to the subject even if it requires compressing or expanding the original text to try to convey the author's intention. Literary texts present peculiar challenges to the translator. As Parks notes, they are "famous for their complexity and ambivalence" and, therefore, difficult to translate convincingly without sounding banal or even ridiculous.

Adultery & Other Diversions is a collection of pieces that Parks describes as "odd hybrids" that "evade the distinction between narrative and essay." Since Parks does not tell the reader which are the narratives and which the essays, it would be dangerous to assume that the "I" in any given piece is the author. Throughout the collection he speaks about himself, his writing, and his motivations—his need to tell stories, his need to seduce the reader, and his need to be recognized. The essay "Rancour" begins: "What the gods most required of man was recognition," and then the writer's "unslakable thirst for recognition." Despite the danger of assuming the "I" in these pieces to be Parks, it is impossible not to read many of them as autobiographical. In "Rancour" he quotes Marcel Proust—"Style is the transformation thought imposes on reality"—and concludes:

Tim Parks, circa 1998 (photograph by Basso Cannarsa; from the dust jacket for the American edition of Europa*)*

I'm at my desk. About to start again. To attempt that transformation again. . . . Writing, I tell myself, staring at the screen, involves a complex movement of the spirit in which one is simultaneously aware of the most sublime and the most base.

In a similar way, in "Prajapati" he analyzes some of the processes of translation, including the way the translator arrives at just the right word and the right shade of meaning. He is frank about why he translates: "to earn money to pay bills and feed my family. Attractive as it may sound, I don't live in a situation where 'there is only the mind.' There are also electricity bills, phone bills, Kellogg's cornflakes." And yet, he adds, "Nothing is more present to me, for better or worse, than my mind . . . I translate therefore I am." As for translation itself, it is the "constant attempt to grasp difference, to overcome it, if only for a few moments, if only on the slippery surface of a text, to appropriate, but also to expand." Further,

the undefined yearns for the defined, the mind for substance. . . . Translation too is this, leaving the definition, the apparent definition, of the original, going through a state of indefinition, perhaps more original . . . than the original, a state where ideas are somehow held wordless, or almost . . . in my mind . . . thence to reappear, gradually recompose themselves, from fuzz to clarity, or almost, in my own language.

The ideas he expresses in *Translating Style* and again in this piece are at the root of his success as a translator.

Translating has been an important element in Parks's writing life. For several years in the early 1980s he translated for trade magazines; since then he has translated literary texts. Parks describes his growing need to put himself into his translations to the point where, as he says in *Adultery & Other Diversions,* "I just want to make [the] text mine, swallow it up, and regurgitate it in an entirely new form." In an onstage interview at the 1998 Toronto International Authors Festival he said, "You feel the drag towards your style in translation, the need to insert an adverb." He describes translation as in part a process of self-discovery, an enriching process, inseparable from and embracing his whole Italian experience: "You learn about yourself when you're translating. Then you also learn how the text operates in the context of its people."

The first book Parks translated, Alberto Moravia's *Erotic Tales* (1985), came his way when another translator rejected the job because of explicit subject matter of the work. Since then, in addition to more Moravia, he has translated works by Antonio Tabucchi, Fleur Jaeggy, Giuliana Tedeschi, Roberto Calasso, and Italo Calvino, with increasing critical recognition. His translation of Calasso's *The Marriage of Cadmus and Harmony* (1993) was awarded the Italo Calvino Prize, and his translation of Calvino's *The Road to San Giovanni* (1993) received the John Florio Prize.

Parks returned to the novel form in 1999 with *Destiny,* his best work of fiction to date. *Destiny* is ambitious and uncompromising, making the reader work hard to reach the level of understanding that the author expects. Its language is complex, with long and convoluted sentences that are reminiscent at times of Henry James and Virginia Woolf. Critics have drawn attention to its stream-of-consciousness technique, as it follows the fragmentary thought patterns of Chris Burton, the main character. The story takes place in seventy-two hours, as Chris and his wife journey to bury their son. It is intense, beginning with a suicide and the decision to end a thirty-year marriage. The novel includes emotional tension and intellectual dilemma, the difficulty of living between two languages and two ways of seeing the world, and the ensuing clashes and chaos. It is about grief and tragedy, reminiscence and anticipation, weakness and forgiveness, and the real responses, contradictory and even callous, that people make. Critics have praised *Destiny* as "a dazzling and sustained tour-de-force," "enthralling . . . structurally accomplished," and "brilliant . . . and powerfully affecting" and have compared Parks to James, Vladimir Nabokov, and William Faulkner, while deploring the fact that it was not even short-listed for the 1999 Booker Prize.

Parks is also a reviewer, journalist, and essayist of note. He has written for *The New Yorker, Granta, The Los*

Angeles Times, The London Review of Books, The New York Review of Books, The Spectator, The Times (London), the *Independent,* and several Italian magazines and newspapers. A piece in *The New York Review of Books* (4 February 1999), nominally a review of Eugenio Montale's collected poems, gives not just a literary analysis of the poetry but also a critique of Montale's place in Italian literary history—Montale in the context of Giacomo Leopardi and Gabriele D'Annunzio, his predecessors in Italian poetry; Montale and the Fascist movement; and a comparison and evaluation of this translation with previous translations and with the original Italian. By showing what he, as translator, might have done, in the end Parks makes his readers want to read not his or any other translation but the original:

> The original . . . has a great deal of internal rhyming, some of it at least potentially significant—*cartone/padrone* (cardboard/master) *rovina/incrina* (destroy/crack) and the weighty half-rhyme *svolacchia/fumacchi.* These latter are difficult words to translate. The rare *svolacchiare,* borrowed perhaps from D'Annunzio, whom Montale at once rejected and ransacked, suggests sudden clumsy flight, while a *fumacchio* is a fumarole or a smouldering log, the one suggesting an infernal connection with those evil spirits, the other giving us a picture of the domestic roofs as themselves alight, the houses slowly burning themselves out, as almost everything in Montale's world consumes itself in fire.

Parks is doing more here than discussing what he calls "the inevitable small swings and roundabouts of translation," the ins and outs of poetic diction, or "different approximations to the impossible perfect solution." His textual analysis is of the highest caliber; it is itself clear and beautiful prose. Parks the literary critic is as at home with the words and ideas of Leopardi, whose "writing fizzes with the excitement of what may best be described as negative epiphany," as he is with William Wordsworth, the early years of Fascism—"not a moment for poetry"—or Calasso. He is not afraid to let his own translation stand alongside the others for comparison.

Parks is a novelist with huge powers of imagination, able to transport his readers into strange and frighteningly realistic human situations. He draws attention to the folly of human quirks and weaknesses, the turns of fate that seem to affect human beings indiscriminately, and the complications people create for themselves. He is a master of caricature and punishing wit and makes his readers love and hate the characters he creates. A brilliant storyteller, Parks holds his readers spellbound with the situations he creates; moreover, not only do many of his characters have the opportunity to learn more about themselves, but so do his readers. In a strange way, this process of discovery also occurs with his nonfiction. To read a Parks review or essay is not only to gain information about a book, a place, or an aspect of modern life but also to be given the opportunity to think about one's own life and world. Parks's works are not only entertaining in the broadest sense but also cause the reader to think seriously, however trivial the subject may at first appear.

It is tempting to give Tim Parks the perhaps outdated label of man of letters. In many ways he fits the model exactly: he writes in a variety of genres—novels, short stories, essays, literary criticism, reviews, travel literature, humor, autobiography, and academic discourse. No one genre has, in the past, been enough to sustain him financially, so he has done journalism, broadcasting, translation, and teaching. Parks will undoubtedly be remembered primarily as a novelist, but the significance of his other work cannot be ignored.

Interview:

Jean W. Ross, Interview with Parks, in *Contemporary Authors,* volume 131, edited by Susan M. Trosky (Detroit: Gale, 1991), pp. 353–358.

Ann Quin

(17 March 1936 – August 1973)

Nicolas Tredell
Sussex University

See also the Quin entry in *DLB 14: British Novelists Since 1960.*

BOOKS: *Berg* (London: Calder, 1964; New York: Scribners, 1965);

Three (London: Calder & Boyars, 1966; New York: Scribners, 1966);

Passages: A Novel (London: Calder & Boyars, 1969; Salem, N.H.: Boyars, 1979);

Tripticks, illustrated by Carol Annand (London: Calder & Boyars, 1972; Salem, N.H.: Boyars, 1979).

OTHER: "Eyes that Watch Behind the Wind," in *Signature Anthology* (London: Calder & Boyars, 1975);

"From *The Unmapped Country:* An Unfinished Novel," in *Beyond the Words: Eleven Writers in Search of a New Fiction,* edited by Giles Gordon (London: Hutchinson, 1975), pp. 250–274.

SELECTED PERIODICAL PUBLICATIONS–
UNCOLLECTED: "Every Cripple Has His Own Way of Walking," *Nova* (1965);

"Leaving School–XI," *London Magazine,* 6 (July 1966): 63–68;

"Never Trust a Man Who Bathes with His Finger Nails," *El Corno Emplumado* (1968);

"Mother Logue," *Transatlantic Review,* 32 (1969): 101–105.

Ann Quin, circa 1964 (photograph by Timothy Rendle; from the dust jacket for Berg*)*

In the four novels she published during her lifetime, Ann Quin made increasingly extreme experiments with language and form while pursuing a set of deeply felt and distinctive personal concerns. To some extent, her fiction continued the modernist project of developing style and structure in an attempt to achieve a closer fidelity to the moment-by-moment texture of lived experience; yet, she was also moving toward a postmodernist practice of producing texts comprising fragmentary echoes of other texts. Along with Alan Burns, Eva Figes, and B. S. Johnson, Quin was one of the writers who helped to extend the boundaries of the British novel in the 1960s and perhaps to prepare the ground for the increased variety of British fiction in the 1980s and 1990s. In *The Review of Contemporary Fiction* (Summer 1985), Figes recalled how she, Quin, Burns, and Johnson "had very different talents and preoccupations, but we shared a common credo, a common approach to writing. All of us were bored to death with mainstream 'realist' fiction at a time when, in England, it seemed the only acceptable sort. We were concerned with language, with breaking up conventional narrative, with 'making it new' in our different ways." Quin's desire to "make it new" was coupled with a sense of existential seriousness, a desire to achieve an autonomous identity. The themes and

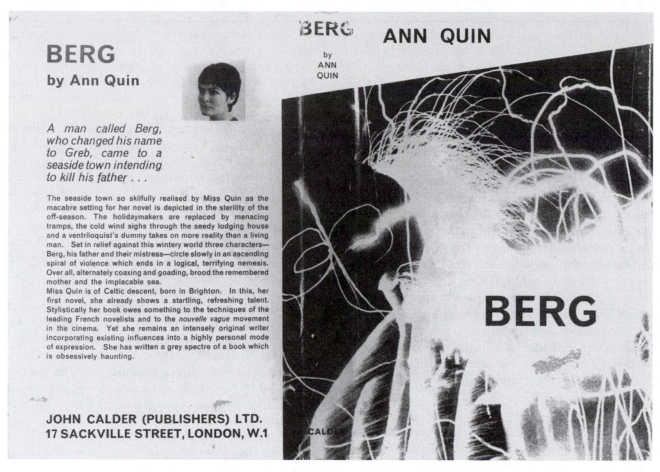

BERG

by Ann Quin

A man called Berg, who changed his name to Greb, came to a seaside town intending to kill his father . . .

The seaside town so skilfully realised by Miss Quin as the macabre setting for her novel is depicted in the sterility of the off-season. The holidaymakers are replaced by menacing tramps, the cold wind sighs through the seedy lodging house and a ventriloquist's dummy takes on more reality than a living man. Set in relief against this wintery world three characters—Berg, his father and their mistress—circle slowly in an ascending spiral of violence which ends in a logical, terrifying nemesis. Over all, alternately coaxing and goading, brood the remembered mother and the implacable sea.

Miss Quin is of Celtic descent, born in Brighton. In this, her first novel, she already shows a startling, refreshing talent. Stylistically her book owes something to the techniques of the leading French novelists and to the *nouvelle vague* movement in the cinema. Yet she remains an intensely original writer incorporating existing influences into a highly personal mode of expression. She has written a grey spectre of a book which is obsessively haunting.

JOHN CALDER (PUBLISHERS) LTD.
17 SACKVILLE STREET, LONDON, W.1

BERG ANN QUIN
by
ANN
QUIN

BERG

Dust jacket for Quin's first novel (1964), about a man who takes on his father's identity (courtesy of The Lilly Library, Indiana University, Bloomington, Indiana)

motifs that recur in her novels include the quest for an independent identity; the persistence into adulthood of the pressure of primary relationships with parents or their surrogates; triangular situations of a familial or quasi-familial kind; the merging of present and past, and of reality and fantasy and dream; role-playing, wearing masks, and dressing up; voyeurism and eavesdropping; and psychoanalytic notions that are treated in a partly parodic and partly exploratory way.

Ann Marie Quin was born in Brighton, Sussex, on 17 March 1936, the daughter of Ann Reid Quin, and former opera singer Nicholas Montague. Her father left soon after she was born. Although not a Catholic, Quin was educated at the Convent of the Blessed Sacrament in Brighton. Her formal education ended relatively early. With aspirations to act, she joined a theater company as an assistant stage manager when she was seventeen, staying only six weeks. She then applied to enter the Royal Academy of Dramatic Art, but felt too nervous to go through with the audition. Instead, she decided to become a writer and

took various secretarial jobs in Brighton and London while completing a novel. Although the novel was rejected for publication, she began another. While working at a summer job in a Cornish hotel, Quin had a serious breakdown. She suffered recurrent bouts of mental illness for the rest of her life. She was able to complete her novel when she returned to London, and in 1964 *Berg* was published by John Calder, a London publishing house with a reputation for promoting avant-garde fiction.

In Britain in 1964, *Berg* certainly seemed avant-garde; it is a black comedy presented in a complex structure and style. Its eponymous antihero, Alistair Berg, comes to a seaside town to find and kill his father, Nathaniel, who deserted his mother when Berg was still a baby (a clear analogy with the disappearance of Quin's own father). The patricide is never performed. The action of the novel is characterized by deferrals, displacements, substitutions, reversals, and repetitions. Berg inveigles his way into the boarding-house where his father lives with his mistress, Judith, but procrastinates when opportunities to kill Nathaniel arise. Instead, Berg displaces his patricidal intent on to a series of substitutes: he kills a cat (possibly Judith's); throws his father's caged budgerigar from the fire escape of a hotel where his father is staying; and strangles a dummy made in his father's image that his father intends to take on tour in a vaudeville act. Berg later identifies a body washed up on the beach as his father's, though he knows it is not. As well as putting off the act of patricide by finding substitutes for his father, Berg becomes a substitute for his father at times. While Nathaniel is trying to retrieve the caged budgie his son has thrown from the fire escape, Berg enters the old man's hotel room, shaves, and orders a meal from room service. After misidentifying the corpse as his father, he returns to Judith and takes his father's place. At one point in the novel, Berg even becomes the substitute for Judith: believing the police are after him, he enters Judith's room and disguises himself as a woman by donning her clothes and makeup, only to have his father return and attempt to make love to him. At the end of the novel Berg has taken his father's place in Judith's room, and a man much like his father has moved into the room next door.

Thomas Docherty, in his critical study *Reading (Absent) Character* (1983), claims that "any attempt to describe Berg is defeated in the wavering lack of definition, the surrealistic blurring of Berg's contours." Docherty's statement is not wholly true: "surrealistic blurring" is certainly a feature of the novel, but the attentive reader can nonetheless discern a great deal about the protagonist. It is possible to interpret *Berg* as a text that both demonstrates and deconstructs the way in which fiction creates character and a sense of reality; but the novel has an existential pressure that suggests this interpretation might not be the most appropriate one. If the reader responds to that pressure, *Berg* can be described as the failure of a quest for an independent identity. The main character is still intensely involved with his parents. His mother's words run through his mind frequently—cajoling, wheedling, reproaching, advising, comfortably entrapping. Her voice is "a wooden spoon stirring the mixed murmurings in his head." He is haunted by his father, who has been held up to him as a man whom he can hardly hope to emulate, and as a villain on whom he should take revenge for his mother's sake and his own. Sometimes Berg seems—like Hamlet—to want to perform an action that will end his self-division and free him from the pale cast of thought: "definitely the supreme action is to dispose of the mind, bring reality into something vital, felt, seen, even smelt. A man of action conquering all." This kind of definitive act eludes Berg.

The narrative technique of the novel reinforces the theme of Berg's failure to develop an independent identity. Most of the paragraphs mix first-person and third-person descriptions of Berg's experience with words that could be attributed to other characters in the novel but that are not set off as dialogue by quotation marks or other means. This lack of visible differentiation contributes to the blurring of the boundaries among what Berg hears, remembers, or imagines. Significantly, it is mainly the words of Berg's mother—and occasionally of other members of his family—that are visibly differentiated by being indented and set in smaller type. The unannounced shifts between present and past, and some gaps in the sequence of present actions, increase the sense of a character whose identity is fragile. The sense of instability produced by the narrative structure of *Berg* is enhanced by Quin's style, which employs striking images that draw attention to themselves and are sometimes highlighted by the use of dashes at the start and the end: "Flaked pieces of distemper fell on his head—snow upon a ploughed field—he closed his eyes." Conversely, the mental impression may be presented without punctuation: "His lips dry leaves slowly parted." In both cases, the unconventional presentation of Quin's symbolic imagery contributes to the sense of a world that can change at any moment, one that is both flexible and frightening.

Berg received a considerable amount of attention from reviewers, and the response was largely enthusiastic. In the early 1960s there was a widespread sense in British society that, in the cultural sphere as in other areas, England was behind the times and that change and modernization were needed. In this context, experimental fiction enjoyed a warmer reception than it might have in the previous decade. For example, the reviewer for *The Times Literary Supplement (TLS)* (25 June 1964) called *Berg* "a most impressive debut." While declaring that Quin had "undoubtedly been influenced by such French novelists as Nathalie Sarraute and by the *nouvelle vague* (New Wave) movement in the cinema," the review went on to affirm that *Berg* was "something of a breakthrough in the sense that, for the first time, these techniques have been used to produce a novel that is both wholly English in atmosphere and quite unpretentious." The novel brought Quin two fellowships—the D. H. Lawrence Fellowship from the University of New Mexico in 1964 and the Harkness Fellowship (for the most promising Commonwealth artist under the age of thirty) for the years 1964 to 1967.

After completing *Berg,* and before setting off for the United States, Quin spent time traveling in Ireland and Greece, and also worked on her second novel, *Three* (1966), which explores a different social milieu from that of the seedy boardinghouse in *Berg.*

In an interview conducted by Nell Dunn when Quin was working on *Three,* Quin said she felt that the concern with class differences in the English novel had been overdone, but acknowledged that she was, nonetheless, writing about "two people who have always had money and have always known a certain side of life and never gone beyond and the girl has never known a family life as such and she's very intrigued by it . . . although she hates it." *Three,* as its title suggests, is about a triangular relationship, and its narrative technique matches this theme as it employs a trio of narrative modes. The triangle is composed of Leonard and Ruth, a well-off married couple moving toward middle age, and S, a young woman who stays with them at their house while recovering from an abortion and who finally disappears, leaving a note that suggests that she may have drowned herself. The three narrative modes are closely observed behaviorist accounts of Leonard and Ruth that detail their actions and conversations but do not attempt directly to describe their inner thoughts and feelings; supposed transcripts of tape recordings by S, which are presented in lines of uneven length, like free verse; and extracts from S's journals. In *Three,* Quin employs what critic John Shea has called "the single most significant and prevalent experimental form of the 1960s and 1970s . . . the block form, in which narrative is constructed of discrete 'blocks.' These units are sometimes paragraph-length, sometimes briefer or longer, but always set off conspicuously from each other." Quin continued to develop her use of block form in her next two novels.

From the different narrative styles of *Three,* the reader can infer something of the characters, their relationship to each another, and of the events that led up to the disappearance of S, though gaps and ambiguities remain. The marriage of Leonard and Ruth is not happy; their day-to-day exchanges are characterized by a superficial politeness that progresses constantly into petty bickering. Their sexual life together has ceased: Leonard feels that Ruth leads him and then balks, while Ruth believes Leonard seeks only his own pleasure. Ruth regrets having no children and invests much of her affection in her cat, which Leonard detests. The impression is one of an ordered and protected, but arid, existence. An extract from one of the transcripts of S's tape recordings describes the house of Leonard and Ruth:

Burglar-proofed.
China plates on the wall. Glass doors. Concealed lighting.
　White curtains transparent.
Nursery done in egg-shell blue. Empty.
A special place for the cat. Never used.

Ann Quin, circa 1966 (photograph by Oswald Jones; from the dust jacket for the American edition of Three*)*

Visitors. Change of linen. Every other day.
Existence bound by habit. Hope. Theirs. Nothing to contend with.
The worst effort not to contradict their next movement
At first.

In a sense, S functions as the couple's surrogate child, as Ruth's confidante, and as a kind of fantasy outlet for the thwarted sexuality of both Ruth and Leonard. It is possible that Leonard and Ruth have—not wholly consciously—used S, and finally, by driving her to suicide, sacrificed her to try to maintain the uneasy equilibrium of their own relationship. A suggested motive for the girl's suicide is her sense that she cannot alter the situation in which she, Leonard, and Ruth are involved. Her last journal entry, and the final words of the novel are "I know nothing will change." As Judith Mackrell argued, in her essay on Quin in *DLB 14,* the death of S does change the situation and provokes Leonard and Ruth to question their relationship much more strongly.

Three closes with a range of unresolved ambiguities and can be examined as an exploration of the difficulty, perhaps the impossibility, of arriving at truth. A notable feature of the novel consists of its references to a range of technological means of preserving the traces of people and events: not only tape recordings, but also still photography and home movies. S finds photographs of a girl whom she later identifies as Ruth before she had plastic surgery. After the girl's death, Leonard, when he is with Ruth, inadvertently starts to screen a home movie in which S appears; he quickly takes it off but later watches it on his own, with great distress. Ruth had made a movie of a mime play that Leonard and S wrote, in which the three of them perform on a private outdoor stage, sometimes with masks and garden statues. These plays enact actual and fantasized aspects of the triangular relationship, as S writes in a journal entry: "my favourite one with the masks is just the three of us, two reject one, or one rejects two, or all three reject each other, or equally accept." The mime plays, masks, and statues allude to Greek drama, myth and ritual; and—as reviewers noted at the time—to more recent sources such as Alain Resnais's avant-garde motion picture *Last Year at Marienbad* (1961), the scenario of which was written by a leading exponent of the French *nouveau roman*, Alain Robbe-Grillet.

Despite the close focus of *Three* on the relationship of its protagonists, the novel does not ignore the social and political tensions of the wider world. Indeed, the relationship of Leonard, Ruth, and S can be seen to embody some of those tensions, on a smaller, more concentrated scale. *Three* suggests that Leonard was politically active during the 1930s, and that he was interned during World War II; the novel also demonstrates that even though he has withdrawn from politics, he cannot wholly insulate himself from social change and the threat of disorder. He dislikes the holiday camp near his seaside home and is angry at the trespassers, who he believes may be from the camp, and who break into his garden, damage the plants and statues, and finally assault him when he is taking part in a mime play. Although the social milieu of Leonard and Ruth is different from that of *Berg*, both novels convey a sense of suppressed violence that sometimes bursts forth.

Three received qualified praise from reviewers. Edwin Morgan, writing in *The New Statesman* (27 May 1966), found the novel "alternately irritating and fascinating" and thought that the "disjointed poetry of memories and impressions" of the supposed transcripts of S's tape recordings did not add "as much as it should." He nonetheless affirmed that *Three* "certainly deserved to be read." The reviewer for *TLS* (2 June 1966) called *Three* "intelligent and at times intense," but saw it as "cerebrally-patterned," a novel that had been "made rather than begotten" and that was "forever flirting with an elegant and obscure symbolism." Classifying it as one of those novels "that ferry us briskly from the sociological to the symbolic," the reviewer judged it "a little too diffuse on the sociological plane to be as truly obsessive as may have been the intention."

Quin's third novel, *Passages* (1969), was written while she was traveling in the United States and draws on her earlier European journeys. Insofar as the reader can infer a story from *Passages,* it is about a man and woman who are traveling in an unnamed, probably Mediterranean, country—perhaps Greece after the military coup of 1967—where the political situation is tense, repression is increasing, and the couple fear they are under surveillance. The woman is looking for her brother who has disappeared and who may or may not be dead. Quin once again employs block form in the narrative. *Passages* is divided into four sections; the first and third can be attributed to the woman, and the second and fourth to the man. Mackrell suggests in *DLB 14,* however, that the divisions between the sections blur, and at times there may seem to be a "merging of identity into a single mind or voice." The first and third parts consist of paragraphs separated by two line spaces rather than the one line space employed in standard paragraph breaks. Sometimes a paragraph breaks off before a sentence is completed, and the opening words of the following paragraph complete the sentence, though on occasion these words divert it from its expected course. For example:

> . . . . A pool of light splashed on the marble. That part I entered, where I returned. Again behind glass I saw

> what did I see, for when that scene reappears it merges with a dream, fallen back into slowly, connected yet not connected in parts.

The second and fourth segments of the book comprise the supposed notes the man is making, possibly for a book, journal, or report. His notes are a mixture of aphorisms, gnomic remarks, accounts of events, lists, definitions of words, mythological allusions, bits of dialogue, notes on the woman's fantasies, descriptions of (or fantasies about) her, accounts of dreams, and "cut-up dreams" in which elements of two dream-accounts are spliced together. These fragments vary in length from a phrase, sometimes of less than one line, to a paragraph. They are set out in two columns or, perhaps as a marginal and a main text: the left-hand column includes entries in small type, whereas the entries in the right-hand column are in standard type. A note at the front of *Passages* describes the items written in the left column as the thoughts that provoked the entries in the right, but the reader can choose to link up the left-hand and right-hand columns in different ways so as to generate different meanings.

The relationship between the man and the woman is uncertain and shifting. Each is largely iso-

*Cover for Quin's 1969 novel, about a man and a woman traveling on a train in a Mediterranean country
(courtesy of The Lilly Library, Indiana University, Bloomington, Indiana)*

lated from the other; as the woman wonders at one point: "What are his dreams, needs, obsessions, demands, desires. Fantasies he rarely shares?" Both people play a range of roles. The man identifies the "faces" of the woman: "Mature woman . . . Femme Fatale . . . The Mystic . . . Country girl 'at heart'" and observes: "often she gets pretty high then she forgets which role she had started with, and a delightful mixture of them all appears, leaving the man confused or even more infatuated." At another stage, the man lays out in the right-hand column what may be a list of possible identities for himself—"lover/husband/brother/father/guardian/prophet/mystic/writer/addict/ = demi-god/ = beast"—and the adjacent left-hand column says: "Can be any one of these, according to whim/projection. What is it/shall it be for today."

There are several mythical references in the man's text, especially to Greek mythology. Many of the Greek references are slightly adapted brief extracts from Jane Harrison's *Prolegomena to the Study of Greek Religion* (1903; third edition, 1922), in which Harrison sought to examine Greek ritual as the first step to any

scientific understanding of Greek religion. *Passages* alludes to Aphrodite, Bacchus, Dionysus, the Medusa, the Minotaur, Oedipus, the Sphinx, Orpheus and Pan, and to Satyrs, Centaurs, Sirens, and Kers (According to Harrison, *ker* is "perhaps the most untranslatable of all Greek words," a "shifting and various term," the possible primary meanings of which are "ghost and bacillus" but which also has secondary meanings that include "disease, death-angel, death-fate, fate, bogey, magician"). The mythic fragments in *Passages* form a montage in which disintegration, orgy, riot, madness, violence, and death figure strongly, with occasional hints of possible renewal, rebirth, and upward development. This montage can be linked to the psychological states of the man and the woman, to the condition of their relationship, and to the situation of the country in which they are traveling. An especially effective device is the way in which the mythic allusions in the second section are echoed in the third. For example, the description of the Sirens as creatures who "dwell on an island in a flowery meadow" and whose "song takes effect at midday" is reworked when the woman is with

8

symbolizing the various paths offered in life. At its
center a small stone summerhouse with a highly finished
interior signifying the hastiness of judgment on the
basis of outward appearances.

'That's the orchard over there a fine sight to see
you know,' he said, 'the Cherry picking Festival is held
in June and the public is invited to pick their own fruit,
and over there well we have the Marine Corps Supply
Depot - there we go you know my grandmother or was it
my great grandfather was Celtic see that fireplace well
its modeled after a Scottish war lord's and this well it's
a miniature Railway an authentic replica you know of an
oldtime coal-burning engine and that well that's a photo
of the world's largest jet-missile rocket test centers
and has a 22-mile runway - not open to visitors of course'.
I made the appropriate gestures, remarks, while thinking
of his daughter's petrified face imprinted on fossilized
leaves. Vital secrets of her own wondering aloud while
shopping by Rolls. I was curious to know if she was a
member, like her mother, of the D.R. (Daughters of
the Revolution). I doubted it. Her speciality would
be wooden heads, tightly leather-wrapped. At the moment,
her father reported she was preoccupied with lizards,
which she says 'look like man in certain stages'.

Later at health resort under hot-water geysers we
made it for the first time in the mineral springs and
mineralized mud baths. My mouth searching for hers by
means of siphon pipes. And later that same day I got
a strange blow-job in a parking lot, it was 35 degrees
outside, by a weird woman, two days later I was still
weak at the knees and couldn't think about it. Now I
could try and ease my way out of this by saying I didn't
ask questions, just stated my personality

smart, well-educated	lack of respect for authority
Ambitious	lack of discipline
deep concern for social problems	lack of spiritual and moral fiber

Page from the typescript for Tripticks *(courtesy of The Lilly Library, Indiana University, Bloomington, Indiana)* the man "on an island. A flowery meadow where I picked flowers," and he says: "Can you hear the sirens—listen . . . their song is supposed to take effect at midday." In reading the text, the impression of these echoes is uncanny, giving a sense of the mythic emerging into the everyday world like the trace of an ancient, archetypal memory.

The fragmentation of *Passages* elicited a disapproving response from David Haworth. Reviewing the novel in *The New Statesman* (21 March 1969), he diagnosed its fault as "the elevation of technique above content." While Quin's language could be appreciated "when it touches the poetic," she "dearly loves obscurity" and was beset by "all sorts of stylistic mannerisms." Haworth went on to say that although Quin was "a pioneer," she made "no clear trail" for the reader to follow. The *TLS* review (3 April 1969) was more favorable, the reviewer declaring that despite "a good deal that is irritatingly opaque and elliptical" in *Passages,* the "fusion between what is experienced, dreamt of and thought, a fusion most noticeable and revealing in solitude or on alien territory, is well suggested." The reviewer contended that "The contrast between those passages which use words to elucidate and those which attempt to bypass language in search of some expressive manner more comprehensive and simpler than prose, is what the novel is about."

Quin's last novel, *Tripticks* (1972), which draws on her experiences in the United States, is her most scrambled text, and Carol Annand's cartoon-like, pop-art style illustrations provide a graphic dimension. The novel has a story of sorts, attributed to a male narrator who highlights, in the opening sentence of the novel, his own multiplicity: "I have many names. Many faces." The narrator is being pursued by his first "X-wife" and her lover—or possibly he is pursuing them: "Who was chasing who I had forgotten." The pursuit involves car chases; a sojourn in a motel room next to the room occupied by his former wife and her lover; a stay at a "CENTRE FOR STUDIES OF THE BODY AND THE SOUL"; and finally, a visit to an Indian reservation. The story of the chase is mixed with monstrous, comic, and erotic images and anecdotes of the narrator's relationships with his first wife and her wealthy, grotesque, demanding parents; with his second and third wives; with his own mother and his stepfather; with his aunt; and with a demoniac, dubious guru, named Nightripper.

Concerns of Quin's earlier novels return in *Tripticks* in a more frenetic context. There are, for example, the triangular and quasi-familial relationships that are almost impossible to escape: the narrator resents and wants to kill his father and, at times, his first X-wife and her lover; he recalls or fantasizes an intensely erotic

and emotional relationship involving himself, his second wife, and a woman who will become his third X-wife. Eavesdropping and voyeurism are also prominent. The narrator overhears and looks through a keyhole at his first X-wife and her lover; recalls looking through a keyhole at his second X-wife being whipped with imported kippers; watches his mother and stepfather "from an enclosed lounge with high-powered telescopes"; and can hear "every move, every moan my mother made from my room next to theirs."

Tripticks also incorporates Quin's interest in role play and in fantasized images of the self. The reader hears the *macho* fantasies of the narrator and of others, such as his father who, though thought of as "a quiet guy in a dark suit," becomes, when there is a call for help . . . "the Man of Steel and flies to your side." The interest in fantasy and role play relates to the quest for reality and identity in a world dominated by modern media: "A reel-by-reel search for reality. . . . Can film be truth at 24 times a second? As soon as you start shooting something it becomes something else." Television abolishes distance and difference: "How far, after all, is the moon from the earth? Precisely the same distance as Vietnam—across the living room." The narrator asks: "What was real, what wasn't? All merged into an immense interior region. . . . Dreams were reality. Reality seen through a rear-view mirror." At the end of the novel silence seems the only option if the protagonist wants to preserve a provisional freedom and a fragile sense of autonomy: "I opened my mouth, but no words. Only the words of others I saw, like ads, texts, psalms, from those who had attempted to persuade me into their systems. A power I did not want to possess. The Inquisition."

Tripticks was not well received by critics. The reviewer for *TLS* (5 May 1972) reported that the "method and layout" of the novel presented "thickets of frustration" to the reader and drew "fatal attention to the powerful underlying humourlessness of the whole thing." Barry Cole, writing in *The New Statesman* (16 June 1972), acknowledged that Quin could "write well" but found *Tripticks* bewildering "to the point of complete incoherence," a "piece of self-gratification" displaying "an artist at the end of her tether."

Soon after completing *Tripticks,* Quin suffered another serious mental breakdown and spent a month in a London hospital, unable to speak. Apparently recovering, she started work on her next novel, provisionally titled "The Unmapped Country." Quin still felt that she lacked formal education, and in 1972, she entered an establishment for mature students, Hillcroft College, in order to prepare for entrance to university. The University of East Anglia offered her a place to read English for the following year, but a month before her course was due to begin, she drowned in the sea between Brighton and Shoreham on the Sussex coast. It was thought that she might have committed suicide, but there was no definite evidence to support this theory, and at the inquest, the coroner returned an open verdict. Quin was thirty-seven.

A section of her last, unfinished novel appeared after her death in Giles Gordon's collection of experimental writing, *Beyond the Words: Eleven Writers in Search of a New Fiction* (1975). In a largely realistic manner, the story evokes the experience of a young woman, Sandra, who is convalescing in a mental home after a breakdown. "The Unmapped Country" is an accomplished piece of work, and the novel might have brought Quin a wider audience had she lived to complete it. As it is, posthumous recognition of her work seems to have been small. Quin's novels were kept in print until 1999 by the publishing house of Marion Boyars, but Boyars's death early that year makes the future availability of Quin's books uncertain.

In 1989 Paladin published a paperback edition of *Berg* to tie in with a motion-picture adaptation of the novel, *Killing Dad* (1989). The movie, written and directed by Michael Austin, was not a success. The 1999 edition of *Halliwell's*, perhaps the most influential British movie guide, dismisses it as a "forced and unfunny attempt at a black comedy." In 1997 *Ann Quin— A Turn of Tides*, a play by Christine Fox based on *Berg*, *Three*, and *Passages*, premiered in Brighton.

Literary critics, to whom Quin's work presents many fascinating challenges, have so far given her fiction little sustained attention, though two important exceptions should be noted: Judith Mackrell's entry in *DLB 14* offers a balanced and perceptive appraisal of Quin's fiction and concludes that it "stands as a considerable and highly original contribution to the experimental tradition in English literature." Philip Stevick, in a contribution to *Breaking the Sequence: Women's Experimental Fiction* (1989), sought to define more closely the nature of Quin's originality: "from

the start, she began to invent ways of representing the inner life by drawing on her own troubled mind, by introspection and a set of conventions largely of her own devising, and that is why the representation of consciousness in her fiction seems so different from that of anyone else, classic or contemporary, akin, if anything, to slightly later writers whom she could not have known such as Peter Handke." Quin's unusual combination of existentialist, modernist, and postmodernist themes and techniques makes her work difficult to unlock, but the effort is rewarding.

Interview:

Nell Dunn, "Ann," in her *Talking to Women* (London: MacGibbon & Kee, 1965), pp. 126–153.

References:

Thomas Docherty, *Reading (Absent) Character: Towards a Theory of Characterization in Fiction* (Oxford: Clarendon Press, 1983);

Eva Figes, "B. S. Johnson, *Review of Contemporary Fiction*, 5 (Summer 1985): 70–71;

John Shea, "Modernist Precursors of the Block Form," *Journal of Modern Literature*, 12 (July 1985): 297–310;

Philip Stevick, "Voices in the Head: Style and Consciousness in the Fiction of Ann Quin," in *Breaking the Sequence: Women's Experimental Fiction*, edited by Ellen G. Friedman and Miriam Fuchs (Princeton: Princeton University Press, 1989), pp. 231–239.

Papers:

Many of Ann Quin's manuscripts and much of her correspondence with publishers are held at the Lilly Library, Indiana University, Bloomington. Other manuscripts and letters are in the Robert David Cohen Papers, Modern Literary Manuscripts Collection, Special Collections, Washington University Libraries, St. Louis, Missouri.

Michèle Roberts
(20 May 1949 –   )

Geneviève Brassard
University of Connecticut

BOOKS: *A Piece of the Night* (London: Women's Press, 1978);

The Visitation (London: Women's Press, 1983);

The Wild Girl (London: Methuen, 1984);

The Mirror of the Mother: Selected Poems, 1975–1985 (London: Methuen, 1986);

The Book of Mrs. Noah (London: Methuen, 1987);

Psyche and the Hurricane (London: Methuen, 1990);

In the Red Kitchen (London: Methuen, 1990);

Daughters of the House (London: Virago, 1992; New York: Morrow, 1992);

During Mother's Absence (London: Virago, 1993);

Flesh and Blood (London: Virago, 1994);

All The Selves I Was (London: Virago, 1995);

Impossible Saints (London: Little, Brown, 1997; Hopewell, N.J.: Ecco, 1998);

Food, Sex & God: On Inspiration and Writing (London: Virago, 1998);

Fair Exchange (London: Little, Brown, 1999; San Diego: Harcourt Brace, 1999);

The Looking-Glass (London: Little, Brown, 2000);

Praying Sardines, and Other Stories (London: Little, Brown, forthcoming 2001).

OTHER: *Cutlasses and Earrings,* edited by Roberts and Michelene Wandor (London: Playbooks, 1976);

Licking The Bed Clean: Five Feminist Poets, includes poems by Roberts, Alison Fell, Sted Pixner, Ann Oostvizen, and Tina Reid (London: Teeth Imprints, 1978);

Tales I Tell My Mother, includes contributions by Roberts, Wandor, Zoë Fairbairns, Sara Maitland, and Valerie Miner (London: Journeyman Press, 1978);

Smile, Smile, Smile, Smile, includes contributions by Roberts, Fell, Pixner, Reid, and Oostvizen (London: Sheba Press, 1980);

Touch Papers, includes poems by Roberts, Wandor, and Judith Kazantzis (London & New York: Allison & Busby, 1982);

"Outside My Father's House," in *Fathers: Reflections by Daughters,* edited by Ursula Owen (London:

Michèle Roberts, circa 1992

Virago, 1983; New York: Pantheon, 1984), pp. 89–98;

"The Woman Who Wanted to Be a Hero," in *Walking on the Water: Women Talk about Spirituality,* edited by Jo Garcia and Maitland (London: Virago, 1983), pp. 50–65;

"Questions and Answers," in *On Gender and Writing,* edited by Wandor (London: Pandora Press, 1983), pp. 150–172;

"Write, She Said," in *The Progress of Romance: The Politics of Popular Fiction,* edited by Jean Radford (London: Routledge, 1986), pp. 221–235;

More Tales I Tell My Mother, includes contributions by Roberts, Fairbairns, Wandor, Maitland, and Miner (London: Journeyman Press, 1987);

"Post-Script," in *The Semi-Transparent Envelope: Women Writing—Feminism and Fiction,* edited by Roberts, Sue Roe, Susan Sellers, and Nicole Ward Jouve (London & New York: Marion Boyars, 1994), pp. 169–175;

Mind Readings: Writers' Journeys through Mental States, edited by Roberts, Sara Dunn, and Blake Morrison (London: Minerva, 1996).

Michèle Roberts, whose novel *Daughters of the House* (1992) won the W. H. Smith Literary Award, has been compared to major modernists such as Virginia Woolf and James Joyce, and her fiction has been studied alongside works by well-known contemporaries such as Jeanette Winterson and Toni Morrison. Despite such critical attention in her native Great Britain, Roberts is relatively unknown in the United States. Most of her novels and collections of poetry have been published in the United Kingdom, and translations of her novels are available throughout Europe, but those works published in the United States have not brought her the public and critical attention she deserves. Perhaps Roberts's stylistic experimentations, her refusal to offer her readers predictable plotlines, and her controversial subject matter have played a role in keeping her books on the margins of contemporary writing. Roberts's fiction explores the tangled and complex relationship between female sexuality and religion, and it does so from a deliberately subversive point of view influenced by the women's movement.

Roberts's heroines typically struggle with definitions of womanhood imposed on them by a dominant patriarchy. Roberts uses the concept of the androgynous mind as an alternative to the gender divisions prevalent in society. Without an integration of the male and female within each individual, her work suggests, relations between men and women remain incomplete and flawed. Another major influence on Roberts's writing is the Catholic Church. In her 1983 essay "The Woman Who Wanted to Be a Hero," Roberts describes Catholicism as "language itself"; throughout her childhood, she prayed to her "constant companion" God, whom she perceived as an androgynous being. As an adult, Roberts distanced herself from religious institutions to explore spirituality as a personal experience. She uses her writing in part as a means to criticize the treatment of women in Judeo-Christian society. She is particularly interested in abolishing the Madonna/whore dichotomy, which she finds is still powerful in society. Roberts also points to a third influence on her art: the idea of loss in general and in particular the loss

of her French-Catholic mother's undivided attention and love. Her fiction and poetry revisit this theme from several angles and suggest that for Roberts the mother-daughter bond is the most complex and engaging of all human relationships.

The daughter of Monique Pauline Joseph Caulle and Reginald George Roberts, Michèle Brigitte Roberts was born on 20 May 1949 in Bushey, Hertfordshire, twenty minutes after her twin sister, Marguerite. She also had an older sister, Jacqueline, and a younger brother, Andrew. Her childhood was spent primarily in England, but she visited her mother's family in Normandy every summer. Her mother, who worked as a teacher, spoke French to her children and raised them in the Catholic faith. Thus, Roberts's upbringing was truly bilingual and bicultural. She wrote in 1983 that she "always wanted to be a writer" and started writing as a young child. Her descriptions of childhood in her later novels emphasize the idea of a lost paradise, an androgynous Eden in which little girls can be anything they want and do as they please. Roberts has described puberty as a "terrible shock," and for many of her heroines the onset of menstruation marks the end of freedom and the beginning of feminine repression by men.

Roberts attended convent school, a place she has revisited in several of her novels. As a child and as a teenager, she wanted to become a nun. She perceived the convent as a safe haven from a world in which women had no freedom of choice and had to submit to confining images of femininity.

Before entering the convent, however, Roberts wanted to see and experience the world in order to make her renunciation more meaningful. Having read Dorothy Sayers's *Gaudy Night* (1935) and "identified strongly" with its writer-heroine Harriet Vane, Roberts chose to attend Somerville College, Oxford, because it was the women's college featured in Sayers's novel. Roberts entered Somerville in 1967 and specialized in the study of medieval literature, particularly attracted by the spiritual content she found in its religious poetry. At Somerville, Roberts also discovered feminism. She has written that the women's movement allowed her to understand that she was not mad, that the inner fragmentation she felt was in fact the consequence of "the psychic dismemberment of the female" in Western culture. Roberts graduated with honors in 1970 and briefly contemplated the idea of pursuing graduate studies at Oxford, focusing on the fourteenth-century mystic Magda of Thagdeburg, but her curiosity about the big city and the desire to be at the center of things led her instead to London.

In London, Roberts's life departed in a radical way from her "nun-like" existence at Oxford. She discovered Marxism and joined a commune in which rooms, possessions, and sexual partners were liberally shared. During this period of political radicalization, Roberts broke completely with the Catholic Church and rejected spirituality as "petit-bourgeois." She studied at the University of London, where she earned an A.L.A. (Associate of the Library Association) degree in 1972. Having become increasingly unhappy in the commune, Roberts then accepted a job with the British Council in Thailand in 1973. She hoped that her removal to Southeast Asia would help her to create a new identity for herself. She did not remain in Thailand long, however; she could not reconcile her Marxist views with the fact that she was well off, white, and—as she said in "The Woman Who Wanted to Be a Hero"—"implicitly supporting American Imperialism."

On her return to London, Roberts became active in the women's movement and began to publish her writing. From 1975 to 1977 she worked as poetry editor for the feminist magazine *Spare Rib,* and she and Michelene Wandor edited a collection of poetry, *Cutlasses and Earrings* (1976), to which she also contributed. With Wandor, Zoë Fairbairns, Sara Maitland, and Valerie Miner, Roberts founded a workshop for feminist writers, and together they published two collections of short stories, *Tales I Tell My Mother* (1978) and *More Tales I Tell My Mother* (1987).

After her return from Thailand, Roberts also began working on her first novel, *A Piece of the Night* (1978). The inspiration for the opening line came to her on a bus during a ride back to London from a visit to her parents. As she later explained in "The Woman Who Wanted to Be a Hero," she spent the next four years "exploring, with a lot of fear, the connections I found I made between Catholicism, sexuality, repression, mothers and daughters." These themes and preoccupations recur in all Roberts's subsequent works.

A Piece of the Night, winner of the 1979 *Gay News* Book Award, received wide critical attention, but the reviews were mixed. The novel, which includes strong autobiographical elements, opens in present-day London and works its way back to the past. As in Roberts's later works, the narrative is not linear. She has described her technique as "cubist"; that is, her narratives typically travel backward, forward, and sideways in time and place, in order to represent reality as she perceives it, as fragmented rather than cohesive. In *A Piece of the Night* a Frenchwoman, Julie Fanchot, who is divorced from her English husband and has custody of her daughter, is living with her lesbian lover and three other women in South London, when she has to return to Normandy to take care of her sick mother. The family visit turns into an inner journey during which Julie uncovers the layers of her past and comes to terms with her wounded, adult self. As in Roberts's subsequent

Dust jacket for Roberts's first novel (1978), which draws on her experiences in convent school (courtesy of The Lilly Library, Indiana University, Bloomington, Indiana)

novels, the Catholic Church occupies a central place in the book. Julie's recollections of her childhood, particularly her strong attachment to—and necessary separation from—her mother, are entwined with the story of Veronica, a nun who taught Julie and her lover, Jenny, at their English convent school. Roberts explicitly connects the female world of the nuns with Julie's life as a lesbian. From wanting to be a nun as a child, Julie has made a brief and unsatisfactory excursion into heterosexuality before settling in a lesbian commune, a sensual "nunnery" of her own choosing.

This first novel includes themes and techniques that Roberts employs again in her fiction. The intrusion of the past into the present in the form of dreams or memories leads to a nonlinear style of storytelling, as if the truth can be achieved only through piecing together fragments of existence. Roberts suggests that Julie's psyche is fragmented until she makes the necessary connections between past and present, feminine and masculine, mother and lesbian: "She is a piece of the night, broken off from it, a lump, a fragment of dark."

Some reviewers found the form of Roberts's first novel problematic. Valentine Cunningham wrote in *New Statesman and Society* (3 November 1978) that the novel was "a runaway chaos of inchoate bits, an incoherence that slumps well short of the better novel it might with more toil have become." In *Feminist Writers* (1996) Tracy Clark quotes a reviewer who described the novel as "full of 'shrieking Lesbian banshees.'" Others considered the novel too obviously geared toward a narrow audience of feminists. Yet, *A Piece of the Night* was praised for the richness of its prose and the poetic quality of its language; one reviewer compared Roberts to Colette. *A Piece of the Night* deals with important issues such as the place of women in the world, relationships between men and women, and the mother-daughter bond, and it does so with passion and honesty. Roberts revisited some of these themes from a slightly different angle in her second novel, *The Visitation* (1983).

With this novel, Roberts set out to investigate the issue of female creativity. As she explained in her 1983 essay "Questions and Answers," she sought "to answer the question: can a woman create art with a gendered voice"? She attempted to do so by looking at female-male twins and by exploring the possibility of nurturing both friendships between women and sexual relationships between men and women. *The Visitation* can be interpreted as a feminist Künstlerroman in which the heroine, Helen, learns what it means to be a woman and a writer in present-day society. The early part of the novel dramatizes in lyrical prose the fall of young Helen from playful and assertive little girl to awkward and weak adolescent following puberty. As a child, Helen feels herself equal to her twin brother, Felix. In this childhood paradise, both children play together, and Helen is an accomplished athlete skilled at various contact sports. When her mother realizes during a Sunday outing that Helen's skirt is stained, the young girl's life changes forever. At this moment Helen perceives that the "family has suddenly divided itself into two camps, male and female, and so far she has hung on to her ignorance of the rules governing entry into the latter." Helen's entry into the female camp is sealed further when Felix points out to her that he has "a bum and a penis" while she has "only got a bum." Felix's triumphant discovery precipitates Helen's fall from the paradise of childhood equality. From this point on Helen is excluded, an exile from the paradise of gender equality she attempts to retrieve as an adult in the course of the novel.

Helen's relationships with men are fraught with deception and betrayal. One lover, George, accuses her of being too intense and at the same time too indepen-

dent and not needy enough. Another, Steven, sees her as a potential wife and mother but not as an individual separate from these restricting gender roles. Her absent brother, who is ever present in Helen's thoughts and memories, works abroad and communicates little with his twin. Only toward the end of the novel does Helen meet a different kind of man, Robert, who listens to her and embraces the idea of true intimacy in a relationship. Helen's love for Robert, however, is presented less convincingly and compellingly than her longtime friendship with Beth, whom she met in college. The friendship between the two women has had its difficulties, but Roberts describes their encounters as if they were lovers. The novel ends with Helen's realization that her psyche is no longer broken up in disconnected pieces; it has become whole, and within herself she possesses both masculine and feminine qualities. This realization allows her to give herself completely to Robert, to accept his love and give him hers in return, without having to lose Beth's friendship.

Reviews of *The Visitation* praised its depiction of relationships between women, the lyricism of its prose, and its nonlinear structure. Laura Marcus wrote in *TLS: The Times Literary Supplement* (27 September 1985) that the "classic 'feminine' conflicts—between work and love, autonomy and dependence—are explored in detail," and Marion Glastonbury noted in *New Statesman and Society* (22 April 1983) that *The Visitation* deserved "to be approached . . . with meditative care." Glastonbury also emphasized the preeminence of imagery over plot in the novel. Like *A Piece of the Night, The Visitation* includes strong autobiographical elements.

Roberts's first two novels may be read as companion pieces. Both works explore autobiographical issues such as the mother-daughter bond, female friendships, and the difficult path to real intimacy between men and women. Roberts's third novel, however, marks a departure from autobiographical concerns while it reiterates some themes and patterns present in the first two novels.

Clark describes the reaction to Roberts's *The Wild Girl* (1984) as "explosive." The novel reads like a primer of New Age philosophy sprinkled with a touch of Virginia Woolf's discussion of the androgynous mind in *A Room of One's Own* (1929) and a strong dose of feminist ideology. In addition Roberts acknowledges that she drew inspiration from the Nag Hammadi manuscripts, also known as the Gnostic Gospels. *The Wild Girl* conflates the figures of Mary Magdalene and Mary of Bethany and follows the destiny of this composite character. As a child Mary is prone to visions, but they end with the onset of puberty. As a young woman she runs away from home to avoid an imposed marriage and, after a brutal rape, she survives as a pros-

Dust jacket for Roberts's 1984 novel, a feminist version of Jesus' relationships with women
(courtesy of The Lilly Library, Indiana University, Bloomington, Indiana)

titute. Later, when Mary returns home to her sister Martha and brother Lazarus, an enigmatic and attractive man named Jesus enters her life. Mary and Jesus become lovers, and Roberts describes their physical union in mystical terms: "As we drew closer and closer towards each other we entered a new place, a country of heat and sweetness and light different to the ground we had explored together before." Jesus preaches spiritual unity between female and male principles and declares that what matters is a marriage in the soul of male and female elements—or, to use Woolf's terms, the androgynous mind. Jesus' physical relationship with Mary profoundly disturbs his disciple Peter. Mary and Peter later clash over Jesus' true message and the nature of his resurrection; the emerging church embraces Peter's version, and Mary chooses exile with Martha and Jesus' mother, Mary. When their boat reaches the southern coast of France, Mary gives birth to Jesus' daughter. Mary ends her life in solitude, writing her life story to express her new understanding of a fusion

between what she has learned from Jesus' teachings and the knowledge she has acquired through her dreams and visions.

As Kate Fullbrook points out in her review for *British Book News* (January 1985), the novel is a "feminist version of the gospel" with the qualities and flaws such a literary endeavor entails. Its subversive retelling of Jesus' story from a woman's point of view offers female readers an intriguing alternative to the official version of the male-dominated church. Roberts strives to criticize and challenge received notions about religious teachings, and her message of spiritual wholeness through inner androgynous reconciliation is compelling, if not revolutionary or subversive. Yet, at times the novel seems too influenced by the women's movement and therefore dated; certain scenes recall the consciousness-raising sessions that were popular among women in the 1970s. Reviews of the novel were mixed. Some reviewers found the book powerful and moving and described it as a tour de force. Critics such as Emma

Fisher in *TLS* (26 October 1984) praised Roberts's passion and intelligence and commented on her "rich use of symbols and metaphor." Others, such as Fullbrook, found the "sentiments" of the novel "fine, even noble," but concluded that "the fiction itself never comes alive." Fullbrook also called the characters flat and predictable, describing Jesus, for example, as an "archetype for the non-sexist male." Reviewers in general found the concept behind the novel more intriguing than the book itself.

In 1986 Roberts, who had been writing poetry since the early 1970s, collected some of her poems in *The Mirror of the Mother: Selected Poems, 1975–1985*. The collection was reviewed widely and for the most part favorably. In *British Book News* (April 1986) Roberts's friend Michelene Wandor praised the book as "strong and assured," while Michael Horovitz wrote in *Punch* (12 November 1986) that *The Mirror of the Mother* "shows a steady maturation of feelings, thought and technique." Peter Porter noted in *The Observer* (9 March 1986) that Roberts "writes with power and conviction." Roberts's poetry rehearses some of the themes and images she expands and explores in greater depth in her fiction. She has produced two further collections of poetry: *Psyche and the Hurricane* (1990) and *All The Selves I Was* (1995).

Roberts's poetic talents are on display in her fourth book of fiction, *The Book of Mrs. Noah* (1987), at times overwhelming its fragile narrative thread. In fact, the book can hardly be described as a novel in the conventional sense of the word. In her daydream-like exploration of the creative process, particularly as it is experienced by women writers, Roberts uses myths, archetypes, and lush poetic imagery to illustrate her message that women have been silenced in history, religion, and literature. Her heroine, Mrs. Noah, arrives in Venice in the company of her husband, who is busy attending professional conferences. Mrs. Noah, who wishes to have a child while her husband rejects the idea, wanders around the city and lets her imagination run free. She invents five sibyls, all writers in various stages of creative paralysis, and embarks with them on a journey of self-discovery aboard an imaginary ark, or, as Roberts puts it, a "salon des refusées." This assembly of outcasts re-imagines stories from the Bible and history, giving back to the female victims their voices and their stories. As in Roberts's previous novels, religion and its condemnation of female sexuality play a large role in Mrs. Noah's visions. As Helen Birch points out in her review for *New Statesman and Society* (22 May 1987), Roberts employs theories set forth by Julia Kristeva: "The women on the ark re-experience what Kristeva calls the 'semiotic': the pre-Oedipal moment before language." The various tales and myths in the novel at times seem disconnected and unnecessarily obscure. Roberts strives to encapsulate the entire history of female repression by patriarchy, and the novel is at times reduced to didacticism and preaching rather than art. At one point her narrator describes narrative as "simply a grid placed over chaos" and suggests that certain writers favor chaos and "prefer to record, rather than interpret, the interlocking rooms and staircases and galleries of this palace, this web of dream images that shift and turn like the radiant bits of glass in a kaleidoscope." This compelling definition of an alternative form of narrative may well describe certain parts of *The Book of Mrs. Noah,* but the novel as a whole includes more obscure chaos than "radiant bits of glass."

The Book of Mrs. Noah was widely reviewed, with critics agreeing that the novel was challenging and cleverly conceived but ultimately flawed. Birch described the book as Roberts's "most ambitious" novel to date, and suggested that her "refusal of a stable subjectivity allows her to explore psychological as well as literary terrain, and to dissolve the borders between the two." Writing for *The Observer* (24 May 1987), Valentine Cunningham pointed out Roberts's debt to *A Room of One's Own* in a scene during which Mrs. Noah vainly searches for the truth about women in the reading room of the British Museum. Cunningham found the novel as a whole narcissistic and deplored the fact that "Mrs. Noah's shipmates are all bourgeois and hyper-literate and therefore aloof from the problems of working-class women." Anna Vaux in *TLS* (24 July 1987) concurred, writing that despite moments of warmth and wit, "for the most part Roberts's devices are so dry that they fail to inspire warmth, and generate a language so private and confessional that it rarely extends beyond self-indulgence or wishful thinking." Vaux also noted that Roberts's characters seem to have been created to mouth theories rather than tell compelling stories. As these reviews suggest, despite its rich imagery and important message about the necessity of psychic unity for one to create, *The Book of Mrs. Noah* collapses under the weight of its good intentions. Unlike Roberts's later efforts, the novel remains chaotic despite its author's attempt to create a coherent pattern.

Roberts's fifth novel, *In the Red Kitchen* (1990), marks a subtle but definitive departure. The novel is arguably her most ambitious, most fully realized, and most cohesive work of fiction to date; it is also her least autobiographical work. The figure of the mother, in turn reviled and venerated in Roberts's previous novels, is treated more evenly in this work and the four narrative strands of *In the Red Kitchen* connect in intriguing and persuasive ways. The novel weaves together the stories of four women: a nineteenth-century medium, Flora Milk, inspired by the real-life medium Florence

Cook; Minny Preston, the deceitful wife of Flora's upper-class benefactor-turned-seducer; Hattie, a modern-day cook and food writer who lives in the house where Flora once lived and seems to have a psychic connection with her; and a pharaoh's daughter whose full name is never revealed, though clues allow readers to identify her as Hatshepsut, the only woman ever to rule as pharaoh in ancient Egypt. Rather than presenting grown women struggling to understand their complex relationships with their mothers, this novel investigates the father-daughter bond and also explores what it means to become a mother—or to fail to do so. Minny Preston writes long letters to her mother about her grief at the loss of her baby daughter; the readers find out later through Flora's powers of divination that Minny killed her daughter for reasons that are left obscure and unexplored. Flora is seduced by Minny's husband, William, who takes Flora to Paris to meet the real-life doctor Jean-Martin Charcot of La Salpetrière, well known in the nineteenth century for his study of hysteria. William abandons Flora when she becomes pregnant; Flora marries a suitor from her own class and abandons her practice as a medium. In present-day London Hattie falls in love with a kind man and becomes pregnant, only to lose the child to a miscarriage. The only character not directly connected to maternity is Hatshepsut, who denies women the power of creating life: she claims that God gave birth to her through her father and that she has become a man herself through her direct connection to him.

The most successful aspects of this novel are the nineteenth-century sections, with Minny and Flora representing two stereotypes of Victorian femininity, the "Angel of the House" and the "Hysteric." Roberts, however, exposes the hollowness of these images and reveals the secrets beneath the traditional exterior of working-class girl and upper-class wife and mother, particularly the latter's hypocrisy. Minny, the supposed angel of virtue, is in fact an adulterer and infanticide while Flora, the presumed impostor, has real psychic powers that almost destroy her. Employing beautifully crafted prose, Roberts convincingly plunges readers into a shadowy world of boudoirs, candlelit séances, and repressed sexuality. As in *The Book of Mrs. Noah,* Roberts gives voice to silenced women and tells their buried stories.

In the Red Kitchen received mostly favorable reviews. In *TLS* (6 April 1990) Louise Doughty praised Roberts's writing as "descriptive, rich and sensual." Doughty also admired Roberts's assured control over her many narrative strands and her successful tackling of issues as varied as the position of women in Victorian society, spiritualism, and antagonisms between women. She calls the book a "truly post-feminist novel."

Roberts in the late 1990s

Birch concurred in her review for *New Statesman and Society* (6 April 1990), calling Roberts an "exquisite writer" and tracing her development from a self-referential to a more ambitious novelist. Birch wrote that Roberts "conjures a delicately spiced repast" from her diverse ingredients, and that her women characters share across time and space "dreams of a common language and experience of incest, hysteria, guilt, death, birth, illusion." Yet, Janet Barron dismissed *In the Red Kitchen* in *The Listener* (22 March 1990) as the journal of a "woman's descent into madness," in which "the air of insanity is so pervasive that the novel becomes oppressive." Barron, however, did find the Victorian sections of the novel successful and would have preferred to have Roberts focus on "this Gothic fantasy of glimmering gaslights, graveyards and ghosts." Reviewers agreed that *In the Red Kitchen* marked a definite departure in Roberts's career, a change of direction she confirmed with her next novel.

Roberts's sixth novel, *Daughters of the House* (1992), received wide critical acclaim. It was extensively reviewed and highly praised. In addition to winning the prestigious W. H. Smith Literary Award, *Daughters of the House* was shortlisted for the Booker Prize, the highest British literary honor. In this novel Roberts returns to her usual themes and preoccupations—the mother-daughter bond, female sexuality, and the Catholic Church—but with a maturity and emotional distance lacking from her earlier efforts. As in her earlier novels, Roberts withholds easy answers from her readers, but the puzzles she presents are more riveting than in her earlier fiction. Autobiographical elements find their way into the book, particularly the detailed descriptions of French country life, but Roberts keeps her autobiographical impulses in check and balances them artfully with the imaginary strands of her story. The novel opens with the imminent return of Thérèse, a nun who has been cloistered for twenty years, to her childhood home, where her cousin Léonie lives with her husband, Baptiste, and their children. As in previous Roberts novels, the past quickly surfaces and takes over the present narrative, as the two women reminisce about traumatic events in their childhood. Roberts also tells the stories of Antoinette, Thérèse's mother, and Léonie's mother, Madeleine, whose secrets still affect the next generation decades later. Family secrets also mirror the larger secret of the village: during World War II Baptiste's mother, Rose, and her husband, Henri, hid a Jewish family in the house, only to be denounced by a traitor. Henri and the Jewish family were shot and killed by the Germans, and their remains were buried at the site of a pagan altar in the woods. Thérèse presumably returns to Blémont to uncover the truth about the betrayal, but her visit brings back to the surface memories of her childhood rivalry with Léonie and of her mother's secret. She also finally admits to herself that the visions of a blue-robed Virgin that she claimed to have received are false and that Léonie's visions were the real ones.

Daughters of the House weaves together the themes of motherhood, spirituality, sibling rivalry, politics, and betrayal in a seamless tapestry. Roberts's prose is assured and rich, and, for the first time in one of her novels, strong elements of mystery and suspense create a riveting plot to supplement her lyrical imagery. The novel dramatizes the limitations of sisterly affection and female betrayal. Family and village secrets revolve around female sexuality, a recurring theme in Roberts's fiction, but also around issues of loyalty, betrayal, and prejudice. Reviews were again mostly positive. In *TLS* (18 September 1992) Roz Caveney wrote that Gothic and detective novels influenced *Daughters of the House* but that "its direction proves profoundly subversive of those genres." She found the novel tragic and moral but applauded Roberts for not letting such heavy elements overwhelm her story. In *New Statesman and Society* (9 October 1992) Judy Cooke praised Roberts for the richness of her "psychological insights" and claimed that *Daughters of the House* deserved to win the Booker Prize. Patricia Craig disagreed, writing in *The London Review of Books* (3 December 1992) that the novel was "overwrought" and accusing Roberts of equating "obscurity with depth." Unlike Caveney and Cooke, Craig did not find the plot compelling and considered

the Gothic elements unappealing. Despite such criticisms, Roberts's sixth novel established her as an author of importance in England.

Roberts followed the critical success of *Daughters of the House* with a short-story collection, *During Mother's Absence* (1993). The stories bear the strong influence of myths, folktales, religion, and feminism. Some stories read like stylistic exercises, games Roberts plays with readers without giving them all the rules. Others seem to be simplified restatings of themes and preoccupations more fully and compellingly explored in Roberts's longer works of fiction. The most story-like piece in the collection is "God's House," a moving tale of a young girl's coping with the untimely death of her mother. The last story in the collection, "Une Glossaire / A Glossary," is more like a personal essay than a short story, with revelations about Roberts's French relatives, and her attachment to the rhythms, language, and culture of her mother's country. Despite its title, this collection includes many stories dealing with mothers and their impact on children's lives. *During Mother's Absence* received sparse critical attention, but the reviews were positive. Trev Broughton, for example, praised the collection in *TLS* (22 October 1993) as a great introduction to the themes and subjects in Roberts's longer fiction. Broughton compared "Une Glossaire / A Glossary" to Gertrude Stein's *Tender Buttons* (1914) and wittily praised Roberts's passions: "sin, sex and saturated fat," playfully arguing that she was worth reading if only for her "promiscuous use of butter and cream" and appetizing descriptions of meal preparations.

Some of the motifs in the stories found their way into Roberts's seventh novel, *Flesh and Blood* (1994). Like *The Book of Mrs. Noah*, *Flesh and Blood* can hardly be called a novel. Better described as a fantasy, the book is an elaborate exploration of female desire in the form of tales within tales, in the manner of Russian dolls. At the center of the novel is the baby's fierce and insatiable desire for the mother's love and breast, expressed in a semiotic-like language: "bébé born crying wanting you mamabébé." The seemingly disconnected tales within tales are linked by the common thread of desire: desire between man and woman, woman and woman, mother and child, and, above all, the child's desire for its mother, the first and most absolute love in anyone's life according to Roberts. As she wrote in her 1994 essay "Post-Script," "the content . . . shapes the form" of her novels, and "only that form can demonstrate that content." The form of *Flesh and Blood* suggests that desire is endless, ever mutable, and ultimately impossible to fulfill. Roberts's usual preoccupations are again present: the Catholic Church and its repressive treatment of women's sexuality, the loss of the mother as perceived by the child, and the polymorphous quality of female

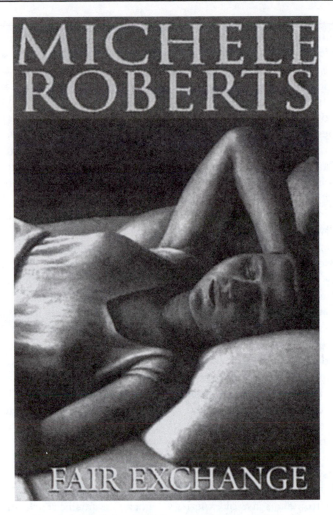

Dust jacket for Roberts's 1999 novel, which includes characters
based on William Wordsworth and Mary Wollstonecraft

sexuality. In one tale an early-modern abbess seduces a nun and encourages "lewd" acts within the confines of her convent. As a result, she is denounced by the patriarchal Church and tried by the Inquisition for heresy. In another, a young convent-bred girl in pre-Revolutionary France is married to an old libertine who makes love to his older mistress in front of his young bride on their wedding day. Yet another story, set in Normandy in 1880, describes the seduction of a young woman by a painter who turns out to be a woman in drag. The painter's seduction does not include intercourse and leaves the young woman panting for more, just as the older libertine tantalizes his young bride without fulfilling her desire. The last two chapters return the reader to the present and to the opening of the novel, giving voice to the mother, who in this case expresses her sorrow after her daughter has run away. In a surprising reversal from her typical preoccupation with the psychological wounds of daughters, Roberts imagines the

trauma of mother-daughter separation from the elder woman's point of view. *Flesh and Blood* is filled with sensual imagery, and vague autobiographical elements are artfully integrated in stories that take place for the most part in a mythical and dateless past.

Roberts received high praise for *Flesh and Blood*. Its language was compared to Joyce's, and its playfulness to Woolf's *Orlando* (1928). Charlotte Moore wrote in *The Spectator* (10 September 1994) that Roberts "constructs her book . . . like a set of Chinese boxes, or Russian dolls" and suggested that the spirit of Angela Carter hovers over *Flesh and Blood*. Moore found the writing sensuous and praised Roberts for her ability to dismiss the usual trappings and conventions of the novel form. Reviewing the novel for *New Statesman and Society* (16 September 1994), Cooke described it as a "wonderful read, if occasionally frustrating" and praised the deliberate construction beneath the seeming discontinuity between the tales. Cooke calls Roberts a "wild original" and saluted the attractive "exuberance" of the book. *Flesh and Blood* further established Roberts as a writer of great imaginative powers and poetic skills.

Impossible Saints (1997) is arguably Robert's most accomplished novel. While it revisits themes already explored in Roberts's earlier fiction—including the lives of nuns and the repression of female sexuality under the patriarchal Church—it does so with maturity, assurance, and creative control. Roberts has reportedly said that she views this novel as a final attempt to come to terms with the influence of Catholicism on her life. In *Impossible Saints* she imagines a different kind of faith, a way of being in which spirituality and sexuality are entwined rather than mutually exclusive. She also criticizes patriarchal religion for its impossible standards for feminine sanctity. Loosely based on the life of St. Teresa of Avila, a sixteenth-century ascetic and mystic, the novel expertly weaves the story of Josephine, an unorthodox nun turned saint despite her forays into fornication with a priest and her heretical views, with clever tales of female would-be saints who have fallen victim to predatory fathers or been destroyed because of their sexuality. Roberts displays irreverent wit in her critique of Church fathers. In one tale Peter is re-imagined as an abusive father; in another a present-day priest finds sensual love in the Israeli desert with his former housekeeper. The tales seem to interrupt the narrative of Josephine's life, but they serve as additional evidence in Roberts's feminist case against organized religion. The novel ends, like several of Roberts's books, with a woman writing as an attempt to make sense of experience: "I invent her. I reassemble her from jigsaw bits and pieces of writing. . . . I make her up. . . . She rises anew in my words, in my story." Like Mary in *The Wild Girl,* Hattie in *In the Red Kitchen,* and other Roberts heroines, Josephine's niece Isabel writes to retrieve the lost voices of women and to understand her place in the world.

Critics were as divided on the merits of *Impossible Saints* as they were about Roberts's previous works. Several reviewers praised *Impossible Saints* for its grace, its idiosyncratic imagery, and its sardonic tone. The reviewer for *Publishers Weekly* (20 April 1998) proclaimed that Roberts "reminds us of the double meaning of passion—both suffering and rapture" in her novel, "which suggests that mortal women might deserve sainthood for seizing the sensory and spiritual world . . . by the throat." Writing for *The New York Times* (20 September 1998), David Guy found the novel fascinating and noted that Roberts's style expertly avoids the dryness of feminist preaching through its intelligence and liveliness. Emma Tristan in *TLS* (25 April 1997) applauded Roberts's parody of Christianity but ultimately decided that the novel as a whole "tries too hard to manipulate

the reader into a conviction of the redemptive power of feminism." Jason Cowley in *The New Statesman* (23 April 1997) described Roberts as a "disarmingly sensuous" writer but deplored her seemingly endless fascination with religion, myths, and fairy tales. He hoped that she would discard "childhood fairy stories and start writing about genuine people in a real society."

Fair Exchange (1999) marks a new departure for Roberts while revisiting earlier themes and preoccupations such as motherhood, the complex bonds between women, and female figures overlooked by patriarchal history. As she does in *The Wild Girl* and *In the Red Kitchen,* Roberts uses well-known historical figures—in this case William Wordsworth and Mary Wollstonecraft, among others. She does so freely and playfully, taking poetic license by changing names and certain biographical facts. In Roberts's creative hands Wordsworth becomes William Saygood and Wollstonecraft, perhaps in a knowing wink to her dignified working-class character in *Maria; or The Wrongs of Woman* (1799), is transformed into Jemima Boote. Roberts is more intrigued by the working-class women who exist on the margins of literary history, however, and the story is told in flashback by the French peasant Louise, who served Saygood's mistress Annette Vallon. The plot hinges around a secret (hinted at by the title) from which Louise must unburden herself before her death. the novel takes place mostly in 1780, when Jemima, after falling in love with poet Paul Gilbert, a character inspired by Wollstonecraft's real-life lover Gilbert Imlay, goes to a small French village to await the birth of her child. There she meets another pregnant woman, Annette, who awaits the return of her lover William Saygood, hoping that he will marry her, The men, however, are more interested in their poetic genius than in their progeny, and the women are left to fend for themselves in the shadow of the French Revolution, which leaves their lives and struggles unchanged.

Critics greeted *Fair Exchange* with mixed reviews. They agreed that Roberts is at her best when describing the French rural landscape she knows well and the details of daily domestic survival, but they suggested that the novel at times slips into didacticism, especially in its treatment of the male characters. In *The Independent* (10 January 1999), Lesley McDowell described Roberts as "expert at the chronicling of daily life, the hard grind of village life," but deplored her choice of Annette Vallon as fictional victim, since she was more survivor than victim in real life: "Annette represents the female sacrifice to men's notions of art and their political ideals, but of all the abandoned women from this period Roberts could have focused on, there are many real victims." McDowell ultimately praised Roberts for making "wonderful play with notions of lineage and history, recalling

Joyce's famous declaration that "paternity is a legal fiction," to show a fond theme, the bond between mothers and daughters." In *TLS* (15 January 1999) Peter Swaab objected to the portrayal of Wordsworth/Saygood, suggesting that a scene of poetry-writing competition between the two new fathers descends "into the style of bad costume drama . . . uncharacteristic of Roberts's precise and spare writing [which] suggests her unwillingness to extend her fictional imagination equally to the men and women." But Swaab also praised Roberts: "The real strength of the book lies in its realization of those parts of life that are stubbornly unaffected by revolution. . . . Roberts brings alive the details of the setting with wonderful density." Swaab concluded that the "scrupulous evocations of village economies . . . are typical of the way [Roberts] brings a world of material constraint vividly to life" and that the novel conveyed its "political conviction" through a "compassionate narrative."

In 1998 Roberts began a four-year term as chairperson of the Literature Advisory Committee to the Literature Department of the British Council, which seeks to promote the work of living writers and the study and teaching of literature. Other members of the committee include prominent literary figures such as Malcolm Bradbury, Penelope Lively, and biographer Hermione Lee. Roberts and painter Jim Latter were married in 1992, and they divide their time between London and France. Roberts's talent is maturing while her literary preoccupations remain patriarchal religion and female sexuality. Roberts's stories and style are too idiosyncratic and personal to appeal to a wide popular audience. She seems likely to continue her journey as a critically praised writer who consistently challenges herself and her readers.

References:

Tracy Clark, "Michèle Roberts," in *Feminist Writers,* edited by Pamela Kester-Shelton (Detroit: St. James Press, 1996), pp. 397–398;

Roger Luckhurst, "'Impossible Mourning' in Toni Morrison's *Beloved* and Michèle Roberts's *Daughters of the House,*" *Critique: Studies in Contemporary Fiction,* 37 (Summer 1996): 243–260;

Susan Rowland, "The Body's Sacred: Romance and Sacrifice in Religious and Jungian Narratives," *Literature and Theology,* 10 (June 1996): 160–170;

Rowland, "Michele Roberts' Virging: Contesting Gender in Fiction, Rewriting Jungian theory, and Christian myth," *Journal of Gender Studies,* 8:1 (March 1999): 35–42;

Sarah Sceats, "Eating the Evidence: Women, Power and Food," in *Image and Power: Women in Fiction in the Twentieth Century,* edited by Sceats and Gail Cunningham (London: Longman, 1996), pp. 117–127;

Cath Stowers, "'No Legitimate Place, No Land, No Fatherland': Communities of Women in the Fiction of Roberts and Winterson," *Critical Survey,* 8 (1996): 69–79;

Rosemary White, "Five Novels as History: The Lives and Times of Michèle Roberts' Prose Fiction," *Bête Noire,* no. 14–15 (1993): 144–157;

White, "Michèle Roberts," *Bête Noire,* no. 14–15 (1993): 125–140.

Nicholas Shakespeare

(3 March 1957 –)

Merritt Moseley
University of North Carolina at Asheville

BOOKS: *The Men Who Would Be King: A Look at Royalty in Exile* (London: Sidgwick & Jackson, 1984);
Londoners (London: Sidgwick & Jackson, 1986);
The Vision of Elena Silves (London: Collins Harvill, 1989; New York: Knopf, 1990);
The High Flyer (London: Harvill, 1993);
The Dancer Upstairs (London: Harvill, 1995; New York: Nan A. Talese, 1997);
Bruce Chatwin (London: Harvill, 1999; New York: Nan A. Talese, 2000).

PRODUCED SCRIPTS: *The Evelyn Waugh Trilogy,* television, Arena, BBC2, 1987;
Cover to Cover, television, BBC2, 1987;
Mario Vargas Llosa, television, Omnibus, BBC1, 1989;
Iquitos, television, Channel 4, 1989;
For the Sake of the Children, television, Granada, 1990;
Return to the Sacred Ice, television, Everyman, BBC1, 1992;
In Search of Bruce Chatwin, television, BBC2, 1999.

OTHER: W. H. Hudson, *Far Away and Long Ago: A Childhood in Argentina,* introduction by Shakespeare (London: Eland, 1982);
Charles Macomb Flandrau, *Viva Mexico: A Traveller's Account of Life in Mexico,* epilogue by Shakespeare (London: Eland, 1990);
Gabriel García Márquez, *Love in the Time of Cholera,* translated by Edith Grossman, introduction by Shakespeare (London: Everyman, 1997; New York: Knopf, 1997);
"Freshwater Fishing," in *The Ex Files: New Stories about Old Flames,* edited by Nicholas Royle (London: Quartet, 1999);
William Faulkner, *The Sound and The Fury,* introduction by Shakespeare (London: Everyman, 2000; New York: Knopf, 2000).

SELECTED PERIODICAL PUBLICATIONS–UNCOLLECTED:
FICTION
"The Statue," *Paris Review,* no. 119 (1991): 52–81.

Nicholas Shakespeare (courtesy of the author)

NONFICTION
"The Art of Backing Into the Limelight," *Sunday Telegraph,* 3 January 1993, p. 11;
"Along the Shining Path," *Daily Telegraph,* 23 September 1995, p. 1.

Nicholas Shakespeare is notable for his versatility. He began his career with two nonfiction books, studies of contemporary history and personality. He then turned to fiction and wrote three well-received novels in five years. During this period of fiction writing, from 1991 through 1998, he worked as well on an authorized biography of travel writer and novelist Bruce Chatwin, which appeared in 1999. Shakespeare has also been an active reviewer, cultural commentator, and literary editor for three different newspapers, and he has written for television. Shakespeare's first novel, *The Vision of Elena Silves* (1989), won a Somerset Maugham Award and a Betty Trask Award; his third, *The Dancer Upstairs* (1995), was commended by the American Library Association; and in 1993 *Granta* magazine named him one of the twenty Best Young British Novelists.

Nicholas William Richmond Shakespeare was born on 3 March 1957 in Worcester, England, the son of John William Richmond Shakespeare and Lalage Ann Mais Shakespeare. John Shakespeare was on the editorial staff of *The Times* (London) at the time of his son's birth and entered the diplomatic service in 1959. Over the next thirty years he filled posts in Paris, Cambodia, Singapore, Brazil, Argentina, Portugal, Peru, and Morocco. Nicholas was being educated in England during much of this time, but he has spoken of working as a cowboy and a peon in Latin American countries where his father was stationed, and it is possible to see the influence of his father's career on the cosmopolitan settings of his novels (none of which is set in the United Kingdom) and his particular interest in Latin America and Portugal. Nicholas Shakespeare was educated at the Dragon School in Oxford and Winchester College and earned an M.A. in English at Magdalene College, Cambridge. From 1980 to 1984 he worked at BBC Television. Then he became, in succession, deputy arts and literary editor for *The Times* (1985–1987), literary editor of *The London Daily News* (1987–1988), literary editor for *The Daily Telegraph* (1988–1991) and in 1989–1991 *The Sunday Telegraph*. In 1989 he was movie critic for *The Illustrated London News,* and in 1991 he left the *Telegraph* organization to work on his fiction and his biography of Chatwin.

Shakespeare's first book is related to a BBC documentary of the same name, for which he conducted the research. *The Men Who Would Be King* (1984) is a rather superficial account of various deposed monarchs, claimants, and pretenders to thrones—including Wallis, Duchess of Windsor, King Carol of Rumania, King Zog of Albania, and other interesting figures. Many of these royals spent time in Portugal, and Shakespeare called on some of them there, including the duke of Bragança, the Portuguese claimant.

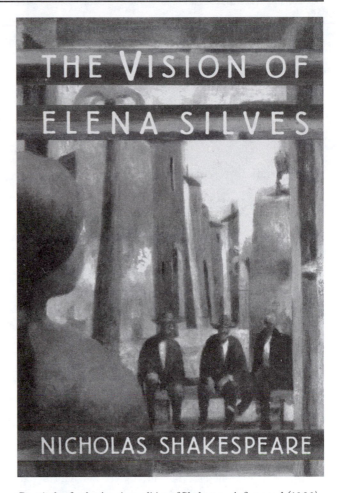

Dust jacket for the American edition of Shakespeare's first novel (1989), which grew out of his unsuccessful attempt to interview Abimael Guzman, leader of the Shining Path guerrillas in Peru

Another work of reportage, *Londoners* (1986) is constructed primarily of interviews with some two hundred Londoners, bringing together obscure people such as taxi drivers and milkmen with well-known Londoners such as author V. S. Pritchett and gangster Reggie Kray. Carol Kennedy, the reviewer for *Books and Bookmen* (November 1986), concluded: "The dominant impression left by Shakespeare's *Londoners* is of a bunch of wily survivors."

In 1989 Shakespeare published his first novel, *The Vision of Elena Silves,* a product of the time he spent in Argentina and Peru during the heyday in Peru of the leftist Shining Path (Luminoso Sendero) guerrillas and their mysterious leader, El Presidente Gonzalo, the *nomme de guerre* of a philosophy professor named Abimael Guzman. The revolution led by Gonzalo left roughly thirty thousand people dead. Both the city and the countryside were full of secret supporters who often declared themselves by using the blood of their victims to paint graffiti on walls. In a 23 September 1995 article for *The Daily Telegraph,* Shakespeare explained, "I wanted to understand the character lurking behind

Nicholas Shakespeare, circa 1990 (photograph © Jerry Bauer;
from the dust jacket for the American edition of
The Vision of Elena Silves)

these actions"; so he set out to interview Guzman, despite the knowledge that forty-two journalists had already been killed for trying to find him. He never succeeded: "I suspected, once the trail petered out, that the grit in my shoe could be extricated only by the device of fiction. Beyond some point, I would have to invent him. It is a curious sensation to be obsessed by somebody one has never met, nor has any likelihood of meeting. I understand it now as the ordinary state of the novelist. For two years, I felt tugged along a narrow path as if I had no say in the matter."

Shakespeare's approach to his novel about Guzman is indirect. It is set in Belén, a little town in the mountains of Peru, where a mysterious man living upstairs in the hotel turns out to be "Presidente Ezequiel," the Guzman figure. The focus of the novel, however, is on Gabriel Rondon Lung, or "Chino," and his beloved Elena Colina Silves. Each has had a vision and is in service to a cause. Chino is a guerrilla, Elena a nun. Their family backgrounds (Elena's family originated in Portugal), their youthful idealism, and the mistreatment they have received from the authorities make up a large part of the book, as do a series of glimpses into the corruption in Peru, especially among the police, the rich, and the Church hierarchy. While such revelations help the reader to understand the motives for revolutionary action, the revolutionaries themselves can

seem almost monstrous in their dedication. At the end of the novel the two lovers are reunited, and, in an ambiguous conclusion, they either escape, or they are killed and thrown in the river. Later they seem to be sighted in the jungle.

The novel seems authoritative on the Peruvian setting and the politics of the Shining Path. Some reviewers were not as impressed by the two central characters, whom Richard Eder called "two lovers separated by two opposite idealisms and rebounding into the arid extremes of each one" (*Los Angeles Times*, 6 December 1990). Eder complained, "Only when they are dead does he manage something of life. The most tangible and believable personages in the novel are Elena's grandparents, who come out of Portugal to settle the back lands; and her parents, who continued their work." In *TLS: The Times Literary Supplement* (27 October 1989), Adam Feinstein said, however, that Shakespeare "laces his writing with geographical and historical detail to provide a convincing picture of a Peru pincered by political and religious extremes." And the novel was well rewarded by literary prizes, winning both the Somerset Maugham Award, which is specifically designed to help writers under age thirty-five enrich their work by spending time abroad, and the Betty Trask Award, which is given for a first "romantic novel or other novel of a traditional rather than experimental nature" written by someone under thirty-five.

Shakespeare was surprised when, in 1992, Guzman was captured by the police and some of Shakespeare's invented details turned out to be accurate. Though Peruvian authorities had declared, and hoped, Guzman was in China, he was, in fact, living in an upstairs room (over a ballet studio rather than in a hotel), and, in confirmation of a detail invented by Shakespeare to explain Guzman's seclusion, he suffered from disfiguring psoriasis.

The High Flyer (1993) is a long, atmospheric, panoramic novel about a failing or failed English diplomat named Thomas Wavery. He is in his fifties and has done well at various diplomatic postings. In fact, he has been thought of as a "high flyer." His next-to-last posting was in Lima, and he anticipated being made ambassador to Portugal for his final assignment. Yet, after the married Wavery falls in love with a woman named Catherine and is seen with her at Heathrow Airport, his marriage and his career are ruined. Instead of Lisbon, he is sent to Abyla, a backwater in Spanish North Africa. His wife divorces him. Before the end of the novel she has remarried, and he is being recalled to London.

Much of the book is about the strange cast of characters who inhabit Abyla. In fact Douglas Hurd (a former Conservative foreign secretary) complained that the main problem with the novel is that the characters in Abyla "are all mad" (*The Daily Telegraph,* 15 May 1993). It is undoubtedly a colorful place. Wavery's main task in Abyla is to prepare for an upcoming visit by the queen, who is coming to mark the opening of a tunnel linking Abyla to Gibraltar—a potent symbol, as all of Abyla looks toward Europe, not least Wavery, who longs for Portugal, Catherine, and all that he has lost. As it happens, the tunneling is suspended (after six years of work) when the workmen find an ancient burial site. The royal visit is canceled, along with Wavery's promised knighthood, becoming one more event in the continuing collapse of everything in Wavery's life. During a big bullfight originally arranged to celebrate the tunnel, everybody, including Wavery, drinks too much, and he sets off to swim to Gibraltar. His thoughts shortly before beginning this impossible attempt indicate his despair: "The drink was working its extravagant effect on Wavery. Magic. Love. They had nothing to do with knowledge, he reminded himself at the bar. They were illusions. Just as his career had been an illusion. Just as Abyla was an illusion. . . ." His disillusionment with the diplomatic service set in earlier as he pondered "The years spent working with great effect on matters of no national importance whatever; the years during which it came to him that his own Service was the enemy, that all of it was about betrayal, that no one cared a damn what the Berbers were thinking."

Hurd, not surprisingly, insisted that "the routines of diplomatic life are not as seedy as Mr Shakespeare describes," and Michael Kerrigan concluded in *TLS* (21 May 1993): "While the novel may venture boldly into the philosophical unknown, its bland, inert protagonist is signally unequal to the existential challenge set him." A more sympathetic interpretation might see Wavery's inertia as a result of the collapse of his life, if not of actual depression. Part of his downfall has been his failure to be bland enough, though he is trying. He is an interesting psychological study of a personality in decline.

In 1995, inspired by the arrest of Abimael Guzman and the discovery that he was actually quite a bit like the fictional character Shakespeare had created in *The Vision of Elena Silves,* Shakespeare returned to his subject in *The Dancer Upstairs.* This novel is a retrospective account of the capture as filtered through the consciousnesses of an English reporter named Dyer and policeman Agustín Rejas, the man who actually captured El Presidente Ezequiel. Dyer's job has been terminated because English readers are no longer interested in Latin America, but he negotiates some paid leave and plans to write a major story, based on getting an interview with Tristan Calderon, a big power in the antiguerrilla struggle. Instead, in Para, Brazil, Dyer meets

Rejas. They are brought together by coincidence. The only two people in a café, they are reading the same book. "'The Most wanted man in the world.' Headlines had debased the phrase, but for twelve years it might have applied to the philosophy professor, Edgardo Vilas—or, as he became known, President Ezequiel. Sitting less than three feet away, so near that Dyer could, if he wanted, touch his sleeve, was the man who had captured the Chairman of the World Revolution."

The remainder of the book, except for a little coda and the occasional linking piece, is Rejas's account of his pursuit of Ezequiel. It turns out that Ezequiel has been living upstairs from the dance studio where Rejas's daughter takes lessons. The police finally catch Ezequiel after they get a videotape on which his face is seen briefly along with a street sign. As Rejas comments, "It would last less than a second. It was no more, really, than a trivial act of clumsiness. But our smallest gesture is never so small as we think. You hand over a camcorder, you rub a crumb from someone's mouth. The consequences are incalculable."

The novel does a good job of conveying the power and mysteriousness of Ezequiel: "This name repeated itself in valley after valley. Whoever this Ezequiel was, he was everywhere. At the same time, he was nowhere. He had published no manifesto. He never sought to explain the actions taken in his name. He scorned the press. He would apparently speak only to the poor." The provocations to revolution are also vivid. Both the army and the rebels are guilty of massacres. City people feel disdain for country people and Indians. Rejas is rural, from the mountains, a speaker of a regional language, and presumably an Indian. He has a lover, Yolanda, a dancer who is interested in folk material from his home region, which she wishes to incorporate into a dance to commemorate some dancers killed by the army. Though he knows of her sympathy with the rebels, Rejas is unaware of her close ties with Ezequiel for most of the novel: "We know so little about people. But about the people we love, we know even less. I was so blind with love for her I hadn't been able to see. . . . there must be thousands of poor bastards who don't know what's going on in their women's minds." In the end the various stories come together. Ezequiel signs a statement of support for the government, and Dyer decides to stay in Peru and write a book about the Indians.

The Dancer Upstairs was well received; blurbs on the cover compare Shakespeare to Graham Greene and Joseph Conrad, and Peruvian novelist Mario Vargas Llosa wrote, "I cannot think of any other contemporary foreign writer who has ventured with such curiosity and such sure instincts into the labyrinth of the politics of my country and acquitted himself so well." Review-

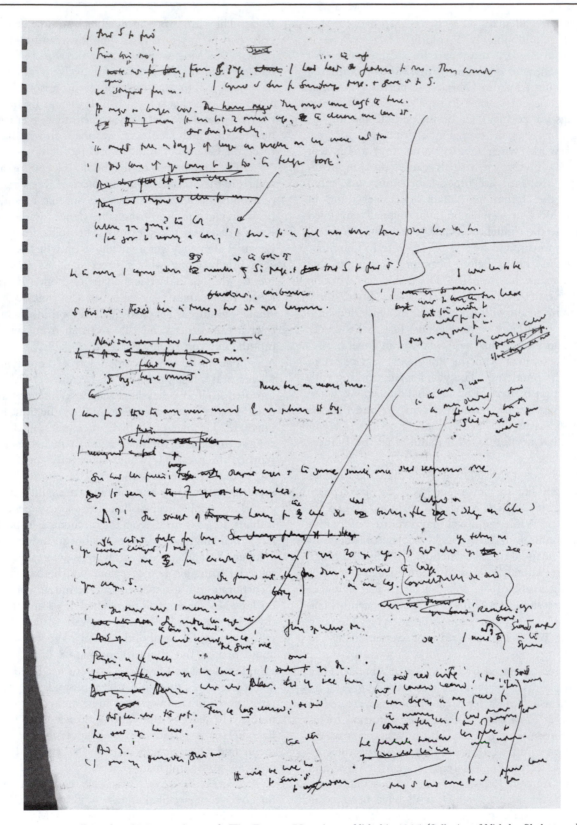

Pages from Shakespeare's notes for The Dancer Upstairs, *published in 1995 (Collection of Nicholas Shakespeare)*

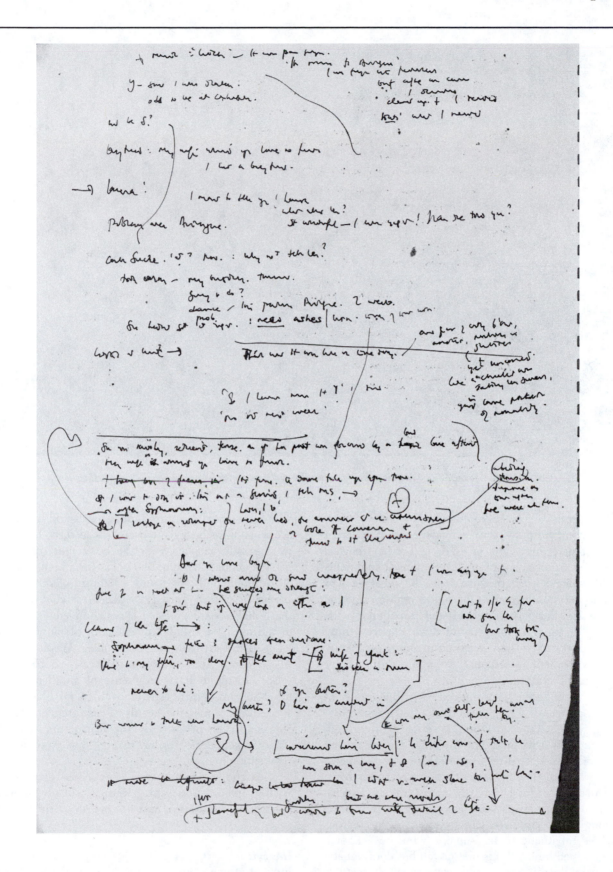

Dust jacket for Shakespeare's 1999 biography of the novelist and travel writer who helped him with his first novel

ing the novel for *The Independent* (11 November 1995), Colin Greenland pointed to coincidences and apparent miracles, detecting signs of Latin American magical realism but adding that when "Dyer himself comments on the coincidences, they cease to be fantastic and dwindle into contingency. Of magical realism, nothing remains but the pellucid, attenuated romanticism: the sense, perhaps, of a spirit, wounded and elusive, whose exact features have been rendered incommunicable by atrocities; something essential, to be pursued by other means than literalism."

In 1999 Shakespeare published his biography of Bruce Chatwin, a writer who died of AIDS in 1989, having given out the story that he was suffering from a rare fungal disorder picked up in China. During the ten years since his death there had been considerable speculation over whether he was not a minor writer overrated because of his charm, his many friends, and his ability to make himself seem fascinating. *Bruce Chatwin* is a long, densely researched biography. Shakespeare is clearly sympathetic to his subject (who, he acknowledges, helped him with his first novel) but does not shy away from the difficult, in some cases repellent, features of Chatwin's life: his mistreatment of his long-suffering wife; his dishonesty and willingness to betray people

who had helped him; his snobbishness and misleading accounts of his background and social class. Reviewers were mostly satisfied with the book, but some complained about its length: 550 pages for a man who died at forty-nine and wrote only a handful of short books. In *The Observer* (4 April 1999) Robert McCrum judged that "Shakespeare's *Chatwin* is not completely successful in the most basic biographical duty of pinning down what so-and-so was not actually like." Writing for *The Independent* (3 April 1999) Sara Wheeler concluded, "It is so difficult to have any sense of another person's inner life, but in this vastly enjoyable book Shakespeare successfully shines the beams of his torch onto a psychic landscape peopled by the fearful monsters that Chatwin kept mostly at bay by continually moving and reinventing himself."

Nicholas Shakespeare is expected to return to writing fiction, and such a return will undoubtedly solidify his reputation as a noteworthy British novelist.

Interview:

Judy Stoffman, "From Cambridge to Peru's Politics: British Novelist's Obsession Led to Two Gripping Books," *Toronto Star,* 28 October 1996, p. E5.

Tom Sharpe

(30 March 1928 –   )

Merritt Moseley
University of North Carolina at Asheville

and

Simon Edwards
Roehampton Institute

See also the Sharpe entry in *DLB 14: British Novelists Since 1960.*

BOOKS: *Riotous Assembly* (London: Secker & Warburg, 1971; New York: Viking, 1971);

Indecent Exposure (London: Secker & Warburg, 1973; New York: Atlantic Monthly Press, 1987);

Porterhouse Blue (London: Secker & Warburg, 1974; Englewood Cliffs, N.J.: Prentice-Hall, 1974);

Blott on the Landscape (London: Secker & Warburg, 1975; New York: Vintage, 1984);

Wilt (London: Secker & Warburg, 1976; New York: Vintage, 1984);

The Great Pursuit (London: Secker & Warburg, 1977; New York: Harper & Row, 1977);

The Throwback (London: Secker & Warburg, 1978; New York: Vintage, 1984);

The Wilt Alternative (London: Secker & Warburg, 1979; New York: St. Martin's Press, 1979);

Ancestral Vices (London: Secker & Warburg, 1980);

Vintage Stuff (London: Secker & Warburg, 1982; New York: Vintage, 1984);

Wilt on High (London: Secker & Warburg, 1984; New York: Random House, 1984);

Grantchester Grind: A Porterhouse Chronicle (London: Deutsch / Secker & Warburg, 1995);

The Midden (London: Deutsch, 1996; Woodstock, N.Y.: Overlook Press, 1997).

Collections: *Riotous Assembly; Wilt* (London: Chancellor, 1984);

Indecent Exposure, The Great Pursuit, Porterhouse Blue, Blott on the Landscape (London: Secker & Warburg, 1986);

The Throwback, Ancestral Vices, Vintage Stuff (London: Pan / Secker & Warburg, 1994);

Tom Sharpe, circa 1984 (photograph © Jerry Bauer; from the dust jacket for the American edition of Wilt on High*)*

Wilt, and Wilt on High (London: Pan / Secker & Warburg, 1994);

Tom Sharpe Treble: Blott on the Landscape, The Wilt Alternative, The Great Pursuit (London: Pan, 1995);

257

Wilt in Triplicate: Wilt, The Wilt Alternative, Wilt on High (London: Secker & Warburg, 1996).

PLAY PRODUCTION: *The South African,* London, Questors Theatre, 1961.

PRODUCED SCRIPT: *She Fell Among Thieves,* television, adapted by Sharpe from Dornford Yates's novel, BBC, 1977.

Tom Sharpe's fertility of invention, comic brio, and savage satire have made him a popular writer whose books sell in large numbers in Great Britain and, since the middle 1980s, in the United States. After ten years working as a teacher and a photographer in South Africa (which gave him the material for his first two novels) and nearly another decade teaching in England, he began writing fiction at the age of forty-one. His outrageously farcical novels share cultural and intellectual concerns with those of earlier comic novelists such as Thomas Love Peacock and Aldous Huxley, and at his best Sharpe may be compared with the great Augustan satirists, such as Jonathan Swift and Alexander Pope; yet, his fiction can also decline into the repetitively mechanical. While reviewers generally praised his early novels, many later criticized his lack of sympathy for his characters, his repeated use of excremental humor and violent fantasy, and his lack of a broad perspective on human behavior. In a 1989 interview with Jean W. Ross, Sharpe suggested that the failure of critics to appreciate his work resulted from the difference between his knowledge of life and that of literary critics: "My experiences have been in a world so far removed from theirs that I seem to be fantasizing. People in British universities may read about torture in the papers, but it's still abstract and theoretical."

Thomas Ridley Sharpe was born on 30 March 1928 in the Holloway section of London, to George Coverdale Sharpe, a fifty-eight-year-old Unitarian minister, and his wife, Grace Egerton Sharpe. He spent his early childhood in Croydon and was then sent to boarding schools. After running away from the Bloxham School in Buckinghamshire, he attended Lancing College. A onetime socialist, George Sharpe had become a fascist and passed on his Nazi sympathies to his son, but when he learned about the German death camps, Tom Sharpe discarded his father's political views. He now describes his politics as "Anti-totalitarian and anti-ideological" and his religion as "Unitarian agnostic."

After serving aboard HMS *The Duke of York* during two years of national service in the Royal Marines (1946–1948), Sharpe entered Pembroke College, Cambridge, earning a degree in history and social anthropology in 1951. Through family connections he found a job with a finance corporation in South Africa, but he quit that job after a few months to become a welfare worker with the Department of Non European Affairs in the black township of Soweto, outside Johannesburg. In 1952 he took a teaching job at a school for white children in Pietermaritzburg, Province of Natal. He left teaching in 1956 and opened a photographic studio in Pietermaritzburg. Throughout this period Sharpe was writing political plays. When *The South African,* the only one of his nine plays to be staged, was produced at the Questors Theatre in London in 1961, its message angered the South African government. The Special Branch of the South African police arrested Sharpe, who was imprisoned and then deported to England.

After teaching for a few months at Aylesbury Secondary Modern School, Sharpe returned to Pembroke College for teacher training. In 1963 he became a lecturer in history and liberal studies at the Cambridge College of Arts and Technology. His eight years there are the background for his first campus novel, *Wilt* (1976). Comparing himself to the title character, Henry Wilt, a lecturer in liberal studies at the Fenland College of Arts and Technology, Sharpe told Ross, "His teaching routine and his views on it were exactly mine." After the success of his first novel, *Riotous Assembly,* in 1971, Sharpe left teaching to become a full-time writer. He married Nancy Anne Looper, an American, on 6 August 1969. They have three daughters and live in Cambridge.

Sharpe's first two novels, *Riotous Assembly* and *Indecent Exposure* (1973), are set in the fictional South African town of Piemburg, an English enclave within Afrikaans territory that is clearly modeled on Pietermaritzburg, and some characters appear in both books. The novels may be interpreted as satiric commentaries on a remark made in *Riotous Assembly* about a mental hospital where the inmates perform a masque reenacting the history of South Africa: "There didn't seem to be any significant difference between life in the mental hospital and life in South Africa as a whole. Black madmen did all the work, while white lunatics lounged about imagining they were God." Both novels target contemporary psychiatry and other aspects of modern medicine, such as heart-transplant surgery, which was first performed in South Africa. The novels also express Sharpe's view that sexual deviation is distorted human energy, while revealing his indebtedness to modern psychological theories about the relationships of sexuality to political and social power, both of which he portrays as distorted in South African institutions. Both novels focus more on tensions between Boer and English settlers rather than those between

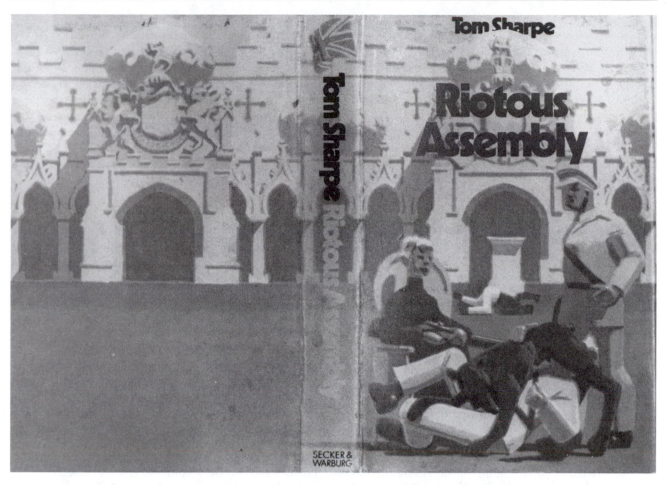

Dust jacket for Sharpe's first novel (1971), set in a town that resembles Pietermaritzburg, South Africa, where Sharpe lived from 1952 until 1961 (courtesy of The Lilly Library, Indiana University, Bloomington, Indiana)

blacks and whites, but Sharpe does illustrate how Boer-English conflicts influence black-white tensions.

In *Riotous Assembly* the Boer-dominated police force investigates the murder of a black cook at Jacaranda Park, the great house of the Hazelstones family, and uncovers violations of the Apartheid laws forbidding interracial sexual relations. The elderly Miss Hazelstones, daughter of the insane general Sir Theophilus, has been having an affair with the cook and claims responsibility for his murder, but in reality her drunken brother, Jonathan, Bishop of Barotseland, seems to have buggered the cook to death.

The Boer policemen are generally repulsive. Konstabel Els, in particular, is a brutal thug whose pleasure in killing and torture disproves the hateful racial theories that his superiors consider the basis for civilization. In the climactic scene Els, who has established himself in an impregnable pillbox at Jacaranda Park with an amazing array of weapons, tries to eliminate singlehandedly the whole invading local police force and army. The battle is depicted dispassionately, as in this descrip-

tion of an armored car that Els has blasted to pieces: "its occupants trickled gently but persistently through a hundred holes drilled in its side." Such treatment pointedly reverses whites' inclination to regard black Africans as merely objects, creating a sort of black humor that satirizes the insanity of South African Apartheid. Another strain of black humor is also apparent in the tortured religious speculations of the bishop of Barotseland, who is eventually sentenced to death. Konstabel Els is the hangman, and his superior, the Anglophile Kommandant van Heerden, negotiates for a transplant of the bishop's heart, hoping to acquire some of the English characteristics he so admires.

Indecent Exposure extends the rivalry between van Heerden and another character from the *Riotous Assembly,* Luitenant Verkramp, who considers all Englishmen possible communist subversives. In *Indecent Exposure* Verkramp brings in Dr. von Blimenstein to conduct aversion therapy on the Piemburg policemen, who regularly break the law against black-white sexual relations. While Dr. von Blimenstein has the local policemen's penises wired to electric-shock machines and is showing them photographs of naked black women, Verkramp arranges for twelve *agents provocateurs* to create a series of outrages in Piemburg—including the release of a herd of exploding ostriches—to frame English residents and justify mass arrests. Verkramp's excesses are possible because van Heerden is away living out his Anglophilic fantasies of upper-class British life with a group of English expatriates at a country house called White Ladies. The two plots come together when the local police, who have completed Dr. von Blimenstein's therapy, attack the country house because they have been led to believe that the people at White Ladies are the perpetrators of the recent sabotage. Konstabel Els, who has been undercover as a servant, ends up chasing van Heerden, who is masquerading in women's clothing, in a brutal parody of an English fox hunt. *Indecent Exposure* includes many such wild reversals, particularly of sexual roles and identities. Without being overtly moral, Sharpe's questioning of the basic nature of reality saves the book from merely mechanical humor. Furthermore, his politically weighted critique of South Africa in his first two novels suggests a political radicalism that is challenged in his next novel, *Porterhouse Blue* (1974).

Sharpe's third novel is set at Porterhouse, a Cambridge college where the faculty is resisting the attempts at modernization initiated by a new master, Sir Godber Evans, a retired Labour cabinet minister. Among the resisters are the aristocratic Sir Cathcart D'eath, who stands for much of the conservative inertia prevalent in English social and political life, and the "populist" hero of the novel, Skullion the college porter. By the end of the novel, Sir Godber has died—after having been educated about the limitations of his crudely Benthamite liberalism—and Skullion, who has suffered a stroke and been confined to a wheelchair, becomes the new master of the college, which may be seen as a microcosm of contemporary England. Skullion's opposition to change has made him a national celebrity. Although he started out as a servile grotesque, he has developed a self-critical moral intelligence.

The novel suggests that men like Skullion, with their admirable though corruptible resourcefulness, are a central part of the power struggles throughout English history. Yet, such men are mostly ignored by the ruling class. One of Skullion's last observations in the novel is the thought that "there were no just rewards in life, only insane inversions of the scheme of things in which he had trusted." This note of illusion and betrayal is characteristic of Sharpe's later work. Skullion's conservative "populism" defies conventional political pigeonholing, a refusal suggested by the side of the body paralyzed by Skullion's stroke: "There were no contradictions now between right and wrong, master and servant, only a strange inability to move his left side."

Sharpe's next novel, *Blott on the Landscape* (1975), continues to examine progress and populism, this time in the context of politicians, bureaucrats, and property development. Skullion's role is assigned to Blott, a German alien who was a prisoner of war in England during World War II and is now a gardener for Lady Maud Lynchwood. The Lynchwoods' marriage suggests a division of modern venture capitalism versus traditional resistence to change within the British aristocracy. Lady Maud's impotent husband, Sir Giles, wants to be free of her while circumventing a complex reversionary clause in their marriage settlement that will deprive him of his share of her family estate, Handyman Hall, in case of divorce. Through his political and business connections, he arranges to have a motorway routed through the estate, which will bring him handsome financial compensation for the condemned land. The devious Lady Maud, who also wants a divorce—but for other reasons—leads the local campaign against the motorway. Like Sir Godber in *Porterhouse Blue,* the bureaucrat Dundridge, who is in charge of planning the motorway, initially represents impersonal progress. His enervated meliorism stands in sharp contrast to the Lynchwoods' two versions of the ruthless "laws of nature." Sir Giles's "dog-eat-dog" justification of his capitalist enterprise echoes his masochistic sexuality, while Lady Maud invokes a Social Darwinian "law of the jungle" in her battle with the developers. She is assisted by the brooding gardener Blott, whose violent resistance to change is based in popular English histories, including the works of Sir Arthur Bryant. Sir Giles is eaten by lions in the safari theme park Lady Maud is establishing on the estate, while Dundridge is forced to conduct the motorway construction as a military campaign. Blott successfully defends the estate during a prolonged siege and eventually marries Lady Maud. Their union demonstrates the way in which the English ruling class has managed to perpetuate itself by encorporating disparate elements.

In previous generations ruthless nineteenth-century industrialists had already been grafted to Lady Maud's family tree of decayed landed aristocrats, and her marriage to Sir Giles was clearly an attempt to add a new component of the social and political power base: the property developer. Blott is a more disturbing character than Skullion, in part because "not knowing who he was" he has "tried out other people's personalities." As a defense of what it means to be English, the novel can be alarming, particularly with the emergence of something that resembles genetic typing as an explana-

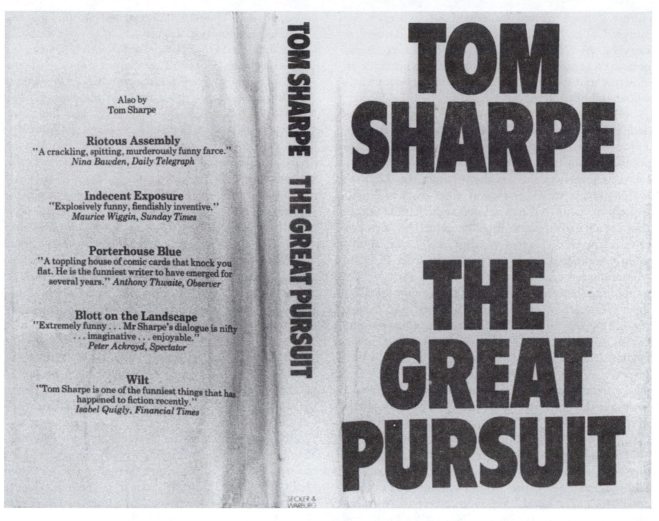

Also by
Tom Sharpe

Riotous Assembly
"A crackling, spitting, murderously funny farce."
Nina Bawden, Daily Telegraph

Indecent Exposure
"Explosively funny, fiendishly inventive."
Maurice Wiggin, Sunday Times

Porterhouse Blue
"A toppling house of comic cards that knock you
flat. He is the funniest writer to have emerged for
several years." *Anthony Thwaite, Observer*

Blott on the Landscape
"Extremely funny . . . Mr Sharpe's dialogue is nifty
. . . imaginative . . . enjoyable."
Peter Ackroyd, Spectator

Wilt
"Tom Sharpe is one of the funniest things that has
happened to fiction recently."
Isabel Quigly, Financial Times

TOM SHARPE
THE GREAT PURSUIT

SECKER &
WARBURG

TOM
SHARPE

THE
GREAT
PURSUIT

Dust jacket for Sharpe's 1977 novel, a response to F. R. Leavis's dictum that novels should be morally uplifting

tion of character. For example, Lady Maud's remark that "evidently the blood of her ancestors ran in her veins" does not seem wholly ironic.

Sharpe's next protagonist, the title character of *Wilt,* is a far more self-consciously intellectual version of the "populist" spirit than Blott. A lecturer at a technical college, Henry Wilt is opposed to the trendy defeatism of his colleagues and oppressed by the bored industrial apprentices in his literature class. His old-fashioned cynicism seems more like that of the "angry" novelists of the 1950s than the views of his contemporaries. After an inflatable life-sized plastic doll is mistaken for the corpse of Wilt's vulgar, sexually voracious, and overweight wife, Eva, Wilt is arrested for her murder. The scandal threatens the future of Fenland College, creating scenes of intellectual pretentiousness and administrative panic. The most compelling part of the novel is Inspector Flint's attempt to force Wilt to confess to a murder that has not been committed.

Wilt's resilience during confinement belies his name. He begins to realize that the world is perverse, silly, and random—a knowledge that liberates him from his doubts about reality and justice. His confinement also gives him a new rapport with the working-class butchers' apprentices to whom he teaches a literature course jokingly known as "Meat One." Having developed a respect for his students' instinctive knowledge of human limits, he decides to teach them practical skills rather than the literature on which the "culture of the word" places too high a value.

The Great Pursuit (1977) confronts directly the questions of literary value and cultural significance that are raised in *Wilt,* treating explicitly the issue of the writer's responsibility. The title alludes to F. R. Leavis's *The Great Tradition* (1948) and *The Common Pursuit* (1952), critical books demanding that novels present moral values uplifting to society. *The Great Pursuit* attacks this requirement in the name of a literary culture "where people write without hypocrisy for money." Yet, this position is as indefensible as Leavis's. As *The Great Pursuit* depicts the economic pressures at work in book publishing, it becomes an indictment of the structure of capitalist production as a whole and of contemporary culture.

In *The Great Pursuit* an aging Cambridge academic, Dr. Louth, is the author of *Pause O Men for the Virgin,* an appalling work of pulp fiction, which she has published anonymously because it directly violates the Leavisite principles she has always espoused. After the foul-mouthed American tycoon who has bought the paperback rights to the novel demands that the author conduct a personal sales campaign in the United States, Frensic, the literary agent to whom Dr. Louth anonymously submitted her book, persuades Peter Piper, to whom she has served as mentor, to act the part. An unpublished novelist of incapacitating literary integrity, Piper is seduced by the tycoon's wife, Baby, and the two run off together to the Deep South, where they end up in an isolated town significantly named Bibliopolis. Charles Dickens's novel, *Martin Chuzzlewit* (1844), which reflects his American tour, echoes throughout the pages of *The Great Pursuit.* For example, the swampy Bibliopolis recalls the new town of Eden in which the younger Martin Chuzzlewit is "born again," just as Baby has become a born-again Christian in Bibliopolis.

In Bibliopolis, Piper opens a School of Logosophy, which defines the world as Logos (The Word) and espouses the tenets expressed in Dr. Louth's most influential work, *The Moral Novel.* Frensic eventually discovers the true author of *Pause O Men for the Virgin,* and Baby terrifies him into publishing under his own name Piper's dreadful novel, *Search For A Lost Childhood,* which Piper has spent a lifetime rewriting. Although the novel has previously been considered unpublishable and probably unreadable, when it finally appears as Frensic's work, it meets universal acclaim.

Disillusioned by his discovery of Dr. Louth's authorship of the pulp novel, Piper thinks, "The age of the great novel was over. It remained only to commemorate it in manuscript. And so while Baby preached the need to imitate Christ, Piper too returned to traditional virtues in everything." Using quill pens, "the original tools of his craft," Piper begins to write: "'My father's family name being Pirrip, and my Christian name Philip, my infant tongue could make of both names nothing longer or more explicit than Piper. . . .' He stopped. That wasn't right. It should have been Pip. But after a moment's hesitation he dipped his quill again and continued." That is, he is rewriting Dickens's *Great Expectations* (1860–1861).

Leavis and his disciples, in fact, celebrate this sort of reversion to tradition. Yet, even though it confronts postmodernist questions of origins, attribution, and meaning in literature and culture, *The Great Pursuit* is closer to a Leavisite text than to the work of a postmodern writer such as Jorge Luis Borges. Sharpe's "populism" may even have Leavisite roots. *The Great Pursuit* fulfills the Augustan criteria for mordant wit and moral purpose. As Sharpe's finest achievement, the novel bears comparison with Evelyn Waugh's *A Handful of Dust* (1934)—to which Sharpe alludes in the closing pages of *The Great Pursuit*—as well as with the satires of Orwell and Swift.

In *The Throwback* (1978) Sharpe returned to the familiar materials and devices of the novels that precede *The Great Pursuit.* Sharpe has said that the extraordinary rhetoric of Old Flawse, one of the central characters in *The Throwback,* has its roots in his father's speech habits, and in an autobiographical reading, the novel may be considered an attempt to exorcize George Sharpe's fascist ideology, with the elderly character's name suggesting "old flaws." The latter part of the book is haunted by the monstrous old man's thundering voice, spouting a vulgarized mixture of nineteenth-century ideologies, but that voice comes from a tape recording played by Old Flawse's mentally ill grandson, Lockhart, after his grandfather's death. The setting of Sharpe's novel, a vast feudal estate in contemporary Northumberland, and some of its characters owe a debt to Sir Walter Scott, whose first biographer was his son-in-law John Gibson Lockhart. Like Scott's fiction, Sharpe's novel is both serious and popular, and in its mixture of sentimentality and the overtly shocking, the novel may also be linked to contemporary imitations of Scott such as Catherine Cookson's popular Mallen trilogy (1973–1974) and parodies such as Stella Gibbons's *Cold Comfort Farm* (1932). While Sharpe says he admires Scott and Gibbons, he says he writes from experience. What he means by *experience,* however, is problematic. Sharpe admits that writing the central sequence of the novel was his most tedious exercise in ingenious plotting.

The illegitimate son of Old Flawse's daughter, Lockhart has been brought up by his grandfather in total sexual innocence and with a system of morality that Old Flawse has based on the hodgepodge of philosophical works he has read. Justifying the use of violence, this morality also lies beneath his hostility toward the twentieth century. Old Flawse is afraid that he might have fathered Lockhart during an act of drunken incest, and Lockhart's discovery at the end of the novel that he is not Old Flawse's son is part of the process of exorcism. The novel ends with another of Sharpe's crazy and violent sieges. Earlier Lockhart has evicted the tenants of his wife's estate in the London suburbs so that he can sell it and use the profits to restore Flawse Hall, his family's ancestral home in Northumberland.

Now as Flawse Hall is surrounded by tax inspectors, who Lockhart fears are seeking payment of taxes due on the sale of his wife's estate, Lockhart frightens off the tax men with the aid of amplified tape recordings of military maneuvers, while the tape-recorded voice of his grandfather resounds through the house, driving Old Flawse's widow (actually the mother of Lockhart's wife) to flight and violent death.

The moral and philosophical dimensions of this novel are imaginatively represented in a comic scene when a group of retainers and clients of the Flawse estate gather together to socialize, but Sharpe fails to integrate its morality into the format of the novel. Other aspects of the novel are less attractive, especially the depictions of Old Flawse's violent sexual appetites and the coy innocence of Lockhart's wife throughout their unconsummated marriage.

The Wilt Alternative (1979), another siege novel, may be seen as an attempt to achieve broad significance and to confront contemporary political issues, as in Sharpe's South African novels. Henry Wilt has become a department head at Fenland College, has been tentatively reconciled with Eva, and is now the father of quadruplet daughters, when he arrives home to find his house occupied by international terrorists and surrounded by army personnel and local police. While trying to get his children out, Wilt is taken hostage as well, but he succeeds in confusing the telephone negotiations between terrorists and authorities, who are willing to sacrifice the Wilts to get the terrorists, and rescues his children during the resulting chaos. As in *Wilt,* the impractical Henry Wilt improvises a practical achievement, a result that once again illustrates Sharpe's mistrust of authority and his hostility toward theoretical knowledge. Thus, a left-wing colleague of Wilt's is lumped into the same category as the terrorists, who are jet-set playboys led by a beautiful and intelligent German girl: they are all "doctrinaire shits." This phrase is part of a developing scatological vein in Sharpe's humor, an Augustan element that is rare in his earlier novels. In *The Wilt Alternative* this vein includes a running joke about organic waste disposal and the recycling of human feces, and it reappears in Sharpe's next novel, *Ancestral Vices* (1980), in the representation of Victorian plumbing.

The Wilt Alternative appears to endorse a flight from ideology and "all the -isms," but such an attitude can turn into the dangerous sort of social and sexual anti-intellectualism that the novel purports to oppose. As an expert satirist, Sharpe represents this paradox through his presentation of Henry Wilt.

Ancestral Vices is another excursion into the excesses of the English upper classes. The Petrefact family of the Vale of Bushampton resemble Sharpe's

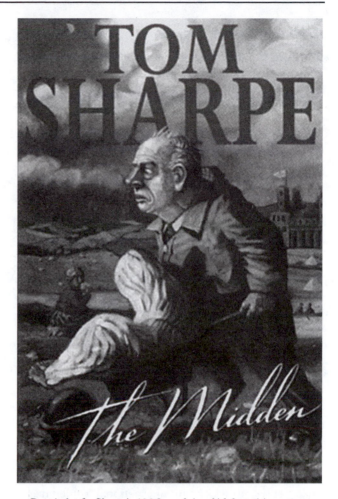

Dust jacket for Sharpe's 1996 novel, in which he satirizes corrupt policemen, overzealous social workers, the decaying aristocracy, and the "political catechism of Thatcherism"

earlier representations of their class: they are in conflict with the modern world, which in this novel is mainly represented by a left-wing American professor, Walden Yapp, who teaches demotic historiography at Kloone University and has been hired to write a history of the Petrefacts. They have a guilty secret that they attempt to conceal from Yapp, providing much of the comedy in the novel.

Yapp renders all experience in social-scientific jargon; the Petrefacts are aristocratic grotesques. The dual satire on left-wing trendy academic nonsense and right-wing aristocratic privilege is reminiscent of the two-pronged attack of *Porterhouse Blue.* Reviewers of *Ancestral Vices*—some of them perhaps believing that satire ought still to ground itself in some sort of moral standards against which grotesque deviations can be gauged—had a mixed response. Writing in *The New Statesman* (7 November 1980), Nicholas Shrimpton called Sharpe's satire "astonishingly, at times almost worryingly, even-handed. . . . Occasionally he comes close to direct contradiction. . . . The truth is that everything is grist to Mr Sharpe's comic mill and he doesn't believe in thinking too hard about his raw material before he tosses it in." Writing in *The Spectator* (20 December 1980), Mary Hope was more favorably impressed: "The moral is that the world is a random place, a constant struggle between conflicting and dangerous idiocies, opposing certainties which are equally blind to the vagaries and unpredictabilities of the real world."

In *Vintage Stuff* (1982) Sharpe returned to satirizing the excesses of education, as well as those of the wealthy and privileged. The "hero" of this novel is Peregrine Roderick Clyde-Brown, a stupid boy who takes everything literally. Having been sent to a worthless public school called Groxbourne, he comes under the sway of a master called Glodstone, a romantic dreamer of the fascist variety, who has fantasies of Bulldog Drummond–type adventures. As a result of a rivalry between Glodstone and another master, Slymne, Glodstone and Peregrine are dispatched on a fraudulent mission to rescue "the Countess," the mother of another pupil and actually a low-born Englishwoman with a chateau in France. Eventually, Slymne and another master, Major Fetherington, are sent to find Peregrine; they are captured and vigorously interrogated by French security forces, as a result of which Slymne apparently loses his mind. Meanwhile, the assault on the chateau—which is actually a sort of hotel and conference center in which an international conference is under way—leads to humiliation for Glodstone and triumph for Peregrine. The two of them escape with the Countess and some gold bars.

Several of Sharpe's favorite themes recur in *Vintage Stuff,* including suspicion of most educational theory and practice. Peregrine's education at Groxbourne is worthless; he passes his O-levels by memorizing the answers, which are supplied to him by a dishonest crammer. Aristocracy, real or imitation, and ignorant worshippers of it are satirized. Husbands and wives generally despise one another, and the humor is often coarse and violent. In one disturbing joke Peregrine confuses crampons (or climbing irons) and tampons, and his assault on the chateau results in his killing the American delegate and shooting off the end of the Russian delegate's penis. Such developments encouraged Stanley Reynolds, who reviewed the novel in *Punch* (3 November 1982), to call Sharpe "Britain's leading practitioner of black humour."

Sharpe's next novel, *Wilt on High* (1984), revisits Henry Wilt and the Fenland College of Art and Technology. In this novel Wilt becomes involved in a typically fantastic plot and is persecuted by the Cambridgeshire police, American security agents, his wife (unsatisfied with his sexual prowess), and his quadruplet daughters, who have become repellent teenagers—knowing, sexually curious, scheming, and even criminal. Wilt has been tutoring an imprisoned criminal, and through this criminal connection, he becomes a suspect in the investigation of a drug ring. The police plant transmitters in Wilt's car; and when he goes to a nearby U.S. Air Force base, where he is also teaching a group of students, the American security force finds the transmitters and suspects him of spying. As usual with Sharpe, the police are bumblers who are outwitted and exasperated by Wilt. In the end the Americans have to give him £250,000 as compensation for his mistreatment; he uses the money to buy books for Fenland College, a donation that does not please the principal, who frowns on Wilt's "attempt to change the curriculum to more practical matters, like how to fill in Income Tax forms, claim Unemployment Benefit, and generally move with some confidence through the maze of bureaucratic complications that had turned the Welfare State into a piggy-bank for the middle classes and literate skivers, and an incomprehensible and humiliating nightmare of forms and jargon for the provident poor."

Marital and familial relations also come in for harsh treatment. For example, after Eva gives Wilt an overdose of an aphrodisiac, he is disabled by an incorrigible erection and has to wear a cricket box to avoid embarrassment. Lord Lynchknowle, father of a student who has taken a drug overdose, continues dining with his friends even after receiving the news that his daughter has died, and reflects that his wife "was going to kick up the devil of a fuss about it afterwards. He sat on over the Stilton in a pensive mood wishing to God he'd never married her"—a classic Sharpe passage. At the end of the novel Wilt, whose primary program is simply to assert himself and "be Wilt, whatever that was," indulges in some uncharacteristically apocalyptic reflections based on the notion that the U.S. airbase, in its "banal enormity," is similar to a concentration camp and makes a final, rather wrenched, connection back to the idea that "it was all insane, childish and bestial. But above all it was banal. As banal as the Tech and Dr. Mayfield's empire-building and the Principal's concern to keep his own job and avoid unfavourable publicity, never mind what the staff thought or the students would have preferred to learn." The connection among the American military, the college administration, and the Nazis (and the police) seems to be their shared, mindless bureaucratic power, and Sharpe's almost anarchistic attitude toward such power is on display in this passage.

In 1995 Sharpe set a second novel, *Grantchester Grind,* at Porterhouse College, Cambridge, which is in dire financial straits. Lady Mary Evans, the widow of

Sir Godber Evans, is convinced that Godber was murdered and establishes the Sir Godber Evans Memorial Fellowship at Porterhouse, intending the fellows to discover the truth about her husband's death. The first fellow is Purefoy Osbert of Kloone University (academic home of Yapp in *Ancestral Vices*), author of "The Crime of Punishment," who believes that the criminal-justice system, not criminals, is responsible for crime. In another plot strand, the bursar of Porterhouse, desperate to raise money, becomes embroiled with a company called Transworld Television Productions, which needs a location for filming. The spokesman for the television company is Karl Kudzuvine, a crudely caricatured American, both born-again Christian and foul-mouthed vulgarian, from Bibliopolis, Alabama. The head of the company, Edgar Hartang, is a mysterious figure of no particular nationality.

After a series of comic mishaps and improbable occurrences, Skullion is deposed and replaced by Hartang, who has a stroke and dies at his first feast. His successor is the odious old Porterhousian Jeremy Pimpole. The college becomes financially secure, but intellectually, culturally, and morally it is—as it always was—negligible.

Sharpe is quite clear on the shortcomings of most of the characters in this novel. One odd feature is that the Praelector, an ancient fellow who had only a tiny role in *Porterhouse Blue,* becomes quite active in forwarding the plot of *Grantchester Grind,* particularly in the events that save the college. He is described, in a somewhat uncharacteristically sentimental passage, as "sitting and contemplating with sad perception that great past when corruption and lying were not accepted social norms." While the narrator acknowledges that such vices have always existed, he asserts,

> It had taken war, two Great Wars in which millions had died fighting for promises that had never been kept, to bring England to its moral knees. And men like Hartang to the top. The Praelector would readily die to prevent Hartang and his ilk destroying Porterhouse and the romantic virtues it had stood for. Even so he smiled. Englishmen had been clever in their time and he himself was still no fool. He just left it to other people to think he was.

The suggestion that Porterhouse has stood for romantic virtues is oddly inconsistent with the picture of the college built up through most of two novels. The little-England tone of the Praelector's thoughts is the counterpart of the characterization and conversation of the American grotesque, Kudzuvine. Reviewing *Wilt on High* for *The Washington Post* (3 March 1985), L. J. Davis commented on Sharpe's "by no means exclusively Brit-

Tom Sharpe, circa 1997 (photograph © L. M. Palomares; from the dust jacket for the American edition of The Midden)

ish belief that once you know a foreigner's nationality, you know something useful about him."

The Midden (1996) has perhaps the most complicated plot of any of Sharpe's novels. Miss Midden (whose surname means dunghill) has inherited a farmhouse and a large house called the Middenhall, where—according to the terms of the will—she must provide lodging to anybody named Midden. As a result she is overrun by worthless spongers of "good family" who complain endlessly and expect servants to care for them. After Timothy Bright, the feckless offspring of another old rich family, wrecks a motorcycle and is catapulted into the bed of the wife of the local chief constable, Sir Arnold Gonders, Gonders assaults him nearly to death and then plants him in Miss Midden's home. Gonders then phones in an anonymous tip about child molestation at the Middenhall, leading to a gigantic undercover police operation and a deadly conclusion.

Somewhat like the Praelector in *Grantchester Grind,* Miss Midden is Sharpe's good person in *The Midden.* She is intelligent, unimpressed by nonsense, suspicious of Gonders, and resourceful. The novel includes considerable topical satire. Gonders presides over a corrupt force obviously meant to suggest the West Midlands Serious Crimes Squad. As the novel opens, Gonders's men have been unconvincingly exonerated for "falsifying evidence, fabricating confessions, accepting bribes, the use of unwarranted violence, and wholesale perjury, which crimes had sent several dozen wholly innocent individuals to prison for sentences as long as eighteen years while allowing as many guilty criminals to sleep comfortably at home and dream of other dreadful crimes to commit." Another target is British hysteria about child sexual abuse. Sharpe's most serious denunciation is reserved for the Child Abuse Trauma Specialists, who, triggered by Gonders's false report of pedophile activity at the Middenhall, swarm there in huge numbers:

> They came from all over Britain and had been attending a conference in Tween devoted to "The Sphincter: Its Diagnostic Role in Parental Rape Inspections." There were witchcraft experts from Scotland, sodomy specialists from South Wales, oral-sex-in-infancy counsellors, mutual masturbation advisers for adolescents, a number of clitoris stimulation experts, four vasectomists (female), and finally fifteen whores who had come to tell the conference what men really wanted. . . . A miasma of mixed emotions and bitter hatred of anything faintly fond or normal seemed to hang over them. Cruelty and sadism were their specialties and they were infected with them. Suffused with guilt about massacres and droughts in faraway places, they appeased their worthless consciences by doing worthless things. And blamed society for everything. Or god. Or men and parents who loved and disciplined their children to be polite and civil and to work at school.

Sharpe's punishment for the various groups of distasteful people in the novel is straightforward: though the Child Abuse Trauma Specialists are spared destruction, thirteen police are killed by gunfire and ten Middenhall inhabitants die when the building burns down.

Timothy Bright is the residue of a despised aristocracy—"what wars and their own preference for playing games and killing birds instead of thinking and working hadn't done, death duties and indolent stupidity had." Yet, he is more or less redeemed at the end of the novel. Despite the soberness of Sharpe's jeremiad against interfering social workers, his satire strikes in both directions: against not only left-wingers in the social welfare system but also the police, the gentry, and Gonders's "political catechism of Thatch-erism," in which "only money mattered and preferably the newest money that talked about little else and cared for nothing."

The reviewers of Sharpe's novels praise them for their comedy—sometimes black comedy—but they have missed much of his real importance, tending to see each novel as a joyously anarchic squib and calling Sharpe a remarkable intelligence making welcome use of an accessible popular form. In fact, taken together, his novels create a troubled world, brooding on humankind's tenuous reproduction and survival. The novels are apocalyptic, haunted by recurring motifs of sterility, impotence, and moral and physical perversion. Writing for *The Spectator* (10 November 1984), Francis King expressed reservations about Sharpe but was accurate in specifying that "Mr. Sharpe's speciality is not human comedy but inhuman farce. It is a cold eye that he casts on the pitiful absurdities of existence and a rough hand with which he manipulates the puppets chosen to demonstrate those absurdities." Closer to Kurt Vonnegut than to P. G. Wodehouse, Sharpe is a novelist with whom criticism of contemporary literature and culture must come to terms if only to explore the relationship between the intelligentsia and popular cultural forms. Sharpe's novels, regardless of setting, form a vast and grotesque counterpastoral of contemporary English life. As much concerned with myths as realities, he has created a history of England at once cruel and sentimental.

Interview:

Jean W. Ross, "*Contemporary Authors* Interview," in *Contemporary Authors,* volume 122, edited by Hal May and Susan Trosky (Detroit: Gale Research, 1989), pp. 417–421.

References:

Bernard E. Dold, *Two Post-1945 British Novelists: Olivia Manning and Tom Sharpe* (Rome: Herder, 1985);

Raymond G. McCall, "The Comic Novels of Tom Sharpe," *Critique: Studies in Modern Fiction,* 25 (Winter 1984): 57–65.

Adam Thorpe

(5 December 1956 –   )

Michael Hayes
University of Central Lancashire

BOOKS: *Mornings in the Baltic* (London: Secker & Warburg, 1988);

Meeting Montaigne (London: Secker & Warburg, 1990);

Ulverton (London: Secker & Warburg, 1992; New York: Farrar, Straus & Giroux, 1993);

Still (London: Secker & Warburg, 1995);

Pieces of Light (London: Cape, 1998; New York: Carroll & Graff, 2000);

From the Neanderthal (London: Cape, 1999);

The Ox-Bow's Heath (London: Ulysses, 1999);

Shifts (London: Cape, 2000).

PLAY PRODUCTION: *Couch Grass and Ribbon,* Newbury, Berkshire, Watermill Theatre, 10 September 1996.

PRODUCED SCRIPTS: *Just Not Cricket,* radio, BBC, 1988;

The Fen Story, radio, BBC, 1991;

Offa's Daughter, radio, BBC, 1993.

OTHER: Barney Cokeliss and James Fenton, eds., *Jellyfish Cupful: Writings in Honour of John Fuller,* includes a poem by Thorpe (Oxford: Ulysses, 1997);

Nick Gammage, ed., *The Epic Poise: A Celebration of Ted Hughes,* includes an essay by Thorpe (London: Faber & Faber, 1999).

SELECTED PERIODICAL PUBLICATION–
UNCOLLECTED: "Sur le mal de pays," *Villa Gillet,* no. 4 (May 1996): 95–119.

Adam Thorpe's first book, *Mornings in the Baltic* (1988), a poetry collection, was published to critical acclaim and shortlisted for the 1988 Whitbread Award for Poetry. In 1990 Thorpe began writing full-time and since then has produced an impressive and comprehensive body of work, including three additional books of poetry, three novels, three radio plays for BBC, a stage play, and a collection of short stories. Thorpe began his

Adam Thorpe, circa 1995 (photograph by Jason Shenai; from the dust jacket for Still)

writing career primarily as a poet and enjoys a solid reputation in that field. As a novelist, however, he is proving controversial. His novels are not determined by a rational, prosaic voice but by a poet's voice—sensuous, responsive, and suffused with epiphanic moments.

Adam Thorpe was born in Paris on 5 December 1956 to Sheila Greenlees Thorpe and Bernard Naylor Thorpe. His mother had met his father while she was working for NATO in Paris and he, having served in the Royal Air Force (RAF) during World War II, was Station Manager in Brussels for Pan Am. His father's subsequent postings created a peripatetic lifestyle and Thorpe was brought up in Beirut, Calcutta, Cameroon, and the south of England. Thorpe completed his secondary education at Marlborough—the traditional

English public school—then matriculated at Magdalen College, Oxford. Thorpe's tutor was the poet John Fuller; he was also taught by the eminent scholar Emrys Jones and poet Bernard O'Donoghue.

After graduating in English with first class honors in 1979, Thorpe cofounded Equinox Travelling Theatre. For six years the company toured the Berkshire-Wiltshire area performing Thorpe's adaptations of local stories, folktales, and myths using actors, puppets, and mime. The troupe performed in halls and schools and conducted drama workshops and youth theater courses at the Arts Workshop in Newbury. At that time, Thorpe also studied mime and physical theater with Philippe Gaulier, John Wright, Peta Lily, and Toshi Tsutitori at the Desmond Jones School of Mime. In 1984 Equinox won the *Time Out* Mime Street Entertainer of the Year Award. Thorpe has taught physical theater at City and East London College, Stepney, and the Modern British Theatre at the Polytechnic of Central London. On 23 November 1985 Thorpe married Joanna Wistreich, a teacher; he now lives in France with his wife and their three children.

Thorpe's first novel, *Ulverton* (1992), is the fictional history of a rural English village from 1650 to 1988. Both Thorpe's subsequent novels also relate in some way to this Wiltshire-Berkshire location situated in the environs of the real village of Avebury with its ancient stone circle dating back to 1800 B.C. The book comprises twelve chapters set at twelve points in history. By carefully selecting a range of narrators the novel explores different social roles and their implications from each period. Although each chapter is individually peopled, the spirit of the place and the mystery of human communication binds the stories into a unity as securely as any conventional action- or character-driven novel.

"Here. 1988," the final chapter, takes the form of a script for a television documentary titled "Clive's Seasons." Clive Walters is a predatory land developer who gets permission from the parish councilors to erect one housing development in Ulverton, resulting in ugly prefab houses ruining the landscape, and then maneuvers to develop a second. Resisting his application are the village conservationists, among them a character called Adam Thorpe, whose crawler caption for the documentary reads "Local Author and Performer." Walters's appeal is successful, but in digging the foundation workers find the remains of a body clutching ribbons and accompanied by gold coins, which, from their position in relation to the skeleton, seem to have been swallowed. What was hidden in the first chapter comes in the last into the light.

The opening chapter, "Return. 1650," commences with the sentence: "He appeared on the hill at first light." The "he" is Gabby Cobbold, returned from fighting with Oliver Cromwell in Ireland, and the narrator is the shepherd William. Gabby, driven by poverty, went to the wars and has returned with ribbons for his wife, Anne, and the money "to set it right"—meaning his farm. Meanwhile, however, Anne has married the surly, drunken Thomas Walters, who has also taken over the farm. Time passes, and no more is heard of the returnee. When the shepherd calls at the farm he is told that Gabby has gone away. During his lonely watches with the sheep, William has waking dreams of the massacres at Wexford and Drogheda and sexual images mingling Anne, the image of the Virgin, and his wife, Ruth, who will no longer sleep with him. To clear the confusion in his mind he goes to the church, where Cromwell's soldiers have concealed the biblical wall paintings by whitewashing over them. Anne follows him inside, and he intuitively speaks her guilt—that she and Walters have murdered Gabby. Anne then lures him from the church to Bailey's Wood where, in a deserted woodman's shelter, they begin a sexual relationship that lasts until she dies.

This story is in direct descent from Richard Jeffries, whose first newspaper articles were about the hardships of Wiltshire shepherds, and W. H. Hudson's *A Shepherd's Life* (1910). But, unlike the other stories in *Ulverton,* "Return. 1650" does not deploy, as Thorpe stated in a 1995 interview, "the authentic manner, the authentic text and the style of the period." The chapter was originally written as a separate story. Later, after he wrote the other chapters, Thorpe admits the problem of incorporation arose. The solution, voiced in the last chapter, was to align Clive Walters's greed with Thomas Walters's greed, and when the story of Gabby Cobbold appears in *The Wessex Nave* Clive is, to the satisfaction of the fictional Thorpe, considerably angered. The story aligns the real Thorpe with a rich tradition of rural writing that allows him to give utterance to forgotten voices and hidden histories. As to the actuality of *The Wessex Nave,* it is whitewashed over—like the biblical narratives on the walls of Ulverton Church.

In "Friends. 1689" Minister Brazier is attempting to explain in an exculpatory sermon to his parishioners why, on the journey home from Reverend Josiah Flaw's funeral, the clerk and the curate froze to death in a snowstorm while he returned safely wearing the curate's clothes on top of his own, and why the three were found to be sheltering near "our comforting protuberance . . . called thereby the Devil's knob." The theme underlying the comic hilarity of this chapter is the real seventeenth-century struggle to grasp the nature of true religion. The breakup of Christianity, of which the Pilgrim Fathers were a symptom, resulted in some 180 sects. At one extreme was the established

Dust jacket for Thorpe's first novel (1992), about a fictional village near Avebury over a period of more than three centuries

church with its emphasis on forms of observance, common prayer, and ritual. At the other extreme were sects such as the newly formed Quakers (or Friends) with their emphasis on direct individual communion with God, devoid of ministers and religious show.

The Reverend Brazier, who emphasizes form, opposes the curate Mr. Kistle. When Brazier describes the farcical scene in which Kistle divested himself of his clothes and threw away the sacred book shouting "worms might have God's Word for supper, I say! Welcome the Resurrection!" he is illustrating Kistle's assertion that pious words must be validated by lived experience, not simply mouthed in pious social show. Often in Thorpe's work the moral center is in the seemingly irrelevant detail: of the ironically named Josiah Flaw, the self-important Brazier eulogizes, "His assiduousness did cause his death." He died serving his flock one stormy evening.

"Improvements. 1712" is Farmer Plumm's journal of agricultural experiments and improvements to make his land more fertile—intertwined with the personal story of his lack of a son. His wife gives birth only to "sickly daughters who do not live." After the last still-birth his wife becomes mentally distraught and physically estranged. From physical need and want of an heir Plumm turns to the more willing maid: "in the dairy . . . I sought to seed my heir, against a full churn." The maid grows big with child, and Plumm's wife hangs herself. A robust baby is born; it is a girl. "Leeward. 1743" is the letters of Lady Anne Chalmers to her lover William Sykes, who may be the father of her child. Leeward is the name of a young black boy whom Lady Anne receives as a present from her sister. The boy, together with a loyal gardener, Elizah Mabberley, carries her love messages to Sykes. Eventually the two messengers are discovered and receive severe punishments. Mabberley may be hanged and Leeward, after a severe beating, is to be sent to the West Indies and slavery.

So far in *Ulverton* the narrative voices have been authentic to the social positions of the speakers or, as in the first story, to the fictionalized author. To make the narratives fully representative of the forgotten voices, "the hidden history" as Thorpe says, he extended the range of characters to the illiterate and the inarticulate.

While a subtheme of the early stories is sexuality and birth, in "Dissection. 1775" the focus is on motherhood. Francis, the disreputable son of the illiterate widow Sarah Shail, is awaiting hanging for stealing a hat. Sarah dictates letters for Francis to John Pounds, a barely literate tailor, who adds postscripts of his own that reveal an increasing tension between Francis and John over his rival relationship with Sarah. The son's letters are absent, but their tone can be inferred from John's patronizing postscripts: for example "yo al wais wer a dail too cokk shore." After his hanging, the son's body is to be handed to surgeons for experimental dissection. Sarah wants the body for sentimental reasons, but she also wants it so she can lay her dead son's hand on her breast to cure a black cancerous spot. This circumstance reveals something of the town-and-country relationship of the period. In a twist of fate, the final letter is written by the curate celebrating, to mixed reactions, the son's pardon.

"Rise. 1803" is the rambling account of the old carpenter Samuel Daye, who, to the accompaniment of free drinks, tells a passing traveler the story of his working life. Though never a master craftsman like his master Abraham Webb, Samuel has two claims to fame. One day he hid in a tree and pretended to be the voice of God, telling Abraham to let his workers go by eight o'clock at night–which Abraham did. Samuel's other claim is a gate he made. It later hangs reliably and becomes the work of an unknown joiner giving good service long after Samuel is dead.

The apotheosis of the forgotten voices comes several chapters later in "Stitches. 1887." In an excellent, authentic rendering of the dialect of southwest England, Jonas Perry's monologue, as he rambles through Ulverton, reflects on places geographic, social, and personal. Intimations of the end of the old world have already been given in "Deposition. 1830," an account of some laborers' failed revolt against the introduction of machinery, and in "Shutter. 1859," a series of descriptions of photographic plates taken in and around Ulverton by an unnamed female photographer. Among the plates are also some from an excavation site in Egypt, which suggest that, even as they record the moment, photographs divest it of its human complexity.

The last authentic voice of the old Ulverton is that of Jonas Perry. The remaining voices–the retired colonial civil servant George Fergusson in "Treasure. 1914," the secretary Violet Nightingale, and the television script–are those of "in-comers." In its allusiveness, local knowledge, energy, and melancholy, "Stitches. 1887" gives voice to the familiar world of the novel and to the inchoate experiences it invokes. Perry's auditor is young Dannul, but the continuity between old and young is broken after the boy dies from a chill he got on

his rambles with Jonas. There is no one to hear Jonas's voice except the reader who struggles to understand what he says and how he relates to "real life."

In "Treasure. 1914," a tale of World War I, the Squire's excavation of one of the ancient barrows is counterpointed by an enthusiastic recruitment drive. One voice, Percy Cullerne, refuses to disturb the dead by joining the excavation or to join the war by enlisting. Cullerne's neighbors refuse to speak to him, and he becomes an outsider in the village. As the war progresses and the numbers of Ulverton's dead and wounded mount, Cullerne is proved right to have said he would "rather bide at home." The Squire sinks into despair, and, in 1923, still blaming himself for the deaths of the young men of the village, he kills himself. In "Wing. 1953," a story of the aftermath of World War II, the sense of the present as perpetually deferred is even more marked. Violet Nightingale has, for thirteen years, been secretary to the self-important artist/cartoonist Herbert Bradman. Her growing affection for him is ignored, and she finally realizes he has always seen her as a somewhat ridiculous figure. As part of the 1953 coronation celebrations for Queen Elizabeth II, Bradman plans to bury some twentieth-century artifacts, particularly his autobiography and a collection of his drawings. In a moment of revolt Violet throws three suitcases of drawings on the coronation bonfire–a gasp of life, if only momentarily, retrieved.

Ulverton was nominated for the prestigious Booker Prize and highly praised by the novelist John Fowles, who declared in *The Spectator* (20 November 1993) that the novel is a true portrait "of the complex nature of our rural past." Except for chapters "Return," "Friends," and "Treasure," the others were written abroad, completing Thorpe's family progression from rural Wiltshire to urban London with a move to France. This distancing perspective, or self-exile, helps crystalize the enquiry into what *English* means, both as a nationality and as a language.

Thorpe's next novel, *Still* (1995), is the stream of consciousness of someone dislocated from context and language and rather desperately seeking to connect with reality. The narrator/protagonist is the Englishman Richard Arthur Thornby, preferred name Ricky, Ratty to his brother Des, and variously Rick, Dick, Dicky, and "to a select few, mostly dead, Richard." The novel opens midsentence while Ricky is in flight back to England for his sixtieth-birthday celebration, which occurs on the eve of the new millennium. The time frame of the novel appears to be the twenty-four hours from midflight to the end of the party on New Year's morning. At the party Ricky intends to show his twelve-hour masterpiece–"a film without pictures." In Ricky's search for reality word replaces film, as he tells his son

Greg, a successful artist, "It's about us. . . . I mean us as in our roots, our genes, our blood, our memory bank and all that."

Ricky's stream of consciousness consists of three interlocked narratives: his autobiography, his motion picture, and his immediate responses to the day of the party. While not sequential, his autobiography reveals the development of a sensibility. Growing up as a child of the 1940s and early 1950s, Ricky was largely shaped by the cinema. Ricky particularly recalls in vivid physical detail the stills outside the Enfield Ritz advertising the movies. The stills were not better than the movies but they crystalized an intensity of "that feeling, that feeling." Already for Ricky, pictures rather than words were associated with articulating powerful but inchoate feelings.

On graduating from Cambridge University, Ricky settled on a career in the movie business, but his early promise as a director faded, and at forty-two he took a dispiriting job teaching film studies at the pedestrian Houston Center for Dramatic and Visual Arts. At sixty his judgment on his career is harsh but accurate; he perceives his movies as "deliberately B. B as in Bad. B as in Bloody. B as in Bollocks. B as in Boring. In other words, they were lifelike, they were exactly like life. Not like life out there, I mean life as filtered by your Brain. Life out there is by Fellini, OK? But life in here is by me. You wouldn't believe what my Brain gets up to." His saving grace is that his novel lays it bare, with scorching honesty.

His relationships are similar failures. The reader can detect that the source of his difficulties with women is his failure to see other people as lives in progress. Zelda, the continuing object of his desire, is fixed in his sentimental and sexual experience of her, and he cannot, as she says, "Just shut up. Just let the whole thing roll on its own. Trust it. Dare."

Ricky talks little about his parents. One of Oswald Mosley's fascists, Ricky's father was a street trader descended from a long line of dealers in urban detritus—even dog-turd collectors for the leather-tanning trade. He lives on, a disreputable old reprobate in a south-coast retirement home. Ricky's mother, who is dead, is a shadowy figure remembered for her kindness and acquiescence. The most experimental strand of narrative in the novel, however, centers around her family, the Trevelyans.

In 1913, on the eve of World War I, the Trevelyans enjoyed the prosperous Edwardian lifestyle provided by their disinfectants business. Presented as a combination of stills, a motion-picture treatment, and shoot in progress, the inciting incident is the expulsion of Ricky's grandfather's younger brother from Randle Public School for painting fellow pupils naked. The nar-

rational style draws a rich portrait of family life. Ricky's choice of portrayal tells the reader a great deal about Ricky.

The most intermittent and the most inclusive narrative is Ricky's account of the day of the party. A mixture of assertive and humble, querulous and sentimental, comic and coarse, he speaks in a heterogeneity of voices. Typical is his parody of an estuarine accent, the self-deprecating voice of the Cambridge-educated Enfield boy of mixed-class origins who lacks a voice of his own. A moviemaker, whose last picture was the routine, 1988 "Clive's Seasons" featured in *Ulverton,* he lacks, as he admits, a visual sense. Somewhere in search of roots he found his place of origin abandoned. A man of failed relationships, he exists essentially alone at the end of the twentieth century.

Ricky's distress in *Still* engages the problems that arise from a relationship to the world being mediated through photographic images. His implied interrogation of the various forms of photographic image, whether zoetrope, cinefilm, microfiche or photocopy, brings with it his re-assertion of the power of words and the possibility of a renewed connection to the real.

Reviews for *Still* were decidedly mixed. Fowles was again effusive in his praise, writing in *The Spectator* (29 April 1995), "We haven't been exposed to such a Rabelaisian gusto of language, such an endless jacuzzi of slang, film-crew jargon and erudition since *Ulysses* and *Finnegans Wake:* so much quirky humour since *Tristram Shandy.*" In *TLS* Tom Shippey called *Still* "a 584-page rant," and Laurence O'Toole in *The New Statesman* complained about "the kind of puzzled, literary complexity that gives modern fiction a bad name." The critics are correct in suggesting Thorpe's books are not easy reading; the complexity of his style and technique makes the reader work.

In a 1995 interview with Sabine Hagenauer, Thorpe responded to her comment that she found his second novel somewhat confusing: "Yes, but, what's interesting is that people who've re-read it say that it becomes clear. I think in many ways in *Still* I am trying to make it new, and I think reviewers were not ready to accept the newness or the radical nature of the novel. They are reading it in a certain way, which is a conventional way, and they're not willing to really start from scratch, which is what you've got to do with the novel: . . . to start . . . completely fresh, without any conventional models in your head." Thorpe went on to say, "The problem with reviewers is that when they judge a book for the first thirty pages, and they are having problems . . . and they haven't got much time, what they'll then do is spend a couple of days just skipping it." He added, "I don't see much point in writing a novel unless the reader works because there's so much

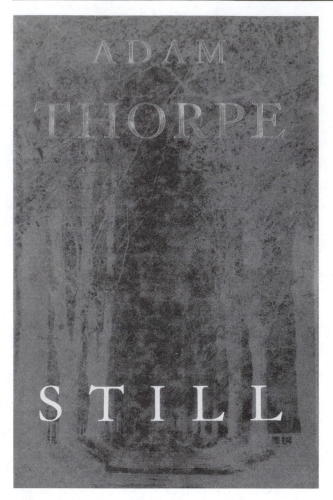

Dust jacket for Thorpe's 1995 novel, about a second-rate movie director whose "masterpiece" is a twelve-hour "film without pictures"

in life and in culture at the moment that's just for easy consumption. Writing difficult books is not particularly popular, perhaps, with publishers, because they don't sell as well—although *Ulverton* is selling well and is continuing to."

Thorpe returned to a more conventional form in his third novel, *Pieces of Light* (1998), which explores the dangers to the individual of imposing a false closure. The reader follows an English boy from an African childhood, through a return to the mythopoeic landscape of Ulverton, to his seventies in an asylum. From the 1920s to the 1990s feelings clash in his psyche with the one thread of hope being, as the epigraph from William Wordsworth reads, to give "while yet we may, as far as words can give. A substance and a life to what I feel."

As usual in Thorpe's work there are various textual modes but this time only two narrational voices, the protagonist, Hugh Arkwright, and the collection of letters written by his mother, Charlotte. The opening is

Hugh's memoir of his childhood, written—the reader subsequently learns—at the suggestion of his former psychiatrist Dr. Wolff. There follows a series of Hugh's diary entries at the age of seventy, on his retirement from the theater. These two texts are followed by an account of the intervening years, written in the form of a letter-journal to his mother, again at the request of a psychiatrist. The novel concludes with Charlotte's letters.

Hugh is born in a remote part of the mandated African territory of Cameroon on the banks of a crocodile-infested, malarial river in the heart of an equatorial forest, an improbable setting for "what I sometimes think of as my golden age, before the fall." For the young Hugh it is Eden. Under the guidance of Quiri, the African houseboy, Hugh absorbs a traditional African worldview, learning the inner meaning of signs, dreams, animals, and places. The all-pervasive presence of the forest creates a "belief in the realness of this world just beyond my own."

But the signs of cultural schism are present; his parents stop him from speaking pidgin, and when his father asks if he is still learning Quiri's language Hugh answers no, realizing he must keep his knowledge hidden. As he approaches seven Hugh fears he is to be sacrificed, and in a sense he is: he is sent back to England to be educated, protected only by the circle with inset cross that Quiri has cut in his neck and rubbed with ashes to make a permanent fetish mark of the Fula forest spirit Yolobola.

In England he lives near Ulverton with his mother's brother Edward. Life in England is a parody of the animistic beliefs he absorbed in Cameroon: his uncle engages with the past believing in reconstructed Druidic practices and signs. Moreover, he protects a small wood reputed to be part of the great forest once covering the south of England. One day, from this small remnant, Edward expects the forest to regenerate. Hugh's memoir breaks off abruptly with the enigmatic disappearance of Hugh's mother into the jungle.

Hugh's diary reveals that at seventy he is still searching for his "lost" mother. His career has been in a highly disciplined practice of theater, emphasizing control and ritual, obviating an inner life on the edge of chaos, and engaging with the Shakespearean past to avoid turning inward. He returns to Ulverton, where his uncle's house, empty for twenty years, needs putting in order. Hugh's diary breaks off abruptly after a reference to his father's leopard skin and its implicit evocation of leopard men who absorb the vengeful spirit of the animal whose skin they wear.

The second psychotherapeutic series of writings fills in the gap between the first two texts, taking the form of Hugh's letters to his mother. Hugh records his service in World War II, performed away from masses of people—first in an anti-aircraft battery and subsequently in a bomber. This section also documents the beginning of his interest in working in the theater. But most important is his love for Rachael. This love promises to reconfigure his love for his mother—"I sometimes think you must have been very like her when you were nineteen"—and allows him to live in the present, realizing in a contemporary form his childhood dream "to have myself marked as the others were, to marry a fertile and beautiful wife and bring forth a crowd of healthy children." Just as his antiquarian interests eviscerate the vital spirits of the past, Edward's taking Rachael from Hugh deprives him of the chance to evolve his inner life, rendering him sterile—a sterility matched by Ulverton, which looks as "if someone's run off with the real thing, leaving a fake."

The climax, occurring after the diary ends, results in a bizarre and horrific murder in the wood, involving the leopard skin and having all the appearance of a blood sacrifice. Hugh's involvement is ambivalent—he is arrested and then released when someone else confesses. The account ends with him in an asylum, planning a trip to Africa, and making a resolute declaration that the copies of his mother's letters are forgeries perpetrated by his uncle in one more betrayal. The letters themselves follow.

Where Hugh struggles to make sense with culturally inappropriate symbols and archaic signs, Charlotte's letters in their no-nonsense perception and liveliness reveal a modern young woman who refuses to be "engulfed by psychological creepers, too heavy for my slender trunk." Her robust practicality is complemented by her good heart. In the last letter the reader learns that she and James are not Hugh's birth parents but willing replacements for his ill-assorted progenitors.

Thorpe's novels explore the reader's relationship to real life, a relationship that is endlessly re-invented by poetry. *Ulverton* explores the past, its continuances and its closures. *Still* focuses on the twentieth century, recognizing displacements and interferences that have obscured the relationship. In *Pieces of Light* Thorpe investigates the psychology of rupture in the final "Letters," nursing the words back to health.

Thorpe's first short-story collection, *Shifts* (2000), is ostensibly about different kinds of work. The stories are monologues unified by the theme of loss. In "Iron" and "Sawmills" limbs are accidentally amputated; in "Stonework" and the title story characters are exiled from their familiar environments. Marcus, the narrator of "Shifts," is an African immigrant living in England who in order to get employment has to pretend to be his absent friend Chukufidu: "I could change persona like my socks. I could speak my lines in Ga or Pidgin or English." Alienation always exacts its price.

Thorpe's fiction explores the nature of language in relation to life. *Ulverton* looks at the past, its continuances and its closures. *Still* focuses on the twentieth-century recognition of the displacements and interferences that have obscured language, a theme expanded in physical and geographical scope by *Shifts*. In *Pieces of Light* Thorpe investigates the psychology of rupture, in the final section nursing words back to health. As both poet and novelist, Thorpe fulfills Boris Pasternak's aim for literature: "it proceeds in history and in co-operation with real life." Thorpe recognizes and articulates the past and gives utterance to the dissociated and elusive present.

Interviews:

Sabine Hagenauer, "An Interview with Adam Thorpe," 10 November 1995, Erlangen Centre for Contemporary English Literature website, <http://www.ph-erfurt.de/~neumann/eese/artic96/hagenau/3_96.html>;

Nick Rennison, "The Question of England," *W* [Waterstone's Bookshop Magazine] (September 1999).

Colin Thubron

(14 June 1939 –   )

Merritt Moseley
University of North Carolina at Asheville

See also the Thubron entry in *DLB 204: British Travel Writers, 1940–1997.*

BOOKS: *Mirror to Damascus* (London: Heinemann, 1967; Boston: Little, Brown, 1968);

The Hills of Adonis: A Quest in Lebanon (London: Heinemann, 1968; Boston: Little, Brown, 1969);

Jerusalem, text by Thubron, photographs by Alistair Duncan (London: Heinemann, 1969; Boston: Little, Brown, 1969);

Journey Into Cyprus (London: Heinemann, 1975; New York: Atlantic Monthly Press, 1990);

The God in the Mountain: A Novel (London: Heinemann; New York: Norton, 1977);

Emperor: A Novel (London: Heinemann, 1978);

Istanbul, by Thubron and the editors of Time-Life Books (Amsterdam: Time-Life Books, 1978);

The Venetians, by Thubron and the editors of Time-Life Books (Alexandria, Va.: Time-Life Books, 1980);

The Ancient Mariners, by Thubron and the editors of Time-Life Books (Alexandria, Va.: Time-Life Books, 1981);

The Royal Opera House, Covent Garden, text by Thubron, photographs by Clive Boursnell (London: Hamilton, 1982; New York: Schocken, 1983);

Among the Russians (London: Heinemann, 1983); republished as *Where Nights Are Longest: Travels by Car Through Western Russia* (New York: Random House, 1984);

A Cruel Madness (London: Heinemann, 1984; Boston: Atlantic Monthly Press, 1984);

Behind the Wall: A Journey Through China (London: Heinemann, 1987; New York: Atlantic Monthly Press, 1988);

The Silk Road China: Beyond the Celestial Kingdom (London: Pyramid in association with Departures, 1989); republished as *The Silk Road: Beyond the Celestial Kingdom* (New York: Simon & Schuster, 1989);

Falling (London: Heinemann, 1989; New York: Atlantic Monthly Press, 1991);

Colin Thubron (courtesy of the author)

Turning Back the Sun (London: Heinemann, 1991; New York: Burlingame, 1991);

The Lost Heart of Asia (London: Heinemann; New York: HarperCollins, 1994);

Distance (London: Heinemann, 1996);

In Siberia (London: Chatto & Windus, 1999; New York: HarperCollins, 1999).

SELECTED PERIODICAL PUBLICATION–
UNCOLLECTED: "Second Thoughts: Forever Young in Rome: Colin Thubron on the Ageless Characters at the Centre of his Novel Set in Rome, *Emperor,*" *Independent* (London), 9 June 1990, p. 31.

Colin Thubron is an example of the doubly talented writer. He is best known as a travel writer. In fact, according to Jeremy Atiyah, Thubron is "the greatest travel writer of his generation" (*The Independent,* 10 October 1999). He was awarded a fellowship in the Royal Society of Literature in 1969, before any of his fiction had been published, and his travel books have a much stronger history of publishing success in the United States. But he is also a powerful novelist, author of six varied works ranging from a novel about the conversion to Christianity of the Emperor Constantine to a love story set in and around a small-time traveling circus in England. There are several connections between the two sides of his career. Penny Perrick prefaced her 1991 interview with Thubron for *The Sunday Times* (London) with the observation that "the word 'distress' attaches itself to everything Colin Thubron writes," explaining that his travel books are about trips to harsh and forbidding places while his novels "are tense and enlightening accounts of men trapped in places not of their own choosing." Though he always chooses his own destinations and is not trapped in them, the places Thubron writes about in his travel books are neither comfortable nor familiar. Having recorded his encounters with the people and landscapes of central Asia, Siberia, China, and war-threatened Lebanon, he has said that "the very frightfulness of a place is compelling." In his fiction he addresses frightful places as well, though they are as likely to be places of the mind and spirit as locations on a map. As he told *Contemporary Authors* in 1998, "In fiction I've stayed obsessed by extreme states."

Colin Gerald Dryden Thubron was born in London on 14 June 1939 to Brigadier Gerald Ernest Thubron and Evelyn Dryden Thubron, a descendent of the seventeenth-century poet laureate John Dryden. Brigadier Thubron was military attaché to Canada, and the family home was in Ottawa. At age seven Colin was sent to boarding school in England, returning to Ottawa only for school vacations. He commented to Perrick in 1991 that "Being sent away from home means that there's always something independent about you, always an element of isolation or self-sufficiency." He went on to Eton College, which he left at eighteen. Though he already wanted to travel and write, he did not at that time see his way clear to being a travel writer, so he took a job as an editor with Hutchinson, a London publishing firm, where he worked from 1959 to 1962. After two years as a freelance television moviemaker, he worked for the publisher Macmillan in New York in 1964 and 1965. Aside from those positions he has been a full-time traveler and writer. He lives in London.

His first extended trip occurred in 1965, when he took all his savings and spent a year in Damascus. He lived with Arabs and penetrated the secrecy of their society. The result was his first book, *Mirror to Damascus*

(1967). After this book on Syria, Thubron fairly quickly wrote books on Lebanon, Jerusalem, and Cyprus. He then published his first two novels, *The God in the Mountain* (1977) and *Emperor* (1978); three Time-Life books, *Istanbul* (1978), *The Venetians* (1980), and *The Ancient Mariners* (1981); and a nonfiction book on the Royal Opera House. Five travel books, interspersed with four novels, followed. The virtues of Thubron's later travel writing have been defined by James Eve as "coolness, precision and detachment" (*The Times,* 7 October 1999), and Atiyah has commented on Thubron's "meticulous preparation": "Thubron has taken the time to learn sufficiently good Russian and Chinese, for example, to be able to conduct insightful conversations with almost any resident of northern or eastern Asia. Russian drunks, Siberian fishermen, Uzbeki poets, Mongolian nomads, Shanghai Buddhists and Cantonese restauranteurs (to name but a few) have all enjoyed shooting the breeze over the years with this remarkable Englishman."

The virtues of Thubron's travel writing are also visible in his fiction. His interest in, and knowledge of, the eastern Mediterranean is most vivid in his first novel, *The God in the Mountain.* This long and complex story is at the same time a love story, a study of a specific culture and its needs, and a rumination on modernization, violence, and cultural imperialism. The novel is set in a place called Kalepia in an unnamed republic somewhere at the eastern end of the Mediterranean. It is not in Greece, but the people are Greeks and the religion Orthodox. The central character is Julian Alastos, whose divided nature symbolizes the forces pulling and pushing at the republic. Alastos is half-Greek and half-English. Having left the republic with his English mother, attended an English university, and become a mining engineer, he has returned to Kalepia and has ended up taking a job supervising open-cast copper mining for The Company, run mostly by Americans of surprising arrogance. Alastos has high hopes that The Company can advance prosperity, end superstition, and improve education in Kalepia. Early in the novel he reacts to the ugliness of the town and thinks: "these people were a good people, at heart intelligent and proud. The people of Pericles. One day something would happen and they would be restored. They simply needed money, education. Education would transform them."

Events of the plot are catalyzed by The Company's plans to buy a mountain adjacent to the city and open an enormous new mine there—a move that will require the destruction of a grove of olive trees that is an important source of food for the poor and changes in the port that will ruin fishing and mean removing some fishermen's and dockers' houses. It

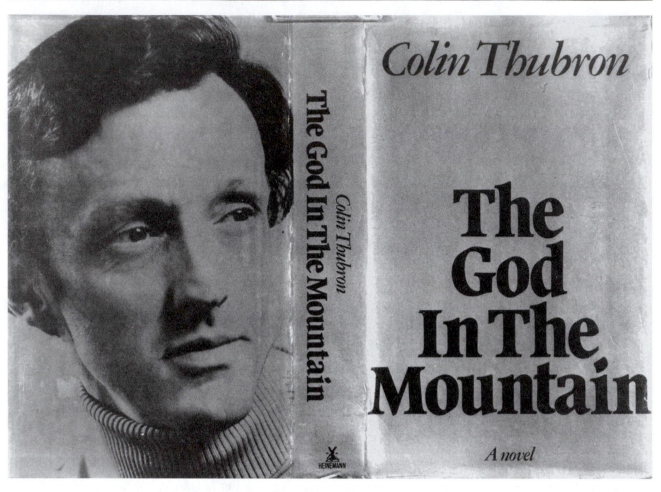

Dust jacket for Thubron's first novel (1977), for which he drew on his knowledge of eastern Mediterranean culture (courtesy of The Lilly Library, Indiana University, Bloomington, Indiana)

will also destroy a shrine to St. Vichinos, the local saint, which makes the mountain holy ground. The Company suggests relocating the shrine onto a slag heap and secures the cooperation of the local religious official, the archimandrite, but most of the common people, led by a rebellious priest, oppose the move and begin staging protests.

Alastos, an idealist, is torn between Kalepian ideals and those of the industrialized "west." (As perhaps his name, divided between Latin and Greek, suggests, along with its possible reference to Julian the Apostate). Finally turning against The Company and quitting in protest, Alastos becomes a teacher but can make no headway because the pupils are politicized and divided between the children of miners and the children of fishermen.

The God in the Mountain has a brooding air of impending catastrophe. The increasing tensions have social, religious, and geopolitical, as well as sexual and economic, roots. Briefly giving allegiance to a radical element in the opposition to the mine, Alastos helps

blow up a bridge, accidentally killing a German engineer who works for The Company. The event shocks Alastos out of his theoretical acceptance of violence: "All theory, all thought, had been cleaned from his mind by the mangled shape in the dust, the individual man, defiled, ended for ever. Alastos had no ideas left. He knew only that he had been wrong, and that nothing must stay as it was. To accept things unchanged was to accept this too: a people which killed." He decides too late to prevent the violent confrontation between the forces favoring and opposing "progress" and, in a perhaps too-neat development, is crushed between the two forces.

The God in the Mountain is a distinguished first novel, building a compelling plot on the cultural knowledge Thubron developed during his travels in the Levant. In the following year he produced a short novel entirely different in almost every way, *Emperor* (1978). This unusual little book tells the story of a short period from August to October, 312 A.D., during which the Emperor Constantine becomes a convert to Christianity. The novel begins with a letter written in Constantinople in 338, in which Melitius, lately master of studies to the Augustus Constantine, sends some documents he has discovered after the emperor's death to Celsus, a professor of rhetoric. Melitius explains, "The result of my findings has not the clarity of state propaganda. But it has, I think, the complexity of truth. Do you think that posterity would condemn me for bringing these things to the light? or is the truth better lost for ever? Should we be blind and happy, or honest and disillusioned? An old debate." Celsus apparently likes the first choice: he sends back unread the documents that constitute the body of the novel.

Among them are Constantine's journal; some letters from his emotionally estranged wife, Fausta (the sister of Maxentius, whom Constantine is seeking to overthrow); letters from Fausta's silly lady in waiting; and the commonplace book of an aged Greek rationalist, Synesius, who is master of the sacred memory, the emperor's private secretary, and the father of Melitius, who eventually discovers the documents that make up the novel. These differing accounts, supplemented with reports from a spy called Geta and an illiterate servant named Cecrops, offer various perspectives on the story.

The novel is set during Constantine's successful invasion of Italy, during which he has a vision at Verona that persuades him to fight under the sign of the cross. He goes on to defeat his rival emperor, Maxentius, at the battle of the Milvian Bridge. Thubron gives rather brief attention to military affairs, being more interested in mental and spiritual alterations. As the novel begins, Constantine is a worshipper of the sun god, but as he travels, his confidence in his god attenuates, and he becomes more interested in Christianity, which he discusses with a Spanish bishop, Hosius, who travels with the army. Constantine becomes unsettled by the setting of the sun, his god, and thinks, "I no longer know how to act. I simply continue as I first intended, and seem not to have a choice but to march against the elder gods of Rome beneath a Sun which has turned cold." Finally, after his fateful vision, during which he falls from his horse and sees a shining cross, he announces to his officers that they will henceforth conquer under that symbol and the god it represents.

Constantine's thoughts on religion are accompanied by his conversations with Hosius the Christian and Synesius the Greek rationalist, as well as by arguments between those two adversaries, arguments in which Synesius usually seems to be superior. He has no religion himself and nothing but scorn for Christianity because it is irrational and because he has disdain for the kinds of people it attracts. As a traditionalist he prefers Constantine before his conversion and has to watch as Constantine disappoints him further.

Emperor is original and persuasive. It raises questions about tradition versus innovation, reason versus emotion, and even cultural imperialism, as Constantine (an Illyrian peasant, by Synesius's lights, and a follower of an alien religion) conquers the empire and the old gods. It is impossible to judge the accuracy of Thubron's ideas about Constantine's beliefs and insecurities, but they are credible and provide a sophisticated psychological subtext to the known facts of his life. Looking back on the novel more than ten years later, Thubron commented in a 9 June 1990 article for *The Independent* (London):

In all historical fiction there lurks an ambivalence for writers. It is not enough to say "These people were fundamentally like us," and to write accordingly. They often weren't like us at all. Yet if the narrative carries no empathy, it sinks into costume drama. Constantine was the son of an Illyrian peasant, and *Emperor* is the story of his crisis of faith in God and in human love—the love of his empress, whom he eventually had killed. Yet I realise that I invested much of myself in the dilemma of these distant people. Where history is silent, they became the creatures of my own unease.

Neither of Thubron's first two novels was particularly noted. His third, *A Cruel Madness* (1984), was widely reviewed. In *The Spectator* (1 September 1984) Francis King praised the novel, contrasting its convincing representation of a disturbed mind with Thubron's reasonable travel writing. John Wheatcroft, writing in *The New York Times Book Review* (10 November 1985), compared its author with Thomas Mann, Alexander Solzhenitsyn, and Ken Kesey, stating: "Among such distinguished company, Mr. Thubron's novel holds its own."

A Cruel Madness opens at a mental hospital in Wales, where the narrator, Daniel Pashley, says he started out "as an occasional volunteer worker years ago" and teaches English to the patients in the Faraday ward. (These patients are called the Acutes, as contrasted with the Chronics.) One day he looks out a window and sees Sophia, a woman with whom he once had an intense but sexless relationship, in the garden. Before going down to talk to her, he thinks, "I was no longer even sure which of us should have forgiven the other. Or even precisely what there was to forgive. Except there was this resurrected ache; and a feeling that it was all immeasurably long ago, longer than its ten years, another incarnation." He first believes she is treating a patient, but then, when he tries to speak to her, he realizes that she is a patient, and he cannot be sure she knows who he is. After this abortive conversation the narrator has a flashback to how he met Sophia, after an

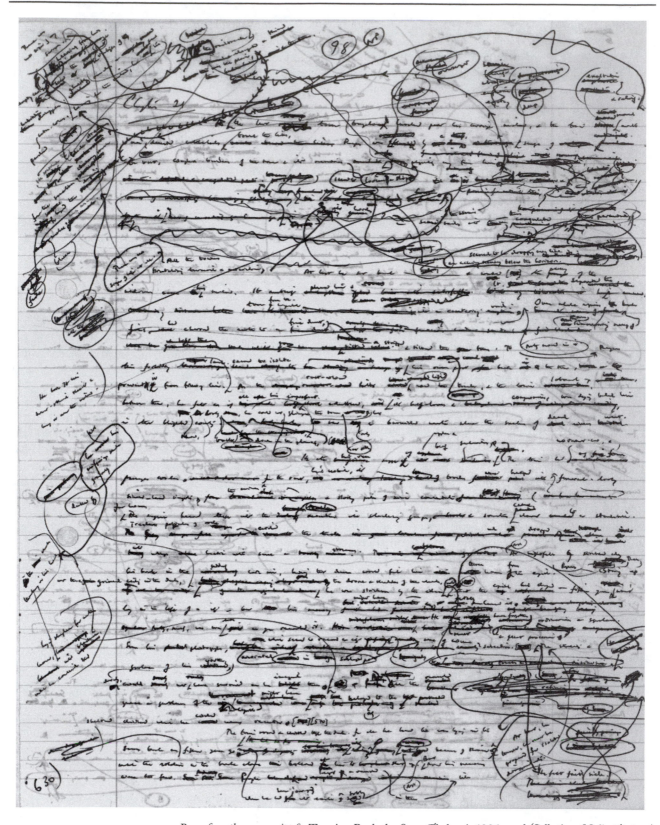

Pages from the manuscript for Turning Back the Sun, *Thubron's 1991 novel (Collection of Colin Thubron)*

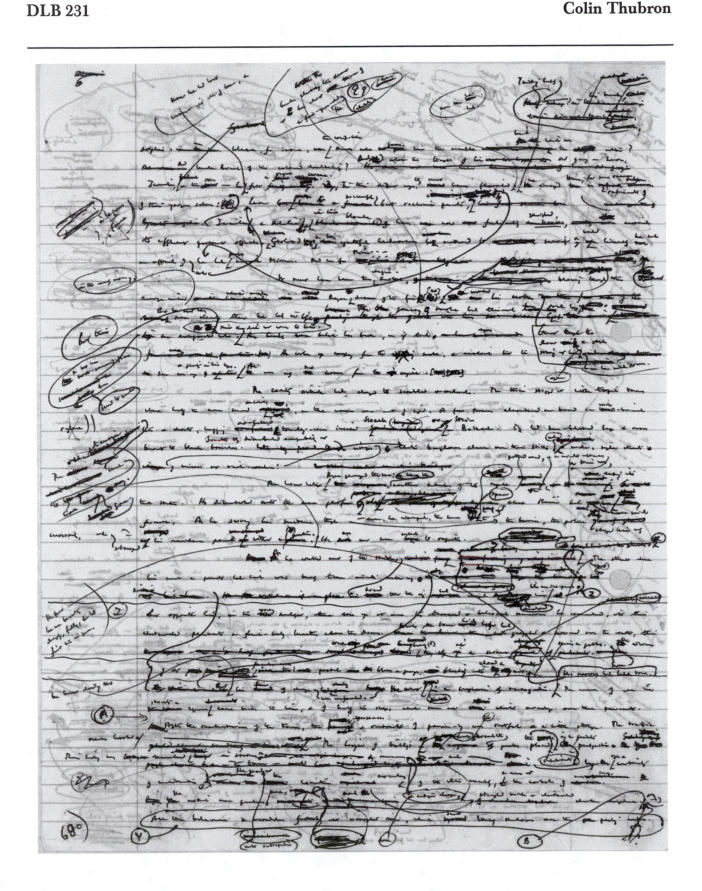

accidental encounter at his doctor's, and fell in love with her immediately.

The novel proceeds with an interleaving of scenes set in the mental hospital and flashbacks and recollections about Sophia. Daniel explains, "I sank into a delirium with her, and slowly lost myself. My frustration disintegrated into a prolonged oblivion," and he narrates a climactic experience when, on a picnic, she told him she was leaving : "I realised—perhaps I had always known—that after all I could keep her, keep her here with me for ever, yes, always. And all the transient warmth of her was suddenly close, there, beautiful near my hands again, this sublime thing. Now my fingers inside the picnic basket were clasping the knife's ivory handle."

In the "contemporary" world of the hospital, Daniel pursues various stratagems to meet Sophia, who usually ignores him. He asks her to write an autobiographical story for him and informs the reader that she writes two different ones, the first full of love for him, the other full of contempt. In fact, Daniel has written both these accounts. As his narrative becomes more and more disconnected and his mental disturbance becomes increasingly obvious, the reader develops a growing awareness of Daniel's unreliability as a narrator. When he looks for her file in the office, it is not there. Then, in a moment of revelation, he adds: "I dipped a hand tiredly into mine (because I am a patient), and found my admission form. It was covered in little squares with ticks or lines through them. Against 'Diagnosis' I read '*Chronic dissociative state. Depersonalisation syndrome.*'" He has stopped taking his medication, saying he needs his strength to help Sophia escape. In a conversation with a psychiatrist, Daniel pleads for Sophia to be helped out of the Chronics section and is told that she is not a patient there.

The novel ends with Daniel's phantasmagorical account of an escape attempt, in which "Sophia" meets him outside on the hospital grounds, then turns and goes back up the fire escape toward the women's quarters. He reenacts, or re-remembers, a knifing scene to which his earlier memories kept leading up (and which the two letters from "Sophia" both describe) and wakes up in the Disturbed ward, having been found asleep on the women's fire escape.

Thubron's use of an unreliable narrator aroused some hostility among reviewers—Stephen Koch in *The Washington Post Book World* (17 November 1985) called it a "cheap trick"—but satisfied others. Wheatcroft commented on the way the novel "compels us to try to discover what actually had happened and what really is happening. As we do so, all the apparently solid ground on which the narrative has built begins to shift, to reveal gaps and inconsistencies." In *The Los Angeles Times*

Book Review (6 October 1985) Sharon Dirlam called it "a gripping tale of passion, however misspent," and said that "the failure of an entire set of characters to come to grips with life seems not as distant from 'normal' as one might think, but simply a look deeper into the mind than most of us dare to probe."

Before Thubron published his next novel five years passed, during which he traveled in China and wrote *Behind the Wall: A Journey Through China* (1987), which earned him a prestigious Hawthornden Prize and a Thomas Cook Travel Award. *Falling* (1989) is a short, atmospheric novel that, like its predecessor, is about obsessive love, killing, and incarceration. It begins with journalist Mark Swabey entering prison and ends with his release. In between there is considerable detail about prison life, including relations between prisoners and guards, drug deals, and hopes for escape. But most of the novel is about why and how Mark Swabey came to be imprisoned. *Falling* has five narrators: Swabey, the prison chaplain, Swabey's cellmate Morgan, Swabey's faithful girlfriend Katherine, and Clara the Swallow, a circus trapeze performer. As features editor of the *Hampshire Times,* Swabey had gone to report on a small-time, failing circus and fallen in love with Clara. This love assumes control over his life, and he follows the circus around to see and sleep with Clara. His love for her is undermotivated; but it has a great deal to do with her daring on the high trapeze. Variations on the theme of falling run through the book. There is the fear of falling that makes the trapeze work thrilling; Katherine, a stained-glass artist, creates a window illustrating the fall of Lucifer; most crucially Mark falls in love. After Clara falls from her trapeze and is paralyzed, Mark helps her commit suicide and is sent to prison for his role in her death.

Falling is a lesser work than *A Cruel Madness,* but it is an interesting study of an eccentric mental state. One of the strongest features is Katherine's attempt to understand Mark's obsession with Clara. Having become aware of his affair with the Swallow Girl, she visits the circus to see Clara and reports, "I felt a physical sickness, not because of her—she was just an ordinary trapeze girl—but because this glittering absurdity was Mark's beloved." Katherine's incomprehension seems a demonstration of the difficulty anyone has in understanding completely what anyone else thinks: a form of psychological alienation or imprisonment that parallels the physical imprisonment or restraint binding the characters in *A Cruel Madness, Falling,* and Thubron's next novel, *Turning Back the Sun* (1991).

Widely reviewed and mostly praised, *Turning Back the Sun* was short-listed for the Booker Prize in England. The novel marks a return to the level of virtuosity Thubron achieved in *A Cruel Madness.* Writing in *The Literary*

Review (September 1991), Janet Barron compared him with Graham Greene and called *Turning Back the Sun* "an immensely impressive fiction, filled with the joy of survival behind the walls of its sombre reflections. It is a novel which stays in the mind, touching in its tender eroticism, a proof of hope always triumphing over experience. There is never a word out of place in this masterpiece of a book." In a review for *The Sunday Times* (15 September 1991), Nick Hornby wrote that it was "an awesomely accomplished piece of work. Thubron's prose has qualities one was beginning to fear had disappeared from the English novel: he writes with a cool, unmannered precision and a genuine and welcome self-effacement, as if he really believed that what is on the other side of the window is of more interest than the glass itself. The result is an old-fashioned literary novel of depth, complexity and deceptive power. . . ."

Thubron told Perrick in 1991 that "The original intent of *Turning Back the Sun* had to do with somebody enduring the here and now, enduring life. It's a little bit odd that I should write of such things, because I'm extraordinarily free, no restrictions at all." It is set in an unnamed country that seems somewhat like Australia but with a centralized dictatorial government. Others have detected traces of South Africa or Argentina, and Thubron told Perrick that he connected his setting with "the system I saw operating in northwest China, where people were forcibly sent to outlying towns." The main character, a doctor named Rayner, is just such a person. He practices medicine in a dusty provincial city a thousand kilometers from the capital, where he grew up. He longs for a summons back to the capital, and worries about the security system, embodied by his old schoolmate Ivar, who keeps things under control for the military government. On the frontier, society is dramatically divided between the white inhabitants, all of whom have come from somewhere else, and the aboriginal population, who call themselves "blackfellers" and live in poverty in and near the town.

The fears of the whites are aroused by a series of murders attributed to the aborigines and by a skin disorder which causes a brown discoloration that seems to threaten to turn white people into blacks. In a state of lurid suspicion, Rayner, whose job it is to treat the people with the skin condition, tries ineffectively to calm fears and assert reason. Meanwhile Ivar tries to keep order by torturing and threatening people. Rayner is quite fascinated by the aborigines though he does not doubt that they may be responsible for murdering whites. When the opportunity to return to the capital finally comes, Rayner finds it strangely disappointing. As Thubron told Perrick, Rayner finds the city "thinner, sweeter. He's sickened by it and thinks the people

there are like children, they haven't learnt anything." He returns to the frontier.

This extraordinary novel has many strengths. As one would expect from one of the best living travel writers, the novel reveals an exquisite mastery of location. Wherever the setting, it is carefully created and believable. Though it may not be—as Carolyn See, the reviewer for *The Los Angeles Times* (27 July 1992), called it—"an allegory on racism," *Turning Back the Sun* does examine racial difference and domination, and the fascination of the aborigines in a way that sometimes reminds a reader of Bruce Chatwin's *The Songlines* (1987). *Turning Back the Sun* is also a subtle examination of nostalgia and memory; the atmosphere of menace and potential catastrophe is impressively maintained.

Another impressive aspect of the novel is the vivid characterization of a dancer at a seedy club, Zoe, with whom Rayner has an affair. Another exile from the capital, Zoe withholds cooperation from the regime by refusing to try to please audiences with her dancing, and she becomes unpopular with the patrons of the club. In his *Sunday Times* review, Hornby worried that the exotic Zoe came too close to the colorful Clara in *Falling:* "the author's women are beginning to appear as if they belong in a different world, where the exotic and the extraordinary exist in splendid metaphorical isolation, just out of the grasp of those stuck with more mundane lives." Perrick, on the other hand, praised exactly the same quality, calling both heroines "vibrantly alive" and calling Zoe "'all colour and bite,' with lashing of make-up and glittering leotards." Thubron told Perrick that Zoe is based on a real woman: "I fell in love with such a woman once, somebody who was out there performing, glamorised and beautiful. The tension between the stage persona and the real person is exciting, a sort of teaser." He also commented that he preferred such women to upper-middle-class women of his generation, "who all went on cookery courses, or something like that."

Hornby's concern that "women readers may feel a little alienated by this masculine vision of femininity, in which girls earn a living by dressing up and leaving real life behind" also overlooks the strong character Katherine in *Falling,* the normal, perhaps even upper-middle-class, alternative to Clara. In Thubron's next novel all the characters (bizarre mishaps aside) are more conventional. Yet, as in *Falling,* the main character is pulled between two women representing different human possibilities.

Distance (1996) begins with Edward Sanders "coming to" or waking up from a blacked-out spell. He has no recollection of his past two years and is living with a woman, Naomi, whom he does not recognize. During the course of the novel his memory gradually returns to him; after a while he can remember all but, say, the past eighteen months; then all but the past year. Edward is an astrophysicist, a postgraduate research student in astronomy, who is researching black holes.

Distance is a fascinating study of amnesia, but it is less powerful than *Turning Back the Sun,* and the astrophysical details do not greatly contribute to the overall effect of the novel. In a 15 September 1996 review for *The Observer* (London), Anthony Quinn objected to the "coldness at its heart" but concluded that "the writing is spare and unfussy, and in the book's closing stages the basic thriller mechanism—what horrible secret lurks in memory's locked attic?–is screwed tighter with each page." Michael Arditti's review for *The Independent* (1 September 1996) strongly connected *Distance* with *Falling,* suggesting that in both books the protagonists "are torn between two archetypal women, the light and the dark. . . . in *Distance* they are Naomi (once again an artist) and Jacqueline, who consciously defines herself as Edward's 'dark companion'–that is, the black hole which accompanies a star."

In 1999 Thubron, at age sixty, talked to Atiyah about his future travel plans. "For me," he explained, "travel has nothing to do with escape. . . . To travel is to meet the world, not to escape it. Staying in my cosy flat in London—that would be escapism. . . ." After Siberia, he was pondering the appeals of India and Iran. Wherever he goes next it seems likely that he will continue to contribute to the world of letters explorations of both external and internal spaces: travel books recounting encounters with the extreme and incisive, elegant literary novels of depth, complexity, and power.

Interviews:

Malise Ruthven, "Guardian Conversations: Colin Thubron," videocassette, ICA Video, 1980;

Penny Perrick, "The Distressed Gentleman," *Sunday Times* (London), 8 September 1991, p. 5;

James Eve, "I couldn't imagine that as an adult I wouldn't go everywhere on the map," *Times* (London), 7 October 1999;

Jeremy Atiyah, "Colin Thubron: In Search of Lone Comforts," *Independent* (London), 10 October 1999, p. 2;

Gayle Feldman, "Colin Thubron: The Art of Traveling Well," *Publishers Weekly,* 247 (28 February 2000): 54–55.

Reference:

John Docherty, "George MacDonald's 'The Portent' and Colin Thubron's *A Cruel Madness,*" *North Wind: Journal of the George MacDonald Society,* 13 (1994): 19–23.

Mary Wesley

(24 June 1912 –   )

Stacey Short
Texas A&M University

BOOKS: *The Sixth Seal* (London: Macdonald, 1969; New York: Stein & Day, 1971; revised edition, London: Dent, 1984; Woodstock, N.Y.: Overlook Press, 1993);

Speaking Terms (London: Faber & Faber, 1969; Boston: Gambit, 1971);

Haphazard House (London: Dent, 1983; Woodstock, N.Y.: Overlook Press, 1993);

Jumping the Queue (London: Macmillan, 1983; New York: Penguin, 1988);

The Camomile Lawn (London: Macmillan, 1984; New York: Summit, 1984);

Harnessing Peacocks (London: Macmillan, 1985; New York: Scribners, 1986);

The Vacillations of Poppy Carew (London: Macmillan, 1986; New York: Penguin, 1988);

Not That Sort of Girl (London: Macmillan, 1987; New York: Viking, 1988);

Second Fiddle (London: Macmillan, 1988; New York: Viking, 1989);

A Sensible Life (London: Bantam, 1990; New York: Viking, 1990);

A Dubious Legacy (London: Bantam, 1992; New York: Viking, 1992);

An Imaginative Experience (London: Bantam, 1994; New York: Viking, 1995);

Part of the Furniture (New York: Viking, 1996; London: Bantam, 1997).

Collections: *Magic Landscapes: A Mary Wesley Omnibus* (London: Dent, 1991)–comprises *Haphazard House, Speaking Terms,* and *The Sixth Seal;*

Three Novels: Jumping the Queue; The Camomile Lawn; Harnessing Peacocks (London: Macmillan, 1992);

Omnibus II (London: Macmillan London, 1993)–comprises *The Vacillations of Poppy Carew, Not That Sort of Girl,* and *Second Fiddle.*

PRODUCED SCRIPT: *Harnessing Peacocks,* television, Thursday Friday Saturday Productions, 1992.

Mary Wesley, circa 1990 (photograph by Kate Ganz Dorment; from the dust jacket for the American edition of A Sensible Life*)*

SELECTED PERIODICAL PUBLICATIONS–UNCOLLECTED: "The Ideal Summer," *Country Life,* 112 (25 June 1998): 98;

"Continental Drift," *Times Educational Supplement,* 21 August 1998, p. 24.

Mary Wesley is a novelist known for her controversial subjects and sarcastic, often darkly humorous style. Although she considers herself a literary late bloomer–she began her career in writing at the age of fifty-seven–she has been a prolific writer, publishing three children's novels and ten adult novels as of 1996. Wesley is more well known in Britain, where motion-picture adaptations of several of her novels have aired on BBC networks. While Wesley enjoys a diverse audience and a general popularity, she has received little academic or scholarly attention.

Wesley was born Mary Farmar on 24 June 1912 in Englefield Green, England, to Harold Mynors Farmar, an army colonel, and Violet Dalby Farmar. Her family moved frequently to a series of countries because of her father's military postings. The moves meant that Wesley was taught by a succession of governesses, tutors, and military schools, leaving her with little formal education. To supplement what she perceived as her poor schooling, she attended Queens College in London from 1928 to 1930 and then the London School of Economics and Political Science in 1931–1932. In January 1937 she married a baron, Charles Swinfen Eady, Lord Swinfen. Wesley often draws from her experiences as wife to a baron in her later novels, making fun of upper-class British conventions. They had two sons, Roger Mynors Swinfen Eady and Hugh Toby Eady, before they divorced in 1944. In the early years of World War II, from 1939 to 1941, Wesley worked in the War Office on secret documents and lived in Cornwall. In 1941, she left her first husband and moved in with journalist Eric Siepman, who eventually became her second husband. Wesley has recalled strangely fond memories of the war years as a time when conventions were set aside, and her experiences from that period have profoundly influenced her writing.

Wesley and Siepman had one son together, William, and eventually married in 1952. The marriage was happy despite difficulties caused by Siepman's bipolar disorder. Mood swings from mania to depression left him unable to keep a steady job or hold onto money. Wesley converted to Roman Catholicism after her second marriage, and despite her unorthodox subjects, her religion has been an important influence on her writing. Siepman and his friend, novelist Antonia White, first encouraged Wesley in her writing, though she had written privately for herself since she was a young girl. Siepman often used her translations and sometimes turned in as his newspaper articles that she had written. Her first published works were those she wrote to read to him when he was bedridden with Parkinson's disease. When she began to publish, she took for herself the pen name "Mary Wesley." Siepman died of Parkinson's in 1970, leaving Wesley to manage on social security until she received an advance for *Jumping the Queue* (1983) and became able to support herself with her writing.

Wesley's first publications were three science-fiction novels for children, *The Sixth Seal* (1969), *Speaking Terms* (1969), and *Haphazard House* (1983). Although most of the blurbs on the dust jackets of her books state that she published her first novel at the age of seventy-one, her children's novels came out years before; she obviously does not consider them in the same class as her adult fiction. *The Sixth Seal* clearly reflects the cold-war paranoia of its time of publication. Set in a post-apocalyptic dystopia, it follows the typical formula for the genre. One night while Muriel, her son Paul, and his friend Henry sleep out in a pit in the backyard, a strange plague of "black snow" falls over the earth, obliterating all life that it touches. Only people who were underground were spared, and in the morning they discover that they are almost the last people on earth. This catastrophe turns out to be somewhat of a blessing for Muriel, who had been unable to pay her bills and now will not have to. The rest of the novel depicts the search for more survivors and the coming-of-age of Paul and Henry. By the end of the novel, enough people have been found to form a community, and at Muriel's suggestion they elect Henry as their leader. *The Sixth Seal* is an unremarkable work, and it received fairly lukewarm reviews.

Speaking Terms also has a predictable plot but shows Wesley's style maturing and her skills sharpening. The novel, about talking animals speaking up about the mistreatment of their kind, takes a clear stand in favor of animal rights. It is narrated by Kate, a schoolgirl whose bullfinch, Mr. Bull, starts talking one morning after eating the buds off her father's almond tree. Soon, more and more animals begin talking, and they recruit Kate, her sister Angela, and a couple of local boys to help save some otters from hunters. This action begins a rather predictable series of events to free animals and protect them from human exploitation and extermination. By the end of the novel, Kate and Angela's parents, as well as other adults, are converted to work for more comprehensive animal rights. As had Wesley's first novel, *Speaking Terms* received mixed reviews, some pointing out the stilted dialogue and uninspired plot.

Haphazard House is the most successful and popular of Wesley's children's books. Nominated for the Carnegie Medal for children's literature and the *Observer* Prize for children's fiction, it differs markedly from Wesley's first two books. Published more than ten years after these works, the novel shows the maturing of Wesley's style, and her confidence in writing a much different kind of children's fantasy anticipates the unorthodox plot twists, characters, and topics of her later writing.

Haphazard House is narrated by eleven-year-old Lisa, who attends her painter father's first show of his own work. On the way, he purchases a magic panama hat to help disguise his real identity from

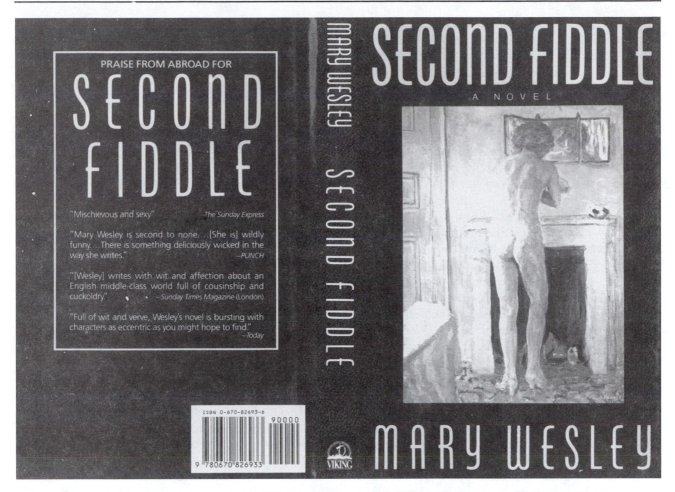

Dust jacket for the American edition of Wesley's 1988 novel, the sequel to her Not That Sort of Girl *(1987)*

patrons at the gallery. Upon reaching the gallery they discover her father has sold every work in the exhibit. Fearing commercial success, her father bets his entire earnings on a long-shot horse Lisa chooses, False Start. Apparently because of the magic hat, the horse wins, and Lisa's family becomes incredibly rich. While waiting at the dentist's office, Lisa and her father peruse old *Country Life* magazines and find in them a mysterious country house they decide to buy with their new money. The family and a motley entourage of animals and random strangers—a meter attendant, three squatters, and a baby—all move to the country estate of Haphazard House.

Once at the house, strange events begin to occur. Lisa's parents and grandfather become younger, there is a mysterious disappearing man in an identical panama hat, and an invisible gardener. Lisa comes to understand that time at Haphazard House is not linear but random, and depending upon the person and the hat, people can be in any time between 1666 and the future.

Eventually, she makes for herself a future with a Haphazard House resident from 1949, Haphazard Hayco.

Haphazard House is a coming-of-age story as well as a science-fiction story about time travel. The novel manages to blend an interesting and improbable tale with important lessons about growing up. As the narrative progresses, Lisa witnesses older people becoming young and finds herself in an adult body. She is at first puzzled by her mother's swiftness as a young woman, her grandfather's striking good looks as a middle-aged man, and the fear of a young couple who return to grade-school age, while their infant son disappears entirely. Lisa learns that time is relative for every person, that all older people were once young, and young people will eventually grow old. Wesley treats with sensitivity and humor the adolescent epiphany that adults were once children themselves. Critics applauded Wesley's creativity and imagination, but some were disgruntled by her refusal to provide explanations of the nature of Haphazard House and the magic hat.

Wesley's first novel for adults, *Jumping the Queue,* was published the same year as was *Haphazard House* but has an entirely different tone, genre, and intended audience. In an interview with Clare Boylan for *Publishers Weekly* (6 July 1990), Wesley stated that she began writing the novel "as a means of working out despair" after the death of her second husband. Wesley's despair, feelings of isolation, and alienation are evident at the start of the novel, as the protagonist, Matilda Poliport, a widow, carefully sets the stage for her suicide. After cleaning up her home and giving away her pet goose, she heads to the beach with a picnic basket of rolls, cheese, and Beaujolais, intending to take an overdose of pills and wade into the ocean. Matilda feels overwhelmed by the bombardment of information from the various media of television, radio, and newspapers, particularly stories of "the Matricide," a man who beat his mother to death with a serving tray and then seemingly disappeared. Matilda puts off her own suicide to prevent a young man, who turns out to be the Matricide, from also jumping off the bridge. Matilda then brings the young man, named Hugh Warner, back to her isolated home.

Most of the novel takes place in Matilda's house, where she and Hugh try to learn more about each other and use each other to find a reason to keep going. Their isolation from their communities and families becomes quickly evident. Matilda has seen each of her four children only once in the past three years, and obviously dislikes the people they are. She reveals to Hugh stories of meanness, selfishness, greed, and incest that make each one of the Poliports, children and parents alike, seem distinctly unlikable. Hugh, having admitted killing his mother, has only one remaining relative, a missing brother. As Hugh points out to Matilda, when discussing the stray dog they rescue during the flight from the bridge, she seems to love and have intimate connections only with animals.

One important recurring theme in *Jumping the Queue* is the comparison between the love and loyalty of animals and that of human companions. Matilda often likens her relationship with her dead husband, Tom, to that of swans, who mate for life. Gus, the pet goose, is also extremely loyal and runs away from his new home to return to Matilda. It becomes clear as the novel progresses that Gus is far more loyal to Matilda than Tom ever was, leaving a harem of geese to return to Matilda, in stark contrast to Tom's infidelities, including incest with their eldest daughter. Hugh turns out to be just as disloyal as Tom and every other person in Matilda's life. Leaving in the middle of the night after attempting to rape her, Hugh assures himself of Matilda's well-being by leaving the stray dog, Folly, with her. Hugh fails to notice that Folly loyally follows

him out of the house and down the road and is struck by a car. The deaths of Folly and Gus, in addition to Hugh's leaving, frees Matilda again of ties and obligations, and she returns to the beach, this time successfully completing her suicide.

Jumping the Queue was Wesley's first successful novel and also marks the first time she was able to make any substantial money from her writing. After its publication she was able to live a more comfortable and financially secure life. Despite this success, however, *Jumping the Queue* is one of Wesley's more controversial works, mostly because of her clear advocacy for euthanasia and the lack of any kind of moral or ethical stand in the narration. In this novel, as in her other works, the narrator is an omniscient yet dispassionate outside observer. Wesley uses third-person narration to treat subjects such as incest, euthanasia, and violence in a nonjudgmental, objective manner that has displeased some reviewers.

Because of the controversial nature of the issues Wesley addresses in *Jumping the Queue,* she requested that there be no publicity for the novel. She was concerned that her novel would offend those close to her, but her desire to keep a low profile may have resulted in the book receiving little critical attention when it was published. What commentary it has received has been consistently mixed, dependent mainly upon the critic's wish for a clear moral judgment, or alternatively, satisfaction with having the difficult questions raised and brought into the open to think about. Reception for *Jumping the Queue* after its publication in the United States was similar, with some critics offended by plots of incest and suicide and others admiring Wesley's edgy, sardonic style and the complexity of the narrative. Eventually, as Wesley's popularity increased, *Jumping the Queue* was made into a two-part television movie by the BBC.

Wesley's second novel for adults, *The Camomile Lawn* (1984), is the first written in what has become her signature style of tragicomic romance peppered with stingingly witty commentary on social mores and convention. The novel begins at a dinner party on the eve of World War II, with five cousins meeting some new neighbors, German Jewish refugees, at the house of their childless Uncle Richard and Aunt Helena. The new neighbors, Max and Monika, are hoping for war, as their son is in a concentration camp, and the cousins also long for the excitement of war. As the novel progresses, the reader discovers that the early narrative is really a flashback, and that the major players are reminiscing on their way to attend Max's funeral, more than forty-five years after the initial dinner party.

Although the war plays an important role in the narrative, it is not central to either the characters or the action of the story. *The Camomile Lawn* is a romance, and the action of the narrative lies within the shifting relationships of and between the main characters—the nine people who attended the dinner party. Wesley, whose own life was radically affected by the events and conditions of World War II, uses the novel to explore the ways in which wartime allows people to throw off conventional social mores and sexual ethics and—in the fear that each encounter could be their last—to explore their passions freely. Although she denies that her novels are autobiographical, in *The Camomile Lawn* in particular, there are many parallels between the characters' choices and actions during the war and those of Wesley herself.

The Camomile Lawn unfolds a highly complicated set of relationships, including several love triangles, shared sexual partners, and in one case, wife-swapping. In an interesting twist, some of the love triangles dissolve while others become a kind of permanent ménage à trois. Another unusual angle to the narrative is that not only the younger generation explores unconventional relationships; the war allows the older members of the party to discover their own passions as well. As the story evolves, the characters continually relate back to the dinner party as a touchstone to their prewar selves. By the end of the novel, the characters are universally grateful to the war for allowing them the freedom to explore opportunities they would not have had if the war had not intervened in their lives.

The characters in *The Camomile Lawn* return to make appearances in Wesley's later novels, particularly Calypso Grant, the cousin who marries for money and then later discovers that she has fallen in love with her rich husband, who has always loved her. Calypso makes a brief appearance in *Harnessing Peacocks* (1985) and then plays a larger role in *The Vacillations of Poppy Carew* (1986), as the aunt to Willy the pig farmer. Some critics have suggested that Calypso serves as a kind of alter ego for Wesley.

Like *Jumping the Queue*, *The Camomile Lawn* had little impact on the critical community, which was still mostly unaware of Wesley's work. In general, critical response was gently positive but not overly enthusiastic. As Wesley's work became better known, *The Camomile Lawn* also became more popular, and the book was adapted into a television miniseries for the BBC in 1992.

Some critics have referred to Wesley as a modern Jane Austen because her novels often make fun of class distinctions, social convention, and mores. This thematic interest is certainly expressed in Wesley's next novel, *Harnessing Peacocks*. The novel focuses on the humorous indecision of the protagonist, Hebe, over whether it is better to be "nice" or "the wrong sort" of person. Hebe, who is from an upper-class background,

MARY WESLEY
PART OF
THE FURNITURE

Dust jacket for Wesley's 1996 novel, about life on a North Country farm during World War II

runs away from her grandparents' house when she learns that her grandfather has arranged for her to abort her illegitimate child. The family's concern is entirely for their name and the political and social position of the men. The story picks up again twelve years later, as Hebe is working as a special cook for old women and as a part-time prostitute, or "tart," as she refers to herself. With the money she makes from cooking and prostitution, Hebe has been able to send her son, Silas, to the right kind of prep school, and she hopes to eventually send him to Eton. Aware of the inconsistency between her disgust for her family's classist ideals and her desire for the possibilities of that life for her son, Hebe agonizes over whether or not she is doing the right thing for Silas.

Several scenes involving the clash between classes evoke Austen's witty and pointed jabs at social convention and illustrate the theme that money and family do not necessarily guarantee true social grace. In particular, Silas's experience at the Reeses' summer cottage highlights the vulgarity of the upper classes. The

Reeses are parents of a school friend, Michael, who has invited Silas to spend three weeks of summer holiday sailing. Hebe hopes Silas will eventually mix with this sort of social class. It turns out, however, that Michael is a fickle friend, and the Reeses' loud vulgarity, pointed rudeness, and taunting eventually lead to Silas's escaping back home after throwing a glass of wine at Mr. Reese. Such portrayals are in stark contrast to the friendly families of Silas's working-class neighborhood and to his friend Giles.

Throughout *Harnessing Peacocks* Wesley makes reference to the myth of Hebe, the Greek goddess of youth, for whom the protagonist is named. According to Greek mythology, Hebe was the cupbearer to the gods on Mount Olympus. She was the daughter of Zeus and Hera and helped Hera with her chariot, pulled by a team of peacocks. In the novel, the peacocks are Hebe's clients, the Syndicate, whom she harnesses through sex.

Like her Greek goddess counterpart, Hebe only finds happiness when she stops catering to the elite classes and focuses on what will make both her and Silas happiest in the long run. Real happiness for each character is only attainable once they have rejected their ties with or pretensions to the upper classes. Hebe realizes that Silas is not happy at his expensive public school and would prefer to go to school locally. In telling Silas about her own background, she comes to understand that she should stop trying to live according to the conventions, rules, and mores under which she was reared. At the same time, she and Silas, now much closer, decide that ultimately class does not matter as much as each had thought and that the elite seem more concerned with how people talk than with how they act. The novel wraps up in the tradition of a Shakespearean comedy, with a series of connections and odd circumstances bringing couples together, including Hebe and Silas's previously unknown father.

Critical response to *Harnessing Peacocks* was positive. Some critics had problems with the complex and implausible plot and with the theme of the "happy prostitute" that Hebe represents. Overall, however, reviewers appreciated Wesley's wit, humor, and skills with narrative that keep the novel fast-paced, no matter how impossible the plot. Virtually all reviewers lauded Wesley's pointed social commentary and satirical wit.

The Vacillations of Poppy Carew, which was published the year after *Harnessing Peacocks,* is a light and funny romantic comedy. It follows the foibles of a group of people brought together by the death of Bob Carew, father of the title character, Poppy. The novel begins with Poppy's visit to her father on his deathbed to tell him that she has been left by her boyfriend, Edmund, over whom they have fought for the last eight years.

Hearing that Edmund is out of Poppy's life, Bob literally dies laughing. As Poppy makes the arrangements for her father's funeral—hiring the mortuary, Furnivals Fun Funerals, that her father requested—she meets a variety of characters associated with her father and the participants in the service.

In the tradition of carnival comedy, many misunderstandings, mistakes, and mix-ups happen before all the characters can be paired up with their true loves. Fergus Furnival discovers that the baby he has been deriding is actually his, and he gets together with the mother. Victor, Fergus's cousin, reunites with his former wife, and Poppy promises to marry Willy, the pig farmer who fell in love with her at first sight at the funeral. In this way, the novel is typical of Wesley's style, as the connections between characters and a complex web of coincidences lie at the heart of the narrative. Unlike most of Wesley's novels, however, *The Vacillations of Poppy Carew* lacks her stinging commentary on class conflict and outdated sexual mores.

Critical reception for *The Vacillations of Poppy Carew* was rather cool. While critics still appreciated Wesley's wit, they were put off by the uninspired plot and predictable ending. Many reviewers disliked the characters, suggesting that young people are not a suitable topic for Wesley, and called the dialogue occasionally strained and unnatural.

Not That Sort of Girl (1987) is similar in style to *Harnessing Peacocks* and *The Vacillations of Poppy Carew.* Another light romantic comedy intermingled with satirical comment on the conventions and mores of the British upper class, *Not That Sort of Girl* focuses on the long, mostly illicit, romance between Rose Freeling and Mylo Cooper. The novel begins with the death of Rose's husband, Ned, and tells the story of Rose and Mylo in flashbacks through Rose's eyes, beginning with the day they met, before either of them were married, and ending with their reunion almost fifty years later, free at last to begin their lives together. In the interim, they manage an intermittent affair through World War II and into their middle years, until they are both in their late sixties and have outlived both of their spouses.

In many ways *Not That Sort of Girl* could be taken as a general criticism of marriage and a condemnation of the reasons people have for getting married. Wesley presents no marriage in which both partners are happy or faithful. Rose's parents hate each other, though they pretend not to, and when Rose's father dies, her mother breaks out of her shell and begins to live happily for the first time. Rose and Ned's marriage is one of security on her part and convenience on his. While Mylo tells Rose that his parents' marriage was happy, his own marriage to Victoria is based on pity. The couples who seem happiest are the ones not married, like the Farthings, the devoted couple who tend Ned's ancestral home, and Nicholas and Emily, an incestuous pair of twins.

The title of the novel at first seems to refer to the protagonist, Rose, who everyone assumes is "not the sort of girl" to have affairs, think for herself, or have secrets. Most of the women in the novel, however, turn out to be "not the sort of girl" everyone assumes. Rose's mother turns out to be not the mousy, patient woman she seemed while married but a level-headed business manager who hates children and procreation in general. Emily Thornby appears to be just the sort of girl to have affairs and sleep around, but nobody suspects that her daughter is the result of incest.

Not That Sort of Girl was well received in Britain, where it was a finalist for the *Sunday Express* Book of the Year Award. Partially because of its success in Britain, the novel was published in the United States in 1988, along with American editions of *Jumping the Queue* and *The Vacillations of Poppy Carew.* The reviews in American publications were not as positive, however, as several critics had problems with the plot, finding it strained in believability and overly sentimental.

Second Fiddle (1988) is a sequel to *Not That Sort of Girl,* telling the story of Laura, the daughter of Emily Thornby, probably the product of the incestuous relationship between Emily and her twin brother, Nicholas. The book follows Laura, now in her forties, through a relationship with Claud Bannister, who is struggling to write his first book. With Laura's help he moves out of his mother's house into his own loft and supports himself by selling junk at a market stall. Surprising Laura, Claud is successful both at the stall and at his novel, which eventually gets published. Laura meantime moves back and forth between her hometown with Claud and her parents and London, where she has a separate, private life. By the end of the novel, Laura has dissociated herself from any kind of connections, either familial or romantic.

In the course of telling Laura's story, *Second Fiddle* updates readers on the lives of the main characters of *Not That Sort of Girl.* Wesley reveals that Rose and Mylo are happily married and that Emily and Nicholas have become pathetically nasty old people and are referred to by villagers as "poisonous." For the most part, however, *Second Fiddle* is a novel about the strange alienation that can evolve between parents and children and the trials and tribulations that assail new authors. The title refers to Laura's feeling that she plays second fiddle to Claud's fictional heroine, but as the novel progresses, it becomes clear that Laura comes second in many other lives. Emily and Nicholas, for example, are far more concerned with each other than with her. The theme of

incest is disturbingly prominent in this novel, though it remains a subplot to the central action.

Critical reception for *Second Fiddle* was positive, notwithstanding concerns over the continual references to incest. Critics were uniformly appreciative of Wesley's prose style and enjoyed her dark wit and her unusual but likable characters. British critics seemed more enthusiastic than American critics, who were more disturbed by the dark undertones of the novel.

Wesley followed *Second Fiddle* with another semiromantic coming-of-age narrative, *A Sensible Life* (1990). On the surface, *A Sensible Life* seems more like the lighter romances of *The Vacillations of Poppy Carew* and *Not That Sort of Girl,* but in tone is far darker, more similar to *Jumping the Queue.* The novel follows the life of Flora Trevelyan, who has been emotionally abandoned by her parents since birth, and then completely abandoned during her adolescence, when she is left at a home school in England year round. Pitied by the acquaintances she comes into contact with, Flora is invited to join other families' activities as a sop to middle-class matrons' consciences. At the age of ten, on a picnic, Flora falls in love with three of the young men—Felix, Cosmo, and Hubert—and the novel recounts her various encounters with them throughout her adolescence and adulthood. Eventually, for different reasons, Flora snubs all three and makes her own way in the world.

A Sensible Life parallels the themes of *Jumping the Queue* in exploring the alienation between parents and children, as well as the dissociation of an individual from society. Wesley's biting portrayal of Flora's self-absorbed parents continues her criticism of middle-class mores and the importance placed on seeming to do the right thing. Flora's parents, Denys and Vita, are an even more narcissistic couple than are Nicholas and Emily Thornby in *Not That Sort of Girl* and *Second Fiddle.* Denys and Vita come to represent everything gone wrong with the middle class—social pretensions, self-absorption, and putting image before substance. Flora is the result of their neglect: a child who rejects her privileged background for the anonymity of the servant class, preferring to work for a living rather than allow herself to be swept into a convenient marriage. The reader is meant to admire Flora for her courage in refusing her mother's life for one in which she is in control of her own destiny.

The critical reception for *A Sensible Life* was mixed. While sales figures were high and some critics applauded the satire, others were put off by the choppy plot and forced romantic ending. Several critics noted Wesley's unusually sympathetic portrayal of Flora and remarked that *A Sensible Life* had a deeper and less arch tone than Wesley's previous work.

Mary Wesley, at the time of Part of the Furniture
(photograph by Jane Brown)

A Dubious Legacy (1992), Wesley's version of Charlotte Brontë's *Jane Eyre* (1847), revolves around the estate manor, Cotteshaw, and its eccentric owner, Henry Tillotson. Henry, upon the dying advice of his father, marries Margaret out of pity. She turns out to be insane, staying in her bedroom, which she continually has redecorated around her, and leaving only occasionally to cause some kind of destructive scene. Two couples, James and Barbara Martineau and Matthew and Antonia Stephenson, become engaged at and later move into the manor with the Tillotsons and their entourage. Life there is punctuated by Margaret's malicious episodes—setting a bird on fire then beheading it, pouring perfume on two dogs, and attempting to drown a little girl. There are hints that during their residence at Cotteshaw, Antonia and Barbara become pregnant by Henry, who is continually saving someone from harm at his wife's hands. Calypso Grant also reappears in this novel, with husband Hector, to make comments on marriage and children.

In *A Dubious Legacy* Wesley speculates about what traits, habits, and psychologies children inherit from their parents. Many characters in the novel come from uncertain patrimony, and those that appear certain, Henry and Margaret for example, do not seem to have inherited anything enviable or useful. The central characters seem to inherit only basic personality traits of uncertain advantage. The tangible legacies of the manor and money are downplayed in the novel in favor of exploring more abstract ones.

Like many of Wesley's later novels, critical reception for *A Dubious Legacy* was mixed, though more positive than the previous novel. The most notable complaints in reviews of *A Dubious Legacy* were directed at the quality of the writing and the veracity of the settings. A few reviewers felt that Wesley was not up to her usual form in this novel and was beginning to get sloppy with her writing—pointing out plot flaws, anachronisms, and the lack of a clear central point. Several critics missed the lighter tone of the earlier comedy of manners novels, and did not understand Wesley's switch in genres.

An Imaginative Experience (1994) is a romantic comedy with Wesley's usual dark undertones. The story follows two people who have recently suffered a loss: Sylvester Wykes, a writer whose wife has just left him, and Julia Piper, whose former husband and young son were killed in a car crash. Sylvester has a hard time keeping people out of his life and getting privacy, whereas Julia is almost alone in the world, with the exception of the Patels, who own a corner shop, and a mongrel dog. Julia's mother, Clodagh, is alive but blames Julia for the deaths of her grandson and Julia's former husband, who was also Clodagh's lover. Alienated from her family and her neighbors, Julia grieves alone until the Patels come to take care of her. Once on her feet, Julia goes back to her work of cleaning houses, and in a typical Wesley plot twist, ends up working as Sylvester's cleaning lady, though they communicate only through notes and the Patels. They eventually meet when Julia stays overnight in Sylvester's supposedly empty house and he returns home unexpectedly.

Julia and Sylvester are spied on by Maurice Benson, a bird-watcher and former private detective. Maurice is a strangely sinister character who ferrets out information and then uses it to torment Julia. He also has a grudge against Sylvester but is too scared to harass him as he does Julia. Maurice seems to disappear once Sylvester and Julia come to an agreement on a relationship, although he is unlikely to abandon his obsession forever.

An Imaginative Experience is much like Wesley's earlier romantic comedies, only this time it is the new middle class of yuppies that are held up for satire. The work also focuses on Wesley's usual themes of individual isolation and parent/child alienation. Despite Julia's dark background and the evil menace of Maurice, *An Imaginative Experience* has a lighter tone than most of Wesley's later work and is more similar in plot and tone to *Harnessing Peacocks* and *The Vacillations of Poppy Carew*. Like the earlier romantic comedies, *An Imaginative Experience* relies on an intricate series of implausible coincidences to bring characters together. Perhaps responding to those reviewers who have criticized this aspect of her work,

Wesley includes a conversation between Julia and Sylvester about the coincidences they have experienced that would not be believed if Sylvester included them in one of his novels.

The critical response to *An Imaginative Experience* was tepid to negative. Critics familiar with Wesley's work were disappointed with the generally upbeat tone and lack of sarcastic humor and accused Wesley of losing the sharp edge that had characterized her earlier works. Critics were also unhappy with the plot based on unlikely coincidences, just as they had been with *Harnessing Peacocks* and *The Vacillations of Poppy Carew*. They pointed to the character of Maurice as a weak plot device and speculated that he was simply there to shore up an otherwise rickety plotline. Unusually, reviewers were also disappointed with the characters, feeling that they were not well-defined and that in general the writing was not up to Wesley's usual quality.

In *Part of the Furniture* (1996), Wesley returns to her most successful formula: a romantic comedy set in World War II England. *Part of the Furniture* is a mixture of coming-of-age story and quest romance. The novel traces the wartime experiences of Juno Marlowe, a seventeen-year-old girl who has fancied herself in love with two older boys from her village since she was a child. The boys, seven years older than she and self-absorbed and opportunistic, first exploit her affection by taking advantage of the free labor she represents; then, on the eve of leaving for war, they use her to experiment with sex, leaving her alone at the train station to watch their departure afterwards. During an air raid, Juno encounters Evelyn Copplestone, who is dying from mustard-gas lung damage from World War I. He sympathizes with her plight—not wanting to join her newly remarried mother in Canada—and writes her a letter of introduction to his father, Robert, who lives on a North Country farm.

Juno stumbles upon a warmth and welcome at Copplestone farm; when she discovers she is pregnant, the farm occupants are delighted and help her deliver twins, evidently fathered by both of the two boys. Juno and the twins thrive on the farm, and eventually Robert and Juno admit to a May-December romance and are married.

Part of the Furniture is one of Wesley's funniest novels, a comedy of manners revolving around Juno's pregnancy and the various people it eventually involves. Less dark than previous novels, Wesley still presents a picture of alienation between parent and child in the case of Juno and her mother, but this portrayal is mitigated by the good parent-child relationships of Juno and her twins, Robert and Evelyn, and Aunt Victoria's boarders and their beloved daughters. Juno's quest, not just for self-discovery, but to find connections to someone who values her, is more than achieved at Copplestone, where she is loved and doted on by virtually every inhabitant of the farm, humans and animals alike.

Part of the Furniture was received well, and though some critics still complained that Wesley was losing her cynical edge, most enjoyed the comic elements and Wesley's broad jokes about the British preoccupation with breeding and family. Unlike her two previous novels, critics found the narrative engaging and the plot cohesive, if somewhat melodramatic and almost too romantic.

Wesley's best fiction presents an interesting picture of life during World War II and satirizes conventional British society. Her nonjudgmental treatment of controversial subjects continues to attract new readers.

Interview:

Clare Boylan, "Mary Wesley," *Publishers Weekly*, 237 (6 July 1990): 51–52.

Nigel Williams

(20 January 1948 –   )

Michael C. Prusse
University of Zurich

BOOKS: *My Life Closed Twice* (London: Secker & Warburg, 1977);

Class Enemy, Methuen New Theatrescript, no. 14 (London: Eyre Methuen, 1978);

Jack Be Nimble (London: Secker & Warburg, 1980);

Line 'Em (London: Eyre Methuen, 1980);

Sugar and Spice; &, Trial Run: Two Plays, Methuen New Theatrescript, no. 28 (London: Eyre Methuen, 1980);

Johnny Jarvis (London: Penguin, 1983);

W.C.P.C. (London: Methuen, 1983);

Charlie (London: Severn House, 1984);

My Brother's Keeper?: A Play (London & Boston: Faber & Faber, 1985);

Star Turn (London & Boston: Faber & Faber, 1985);

Country Dancing (London & Boston: Faber & Faber, 1987);

Witchcraft (London & Boston: Faber & Faber, 1987);

Black Magic (London: Hutchinson, 1988);

Breaking Up (London: Faber & Faber, 1988);

The Wimbledon Poisoner (London & Boston: Faber & Faber, 1990);

They Came from SW19 (London & Boston: Faber & Faber, 1992);

East of Wimbledon (London & Boston: Faber & Faber, 1993);

2 ½ Men in a Boat (London: Hodder & Stoughton, 1993);

Scenes from a Poisoner's Life (London & Boston: Faber & Faber, 1994);

From Wimbledon to Waco (London & Boston: Faber & Faber, 1995);

Harry and Me (London & Boston: Faber & Faber, 1996);

William Golding's Lord of the Flies (London & Boston: Faber & Faber, 1996);

Stalking Fiona (London: Granta, 1997);

Fortysomething (London: Viking, 1999);

Collection: *The Wimbledon Trilogy* (London: Faber & Faber, 1995)—comprises *The Wimbledon Poisoner, They Came from SW19,* and *East of Wimbledon.*

PLAY PRODUCTIONS: *Double Talk,* London, Square One Theatre, 1976;

Snowwhite Washes Whiter and *Deadwood,* Bristol, 1977;

Nigel Williams (photograph © Jerry Bauer)

Class Enemy, London, Royal Court Theatre, 4 April 1978; New York, 1979;

Easy Street, Bristol, 1979;

Line 'Em, London, Cottesloe Theatre, 1980;

Sugar and Spice, London, Royal Court Theatre, 9 October 1980;

Trial Run, Oxford, Oxford Playhouse Company, and London, Young Vic, 25 February 1980;

W.C.P.C., London, Half Moon Theatre, 29 April 1982;

The Adventures of Jasper Ridley, Hull, 1982; London, 1983;

My Brother's Keeper? London, Greenwich Theatre, February 1985;

Deathwatch, adaptation of a play by Jean Genet, Birmingham and London, 1985;

Country Dancing, Stratford-upon-Avon, The Other Place, 12 November 1986;

As It Was, adaptation of a book by Helen Thomas, Edinburgh, 1987;

Nativity, London, 1989;

Harry and Me, London, Royal Court Theatre, 21 March 1996;

William Golding's Lord of the Flies, adaptation of William Golding's novel, Wimbledon, King's College Junior School, 3 December 1991; Basingstoke, Haymarket Theatre, 1 December 1998.

PRODUCED SCRIPTS: *Talkin' Blues,* television, BBC 2, 1977;

Real Live Audience, television, 1978;

Baby Talk, television, BBC 1, 1981;

Let 'Em Know We're Here, television, 1981;

Johnny Jarvis, television, 1983;

"George Orwell," television, *Arena,* BBC, 1983;

Charlie, television, ITV, 1984;

Breaking Up, television, BBC 2, 9 November–10 December 1986;

Centrepoint, television, 1990;

The Storyteller: Greek Myths, television, TVS, 1990;

The Kremlin Farewell, television, 1990;

The Last Romantics, television, 1991;

Skallagrigg, television, BBC, adaptation of a novel by William Horwood, 1994;

The Wimbledon Poisoner, television, BBC, 1994;

It Might Be You, television, BBC, 1995.

Nigel Williams has published seventeen plays and fifteen novels to date. He has also written several television plays and produced documentaries (mainly on authors) for the British Broadcasting Corporation (BBC). Outside England, Williams is best known for his plays, especially *Class Enemy* (1978), which provided the source material for the German motion picture *Klassen Feind* (1983). The play, in which six teenage boys wait in a bare classroom for a teacher who never shows up, has been compared to Samuel Beckett's *Waiting for Godot* (1952); the hopelessness of the boys' lives and the black humor of the dialogue suggest further similarities to Beckett's work. In his fiction Williams has focused on relationships and families and the struggles they go through. The middle-class suburbs of London, Wimbledon and Putney, provide the setting for most of his novels. In a world in which suburban life is an experience shared by a growing number of people, Williams's careful analysis of life and manners in residential areas gains a certain universality. In his best books he offers serious commentary on contemporary life while utilizing satire and humor that exposes and exaggerates the grotesque behavior of suburban residents.

Born in Cheadle, Cheshire, on 20 January 1948 to David Williams, a headmaster and teacher of modern languages, and Sylvia Hartley Williams, a teacher specializing in the training of nurses for preschool children, Nigel Williams was the youngest of three brothers—born in 1942, the eldest brother, John Hartley Williams, is a well-known poet who teaches at the Free University of Berlin, and the middle brother is an executive with a video company. Williams was educated at Highgate School in London and then went on to read history at Oriel College, Oxford. He worked at the Playhouse, as he told Sheridan Morley in *The Times* (London), "putting together apparently conventional undergraduate revues, in which suddenly everyone got murdered, until the manager there said that I was the kind of dramatist whose plays should be read privately in lavatories." When Williams graduated with a B.A. in 1969, he joined the BBC and worked on Melvyn Bragg's book program, *Read All About It,* and on *Arena.* Subsequently, he became executive editor of *Bookmark* and produced documentaries. His career as a writer did not really begin until he was thirty years old. Williams has expressed the conviction that he needs another job besides writing: "If I tried to be a full-time writer I'd end up down the pub all day." In 1972 he married Suzan Harrison, and they have three sons, Ned, Jack, and Harry. He lives in Putney, London, and works as a writer and as a BBC television executive.

Williams's first novel, *My Life Closed Twice* (1977), consists of the journal in which the compulsive novelist Martin Steel records the progress of his seventeenth work—the previous sixteen are all unpublished, and hence, he is also a collector of rejection slips. Martin, who works for the BBC, consistently fails to create fiction, instead coming up with versions of his own life as he tries to exorcise his obsession with another woman. When his wife, Ellen, and his friends discover the manuscripts, they are either offended or bored. The couple shares their flat with a journalist, Oswald, who accompanies Martin to the pub and acts as go-between in the developing marital strife. Ellen is fed up with his novel-writing antics—Martin complains about every noise, forgets his lunch, and is generally a nuisance to live with—and, eventually, she and Oswald move out. As a result of the separation, Martin instantly suffers from writer's block. Sacrificing his novel to regain Ellen, he eventually realizes that his journal (which he keeps secret from his wife) is better than his fiction.

In his journal Martin offers wry commentary on the writing life, for instance by imagining blurbs for his

Dust jacket for Williams's 1977 novel, written as the
journal of an obsessive, would-be novelist

novels that provide a comic twist to the hackneyed phrases often employed by newspaper book reviewers: "Mr Steel's characters have the quality of men and women trapped in wet cement. *The Guardian*." Much humor arises from the desperate measures that Ellen takes to force Martin to face life. To some extent, these details might be autobiographical; as Williams confided to Morley, he was "an obsessional writer" from the age of fourteen onward: "When we first got married we used to go every weekend to my mother-in-law's and I'd spend all Saturday and all Sunday in an upstairs bedroom writing a short story which I'd read to my wife on the train back to London and then, when we got to Victoria, I'd throw it in the rubbish bin." Williams added that he kept this habit up for four years until his wife began to doubt his sanity.

Although he commended the author on his "sharp ear," Michael Neve, writing in the 15 July 1977 issue of *TLS: The Times Literary Supplement*, did not like

the novel and complained of its lack of astringency. Others were far more generous with Williams's first work: the reviewer for *The Sunday Times* (London) admired the writer's "wit and energy" and called him "a splendid debunker, a talent that should take him far." Reviewing Williams's next novel in *TLS* (14 March 1980), A. N. Wilson praised *My Life Closed Twice* in retrospect by saying that it had established the writer "as an effortless verbal jokester, a master of timing and of the unexpected phrase." The novel was declared joint winner of the Somerset Maugham Award in 1978.

Jack Warliss, the protagonist of Williams's second novel, *Jack Be Nimble* (1980), is similar to Martin Steel. He sports the same linguistic aggression twinned with a "physically passive approach to the universe," as Wilson characterized him. A notorious liar with many identities, he is married to Annie Warliss and has a son, Egbert, with his mistress, Lucy, a neurotic feminist poet. Jack writes plays and sitcoms that he publishes under various pseudonyms—a precautionary measure that reflects the contempt he feels for a series such as *The Wheebles:* "They were a lethal mixture of situation comedy and soap opera, combining the worst elements of both." Then there is upheaval in his private life: his friend from school days, Mikey Snaps, is in love with Annie and leads her to Lucy. Caught in flagrante delicto, Jack runs away and has an affair with Mikey's wife, Nelly. The various adulteries result in a series of shifting relationships in which characters change their living arrangements. Eventually, Lucy and Jack reconcile, and Nelly gives birth to a child. The childbirth figures as an epiphany that propels the young adults toward greater maturity.

Jack's lying and his polygamy are treated as subjects for farce and slapstick. Despite the hilarious setup and frequent puns, the novel has an undertow of seriousness, raising topics such as the war between the sexes, adultery, politics, and race riots. Williams manages to evoke the early 1970s extremely well: there are hippies and communists, and all the protagonists are on a quest for identity. Jack in particular experiences birth as a rite of passage that makes him accept his role as father and husband. Not all critics were convinced: Desmond Hogan in *The New Statesman* (7 March 1980) described the ending as "hollow sounding." Wilson, on the other hand, enthusiastically commended the satire, which he considered more disturbing than in *My Life Closed Twice*. "This novel would be remarkable alone for its humorous exploration of the misuses to which we subject our language," Wilson wrote, praising Williams as "a warmly rich comic inventor."

Whereas *Jack Be Nimble* deals with immature adults, Williams's next novel, *Johnny Jarvis* (1983), was written with young readers in mind and describes the difficulties teenagers experience growing up. The narrator, Alan Lipton, lives with his mother on a South London council estate. The flat below them is inhabited by the Jarvis family, whose son Johnny goes to the same class as Alan at the local comprehensive school. Alan is envious of Johnny, the model of a hard-working teenager, particularly because the latter has a father who takes him along to football matches. Alan, by contrast, works only sporadically, obtains money in dubious transactions with his mysterious father, and moves out to live with a punk girl, Stella, in a squat. Stella is impressed when Johnny begins an apprenticeship and plans his further education, and, fed up with Alan's inactivity, she deserts him for the better life promised by Johnny. After some time spent sleeping in parks and hostels, Alan eventually helps found a band and becomes a famous songwriter. A subplot involving Jake, Alan's presumed father, and the Colonel, who is sometimes Jake's friend and sometimes his enemy, introduces thriller elements into the narrative.

Alan, in many ways reminiscent of Holden Caulfield, the protagonist of J. D. Salinger's *Catcher in the Rye* (1951), is initially naive but grows up quickly. "Suddenly corruption seemed an inevitable part of growing older, something you couldn't escape." Johnny's fate, by contrast, symbolizes the decline of the old industries and virtues in England under the government of Margaret Thatcher. When he marries Stella, they seem ready to climb the social ladder, but Johnny is made redundant, and their dream collapses. Alan recognizes that Stella and Johnny are doomed because of their commitment to the way of life of their parents' generation. Williams successfully portrays an era of change by cleverly connecting the pains of growing up with radical social and political change.

Two elements from *Johnny Jarvis*—the South London setting and the thriller plot—resurface in *Charlie* (1984), a detective story in four parts, which was originally written for television. Charlie Alexander, a divorced private eye, comes across a dead body in a council flat. His investigations do not follow any rational pattern and are clearly modeled on the way Sam Spade and similar American detectives handle inquiries. He is involved in car chases, beaten up, and even kidnapped. Williams parodies traditional detective stories, however, by having Charlie involved with boring union conferences, strikes, and scheming functionaries. Hence, the traditional brutality of the genre erupts in an effective and surprising fashion in an otherwise unheroic English setting. The author deflates the impact of the violence with his choice of metaphors: "He flew up into the air with the speed and ease of a helium balloon ripped out of a child's hand. He hit the pavement with a monstrous, percussive crack."

Charlie is a self-conscious narrator who is aware of the fact that he acts a part and even warns his readers not to believe everything he tells them. He knows that he is not really the tough American private eye who stoically accepts misfortune: "If you live your life by the conventions of pulp fiction, don't expect to complain of the endings it dishes out to you. We get the clichés we deserve." By parodying American detective stories, Williams implicitly criticizes the social upheaval caused by the American model of laissez-faire capitalism of the Thatcher era.

Amos Barking of *Star Turn* (1985) also can be categorized as an unreliable narrator. Amos writes his incredible memoirs while working for the Ministry of Information (MOI) toward the end of World War II. The basic plot consists of the relationship between Amos, who grows up in the East End of London, and classmate Isaac (Zak) Rabinowitz, whom Amos admires for his superior attitude, strength, and coolness. They become close friends who manifest diametrically opposed attitudes toward life. Amos has artistic ambitions and enjoys the role of detached observer while Zak, fascinated by power and wanting to exert influence, chooses politics. Like Fabrizio in Stendhal's *The Charterhouse of Parma* (1839), Zak and Amos materialize where history is being made. D. H. Lawrence, Field Marshal Douglas Haig, Marcel Proust, Virginia Woolf, Sigmund Freud, Josef Goebbels, Winston Churchill, the Nazi propaganda broadcaster Lord Haw Haw (William Joyce), and the British fascist Sir Oswald Mosley are among the historical figures they encounter in the course of their adventures. Acting as Mosley's double, Zak is beaten up and killed in a scuffle. Amos is forced by his superior at the MOI to observe the notorious Dresden bombing raid in order to understand the evil nature of man.

In *Star Turn* Williams is concerned with the nature of evidence in the face of the distorting capacity of both private and public memory. His characters frequently discuss history and, in an allusion to James Joyce's novel *Ulysses* (1922), Amos states that he does not understand his own history or that of his times: "It is some kind of nightmare for me, from which I am unable to awake." In his position as a writer of propaganda, Amos is well aware of how history can be "corrected," and he is not sure that history will ever judge criminals. By debunking history and memory and by pointing out how volatile evidence is, Williams states that the counterfeit and the authentic are equally absurd and ridiculous. The author thus joins ranks with postmodernist writers who question the validity of "history." Amos only drops the mask of cynic when he has truly experienced history himself, having seen the results of the bombing of Dresden.

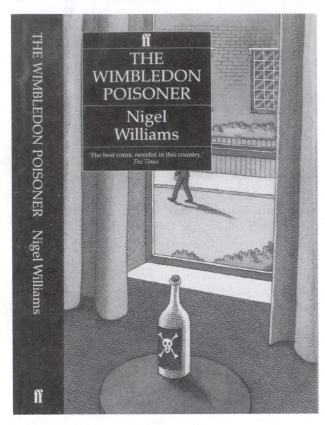

Dust jacket for Williams's 1990 novel, about a man who believes he is a murderer

Reviewing the novel in *TLS* (1 February 1985), Peter Kemp declared that *Star Turn* was "stronger on farce than finesse." Neither did he think the ending credible, stressing "Williams's saturation bombing of his narrative with burlesque and derisive extravaganza." By contrast, Richard Deveson, writing in the 1 February 1985 issue of *The New Statesman,* praised the novel as "a clever book" and added that it was "hard not to be impressed by its showy intellectual energy." Andrew Sinclair concluded in his 24 January 1985 review in *The Times* (London) that Williams was "the best young comic novelist in this country."

With *Witchcraft* (1987) Williams created a more experimental novel. Jamie Matheson is frustrated by his marriage and, during research for a television series on the English Civil War, suffers a nervous breakdown. While recovering, he attempts to chart the evolution of his schizophrenia. Another unreliable narrator, Jamie lives with his wife, Meg (who also has psychological problems), their three daughters, and his mother-in-law, Juliet, in Putney. In the British Library he comes across a pamphlet by Ezekiel Oliphant, a fanatical witch-hunter in Oliver Cromwell's New Model Army who denounced his own wife as a witch and had her hanged. Oliphant was later involved in a conspiracy against the Lord Protector; he was accused of consorting with the devil and ultimately condemned to death. Jamie is helped in his research by the attractive and promiscuous Anna, with whom he has a passionate affair. The researcher increasingly becomes obsessed with the idea that Oliphant's spirit is alive and gaining possession of his own mind. He eventually believes that he has strangled Anna and killed his stepmother.

Williams uses the doppelgänger motif in his own fashion, and yet the novel reminds the reader of Robert Louis Stevenson's *Dr. Jekyll and Mr. Hyde* (1886) and of Fyodor Dostoyevsky's novella *The Double* (1845). The possibility that Oliphant may take over the researcher's mind is psychologically rooted in the protagonist's ambiguous vision of life and his vivid imagination: Oliphant's "legs, chest, belly, neck, head and thighs eased themselves into me, pushing in through veins and arteries until they bumped against the skin like a rowing boat against a jetty." The dualism is apparent in the plot, as well: Oliphant's wife and mistress have the same names as Jamie's; several events are repeated; and the same setting is also frequently used in both past and present. All these intersections help connect Oliphant's story with Jamie's, and the novel presents the two lives alternately. As the narrative proceeds, Jamie assimilates a great deal of Oliphant's old-fashioned vocabulary, and the borderline between past and present as well as between fictional reality and hallucination begins to disappear. In *Witchcraft* Williams is concerned with misogyny and, since the boundaries between fact and fiction appear to be indistinct, with the unreliable nature of history as well as its researchers.

The novel drew a positive response from critics, including Elaine Feinstein in the 28 March 1987 *Times* (London), who praised it as "marvellously funny" and "utterly contemporary in its unnerving humour." Douglas Dunn, in *The Observer* (24 May 1987), considered its "revelation of maggoty skulls beneath the modern facelift . . . truly terrifying." Feinstein pointed out that the narrative is concerned with "the shifty present" and throws light on contemporary life in London. "*Witchcraft,*" wrote John Melmoth in *TLS* (12 June 1987), "demonstrates that apparently remote and bizarre events can be squeezed until they yield comedy and contemporary significance."

The novella *Black Magic* (1988) resembles *Witchcraft* in that it also has two narrative levels. After a quarrel with his wife, Jane, the narrator, James, drives his three sons home and tells them the first installment of a fairy tale. Although the story relates the struggle between white and black magic, it is intertwined with reality, with certain symbols corresponding to real-life issues. The white magician owns a humming, light-radiating pebble, which is stolen by the black magician, who wants to put it to evil use. These events are related to the king, who is intent on laying his hands on such superior power. Later, Jane offers a detailed interpretation of the allegory, drawing the connection between the magic pebble and nuclear energy and weapons, which she had observed a women's group protesting at Greenham Common; the narrator is subsequently afflicted with writer's block, which is broken only as his relationship with Jane worsens dramatically: "I don't want to share food with you, you see. I don't want to share stories with you. I don't want to share my life with you. I don't want you anymore." Although the narrator finds an ending for his tale and recognizes the true state of their marriage, he is too late: he is divorced, tearfully takes leave of his children, and writes the story down.

The narrative deals with problems similar to those raised in Williams's previous fiction. The narrator's dilemma is reminiscent of Martin Steel's choice between marriage and fiction. His inability to shoulder the responsibilities of life are well expressed in Jane's reproach that he has always been a "child father" who enjoyed the nice bits and amused himself and his sons with stories. The novella both affirms and questions the power of storytelling. On the one hand, readers and the narrator's sons are captivated; on the other hand, its power fails to heal the rift between the narrator and his wife. "Storytelling, of course, is as much about withholding information as imparting it. If the storyteller is to have any power at all he must retain control of his material." Through his narrator, Williams also delivers jibes against "anti-racist, non-nuclear, post-feminist" fathers and mothers.

In 1990 Williams published his most successful book, *The Wimbledon Poisoner,* the first part of his Wimbledon trilogy. Its protagonist is Henry Farr, a fat solicitor in his forties, who hates his wife, Elinor, because of her feminism, her tendency to send him to do the shopping, and her preference for healthy food. Henry loves his fat daughter, Maisie, whom he spoils with chocolate bars and stories. His plan to poison his wife goes badly wrong—he serves her chicken laced with thallium, but she passes the poisoned piece on to his friend Donald Templeton, an incompetent physician who becomes Henry's first victim. At Donald's funeral Henry causes four further deaths by adding bleach and other poisonous cleaning liquids to the punch. A policeman, Rush, seems to suspect Henry, visiting him often. Henry believes that Rush is watching him, waiting for him to make a mistake so that the policeman can arrest him. Elinor's psychiatrist is a predictable victim—he dies of a poisoned red apple, reminiscent of Snow White—and, in turn, is followed by Karim Jackson, the publisher who rejected Henry's *Complete History of Wimbledon;* Karim dies of strychnine on his salad dressing. To his astonishment Henry later finds out that he did not kill anybody; rather, there is a far more ruthless killer at work. Inspector Rush informs Henry that he "couldn't poison a . . . fruit cake" and that the inspector himself had murdered the people Henry considered his victims. The real poisoner commits suicide on the Wimbledon windmill and Henry returns to Elinor, whom he has learned to love.

Although Williams began *The Wimbledon Poisoner* in a spirit of wrath at Thatcherism, he chose to express this anger comedically. The humor results from the juxtaposition of grotesque events and an ordinary setting. The boring suburb clashes with the violence of the crimes and Henry's fatuous outside jars with his interior ambitions to become an interesting person, a poisoner.

Although *The Wimbledon Poisoner* was extremely successful, it also generated hostile reactions from reviewers who found it in questionable taste. Danny Karlin, writing in *The London Review of Books* (8 March 1990), suggested that "Perhaps it is unEnglish of me to find all this unfunny." The anonymous reviewer in *The Observer* (24 February 1991) was less equivocal, rejecting the novel as "misogynistic, morally unconvincing and often downright unpleasant." Reviewing the novel for *TLS* (9 March 1990), Patricia Craig observed that "as a commentary on suburban life, *The Wimbledon Poisoner* has much to recommend it" but found it "a worrying book none the less."

While there are not many autobiographical moments that can directly be identified in Williams's fiction, he has acknowledged that the second part of the Wimbledon trilogy was created in reaction to the death of his father. *They Came from SW19* (1992) is permeated by an immense sense of loss, felt by Simon, the fourteen-year-old narrator, when he learns that his father has died. Melancholy scenes—"the sun was going gently, winking back at me from the windows of the neighbours' houses in the way it can do, even when someone you care about dies"—combine with comedy, for instance, when Simon's mother tries to get some coffee from the machine at the hospital where she attends his father: "It gave me soup which turned out to be oxtail. And while I was getting my change back he had a second coronary thrombosis." Apart from dealing with the usual difficulties of adolescence, the narrator also has to contend with the congregation of the First Church of Christ the Spiritualist, South Wimbledon, to which his parents belong. More interested in UFOs, Simon is surprised when his friend, the ufologist Mr. Marr, disappears and his dead father appears outside his bedroom window. Simon develops confusing theories to explain these strange events, but the novel ends with a perfectly rational explanation.

Dust jacket for Williams's 1997 novel, in which a woman attempts to determine which of her coworkers raped her

Disgusted with the bizarre beliefs entertained by people who seem to act perfectly normal in ordinary life, Simon comes to his own, premature conclusion: "No one gets close to me. Not ever." Williams is good at analyzing teenage cynicism as a reaction to a childish adult world, which, as he demonstrates, has eccentric cults flourishing beneath the pleasant surface of the leafy suburban lanes. Reviewing the novel in the 16 July 1992 issue of *The Times* (London), Alison Roberts was appreciative of the "rather more serious undercurrent" to the work and pointed out that "the reversal of values prevalent throughout takes on a nastier hue" with Simon's conclusion. Hilary Mantel, by contrast, writing in *TLS* (3 July 1992), admonished that "the comedy itself tends to run out of control," whereas Andrew Billen in *The Observer* (5 July 1992) is happy with Williams "not sniggering at the conclusion" the narrator draws from the events.

A key moment in *They Came from SW19* is Simon's talk to the congregation of his parents' church. The desperate speech in front of an amazed audience,

interjected with the frantic working of the orator's mind, is one element that links all three volumes of the Wimbledon trilogy. In *The Wimbledon Poisoner,* Henry addresses the mourners at Donald's funeral and utters a four-letter word. In *They Came from SW19,* Simon manages to convince the sect that "Wimbledon was being invaded by aliens from another planet." Robert Wilson, the protagonist of the third book in the trilogy, *East of Wimbledon* (1993), has lied himself into a teaching job at the Wimbledon Islamic Boys' Day School by pretending to be a Muslim and is asked to tell the assembled boys about his conversion: "I became a Muslim . . . at four-thirty on Wednesday the twenty-third of July. On Wimbledon Station." The acute embarrassment of the speaker who stumbles from elation to depression according to the reactions of his listeners provokes pity and derision.

Robert, who calls himself Yusuf Khan, is another persistent liar who finds it increasingly difficult to extricate himself from the predicaments he has gotten himself into. He loves Maisie Pierrepoint, who becomes interested in Robert because he has converted to Islam. She is even more fascinated, however, by Mr. Malik, Robert's employer and headmaster of the school, whom she eventually marries. Malik is a charismatic swindler and businessman who achieves success as a result of his ability to persuade people. Robert, who has also pretended to have a degree from Oxford, gets into trouble with the Wimbledon Dharjees—an Islamic sect whose members wear only one shoe. The protagonist's attempt to regain Maisie by admitting his lies fails—he offends the Muslims, runs away, and is run over by a truck. While the Muslims succeed in finding a place within the community, and the school prospers, Robert remains an outsider. Robert Irwin, who reviewed the novel in *TLS* (9 July 1993), was reminded of the "very English tradition of pathetic and charmless comic anti-heroes," such as Kingsley Amis's Jim Dixon, and praised *East of Wimbledon* as "a sunny, good-natured book."

In the same year Williams published the first of his two travel books, *2 ½ Men in a Boat* (1993), in many ways a parody but also a modern adaptation of Jerome K. Jerome's *Three Men in a Boat* (1889). Williams keeps the Victorian short summary at the beginning of each chapter but adds footnotes, which he uses to introduce manifold diversions of the sort that the rambling Jerome integrated in his text. This technique culminates in chapter 18, which consists of two short sentences followed by a footnote taking up three pages—Williams here seems to allude to Laurence Sterne's *Tristram Shandy* (1759–1767). Williams and his friend JP—an experienced explorer who has climbed the Himalayas and visited the Amazon Indians—row up the Thames and longingly await the arrival of the third man, Alan, a BBC television producer who cannot live without his mobile phone. The journey allows Williams to remark upon his own middle age, to create some beautiful vignettes about the absurdities of contemporary life—he lovingly describes Alan's rushing from one useless meeting to another—and to re-create the atmosphere of Jerome's original work.

In *Scenes from a Poisoner's Life* (1994) Williams returns to the character of Henry Farr and observes him at eleven significant dates throughout the year. St. Valentine's Day, April Fools' Day, Halloween, and New Year's Eve figure in the comic short stories, as does a disastrous excursion to the Lake District, in which Williams satirizes the countryside fantasies of suburban Londoners. In a review in *TLS* (11 November 1994), J. K. L. Walker pronounced the book "artfully" constructed and expressed his pleasure with the way each episode concludes with a comic twist "in the classic style." For Kemp, reviewing the novel in the 6 November 1994 issue of *The Sunday Times* (London), the book

"makes an enjoyable and sometimes hilarious addition to the fictional annals of the present-day suburb."

The Williams family's first trip to the United States is chronicled in *From Wimbledon to Waco* (1995). As in *2 ½ Men in a Boat* Williams begins by outlining the chaos of departure and then records his impressions of traveling. He dives into many of the classic clichés about the United States. His initial enthusiasm for American friendliness soon wanes when he realizes that it has a mercenary motivation. Business pervades every aspect of their American experience, whether they visit the dream factories of Hollywood or the Navajo and Hopi Indians on their reservations. The family reacts with disgust to Las Vegas and finds Yosemite National Park unbearable because of the ubiquitous park rangers who warn tourists about bears. Williams is clearly keen on debunking various American myths, particularly the popular conception of San Francisco as a counter-culture mecca. In the end Williams asserts that he has not realistically portrayed his family and acknowledges that his title for the work is inaccurate, since their route does not take them to Waco. "Even when I am writing non-fiction as in the travel books, I am writing as a novelist and therefore feel an urge to transform things, to change them."

There is a marked change of tone in *Stalking Fiona* (1997). Although Williams initially intended to write a comedy, he turned the novel into a thriller, professedly frightening even himself as he wrote it. Fiona, the twenty-three-year-old narrator, has a degree in English literature and works in an office in London's City with three accountants, Peter, Paul, and John, whose names seem intended to evoke the apostles. One of them is a fraud who, wearing a balaclava and yellow rubber gloves, has raped Fiona in her apartment. The rapist leaves a boastful confession on a floppy disk, which is dispatched to Fiona. She is now faced with a variety of texts—apart from the disk there is a letter from Paul (whom she loves), her own diary, and a journal by Peter, who attempts to expose the office embezzler. The reader is presented with this material as Fiona reads through it, switching from one document to the other, which results in a palimpsest of texts. Fiona approaches her investigation as a form of literary criticism: only by studying the written evidence in detail can she unmask her stalker: "Look at the style as if you were a critic and this were a text." This method raises serious questions as to whether style reveals identity and about the trustworthiness of the narrative voice. Eventually, she kills the man she suspects, Peter, and is united with Paul. Her ultimate conclusion, however—that murderers "don't look any different from you and me. Perhaps they aren't different"—leaves unresolved the worrying question of whether her reading of the different texts is the correct one.

Stalking Fiona provoked considerable controversy among critics. In the 25 January 1997 *Times* (London), Peter Millar was certain that the novel would create "a new craze for the epistolary novel" and added that "Alfred Hitchcock would have adored it. This is one of those rare, treasured books in which I wanted to cover up the bottom of each page to stop my eyes cheating by jumping ahead." There were also dissenting voices, however, as indicated by the contentious headline in the *London Evening Standard* portraying Williams as "The Man Who Makes Comedy Out of Rape." Julie Myerson in the *Mail on Sunday* called the novel a "collision of misogynistic, masturbatory criminal fantasy and sitcom farce." To those who objected to the structure of the novel, Nicholas Royle replied in *The Literary Review,* "to complain that *Stalking Fiona* often seems over-contrived would be a bit like sending back your vindaloo for being hot and spicy. Of course it's contrived: that's the whole point."

Williams intended to follow *Stalking Fiona* with "The Border Collie Book of Management," a satirical fable along the lines of George Orwell's *Animal Farm* (1945), dealing with modern management theories. Williams decided that the novel did not work, however, and abandoned it in favor of *Fortysomething* (1999), in which he quite possibly included material from the rejected project. Paul Slippery's diary about the last six months before turning fifty is replete with the chaos caused by management upheavals at the BBC, where Paul works as an actor in the radio soap *General Practice.* Since his character, Dr. Esmond Pennebaker, is about to be killed off in a sinister conspiracy among the managers (who are either transsexual, idiotic, or both), Paul is worried about securing his income. He is also troubled that he cannot remember the last time he had sex with his wife, Estelle, who is completely absorbed by her recently discovered talent for producing little men made out of dough. Meanwhile, Paul watches his three sons, Ruairghy, Jakob, and Edwin, live through their own difficult times in their relationships with women. As his surname suggests, Paul is a slippery character whose obsession with sex and his family is meant to convey a picture of Williams's typical middle-aged male strug-

gling to make a living in "the giant suburb that the world is slowly becoming."

Fortysomething offers vignettes that beautifully explore questionable developments in contemporary society. There are penetrating insights into parenthood and marriage, into eating habits and charities for the homeless, as well as some devastating comments on political correctness. Other elements of the novel, such as Paul's inability to spell the Celtic name of his eldest son correctly, irritated several critics. Antoinette McMillen, writing in *The Irish News* (27 September 1999), likening the novel to a sitcom, could not decide whether the resemblance was a strength or a weakness: she feared that the novel is "just a tired outing" for an already established author. Bryony Bowden, reviewing the book in the 3 September 1999 *TLS,* asserted that "the general effect of overdoing must . . . be laid at the novelist's door" and concluded that the author may well "fatigue his readers."

Williams is an author who writes on the critical borderline between serious intention and comic expression. As a consequence of the many possible interpretations, he appears to be exposed to the same kind of criticism as Jonathan Swift: he is suspected of misogyny and assumed to endorse the views expressed by some of his protagonists. The danger of being misread is part of the risk a satirist takes, however, and thus the novels of Williams will probably continue to be read as controversial. In any case, they contribute to understanding and recording life and manners in contemporary suburban England.

Interview:

Sheridan Morley, "Writing Crazy," *Times* (London), 28 April 1982, p. 10.

References:

Bernard Gilbert, "Nigel Williams—*The Wimbledon Poisoner* ou le Reno uveau du Crime Anglais," *Études Britan–Niques Contemporaines,* (9) 1996: 31–40;

Ulrike Kahle, "Lüge mit Überschlag," *Theater Heute,* 96 (1996): 22–23;

Ansgar Nünning, "Nigel Williams. *Witchcraft,*" in *Kindlers Neues Literatur Lexikon,* volume 17, edited by Walter Jens (Munich: Kindler Verlag, 1992), pp. 699–700.

Raymond Williams

(31 August 1921 – 26 January 1998)

Seán Matthews
University of California, Los Angeles

See also the Williams entry in *DLB 14: British Novelists Since 1960.*

BOOKS: *Reading and Criticism* (London: Muller, 1950);
Drama from Ibsen to Eliot (London: Chatto & Windus, 1952; New York: Oxford University Press, 1953); revised as *Drama from Ibsen to Brecht* (London: Chatto & Windus, 1968; New York: Oxford University Press, 1969);
Drama in Performance (London: Muller, 1954; Chester Springs, Pa.: Dufour, 1961; revised and enlarged edition, London: Watts, 1968);
Preface to Film, by Williams and Michael Orrom (London: Film Drama, 1954);
Culture and Society, 1780–1950 (London: Chatto & Windus, 1958; New York: Columbia University Press, 1958); republished with a postscript by Williams (Harmondsworth, U.K.: Penguin in association with Chatto & Windus, 1963; New York: Columbia University Press, 1983);
Border Country: A Novel (London: Chatto & Windus, 1960; New York: Horizon, 1962);
The Long Revolution (London: Chatto & Windus, 1961; New York: Columbia University Press, 1961);
Communications, Britain in the Sixties Series (Harmondsworth, U.K.: Penguin, 1962; revised edition, London: Chatto & Windus, 1966; New York: Barnes & Noble, 1967; revised again, Harmondsworth, U.K.: Penguin, 1976);
The Existing Alternatives in Communications, Socialism in the Sixties Series (London: Fabian Society, 1962);
Second Generation: A Novel (London: Chatto & Windus, 1964; New York: Horizon, 1965);
Modern Tragedy (London: Chatto & Windus, 1966; Stanford: Stanford University Press, 1966; revised edition, London: Verso, 1979);
The English Novel from Dickens to Lawrence (London: Chatto & Windus, 1970; New York: Oxford University Press, 1970);

Raymond Williams climbing in the Black Mountains of southeast Wales (from Tom Pinkney, Raymond Williams, *1991)*

Orwell (London: Fontana, 1971; New York: Viking, 1971; revised and enlarged edition, London: Fontana, 1984);
The Country and the City (London: Chatto & Windus, 1973; New York: Oxford University Press, 1973);
Television: Technology and Cultural Form (London: Fontana, 1974; New York: Schocken, 1975);

Drama in a Dramatised Society: An Inaugural Lecture (Cambridge & New York: Cambridge University Press, 1975);

Keywords: A Vocabulary of Culture and Society (London: Fontana, 1976; New York: Oxford University Press, 1976; revised and enlarged edition, London: Fontana, 1983; New York: Oxford University Press, 1985);

Marxism and Literature (Oxford: Oxford University Press, 1977);

The Volunteers (London: Methuen, 1978);

Politics and Letters: Interviews with the New Left Review (London: New Left Books, 1979; New York: Schocken, 1979);

The Fight for Manod (London: Chatto & Windus, 1979);

The Welsh Industrial Novel: The Inaugural Gwyn Jones Lecture (Cardiff, U.K.: University College Cardiff Press, 1979);

Problems in Materialism and Culture: Selected Essays (London: Verso, 1980; New York: Schocken, 1982);

Culture (London: Fontana, 1981); republished as *The Sociology of Culture* (New York: Schocken, 1982);

Democracy and Parliament, introduction by Peter Tatchell (London: Socialist Society, 1982);

Socialism and Ecology (London: Socialist Environment and Resources Association, 1982?);

Cobbett (Oxford & New York: Oxford University Press, 1983);

Towards 2000 (London: Chatto & Windus, 1983); republished as *The Year 2000* (New York: Pantheon, 1984);

Writing in Society (London: Verso, 1984);

Loyalties (London: Chatto & Windus, 1985);

Country and City in the Modern Novel: W.D. Thomas Memorial Lecture: Delivered at the College on 26 January 1987 (Swansea: University College of Swansea, 1987);

The Defenders of Malta, by Williams and Maureen Williams (Newby Bridge, U.K.: Raymond Williams, 1988);

Raymond Williams on Television 1921–1987, edited by Alan O'Connor (London & New York: Routledge, 1988);

Resources of Hope: Culture, Democracy, Socialism, edited by Robin Gable (London & New York: Verso, 1989);

What I Came to Say (London: Hutchinson Radius, 1989);

The Politics of Modernism: Against the New Conformists, edited by Tony Pinkney (London & New York: Verso, 1989);

The People of the Black Mountains, 2 volumes (London: Chatto & Windus, 1989, 1990)—comprises volume 1, *The Beginning . . .* (1989) and volume 2, *The Eggs of the Eagle* (1990).

PRODUCED SCRIPTS: *A Letter from the Country,* television, BBC 2, 1966;

Public Inquiry, television, BBC 1, 1967;

The Country and the City, television, 1979.

OTHER: D. H. Lawrence, *Three Plays,* introduction by Williams (Harmondsworth, U.K.: Penguin, 1969);

The Pelican Book of English Prose, volume 2, *From 1780 to the Present Day,* edited by Williams (Harmondsworth, U.K.: Penguin, 1969);

Charles Dickens, *Dombey and Son,* edited by Peter Fairclough, introduction by Williams (Harmondsworth, U.K.: Penguin, 1970);

Lucien Goldmann, *Racine,* translated by Alastair Hamilton, introduction by Williams (Cambridge: Rivers, 1972);

D. H. Lawrence on Education, edited by Williams and Joy Williams (Harmondsworth, U.K.: Penguin Educational, 1973);

George Orwell: A Collection of Critical Essays, Twentieth Century Views Series, no. 119, edited by Williams (Englewood Cliffs, N.J. & London: Prentice-Hall, 1974);

English Drama: Forms and Development: Essays in Honour of Muriel Clara Bradbrook, edited by Williams and Marie Axton (Cambridge: Cambridge University Press, 1977);

Roger Sales, *English Literature in History, 1780–1830: Pastoral and Politics,* edited by Williams (New York: St. Martin's Press, 1983);

John Clare: Selected Poetry and Prose, edited by Williams and Merryn Williams (London & New York: Methuen, 1986);

L. J. Jordanova, ed., *Languages of Nature: Critical Essays on Science and Literature,* foreword by Williams (London: Free Association Books, 1986);

Edward Timms and Peter Collier, eds., *Visions and Blueprints: Avant-Garde Culture and Radical Politics in Early Twentieth-Century Europe,* introduction by Williams (Manchester: Manchester University Press, 1988).

Raymond Williams was among the foremost cultural critics of his generation. As his record of publications suggests, Williams's legacy is primarily that of the public intellectual. His work, a massive and interdisciplinary effort of teaching and writing stretching over forty years, redefined the idiom and priorities of literary criticism, determined much of the foundation and early formation of cultural and media studies, and generated new methodologies for a sociology of literature. A central figure in the first British New Left movement of the 1950s, his life was a pattern for the role of

Williams with his future wife, Joy Dalling, in 1940 (photograph by Michael Orrom)

engaged, socialist intellectual, combining articulate political commitment with an activism that was both theoretically sophisticated and of practical force.

Nevertheless, Williams always maintained that he viewed himself, above all, as a novelist, and he insisted on the importance of the novel form in cultural practice. He declared that the writing of fiction had always taken priority in his work. When he retired early from his position as professor of drama at Cambridge University in 1983, it was to address the enormous project that was eventually published, posthumously, in two volumes as *The People of the Black Mountains* (1989, 1990). Despite his convictions, however, critical attention to Williams's seven novels has remained sporadic and uneven. Unfashionable in content, idiosyncratic in form, resistant to conventional categorization, the fiction has only rarely been properly addressed as literary work. Its significance appears marginal, most commonly mined for biographical data or to illustrate arguments made more succinctly in the criticism. Tony Pinkney remarked, "*The Long Revolution* is evidently the tea-bag from which the swirling draughts of *Second Generation* are brewed." Yet, the novels do retain popular readership, and their value is more than historical. They continue to develop that classic, provincial tradition of realist fiction that extends back through D. H.

Lawrence, Thomas Hardy, and George Eliot, demonstrating the necessity of that form for the articulation of important aspects of contemporary experience.

The main themes of Williams's fiction derive from his history. He was convinced that much of his experience was in important ways ordinary (one of his first publications was the polemic essay "Culture Is Ordinary"), that his life was typical, common, even representative of his generation and class. This conviction was reinforced by his extensive knowledge of local and national history: tensions between these two forms, which he engaged both intellectually in his academic work and personally as a member of the Welsh working class, particularly inform his later novels. Experience was the ground of the peculiar unity and consistency that mark his work, and he drew from it the authority for a whole framework of moral and evaluative priorities. Although some critics point out that his life was in many ways more distinctive than he allowed, the examples of his work, and above all his fiction, remain a key reference for modern debates around the representation of identity.

Raymond Henry Williams was born on 31 August 1921 in Pandy (near Abergavenny in Wales), a rural village in the mountainous border between Wales and England, to Gwendolen (Bird) Williams and Harry

Williams. Raymond's father was a railway signalman, union representative, and Labour Party activist. Political and social conflicts of the 1920s and 1930s were thus defining elements in Raymond's childhood, and his writing returns insistently to the General Strike of 1926, to the first Labour Government (1929) and the Depression years, and to the period of the Spanish Civil War and the Popular Front. This vivid political education, however, was not acquired at the cost of conventional academic progress, although such achievement brought further pressures. Williams would not have been able to enter secondary education without the state scholarship he won in 1932 to the prestigious King Henry VIII Grammar School, Abergavenny. His was a new generation, advanced by recent educational reforms, of "scholarship boys" from the working class. For many such boys (and girls) there were difficult tensions between the habits of home and community and the conventions and assumptions of the educational system—strains that Williams examines intently in his writings. Nevertheless, he was a brilliant student, and at seventeen he was placed first in the region's Higher Certificate Examinations. According to Fred Inglis, Williams's biographer, during the school's prize-giving ceremony a visiting dignitary wondered "if we should ever get to the end of prizes for Raymond Williams."

In 1939, garnering further scholarships, Williams was accepted to read English at Trinity College, Cambridge, a rare achievement for one from his background. Once there, though, he threw himself with extraordinary energy and confidence into university life. He established himself at the Socialist Club, the Cambridge Union, then in its heyday, and the student newspapers. He joined both the Communist Party and the Officer Training Corps (not so unusual a combination for that time and place, if again symptomatic of the contradictions in loyalties he was to explore later). He left the Communist Party when the leadership criticized his choice of girlfriend, and he later left the army in opposition to the Korean War. At Cambridge he also met Joy Dalling, a student from the London School of Economics (which had been evacuated to Cambridge), whom he married on 19 June 1942. The couple eventually had three children: Merryn, born in 1944; Ederyn, born in 1947; and Gwydion Madawc, born in 1950.

From 1941 to 1945, Williams served as an officer of the Guards Armoured Division, rising to the rank of captain in his tank battalion, and participated in the Normandy landings and the final Allied offensives. After returning to Cambridge to complete his degree (with first-class honors), he took the position he held for the next fourteen years, as tutor in English for Oxford University's Delegacy for Extra-mural Studies, the department for adult and continuing edu-

cation. During this period he established his reputation as a writer and critic.

Williams's first published novel was *Border Country* (1960), written at the same time as the series of critical books that first brought him to public attention, most notably *Culture and Society, 1780–1850* (1958) and *The Long Revolution* (1961). Reviewing *Culture and Society,* Frank Kermode commented in *Encounter* (January 1959), "This is a book of quite radical importance, and even a reader who dissents from its conclusions may have to accept a substantial alteration in his mental habit." Despite such plaudits Williams had already established the writing of fiction as his true priority and preference. He stressed in *The Long Revolution* that *Border Country* had "an essential relevance to the two general books. I have completed a body of work which I set myself to do ten years ago." It had taken a long time to complete; from first draft as "Brynllwyd" (1947–1949), the novel went through a series of seven rewritings before it was published in 1960. During the same period, Williams wrote three other unpublished novels ("Rideyear," 1948; "Adamson," 1950; "The Grasshoppers," 1951) and an unpublished play ("King Macbeth," 1957). Even if it gained less public attention, the writing of fiction was the central and most time-consuming element in his work.

Border Country has a double plot in which past is interleaved with present. Matthew Price, a young university lecturer in economics, leaves his wife and sons in London and makes the long journey back to the Welsh border village of Glynmawr, where his father, Harry, a railway signalman, has suffered a heart attack. The present narrative portrays Matthew struggling to readjust to the rhythms of his family and native community, realizing intensely the alienating effects of his migration, education, and chosen profession. His memories of childhood and adolescence, which form the past narrative, reveal how much the early formation of his character and relationships are in tension with the metropolitan English habits he has adopted. Gradually he begins to resolve these contradictions, above all through the effort to understand Harry's experiences and choices and his own relationship to them. Although Harry seems to recover, he eventually worsens and dies. The novel ends with Matthew again in London: "Only now it seems like the end of exile. Not going back, but the feeling of exile ending. For the distance is measured, and that is what matters. By measuring the distance, we come home."

The title of the novel, *Border Country,* provides an image that nicely suggests something of Williams's habits of thought and technique: the idea of the border, the liminal state, is a recurrent feature throughout his work. His writing explores ostensibly sharp oppositions and contrasts, repeatedly demonstrating the complexity and confusion of these elements in experience. Matthew Price, for instance, inhabits an intellectual and emotional border region between strongly differentiated ways of life. He is known as "Will" in Glynmawr but "Matthew" in England. When he talks to his wife on the phone from Glynmawr she immediately notes a shift in his accent and idiom. His research work, which deals with "population movements in Wales during the industrial revolution," places him at a critical, scrutinizing distance from his parents and friends, whose labor is essentially manual. As an exile living in London, his urban habits are at odds with slower country customs. These alienating oppositions are gradually overcome through Matthew's rediscovery and acceptance of the human meanings of community in Glynmawr, a process at once incidental, as in the small details of neighborly kindness and support, and overt, especially in the great set piece of solidarity, the General Strike. When Matthew reappears in *The Fight for Manod* (1979), his work is praised for altering the practice of economic history in just such terms: "Just because it was a book on population movement it wasn't only . . . the statistics. You had the statistics, but you turned them back into people. . . . A human movement, the flow of actual men and their families into the mining valleys." For Williams, fictional realism similarly provides the opportunity to turn facts and statistics "back into people."

Williams characterized the importance of great realist fiction as a revelation of "knowable community," a demonstration of the range and power of social relations. The *Border Country* is the account of the early married life of Harry and Ellen Price as they settle in Glynmawr (the difficulties of "settlement" are a key theme for Williams); of their friendship with Morgan Rosser; of the tensions between the men during the General Strike; of the adjustments between Harry and Morgan when Morgan shifts his allegiance to business; and, throughout, of Harry's stubborn but strong attachment to ideals of life and work that, however independent, are inextricably implicated in that "knowable community." These depictions demonstrate Williams's commitment to this realist tradition. A comment he makes on D. H. Lawrence, in *Culture and Society,* is just as applicable to his own fiction:

> The early chapters of *Sons and Lovers* are at once a marvelous recreation of this close, active, contained family life, and also in general terms an indictment of the pressures of industrialism. Almost all that he learned in this way was by contrasts, and this element of contrast was reinforced by the accident that he lived on a kind of frontier, within sight of industrial and agricultural England.

Williams at Cambridge University, 1941 (from Tom Pinkney, Raymond Williams, *1991)*

The affinities with Lawrence—of origin, social critique and the ambiguous predicament of the self-exile socially poised between two cultures—are especially evident in Williams's next novel, *Second Generation* (1964), where the influence of Lawrence's *Sons and Lovers* (1913) is particularly strong. *Second Generation* is set in Oxford in the early 1960s and deals with the parallel and interacting lives of two generations. Two Welsh émigré working-class couples form the older generation: Harold and Kate Owen, and Harold's brother, Gwyn, with his wife, Myra. The brothers left Wales together to work in a car factory and are neighbors. Harold's son, Peter, is a research student in sociology at the university, and since early childhood Peter and Beth, Myra's daughter from a first marriage, have been unofficially engaged. Kate and Harold are militant socialists, she on Labour Party committees and he on the shop floor of the factory. Peter's academic work, concerned with growth and tensions in industrial communities, is also grounded in socialist principles. Gwyn and Myra, by contrast, are politically apathetic, focused more immediately on

Williams (right) while he was serving as an officer in the 21st Anti-Tank Regiment of the Guards Armoured Division during World War II (from Tom Pinkney, Raymond Williams, *1991)*

their home life and, in Gwyn's case, his gardening; Beth works as a bank clerk. The novel is dominated by events in the factory, culminating in a strike led by Harold and a large public protest march through the city organized by Kate. During these events, Kate and Harold gradually become estranged, and Kate has an affair with an Oxford don from one of her committees. At the same time, Peter, experiencing difficulties in his own work, deserts Beth for a previous girlfriend, whom he meets again at the house of his thesis supervisor, Robert Lane. When Harold and Beth learn of these betrayals, there is a crisis and Peter leaves home, staying first with relatives in Wales and then settling alone in Oxford. The novel eventually closes on an uneasy note of harmony: work resumes at the factory; Kate is reunited with Harold; Peter marries Beth and, completing his thesis, determines to pursue a wholly new kind of academic project.

Second Generation differs from *Border Country* in its more extended range of relationships and in the spe-

cifically contemporary issues it addresses, though it does rework many of the concerns of the earlier novel: the tensions between working-class parents and a child educated to different perspectives and values; the difficulties of migration from a close, rural community to the more anonymous relations of the industrial city; the day-to-day bitterness of working conditions under capitalism; the deep but threatened structures of community; the obstacles to principled academic work within the available institutional and methodological conventions. These themes are further complicated with new issues of sexual politics and morality, an interest that places the novel historically on the cusp of the 1960s sexual revolution. The influence of *Sons and Lovers* is clearest here, in the difficult exchanges between Kate and Peter, paralleling those between Mrs. Morel and Paul, and in Peter's involvement in a series of relationships that repeat the Paul-Miriam-Clara triangle. The consummation with Beth is overtly in the Laurentian mode:

Peter touched and knew her whole body, and he held him close to her, knowing him again as they touched. Slowly, as they moved, came a new feeling, that seemed in the warmth, in the actual change in their bodies, a change of tissue and substance so that they felt quite newly alive, newly capable of life. They responded, wondering, to this transformation, and again it seemed a deep recognition. The known features were blurred and their separateness lost, yet in the change they were more deeply known. The touch between them was warm and moving, and yet reached beyond them, to a felt consummation, that would again flow and continue, beyond itself, into sleep and into life.

The relation between Williams and Lawrence is, though, one of argument as well as affinity. Whereas Paul Morel strikes out for the lights of the city at the end of *Sons and Lovers,* using educational opportunity as a way beyond the deadlock of the working-class home, Peter Owen chooses to work alongside his father in the factory, making a difficult commitment to study the industrial relations that generated his original values and loyalties from within. A further refusal of the Laurentian pattern is in Williams's insistence on generational continuity, and through that to the process of history. He criticized *Women in Love* (1920) for the limitation of the narrative to a single generation, which he saw as a simplification, a failure of imaginative consciousness. His characters' relations to history, figured as influences and residues of earlier events, people, and examples, are crucial to Williams. Just as Matthew Price must bring his Welsh and English experience into relation, so Peter argues fiercely with Robert Lane against the suppressions of vital connections in his life by academic conventions:

This is my real situation. What I'm trying to say to you is a kind of truth. The connections are deeper than we ever suspected: between work and living, between families, between cities. You surrendered by breaking the connections, or by letting them atrophy. We shall try not to do that, in this generation. We shall hold to the connections and ride our history.

Williams's work reveals how it is also, preeminently, in the tradition of the realist novel that such connections are most powerfully articulated and represented.

Williams's third novel, *The Fight for Manod,* is a more overtly combative book than its predecessors. It figures a shift in Williams's preoccupations, brought on by his increasingly urgent sense of the threatening right-wing political environment in Britain. During the long interval after *Second Generation,* he moved to Cambridge to accept a conventional academic lectureship (he became professor of drama in 1974), with an increase in committee work and institutional responsibility. He

also became more involved in public political projects, including active membership in the Labour Party (1961–1966), leadership of the May Day Manifesto Group (1967–1969), and alignment with various protest movements. During the furor surrounding the case of Rudi Dutschke, the West German student leader expelled from Britain in 1971, Williams strikingly articulated his feelings of anger and dread about contemporary trends. Evidence brought by the government to show that Dutschke was a threat to national security was, Williams argued in the *Cambridge Review* (29 January 1971), "all of a kind which could be adduced against many of us: in our work and contacts inside the university, to say nothing of any more general public life." In the three works of Williams's middle period—*The Fight for Manod, The Volunteers* (1978), and *Loyalties* (1985)—such an atmosphere of menace provides the context for more dramatic acts and scenes of resistence than occur in the earlier works.

The Fight for Manod brings together characters from the previous two novels, and thus forms a conclusion to what has been called Williams's "Welsh Trilogy." Robert Lane, now working for the Labour government in the Department of the Environment, invites Matthew Price and Peter Owen to serve as consultants on a project to create a new town in a depopulated area of Welsh borderland around the village of Manod. They are to report on the "human factor," the impact that the planned transformations would have on the local communities. Matthew and his wife, their sons having grown up and left home, move to Manod for a year and are eventually joined by Peter and Beth, who is pregnant. Peter's suspicions about the project are confirmed when Matthew clashes with local developer John Dance. Peter and his family leave Manod to do further investigation in London and then Brussels, finding that the project is a conspiracy involving supranational Anglo-Belgian corporations, property speculation, and possible misappropriation of government funds. At a decisive meeting with the minister of the environment, Peter resigns and takes the story to the news media. Matthew, still arguing that some development is necessary and valuable, suffers a heart attack. The novel ends with Matthew settled once more in Wales, directing a new Institute and Library of Industrial Wales and continuing his efforts to influence government development policy. Beth rejoins Peter in London as he begins his book exposing the scandal. The Manod project proceeds: it is unclear whether the fight has had much practical effect.

The Fight for Manod explores a direct confrontation of Leftist intellectuals with capitalist forces and has less of the brooding, discursive, and introspective material of the earlier two novels. Written at the same time as the political

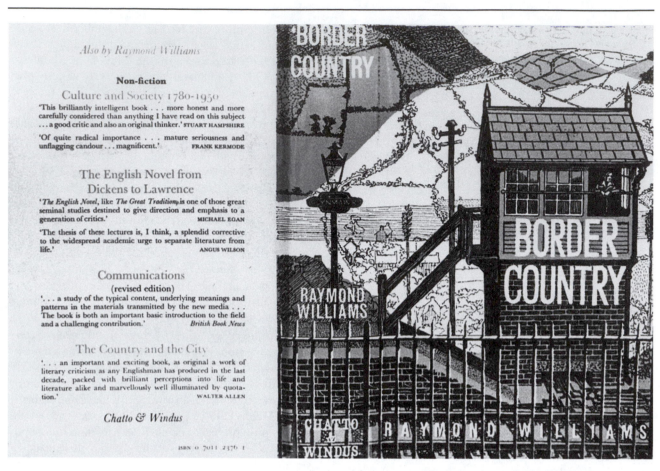

Dust jacket for Williams's first novel (1960), in which a Welshman living in London returns home to visit his dying father

thriller *The Volunteers,* it shares with that work a quicker narrative pace, deriving from the detective mystery aspect of the story and the practical mechanics of a more complex plot. The sophisticated and diffuse nature of late-twentieth-century capitalism, the facelessness of the "enemy," presents imaginative difficulties of which Williams is clearly aware, but the moral and political value of realism is that it allows just such conventionally hidden or suppressed aspects of experience to be explored. As Matthew explains in the novel:

> The companies. And then the distance, the everyday obviousness of the distance, between the lane in Manod, all the immediate problems of Gwen and Ivor and Trevor and Gethin and the others: the distance from them to this register of companies, but at the same time the relations are so solid, so registered. The transactions reach right down to them. Not just as a force from outside but as a force they've engaged with, are part of. Yet still a force that cares nothing about them, that's just driving its own way.

Williams's achievement is to demonstrate the subtle implication of such forces in the familiar, unexamined texture of everyday existence. As is apparent from the closing scenes, *The Fight for Manod* is, if not actually pessimistic, a bleak meditation on the efficacy of political activism. Even a sympathetic Robert Lane characterizes Matthew's confrontation with the minister as "heroic absurdity." His heart attack, brought by the pressures and strains of his work, is paralleled by the strains on Peter and Beth's marriage. The emotional and physical costs of socialist commitment under capitalism are again revealed to be extreme. As Kate Owen remarked in *Second Generation,* "We used to say, be humane and tolerant, make a better life. But to be humane now we can't be tolerant. We have to break and fight, and go dry and hard in the process. All that's left to us now is this struggle." This further theme, of the draining and ultimately disabling nature of the struggle against structures of inequality and exploitation, becomes a predominant element in Williams's next two novels.

The Volunteers marks a departure from the realism of "knowable community" that typifies the Welsh Trilogy. The novel is a thriller set in 1988. During a period of world economic recession, an authoritarian coalition has taken power in Britain. The book opens with the shooting of Buxton, a right-wing government minister, during a visit to a Cardiff folk history museum. Buxton has become a target because of his earlier deployment of troops to break up a strike at Pontyrhiw, in the Welsh coalfields, that resulted in the death of a young miner. Lewis Redfern, a cynical analyst of the political underground for the international satellite television news agency Insatel, is sent to investigate. He uncovers an international network of leftist activists working secretly from within to destabilize capitalist governments and he eventually confronts the controlling mind in the Welsh-British context, a charismatic former Labour politician, Mark Evans. Evans, however, convinces Redfern not to expose the organization. Redfern leaves Insatel and at a public inquiry chooses to protect the conspirators, revealing instead details of governmental malpractice. He realizes he has left behind the pose of objectivity that marked his journalism to become, himself, a volunteer.

The change of genre grants further perspectives on Williams's central themes. Through the device of a first-person narrator, he continues to explore the implications of the individual's necessary involvement in relationships and communities. The conventions of hard-boiled writing, particularly with respect to the hero's sad, cynical and lonely integrity, are subverted by Redfern's ultimate rejection of isolation, his recognition of the practical, political ramifications of his moral responsibility and of the complicit nature of his supposed detachment and objectivity. Further, locating the scenario in the near-future permits a suggestive presentation of technological and political trends that cannily prefigures the manipulation of an increasingly global news media. *Second Generation* had introduced this theme in an account of the making of a documentary about the strike. With *The Volunteers*, Williams's preoccupation with intellectual alienation, the struggle against institutions, methodologies, and intellectual forms inherently inimical to many aspects of common experience is thus extended to include the context of new and emerging media.

The Volunteers also heralds the concentrated scrutiny of issues around the representation and ideological control of the historical record that dominates Williams's later work. The events at the folk museum provoke Redfern to speculate about the ideological conditions of such a project. He notes that the selection and organization of artifacts constructs the image of a primarily rural Wales, suppressing the widespread impact of mining and heavy industry: "The idea the museum embodies is of an old Wales, still in part surviving, but with all modern

Williams reading from his novel Second Generation, *in Cardiff, circa 1964 (from Tom Pinkney,* Raymond Williams, *1991)*

realities left outside in the car park, or brought inside only in the toilets which have replaced the privies. Folk is the past: an alternative to People."

Equally, the museum effaces much of the political and economic context of Welsh history, a history of colonization and exploitation. Set in the grounds of the castle of a conquering Norman overlord, the project physically obscures the real conditions of oppression under which people lived. Redfern comes to see the shooting of the minister on the museum grounds as a specific and symbolic continuation of Welsh struggles for self-definition against external rule:

In the tidied farms, among the casks and presses, you could forget this history, on an ordinary day. But today was not ordinary. Today made these other connections: the connections to Pontyrhiw. What had started there had come back to this folk museum, not as an exhibit but an action, bursting in on its peaceful and arranged order.

Williams and critic Frank Kermode, Cambridge, 1981 (photograph by Times Newspapers Ltd.)

The recovery and revaluation of such historical connections is at the heart of Williams's next novel. As the plural form suggests, *Loyalties* is a drama of the conflicts generated among differing forms of loyalty. The narrative explores difficult, defining choices between competing, even contradictory, commitments: to lovers, friends, family, community, class, nation, and political and moral ideals. Again, the figure of a young researcher faced with the impossibility of separating public from personal history, of making moral distinctions between political and private actions, is at the center of the plot. Jon Merritt is working on a television documentary about a Cambridge spy ring. He finds that the ramifications of the story implicate his own family and friends, stretching into a complicated network of relationships dating back more than fifty years. The investigation begins with a Popular Front meeting in Danycapel, Wales, in 1936. Student communists and working-class activists come together to protest against the rise of fascism. Jon's grandfather, Norman Braose, a brilliant Cambridge mathematician and ardent communist, fathers a child, Gwyn, by a local girl, Nesta Pritchard. Braose, however, immediately leaves for the Civil War in Spain and never returns to Nesta, though

his sister Emma maintains a friendship with her. Nesta eventually marries the miner Bert Lewis who volunteers to fight first in Spain and then in World War II, where he is badly wounded. Bert brings up Gwyn as his own son. Braose also marries and has another child, Alex, Merritt's mother. During the war, Braose and his close university friend Monk Pitter work for the British government, secretly developing computers. They are later suspected of having passed information to Russia: Pitter loses his job at an American university, and Braose is pushed toward early retirement. When Gwyn applies for an important government post in 1984, because of his connection to Braose and his own left-wing convictions, his loyalty is questioned at a security interview. As Merritt gradually uncovers these facts, he struggles to organize the material, recognizing the complex judgments involved. In a further suspicious twist, his superiors abandon the documentary, and he is moved onto another project.

A short summary can only hint at the fascinating and complex pattern of relationships sustained in this work. *Loyalties* is a more ambitious and sophisticated novel than its predecessors in terms of both range of characters and sweep of historical action, though the thematic preoccupations remain distinctively Williams's own. Typically, the effect of the novel is to emphasize the close implication of the characters' life histories with political and social upheavals such as the Spanish conflict, the Suez crisis, the Vietnam War, and the miners' strike of 1984. Williams shows that the experience of these events—of fighting, of marching in a protest, of sustaining a strike—differs, often in significant ways, from what is conventionally recorded. He retrieves central aspects in the lives of common people that are often ignored or downplayed. Decisions and actions taken during such crises figure deep affiliations and customs often alien, invisible, or inaccessible to historians, yet still commonly sustained through family and community narratives.

As with *Border Country,* there is an insistence on the moral strengths derived from the experience of growing up in a working-class community, a "knowable community," even as this is contrasted with the confident social and intellectual mobility of the more upper-class characters. Gwyn, for instance, goes away like Matthew Price to Cambridge for his formal education and is most explicitly confronted by this experience of social and intellectual difference. At the climax of the novel his natural father, Braose, argues that they are both caught in an inevitable and permanent process of internal conflict: "You grew up with others, and you love them, as you must. And then within that love you try to see the world in their way, though you are already in practice removed from it. So that you cling to these old and useless ideas, as a way of clinging to those people." Nesta makes the same point, but from the other side, when she shows Gwyn her secret picture of Bert, painted after his return from Normandy. Gwyn remarks that it is "in its way . . . intensely beautiful." She reacts angrily against such an abstracted, aesthetic reaction: "'It is not beautiful!' she cried again. 'It's ugly, It's destroying! It's human flesh broken and pulped!'" Gwyn's intellectualized response is symptomatic of a distance of education and social custom between him and his mother, indicating how issues of loyalty become inevitably caught in problems of articulation, of what Williams defines in *Marxism and Literature* as the generational "structure of feeling."

The greater range and confidence that Williams demonstrates in *Loyalties* suggest that retirement from Cambridge at last gave him the time, energy, and space—he bought a cottage near the village of his birth—for more substantial projects in fiction. With his final work, he moved beyond the more conventional modes of his other novels to attempt an unprecedented historical synthesis. This unfinished piece, *The People of the Black Mountains,* was conceived as a monumental trilogy tracing episodes in the history of the border region from 23,000 B.C. to the present day. The work was posthumously published in two volumes, completed in this form by his widow, Joy, who had assisted in the research and editing of Williams's work throughout their life together.

The People of the Black Mountains depends on a unity of place, rather than of personae. Pinkney, in his 1991 book, includes a letter from Williams to his patient publisher, "It will be what I call a historical rather than a period novel: showing how different people lived in and used a particular beautiful place, my native Black Mountains." The material is loosely connected by the course of Glyn Parry's search over the mountains for his grandfather, Elis, who is late returning from an afternoon walk. As Glyn retraces Elis's route across the familiar terrain, the landscape seems uncannily altered in the moonlight, and he struggles to find his way. Some historical spirit of the place oddly moves him. As a child "he had often walked into one of these hollows and closed his eyes, trying to feel its generation of life. Sometimes what he knew and what he sensed came briefly together." As he walks on, this childhood sensation, his powerful historical imagination affects him strongly, and he feels the "old and deep traces along which lives still moved." In this strange state he remembers or imagines episodes in the long and confused history of the area. Although the Glyn and Elis element of the novel was to have been developed more substantially, implicating the two men still more closely in the historical landscape, it subsists as little more than the suggestive connecting device. The strength of the work is in the dense, thickly layered portrait that emerges of the Black Mountains and its people. In an opening appeal to the reader's own historical imagination, Williams evokes a relationship to the land similar to Glyn's, inviting us to share his intense and physical appreciation of the power of the place: "Press your fingers close on this lichened sandstone. With this stone and this grass, with this red earth, this place was received and made and remade. Its generations are distinct but all suddenly present."

The formal coherence effected through the Glyn/Elis motif and the unity of place is augmented by the reworking of many of Williams's familiar themes. The recurrent pattern of his interests across the sequence of settlements also serves as a unifying element. His concern for power relations and political processes, for instance, is frequently evident. Narratives of the brutal workings of feudal power are contrasted with explorations of other more peaceful and equitable modes of governance and community. Given the equal evidence of their historical actuality, these systems are shown to be neither inevitable nor eternal. Similarly, the problems around learning, sophistication, and intellectual

Williams with his portrait by John Bratby, circa 1987 (photograph by Mark Gerson)

work that figure throughout Williams's novels are here set within new and illuminating contexts. "The Coming of the Measurer" offers a meditation on how the pursuit of knowledge becomes separated from day-to-day concerns. In "Oldcastle to Oldchon" the problematic links between state power, religion, and learning are dramatized. The reiteration over time of these common patterns of action and feeling figures again the deep historical connections that are always at stake in Williams's novels, but in this last work there is a much more open commitment to such contrasts and counterfactual situations.

The People of the Black Mountains consists of striking innovations in Williams's writing practice. Fresh qualities of lyricism, humor, and even mysticism are revealed in his narrative voice. Episodes stand independently as well-wrought short stories, settling within a loose overall conception free of the weight of significance and implication that typifies the other novels. This late style recalls ancient annals and local legends, the language blending colloquial idiom with a more portentous, magisterial voice suggestive of the King James Bible or native Welsh stories of *The Mabinogion*. Indeed, *The People of the Black Mountains* parallels such heterogeneous texts in its compound, cumulative force. Places are named and renamed, events resonate and repeat across first centuries, then millennia, and the memories of one community become the legends of another. The result is an impressive chronicle, the more poignant for the insistence on a narrative perspective grounded in the experience of those who inhabit the region, rather than those who merely own, rule over, or dispose of it.

Williams's current reputation as a novelist is equivocal. The power and significance of his cultural criticism will perhaps always surpass that of his fiction. Critics of the novels have praised his moral seriousness and polemical political commitment while also suggesting that these purposes are too obvious, too crudely realized. Although his adherence to realist modes is far from rigid or doctrinaire, set against the variety of formal experiment undertaken by his contemporaries, his writing often seems conventional, even old-fashioned. His campuses are a world away from those of Malcolm Bradbury and David Lodge, his Welsh characters often seem of a different race to the exuberant, bitter, iconoclastic inhabitants of Kingsley Amis's Wales, his moral compass lacks the range and sensitivity of those of Iris Murdoch or Doris Lessing. Williams's distinctive strengths should not be neglected, however. His painstaking, often moving representation of disregarded aspects of common life and the stubborn articulation of drama in quite ordinary experience is characteristic of his fiction as much as his criticism. His effort to give a contemporary voice to these concerns is an essential element of the postwar scene. As Glyn remarks in *The People of the Black Mountains,* rehearsing once more the conflict between differing forms of knowledge and history, different ways of seeing and articulating, "Only the breath of the place, its winds and its mouths, stirred the models into life."

Interviews:

"Two Interviews with Raymond Williams," *Red Shift* (Cambridge), no. 2 (1977): 12–17; no. 3 (1977): 13–15;

Terry Eagleton, "The Practice of Possibility," *New Statesman* (7 August 1978): 19–21; republished in *Raymond Williams: Critical Perspectives,* edited by Eagleton (Oxford: Polity Press, 1989), pp. 176–183;

"Television and Teaching: An Interview with Raymond Williams," *Screen Education,* no. 31 (Summer 1979): 5–14; republished in *Raymond Williams on Television,* edited by Alan O'Connor (Toronto: Between the Lines Press, 1989), pp. 203–215;

"Nationalisms and Popular Socialism: Phil Cooke Talks to Raymond Williams," *Radical Wales,* no. 2 (Spring 1984): 7–8;

Writers in Conversation: Raymond Williams with Michael Ignatieff, ICA Video, 1985, videocassette;

Stephen Heath and Gillian Skirrow, "An Interview with Raymond Williams," in *Studies in Entertainment: Critical Approaches to Mass Culture,* edited by Tania Modleski (Bloomington & Indiana: Indiana University Press, 1986), pp. 3–17;

"'People of the Black Mountains,' John Barnie Interviews Raymond Williams," *Planet,* 65 (October/November, 1987): pp. 3–13;

Biography:

Fred Inglis, *Raymond Williams* (New York & London: Routledge, 1995).

References:

Terry Eagleton, ed., *Raymond Williams: Critical Perspectives* (Oxford: Polity Press, 1989);

Jan Gorak, *The Alien Mind of Raymond Williams,* Literary Frontiers Editions, no. 32 (Columbia: University of Missouri Press, 1988);

Katie Gramich, "The Fiction of Raymond Williams in the 1960s: Fragments of an Analysis," *Welsh Writing in English: A Yearbook of Critical Essays,* 1 (1995): 62–74;

Stephen Knight, "'A Local Moment': Raymond Williams's *The Volunteers* as Crime Fiction," *Welsh Writing in English: A Yearbook of Critical Essays,* 2 (1996): 126–137;

Bronwen Levy and Peter Otto, eds., *Southern Review,* special Raymond Williams issue, 22 (July 1989);

Alan O'Connor, *Raymond Williams: Writing, Culture, Politics* (Oxford: Basil Blackwell, 1989);

Tony Pinkney, *Raymond Williams* (Bridgend, U.K.: Seren, 1991);

Pinkney, ed., *News from Nowhere,* special Raymond Williams issue, 6 (February 1989);

J. P. Ward, *Raymond Williams* (Cardiff: University of Wales Press, 1981);

"Raymond Williams as Inhabitant: The Border Trilogy," *New Welsh Review,* 1, no. 2 (1988): 23–27.

Books for Further Reading

Acheson, James, ed. *The British and Irish Novel Since 1960*. New York: St. Martin's Press, 1991.

Adelman, Irving, and Rita Dworkin. *The Contemporary Novel: A Checklist of Critical Literature on the British and American Novel Since 1945*. Metuchen, N.J.: Scarecrow Press, 1972.

Allen, Walter. *The Modern Novel in Britain and the United States*. New York: Dutton, 1964.

Astbury, Raymond, ed. *The Writer in the Market Place*. London: Bingley, 1969.

Bell, Ian A., ed. *Peripheral Visions: Images of Nationhood in Contemporary British Fiction*. Cardiff: University of Wales Press, 1995.

Bergonzi, Bernard. *The Situation of the Novel*. London: Macmillan, 1970.

Bergonzi, ed. *History of Literature in the English Language*. Volume 7: *The Twentieth Century*. London: Barrie & Jenkins, 1970.

Blair, John G. *The Confidence Man in Modern Fiction: A Rogue's Gallery with Six Portraits*. London: Vision, 1979; New York: Barnes & Noble, 1979.

Bloom, Clive, and Gary Day, eds. *Literature and Culture in Modern Britain*. Volume 3: *1956–1999*. Harlow, U.K.: Longman, 2000.

Booker, M. Keith. *The Modern British Novel of the Left: A Research Guide*. Westport, Conn.: Greenwood Press, 1998.

Bradbury, Malcolm. *Dangerous Pilgrimages: Transatlantic Mythologies and the Novel*. London: Secker & Warburg, 1995; New York: Viking, 1996.

Bradbury. *The Modern British Novel*. London: Penguin, 1993.

Bradbury. *No, Not Bloomsbury*. New York: Columbia University Press, 1988.

Bradbury, ed. *The Novel Today: Contemporary Writers on Modern Fiction*. Manchester: Manchester University Press / Totowa, N.J.: Rowman & Littlefield, 1977.

Bradbury, ed. *Possibilities: Essays in the State of the Novel*. London & New York: Oxford University Press, 1973.

Bradbury and Judy Cooke, eds. *New Writing*. London: Minerva, 1992.

Bradbury and David Palmer, eds. *The Contemporary English Novel*. London: Arnold, 1979; New York: Holmes & Meier, 1980.

British Council. *The Novel in Britain and Ireland Since 1970: A Select Bibliography*. Third edition. London: British Council, 1994.

Burgess, Anthony. *Ninety-nine Novels: The Best in English Since 1939. A Personal Choice.* London: Allison & Busby, 1984; New York: Summit, 1984.

Burgess. *The Novel Now: A Guide to Contemporary Fiction.* London: Faber & Faber, 1967; New York: Norton, 1967.

Burns, Alan, and Charles Sugnet, eds. *The Imagination on Trial: British and American Writers Discuss Their Working Methods.* London & New York: Allison & Busby, 1981.

Cassis, A. F. *The Twentieth-Century English Novel: An Annotated Bibliography of General Criticism.* New York: Garland, 1977.

Cope, Jackson I., and Geoffrey Green, eds. *Novel vs. Fiction: The Contemporary Reformation.* Norman, Okla.: Pilgrim, 1981.

Crosland, Margaret. *Beyond the Lighthouse: English Women Novelists in the Twentieth Century.* London: Constable, 1981; New York: Taplinger, 1981.

D'Haen, Theo, and Hans Bertens, eds. *British Postmodern Fiction.* Amsterdam & Atlanta: Rodopi, 1993.

Federman, Raymond, ed. *Surfiction: Fiction Now . . . and Tomorrow.* Chicago: Swallow Press, 1975.

Firchow, Peter, ed. *The Writer's Place: Interviews on the Literary Situation in Contemporary Britain.* Minneapolis: University of Minnesota Press, 1974.

Fletcher, John. *Novel and Reader.* London & Boston: Boyars, 1980.

Gerard, David. *Fallen among Scribes: Conversations with Novelists, Poets, Critics.* Wilmslow, U.K.: Elvet Press, 1998.

Gindin, James. *Post-War British Fiction: New Accents and Attitudes.* Berkeley & Los Angeles: University of California Press, 1962.

Glicksberg, Charles I. *The Sexual Revolution in Modern English Literature.* The Hague: Martinus Nijhoff, 1973.

Gray, Nigel. *The Silent Majority: A Study of the Working Class in Post-War British Fiction.* London: Vision, 1973.

Gunn, James. *Alternate Worlds: The Illustrated History of Science Fiction.* Englewood Cliffs, N.J.: Prentice-Hall, 1975.

Hall, James. *The Lunatic Giant in the Drawing Room: The British and American Novel Since 1930.* Bloomington: Indiana University Press, 1968.

Hassam, Andrew. *Writing and Reality: A Study of Modern British Diary Fiction.* Contributions to the Study of World Literature Series, no. 47. Westport, Conn.: Greenwood Press, 1993.

Hawthorn, Jeremy, ed. *The British Working-Class Novel in the Twentieth Century.* London & Baltimore: Arnold, 1984.

Hazell, Stephen, ed. *The English Novel: Developments in Criticism since Henry James.* London: Macmillan, 1978.

Hosmer, Robert E., Jr., ed. *Contemporary British Women Writers: Narrative Strategies.* New York: St. Martin's Press, 1993.

Jameson, Storm. *Parthian Words.* London: Collins/Harvill Press, 1970.

Josipovici, Gabriel, ed. *The Modern English Novel: The Reader, the Writer, and the Work.* London: Open Books, 1976.

Kaplan, Sydney Janet. *Feminine Consciousness in the Modern British Novel.* Urbana: University of Illinois Press, 1975.

Klaus, H. Gustav, ed. *The Socialist Novel in Britain: Towards the Recovery of a Tradition*. Brighton, U.K.: Harvester, 1982; New York: St. Martin's Press, 1982.

Korte, Barbara, and Klaus Peter Muller, eds. *Unity in Diversity Revisited?: British Literature and Culture in the 1990s*. Tubingen, Germany: Narr, 1998.

Lee, Alison. *Realism and Power: Postmodern British Fiction*. London & New York: Routledge, 1990.

Lewald, H. Ernest, ed. *The Cry of Home: Cultural Nationalism and the Modern Writer*. Knoxville: University of Tennessee Press, 1972.

Lodge, David. *After Bakhtin: Essays on Fiction and Criticism*. London & New York: Routledge, 1990.

Lodge. *The Art of Fiction: Illustrated from Classic and Modern Texts*. London: Secker & Warburg, 1992; New York: Viking, 1993.

Lodge. *Language of Fiction: Essays in Criticism and Verbal Analysis of the English Novel*. London: Routledge & Kegan Paul / New York: Columbia University Press, 1966; revised edition, London & Boston: Routledge & Kegan Paul, 1984.

Lodge. *The Modes of Modern Writing: Metaphor, Metonymy, and the Typology of Modern Literature*. London: Arnold, 1977; Ithaca, N.Y.: Cornell University Press, 1977.

Lodge. *The Novelist at the Crossroads and Other Essays on Fiction and Criticism*. London: Routledge & Kegan Paul, 1971; Ithaca, N.Y.: Cornell University Press, 1971.

Lodge. *The Practice of Writing: Essays, Lectures, Reviews and a Diary*. London: Secker & Warburg / New York: Viking, 1996.

Lodge. *Working with Structuralism: Essays and Reviews on Nineteenth- and Twentieth-Century Literature*. London & Boston: Routledge & Kegan Paul, 1986.

Madden, David. *A Primer of the Novel: For Readers and Writers*. Metuchen, N.J. & London: Scarecrow Press, 1980.

Massie, Allan. *The Novel Today: A Critical Guide to the British Novel 1970–1989*. London & New York: Longman, 1990.

McEwan, Neil. *The Survival of the Novel: British Fiction in the Later Twentieth Century*. London: Macmillan, 1981.

Middeke, Martin, and Werner Huber, eds. *Biofictions: The Rewriting of Romantic Lives in Contemporary Fiction and Drama*. Columbia, S.C.: Camden House, 1999.

Miles, Rosaline. *The Fiction of Sex*. London: Vision Press, 1974; New York: Barnes & Noble, 1976.

Morris, Robert K. *Old Lines, New Forces: Essays on the Contemporary English Novel, 1960–1970*. Rutherford, N.J.: Fairleigh Dickinson University Press, 1976.

O'Connor, William Van. *The New University Wits and the Ends of Modernism*. Carbondale: Southern Illinois University Press, 1963.

Palmer, Helen H., and Anne Jane Dyson. *English Novel Explication: Criticism to 1972*. Hamden, Conn.: Shoe String Press, 1973.

Parker, Peter. *The Reader's Companion to the Twentieth Century Novel*. Oxford: Fourth Estate, Helicon, 1994.

Philips, Deborah, and Ian Haywood. *Brave New Causes: Women in British Postwar Fictions*. London & Washington, D.C.: Leicester University Press, 1998.

Ross, Stephen D. *Literature and Philosophy: An Analysis of the Philosophical Novel*. New York: Appleton-Century-Crofts, 1969.

Schlueter, Paul, and Jane Schlueter. *The English Novel: Twentieth Century Criticism*. Volume 2: *Twentieth Century Novelists*. Chicago & London: Swallow Press, 1982.

Shaffer, Brian W. *The Blinding Torch: Modern British Fiction and the Discourse of Civilization*. Amherst: University of Massachusetts Press, 1993.

Shapiro, Charles, ed. *Contemporary British Novelists*. Carbondale: Southern Illinois University Press, 1965.

Smith, David J. *Socialist Propaganda in the 20th-Century British Novel*. Totowa, N.J.: Rowman & Littlefield, 1978.

Spilka, Mark, ed. *Towards a Poetics of Fiction*. Bloomington & London: University of Indiana Press, 1977.

Staley, Thomas F., ed. *Twentieth-Century Women Novelists*. London: Macmillan, 1982.

Stevenson, Randall. *The British Novel Since the Thirties: An Introduction*. Athens: University of Georgia Press, 1986; London: Batsford, 1986.

Sutherland, John. *Fiction and the Fiction Industry*. London: Athlone Press, 1978.

Swinden, Patrick. *The English Novel of History and Society, 1940–80*. New York: St. Martin's Press, 1984.

Swinden. *Unofficial Selves: Character in the Novel from Dickens to the Present Day*. London & New York: Barnes & Noble, 1973.

Taylor, D. J. *After the War: The Novel and English Society since 1945*. London: Chatto & Windus, 1993.

Taylor. *A Vain Conceit: British Fiction in the 1980s*. London: Bloomsbury, 1989.

Todd, Richard. *Consuming Fictions: The Booker Prize and Fiction in Britain Today*. London: Bloomsbury, 1996.

Weiand, Hermann J., ed. *Analyses of Twentieth-Century British and American Fiction*. Frankfurt am Main: Hirschgraben-Verlag, 1981.

Werlock, Abby H. P., ed. *British Women Writing Fiction*. Tuscaloosa: University of Alabama Press, 2000.

West, Paul. *The Modern Novel*. London: Hutchinson, 1963.

Wheeler, Kathleen, ed. *A Guide to 20th-Century Women Novelists*. Oxford & Cambridge, Mass.: Blackwell, 1997.

Wicker, Brian. *The Story-Shaped World: Fiction and Metaphysics*. London: Athlone Press, 1975.

Wilson, Colin. *The Craft of the Novel*. London: Gollancz, 1975; Salem, N.H.: Salem House, 1986.

Ziegler, Heide, and Christopher Bigsby, eds. *The Radical Imagination and the Liberal Tradition: Interviews with English and American Novelists*. London: Junction, 1982.

Contributors

Andrew Biswell . . . . *University of Warwick*

Geneviève Brassard . . . . *University of Connecticut*

Henry L. Carrigan Jr. . . . . *Otterbein College*

Simon Edwards . . . . *Roehampton Institute*

Martine van Elk . . . . *California State University, Long Beach*

Gillian Fenwick . . . . *University of Toronto*

Nicholas Freeman . . . . *University of Bristol*

Ann-Barbara Graff . . . . *University of Toronto*

Graeme Harper . . . . *University of Wales, Bangor*

Michael Hayes . . . . *University of Central Lancashire*

Cecile M. Jagodzinski . . . . *Illinois State University*

Seán Matthews . . . . *University of California, Los Angeles*

Merritt Moseley . . . . *University of North Carolina at Asheville*

Michael C. Prusse . . . . *University of Zurich*

Susan Rowland . . . . *University of Greenwich–London*

Stacey Short . . . . *Texas A&M University*

Nicolas Tredell . . . . *Sussex University*

Cumulative Index

Dictionary of Literary Biography, Volumes 1-231
Dictionary of Literary Biography Yearbook, 1980-1999
Dictionary of Literary Biography Documentary Series, Volumes 1-19

Cumulative Index

DLB before number: *Dictionary of Literary Biography,* Volumes 1-231
Y before number: *Dictionary of Literary Biography Yearbook,* 1980-1999
DS before number: *Dictionary of Literary Biography Documentary Series,* Volumes 1-19

Cumulative Index

ISBN 0-7876-4648-2

90000

9 790787 646485